SMUTS

THE FIELDS OF FORCE

1919–1950

Smuts
The Sanguine Years, 1870–1919
by W. K. HANCOCK

Cambridge, 1962

SMUTS

The Fields of Force

1919-1950

BY

W . K . HANCOCK

CAMBRIDGE

AT THE UNIVERSITY PRESS

1968

Published by the Syndics of the Cambridge University Press
Bentley House, 200 Euston Road, London, N.W. 1
American Branch: 32 East 57th Street, New York, N.Y. 10022

© Cambridge University Press 1968

Library of Congress Catalogue Card Number: 65-2414

Printed in Great Britain
at the University Printing House, Cambridge
(Brooke Crutchley, University Printer)

IN MEMORY OF

THOMAS BENJAMIN DAVIE

CONTENTS

Contents

LIST OF ILLUSTRATIONS

ix

PREFACE

ACCORDING to Smuts everything and every idea had its field of force, like the fields of force in electromagnetism. Events took place, he said, not by the cause-and-effect impingement of one separate thing upon the other but by their reciprocal action upon each other within their inter-penetrating fields of force. A man could no more live to himself than a plant could; he lived and moved and had his being inter-dependently with nature, with other human persons and with God.

Smuts lived his life on so many fronts that one is moved to write in the plural about his fields of force—for example, his personal, philosophical, political and military fields. Their collisions with the fields of other persons—of Hitler, for example—produced some spectacular explosions. Conflict dominates the action recorded in this book. By contrast, a vision of harmony in the cosmic process and in human destiny dominates Smuts's thought. His life can be seen from one point of view as a sustained striving towards the reconciliation of these opposites.

The story is richly documented. For almost every week from 1919 until his last illness in 1950 there has survived at least one long letter from Smuts to one or other of his friends. He wrote to them almost always in his own hand, not for the historical record but simply to exchange news and views with them about family affairs, books old and new and the ideas which they suggested, politics at home and overseas, mountain climbing, botanical and archaeological excursions, the state of the world, of the nation, of the weather. A vast pile of public print reinforces these intimate revelations. Consequently, I have been able to tell my story in terms of the contemporary record. I have imagined at times that the story was telling itself.

Nevertheless it is not the final or—as some people like to say—the 'definitive' story. Finality exists in mythology, not in history. I drafted a chapter on the mythology of Smuts but decided not to publish it because every myth in my fascinating collection turned out to be nothing more than a label; my readers, I foresaw, would expect me to end the chapter by producing a label of my own, which was the last thing I wanted to do. I want the inquiry to continue. This volume explores a period of South African history which deserves to be called a Dark Age, because it has been so little illuminated by historical study. Still, the prospect is brightening. A few historians are at work on the records of industries and trade unions, of political parties and parliamentary elections. A few economists and sociologists have made and are making valuable contributions to historical knowledge. An extension of the 'open' period of the official archives may be granted before long in South Africa, as in Britain. I hope that the next few decades of historical endeavour may prepare the way for a new biography of Smuts.

Meanwhile, I owe some explanations to readers of this biography. I have tried not to write about Smuts *and* his times but I have had to write about him *in* his times. He carried a heavy burden of history which I have seldom felt free to shed. For example, he was called the Butcher of Bulhoek, but many of my readers have never heard of Bulhoek; consequently, I have felt constrained to tell the story of what happened there. On the other hand, I have dealt briefly with some important stories—such as the proceedings of the joint parliamentary session of 1936 and the main strategical decisions of the Second World War—which other writers have already told at sufficient length.

In writing this book I have envisaged an audience seated in concentric circles. In the outer circles I see people of many nations whose concern is with the experience of all mankind in this brilliant and tragic century. In the inner circles I see my South African friends and critics. At the centre of the first row I see a fellow-craftsman of the University of Stellenbosch, where Smuts received his broad-based (and, in those far off days, his English-based) education. If my Afrikaner colleague finds fault with my craftsmanship I shall consider this book a failure.

I apologize for having taken so long a time to produce the book; but my task—starting fifteen years ago with the effort to recover widely scattered documents and to teach myself Dutch, Afrikaans and a little philosophy—has been arduous. I have, besides, been closely committed to my academic duties in Australia. On the other hand, the Australian National University has given me its unfailing support. I have also enjoyed opportunities for concentrated bursts of work as the guest of the Rockefeller Foundation at the Villa Serbelloni on Lake Como; as Le May Fellow at Rhodes University in Cape Province; as a visiting Fellow both at Churchill College, Cambridge, and All Souls College, Oxford. In March 1964 I began to write this volume at the Villa Serbelloni; in December 1966 I finished it at All Souls, where forty-two years earlier I had finished my first book.

It remains my practice as an historian to hew my own wood and draw my own water; but, given the limited periods of my residence in South Africa, I found it impossible to complete some necessary investigations, even with the aid of microfilm. The gaps have been filled by memoranda written for my use. At the appropriate places in this book I acknowledge my debt for this assistance. I shall not here attempt to thank by name all the friends and colleagues to whom I owe stimulus and criticism, but I gratefully acknowledge my particular debt to the following: in Australia, to Mrs Joan Lynravn; in England, to Mrs Cato Clark, General Smuts's daughter, and to Mrs Peggy Inman; in Kenya, to Mr Jan Gillett; in South Africa, to Dr Rodney Davenport, Professor Noel Garson, Miss Winifred Greenshields, Mrs Knapp-Fisher (formerly Miss Joan Bradley), Dr E. G. Malherbe, Mr Donald Molteno, Q.C., Miss Clodagh O'Dowd, Professor D. Oosthuizen. To this list of friends and helpers two special additions must be made. Mr J. C. Smuts, the son and literary executor of General Smuts, the donor to his country of a great collection of papers and the author of a valuable biography, has given me his trust and friendship. Dr Jean van der Poel of the University of Cape Town has been for fifteen years my friend and my co-worker in an enterprise which goes far beyond the production of this book.

I appreciate the gracious permission granted to me by Her Majesty the Queen to pursue research in the Royal Archives at Windsor and to quote from documents in that superb depository.

It has been a pleasure for me to work with the Cambridge University Press and I am grateful to my helpers there. I am grateful for the help with illustrations generously given to me by Mrs Phyllis Lean of Johannesburg and the General Smuts War Veterans Association.

Last year I published a lecture provocatively entitled *Are there South Africans?* The dedication of this book answers that question. It commemorates a Vice-Chancellor of the University of Cape Town to whom I owe much, a wise and brave academic leader and a South African patriot.

W. K. HANCOCK

Canberra
28 August 1967

PART I

PRIME MINISTER, 1919–1924

CHAPTER I

THE WIDE WORLD AND SOUTH AFRICA

WHEN Louis Botha died in August 1919 friends and enemies alike took it for granted that Smuts would succeed him as Prime Minister; but some even of the friends doubted whether Smuts alone would be able to give his people the leadership which Botha and he together had given them. Botha's contribution to the partnership, they said, had been common humanity; Smuts's contribution had been uncommon brains. They hoped, but they did not feel sure, that Smuts would prove himself a big enough man in heart as well as in head to govern South Africa.

These commentators would have been more helpful if they had been more specific. They tried to identify some temperamental disabilities which Smuts might find it hard to conquer but they failed to probe his disqualifications of training and experience. Two at least of these could prove troublesome to him. Twenty-one years had passed since Kruger had made him State Attorney of the South African Republic; but in all those years he had never once belonged to a parliamentary opposition or shared the experiences of the ordinary M.P. Three and a half years had passed since he had set out for service overseas; but now he found himself Prime Minister of South Africa after being back there for no more than three weeks. In the eyes of his enemies, such a long absence was by itself the proof that he was alienated from his own country and thereby disqualified from leading it.*

The absence, however, had been imposed upon him as a duty. He had not sought the command in East Africa: on the contrary, he had refused it when it was first offered to him and when the offer was renewed he had accepted it 'with many a pang and many a grave misgiving' under the strong urging of his South African colleagues. He had not wanted to go to London to attend Lloyd George's Imperial War Cabinet: on the contrary, he had told Botha that he should go himself. Botha could not or would not go. Yet somebody

* He had been away from February 1916 to August 1919, except for one week at home between his military service in East Africa and his political service in London.

had to go. Smuts accepted service in London upon the insistent urging of Botha and the full South African Cabinet. He retained their full support up to the time of his return home.

Botha and Smuts were completely of one mind upon South Africa's military and political participation in the war. From the start of the war to its finish they held constantly in view two paramount objectives: national security, national status.

From Kruger and Rhodes and even from their former British conquerors* they had inherited an expansionist concept of security—wider frontiers for the Union and an economic and political hegemony extending beyond those frontiers far into equatorial Africa. Their immediate objectives were sovereignty over German South West Africa, which they had conquered in a joint campaign, and over Delagoa Bay, which they hoped to gain from the Portuguese in exchange for some of the territory conquered by Smuts in East Africa. In the event, they had to be content with a C Mandate over South West Africa. Smuts hoped for bigger things later on.†

The struggle for status was at a critical stage when Smuts reached London in March 1917. The protagonists of Imperial Federation, inspired by Lionel Curtis and other zealots, were making their supreme bid for victory. In 1911, Botha had resisted them; in 1917, Smuts routed them. As one of his South African colleagues inelegantly expressed it, he 'put the lid on Messrs Lionel Curtis & Co.'. Next year, in partnership with Borden of Canada and Hughes of Australia, he asserted the right of each self-governing Dominion to take its place at the Paris Peace Conference among the sovereign nations of the world. At Paris, South Africa's signature upon the Treaty and her original membership of the League of Nations became the outward and visible signs of her sovereignty in international law. Back in South Africa, the Nationalists derided it as a sham sovereignty; but they were wrong. Smuts might have convinced even them that it was real—despite the need for a thorough tidying-up of the law, which he had just as much in mind as they did—if he had felt free to publish two letters to Lloyd George which he had drafted and Botha had signed in May 1919. The occasion of this correspondence was

* Chapter VI of the Selborne Memorandum contains a programme of South African expansion comparable in its exuberance with the most ardent propaganda of Manifest Destiny in nineteenth-century America. The Memorandum was drafted by Lord Milner's young men and endorsed by Lord Selborne as a sustained argument for South African Union.   † See pp. 151–3 below.

the British offer to France of a treaty of military guarantee. Botha and Smuts exacted from Lloyd George the admission that such a treaty would be binding upon Great Britain alone. Then they pointed the moral.

One result of the perfectly correct exclusion of the Dominions from the obligation which it is proposed to lay on the British people may well be that in some future continental war, Great Britain may be at war and one or more of the Dominions may stand out and maintain their neutrality. But that result is inevitable, and flows from the independent nationhood of the Dominions.[1]

General Hertzog could have said no more than that. The Nationalists, Smuts told his wife, were making a great noise about South African independence, while all the time Botha and he were winning it.

As a political calculator, Smuts bore Cavour's stamp. He calculated that South Africa no longer had anything to gain by challenging the British Empire, as Hertzog tried to do at the Paris Peace Conference, but that she had everything to gain in combination with the free nations who were transforming the Empire into a Commonwealth. Smuts was shrewd—*slim*, as they said in South Africa.

But he was also simple. To the end of his life he never forgot the simple question which he had put to Campbell-Bannerman on 7 February 1906:

Do you want friends or enemies? You can have the Boers for friends, and they have proved what quality their friendship may mean. I pledge the friendship of my colleagues and myself if you wish it. You can choose to make them enemies, and possibly have another Ireland on your hands.

That same night, Campbell-Bannerman made his choice of having the Boers for friends. Eight years later, Smuts made his choice of proving what Boer friendship could mean.

A few people in Britain—most notably, perhaps, L. S. Amery—understood his shrewd calculations. British people in general responded to his simplicity. But they did not understand it. They saw him as a romantic figure. To be sure, he sometimes saw himself that way. He told his wife in March 1917 that a journalist had written his life story and had described him as the most romantic figure now in the country: yes, he reflected, his story was indeed romantic—the lonely Cambridge undergraduate, the enemy of the British and their Empire now returning to help them in their hour of need. But the truth was not so simple as that. Even while he was establishing the

5

Royal Air Force and imposing an order of priorities upon British war production, victory for Britain was never his final purpose but merely his incidental or instrumental purpose. Jingo imperialists had good reasons, from their point of view, for smelling him out as a traitor. He held heretical ideas about the British Empire. Of course, the time was long since past since he had denounced it as an ungainly and brutish mastodon, whose predestined doom could not, for him, come quickly enough. Nowadays, he looked at it with a philosophical eye. Like all the other empires, he said, it had once possessed an ephemeral justification in human history; but henceforward its only justification would be the metamorphosis which was giving it a new name and a new nature.

Nations in their march to power [he wrote] tend to pass the purely national bounds; hence arise the empires which embrace various nations, sometimes related in blood and institutions, sometimes again different in race and hostile in temperament. In a rudimentary way all such composite empires of the past were leagues of nations, keeping the peace among the constituent nations but unfortunately doing so not on the basis of freedom but of repression. Usually one dominant nation in the group overcame, coerced and kept the rest under. The principle of nationality became over-strained and over-developed, and nourished itself by exploiting other weaker nationalities. Nationality overgrown became imperialism, and the empire led a troubled existence on the ruin of the freedom of its constituent nations. That was the evil of the system, but with however much friction and oppression, the peace was usually kept among the nations falling within the empire. These empires have all broken down, and today the British Commonwealth of Nations remains the only embryo league of nations because it is based on the true principles of national freedom and political decentralisation.

Those sentences came early in 'the great State Paper', as Lloyd George called it, which Smuts wrote on the League of Nations. They pointed forward to three exuberant sentences of its concluding paragraph.

For there is no doubt that mankind is once more on the move. The very foundations have been shaken and loosened, and things are again fluid. The tents have been struck, and the great caravan of humanity is once more on the march.

Back in South Africa, the Opposition labelled Smuts an imperialist.

That label half stuck. In the mid-1930s the Nationalists and a small Marxist remnant were still insisting that it fitted him. But the Dominion party was accusing him of selling the Empire down the river. To have found any label that fitted him would have been a hard task. During the First World War most people could be known by the company they kept; but not Smuts. Throughout his working week he moved in a masculine and military society; but the society which he frequented at week-ends was feminine and pacifist in tone. His immense administrative competence made him immediately at home with Hankey, Amery and the other administrators working for the War Cabinet. He quickly found his way through the intricacies of Whitehall and established easy, matter-of-fact relationships with the chiefs of the armed services. He conversed and corresponded with political leaders in the various parties on a surname basis. Nevertheless, he rejected every proposal, beginning with Lloyd George's proposal of a seat for him in parliament, which could possibly involve him in British politics. He rejected just as decisively the natural intimacies of British political society. With one or two exceptions he never visited the associates of his working week in their own homes.* At week-ends he hurried away to stay with his friends the Gilletts in their home at 102 Banbury Road, Oxford, or in the gamekeeper's cottage which they rented in the Berkshire Downs south of the Thames near Moulsford. He and the Gilletts called the cottage and its encircling beeches Paradise Plantation—more frequently, Paradise.

Arthur and Margaret Gillett both belonged by birth, upbringing and conviction to the Society of Friends. As undergraduates at Cambridge during the Anglo-Boer war they had both been passionate pro-Boers. After the war, she had gone to South Africa to help Emily Hobhouse in her work for Boer women and had made close friendships in the Steyn, Smuts and some other Boer families. By steady conviction she remained a pacifist. Her husband took the opposite side during the First World War but this difference did not create dissension between them. Husband and wife remained united with each other and with the far-flung clans of Gillett and Clark in their radical and anti-imperialist politics, their practical good works and their longing for a better ordering of the world after the war. Most appropriately, it was in his bedroom at 102 Banbury Road, where he was fighting influenza just after the Armistice, that Smuts wrote *The League of Nations: A Practical Suggestion.*

* Amery and Churchill were exceptions. When Smuts wrote to them after the war he usually sent greetings to their wives. Churchill once reminded him, in Botha's phrase, that they had 'been out in all weathers'.[2]

During his week-ends with the Gilletts he sometimes discussed philosophy. He had brought with him to England the typescript of his *Inquiry into the Whole*, a book which embodied his feeling and thought about the universe and man's place within it. Only two people had hitherto seen the book, his wife and his eccentric friend H. J. Wolstenholme,* who thought it so bad that he could not bear to read it through. Smuts nevertheless believed in it and looked forward to revising it for publication. Meanwhile he found at Oxford or in the Downs two new readers for it, Agnes Murray, Gilbert Murray's daughter, and Alice Clark, Margaret Gillett's sister. Among his friends Alice Clark came as close as anybody ever did to understanding him. She understood his obstinate endeavour to find significance and hope for the fleeting generations of man amidst the immensities of Space, Time and Deity. She criticized his personal shortcomings and his philosophical fumblings; but she knew what he meant by calling himself a holist.

That was a word of his own minting which had not yet found its way into the dictionaries. One at least of his scholarly friends thought it an unpleasing word but conceded its etymological and logical appropriateness to his system of thought.† Two of his younger contemporaries, whose systems were in some respects similar to his, met with no better success than he did in finding elegant names for themselves as thinkers: Julian Huxley called himself an evolutionary humanist; Pierre Teilhard de Chardin called himself a terrestrial.[3] But Smuts had the bad luck of being a politician with enemies waiting for the chance to give his words a political twist. To these enemies, holism spelt imperialism. They asserted, and possibly they believed, that his philosophical cosmology was camouflage for his obsession as a politician with sheer size—the Union, the Empire, the League; always something bigger.‡

But the opposite was true. The evolutionary process, as Smuts envisaged it, was a movement from outwards inwards, from the universal to the particular—this nation, this person, this moment in time. Whether it was profitable to him as a politician to see his own time in the perspective of evolutionary time was disputable. Like other politicians, he was fallible in his appreciations of immediate

* Wolstenholme died in December 1917.
† See pp. 188–9 below.
‡ For a discussion of this misunderstanding see pp. 193, 197, 234 below.

situations. It was his sanguine temperament, not his philosophical understanding, that prompted him to exclaim in December 1918 that the tents were struck and the great caravan of humanity once again on the march. His mood that December day was assurance of victory—not the impermanent military victory which the western allies had already won, but a permanent victory now to be won by the practical reason of humanity. He looked forward with sanguine expectations to the Paris Peace Conference. He expected it to establish a new political order which would give the suffering nations at long last liberty and peace. He expected it to build a sound foundation for this new order by making a prudent and magnanimous peace treaty, just like the pledge from man to man which he and Campbell-Bannerman had made with each other. The event shattered his expectations. He considered the draft treaty both imprudent and vindictive. In May 1919 he launched a furious assault against it. In June he declared that he would never sign it. But in the end he signed. In a violent revulsion of mood he told Alice Clark that he was no better than the others and must stand in the dock beside them. He confessed himself a failure and saw himself slinking home like a wounded animal.[4]

During the last months at Paris his longing for home had become almost more than he could bear.* He told his wife that he often saw the farm in his dreams.

Santa and Cato are already big girls, the little ones are also growing up, the trees are getting big. Yes, I shall see changes after 3½ years of absence...

I wonder how the farm looks now? May is always a very pleasant month in the Transvaal, when the heat is past and the sharp cold has not yet come. I hope it is well with all the animals and also the cattle...

My wish, my ardent wish, is to get out of it as soon as possible and to return to home and country...My most fervent wish is to go back to you, and only the most extreme and bitter fate will keep me from it...[5]

When he wrote those sentences he was still asking himself whether it was not his duty to stay in Europe to launch a crusade against the peace treaty. The confession that his place was in the dock with the others came a few weeks later.

After that confession his mood changed again. He could not bring

---

* Letters to and from Doornkloof at this time were still in Dutch; ten years later they were in Afrikaans.

himself to believe that the agony and effort of the past four years had been altogether in vain. Prussianism had been overthrown. The League had been established. The real peace of the peoples would follow, complete and amend the peace of the statesmen. In a message of farewell to the British people he set out his ideas of how this could be made to happen. His letters to his English friends on the voyage home revealed him as a warrior still licking his wounds but already looking forward to new battles. He began to enjoy the first weeks of rest that he had had for many years. He began to see himself again in a romantic light. He allowed the picture of his wide wanderings to pass across his eyes—river after river and range after range from north to south in German East Africa; Flanders and its mud; Egypt and its sunshine; London, Edinburgh, Tonypandy, the Downs; Paris, Budapest, Prague. He felt like Ulysses coming home at last. 'But what will Ulysses do', he asked, 'in his little Ithaca?'[6]

His enemies said that he found his own country too small for him. That was a catch cry; but it had some plausibility. The wide world was still in his mind even when he was fighting a hard political campaign among the little dorps of the western Cape where twenty years earlier he had fought a military campaign. Meanwhile his friends overseas were giving him no chance to forget the sufferings of Europe. Hardly a mail arrived in South Africa without his receiving letters from Emily Hobhouse, who was engaged on relief work in Leipzig, or from Hilda Clark, who was doing similar work in Vienna, or from liberals in England—Gilletts, Clarks, Courtneys, Murrays— all lamenting the distressful condition of humanity. He shared their griefs and anxieties.

I sometimes fear that this war [he meant the war just over] is simply the vanguard of calamity and that the Great Horror is still to come...

It is an awful thought—that the great storm has not merely blown off the rotten and weak branches of the human tree, but affected the tree itself, and that in future it will for generations have only a stunted growth. I believe in God and I believe in Good. But, dear Alice, I am often very low and despondent over it all. Only a few years ago we still saw the vision of the New Earth. In Paris that vision vanished. And now arises that other vision of human decay—when God rings down the curtain and darkness settles down once more on human destiny...

What is in store for us all?...Have we passed through one great historic cycle and are we entering upon a very different one—perhaps much worse?[7]

But his audiences in Namaqualand and the western Transvaal were not troubling their heads about historical cycles or fading visions of the New Earth. What interested them were the arguments for and against the Republic and the prices they were getting—or thought they ought to be getting—for their wool.

The tone of his letters troubled Alice Clark. She told him that he was not close enough in sympathy to his own people. She told him further that his lamentations over humanity's sad state were doing no good either to humanity or to himself. Her prescription for him, as for herself, was a quiet trust in God and the daily round of duty.

But however much the heathen rage and the people imagine vain things [she wrote] for us our duty is clear; to go forward with the work that is given us, knowing that God is good and is all, and that in love, goodness and truth is eternal life—and therefore fearing no evil. It is the fear of evil that leads people to waste their strength in a barren struggle to overcome it—with evil—instead of devoting themselves to doing good.

He agreed with her up to a point but said that things were not so simple as they seemed to her good Quaker soul.

Often and often [he wrote] I think of you and of the sources of Goodness and Power in the nature of the Whole. You have really assimilated the central idea of Holism...I see M. Coué has raised a sort of revival in England. I suppose it is the same thing—the healing influence of faith in goodness and betterment. The real trouble begins when you try to reconcile this central idea with the sea of misery and suffering in which all living creation is moving. The Goodness of God and the existence of Evil still remain the great religious and metaphysical problem. And we shall never solve it theoretically because as partial beings we cannot grasp the whole where these antinomies disappear.

Thus their debate continued on the nature of good and evil. He did not challenge her faith in 'Love and Truth and Life and the other Great Capitals' but he told her to look at the world as it was now and to ask herself whether she could still remain an optimist. His own deepest beliefs, he protested, were the same as hers—

but I also believe that as the flowers grow on a granite soil, so life with all its beautiful flowerings rests at last on a granitic foundation. Unless society is to go to pieces there must be the solid guarantee of force in the background, and this will remain so until human nature has undergone a thorough change.

He wrote those last sentences during the aftermath of revolution on the Rand.[8]

But even in the worst times 'the soul of goodness in things evil' remained for him the positive principle of the universe and of human history. He affirmed that principle in a correspondence which arose unexpectedly between himself and James Ward, a trained philosopher who had been a professor at Cambridge when he was an undergraduate there. Ward opened the correspondence with an anxious letter about some unfavourable comment which he believed that Smuts had made on his book, *The Realm of Ends*. Smuts replied that he had made no such comment: on the contrary, he had found the book absorbing when he first read it on the slopes of Mount Kilimanjaro, during his East African campaign, and he had read it twice since then with deepening admiration. He discussed some of Ward's themes and some of his own difficulties. If only it were possible, he exclaimed, to disentangle from their archaic setting the great truths discovered by the spirit of man in past ages! If only it were possible to reaffirm these truths in language in key with the experience and mental habit of modern man! In a resonant phrase, which Alice Clark would have approved, he made his own attempt: 'I believe', he declared, 'in spite of the war and everything, that this is a Friendly Universe, and that what is best in us is also deepest in it.' Eleven years later, in his presidential address to the British Association, he repeated almost in the same words the same declaration of faith.*

Ward volunteered to take over the service which Wolstenholme had formerly rendered of compiling reading lists and ordering books for him. Smuts did not need this help because he was getting it already from Mrs Gillett, but he asked Ward to send to her any suggestions which might occur to him. Thus the stream of books kept flowing to Doornkloof.[9]

They were not books that a man might comfortably read with his feet on the mantlepiece. Mrs Gillett warned him once that her last parcel contained three treatises which he could hardly hope to understand. He replied to her after his return from a speech-making tour in the western Transvaal—

Well I took what appeared the most difficult of the three with me and read it through on the journey, and I believe thoroughly mastered it. That was Einstein's book on Relativity. I enjoyed it immensely, my knowledge of Dynamics making it comparatively easy for me to follow it. So don't you belittle my intelligence too much.

* See p. 234 below.

For a politician to read Einstein in between the speeches he had to make about secession and the price of wool was a phenomenon that his audiences, had they got wind of it, might have found puzzling.[10]

He told Alice Clark that he was never 'meant for a politician'. In the world of action, he said, and also in the world of thought—but politics belonged to neither—he felt happier, surer and more himself than he would ever feel in political life. He called politics a futile game. He said they were no life for a Christian. He protested that he would rather herd pigs. He prayed General Hertzog to give him his release from politics at the next elections.

It is really a terrible thing, this chain of responsibility round one's neck—not for a few weeks or months, but practically for a lifetime. I pray General Hertzog to release me. . .

With me the anthropophobia (what a word!) sometimes amounts to something active and fierce. There is no pressure like that of humans on our personalities and in the end we rebel. And I rebel. Only it is a vain rebellion from which one does not even get away in sleep or dreams.

If that had been his mood always, he would have done well to quit politics for good before they broke him.[11]

But it was his mood only intermittently. His eruptions of rebellion were violent when they broke out but he always kept them hidden except from a few friends and most of the time he remained submissive to the political grind. It was hard for him to have to learn in his fifties* what the grind really meant. In all his years of political life from June 1898 to August 1919 he had fought only three elections, but in the next nineteen months he raised that figure to five. Of all those twenty-one years in politics he had spent only eight as a fully participating member of parliament,† but now he considered it his duty to be in his seat on every day of every session. Between sessions he gave himself no rest from political campaigning. Seldom if ever was he able to stay at home for more than a few days at a time. He felt his homesickness most bitterly during the months that he had to spend in Cape Town when parliament was in session. He thought it a wonderful thing when his wife was able on one occasion to stay with him there for seven continuous weeks. In the

* He turned 50 on 24 May (Empire Day) 1920.
† As State Attorney of the South African Republic he had not held a seat in the Volksraad, although it was his duty to attend it when summoned.

twenty-four years of their married life, he reflected, they had scarcely ever had so long a time together.[12]

Continuity was his craving; a fragmented life was his fate. Yet he had unusual recuperative powers. He felt himself a whole man again whenever he could retreat to the solitude of his study, or exchange the press of people for the society of a few friends and walk with them in the mountains, or walk alone. One July day in 1920 he had the joy of revisiting the mountain-shadowed farm in the Swartland where he had grown up.

I enjoyed myself [he wrote] very much yesterday. I took a walk by myself over the farm humming my monotonous tune to myself to the accompaniment of a gentle rain most of the time, and I felt uplifted once more. Those hills of my beginnings always have a great effect on me. 'The land of sacrament' you once called the hills at Street. My native country too is very close to me and fills me with indescribable feelings. The places where I looked after sheep or cattle, or picked up tortoises, or dug out edible roots in the Bushman fashion, the hills where dim unformed aspirations began to surge up; where I used to sit for half a day under a 'skerm' in the rain while a roaring fire burnt in front—how close they are to me even at this great age of 50! And the hopes and the dreams of that birth time![13]

The hopes and dreams ranged wider now; but South Africa was still their centre. He thought South Africa a fortunate country with a splendid future. He tried to persuade the 'little family' in Oxford to pull up their English roots and settle there.*

Even politics seemed an endurable evil to him when he could get a day off to climb mountains. He enjoyed the physical exercise of climbing and in August 1921 astonished the white colonials of Sierra Leone, who were used at most, he said, to a languid meandering between their homes and offices, by rushing up the mountain above Freetown.[15] He told them that it was only 2,000 feet high and altogether insignificant in comparison with his own South African mountains. *They* were a real challenge to any man to keep his body fit by hard exercise and copious sweat. But to him they meant more than that. Their appeal to him was romantic, poetical, religious. One Sunday morning early in 1923 he unveiled the Mountain Club War Memorial at Maclear's Beacon on the summit of Table Mountain.

* They went so far as to send money out so that he could buy a farm for them; their relation, Malcolm Reynolds, came out to work it.[14]

1. At Maclear's Beacon, February 1943

The sons of the cities [he said in his oration] are remembered and recorded in the streets and squares of their cities and by memorials placed in their churches and cathedrals. But the mountaineers deserve a loftier pedestal and a more appropriate memorial. To them the true church where they worshipped was Table Mountain...Here in life they breathed the great air; here in death their memory will fill the upper spaces...Here for a thousand years their memory shall blend with these great rock masses and humanise them...

Geologists tell us that in the abyss of time Table Mountain was much more of a mountain than it is today. Then it was more than 18,000 feet high, of which barely one-fifth remains today. And in another million years no trace may be left of it. Here there is no abiding city, neither is there an abiding mountain. Human life itself may be but a passing phase in the history of this great globe. But as long as human memory lasts...so long...the memory of the great sacrifice here recorded will endure as part of it...

The Mountain is not merely something externally sublime. It has a great historic and spiritual meaning for us...From it came the Law, from it came the Gospel in the Sermon on the Mount. We may truly say that the highest religion is the Religion of the Mountain.

What is that religion? When we reach the mountain summits we leave behind us all the things that weigh heavily down below on our body and our spirit. We leave behind all sense of weakness and depression; we feel a new freedom, a great exhilaration, an exaltation of the body no less than of the spirit. We feel a great joy. The Religion of the Mountain is in reality the religion of joy, of the release of the soul from the things that weigh it down and fill it with a sense of weariness, sorrow and defeat...

We must practise the religion of the mountain down in the valleys also. This may sound a hard doctrine, and it may be that only after years of practice are we able to triumph in spirit over the things that weigh and drag us down. But it is the nature of the soul, as of all life, to rise, to overcome, and finally to attain complete freedom and happiness...To this great end Nature will cooperate with the soul.

He sent Mrs Gillett a copy of his oration and told her that it was a 'bit of me and not merely a speech'.[16] For that very reason, he may have made a mistake when he allowed it to be published. Roy Campbell, that master of satirical verse, always loathed his prose-poetical flights.* Most philosophers and theologians—though not all†—disliked his nature-mysticism. To be sure, poets, philosophers and theologians were not conspicuous that Sunday morning in the gathering at Maclear's Beacon. Smuts was speaking to mountaineers and to the friends of dead mountaineers. His words touched their hearts.

* See p. 100 below.   † See p. 196 below.

Sardonic persons said that his head was always too much in the clouds. Yet his eyes were on the ground most of the hours that he spent on the highveld or among the mountains. He had taken to his botany again. He was collecting specimens to send to Marloth, the grand old man of South African botany, who thirty years ago at Stellenbosch had trained him in taxonomy. He was collecting more specimens for the Bolus herbarium in Cape Town. He was in correspondence with Hill, the Director of Kew, about finding a young South African for the herbarium there. He was in close discussion with Pole-Evans, a grasses expert of the Agricultural Department and his near neighbour at Doornkloof, about the botanical education of his daughter Santa. He was searching the gorges of Table Mountain for rare timber trees. He was raising money to publish Marloth's book. He was planning a botanical holiday with Pole-Evans. 'In all my troubles', he wrote at a distressful time, 'I don't forget my grasses.'[17]

He studied his grasses microscopically but he also saw them as products of evolution and assigned to them their appropriate place in his macroscopic cosmology. He reserved the pre-eminent place in his cosmology for homo sapiens, whose pre-history he was beginning at this time to see in the context of the great climatic cycles.[18] Some years were still to pass before he discovered that South Africa itself was a treasure house of pre-historical record.* Nevertheless his vision of his own landscapes—a vision at one and the same time poetical, scientific, historical—was year by year growing deeper. Between his philosophy of the Whole and his love of country no conflict arose. He saw universal nature revealed in his own particular place.

A comparable mingling of the universal and the particular informed his political vision. He looked forward to the 'convergence'— although that word was not his own†—of all the particular peoples comprised within the universal human family. In December 1920 he wrote to Arthur Gillett: '"The Poet hath said Dear City of Cecrops and shall we not say Dear City of God?" That was Marcus Aurelius.'‡ He was too much the pre-historian and, no doubt, too

* See p. 175 below.

† 'Convergence' was a favourite, although still unpublicized, word of Pierre Teilhard de Chardin.

‡ He repeated the phrase in his speech in 1926 at Bloemfontein when Emily Hobhouse's ashes were buried at the foot of the Vrouens Monument. But his quotation was not quite correct. 'Dear City of Zeus' was what Marcus Aurelius wrote.

much the South African to expect the City of God to come quickly. He expected its realization to take centuries, if not millenniums of purposeful striving. Nevertheless, he rated high the achievements and opportunities of his own time. To him, the British Commonwealth of Nations seemed a secure toe-hold which humanity had already won upon the cliff of world unity and freedom. The League of Nations was a second toe-hold—if only it could be made secure—higher up the same cliff. He saw these two institutions as fortresses of human solidarity. But he also saw them under threat. 'It is curious', he wrote, 'how this nationalist wave in the world is reaching its climax just as we are entering on the great international order of the world.'[19]

He made a distinction between national sentiment and nationalism. To him, national sentiment connoted a man's proper pride in his own place and people; it was unaggressive, and consequently compatible with membership of free societies such as the Commonwealth and the League. Nationalism seemed to him the perversion of this proper pride; it was xenophobic, and consequently the enemy of international order in any form. He never expounded this distinction systematically; nor did he explore the roots of nationalist pathology. Nevertheless, he correctly diagnosed its danger for Europe. A similar danger, he believed, threatened South Africa. While the Peace Conference was still in session, General Hertzog had arrived in Paris to demand liberation from the British connection—if possible, for the entire Union of South Africa; failing that, for the two former Boer Republics; failing that, for the Orange Free State. These demands, in Smuts's view, typified disruptive nationalism at its worst. He returned to South Africa to fight them.*

No sooner had he become Prime Minister than he flung himself into the fight.

I returned last night [he wrote on 4 October 1919] from a fortnight's tour through the North Western Districts of the Cape Province, having travelled over 700 miles by motor over bad roads mostly (and generally doing my own driving) and visiting 13 or 14 towns and making innumerable speeches and attending endless functions. I am glad it is over; it has been a most trying time. But not without the greatest interest and keen enjoyment. I was there last eighteen years ago in command of the republican

---

* It is arguable that Hertzog, who in any case was pushed by Tielman Roos, merely intended to demonstrate the difference between Dominion status and the Wilsonian principle of self-determination; but Smuts took Hertzog's words at their face value.

forces, calling upon the population to join me. And now I was calling upon them to drop all agitation for the republic and abide in the British Connection. Such is my fate. And yet I do not feel inconsistent. But it is somewhat mystifying to the plain man on the veld.[20]

To clear that mystification up would have been a daunting task. He might perhaps have given his version of world history during the past quarter-century, explaining how imperialism and nationalism— which he saw as the opposite sides of the same coin—had both be- come incompatible with the peace and liberty of nations. But many people in his audiences would have disputed that version. He might perhaps have made the story personal, starting in 1899 with his own *A Century of Wrong*, a nationalist tirade more virulent by far than any that Hertzog had ever uttered. That would have brought Milner into the story, and he would have had to explain how it had come to pass that Milner, who was still alive, had now become a different Milner from the man who twenty years earlier had stung him into writing his pamphlet.* Then he would have had to explain how Campbell- Bannerman and Botha, although they were physically dead, were still living in their work; and how their work had become his work. He would have had so many things to explain. But he did not want to make explanations. He did not want to spend time on demon- strating his own consistency. He had a more urgent task—to tell his people where he stood now.

He saw secession from the British Commonwealth as the immediate issue. Hertzog had raised it at Paris and many of his followers in South Africa were clamouring for it. Smuts denounced it as a blow to human solidarity, to the Commonwealth, to South Africa herself.

For secession means not only secession from the British Empire [his opponents had not yet accepted the name Commonwealth], it means also secession of Dutch-speaking from English-speaking South Africans, who made together a solemn pact at the Union. It means secession of one province of the Union from another, and the break-up of the Union which is the noblest legacy of our great statesmen, the consecration of all the sacrifices of the past. It means the secession of the natives, whose devotion to the British connection is historical. It means the complete isolation of Dutch-speaking Africa and in that isolation its stranglement and decay. It means the blasting of all the great hopes which have sustained our

---

* In June 1921, when he heard the news of Milner's departure from the Colonial Office, he wrote, 'I am really sorry Milner is gone. He had found salvation at the last.'[21]

people in the past. It means that a civilised South Africa becomes a dream, and that the white people of this country have decided to commit political suicide.*

Some items of that declaration were open to argument even when Smuts made it. Before he died, thirty years later, some other items of it had become arguable. Nevertheless, on the day that he made the declaration, 3 December 1920, he was talking sense to South Africa's white people.

It was a fighting declaration. He kept telling his friends that fighting was no use and that he proposed to give it up; but they knew him too well to believe him. Emily Hobhouse reminded him how he had told her nearly twenty years ago, just when he was starting his big political fight against Milner, that he proposed to read philosophy and water his orange trees and give up politics for good. And now once again he was saying the same thing, not only to her but to other people. The world today, he was saying, was just like the Roman world in its decline. Only a spiritual revival could save it. The revival would have to come in the hearts and homes of ordinary people. Nothing that he or any other politician did would make any difference. He, J. C. Smuts, might just as well quit politics.

And yet he could not quit politics. Sooner or later he always swung back to that brute fact.

Arthur writes in his last letter [he told Margaret Gillett] that he finds the trouble of the world beyond him and falls back more and more on the philosophy of home life. The greatest and truest of all philosophies in my humble opinion. It only shows that Arthur is wiser than I and others who toil at problems beyond our powers. And yet what can one do? Is it possible for those who occupy positions of leadership to fold their hands and admit defeat?...We may feel that something far more fundamental is required than has yet appeared. It is a new spirit, a new heart, in fact a new religion that is wanted...And yet we cannot wait till the new religion appears, till the Great Word is spoken by some authority greater than any among us today. And so we have to labour on with our little palliatives and keep the show going with some appearance of human decency.

In a letter to Alice Clark he said the same thing in one terse sentence —'We are not consulted in these matters'.[23]

* The occasion of this emphatic declaration was a statement by Bonar Law, speaking in the House of Commons on the Government of Ireland Bill, to the effect that the right of secession existed in practice.[22]

Prime Minister, 1919–1924

As a signatory of the Treaty of Versailles Smuts bore some responsibility for keeping the show going in the western world. As Prime Minister of the Union he bore the main responsibility for keeping it going in South Africa. He could not shuffle that responsibility off. Nor did he want to, even in his moods of rebellion. He had said that he prayed General Hertzog to release him at the next elections, but when they came he fought furiously for his political life. He perambulated the Union from city to city and town to town making speeches to immense crowds in the open air. He made speeches until he tore his vocal cords. Then he went on from city to city and town to town still making speeches with his throat bleeding.[24]

CHAPTER 2

HOME POLITICS

NOBODY in South Africa thought it strange to see Smuts concentrating his energies upon an argument with his fellow Afrikaners about their proper relationship with English-speaking South Africans and with the British Commonwealth of Nations. Up to the mid-1920s, that argument by common consent held priority over the argument about the proper relationship between South Africa's whites and blacks. In the political vocabulary of that time, the word racialism seldom if ever referred to the colour question; the racialist was a Briton who wanted to make his section of the white population top dog in South Africa, or a Boer who wanted to make his section top dog. Smuts had run no risk of being misunderstood when he told W. T. Stead in March 1907 that he saw a wonderful opportunity 'to work away from racialism'. He meant that he saw the chance at long last of establishing a creative partnership between Boers and Britons.[1]

Smuts was announcing the final overthrow of Milner's racialist régime. Before, during and after the Anglo-Boer war Milner had pursued the single aim of British domination. In December 1900 he wrote: 'If, ten years hence, there are three men of British race to two of Dutch, the country will be safe and prosperous. If there are three of Dutch to two of British we shall have perpetual difficulty.' To achieve his aim Milner needed first of all to make British power supreme throughout South Africa. He did that by war. He needed secondly to make English the sole official language and as near as might be the sole language of the schools. The Treaty of Vereeniging did that. But afterwards? A flood of British immigrants to swamp the Boer population? That hope foundered on the rocks of economic and demographic fact. A campaign of linguistic and ideological denationalization among the children? That project foundered on the rock of Boer resistance.

Botha and Smuts led the resistance and led their defeated people out of the valley of the shadow of death. Two and a half years after the Boer capitulation, they established Het Volk, a political party and something far more; L. S. Amery recognized it as a whole people in action on the field of politics. Four and a half years after the capitulation, Het Volk was ruling the Transvaal. Eight years after the capitulation, Het Volk and its associates in the other Provinces were ruling the Union of South Africa.

To Milner, those events signified the triumph of an Afrikaner racialist conspiracy. To Milner's successor, Lord Selborne, in his early months of office, their significance seemed the same; the Boers, Selborne declared, were fighting to regain in the political arena what they had lost on the field of battle.* The idea that Afrikaner rebels would someday make England's danger South Africa's opportunity had its adherents in the Colonial Office. As the event showed, that idea was not fantastic; but it had no lodgement in the minds of Botha and Smuts.

Conciliation was their watchword. It expressed both the idealistic and the realistic elements of Smuts's temperament and thought. In the golden age of Onze Jan Hofmeyr he had grown up with it; in the aftermath of the Jameson Raid he had repudiated it; in the last months of his guerilla campaign in the Cape he had returned to it. In January 1902 he told W. T. Stead that the two white races were fighting a fratricidal war and must combine their forces to found a Commonwealth in which they could both feel proud to be partners. That, by implication, was the concluding plea of his great speech at Vereeniging. It became the recurrent theme of his letters from Vereeniging. 'Let us try so to arrange our politics', he told T. L. Graham in August 1902, '...that when eventually we become politically independent (as we necessarily must, in course of time, and who knows how soon) we shall no longer be at our old battle of the Kilkenny cats but shall be united within and present a united front to the outside world. Then this war which we have gone through will remain for *all* South Africa as a memory and heritage of glory and not as a nightmare.' In that spirit he spoke at the unveiling of the Women's Monument at Bloemfontein on Dingaan's Day 1912. It was a passionately patriotic spirit.

It was, at the same time, politically realistic. The figures of the 1904 census made it plain that Afrikaners by themselves had no

* I have particularly in mind Milner's letter of 14 April 1905 to Selborne, and the latter's memorandum of 23 December 1905, both of which are cited by N. G. Garson in his study of Het Volk.

chance of achieving political power. Afrikaners in the Transvaal amounted to barely half of the white population and to far less than half of the potential voters.* In these circumstances, their leaders needed a policy which would unite their own people and divide English-speaking South Africans. The conciliation policy served those purposes. On the one hand, it healed the feuds of 'bitter-enders', 'hands-uppers' and 'national scouts'; on the other hand, it divided English-speaking South Africans along the lines of economic and ideological cleavage. Het Volk beat the anti-capitalist drum† and made bargains with the English-speaking radicals. It honoured those bargains. On the morrow of victory in the 1907 elections, Smuts wrote, 'I am most anxious *not* to have a pure Het Volk Ministry. On our policy of racial peace we carried many English constituencies with us, and I think we should continue in that policy night and day.'

The conciliation policy justified itself as an instrument—as *the* instrument—of state-building. It opened the way to a self-governing and united South Africa under Afrikaner political leadership. Thereby it provided a 'protective shield' for the reconstitution of a healthy and self-respecting Afrikaner society. Both chronologically and logically, the conciliation policy and the Afrikaner cultural renaissance went forward together.[2]

Nevertheless the policy entailed certain costs which made it, as time went on, a liability to its main promoters. It put political power into the hands of Afrikaners; but the symbols of that power were British; the King, the Flag, the Empire—they were all British. Botha and Smuts did not object to that; freedom, they said, was the thing that mattered, not its symbols; but many Afrikaners wanted their old freedom back with its old symbols. At the same time, they wanted quickly to achieve the tangible blessings of cultural, social and economic equality with English-speaking South Africans. While the conciliation policy opened the road to that end, it also put some brakes

* To be precise, Afrikaners would be far less than half of the voters *unless* Het Volk's advocacy of 'representation by population' proved successful, which in the event it did not. Boers (members of the Dutch Reformed Churches, as enumerated in the census) constituted 49·32 % of the total population but only 32·07 % of adult male whites.

† In the memorandum which Smuts took with him on his historic mission to London in December 1905, he insisted that responsible government would be a failure if its effect was simply to substitute the mine-owners for the Colonial Office as the real power in the Transvaal. In April 1905 Het Volk made a pact with the Responsible Government Association; in September 1906 it made one with that body's successor, the National Association. The objective was a combined front against the Progressive Party, whose capitalist affiliations were caricatured in D. C. Boonzaier's cartoons of Hoggenheimer.

on the rate of progress along the road. For example, Het Volk's electoral pact with the National Association made it impossible for Smuts to produce an Education Act so thoroughly egalitarian in its stipulations for the use of Dutch and English as was the Act which Hertzog produced in the Orange Free State: among impatient Afrikaners, that contrast signified a bad mark for Smuts.* Again, the conciliation policy imposed restraint upon Botha and Smuts in the steps they took to redress the Milnerite preponderance of the English language in public administration. By making proficiency in both languages a condition of promotion, at a time when English-speaking South Africans considered it their natural right to master no other language than their own, they made the civil service a sheltered industry for Afrikaners; but the linguistic transformation was bound to take time. Meanwhile, Afrikaans-speaking farmers received instruction from a predominantly English-speaking Agricultural Department, and poverty-stricken Afrikaners looking for jobs in the cities felt themselves to be lost among foreigners—foreign employers, foreign labour leaders, foreign officials.

Hertzog made himself the mouthpiece of Afrikaner disillusionment. Up to 1907 or thereabouts he too had been a conciliator; but he moved thereafter into a new phase of policy. In his De Wildt speech of 7 December 1912 he called conciliation an idle word which deceived nobody. A schism in Afrikanerdom followed. In January 1914, Hertzog became the leader of a new political organization, the National party.† Its methods were constitutional; but its membership was exclusively Afrikaner.

Hardly less than the Afrikaner nationalists, the English-speaking radicals felt disillusionment with Botha and Smuts. In particular, the Labour party accused them of having gone over to the side of Hoggenheimer.‡ That accusation had some force. Political responsibility had taught Botha and Smuts to recognize the mining industry

---

* Hertzog's party in the Free State, Orangia Unie, was unfettered by any such pact, which would indeed have been superfluous, seeing that the white population there was 90 % Afrikaans-speaking.

† Members of the National party were often called—and called themselves—Nationalists. That appellation had first belonged to the English-speaking allies of Het Volk in the Transvaal elections of 1907. In the Union elections of 1910 the followers of Botha and Smuts, Merriman and Hertzog had called themselves the South African National party; but by a formal decision of November 1911 they became simply the South African party. Consequently, the way was open to Hertzog to appropriate the word National, which the S.A.P. had discarded.　　　　　　　　　　‡ See note on p. 64 below.

for what it was, namely, South Africa's power house for economic development. Trade Unionists, on the other hand, expected the industry to pay its white workers at ten times the rate for black workers, and the Labour party achieved the distinction of being the first political organization in South Africa to make racial segregation a plank of its platform. Given the accelerating movement of Afrikaners into mining and industrial employment, the conditions appeared propitious for a pact between the Nationalists and Labour. That might well have been the sequel to the government's handling of the great strikes of 1913 and 1914, had not war broken out.

On the war issue, the National party and the Labour party went opposite ways. Labour—excepting Andrews's 'war on war' faction—supported the war policy of Botha and Smuts; the Nationalists opposed it. As leader of the opposition, Hertzog kept himself and his party on the constitutional path; but he refused to condemn the Afrikaner uprising of 1914. In the course of time, he drew political advantage from its emotional backwash. Before the war, his National party had had only five representatives in parliament; but the elections of 1915 revealed its rapid growth in the constituencies.

South African party	54
Unionist party*	40
National party	26
Labour party	4
Independents	6

Those figures of parliamentary representation did less than justice to the Nationalists. Their poll of 78,000 votes was nearly one-third of the total vote; it was 18,000 above the Unionist poll and only 16,000 short of the S.A.P.'s poll. Since many English-speaking voters supported the S.A.P., the Nationalists might fairly claim to have won half the Afrikaner voters to their side. In particular, they had made themselves the predominant party in the country districts which had seemed in 1910 to be Botha's impregnable fortress.

Smuts felt certain that the 1915 elections were their high water mark; but it proved not to be so. In by-elections during the four-year period 1915–19 they gained one seat and the S.A.P. lost one; Labour gained two seats and the Unionists lost two. Throughout this period, the S.A.P. government held office by grace of the Unionist

---

* Since 1910, this had been the name of the former Progressive party (or rather the Progressive parties in the various colonies).

party. That arrangement, although irksome to the Unionists, was
stable so long as the war lasted; but it could not be expected to survive
indefinitely when peace came. One way or another, the political
parties would have to be reshuffled.

The South African party still stood firm for the conciliation policy,
by which it meant an equal partnership of the two language groups
in the tasks of nation-building. It accused the Nationalists of 'racialism', by which it meant an exclusively Afrikaner conception of
South African nationhood.* Hertzog rejected that accusation. He
claimed to stand simply for the sovereign independence of South
Africa, both in its domestic and in its foreign policy. While asserting
South Africa's right of secession from the British Empire, he said
that the right would not be made effective except 'upon the broad
basis of the national will'.† His conception of nationality, like that
of Smuts, postulated an equal partnership between Afrikaners and
English-speaking South Africans, with firm foundations in a reso-
lutely bilingual system of education. Possibly, his main difference
from Smuts had its root in his estimate of the time factor: it would
be time for the two communities to come together, he seemed to
think, when the Afrikaans-speakers had achieved substantial equality
with the English-speakers: until then, let the life of each community
flow in its own separate stream. But Smuts believed that the time
for their coming together was now; if not now, it might prove to be
never.

Hertzog was studiously moderate in his prepared political statements; but his platform performances were too often vituperative
and incoherent. On these occasions, his emotions appeared to gain
the upper hand over his reason. He very quickly took colour from
his audiences. Consequently, it was hard to know for certain what he
stood for. Possibly, Hertzog himself did not clearly know. But he had
in his political following men who knew with complete precision
what they stood for.

In May 1918 the Afrikaner Broederbond constituted itself.‡ It was

---

* The contending concepts of South African nationality can be expressed in Afrikaans
as *Suid-Afrikaanse Volkseenheid* and *Afrikaner Volkseenheid*.

† 'op die breë grondslag van die volkswil'.

‡ The birthday of the Afrikaner Broederbond (as of Queen Victoria and Smuts) was
24 May, although on that date in 1918 the fourteen original members called their association Jong Suid-Afrika. The change of name to Afrikaner Broederbond was made within
the next four weeks.[3]

an *élite* dedicated to the service of the Afrikaner Volk. It recognized
no other nation in South Africa. In 1921 it took two fundamental
policy decisions—to maintain absolute secrecy and to fight for unilingual schools. The latter decision was just as much a challenge to
Hertzog as it was to Smuts; but more than ten years went by before
Hertzog accused the Broederbond of propagating a false doctrine of
nationality.* Probably, he had missed the significance of the Broederbond's inauguration and of its growth to greatness behind the screen
of his political leadership.

Whether or not Smuts knew anything about the Broederbond, he
did know that he would have to pay close attention not merely to the
transitory attitudes of Nationalist politicians, but also to the deep
forces operative in long term within the Nationalist movement.

On 6 September 1919 Smuts faced Parliament for the first time as
Prime Minister. In a special session of barely two weeks he guided
the debate on his resolution praying the King to ratify the peace
treaty on behalf of the Union of South Africa. He expounded South
Africa's sovereign status in the emergent order of League and
Commonwealth and sounded the call for the march forward.

Let us not mope over the past. Today we have every opportunity to build
our nation; and I am standing here to make the strongest, the most
urgent appeal to this House and the country to live in the present and the
future. Let us get off our ant-heap of grief and let us concentrate on the
great things which the future holds for us.

It was time, he pleaded, for a new beginning, time for both sections
of white South Africa to bury their feuds, close their ranks and work
together for their joint survival and greatness as a nation: 'I say woe
to the man or the party who stands in the way...Woe to me if I stand
in the way.' He affirmed three fundamental principles: first, agreement to abide by the British connection; secondly, co-operation
between the two white races; thirdly, the industrial development of
South Africa.[4]

In affirming those principles at that time he had a tactical purpose.
On his return to South Africa he had found under way a movement
for *hereniging*—that is to say, for a reunion of the two political camps
of Afrikaners. From 1915 onwards well-intentioned Afrikaners in

* See pp. 287–8 below.

both camps had been meeting each other at intervals in reunion congresses. During the first half of 1919 they had held two such congresses and they had agreed to hold a third at Paarl in the first week of October. Since the Paarl congress seemed likely to prove decisive one way or the other, Smuts thought it essential to make a clear statement of his terms for reunion. If the terms proved acceptable, a strong central party would probably take shape;* if they proved unacceptable, alternative means would have to be explored for achieving political stability. The Paarl congress failed to reach agreement on Smuts's terms. Specifically, it broke down on the issue of the British connection. A fortnight later, Hertzog baulked at the same issue when he gave his answer to Smuts's appeal for national unity. Speaking on 16 October at the Free State Congress of the National party, he declared that South Africa was faced with two alternatives: independence,† or a decline to the status of a Crown Colony. He admitted that the time was not yet ripe for achieving the country's independence; but he asserted the right of Afrikaners to work for independence until at last the day should come when they could say, 'The time has now arrived.'5

Smuts faced the fact that his terms for reunion had been rejected. The obvious alternative open to him was to seek a political deal with the Unionists. Such a deal, however, might become the occasion of a dangerous seepage of his Afrikaner followers into the Nationalist camp. He was not yet ready to run that risk. At a conference of his party in Bloemfontein on 11 December 1919 he announced his government's decision to hold a general election. 'We are going into the election', he declared, 'on our own legs without any understanding or pact with any other organization. My appeal is to the moderates of all parties.'

Polling day was fixed for 10 March 1920. Throughout the three months of strenuous campaigning, Smuts and his supporters never ceased to insist that secession was the crucial issue. They painted a lurid picture of the damage which secession would do to the peace

* No doubt this central party would have been harassed on both flanks by rival bands of irreconcilables, as happened when Hertzog and Smuts achieved reunion fourteen years later.

† Hertzog at that time equated independence with secession; he had not yet reached the conception of independence within the Commonwealth. Similarly, *Die Burger* (editorial of 7 February 1920) took it for granted that *onafhanklikheid* (independence) and *die Britse konneksie* (the British connection) were irreconcilable opposites.

and prosperity of South Africa. The Nationalists showed tactical
skill in blunting the force of this thrust. They stuck to their principles;
but they also pledged themselves to patience in applying them.
Independence, they insisted, must come some day; but the day was
not imminent. It would not dawn until a decisive majority of the
white population had been converted by constitutional means to
the cause of the republic.[6]

Large sections of the electorate shrugged off the secession issue.
Their mood and preoccupations were different. They were tired of
the party which had held office continuously for ten years. They believed that they were suffering severe economic hardships which were
due, they said, to the ineptitude of the government: in particular,
they attacked the government for its failure to redress the high cost
of living. Actually, the hardships of white South Africans during and
after the war were negligible in comparison with those of most other
nations; it was the black people who suffered most, because they did
not share the powers of collective bargaining or the other powers
which gave white people a fair chance of keeping their incomes in
alignment with prices. Apart from that, the rise of prices in South
Africa since 1914 had been below the world trend. But Smuts and
his party were out of luck; there was a steep rise in the year preceding
the election.*

As the campaign approached its climax Smuts realized that he
had little to hope for. On 8 March he wrote to Alice Clark:

Two days before the poll!...I am fighting very hard against the Nationalist
republican movement which is in essence a racial anti-British movement.
But during the war it attained to a surprising strength...I hope to be
able to hold my own...I am afraid in any case there is before me the
ugly prospect of going or forming a Coalition Government with the

*

*Cost of living index (food, fuel, light, and rent)
in nine South African towns 1914–20*

Year	Weighted average
1913	1000
1914	1092
1915	1126
1916	1158
1917	1248
1918	1289
1919	1376
1920	1698

Prime Minister, 1919–1924

Unionist Party (the old Jingo party now much sobered down). So you can realise my difficulties.[7]

His difficulties proved even more daunting than he had feared.

On polling day 284,312 electors (= 68·58 per cent of the 414,575 electors on the register) cast their votes. The results were as follows:

Candidates returned

South African party	National party	Unionist party	Labour party	Independents
41	44	25	21	3

The National party had gained seventeen seats and the South African party had lost twelve; the Labour party had gained fifteen seats and the Unionists had lost thirteen; the number of Independents had been halved. The Nationalists had won nearly all their victories in straight fights against the S.A.P. in country constituencies. The Labour party had won nearly all its victories—although not in straight fights—at the expense of Unionist candidates in urban constituencies.

Votes[8]

South African party	National party	Unionist party	Labour party	Independents
90,357	100,583	45,720[8]	39,943	9,610

Votes cast as a percentage of the total

31·57	35·14	15·97	13·96	3·36

For Smuts it was a catastrophic defeat. His once all-conquering party was now second to Hertzog's party both in its parliamentary representation and in the number of its supporters. The Nationalists had long since conquered the country districts of the Free State and were now conquering them in the western Cape and the Transvaal. In the cities, they had not yet made themselves dangerous challengers; but the great swing from the Unionists to Labour favoured them. Although Labour still remained schizophrenic in its attitude towards Smuts, he had to face the fact that it might at any time join with the Nationalists to pull him down. His government had no assurance of survival unless the twenty-five Unionists and the three Independents remained willing to vote on questions of confidence with the forty-one S.A.P. men. On that assumption, his parliamentary majority was four.

On that shoe string he governed for the next eleven months. He governed efficiently. The Governor-General's speech of 19 March 1920 announced a forthright programme of legislation and administration: to prevent profiteering in foodstuffs, to establish fair rents, to provide more houses, to reform the banking system, to foster agricultural and industrial expansion, to develop and improve the transport system, to make better provision for settling industrial disputes, to make important innovations in Native administration. The government kept parliament hard at work throughout the session in passing legislation which in large measure made these promises good. In mid-August Smuts wrote:

We are now in the last days of the session and next week the shutters will be up in the National Talking Shop. On the whole I have succeeded in putting through a great deal of excellent work. It is really curious to see what one can do with a parliamentary minority. We have done more and better work than the strongest government relying on a powerful majority has attempted. But my position remains precarious and insecure, and some reform of the government will be necessary before parliament meets next January.[9]

Ever since the elections, Smuts had had this need in mind. His position as a negotiator was now much weaker than it had been; but he showed no sign of admitting it. His first move was to propose a national government representing all four parties; but the Labour party and the National party both rejected the proposal. Hertzog then proposed an agreement between the National party and the S.A.P., on the basis of no secession now, but freedom for secessionist propaganda. Smuts rejected that bargain. Its consequence, he said, would be an Afrikaner bloc against English-speaking South Africans and a return to the reactionary politics of racialism.*

Nothing daunted, the zealots for reunion called a new congress at Robertson in May 1920. This congress proposed a national reunion conference—of 550 delegates from Hertzog's and Smuts's parties together—to meet at Bloemfontein on 22 September. It also approved thirteen articles as the basis of reunion. Most of the agreed articles

* een doorgaans anti-Engelsche combinatie en een terugkeer naar de rassenpolitiek die Zuid-Afrika reeds voor goed ontwassen is.

were uncontroversial; but article 3 had a more positive slant to secession than Smuts would accept. Following a meeting in June of his party's head committee, he wrote an open letter, spelling out the conditions for reunion in unambiguous words:

(1) The people of South Africa does not desire to limit its future political development as a free people, and leaves the door open for the evolution of that freedom under Divine Providence. It recognizes, at the same time, that any far-reaching change in our form of government can only rest, just as the establishment of our present Constitution by the National Convention, on the broad basis of the united will of the whole people—namely, on the co-operation of all sections of the white population, and not merely on a parliamentary majority.

(2) With a view to giving effect to the strong desire of the people for peace and unity, and having regard to the sharp division of opinion on constitutional questions, it is accepted that it is not in the best interests of South Africa to agitate for any change in our form of government as laid down in the Constitution; and that our constitutional development shall be left to the natural course of circumstances.

(3) No obligations or responsibilities towards other parts of the British Empire, or other countries, shall be undertaken which are contrary to the interests of South Africa or which detract from the existing status of South Africa.

(4) In application of the above fundamental principles, no distinction of race as regards the European population is recognized, but all who wish to co-operate on this basis are welcome in the reunion movement.[10]

F. S. Malan led the S.A.P. delegation at Bloemfontein. On the first day of the conference (22 September 1920) the Robertson proposals were moved as a resolution. On the second day F. S. Malan moved as an amendment the four propositions of Smuts's open letter. On the third day the conference broke down. Reunion had foundered once again on the rock of secession.

Five days later Smuts summoned a special conference of the South African party to meet at Bloemfontein on 27 October. The Nationalists, he said, had killed reunion by their insistence upon fanning the fires of secession and driving the European races apart from each other.[11] When the conference met, he put before it an alternative policy which he and Sir Thomas Smartt had recently hammered out.[12] That policy was the immediate and total absorption of the Unionist party into the S.A.P., on the basis of the four principles which Smuts had affirmed in his open letter.

On 27 October the South African party approved the Smuts–Smartt agreement. On 2 November, after some grumbling,* but in the end by a unanimous vote, the Unionist party approved it. Working out the details did not take long. On 25 November 1920 South Africans read in their newspapers that the historic Unionist party was allowing itself to be absorbed *en bloc* into the South African party.

Throughout this rush of events Smuts remained aware that the pace might prove too hot for some of his old comrades:

My people [he wrote in late October] are full of fears if the Unionists join us as a body as I think they will do. But I do not see any other exit out of the present political troubles. I cannot go on with 40 members in a house of 134. If I fail now it means that I am going to be scrapped politically. If I succeed, South African politics will have made a great step forward on the path of racial unity and nationhood. My friends are all somewhat scared by my pressure forward. But I feel necessity is laid on me, as a great man once said.[13]

He reassured his friends by telling them that the Unionists were by now so much changed as to be no longer the party which in the past had done so much damage to South Africa. None the less he was afraid that some old stalwarts of the S.A.P. might be unable to stand the shock of finding themselves under the same umbrella with their traditional enemies. He had good hopes of the younger men, particularly of J. F. H. Hofmeyr, the nephew of 'Onze Jan', whom he was trying at this time to bring into politics. The dissolution of the party of Rhodes and Jameson, he told Hofmeyr, was a glorious landmark on the road of South Africanism; but he could not feel sure that his own Afrikaners would see it in that light.[14]

He launched a whirlwind campaign to win the country to his way of thinking. On 26 November he announced new elections for 8 February 1921. On 3 December he opened his campaign at Pretoria with an onslaught against secession and an appeal for constructive nation building. This time he seized the initiative at the beginning of the campaign and held it right to the end. The Nationalist leaders pleaded, as they had done last time, that secession was not really the issue. They tried to wrest the initiative from Smuts by

* Some Unionists objected to being 'handed over to the S.A.P.'. They felt particular grief at losing their historic name and wanted it to be perpetuated by renaming the S.A.P. 'The United South African Party'. When the cabinet was reconstituted after the general election three ex-Unionists—Smartt, Duncan and Jagger—received portfolios.

denouncing him as an imperialist who was subordinating South Africa to British interests. They painted a lurid picture of the economic damage that he was doing to South Africa. The Labour politicians took up that theme. They denounced Smuts for his subservience to the capitalists and his failure to provide remedies for the economic ills of white South Africans. But he was able to enumerate specific and effective remedies which he had in fact provided during the past eleven months.* Moreover, he was at last enjoying some good luck. He was fighting the election during the short period of calm weather between the inflationary and the deflationary storms.†

It was as hard a fight as any that he ever fought. By Christmas he had a dull pain in his head which warned him that he was going beyond the limits even of his strength. For the last fortnight of the campaign he had a bleeding throat. He believed that he would just manage to reach 10 February without a physical breakdown.

I am fighting [he told Alice Clark] for my political life. If beaten now I shall probably be beaten finally. For I have left no back door, no line of retreat. I hope to win.

And he did win.

The Elections are over [he wrote on 15 February] and I am in command of a majority larger I believe than any P.M. has commanded for a very long time...My throat, which was very bad and bleeding...is right again.

He said that his affairs had prospered beyond all expectations. Not only had he beaten the Nationalists but he had brought the two white races together to a degree which people only a few months earlier would have declared impossible.[15]

In the elections of February 1921 there were twelve unopposed returns as compared with only three the previous March. Of 411,210 registered voters in contested constituencies 277,742 (= 67·54 per cent) cast their votes. The election results, in outline, were as follows:[16]

---

* E.g. the Profiteering Act, the Rent Act, the Housing Act and—of great importance for the South African economy in long term—the establishment of the Central Bank.

†   *Cost of living index* (see p. 29 above)

Year	Weighted average
1920	1698
1921	1494
1922	1320

	South African party	National party	Labour party	Independents and others
Candidates returned	79	45	9	1
Votes cast	139,635	105,039	27,526	3,113
Estimate for uncontested seats	14,349	1,376	1,627	2,191
Total (votes and estimated votes)	153,984	106,415	29,153	5,304
Percentage of total	52·22	36·09	9·89	1·80

Smuts had won an absolute majority of twenty-four seats.* His enlarged South African party had won thirteen more seats than the combined S.A.P. and Unionist total at the previous general election. Those gains, however, were predominantly in the cities and at the expense of the Labour party. In the country constituencies, the National party was still gaining ground. Its total poll was nearly 6,000 higher than at the previous elections, and it had gained one additional seat.

For these and for other reasons Smuts was flattering himself when he hailed the elections of 1921 as the opening of a new epoch for South Africa. All appearances to the contrary, his victory was precarious. Nevertheless it was a remarkable demonstration of his own effectiveness as a political force. He had struggled against a dangerous tide and had fought his way to the shore. He might do the same again. So long as he remained alive, no totally deterministic interpretation of South African politics could be convincing.

* Subsequently, following applications to the courts, two seats which the S.A.P. candidates thought they had won were awarded to their opponents.

3-2

CHAPTER 3

'THE LORD ADVANCES'

FROM September 1920 to February 1921 events moved with a rush: in September, climax and collapse of the reunion movement; in October–November, hot pursuit of the Unionists and their marriage by capture; from December to February, furious electioneering. Throughout these six months Smuts fought his South African battles with fierce concentration of purpose. Nevertheless, he did not forget the troubled condition of mankind. His temperament and training made it impossible for him to envisage South African politics and world politics in isolation from each other.

His picture of South Africa appeared serene in comparison with his world picture. 'Your affairs in the Old World', he wrote in October to an English friend, 'are in an awful mess; Ireland in a state of chaos; England in a great coal strike; the Poles in Vilna; Europe starving; millions in China dying from starvation etc. etc. When will the day dawn again over this scene of darkness?' In letter after letter he recited the lengthening list of the world's woes. On three separate occasions within two months he asked Alice Clark whether she still remained an optimist. Her habitual cheerfulness, he told her, was quite beyond his capacity. Nevertheless he told Professor Ward that human striving to achieve the good was not meaningless but had its firm anchorage in the constitution of the universe.* His affirmative spirit impelled him to action.[1]

To begin with, the action was philanthropic. He was in correspondence with Emily Hobhouse about her relief work in Leipzig and his government contributed on a pound for pound basis to a fund which Mrs Steyn was raising to help the work. Then he conceived the idea of a great Commonwealth fund for European relief. He wrote the draft of an appeal to be made by all the Commonwealth Prime Ministers; it was full of phrases about binding up the wounds of war and restoring the broken unity of the European family—echoes from the letters that he had written to his wife eighteen years earlier from Vereeniging. Prudent officialdom scotched this project but could not

* See p. 12 above.

prevent Smuts from giving his witness as a person. In anticipation of President Wilson's retirement on 4 March 1921 he wrote for the *New York Times* a long article under the heading, 'Woodrow Wilson's Place in History'. 'Wilson erred grievously', he told a friend, 'but he wrought a great work for the world and the future will justify him. I want to tell the Americans something about it and at the same time break a lance for the League.' In his official capacity, he broke another lance for it. Lloyd George's government was cold-shouldering Lord Robert Cecil, one of the architects of the League and its most prominent champion in Britain; but Smuts appointed Cecil as South Africa's representative at the League Assembly. Believing that the Great Powers were endangering the future of the League by associating it with their own interests, he instructed Cecil to press for the admission to the League of Germany and the other ex-enemy Powers. At the same time he was sufficiently a realist to understand that a small power like South Africa could achieve very little by acting in isolation. For this reason he welcomed the news which Lloyd George sent him in November 1920 that next June had been agreed upon as the most convenient time for a conference of 'the Prime Ministers of the Empire'. Smuts hoped that they would hammer out policies to help set the world to rights.[2]

His concept of a world-set-to-rights was essentially simple: free and equal nations peacefully pursuing their purposes within a co-operative international order. This was the concept of the Commonwealth which he had expounded in May 1917; it was the concept of the League which he had expounded in December 1918. He still clung to it, despite his disillusioning experience of national rivalries at the Paris Peace Conference. He still awaited the day when the peace of the peoples would 'follow, complete and amend' the peace of the statesmen. He still envisaged the League as the guardian of national freedom and world peace. If only the Great Powers would give the League the chance of establishing itself! The statesmen of the Commonwealth, he hoped, would guide the Great Powers into the right road.

This outlook and programme had their roots in the political philosophy of Western liberalism. Smuts had the encouragement and support of J. A. Hobson, C. P. Scott, Gilbert Murray and many other liberal friends. However, he had other friends, such as L. S. Amery, who considered his world picture naïvely optimistic. Across the

Atlantic, the United States Senate passed a similar judgment upon President Wilson's world picture. The Senate's repudiation of the League and, in particular, its objection to Dominion representation at Geneva gave fresh ammunition to the opponents of Smuts in South Africa. It encouraged their will to disbelieve the tall story that he was telling them about South Africa's new status among the nations. Alternatively, if that story turned out to be true, it encouraged them to oppose the use that Smuts was making of the new status. Instead of looking after his own country, they complained, he was meddling in European politics. The Americans were more sensible: their motto was 'No Foreign Entanglements'. It ought to be South Africa's motto. Smuts, despite his pious talk, could do nothing effective on the world scale. His vaunted world policy was merely a new disguise for his disastrous imperial policy.

Nationalist politicians after the First World War had a bogeyman—the much-advertised Imperial Conference for 'the readjustment of the constitutional relations of the component parts of the Empire'. The Imperial War Cabinet had resolved in March 1917 that this conference should meet as soon as possible after the war; in June 1920 Lord Milner announced that it would meet the following year. Thereupon the parliamentary Opposition in South Africa launched a determined attack against the Smuts–Milner conspiracy—as they deemed it to be—against South African independence. 'The Conference to be held next year', exclaimed F. W. Beyers, 'had only one aim, that of making the whole of the Empire speak with one voice, and against that the whole of Dutch-speaking South Africa protested, as it did not wish to be tied forever to the British Empire...Where was the country's right of self-determination?' Beyers quoted Article XI of the Covenant of the League of Nations to prove that South Africa was in danger of being drawn into the whirlpool of European politics. He attacked the provision on the Estimates of £20,000 towards the expenses of the League of Nations. Where, he asked, would it end? How could South Africa afford it? His party wanted South Africa to get her independence back. He attacked the appeal to the Privy Council and the King's right of veto—clear proofs, he declared, that South Africa's status was inferior to England's.

Beyers was peppering a wide target. A later speaker in the same debate, C. J. Langenhoven, kept his aim steadier. He declared that parliament and the country were entitled to be informed by the

Prime Minister, definitely and clearly, what the government's policy was towards the scheme for the closer union of the British Empire. He cited two propositions of Lord Milner's recent speech: first, the absolute equality of the Dominions in the management of their internal and external affairs; secondly, the Empire's need to speak with one united voice on foreign policy. Milner, it seemed, was afraid that conflict might arise between these principles of equality and unity, for he had asserted that some stronger means than the Imperial Conference was requisite for the Empire's solidarity in foreign policy. At this point of his speech Langenhoven uttered a warning against secret imperial diplomacy. South Africa, he declared, had a right to be told what was going to be done for and against her. Nevertheless, despite his suspicions and fears, he concluded his speech on a conciliatory note. He gave Smuts credit for having a sincere will to resist encroachments on South African freedom. If South Africa, the other Dominions and Britain were free to form a compact as perfectly equal allies, then let them—Langenhoven declared—be so many sovereign states and constitute the British Empire; but to bind them down by detrimental alliances would bring them to a far worse level than a Crown Colony.

Smuts spoke after Langenhoven. The debate, he said, had been constructive. He dealt systematically with the issues that had been raised. He admitted that the League had made a small and insignificant beginning and he enumerated the reasons, but he believed that it embodied a great hope for the world. He explained how South Africa's contribution had been fixed and saw some chance of its being scaled down; but he did not grudge the £20,000 on the Estimates as his country's contribution towards giving the League the chance of establishing itself. 'Unless the nations could get away from the spirit of exclusion and selfishness', he said, 'they were likely to see a recurrence of those calamities which had come over the world. Let them feel that they were members of one another.' Even now, he went on, economic calamity in distant countries was creating trouble for South Africa. To him, this was tangible proof that South African isolation was a dream. The nation should rather seek its destiny in active co-operation with other nations, both in the League and in the British Empire.

Smuts wanted the British Empire to change its name and call itself a Commonwealth; but the change had not yet been made. He made a list of the changes that still needed to be made in order to establish beyond all possibility of dispute the separate South African nationhood which the Paris Peace Conference had recognized. South Africa's formal correspondence with Britain, like that of the other Dominions, was still conducted through the Colonial Office; this must be changed. South Africa's Governor-General still represented not only the King but the British government; this must be changed. South Africa's relations with foreign countries were still conducted through the British Foreign Office; this too must be changed; South Africa, like Canada, must start appointing her own diplomatic representatives in foreign capitals.* The British Empire, Smuts insisted, could continue to exist only on the basis of complete freedom and equality. A new world had arisen and a new Empire had therefore to be moulded. That was the reason for holding the Constitutional Conference. Its task would be to remove the last vestiges of the old inequality and then, on the basis of total equality, 'to see in what way they could conduct the affairs of the Empire, in which all were interested, on a common basis'. Smuts believed that improved techniques of consultation and conference would prove the sufficient means of achieving unity of decision in foreign policy. Langenhoven had expressed the fear that South Africa would be dragged by a majority vote into imperial policies that were not her business; but Smuts gave him the categorical assurance that this would not happen.

No resolutions should be taken [he declared] without the unanimous consent of all the members of the Empire. Let them look to that as bedrock, and he would never agree to the voice of South Africa being smothered, or the opinion of South Africa being coerced by the majority vote of the rest of the British Empire, and he was sure that the other Dominions would take up the same position. That was the ground that should be taken not only by the Dominions, but by the British government—that no resolution should be taken binding upon any part of the Empire without its free consent. The only method would be the Conference system, and if they could agree to take a resolution, well and good; and if they could not do so, then they would have to go on without agreeing...

* On 10 May 1920 it had been announced both in the Canadian and British parliaments that Canada proposed to appoint a Minister Plenipotentiary to Washington. The terms of the announcement made it clear that the Minister would represent Canadian interests, but without prejudice to the diplomatic unity of the Empire. The appointment was not made until February 1927, three years after the Irish Free State had appointed —without any protestation of the Empire's diplomatic unity—its own Minister at Washington.

It seemed clear that if they wanted to reach their goal and remain in harmony with the British Empire and keep all the parts working together, they must follow this system of free deliberation and consent. The final decision so far as the Union was concerned rested, and would always rest, with one country and one body only—South Africa, the South African Parliament and Government. Let it be clearly understood, that, so far as he was concerned, whatever decision was to be taken and whatever final say was to be said with regard to South African affairs, it would not be said in London, or at any Conference, but by the people, the Parliament and the Government of that country.

The pledge was absolute. Langenhoven accepted it. But Langenhoven was thinking of the constitutional issue. There was also a political issue. Smuts was as insistent as the Nationalists were upon South Africa's sovereign right to decide her own destinies; but he held different ideas from theirs about what the decision ought to be. The major premiss of his speech was that the nations of the world were members one of another and that South Africa's membership of the League and the Commonwealth must be positive, active, co-operative. He said explicitly that he wanted South Africa to exercise her influence in the world. He went on to say that he wanted her to exercise it in association with the other nations of the British Empire —'protecting her own rights and continuing her status', he insisted, 'and determined always to do the best for herself, but never in a selfish way—to co-ordinate her own interests with those of the British Empire and the world as a whole'. This political idealism alarmed Dr D. F. Malan. In the concluding speech of the debate on the Nationalist side, Malan expressed the fear that consultation at Imperial Conferences would drag South Africa into all sorts of imbroglios which the South African people would know nothing about until after war had been declared.[3]

Malan thought, or professed to think, that Smuts was subservient to British policy; but senior civil servants in London thought the opposite. They saw Smuts as a danger to the British Empire, not because he did not care for it—they imputed no ill will to him—but because he did not understand it. The civil servants were custodians of a tradition which maintained that the Empire would stand or fall by its capacity to speak with one voice on the issues of foreign policy. Their predecessors in the 1830s had viewed with alarm the proposal to grant responsible government to the Canadians; in logic, they had argued, self-government must necessarily extend from home affairs to foreign affairs; the King would then receive from his separate governments separate advice on the issues of peace and war; when that happened, the Empire would fall to pieces.[4] To the civil servants of 1920 the day of disruption appeared imminent. In logic—and logic remained a virtue, if not the only virtue, of their calling—they could see one way only of reconciling the Empire's time-honoured diplomatic unity with the expanding autonomy of its several parts: imperial federation was that one way. They recalled the high hopes of imperial federation that had been held early in 1917; they also recalled that Smuts had been principally responsible for killing those hopes. They did not deny that he had had his reasons; but they did reproach him for his failure to produce any constructive alternative. His policy, they complained, was altogether negative. In their eyes, negation meant disruption. They quoted the disruptive letter to Lloyd George in which Botha, prompted by Smuts, had announced South Africa's repudiation of any commitment arising from the proposed British guarantee to France and—to rub salt into the wound—had coolly looked forward to the day when one or more of the Dominions, in exercise of their sovereign rights, might decide to remain neutral in a British war.* Everything that Smuts had said and done since then, they argued, pointed towards that day. In their view, his concept of the Empire was completely separatist, subject only to the separate parts recognizing the same King. That, they recalled, had been the relation of Great Britain with Hanover under the early Georges. Its constitutional, political and military significance was zero.[5]

Their analysis was sharp, but lopsided. Their political masters knew Smuts better than they did and recognized the positive elements of his thought—his emphasis upon the Crown, upon the procedures of consultation and conference, upon the common values and the co-operative will which held the British Commonwealth together. But for how long? British civil servants were not the only people who feared that the diffusion of political sovereignty throughout the Empire would sooner or later destroy its will to survive as one community. Politicians in New Zealand looked back nostalgically to the Imperial War Cabinets of the latter war years and viewed with apprehension their country's separate and exposed position as a signatory of the Peace Treaties and a member of the

* See p. 5 above.

League of Nations. Politicians in Australia took up a half-way position. W. M. Hughes, the Prime Minister, was insistent upon Australia's right to speak with her own voice on everything that touched her interests; but he had no intention of spelling out that right as doctrine. In his view, doctrinaires and codifiers were mischievous people. The Empire, he thought, would continue to rub along very well if only those people would let it alone.

Smuts did not have the option of letting it alone. Both his personal history and his political circumstances compelled him to formulate a doctrine, to promulgate a code. In letters to his wife from London during the last years of the war and from Paris during the Peace Conference he had recalled his fight twenty years earlier for the sovereign independence of the South African Republic; but now, he told her, the prize was far greater—the sovereign independence of united South Africa.* He was bound to make that claim good in his wife's eyes and in his own. He was bound to make it good in the eyes of nationalist Afrikanerdom, in so far as he could persuade its political leaders to recognize the new situation. In an important debate of May 1921 he made one more attempt to persuade them. He announced that he would be setting out early next month with two of his colleagues to attend the Conference of Prime Ministers in London: it would not be, even now, the much-postponed constitutional conference; but it would prepare the agenda for that conference and would also discuss some urgent problems of foreign policy and defence. He called upon South Africans to accept two basic ideas: first, the idea of a self-reliant nation, bearing so far as it was able the burden of its own defence, mistress in its own house, independent in all the essential meanings of that word; secondly, the idea of a co-operating nation, in active partnership with the other nations of the Empire and the League. Two hundred years ago, he said, it might have been possible for South Africans to live their lives in isolation; but, as the world was now developing and amidst the dangers surrounding every country, isolation was no longer possible.

In reply to Smuts's pleadings, Hertzog declared it ridiculous for South Africa to participate in the talks on defence when she did not possess even a small barge of her own. As for her participating in the talks on foreign policy, England's whole object was to get her bound down. He appealed to the Prime Minister to confine himself to the

* Cf. *Smuts: The Sanguine Years* (Cambridge, 1962), pp. 437, 497.

43

affairs of South Africa and take as little part as possible in the affairs of the Empire: let him send some subordinate person to conferences in London, instead of going there himself. Later in the debate, D. F. Malan spoke to the same tune. For good measure he accused the Prime Minister of threatening the South African nation by bringing in immigrants from Britain and he called for a drastic cut* in South Africa's contribution to the League of Nations.[6]

This sterile debate must have convinced Smuts, if he still needed convincing, that the need was now urgent to clear up the obscurities of his country's status. That was the opening argument of a memorandum on the constitutional relations of the British Commonwealth which he took with him to London.

I would emphasize the urgency of the subject [he wrote] and the necessity of as early a settlement as possible. Delay in the settlement of Dominion status is fraught with grave dangers. The British Commonwealth cannot escape the atmosphere of political unsettlement and change which is affecting most other countries. The national temperature of all young countries has been raised by the events of the great war. The national sense, the consciousness of nationhood of the Dominions has received a great impetus from their share in the great war and from the experiences of hundreds of thousands of Dominion troops in the great war. While these experiences have strengthened the common bonds, they have undoubtedly also deepened the Dominion sense of national separateness, of the Dominions as distinct nations in the Commonwealth and the world. And with this sense goes a feeling of legitimate pride and self respect which affects the rank and file of these young nations just as much as their political leaders. Unless Dominion status is settled soon in a way which will satisfy the legitimate aspirations of these young nations, we must look for separatist movements in the Commonwealth. Such movements already exist, notably in South Africa, but potentially in several of the other Dominions also. And the only way to deal with such developments is not to wait until they become fully developed, and perhaps irresistible in their impetus, but to forestall them and make them unnecessary by the most generous satisfaction of the Dominion sense of nationhood and statehood. The warning against always being too late in coming to a proper settlement, which the example of Ireland gives to the whole Commonwealth, is one which we can only neglect at our own peril.

Smuts therefore proposed the promulgation of 'A General Declaration of Constitutional Right'. That proposal had recently been put forward by a young Australian, H. Duncan Hall, in chapter ix of his book, *The British Commonwealth of Nations*. The book had made

---

* Dr Malan thought £15,000 per annum sufficient.

a stir in Great Britain and had attracted considerable attention in South Africa.[7] Smuts himself had studied it closely and believed that foreign statesmen could do the same with profit to themselves.

Foreigners [he wrote] find it difficult to understand the unwritten British Constitution, in which precedents mould and expand the Constitution, and the legal aspect is nothing and the constitutional everything.* Even in America the Senate debates over the reservations in regard to the voting power of the British Empire in the Assembly of the League of Nations are a warning to us. Other people find it difficult to grasp the difference between legal theory and constitutional practice in the Empire and to see how the law of the constitution is moulded and finally abrogated by the practice of the constitution, and how, without a change of the law, a British colony becomes in constitutional fact an independent State. These abstruse matters might be cleared up in some formal way which would show the true nature of the Dominion status as distinct from the legal archaisms. It has been suggested by Mr Duncan Hall in his interesting book on the British Commonwealth of Nations, that a declaration of Constitutional Rights should be made which would explain the new developments in the Dominion Status, remove obscurities, set at rest doubts and abrogate what is obsolete—a declaration, in fact, which would become a precedent and a most important amendment of the unwritten law of the constitution. Such a declaration would set out that, as a matter of constitutional right, the British Parliament has no legislative power in respect of the Dominions; that the King has no more constitutional right of vetoing Dominion Bills than he has in respect of British Bills; and that the King in his Dominion Government has in respect of foreign affairs affecting the Dominions the same constitutional right that he has as King in his British Government in respect of the United Kingdom.

Smuts enumerated some additional items which the declaration would deal with and he proposed a procedure for drafting, passing and promulgating it. He made his meaning clear on one other matter. Decision upon the content of the declaration must not be postponed until next year's constitutional conference. The main principles could and should be decided and published now, even if the final drafting and formal promulgation of the declaration had to wait until 1923.

As Smuts saw the situation, the Prime Ministers of the Commonwealth could go immediately into action because of the commitment they had accepted to draft the agenda for next year's constitutional conference. He wanted them to tackle their task in a positive spirit:

* At the Imperial War Conference of 1917, Sir Robert Borden had heavily emphasized the importance of this distinction between legal and constitutional right.[8]

not merely to make a list of topics, but to propose a series of resolutions.

If this is not done [he wrote] there is every risk that the Conference [i.e. next year's constitutional conference] may resolve itself into a series of academic discussions on some of the most abstruse and intricate questions in the whole range of constitutional law. In that way the Conference might prove abortive and futile, and public opinion in the Dominions might become exasperated. From bitter experience in South Africa extending over about two years of public discussion, I feel that public opinion requires education—it requires a lead—it requires practical suggestions for its guidance through a maze of questions which even technical lawyers find it difficult to follow. If a series of resolutions were passed...as a programme for discussion at the Conference, and if these resolutions were published as soon as possible in order to guide the formation of public opinion all over the Commonwealth, we should go far in ensuring the success of the Conference and in making it the greatest landmark in the history of the Commonwealth. Nay more...the Conference could be made a larger and more representative body and embrace representatives from other parties as well as from the Government...This enlarged Conference, if successful, could then become a precedent for the future and take the place of the present Imperial Conference which is not a very satisfactory body.

Towards the close of his memorandum Smuts emphasized the need for symbolic recognition of the change from Empire to Commonwealth. 'It will no longer be an Empire', he wrote, 'but a society of free and equal sister states.' He proposed that this society should stop calling itself the British Empire and call itself instead the British Commonwealth of Nations. He proposed further that each sister nation of the society should adopt its own distinctive national flag. Meanwhile, he conformed with a good grace to the established usages. For example, although he considered the term Imperial Cabinet to be not merely a misnomer but the cause of dangerous misunderstandings,* he used it once or twice in his memorandum.

---

* Smuts wrote: 'This name is a misnomer, as it is no Cabinet and takes no executive action, nor is there joint responsibility to any Parliament...The Imperial Cabinet is really and substantially a Prime Ministers' Conference...' But L. S. Amery (to Smuts 20 June 1921) made a plea for retaining the name. 'The essence of a Cabinet', he wrote, 'is not that it is executive—the Executive lies in the several Ministers—nor that it is responsible to a single Parliament. It lies in the sense of intimacy and collegiality, and though the name is at this time criticized in one or two quarters, I should be inclined to let it run on concurrently with the name "Prime Ministers' Conference" in the belief that it will, before long, be generally accepted.' The view of Smuts prevailed; but Amery retained a nostalgic affection for the Imperial Cabinet as a concept and as a name.

Indeed, he had left himself no time for niggling at phrases. His memorandum added up to approximately 4,000 words. Its concluding summary demonstrated how much thought he had packed into that small space.

To summarize the above suggestions:

1. The Imperial Cabinet should draft a general scheme of future constitutional relations for the British Commonwealth, and this scheme should take the form of a series of concrete resolutions to be submitted for the consideration of the Constitutional Conference next year, and to be published for general information and public discussion in the meantime.

2. The scope of the resolutions should be the practical recognition of the equality of statehood of the Dominions with the United Kingdom and the methods of conference and consultation to be adopted in future in respect of common policies and concerns of the Commonwealth.

3. The resolutions should provide that legislation of the British Parliament be passed (*a*) giving power of amendment in respect of their Constitutions to the Dominions, (*b*) extending their legislative jurisdiction beyond their territorial limits, and (*c*) abrogating the Colonial Laws Validity Act in its application to future Dominion legislation.

4. The resolutions should further provide that a Declaration of Rights be presented by the Constitutional Conference for the acceptance of the King, providing (*a*) that the British Parliament has no constitutional right of legislation in respect of the Dominions, (*b*) that the Royal veto is in the same constitutional position in the Dominions as in the United Kingdom, (*c*) that the Dominions have direct access to the Sovereign without the intervention of any British Secretary of State, and (*d*) that the international status and right of diplomatic representation of the Dominions is unquestioned.

5. The resolutions should further provide (*a*) that Dominion affairs be removed from the Secretary of State for the Colonies and placed under a Dominions Committee, consisting of the Commonwealth Prime Ministers or their nominees and having direct access to the King; and (*b*) that in future the Governor-General in the Dominion shall be simply and solely a Viceroy, representative of the Sovereign.

6. With regard to the methods of conference and consultation the resolutions should provide that there be (*a*) a quadrennial Commonwealth Congress, (*b*) a biennial Prime Ministers' Conference (in lieu of the Imperial Cabinet), and (*c*) a continuous Dominions Committee; all with scope as above explained.

7. (*a*) To mark the fundamental change in the character of the British Empire, the resolutions should provide that its name be altered to that

of the British Commonwealth of Nations. (*b*) To mark the fundamental change in the status of the Dominions, the resolutions should provide that besides a common Imperial flag (which may be the Union Jack) each Dominion should have its own distinctive national flag.

Smuts's memorandum of June 1921 contained by anticipation the Balfour Declaration of 1926 and the entire constitutional achievement from then until the Statute of Westminster of 1931; but Smuts gained no credit from it. By the irony of fate, he found his plans frustrated by the principle of unanimity, which he himself, when reassuring the distrustful Nationalists, had declared to be 'bedrock' in all the affairs of the Commonwealth. The principle of unanimity made it possible for any Dominion Prime Minister to veto any and every proposal for constitutional change. W. M. Hughes of Australia was determined to do precisely that. 'Leave the Empire alone' was his motto; he had declared it before he left Australia; he declared it on his arrival in England; he declared it again at the first meeting of the Prime Ministers. On every possible occasion he declared himself implacably opposed to constitution-mongering of any kind, either now or later. He saw no sense in making preparations for next year's constitutional conference because he saw no sense in summoning the conference.

It may be that I am very dense [he declared] but I am totally at a loss to understand what it is that the constitutional conference proposes to do. Is it that the Dominions are seeking new powers, or are desirous of using powers they already have, or is the conference to draw up a declaration of rights, to set down in black and white the relations between Britain and the Dominions? What is the conference to do? What is the reason for calling it together? I know, of course, the resolution of the 1917 Conference. But much water has run under the bridge since then. Surely this Conference is not intended to limit the rights we have now. Yet what new right, what extension of power, can it give us? What is there we cannot do now?[9]

Smuts was the target of this rhetoric and he knew it. He also knew that Hughes was carrying the conference with him. Rightly or wrongly, he saw no point in circulating his memorandum until he had prepared the ground for it by a verbal exposition of its principles and proposals.* Even that opportunity was denied him until the

* On his arrival in England he had shown his memorandum to L. S. Amery, who approved his exposition of Dominion sovereignty but wanted him to put more emphasis upon the elements of unity in the Commonwealth, such as the Crown and the common

conference was close to its end. At the 22nd meeting, after the conference had dealt successively with foreign policy in general, the Anglo-Japanese Treaty, and defence, he made his plea for the General Declaration of Constitutional Right. No other Prime Minister supported him. Massey of New Zealand accused him of trying to foist a written constitution on the Empire. He denied it. He persuaded his colleagues to discuss his proposal informally. The informal discussions went no better for him than the formal debate had gone. The final upshot was a resolution repudiating not only Smuts's proposed declaration, but also the constitutional conference which all the Prime Ministers had approved hitherto. It was a crushing victory for W. M. Hughes. He told the Australians on his return home that he had soldered up the constitutional tinkers in their own tin can.

Smuts had been ahead of his time. Five years later, Hertzog enjoyed better luck. Between 1921 and 1926, the Prime Ministers of the Commonwealth became a different constellation. Hughes's star sank. Mackenzie King's star rose. Amery became Secretary of State. Pacemaking Irishmen joined the Commonwealth. But they might not have done so had it not been for some work that Smuts did in June and July 1921.

Smuts was known to his friends, including his Irish friends, as a champion of national freedom for Ireland. In July 1919, on the eve of his return home after his two and a half years' service in Europe, he committed himself publicly to that cause. In his farewell message he told the British people that the Irish wound was poisoning their whole system. He told them that freedom was the only remedy in Ireland, as it had been the remedy in his own country and in other parts of the British Empire. Unless that remedy were applied in Ireland, he declared, the British Empire must cease to exist.*

Throughout the next two years he saw no sign at all of the British government paying heed to his warning. On the contrary, he saw the condition of Ireland drifting from bad to worse. In January 1919 Dáil Éireann issued a declaration of Irish independence and set up

citizenship. Smuts might have redrafted it, had he seen any prospect of getting it seriously considered. Later on, the memorandum gave grist to Hertzog's mill; but Hertzog appeared to think that Smuts should have circulated it officially. See p. 205 below.

* Cf. *Smuts: The Sanguine Years*, p. 547.

a republican government. A native Irish state, with its own courts, its executive departments and its armed forces took shape within the shell of the United Kingdom. In mid-1920 the British government launched a determined campaign to destroy this Irish state by force. In December 1920 the Government of Ireland Act imposed limited Home Rule upon the partitioned areas of Northern and Southern Ireland. Dáil Éireann denounced the Government of Ireland Act as a new British aggression against independent and united Ireland. The fighting grew more savage. An Irish judge called it 'competition in crime'.[10]

Nevertheless, civilized and patriotic men on both sides of St George's Channel continued to work for Anglo-Irish reconciliation. In Ireland, Sir Horace Plunkett and his Irish Dominion League drew inspiration from the concept of the Commonwealth which Smuts had expounded. Their programme, with its strong Irish roots in the political theory of Molyneux, Swift, Grattan and Griffith, offered the hope of a negotiated settlement. Meanwhile a passionate revolt was arising in Britain against the attempt to subdue Ireland by force. Not only the Liberal newspapers but *The Times* and the *Round Table*, not only Labour and the Asquithian Liberals but Lord Robert Cecil and other prominent conservatives denounced British frightfulness in Ireland. King George V let his ministers know that 'the policy of reprisals' was repugnant to him. The government persisted in that policy; but it also began to explore the chances of negotiation. These explorations were secret and, up to the time of Smuts's arrival in London, fruitless.

A good many people were pinning their hopes on Smuts. His fellow-soldier and friend in the East African campaign, Tom Casement—Roger Casement's brother—had for some time past been sending him pamphlets about the rights of Ireland and the misdeeds of Britain. Smuts found waiting for him at Madeira when his ship put in there another batch from Tom Casement. A week later he found waiting for him in London a letter from Lady Courtney, who wanted him to meet Erskine Childers, and a letter from Sir Horace Plunkett, who enclosed some thoughtful proposals for a settlement of the Irish question on Dominion lines.* These three people held

* Amongst these proposals was the 'Memorial of Certain Irishmen', recently addressed to Lloyd George, and a careful exploration of the constitutional problem by A. D. Lindsay of Balliol.

divergent ideas about what needed to be done; but each of them believed that Smuts was the man to do it.

My language is crude [Tom Casement wrote] but when a man has stood through thick and thin and fought for another man he feels he has some slight excuse to bring his own affairs before him. I want you to try and come for a few days to Ireland. I want you to meet the kindliest people in the world and I want you to see the country. You will then grasp what it means to us to have our country to ourselves...Privately, I have always felt that you would some day be a big factor in settling our question. I may be wrong, but I have pinned a lot of faith on you. You went through the mill years ago and see things quite differently from the narrow political point.

In this situation [Sir Horace Plunkett wrote] it occurs to me that you may see your way, on account of the Imperial interests involved, to use your personal influence to promote an Irish settlement. From a pretty full knowledge of my countrymen at home and abroad I can truthfully say that no living statesman would be more acceptable to the majority of the Irish people as a political adviser than yourself.

You will soon find [Lady Courtney wrote] that people *of many points of view* are looking to you to help us about Ireland—in fact you are almost in as dangerous a position as Wilson was when he landed in France: I know you will not, like him, make glorious speeches first and realize or *not* realize their application afterwards.[11]

Smuts landed in England on Saturday 11 June. He made no pronouncement on Ireland but quietly brought himself up to date with the Irish news. He spent the evenings of his first week-end with the Gilletts, who had taken a house in London for the period of his visit. On Monday 13 June, only two days after his landing, he saw and seized an opportunity for action.

On Monday [he told his wife] I was at Windsor Castle for lunch—Smartt, Mentz and I with the King, the Queen and Princess Mary. It was very sociable and pleasant. After lunch the other two went over the palace, but I sat talking with the King until 4.30, especially about Ireland. I am doing my best to do something about Ireland.[12]

That was a modest statement. In their two hours' talk that Monday afternoon King George V and Smuts broke the Irish log jam.

Smuts found the King 'anxiously preoccupied' with thoughts of a duty which his ministers had laid upon him—to open the new parliament of Northern Ireland on Wednesday 22 June. The King had not yet seen any draft of the speech that he would have to make, but he was afraid that his very presence in Belfast would appear as an affront to the majority of his Irish subjects. Lord Stamfordham, his Private Secretary, was indignant with the government's action in sending the King on a mission which might prove to be not only unpleasant but dangerous. Smuts, on the contrary, saw the mission as an opportunity. Could not the King bring a message of peace and hope to all his Irish subjects? At the King's request, Smuts composed a draft of the message. He sent it to the King next morning, together with the copy of a letter, enclosing the draft, which he had written to Lloyd George.[13]

The draft ran as follows:

Declaration

I have come here today not only to open this Parliament but also and especially to testify to my love for and my sympathy with Ireland and the Irish people as a whole. As the Sovereign and Executive Head of the British Empire, I bring to Ireland today a message of good will and sympathy in all the trials and sorrows through which she is passing. My world-wide Empire is a system of human government which rests on certain principles and ideals of freedom and co-operation, which must find their application in Ireland no less than in the other parts. I trust that the establishment of this Parliament for North East Ireland will be found to have removed what has in the past proved an insurmountable obstacle to the realization of this high destiny for Ireland as a whole, and that the path is now clear for a lasting settlement of the age-long misunderstanding and estrangement. God grant that there may be found here too the spirit of wisdom and moderation which under somewhat similar circumstances brought appeasement* and reconciliation to another great portion of my Empire.

In those five sentences Smuts submitted to the King the epitome of his political philosophy and—as he then interpreted it—his political experience. He believed them to be relevant to the condition of Ireland. The King was ready and eager to believe the same; but he was also aware that he could take no official action in Belfast on the advice of Smuts. In everything that affected Ireland, it was his constitutional duty to act on the advice of his government in the United Kingdom.

* On the original meaning which Smuts gave to the word 'appeasement', and on the different meanings given to it in later years, see pp. 271–2 below; see also *Smuts: The Sanguine Years*, pp. 512–13.

Consequently, it was necessary to put Smuts's draft declaration into the proper constitutional channel. Before he left Windsor on the Monday afternoon, Smuts had agreed with the King and with Lord Stamfordham that he would send the draft to Lloyd George, who was at the time staying out of London owing to an indisposition. On Tuesday morning Smuts kept some appointments which Lord Stamfordham had made for him. He had an encouraging talk with Lord Fitzalan, the newly appointed (and the first Roman Catholic) Viceroy of Ireland; but he thought it prudent not to show his draft to the Viceroy before it had reached the Prime Minister. On leaving Fitzalan he called on Sir Edward Grigg, one of the Prime Minister's secretaries. He handed Grigg his draft declaration and its covering letter and received the assurance that they would go down to the Prime Minister by bag that evening. The cautious Grigg laid ponderous stress upon the complexities of the situation and the consequent need to strike a balance between conflicting considerations; but Smuts's argument impressed him. He felt sure that the Prime Minister would give it his whole attention.[14]

In his letter to Lloyd George, Smuts was forthright. He began quietly enough, with a sentence expressing his concern for the Prime Minister in his indisposition and another sentence of apology for troubling him at such a time; but—he went on—his business was of extreme urgency.

I need not enlarge to you on the importance of the Irish question for the Empire as a whole. The present situation is an unmeasured calamity; it is a negation of all the principles of government which we have professed as the basis of Empire, and it must more and more tend to poison both our Empire relations and our foreign relations. Besides, the present methods are frightfully expensive in a financial sense no less than in a moral sense; and what is worse they have failed.

In those three sentences of scorching indictment Smuts dismissed the past and present of Lloyd George's Irish policy. What, he asked, was the next move? In a situation which seemed almost desperate he saw two elements of hope: first, the old stumbling block of the coercion of Ulster had now at last been removed; secondly, the King was going to Belfast next week to open the Ulster Parliament. It was questionable whether he ought to go; but his going would be fully justified if it were made the occasion for declaring a new policy towards Ireland.

The Irish might accept it as coming from the King, and in that way the opening might be given you for a final settlement. I would suggest that in his speech to the Ulster Parliament the King should foreshadow the grant of Dominion Status to Ireland, and point out that the removal of all possibility of coercing Ulster now renders such a solution possible. The promise of Dominion status *by the King* would create a new and definite situation which would crystallize opinion favourably both in Ireland and elsewhere. Informal negotiations could then be set going with responsible Irish leaders...Such a declaration would not be a mere kite, but would have to be adopted by you as your policy, and the King could of course only make it on your advice.

Smuts was insistent upon that constitutional point. Nevertheless, in concluding his letter, he expressed the belief that all the Dominion Prime Ministers would support the British Prime Minister if he took the present opportunity of launching this new policy towards Ireland.[15]

Lloyd George and his British colleagues had barely a week in which to make up their minds. On Thursday 16 June, a committee of the cabinet, with Sir Austen Chamberlain in the chair, considered a draft of the King's speech. Lord Stamfordham was present in consequence of some firm representations that he had made: the King, he had said, 'considered that he had been kept in the dark with regard to the speech to be made on the opening of the Parliament in Belfast...and that...he should be made acquainted with the views of the Cabinet, especially after his recent conversation with General Smuts'. Lord Stamfordham showed no sign of any dissatisfaction with the progress made that day in redrafting the speech; but he took note that the final decisions would be made at a meeting which the Prime Minister was calling the next day at Chequers. The day after that—Saturday 18 June—the Prime Minister would go to Windsor to report the result to the King.[16]

The King's speech, as finally approved, did not contain the five-sentence Declaration which Smuts had drafted on 13 June. Nevertheless it embodied the thought of Smuts and bore the imprint of his style. Words that Smuts had spoken and written at Vereeniging were heard again at Belfast on 22 June 1921. The King prayed that his coming to Ireland that day might prove to be the first step towards the end of strife among the people of Ireland. 'In that hope', he continued, 'I appeal to all Irishmen to pause, to stretch out the hand of forbearance and conciliation, to forgive and forget, and to join in making for the land they love a new era of peace, contentment and good will.'[17]

The King's speech in Belfast achieved all that Smuts had hoped from it. Lloyd George himself felt that. In a letter to the King next day he expressed his deep thankfulness: 'None but the King could have made that personal appeal; none but the King could have evoked so instantaneous a response.' He gave his promise that the government would spare no effort to follow up this great opportunity. The King expected the government to make its effort at once; on 24 June he sent Lord Stamfordham to the Prime Minister to impress on him the need for prompt action. Lloyd George was able to report that he had taken action already. The Cabinet had decided that same morning to invite to London Mr De Valera, as 'the chosen leader of the majority of Southern Ireland', and Sir James Craig, as 'the Premier of Northern Ireland'. The Cabinet had also decided that its best intermediary with the Southern Irish would be General Smuts, who had once been in a position very similar to that of Mr De Valera.[18]

On 28 June Craig and De Valera both replied to the British invitation. The former accepted it; but the latter said that, much as he desired a lasting peace between the English and the Irish, he could see no road leading to peace so long as the English denied Ireland's essential unity and her right of national self-determination. Instead of accepting Lloyd George's invitation to London, he invited Craig to a conference in Dublin. He invited some other representatives of 'the minority' to the same conference. They accepted; Craig refused. Craig and De Valera, on their separate assumptions, were equally logical: if Craig went to Dublin, he would in effect be recognizing De Valera's claim to be the lawful President of a united Ireland; if De Valera went to London—on the terms, at any rate, which Lloyd George had proposed both to him and Craig—he would in effect be recognizing Craig as co-equal with himself in a partitioned Ireland. It looked like an impasse.

When the King received this disappointing news his first thought was that Smuts must move at once into action. Lord Stamfordham explained the King's wishes to Grigg, who replied that Smuts was waiting until the time was ripe. Lord Stamfordham made a note of his conversation with Grigg and the King wrote in pencil at the bottom of the typescript: 'If De Valera won't come over I hope

Smuts will go to him and make him come.'[19] But Smuts was no longer so impatient for action as he had been two weeks earlier. He realized that the time had come to move cautiously. The prospect of a military truce was emerging from De Valera's talks with the minority spokesmen in Southern Ireland, and their representations to the British government. Smuts himself was having talks with emissaries of De Valera in London. He was resolved on no account to go to Dublin in the guise of a British agent. He was working and waiting patiently for an Irish invitation. It came at the end of June. On 1 July he asked Lord Stamfordham to inform the King that he would be meeting Mr De Valera in Dublin four days later. He explained what his objective would be at that meeting: to ascertain De Valera's views and to try to establish with him some preliminary basis for an agreement, in order to reduce the risk of failure at the conference in London if and when it took place. Smuts asked Lord Stamfordham to express to the King his regret at being unable, 'owing to the peculiar circumstances', to attend the State Banquet on 4 July. He hoped that the King might find it possible to receive him and hear his report after his return from Dublin.[20]

Lord Stamfordham replied the same day:

The King desires me to say how delighted he is that you have accepted Mr De Valera's invitation to visit him in Dublin on Tuesday next. For His Majesty is impressed with the belief that *you* of all men will be able to induce Mr De Valera to be reasonable and to agree to a settlement.[21]

Inducing Mr De Valera to be reasonable, as both the King and Smuts understood that word, proved to be a more complicated and time-consuming task than either they or the British Prime Minister or—for that matter—Irish patriots of the Tom Casement or the Horace Plunkett stamp had ever conceived.*

Smuts tried, but with indifferent success, to keep his mission to Dublin secret.† He travelled *incognito* as Mr Smith—the same designation as he had given himself in December 1917, when he had set out from London to talk peace in Switzerland with Baron Mensdorff, the emissary of the Hapsburg Empire. By mid-morning on 5 July

* Sir Horace Plunkett, in his letter to Smuts of 8 June (see p. 51 above), had claimed, and had cited strong evidence in support of his claim, that a settlement on the Dominion principle would win general acceptance in Ireland.

† On 3 July the *Manchester Evening Chronicle* and the *Morning Post* published news items foreshadowing it. On 5 July the *Westminster Gazette* and some other papers announced, with corroborative detail, his arrival that morning at Kingston.

he was in conference at the Mansion House in Dublin with De Valera and three of his ministerial colleagues. He explained at the outset that he had been determined *not* to come to see De Valera unless De Valera invited him to come. He insisted that he had not come as an emissary of the British government: he brought no proposals from that government: he had no connection with it. He came as a friend who had passed through similar troubles. He could assure them that an intense desire for peace existed in England; that the King shared that desire; that the King's words at Belfast had been spoken from the heart.

It was a good opening; but suddenly the going became difficult. De Valera might be ready to believe the news that Smuts brought of the King's good will but he found it difficult to believe any good of the King's government. He distrusted its invitation to a conference. Lloyd George, he said, wanted to get him and Craig around a table where they would be like two small boys; they would inevitably disagree and the Prime Minister would profit by their disagreement. Smuts replied by telling De Valera that he would be making the greatest mistake of his life if he refused to take part in the proposed discussions; refusal would put him in the wrong in the eyes of the whole world, of America, even of Ireland. Moreover—and here Smuts made a new and important point—there was no need for him to fear sitting at the same table with Craig; he and his colleagues could go by themselves to London as the representatives of Southern Ireland. But De Valera regarded himself as the lawfully elected President of Ireland one and indivisible. He inveighed against the Government of Ireland Act which had partitioned his country. Smuts tried to make him see a different significance in the Act. As he put the matter in the report of the talk that he gave to the King—

General Smuts replied that it was not a partition,* but merely that Ulster, which had always proved the obstacle, is now out of the way. Surely De Valera would recognize this. Both in Mr Gladstone's Bill and in Mr Asquith's the one stumbling block had always been Ulster, with the result that Ulster, which did not want Home Rule, has got Home Rule, and the rest of Ireland is quit of Ulster but is left without the Home Rule she wants: therefore, obviously, the right thing for De Valera is to cease talking or troubling about the Ulster partition, accept what has been done and talk to the British Government about South Ireland.

* No doubt he had in mind the 'Council of Ireland' provided for in the Government of Ireland Act.

Smuts believed that Griffith accepted his line of argument on Ulster, but the others remained silent and Erskine Childers, who had come into the room just then, appeared wrought up and somewhat neurotic.

That was as far as the discussions got in the morning. In the afternoon Smuts opened them by asking De Valera what solution he proposed for the Irish question. De Valera answered, 'A Republic'. Smuts asked him whether he really thought that the British people were likely to agree to it. De Valera replied that Ireland would be prepared to be bound by a Treaty with England. He spoke emotionally and at length in the language of natural right. Smuts answered him in the language of political experience.

I can talk [he said] from experience as to Republics bound by Treaty, for I served as a Minister, Attorney-General, in the Transvaal Republic, under such conditions. The result was, quarrelling day and night over breaches on our part of the Treaty, in which we were very likely to blame; but whoever was to blame the end was a three years' war, at the end of which our country was devastated.

He begged De Valera not on any account to accept a Republic under such conditions, even if the British were prepared to offer it. Then he told the story of his own country's achievement of unity and sovereignty by the path of constitutional evolution. His people had worked both systems. In the recent election, a large majority of them had declared that they did not want a Republic but free membership of the British Empire. 'As a friend', Smuts concluded, 'I cannot advise you too strongly against a Republic. Ask what you want, but not a Republic.' De Valera replied that it was for the Irish people to make the decision. Smuts formed the opinion that De Valera personally was willing to support a decision on Dominion lines. He believed that his visit to Dublin had done some good and that the Irish, despite their suspicions, would accept the invitation to London.[22]

They accepted it just three days later, on 8 July. On 10 July a military truce was signed and proclaimed in Ireland. On 12 July De Valera, accompanied by Griffith and Collins, arrived in London. To the King and to Smuts the auguries seemed good. But disappointment followed. In less than a fortnight the Irish were back in Dublin without having reached any agreement with the British on the basic principles of an Anglo-Irish settlement. All that the negotiating parties had achieved was a clearer view of the wide gap separating them. The British were prepared to offer Dominion status to Ireland, provided the six counties of Northern Ireland were not brought into the new Dominion without their own consent. The Irish were ready to accept the status of a Dominion provided they could have the six counties; but if they could not, they would accept nothing less than complete independence for Southern Ireland. That, in essence, was De Valera's reply to the written proposals which Lloyd George had handed to him. He promised to prepare and submit counter-proposals; but Lloyd George could see little hope of their proving satisfactory.[23]

Smuts, of course, had no part in the Anglo-Irish negotiations; but he remained informally in touch with both negotiating parties. He was due on 5 August to board ship for South Africa. On 4 August he wrote a short letter of farewell to the King, reaffirming his conviction that an Anglo-Irish settlement would in the end be achieved and enclosing the copy of a long letter that he had written the same day to De Valera.

On the immediate issues in dispute he had no more comment to make than he had made in Dublin a month earlier; but he now offered De Valera his reflections on the significance of the time factor in human affairs. His starting-point was the impasse between De Valera and Craig, the former insisting that the North must come within the constitution of United Ireland, the latter taking his stand on the existing constitutional rights of the North. Smuts could see no prospect of De Valera being able to impose his will on Craig; 'Ulster', he said, 'will not agree, she cannot be forced'. He advised De Valera to leave Ulster alone for the present and to concentrate his efforts upon building in the south a strong and free state, which would inevitably, in the course of time, exercise a magnetic attraction upon the six northern counties. He was aware that this advice would be repugnant to De Valera—

But the wise man [he submitted] while fighting for the ideal to the uttermost, learns also to bow to the inevitable. And a humble acceptance of the facts is often the only way of overcoming them. It proved so in South Africa, where ultimate unity was only realized through several stages and over a process of years; and where the republican ideal for which we had made unheard-of sacrifices had ultimately to give way to another form of Freedom.

My belief is that Ireland is travelling the same painful road as South Africa, and is destined to achieve the same success. I do not consider one clear-cut solution of the Irish question possible at present. You will have to pass through several stages, of which a free constitution for Southern Ireland will be the first, and the recognition of Irish unity will be the last ...Irish unity should be the ideal to which the whole process is directed. I do not ask you to give up your ideal, but only to realize it in the only way which seems to me at present practicable. Freedom will lead inevitably to unity.

As to the form of that freedom, here too you are called upon to choose between two alternatives. To you, as you say, the Republic is the true expression of national self-determination. But it is not the only expression: and it is an expression which means your final and irrevocable severance from the British League. And to this, as you know, the Parliament and people of this country [i.e. Britain, which Smuts was leaving next day] will not agree.

Smuts recalled once again the history of his own country, which had discovered, after a start far less promising than Ireland would make, that the Dominion solution of her problems really worked. If Ireland accepted the same solution, he said, she would find support in a great society of sister nations, all sharing and shielding the same freedom.[24]

Hertzog would not at that time have accepted the version which Smuts gave De Valera of South African history. The Afrikaner Broederbond would never have accepted it. De Valera would not and could not accept South African history, in the Smuts version or in any other, as a copy book of wisdom for Irishmen. Besides, De Valera no longer wanted advice from Smuts. Yet he had asked for it. Even if it no longer appealed to him, it still appealed to some of his colleagues. Six months later, when Michael Collins defended the Treaty, he said that it gave Ireland 'not the ultimate freedom that all nations desire and develop to, but the freedom to achieve it'. Collins put into a single sentence the argument which Smuts had developed at length in the Dublin talks on 5 July and in his letter to De Valera on 4 August.

When Smuts boarded ship for home on 5 August, he found waiting for him a telegram from the King bidding him farewell and thanking him for all that he had done.[25] It was a fitting close to his work for Anglo-Irish reconciliation. Thereafter he was merely a distant spectator of the struggle for peace. 'I have brought both mules to the water', he wrote, 'I have pushed their heads right into the trough; but the drinking is their own affair.'[26] He settled down to enjoy his voyage, with a big parcel of books from the Gilletts, some good travelling companions and, before long, the excitement of his ship catching fire; he always enjoyed the spice of danger. When he reached Cape Town the Irish news was still unpromising and he could not help regretting that he was no longer at hand 'to oil the wheels'; but at the most critical time the King oiled them.[27] On 7 September the British government issued a new and tactfully phrased invitation to a peace conference; on 12 September De Valera sent his letter of acceptance. The conference held its first meeting on 11 October and reached its conclusion in the small hours of the morning of 6 December, with the signature of Articles of Agreement for a Treaty between Great Britain and Ireland.

This Anglo-Irish agreement became the prelude to bitter strife among Irishmen. Smuts might have been better prepared for that tragic anti-climax, had he explored more deeply the temperamental and ideological roots of strife among his own people. Even so, he would still have held fast to his conviction that the choice which Griffith and Collins made for Ireland in December 1921, like the choice which Botha and he had made for South Africa in May 1902, was the right choice. The time was to come, although in the immediate aftermath of the Treaty it would have seemed improbable, when De Valera himself would recognize, practise and enlarge the freedom which Michael Collins saw and chose in December 1921— Ireland's freedom to achieve freedom.

That was what the Treaty meant for Smuts when the news of its signature reached him. From Pretoria he could not see the gathering storm in Dublin; he saw only the miracle of Anglo-Irish reconciliation, the resurrection of a nation, the redemption of the Commonwealth. He saw the name Commonwealth written formally into the Treaty, and the British league of free nations recognizing itself at long last for what it was. In so splendid a dawn of hope, the frustration of his plan for a General Declaration of Right seemed to him a trivial setback.

News has just arrived [he wrote] that the Irish question has been settled on the lines on which I advised last August...Washington also seems to be going well and at any rate a naval Disarmament Treaty and a Pacific arrangement will emerge from the present Conference. These are all good things and may well be the beginning of still better things...

'The Lord advances and ever advances', as Walt Whitman says. Why should we assume that just now He is in retreat?[28]

CHAPTER 4

DISASTER ON THE RAND

FOR a good many months past Smuts had been feeling anxious about the economic outlook. In April and May 1921 he had asked himself whether he ought not to stay at home instead of going overseas to the Prime Ministers' Conference; but he had concluded that he might be able to do some economic as well as some political good there, seeing that Europe was the storm centre on the economic weather map. On his arrival in Britain in June 1921 he had found the economic trouble there far worse than it was in South Africa. Many English people, he told his wife, would soon be migrating to South Africa. He even had some hopes of the Gilletts joining them.[1]

Nevertheless he had an anxious homecoming. 'Nature smiles', he wrote, 'but Man scowls.' Despite his establishment the previous year of the Central Reserve Bank he now found many things amiss with South African financial practice.

Here our main problem [he wrote in late September] is created by a drastic process of deflation; the banks have turned off credit on such a scale that there is not sufficient left for the business of the country. It shows how careful one must be even in doing the right thing. The money stringency is such as to create grave political unrest and I am daily meeting deputations from all parts of the country asking for printing of paper money, for a moratorium, for many other impossible things.

This financial sickness, bad though it was, was not his worst worry. He was watching with alarm the opening of a dangerous crack in South Africa's industrial structure.[2]

The massive foundations of that structure were sunk deep into the rock of the Witwatersrand. The gold-mining industry of that fabulous region was the main contributor to the national product, the main employer of the labour force, the main earner of foreign exchange, the main importer, accumulator and investor of capital, the main provider of public revenue, the main subsidizer of agriculture, the main stabilizer of economic fluctuations, the main dynamo of economic energy. The radiation of that energy had brought, or was bringing, to life many new industries—explosives, the railways, coal-mining, cables, engineering—with confident prospects in the near future for iron and steel* and with accelerating development of manufactures and services to meet the demand of great urban concentrations. Smuts, probably, did not make so systematic an inventory as that of the industry's functions within the South African economy; but he knew well enough that the country would face economic ruin if ever the day came when the Witwatersrand failed to produce gold at a profit.

In May 1920 the Low Grade Mines Commission had given warning that the day of disaster was not far off. Costs of production, the Commission reported, were pressing dangerously upon the price of gold. Since the price was externally determined, the industry's prospects, not merely of expansion but of sheer survival, depended upon the success it achieved in cutting its costs. The Commission was unanimous in making that diagnosis; but it split on the question of remedies. The majority proposed total abolition of the industrial colour bar; the minority rejected that proposal.†

The gold-mining industry, thanks to its command of scientific and technological skills, was able to cope efficiently with the material costs of production; but it had far less control over the labour costs. For deeply rooted historical reasons it had to operate two separate labour markets, the one for cheap black labour, the other for dear white labour. In 1921 its wages bill for 21,000 white workers was almost double its wages bill for 180,000 black workers.‡ If and when the day of adversity came, the temptation would prove almost irresistible to cut costs by promoting black workers to positions which white workers had occupied hitherto. After the Low Grade Mines Commission had sent in its report, that day of adversity was for a brief interval postponed; but late in 1921 it approached with a rush.

* In 1919 Smuts had appointed Dr H. J. van der Bijl as adviser to the government in the field of science and industry. He endorsed van der Bijl's plans for the Electricity Supply Commission (ESCOM), established in 1922. He also gave van der Bijl authority to investigate and make recommendations for the iron and steel industry. There followed the Gutehoffnungschütte Technical Commission. Its report, although not presented until after Smuts's fall from power, established the basis for the Iron and Steel Industry Act of 1928 and, consequently, for ISCOR.[3]

† On the Low Grade Mines Commission three representatives of the mine-owners sat with three representatives of the miners under the chairmanship of the chief government engineer. He was Mr (later Sir) Robert Kotze, who in 1891 had been runner-up to Smuts for the Ebden scholarship to Cambridge.

‡ The actual figures, according to the 32nd Annual Report of the Chamber of Mines (pp. 219–21), were: 21,455 white miners earning £10,640,521 and 179,987 black miners earning £5,964,528.

In November 1921 the price of gold fell to 104*s*. In December it fell to 95*s*. and the Central Bank forecast that it would soon fall all the way to gold parity.* According to estimates both of the Chamber of Mines and the Chief Government Engineer, that would mean production at a loss for twenty-seven of the Witwatersrand's thirty-eight mines. The crisis had come.

Throughout the crisis the limelight fell, not upon F. S. Malan, the Minister of Mines at that time, but upon Smuts. As a former Minister of Mines Smuts had already played the major part in codifying† government policy towards the gold-mining industry. In 1911 he had introduced and carried the Native Labour Regulation Act and the Mines and Works Act, which together regulated the two separate labour markets. Before that, he had been the main author of the Transvaal's Industrial Disputes Act of 1909, which offered conciliation as an alternative to the straight-out fight between capital and labour. About the same time he became a main supporter of the determined and in the end largely successful campaign against the scourge of miners' pthysis. From about 1913, if not earlier, he put persistent pressure upon the mine-owners for the recognition, belatedly conceded in 1915, of the white trade unions. These various services to workers on the top side of the colour bar were cumulatively impressive. They went unremembered. Instead, the white miners remembered the misdeeds imputed to Smuts during the industrial struggles of 1907, 1913 and 1914. In their mythology he became Hoggenheimer's hireling and the puppet of the Goldbug.‡

* Before the First World War, when world trade was on the sterling standard and sterling was on the gold standard, the price of gold was invariable: 77*s*. 10½*d*. per fine ounce. During the war the Bank of England received all the gold produced in South Africa at the par price, less 25*s*. per cent for shipping, insurance, etc. From July 1919 onwards the industry became free to sell gold for American dollars. These dollars, converted into South African pounds, raised the price of gold to 130*s*. per fine ounce. But not for long. The so-called gold premium was the measure of the pound's depreciation in terms of the dollar and was bound to diminish *pari passu* with deflation in Britain and the consequent appreciation of the pound sterling and the South African pound.

† Codifying, not establishing: the foundations of labour policy in the mining industry had been established in the time of the South African Republic and had been strengthened during the régime of Lord Milner.

‡ Hoggenheimer was a caricature symbolizing the mining capitalists; the symbol's origin and early development can be traced by using the index to *Smuts: The Sanguine Years*. 'Puppet of the Goldbug' was the caption of an extremely unpleasant cartoon published during the strike of 1922 (see p. 70). Smuts's reputation among white militants on the Rand can be illustrated from an episode of the 1915 election. While he was addressing a meeting in a Johannesburg suburb a woman called Mary Fitzgerald climbed on to the platform with a baby in her arms. 'This is Labuschagne's baby', she shouted, 'the child of the man you shot.' Smuts was lucky to get away from that meeting with his life.

That unenviable reputation was a main impediment to his efforts in 1921–2 to find a way through the crisis with the minimum amount of damage to the country's economic and social fabric. He accepted the economic diagnosis of the Low Grade Mines Commission; but he did not accept the majority's recommendation of a frontal assault on the industrial colour bar. From start to finish of the dispute he insisted on the need to treat as sacrosanct the so-called statutory colour bar, that is to say, the regulations under the Mines and Works Act which guaranteed the absolute security of approximately 7,000 white workers. The security of approximately twice that number* rested upon the conventional colour bar, that is to say, upon the custom of the industry as established and safeguarded by trade union pressure and public opinion. The conventional colour bar had been to some extent eroded during the war by the increasing use of black labour in semi-skilled occupations; but any further movement along that road was blocked by the *status quo* agreement of September 1918. Towards the end of 1921 the Chamber of Mines became convinced that it would have to free itself from that agreement if the industry were to have any chance of getting through the impending crisis.

Smuts made his first intervention in November 1921. So far as it went it proved successful. On the one side, he secured from the president of the Chamber of Mines, in the presence of trade union representatives, an assurance that no general attack was intended against white employment and that the Chamber would be ready if requested to fix a ratio of white employees to black. On the other side, he secured from the trade unionists an important if relatively painless concession, namely, the cancellation of a restrictive practice by the white miners which was wasting three hours or more of the ten-hour underground working day of the black miners. He must have felt pleased with that beginning; but he believed that a good deal more would have to follow. He therefore suggested direct negotiations between the employers and their white employees. Both sides accepted his suggestion and on 15 December a conference opened between the Chamber of Mines and the South African Industrial Federation.

* According to the Secretary of Mines and Industries and the Government Mining Engineer (U.G. 37–1923) daily-paid white workers on the Transvaal gold-mines (i.e. the workers sheltered by the conventional colour bar) numbered 14,658 in June 1921.

About a week later Smuts fell ill with gastric influenza. His doctor ordered him a month's rest and he consented to give himself a few days. So far, he saw no immediate cause for anxiety about the dispute in the gold-mining industry. By common consent the Chamber of Mines and the Industrial Federation had adjourned their discussions until 9 January. Unfortunately, disputes over wages in three other industries—coal-mining, engineering and the power industry—were all coming to a head at that time. In the week before Christmas the representatives of the coal-miners, by a sudden change of front, appealed to Smuts to intervene. On 28 December Duncan, the Minister of Justice, met them on Smuts's behalf and read to them a letter which urged them to accept the wage reductions proposed by the employers.* That same day the Chamber of Mines notified the Industrial Federation of its intention to terminate on 1 February 1922 the *status quo* agreement regulating the employment of semi-skilled labour. That meant a threat of dismissal for approximately 2,000 white gold-miners.

To the officials of the Industrial Federation it seemed on 28 December that the Chamber of Mines was launching a concerted and premeditated assault on white labour. They suspected, or gave the impression of suspecting, that the government was privy to the Chamber's plans. That was not so. In parliament on 24 February, F. S. Malan reproved the Chamber of Mines for its failure to use the procedure of conciliation provided by the Industrial Disputes Act. The Chamber's precipitate denunciation of the *status quo* agreement was possibly a panic response to the accelerating fall in the price of gold; within four weeks in November–December the price fell by 9s. Many mines would soon be working at a loss.

In its reaction to the crisis the South African Industrial Federation was no less precipitate. The Chamber of Mines had given five weeks' notice† of its intention to terminate the *status quo* agreement. That gave the Federation plenty of time for invoking its rights under the Industrial Disputes Act. Instead, it rushed the unions into a strike.

---

* Under the Industrial Disputes Act it had been open to the coal-miners to have their case referred to a Conciliation Board; but from early October to late December they preferred to argue it direct with the Chamber of Mines. At the last minute they said that they would accept arbitration; but South Africa's industrial legislation made no provision for arbitration as distinct from conciliation. Smuts in his letter advised them to accept the proposed wage reductions as the only means of saving the export trade which, with bunkered coal, absorbed approximately one-third of South Africa's coal production.

† The law required four weeks' notice.

The coal-miners went on strike on New Year's Day; the gold-miners, engineers and employees of the Victoria Falls Power Company went on strike on 10 January.

The recent experience of organized labour in Britain might have warned South Africa's labour leaders that their prospects of victory were poor. Indeed, they were far poorer than the prospects of their British comrades had been. Nothing comparable with the Triple Alliance of miners, railwaymen and dockers existed in South Africa. The South African Industrial Federation was a flimsy organization with negligible support outside the Witwatersrand. It had no anchorage in the vast mass of unskilled labour. It was a regionally cramped and racially exclusive organization of the aristocrats of labour. It had no income of its own. It could expect no financial support from its constituent unions, most of which had their own money troubles. It tried to cover up all these weaknesses by raising the cry that white civilization was in danger and by creating an 'Augmented Executive' to represent all the combatant unions. Events were soon to show that the Augmented Executive had little or no control over events.

Even after the ballots had been taken Smuts kept on trying to persuade the leaders to call off the strike. He told them that it would be ruinous to the country and profitless for themselves. Besides, there was no need for it; if they submitted their case to a Board of Conciliation the situation would remain as it was until the Board delivered its report. If nevertheless they insisted on striking he gave them warning not to pin their hopes on intervention by the government. On 10 January the morning papers reported the terms of his warning. 'If a strike were to take place', he said, 'the Government would draw a ring round both parties, do its best to maintain law and order, and let the two parties fight it out.' After the strike was over Opposition speakers quoted that statement as evidence that Smuts had wanted from the very start to see white labour crushed. 'What could be more cruel', Hertzog declaimed in the House of Assembly on 3 April 1922, 'than the spectacle of the government drawing a ring and letting the situation develop?'

In practice Smuts showed no intention of standing aside as a spectator of the fight. On the contrary, he postponed the meeting of parliament from 20 January until 17 February and remained in the north to work for a settlement. The Augmented Executive gave him no help. On the day the strike broke out it asked him to call a conference with the employers on the condition that they should withdraw all their notices. But that would mean their unconditional surrender. Smuts refused to arrange a conference on those terms; but he did propose a conference of seven representatives from each side, meeting each other without any pre-stated conditions and choosing their own chairman. Both sides accepted this proposal and the conference met on 13 January under the chairmanship of Judge Curlewis. He proved to be an understanding and constructive chairman; but on 27 January the conference collapsed in deadlock.

That same day Smuts issued a strong appeal to both sides for 'a spirit of give and take'. He offered his own mediation in their dispute. But neither side was in the mood for compromise. The Chamber of Mines had just dismissed 600 coal-miners* and in its reply to Smuts on 29 January it took a tough line. It began by announcing the abolition of paid holidays on May Day and Dingaan's Day. Then it went on to offer an alternative proposal to cancellation of the *status quo* agreement: the guarantee of a ratio of 1 to 10·5 in the employment of white and black labour on the gold-mines. The ratio, however, was guaranteed for two years only and it would have permitted even more white dismissals than the number originally proposed. The Chamber ended its statement with the warning that it would be unable to provide full employment on the gold-mines when the strike ended.

The Augmented Executive at that time was even more intransigent than was the Chamber of Mines. It made no reply at all to the appeal of Smuts. Instead, it declared war on him. In a resolution of 29 January it accused the government of 'backing the present attack by the employers on the white workers, both in reducing their standard of living and curtailing their opportunities of employment'. It called on the workers and their sympathizers to join forces with the National and Labour parties in their struggle to overthrow the Smuts government and set up in its place a government 'calculated to promote the interests of the White race in South Africa'.

The resolution of 29 January proclaimed the decision of white labour to turn the industrial struggle into a political conflict. Two and a half years later, the decision produced rich dividends; but in

---

* This brusque decision was an immediate cause of the breakdown of the Curlewis conference.

February and March 1922 it brought disaster to the Witwatersrand. Its immediate cause was a surge of anger amongst the strikers against the terms in which Smuts had appealed for peace and offered his mediation. Smuts recited facts about the damage the strike was doing to the gold-mining industry, to the white workers and to South Africa. These facts, or many of them, were visible. Smuts recited more facts about the industry's deep-seated economic crisis and its consequent need to improve its efficiency. These facts, or many of them, had been accepted as true by the workers' representatives on the Low Grade Mines Commission; but the recitation of them at this juncture sparked off an emotional storm. They were facts for the capitalists, the strikers felt, not facts for the white workers; Smuts, when he recited them, was taking sides with the Chamber of Mines.

For the past four weeks and more Smuts had been the target of a vituperative propaganda. Day after day the demagogic orators and scribblers had been flinging mud at him. They denounced him as the paid servant of the Chamber of Mines and the enemy of the workers. They accused him of wanting to turn White South Africa into Black South Africa. They pictured him waiting like a vulture to provoke the strikers to rise in honest indignation so that he could proclaim martial law and crush them. Their mud stuck.

The Opposition parties did not participate in this reckless campaign against Smuts but some of their members did. The party leaders, possibly, deplored its excesses; but they did not deny themselves its profits. They saw in the industrial struggle the makings of a political combination between Nationalism and Labour to overthrow the Smuts government, perhaps not immediately but certainly at the next election. In an official resolution of 14 January the Labour party declared its solidarity with the S.A. Industrial Federation. The National party passed no comparable resolution but its executive committee in the Transvaal demonstrated by word and deed its support for the strikers: after all, they were white, and the majority of them were Afrikaners.* On the Transvaal Provincial Council the two parties in combination pushed through a motion on 22 February voting £20,000 for strike relief. All this support from the Opposition parties encouraged the strikers to bid for more. They took too little

---

* From the time of the 1907 strike onwards there had been a steady influx of Afrikaners into the gold-mining industry, until by 1922 approximately three white workers in every four were Afrikaners. Afrikaans farmers gave indispensable help to the strikers by deliveries of food.

The Puppet of the Goldbug.

PULL THE STRING AND "JANNIE" MOVES!

notice of a reservation which was stated more than once in the party resolutions—namely, that support would cease to be forthcoming for the strikers if they turned to unconstitutional methods of maintaining their just cause.

The strikers had some excuse for not taking that reservation seriously. Some of the politicians seemed not to take it seriously. Tielman Roos, the Nationalist leader in the Transvaal, and R. Waterston, the Labour M.P. for Brakpan,* failed to keep their demagogic impulses under control. Waterston declared on 14 January that the Chamber of Mines was plotting to eliminate 90 per cent of the white labour force. Roos was more intent upon exposing the plots of Smuts: in particular, his plot to use force against the strikers. Even before the strike broke out, Roos was inciting Afrikaners in the Active Citizen Force to disobey the government's mobilization orders when they were issued—he appeared to take it for granted that they would be issued.† On 22 January he accused the government of trying to create the conditions which would give it an excuse to proclaim martial law. About a week later he called together in Pretoria a so-called 'Parliament'—ten Nationalist and five Labour M.P.s, whose ostensible purpose it was to settle the industrial strife. Instead, they inflamed it. On 5 February a mass meeting of strikers on the East Rand carried a resolution calling on the 'Pretoria Parliament' to set up a Provisional Government and proclaim a Republic. Next morning Waterston took the resolution to the Johannesburg Town Hall where 2,000 wildly excited people carried it by acclamation. It ran as follows:

That this mass meeting of citizens is of the opinion that the time has arrived when the domination of the Chamber of Mines and other financiers should cease, and to that end we ask the members of Parliament assembled in Pretoria tomorrow to proclaim a South African Republic, and immediately to form a Provisional Government for this country.

Tielman Roos was profoundly shocked at having so unconstitutional a demand presented to him, for he had been playing politics with no thought of stirring up a revolution. When the real parliament

* Waterston had been one of the strike leaders deported by Smuts in January 1914.
† The incitement was contained in a letter said to have been published by Roos in *Ons Vaderland* on 30 December 1921. That issue of *Ons Vaderland* has apparently disappeared, but the letter was reprinted in *Die Volksblad* on 6 January 1922. It attracted a great deal of contemporary comment.

met he and Waterston took up attitudes of injured innocence.* Nevertheless, they had done serious damage not only to their country but also to the men whom they professed to be helping. The damage might have been less serious if their demagogic bubble had been pricked just a day or two earlier; but, by an unlucky accident of timing, their mischief-making reached its climax—or anti-climax— just when Smuts was making his most determined bid for a negotiated peace. If that coincidence had not occurred, the Augmented Executive would surely have thought twice before it slammed the door on Smuts's proposals.

The Augmented Executive had been having some second thoughts about the wisdom of its anti-government manifesto of 29 January. Only two days after that, the Germiston strike committee passed a resolution in favour of calling off the strike. It followed up this resolution with a telegram to Smuts asking for an interview. Smuts was willing; but a commando surrounded the Germiston strike committee at its headquarters and compelled it to rescind its invitation. To the moderate trade unionists of the Augmented Executive this was an ominous intimation of revolt. On 3 February they asked Smuts and F. S. Malan to meet them. The meeting took place next day. Smuts proposed to them a return to work on the Chamber's terms, if no better ones could be secured, subject to such modification of those terms as might be recommended by an impartial board to be appointed by the government: the report would be submitted to parliament: the miners, if they so desired, could hold a ballot on its recommendations. Smuts also pledged his government to find alternative employment for those miners who might fail to get their old jobs back when the mines started work again. The Augmented Executive rejected those proposals. Thereupon Smuts made his last and his largest bid for compromise and a peaceful settlement. On 5 February he wrung from the Chamber of Mines an undertaking to retain the *status quo* agreement on the higher grade mines, pending final settlement of the points at issue by a parliamentary Commission of Inquiry.† This undertaking marked a big retreat by the Chamber

---

* Waterston protested that he had had no part in moving the resolution. This was strictly true. He had merely 'presented' it to the mass meeting in the Johannesburg Town Hall and pleaded for it in an impassioned speech about blood not flowing in vain.

† This proposal emanated originally from Judge Curlewis. Designation of the higher grade mines, on which the *status quo* agreement would remain in force, was to be entrusted to Robert Kotze as Chief Government Engineer.

from its original position; but when Smuts met the trade union delegates next morning he found that nothing short of unconditional surrender would satisfy them: the Chamber of Mines, they insisted, must withdraw all its pre-strike notices. Thus they threw away their last chance of an honourable and workable compromise. The only alternative open to them from that time onwards was their own unconditional surrender.

Smuts wrote the next day to the Gilletts in a mood of deep depression. He began by acknowledging letters which two of their children had written to him.

Helen is a dear thing and you must give her a kiss from me. And Nico too. I am sorry I have not yet had time to reply to their last letters. But they will understand what a hard time I have over this awful strike. It has now gone on a month, luckily without violence being resorted to. I have spent days at conferences, with no result. The leaders are not in control, as usually happens. And so the accursed thing goes on.[4]

During the next few days he went to work on a new plan for ending 'the accursed thing'. It proved to be a calamitous plan.

Up to the end of the first week of February Smuts had been a persistent and fair-minded mediator.* It had been his duty as Prime Minister to keep his mind in steady focus on the economic crisis of the mining industry and—in consequence—of the country; but he had also done his best to find a workable compromise between economic necessity and a fair deal for white labour. He had not at any time deserved the insults which day by day were flung at him. His proposals of 6 February had contained incontrovertible proof, if it were still called for, that he was not 'the paid agent of the Chamber of Mines'. But now he made an abrupt change of front. Up to the evening of 7 February, when he wrote to Mrs Gillett, he was still an impartial, although by this time a deeply despondent, mediator. By the evening of 11 February, he and his government were direct participators in the conflict.

His announcement of the new policy appeared next morning in the newspapers. It made an assertion, proceeded to an appeal and culminated in a pledge. 'It is clear', he asserted, 'that the continuation of this unhappy state of affairs cannot be tolerated any longer.'

* In defiance of the evidence his biographer, F. S. Crafford (*Jan Smuts: A Biography* (London, 1945), p. 216), repeated the myth of his 'inexplicable inactivity' at this time.

On the basis of that assertion, he appealed to the employers to re-open the mines and to the miners to go back to work. His pledge followed: 'The government', he declared, 'will use all its powers to protect those who listen to this appeal, and the police have instructions, as from 13. 2. 1922, to give protection to all miners who return to their former employment, and I call upon the mine-owners to re-start the mines in all cases where sufficient numbers of men offer to return to work.'

The mine-owners, while protesting that they would never have wished to run their industry under such conditions, gave a prompt and positive reply to the Prime Minister's appeal. The Augmented Executive submitted it to a meeting of the executive committees of all the striking unions. This meeting rejected the appeal and mass meetings of strikers all over the Rand denounced Smuts as the enemy of the workers. That was an old cry; but now, at last, Smuts had made it a plausible one. His promise of police protection for scabs* awakened vivid and angry memories of past conflicts—of traitors slinking back to work, of pickets warning them off, of honest strikers beating them up, of fighting breaking out between strikers and police, of hooligans breaking loose, of death and destruction and the soldiers coming in at last to suppress the workers in the name of law and order.

The event proved that Smuts had underrated the risks of this new policy. He had also overrated the advantages which the government and the country stood to gain from it. The physical assets of the industry were in no serious danger of destruction because 'the officials'—that is to say, the industry's administrators and technicians—had refused to join the strike and were willing to maintain essential services. Still, the current loss of production was inflicting serious economic damage on South Africa and every week the strike dragged on would aggravate the difficulties of getting production started again. If the new policy had the effect of cutting the strike short, there was something to be said for it, not in principle but on pragmatic grounds. It would win fairly wide approval if—but only if—the strikers were in the mood to return to work. By the time

* This ugly slang word of American origin designates a worker who offers his labour in an industry in which the union men are on strike. It can also be used as a verb. Perhaps for this reason, as well as for its venomous sibilant sound, it has, in South Africa and other countries, ousted the English word *blackleg*, which, as a noun, has the same meaning.

parliament met on 17 February, it was plain they were in the opposite mood.

Smuts denied that the government was demanding their unconditional surrender. In his opening statement to parliament he recalled his invitation* to the Industrial Federation and the Chamber of Mines to appoint representatives to an impartial Board: this Board would examine the issues in dispute and recommend terms of settlement to parliament; when parliament had approved the terms they would operate retrospectively. It followed that the men would not prejudice their case by returning to work. On various occasions Smuts had given the strike leaders these same assurances; but they had always brushed them aside in the expectation of getting prompt and effective support from their friends in the Opposition parties. The debate in parliament dashed their hopes. On 22 February Hertzog moved a long and confused resolution which asserted the principle that black labour should under no circumstances be permitted to enter the sphere of employment reserved for white labour: which also asserted that a return of the strikers to work was desirable on the basis of that principle: which asserted further that a Select Committee of Parliament should lay down provisional terms for their return to work: which asserted still further that the Select Committee should appoint a Commission which would both lay down the final terms of their return to work and also make recommendations for a permanent body to settle industrial disputes. In that jumble of proposals only one thing was clear—that Hertzog had nothing to offer the strikers now.

Thomas Boydell, the acting leader of the Labour party,† was more forthcoming. The way to end the strike, he declared, was for the employers to withdraw the 'ultimatum' which had caused it. He praised the self-restraint of the strikers and said that it was due in large measure to their 'commando system'—a new development in industrial warfare which would produce far-reaching effects in other countries. Then he attacked the police for their provocative conduct towards the strikers. Towards the end of his speech he discussed the social and economic issues facing the country. He did not want to see industries built up on cheap labour to the detriment of the white population; he wanted to see civilized conditions of labour. If the

---

* Neither the Federation nor the Chamber had responded to this invitation.
† The leader, Creswell, had lost his seat in the last election.

low-grade mines could not provide those conditions South Africa could not afford to have them. They must close down.*

Smuts, in his reply to Hertzog and Boydell, recorded systematically the origin and development of the strikes in the engineering, power, coal-mining and gold-mining industries. He defended the government's record and underlined its responsibilities. It could not, as Boydell suggested, allow half the gold-mining industry to be squeezed to death between the low price of gold and the high costs of production. The Witwatersrand not only supported the largest industrial population and industry of South Africa but it was also the main market of all their producers: if half of the Witwatersrand were to decay, and the mines were to stop, the result would be a cataclysmic blow to the whole of South Africa. He hoped that they all supported the ideals of white civilization, but if they attempted to establish those ideals on a false economic foundation the result would be a ghastly failure. He insisted that the foundations of the gold-mining industry must be made stronger. He insisted equally that this could and would be done without touching the colour bar.† The *status quo* agreement was a different matter; unlike the colour bar, it had no statutory sanction; it had never been discussed in parliament nor could he conceive that any member would propose to make it the law of the land. He had made it perfectly clear, when negotiations started last year between the Chamber of Mines and the Industrial Federation, that the colour bar† must not be touched. He had said so plainly and it was the bedrock of the whole situation. The dispute was on a narrow issue: whether or not the mine managements should have the right to retrench the maximum number of 2,000 white men, with the retrenchment spread out over a number of years. He disliked retrenchment but the country was faced with a choice between two evils: if the mine managements were denied the right to make their industry efficient, many more than 2,000 white workers would be put out of work.

Smuts defied anybody to study the events of recent months and point out to him what more the government could have done than it had done to prevent the strike. Once the strike had started, he

* At this point of his argument, Boydell quoted Judge Higgins of Australia. Boydell, like Hertzog, called for a system of compulsory arbitration on the Australian model. Smuts rejected that model. He was the advocate of industrial conciliation as practised in Canada.

† I.e. the statutory colour bar; but the strikers were resisting infringements of the conventional colour bar (see p. 65 above).

declared, it was the government's duty to uphold law and order, maintain essential services and protect the peaceful pursuits of the country. He denied that the police had acted provocatively; on the contrary, they had been patient, good humoured and helpful. He was sorry that some politicians had been unable to resist the temptation to make political capital out of the strike. He did not mind at all being called a paid agent of the Chamber of Mines; he was entirely beyond that; but the campaign of slander against the government had frustrated its efforts to extract the workers from their impossible position. Now he had advised them to go back to work. If they did, he insisted once again, they would not prejudice their case, because an impartial tribunal would make its report and parliament would make the final decision. A just settlement of the issues in dispute would be achieved during the present session.

The debate dragged on for four more days. Few if any of the participants shed any new light on the immediately contested issues but some speakers revealed startling attitudes towards the underlying issues. J. X. Merriman considered it an interference with the laws of nature to lay down the principle that because a man was coloured he would never be able to do skilled work. But Merriman was old and eccentric. H. W. Sampson stated the issue as Labour saw it: what, he asked, was of more consequence to the country—the wages the White man spent or the few pence that dribbled through to the Native? Tielman Roos denounced the mines as the graves of a large portion of the cream of South African manhood. He then protested, with reference to his 'Pretoria Parliament' and the republican resolution of 6 February, that he and his party had always been, and would always remain, strictly constitutional republicans.

After an all night sitting the debate ended at 9.30 a.m. on 21 February with a government victory of 69 votes to 53. On the merits of the debate the government deserved its victory; but it did not sufficiently deserve it. Its argument, as Smuts had expounded it, was firmly grounded on fact and rigorously consistent in logic; but the logic was in conflict with trade union principle and in apparent conflict with human sympathy. Smuts allowed his friends to see, but did not allow South Africa to see, that he had bowels of compassion.

It is a very bad business [he wrote to the Gilletts on 23 February]. The men have chosen to be unbending just at a time when all over the world labour has either to bend or to break before the wild economic storm which is raging. I am very sorry, but I feel that if the men win half the gold industry is dead, and if the Chamber of Mines win, they will return to their old dictatorial attitude towards labour.[5]

Of those alternatives the second seemed to him harsh, the first calamitous.

The Chamber of Mines was already returning to its old dictatorial ways. It was waging war against the trade union leaders and attacking the solidarity of the rank and file. Its propaganda was arrogant and intimidatory. Smuts, surely, should have warned it to mend its ways. Had he done so, the strikers might perhaps have paid attention to the warnings he addressed to them. Unfortunately, he made them feel that he was not a just man but a harsh man. He told the coal-miners that they had lost their export trade and were now un-employed. He told the gold-miners that they had had no need to go on strike. Both those statements were true: but Smuts would have done well to add a little sweetening to such bitter pills. Nevertheless, he could have argued in his own defence that when he did add the sweetening neither the strikers nor their political champions took any notice of it. In parliament, when he was repeating his call to the men to go back to work, W. B. Madeley interjected—'On what terms?' Smuts answered: 'On the Chamber's terms. On any terms. Their case will not be compromised because Parliament will finally settle it.' It suited neither the strikers nor the Nationalist and Labour politicians to quote his last sentence. Eagerly and maliciously they seized hold of the stick he had given them to beat him with: 'On the Chamber's terms. On any terms.' Long after he was dead, men who could not forget their hate of him were still quoting half of what he had said.*

At the end of February 1922 his parliamentary victory did not settle the industrial conflict but made it more tumultuous. To begin with, it exposed the tragic miscalculation of the Augmented Execu-tive in its decision on 29 January to commit the strikers' cause to the Opposition parties. Those parties might be able to help their protégés after the next elections; but these in the normal course were not due for four more years and the Augmented Executive would be lucky if it could survive for a few more weeks. Power was slipping from its grasp and the strikers were not in unity with each other about what

---

* Here I have in mind the book by Ivan L. Walker and Ben Weinbren, *2,000 Casualties* (1961). See the General Note on Sources, p. 534 below. In fairness to the two authors it must be said that they gave Smuts credit for having mellowed in his old age.

to do and what leaders to follow. Many of them wanted to give up the fight. On the Witbank coalfield and in the Vereeniging foundries and engineering works they did give it up. Even on the Witwatersrand hundreds of miners drifted back to work and hundreds more would have done so had they dared to defy mass feeling and its physical expressions. Here was a force with deep foundations in the violent history of white labour; here was an aggressive, not a submissive, psychology of the crowd.

The majority of the miners, as they grew more disillusioned, grew more in the mood for a fight to the finish; but right up to the finish they had no notion who would lead them in the fight. The most conspicuous contestant for leadership was the Council of Action, a small group* of militants who had defied the mineworkers' union and after their expulsion from it in July 1921 had published a revolutionary manifesto: 'First, the class struggle: second, the science of revolution: third, the economic and political needs of the Industrial Republic.' W. H. Andrews, the founder and first secretary of the South African Communist party, acted as secretary for the Council of Action. Its propaganda and tactics bore the communist stamp. Communism, however, could not easily adapt itself to the colour bar. The champions of proletarian solidarity felt ill at ease when their pupils in Marxist doctrine refurbished an old May Day banner so that it urged the Workers of the World to fight for a White South Africa. Nevertheless, they temporized. As R. K. Cope, in his biography of Andrews (p. 231), expounded their tactics in retrospect—

Although the cry for a 'White South Africa', which became the chief slogan in the dispute, appears reactionary on the surface, it was nevertheless founded on a sound working class instinct. The 'White South Africa' slogan embodied a defence against capitalist aggression and was a challenge against the capitalist class. That the White workers saw no identity of interest with the Black workers and were not prepared to co-operate with them was a concrete reality of the time, and had to find its expression.†

Those tactics became harder to tolerate when the white workers started to beat up the black workers; but only one communist, S. P. Bunting,

* Its original members were J. Wordingham, E. Shaw, W. Richardson, K. J. van Coller, M. Higgins, R. Annets, F. W. Pate, A. McDermid, D. McPhail and H. Spendiff. P. Fisher, who with H. Spendiff dominated the Fordsburg commando, was the most important latecomer to the Council. During the strike members of the Council acted in close concert with each other rather than by official collective action.

† In the same book, Cope found similar tactical justification for the decision of South African communists in 1940 to advocate—as the Nationalists were advocating—a separate peace with Hitler.

refused from start to finish to tolerate them. Bunting was not permitted—not even once—to speak from a working-class platform. The Council of Action did not want just then to spread the gospel of proletarian solidarity. It wanted to win control of the strike commandos.

The strike commandos, unlike the Council of Action, were a spontaneous growth. They had tough roots in Afrikaner tradition and the experience of war. Three-quarters of the strikers were Afrikaners, many thousands of them were ex-soldiers, all of them soon grew weary of enforced idleness and impatient with the leadership that was getting them nowhere. The Afrikaners were new to trade unionism and it was natural that they in particular should make a ready response when veterans of the 1914 rebellion or of the East African campaign began to suggest that commandos were the thing to hold them together and keep them usefully occupied. The commandos varied in size from 50 to 500. The Augmented Executive would have liked to find a place for them in the trade union structure but they organized themselves regionally and maintained their independence. To begin with, they had nothing much to do except march about and perform simple drill, but by mid-February the drill was including some complicated exercises, such as pulling mounted men off their horses and handling dummy machine guns. Moreover, they now had a recognized function in the strike, namely, to put down scabbing. In performing that function they were bound sooner or later to come into conflict with the police. They grew rougher with the scabs; the police grew tougher with them. Politicians like Boydell might still acclaim them as guardians of law and order and as a model for labour movements elsewhere; but some of the newspapers expressed different views and the government felt worried. On 22 February a government notice announced that gatherings called commandos, which were interfering with people in their peaceful pursuits, were unlawful assemblies under common law and would be dispersed by the police. On 27 February the police dispersed two commandos at Boksburg and took 27 prisoners. Next day the Boksburg commando approached the gaol and refused to disperse. The police fired and killed three men of the commando. That night Johannesburg was in darkness.* Next day an immense crowd attended the funeral of the three dead men.

* The supply of 'clean' coal (i.e. coal that had been mined before 1 January, when the coal-miners went on strike) had given out and on 27 February the workers refused to handle

The police had been heavily reinforced from all over the Union and by successive stages they had been issued with firearms; but after the Boksburg disturbances it became a matter for urgent decision by the government whether peace could be preserved on the Rand without bringing in the citizen soldiers and declaring martial law. Every magistrate on the Rand who later gave evidence before the Martial Law Commission felt certain that the government had acted too tardily, and this retrospective judgment received almost universal endorsement throughout South Africa; but in the first week of March it would have been hotly disputed. Smuts anxiously discussed with his colleagues in the Cabinet the alternative risks of declaring martial law and of not declaring it. In his letter to the Gilletts on 23 February he had expressed the hope that public opinion was, on the whole, behind the government; but he had added: 'You know what an unreliable thing public opinion is.'[5] He could not afford to be ahead of public opinion if and when he declared martial law. South Africans considered martial law an evil thing and had handled Smuts roughly for his part in declaring and executing it in 1914. More than that: many of them suspected him of waiting and plotting to do the same thing again. Even so moderate a paper as *Die Burger* gave expression to that suspicion. Amongst the strikers it was not merely a suspicion: from the very beginning of the strike hardly a day had passed without their making it an accusation. Tielman Roos and other well-known politicians repeated the accusation. The inevitable consequence was to make Smuts most reluctant to proclaim martial law, not because he was anxious for his reputation —as he said in Parliament, he was beyond that—but because he had good reason to doubt whether the country would fall into line behind the government. Not a single M.P. in any party stood up and called for martial law. Up to the very last, the National and Labour members remained hostile to it. And there was a more cogent reason still for delaying its proclamation until the need for it had been demonstrated beyond possibility of doubt. It had no efficacy in itself. If it were to be efficacious, the Active Citizen Forces must be mobilized and ready for action. Yet the government could not be certain that its mobilization orders would be obeyed. In his letter of

'scab' coal. The government took over the power house and was able to restore light, but not power for public transport. In *Historia*, March 1960, C. R. Ould published an article on '"The Boksburg Incident" during the Strike of 1922'.

30 December, Roos had given a plain incitement to disobedience. The conspiratorial junta of commando leaders were counting on active, armed support from the *platteland* when the great day came for them to order their commandos into action. Smuts and his colleagues did not know very much about that plot; but they knew something about it.* They had vivid memories of 1914. They dared not run the risk of issuing a call to arms unless and until they could feel assured that country and town, Afrikaner and English-speaking South Africans, would make a united response to the call.

On the other hand, they were well aware that if they delayed too long the police might lose control of the Rand. If that were to happen the consequences would be grave, but they told each other that peace would be restored within a day or two and that the country would this time make up its mind never again to tolerate revolutionary tumult. After the tumult was over, Smuts, with almost unbelievable frankness, revealed to parliament that strand of the government's thought, along with the other strands.†

In late February and early March the strongest strand was the anticipation of a speedy and peaceful end to the strike. Despite the warning of Boksburg, or perhaps because of it, the moderates were gaining the ascendancy over the militants. So, at least, it seemed. The drift back to work was becoming a rush. On 2 March the Augmented Executive asked the Chamber of Mines to agree to a conference without conditions and with the sole purpose of ending the strike. On 4 March, in an arrogant reply, the Chamber rejected the proposed conference and refused to have any more dealings with the Augmented Executive.‡ Smuts was furious with the Chamber for acting so irresponsibly at the very time when he saw within his grasp the great prize, settlement of the strike by peaceful and constitutional means. Nevertheless his hopes remained predominant over his fears for two days more. The moderate trade unionists, persisting in their effort for peace, formed a new and widely representative body, the Joint Executives, which they hoped the Chamber of Mines would recognize: this body would again ask for a conference: only if the Chamber again rejected it, a general strike would be called.

* Even the Martial Law Commission discovered little about the plot. The evidence of its existence emerged, clearly if only fragmentarily, in trials by the Special Court (see p. 85 below).   † See pp. 85–6 below.

‡ The Martial Law Commission named this provocative letter among the causes of the armed uprising.

But at this juncture the militants seized control. On 6 March the Council of Action and a junta of commando leaders whipped up a mob which besieged the Trades Hall and terrorized the Joint Executives until at 6 p.m. they declared the general strike.

Outside the Witwatersrand the general strike never even got started; but the junta was planning something different, a rising of the Witwatersrand commandos.* On 7 March acts of violence occurred all over the Rand and continued for the next three days until they reached their climax in a general assault on the police. Conspicuous in these acts of violence were murderous attacks on non-Europeans, including the African miners in their compounds. On 9 March the Ministers of Justice and Defence issued the following statement:

During the last few days in Johannesburg and surrounding districts attacks have been made by certain Europeans on natives and coloured persons without the slightest provocation...The Government has information that these deliberate and unprovoked attacks, amounting in certain particular cases to wilful murder, are designed to give the impression throughout the country that a native rising on the Witwatersrand is imminent, and that the lives and properties of Europeans are in danger.

That explanation of the attacks on Africans was consistent with the junta's plans to combine a rising on the *platteland* with the rising on the Rand. However, alternative theories were put forward. Labour spokesmen put the whole blame on the hooligan element. Communist writers like R. K. Cope asserted later on that the Smuts government itself had arranged the attacks on Africans.

In Cape Town on 9 March Merriman moved the adjournment of the House on a matter of urgent public importance, namely the recent developments on the Witwatersrand leading to loss of life among Natives and Indians. W. H. Stuart, the S.A.P. member for Tembuland in the Cape, spoke vehemently in support of Merriman. Boydell followed with an appeal to the Prime Minister to stop trying to settle the dispute by the military machine. Then Smuts rose.

We Whites [he said] are on our trial, and I hope that from this House will go the impression all over South Africa that on all the benches here and on all sides of the House we deplore, and deplore bitterly, what has happened on the Witwatersrand, and not only do we deplore it, we denounce it.

* This statement is based on evidence collected and critically assessed in the two theses cited in the General Note on Sources. See p. 534 below.

In reply to a question he added—

I do not draw any distinction between the black man who is killed and the white man who is killed. We deplore and denounce all these outbreaks.

That same day, 9 March, he issued mobilization orders for the Active Citizen Force. Next day he announced in parliament that martial law had been declared. He also announced that the police were under attack all over the Rand and that the fighting was going badly for them. After making those announcements he went north to assume the command. He came under fire as he entered Johannesburg and at military headquarters he learnt that the commandos were holding almost the entire Rand. But the citizen soldiers had obeyed the government's mobilization orders. In three days of fighting Smuts suppressed the insurrection. According to the Martial Law Commission he used larger forces than were strictly required, but saved lives by doing so. Nevertheless, the casualty lists were grievous.*

After it was all over Smuts continued his exchange of views with Alice Clark about the great ideals. They were, he agreed, the flowering of life, but their roots, he told her, grew in a granite soil.† He wrote in the same mood to her sister, Margaret Gillett.

We have passed through a bad time, and the more I have of it the more I pity the lot of rulers in these days. The commandos, which had been drilling and marching on the Rand, suddenly and mysteriously became armed with rifles and attacked the police, inflicting heavy casualties. So martial law and all the rest of it. And I have earned an additional claim to the titles of butcher and hangman.[6]

Whether or not he had earned those names, he got them.

---

* The Martial Law Commission listed the casualties as follows:

Military forces	176, including 43 killed
Police	115, including 29 killed
Civilians	396, including 81 killed

The Commission had a sub-classification for the civilians:

Revolutionaries	56, including 11 killed
Suspected Revolutionaries	101, including 28 killed
Innocent civilians:	
European	87, including 18 killed
Others	152, including 24 killed

The Commission gave close attention to the cases of six persons who had been reported shot when trying to escape. Among them were three brothers named Hanekom, whose names had become prominent in political controversy.

† See p. 11 above.

On his return from the Rand he announced that martial law would be withdrawn quickly and that accused persons would be tried in the civil courts, except that persons accused of murder would be tried in a Special Court set up under the Riotous Assemblies Act of 1914: two or three judges of the Supreme Court, without juries, would constitute the Special Court. General Hertzog asked for a special commission, consisting of M.P.s, to inquire into the events leading to the proclamation of martial law and the ensuing disturbances, including the excesses alleged to have been committed by the police and military forces. Smuts said that it would be difficult to conduct such an inquiry while the courts were sitting; but later, as a reply to taunts that the government was afraid of the truth, he appointed two judges of the Cape Bench as a commission of inquiry.

Of the various speeches that he made on these and other procedural matters the most important was his speech of 31 March in introducing the second reading of the Indemnity and Trial of Offenders Bill. From such information as the government then possessed* he gave a full and fair account of events on the Rand following the overthrow of the trade union leaders on 6 March. The core of his speech was a defence of the government's action in declaring martial law. He took note that some people blamed it for not declaring martial law soon enough but that other people blamed it on the opposite count. A stenographer took his words down as follows.[7]

There are other people who blame us—they are the people who are dead against Martial Law. And the subtle charge they make against us, I believe it is Hon. Members on the Nationalist benches and their supporters, and they say that this snake-like Government was sitting still. They wanted revolution first to take place in order that they might crush it with violence and lawlessness (MR FICHARDT: You wanted Revolution.) No, the government wanted the situation to develop; the Government took this attitude that they could not agree with either the one or the other

* Examples of mistaken information or interpretation were:

(1) The emphasis laid by Smuts on the theme of a Red Conspiracy aiming at a Soviet Republic. At the time this mistake was understandable, given the propaganda of the Council of Action and incidents such as the spectacular suicides of two of its members, Spendiff and Fisher, before the government forces captured Fordsburg, which was almost the only place where the commandos had fallen under the control of the Council of Action. The relative unimportance of the Council of Action in comparison with the commandos did not begin to be discernible until the trials.

(2) He said that all the commando leaders were Afrikaner Nationalists. Nearly all of them were; but the 'Adjutant-General' (sometimes called 'Commandant-General') was A. A. Sandham. Sandham later admitted convictions for bigamy and fraud.

of these two extreme criticisms, that before they declared Martial Law they were bound in the interest of the country to let the situation develop, naturally, because it was possible that the situation might develop peacefully.

...There was this possibility that the strike which had lasted a long time in a peaceful manner might end peacefully. A similar strike in England had lasted three months and had ended peacefully, and I thought, and my colleagues thought, that if the Government of this country could get through this great industrial crisis without the declaration of Martial Law it would be a great point scored in the interests of the country...

He expounded that line of thought in further detail and said that the police authorities had told him, before he left the Transvaal for parliament, that they could get through without martial law unless something very much larger happened on the Rand than was happening so far.

I had that assurance when I came here to Parliament, and I thought there was a great deal behind it to make me believe that the judgment was correct, that the police having maintained control of the situation so long, would continue to maintain it to the end. But at the same time behind this judgment of the police and of myself I did have the fear that events might take a more fatal turn, and I told my colleagues, and they will bear me out, that the possibility might arise that for a couple of days, if we delayed the declaration of Martial Law and the calling out of the Burghers, that we might lose control of the Rand, and that matters might get out of hand, and that a good deal of outrage and destruction might take place, the very contingency which ultimately did take place, but even with that risk, the Government said 'let us run it. If there are revolutionary forces brewing in this country, if we are continuously walking on the edge of a volcano, let the country see it, let us even at the risk, the very serious risk of a couple days of revolution, delay the declaration of Martial Law and let the situation develop.'

In telling the truth to parliament Smuts had overstepped the bounds of prudence and delivered himself into the hands of his enemy. Hertzog seized on his phrase about letting the situation develop. 'The Prime Minister himself', he declared, 'has been the main cause of the bloodshed...That is my contention, as opposed to the contention of the Prime Minister, and I shall contend that the strikers resorted to violence because of the insults of the Prime Minister, the incitement of the policemen, of the Government, and the policy of the Government of allowing things to develop.' Hertzog tore that phrase from its context. By a Bismarkian masterstroke of selective abridgement* he pushed aside four paragraphs and fastened on three sentences of Smuts's speech. Smuts had revealed and defended the government's hopes for a peaceful development of the strike; with equal frankness, he had revealed and defended its decision to accept the risks of a violent development. The first revelation was of no use to Hertzog; the second was a godsend to him. He quoted the startling words 'If we are continuously walking on the edge of a volcano, let the country see it...let the situation develop'. Nothing, he exclaimed, could be so unfeeling and criminal as that policy. The government had been determined from the very beginning to use military force and it had pushed ahead with its preparations at the very time when the police, as the Prime Minister himself admitted, had the situation firmly in hand. The Prime Minister had been determined from the very beginning to break organized labour and he had imposed upon the peaceful workers a terrible choice: 'either you voluntarily leave and break your unions or I am ready with might of arms to break them'. He had known what the end would be when he ordered the police to protect scabs. He had wanted the situation to develop because he had arranged how it would develop. 'The Prime Minister', Hertzog cried, 'had sat still, incited the men; he had shot them down with one object—that he might sit behind the tortoise to stick his fork into its head when it should put its head out.' If he had wanted peace he could have had it, but peace would have spoilt his plan to break organized labour. Hertzog harped on those words. Why, he asked, had a judicial inquiry been refused into the Boksburg shootings? Simply because the Prime Minister was determined that organized labour must be destroyed. He wanted the situation to develop and did not care whether or not innocent men got shot. At this point the Speaker intervened; but Hertzog had found a new subject to expound, *platskiet politiek*, the policy of shooting people down. As the *Cape Argus* reported the exposition—

General Hertzog went on to refer to the happenings of the past, declaring that everywhere General Smuts had indulged in a policy of shooting down. The passive resistance movement was the first occasion. Then came the shooting in 1913, and then the illegal deportations...Then the rebellion— shooting down and murder. Then the war, which had distracted the Prime Minister's attention. Then the native trouble at Port Elizabeth—

* The reference is to Bismarck's selective abridgement in producing the Ems telegram.

87

shooting again. Then Bulhoek—shooting again; and then the trouble on the Rand—shooting again.

General Hertzog went on to say that the Prime Minister's footsteps dripped with blood—his footsteps would go down to history in that manner.

That was the climax. There followed a reference to the old war comrade—presumably Jopie Fourie—whom Smuts had shot without giving him the right of appeal. Then came a defence of Tielman Roos and a rhetorical question: were they living in a country where they had justice and right or in a country where they were to have murder and assassination? That was the last flare of passion. Hertzog ended his speech quietly.

For Smuts there was no release from strain. The end of 1922 was almost as stormy for him as its beginning. The Special Court sentenced eighteen men to death for murder. On the advice of the Cabinet, the Governor-General confirmed the sentences on four of those men. One of them was Taffy Long, a Welsh miner and an old soldier who had fought on Gallipoli.* Lord Buxton wrote to tell Smuts that he himself would have followed the Cabinet's advice with a clear conscience if he had still been Governor-General; but Taffy Long took his place with Jopie Fourie in the list of martyrs whom Smuts, his enemies said, had done to death.

All the letters at this time from Smuts to his friends bore the imprint of his exhausted spirit. Nevertheless he hoped for better things later on.

So the New Year has come [he wrote on 2 January 1923]. One expects little good in these days, but I have the consolation that 1923 could not be worse than its predecessor. And with luck it may be much better.[8]

---

* Taffy Long was convicted of murdering a grocer. His defence was that he was executing the sentence of a court on a traitor who had been caught signalling to government forces.

CHAPTER 5

BULHOEK AND BONDELZWARTS

WHEN Hertzog said that Smuts's footsteps dripped with blood he threw into his long list of imputed crimes the slaughter at Bulhoek. Henceforward the enemies of Smuts denounced him as the man who had 'fattened up the vultures'. That denunciation took conspicuous liberties with the historical record.

The recorded slaughter was tragic but neither Smuts nor anybody else had willed it. At Bulhoek on 24 May 1921 eight hundred police and soldiers armed with modern weapons faced five hundred black Israelites armed with knobkerries, assegais and swords. The Israelites charged. The white officers withheld so long as they dared the order to fire, but when the firing was over 163 Israelites lay dead and 129 lay wounded on the field. Casualties on the government side amounted to one trooper wounded and one horse killed.*

How and why the tragedy had occurred was hard for contemporaries to understand. The Israelites were members of a 'Separatist Church'; but in the 1920s the scientific study of the phenomena of 'separatism' was as yet only in its infancy. Nevertheless the potential political significance of those phenomena had already been recognized. By the early 1920s Bantu separatist churches could be numbered by scores. One element common to them all was their passionate resolve to break away from the white man's Christianity and to live under their own leaders within their own religious communities. These communities fell broadly into two classes, the Ethiopian and the Zionist. Psalm 68, verse 31, with its vision of Ethiopia stretching out her hands unto God, and Acts 8, verses 27 to 39, with its story of the apostolic baptism of the eunuch who held high authority under Queen Candace, were foundation texts of the Ethiopian churches, suggesting as they did that black men could achieve equality with white men in the Kingdom of God—or achieve the mastery, with a Black Christ holding the keys of heaven. Of heaven only? The

* The figure of 500 Israelites is perhaps too high, but that of 800 on the government side is nearly accurate, as follows: 612 officers and men of the mounted police; a maxim gun troop of 1 officer and 42 other ranks; an artillery detachment (with two field guns) of two officers and 55 other ranks; a medical staff of seven; a small headquarters staff.

Zionist Churches proclaimed the return of Christ to earth, his over-throw of the four beasts and the final victory of his saints, as prophesied in chapter 7 of the Book of Daniel: 'And the kingdom and dominion, and the greatness of the kingdom shall be given to the saints of the most High, whose kingdom is an everlasting kingdom.' Some Zionist preachers intermingled these spiritual prophesies with the earthier vision of Negro liberators arriving from America in fleets of aero-planes to succour Africa's black saints.

Rigorous academic investigators of the mid-twentieth century identified these emotional and ideological elements, but were unable to weigh them comparatively with the other elements of religious life in the separatist churches. Inevitably, white politicians and ad-ministrators earlier in the century fell far short even of this limited understanding. With little or no support from scientific research they had to strike the best balance they could between optimistic and pessimistic guesses. In Natal, pessimism produced a policy of repression; in the Cape, optimism produced a policy of tolerance. Some sentences which John X. Merriman wrote on 25 April 1909 embodied the Cape doctrine:

I am sure that it is not sound policy to repress these religious ebullitions, however inconvenient and absurd they may seem to us. Repression will be like 'the blood of the martyrs—the seed of the church'. When we come to granting church and school sites, it is a different question. Each must be dealt with on its merits...I hope that the Magistrate will recollect Gibbon's account of the Roman attitude in such matters: to the Magis-trates, all religions were equally useful.[1]

Officials in the Cape's Department of Native Affairs accepted these principles with conviction and administered them with common sense. When the Union was formed the Cape tradition achieved the predominance, although not without some struggle, at administra-tive headquarters in Pretoria. Smuts, when he became Prime Minister and Minister of Native Affairs, chose a Cape man, E. E. Barrett, as Permanent Secretary of the Native Affairs Department.

The Cape's tolerance was more humane and probably—provided it was combined with firmness—more prudent than Natal's repres-sion. Unfortunately, the Native Affairs Department, in its dealings with the Israelites of Bulhoek, forgot the proviso. As a separatist church, the Israelites were an amalgam of Ethiopian and Zionist elements. By distant origin in the 1890s they were an offshoot of the

American Negro 'Church of God and Saints of Christ', a religious order which observed the Jewish calendar and ascribed to its leaders the gift of prophesy. Their founder, John J. Msinkya, established his community in the Queenstown district of Cape Province and attracted to it a forceful young man called Enoch Mgijima. When Msinkya died in 1914 Enoch Mgijima succeeded him as 'Bishop, Prophet and Watchman'. In 1918 he was excommunicated from the Church of God and Saints of Christ, allegedly because of two visions which he brought continually into his preaching: the first, of a stone rolling down a mountain and crushing the people at its foot; the second, of two white goats fighting, with a baboon standing by and watching them, until it suddenly intervened and 'broke them both'. In Enoch's interpretation of the second vision the goats represented the two white peoples of South Africa and the baboon the black people.[2]

Not until after the disaster at Bulhoek did the white officials hear this sinister story of Enoch's visions and preaching.* In their eyes, he was troublesome chiefly because he and his followers were persistent squatters on common land. Bulhoek was a sub-location of the Kamastone location near Queenstown. It contained plots held by individual title and common land reserved for the title-holders. Enoch was a title holder; but he could not accommodate on his own plot the hundreds of Israelites who visited Bulhoek year by year for the feast of the Passover. He therefore selected a site on the commonage named Ntabilanga and erected his tabernacle on it. The other land holders did not at first object because Enoch told them that the people would disperse when they had completed the Passover; but in 1920 they failed to disperse and began erecting permanent huts. On various occasions between June and September the Superintendent of the Kamastone location, E. E. Nightingale, remonstrated with Enoch and received his assurances that the intruders would soon go away; but they stayed on. Nightingale called in the police and issued summonses against them; but they took no notice of them. In October 1920, Nightingale received instructions to collect the names of all the people living at Ntabilanga; but the Israelites set guards around their settlement and refused to let him in. On 8 December the magistrate from Queenstown, supported by a force of nearly 100 police, attempted to deal with the situation. He

---

* They gained their knowledge retrospectively through evidence submitted at the trial of Enoch and some of his surviving followers in November and December 1921.

called on the Israelites to register themselves and offered them rations and free railway passes to their homes; but in an eight-hour parley he made no headway at all. God, they told him, did not approve registration. That same evening, messengers from Enoch visited the police camp and told the officer in charge that the prophet ordered him to withdraw his men from the Bulhoek location. The officer obeyed the prophet. It was a pusillanimous and ultimately a disastrous surrender.

At headquarters in Pretoria the high officials refused the proffered help of volunteers from Queenstown—a wise decision—but unwisely refused the magistrate's request for police reinforcements. Instead the Secretary of the Native Affairs Department, accompanied by the Chief Commissioner of Police and a senior military officer, made a personal visit to Bulhoek. He found the permanent Native population of the district incensed against the Israelites and insistent on having them removed. He asked four prominent Natives, including Tengo Jabavu, the editor of *Imvo*, to accompany him to a meeting which he had arranged with the Israelites for 17 December. They thought they might achieve a better result by an independent parley, but it proved fruitless. So did the official meeting on 17 December. Its only outcome was an Israelite request for a meeting with the Prime Minister.

Smuts said that he would grant them an interview as soon as he could. He would have done better to have refused them firmly because there was no prospect of his being able to meet them for a long time to come; for he was in the middle of a fierce election fight and after that had urgent work awaiting him both in South Africa and at the Imperial Conference. His half-promise had merely given the Israelites what they most wanted—an additional excuse for digging in at Bulhoek, bringing in more disciples and erecting more huts, while all the time they paid no taxes, reported no births or deaths and denied recognition of any kind to the officials of the government and the law of the land. Enoch was content to leave things as they were and made no second request for an interview with the Prime Minister.*

Pending the time when he could go himself to Bulhoek, Smuts sent

* Smuts was subsequently blamed for not having met them; but Sir Thomas Graham, the presiding judge at Enoch's trial, said in his summing up that they had felt no sense of grievance on that account.

there his newly appointed Native Affairs Commission.* He had chosen its three members carefully from the best talent and experience available in South Africa. Two of the three, Senator A. W. Roberts and Dr C. T. Loram, had deep roots in the Cape's tradition of tolerance. Roberts by birth was a Scot but had given to South Africa many decades of meritorious service in the fields of Native education and natural science; Loram was South African born, a graduate of Cambridge and Columbia, an educational expert and a pioneer of race relations studies, who in later years achieved a high position at Yale University.† The third member of the Commission was General L. A. S. Lemmer, a comrade of Botha and Smuts in the Anglo-Boer war and ever since then their faithful follower in politics. Smuts doubtless regarded Lemmer's earthy common sense as a counterweight to the academic sophistication of his two colleagues.

On 6 April 1921 the three members of the Commission held a long parley at Ntabilanga with three of Enoch's followers. The Israelites explained that they would like to obey the law, but that Jehovah was more powerful than the law and that they feared to offend him by disregarding his wishes and obeying the wishes of men. On 7 April the Commission held discussions with the chief officials of the district, whom they found dithering between their conviction that the law must be asserted and their reluctance to assert it forcibly. On 8 April the Commission held a second meeting with a delegation of the Israelites, who this time appeared more friendly and even tolerated an inspection of the huts on the commonage. They said that they were simply waiting for the command of God to hear his word through the mouth of his prophet and would then disperse; but General Lemmer had the feeling—so he told parliament afterwards‡—that even an angel from heaven would not persuade them to listen to reason. On 9 June the Commissioners held a meeting in the morning with the settled Natives of the district and another meeting in the afternoon with the white farmers; members of each

---

* See p. 119 below.
† Roberts joined the staff of the Native College at Lovedale in 1883; he was President of the S.A. Science Congress in 1913 and of the S.A. Astronomical Society in 1928; between 1920 and 1930 he was appointed to various commissions of inquiry into Native affairs. Loram was Inspector of Schools in Natal from 1906 to 1917 and Chief Inspector of Native Education from 1917 to 1920. Bishop Sundkler, in *Bantu Prophets in South Africa* (London, 2nd edition, p. 73), calls him 'the famous expert on Native education'. In 1931 he became Sterling Professor of Education at Yale and in 1933 Director of Studies in the Department of Culture Contacts and Race Relations of the Yale Graduate School.
‡ On 22 June.

group attended both meetings and there was a strong consensus of opinion between the two groups. The Natives began by demanding the immediate eviction of the Israelites, but, after the Commissioners had pointed out that this might well lead to bloodshed, they promised to remain patient for a few months more while the Commission worked for a peaceful settlement. The white farmers were not so patient and said that they would take action themselves if the government did not take it soon. On 21 April the Commissioners submitted an interim report to the government. Like the local officials, they wavered between their feeling that force would have to be used and their fear of using it. They recognized that the present situation could not continue indefinitely but asked leave to visit the Israelites again as bearers of the following proposals:

(1) that the Government will furnish rations and free railage to those who have homes, either on private farms or locations, to return to their domiciles;

(2) that on a general dispersal of the Israelites the Government will be prepared to consider an application for a site at Ntabilanga, which could be used for the purposes of the sect, on some such conditions as the following: That such site should not be used as a permanent habitation but only be used by persons attending from time to time the religious festivals observed by the Israelites, and that such persons should not depasture stock on the commonage;

(3) that the Government will endeavour to arrange for the persons who, having sold their land, and are penniless to be accommodated in some Crown location occupied by members of the same tribe.[3]

The concluding reference to penniless persons had sinister implications. As a community, the Israelites had sufficient resources to keep them going only for a few months more. Some members of the community were already begging and others were stealing on the lands of their neighbours, both white and black. Six months earlier, a white farmer had shot at some Israelites whom he had caught trespassing on his land. He had wounded one of them and killed another, and was now awaiting trial for culpable homicide; but the Israelite witnesses, consistently with their principle of recognizing only the laws of God, were refusing the summons to attend court. A warrant was issued for their arrest and the government published a notice which insisted that all South African people, both white and black, must respect the courts of law.

The Commissioners had made arrangements for another meeting

with the Israelites on 11 May. The Israelites received them peaceably but refused their terms for a settlement: if the government could not allow them to remain in peace at Ntabilanga, they said, then the matter was simply an issue between God and the government and they preferred to follow Jehovah. The Commissioners regretfully concluded that further discussion would be fruitless and sent the following telegram to the government:

Commission visited Bulhoek today, discussed situation and placed before Israelites the conditions contained in its report of 21st ultimo. Government's offer was refused, Israelites maintaining fanatical attitude. Commission unanimously of opinion that a force be sent which is sufficiently strong to carry out such instructions as may be issued by the Government regarding illegal squatting of Israelites as well as to effect arrest of defaulting witnesses. Commission urges that such force should be sufficiently strong to overawe natives if possible and so prevent unnecessary bloodshed.

Nobody in South Africa believed that the government could procrastinate any longer in upholding the law. On 17 May *Imvo*, the leading Bantu newspaper, took a firm line against Enoch and his followers. 'The Israelites of Bulhoek', it wrote, 'are a tough lot. They have withstood the blandishments of the Native Affairs Commission and the Government to obey the laws of the country. The Commission has had to give them up in sheer disgust. The next step is with the Government, and the Israelites have left them no other course than that of coercion.' On the same day the General Council of the Transkeian Territories passed a resolution condemning the Israelites and calling on the government to enforce the law, if possible without bloodshed. That, precisely, was the advice which the European newspapers gave. To cite an important example: the Johannesburg *Star*, which after 24 May became strongly critical of the government, was insistent right up to then that force would have to be used to uphold the law—massive force, the *Star* demanded, for then there would be less likelihood of the Israelites resisting it. That was the theme of a *Star* editorial on 10 May and that was the argument of its correspondent in Queenstown, who on 20 May acclaimed the arrival of a 'magnificent force of business-looking police'. There was a general feeling, the correspondent continued, that they would meet with no resistance when they advanced towards the Israelite camp. But next day his report was not quite so confident. 'The overwhelming size of the force at Colonel Truter's command', he wrote, 'is the best security against resistance on the part of the Israelites, but many people hold the view that the hotheads amongst Enoch's leaders will not surrender without a struggle.'

At 8 a.m. on 24 May the Commissioner of Police, Colonel Truter, deployed his force. Before ordering the advance he made one last bid for peace.

I despatched Sergts. Wicks and Boucher, both competent native linguists, to the main body of the Israelites with the following message: 'What are your intentions? Will you allow us to come in and do as we intend to do, or do you intend to fight?'...At 11.30 a.m. Sergts. Wicks and Boucher returned with the following reply from the Israelites: 'Jehovah will not allow you to burn our huts, to drive our people away from Ntabilanga, or arrest the two men you wish to.'

Meanwhile Colonel Truter had ordered Colonel Woon to take up a position facing the main body of the Israelites. Three men advanced to meet him and their spokesman asked him what his intentions were.

He replied that he intended to enter the Israelite village, and informed him that resistance on the part of the natives would be met with force. The spokesman then said if that was the intention...the Israelites would fight, adding: 'If there is a fight God will fight with us on our side.' Col. Woon repeated his advice to lay down their arms. They then asked if the Colonel had anything to add and, on being informed that what Colonel Woon said was final, they said: 'It is finished.'

As soon as the three men had returned the Israelites advanced at a fast run. Colonel Woon ordered the centre troop of twenty-five men to fire one volley. The Israelites still came on. Colonel Woon then ordered the whole of his front line to open five rounds rapid fire. In his evidence at the inquest he said:

It was a very deadly fire—the charging Israelites began to drop in numbers, but it did not retard their charge in the slightest. They continued charging...It was not until about twenty yards from my line that the charge was broken.

He then ordered the cease fire.[4]

There was firing on other sections of the front but it ceased as soon as the charge was broken. An Israelite in a red cloak, supposed to be Enoch, watched the slaughter from a ridge on the left of the front. When all was over the troops found Enoch hiding in a hut in Ntabilanga. They sent him away to Queenstown gaol. They set the other unwounded prisoners to work on collecting the 163 dead Israelites and digging graves for them. When that work was finished the Commissioner of Police permitted the grave-diggers to hold a religious service over the graves. Meanwhile, the small ambulance force of one officer and five other ranks worked throughout the night and far into the next day attending to the 129 wounded Israelites.

On 25 May Smuts rose in the House of Assembly to make a statement about the events of the previous day.* 'No one', he said, 'regrets what has happened at Bulhoek more than the Government— and the attitude of the Government all through for months past has been to prevent what has occurred there.' He laid stress on the policy of tolerance and patience which the government had followed for many months past and explained the reasons which had finally compelled it to enforce the law. Even so, he said, the police had received specific instructions not to use their fire-arms, 'except in the very last resort—the ultimate resort'. In obedience to these instructions they had reserved their fire until the very last moment. 'I am persuaded in my own mind', he declared, '...that there was no alternative for the police but to fire as they did. I am sure that the Government has done its best to avoid bloodshed, and to make it plain to the people that, whether white or black, they have to submit to and obey the law of the land, and...the law of the land will be carried out in the last resort as fearlessly against black as against white.'[5]

He would have done better in his concluding sentences to have expressed grief at the tragic loss of life. Had he been given the opportunity, he might later on have corrected his mistake of emphasis; but he was on the eve of boarding ship in fulfilment of his long-standing commitment to attend the conference of Commonwealth Prime Ministers. He arrived in London on 11 June, three days before his statement was debated in parliament. In his absence, F. S. Malan answered for the government. By this time, criticisms of its action at Bulhoek had found wide expression in the newspapers; but many of the criticisms cancelled each other out. In open contradiction of the opinions which it had expressed earlier, the *Star* blamed the government for sending too large a force to Bulhoek; but it also

---

* Smuts had not yet received final reports from Bulhoek and his statement contained some errors. For example, he spoke of 'thousands of poor deluded Natives' but well-informed contemporary reports make it clear that the total Israelite strength was between 400 and 500.

blamed it for not frightening the Israelites into submission by bombing them from the air.* Again, the *Star* blamed the government for instructing the police to withhold their fire until the very last moment, for this—it said—made the maximum killing inevitable; but the *Star*'s correspondent at Queenstown insisted that the police would have put themselves in the wrong if they had fired earlier. Indeed, the government and its agents at Bulhoek had been caught in a dilemma: as F. S. Malan put it in his reply to the debate on 24 June—

Suppose the natives with their assegais and spears had got amongst the police and a half dozen or more police were killed, and a large number wounded, what would the complaint have been?...So if they took a force they were blamed for slaughter, and if not, and if some of the police were killed, then the complaint would have been on the other side, that it was a careless Government, sending in a small number of police among many armed natives, to their death. He asked, was part of the shock people felt not due to the fact that it was an unequal fight, and on the native side there were killed, and on the ¦police side there were not? He thought so.[6]

Many other people thought the same. On 16 June *Die Burger* expressed the fear that the Natives might come to view Bulhoek in the same light as the Afrikaners viewed Slachter's Nek. Among a minority of Natives this was already happening. On 27 May the South African Native National Congress at Bloemfontein denounced 'the pogrom' at Bulhoek. The Congress found it hard to believe that the government would have taken similar drastic action if South Africans of European descent had been involved in a similar situation. In the Queenstown district, a meeting of Natives, while praising the government for its earlier 'patience and forbearance', deplored 'the carnage' of 24 May and called for a commission of inquiry which would include four Native representatives, including two to be chosen by surviving members of the Israelite community. General Hertzog also demanded a commission of inquiry, although he intended it to be all-white. The majority of the newspapers, including those that normally supported the government, endorsed this demand; but on 15 June F. S. Malan announced the government's final decision not to appoint a commission of inquiry.

For reasons of psychology, in particular of Native psychology, that decision was ill-advised. The government should have seized the

* This criticism was of ill omen: see p. 101 below.

chance of submitting its thoughts and deeds, including its early mistakes of omission, to judicial scrutiny. But in the event—although the government gained no credit thereby—Sir Thomas Graham, as presiding judge at the trial of Enoch Mgijima and more than a hundred of his disciples, brought to light as much truth as any commissioners of that time could have discovered. Graham concluded that the tragedy was inevitable, given what had gone before; but he dealt sternly with the procrastination, hesitations and retreats which had flattered the Israelites into believing that the government was cowardly and they themselves invincible. At the same time he dealt sternly with Enoch and the other Israelite leaders. The evidence submitted to him made it clear beyond all doubt, he said, that they were fanatical, power-drunk and seditious.*

Nearly three decades later, a scholarly and impartial investigator, Bengt G. M. Sundkler of Sweden,† endorsed Sir Thomas Graham's findings and put them into historical perspective. Sundkler measured the rapid spread of separatist churches in South Africa: at the end of the First World War, 76; in 1932, 320; at the end of the Second World War, 800. He traced some typical genealogies of the churches and established useful categories of classification. Not least, he demonstrated the connection between the impulses of religious self-expression, racial protest and—potentially—political insurrection. Although he examined religious separatism as a specifically South African phenomenon, he also showed himself aware of its prevalence elsewhere in Africa. He referred, for example, to two movements closely contemporaneous with the rise of the Israelites—John Chilembwe's revolt at Nyasaland in 1915 and the Watch Tower agitations in Northern Rhodesia at the close of the First World War. Had he wished, he could have recorded half a dozen or more East African movements which were closely akin—sometimes even in their tragic climaxes—to the Israelite movement.‡ Even that range of

---

* Enoch Mgijima, his brother Charles, Gilbert Matshoba and 129 other Israelites were tried in November–December at Queenstown for sedition or, alternatively, for riotous assembly endangering the public peace. Enoch was sentenced to 6 years' imprisonment with hard labour; 30 office-bearers to 3 years' imprisonment; the rank and file to 18 months' imprisonment; the old men and boys to 1 year's imprisonment, suspended for 2 years. One would wish to know whether this last sentence was ever enforced.

† The 1st edition of Bishop Sundkler's *Bantu Prophets in South Africa* was published in 1948. See General Note on Sources, p. 536 below.

‡ Professor D. A. Low, in a note which he has kindly written for my use, refers to the Kamba 'madness' of 1911 in Kenya; the Maji-Maji rebellion of 1904–7 in Tanganyika; the Allah Water and the Nyabingi cults in Uganda between 1911 and 1930; the Dinyi ya

comparison would have been too narrow. The story of Bulhoek was
a variation upon a theme which sociologists of the mid-twentieth
century found constant from Indonesia to Brazil and which historians
found constant from Maccabean zealots in the second century B.C.
to Jehovah's Witnesses in the twentieth century A.D.*

Unfortunately for Smuts, those new insights of sociology and
history came too late. Partisan malice had already branded him 'the
butcher of Bulhoek'.† That mud stuck. Roy Campbell, a poet
temperamentally antipathetical to Smuts, hailed the publication of
Holism and Evolution with four stinging lines.

> The love of Nature burning in his heart
> Our new St Francis offers us his book.
> The Saint who fed the birds at Bondelswaart
> And fattened up the vultures at Bull Hoek.

Those couplets were brilliant satire but their last line was a travesty
of the truth.

'The Bondelzwarts affair', as the Permanent Mandates Commission of the League called it,‡ reached its climax in military operations of late May and early June 1922. The contending forces, unlike
the contending forces at Bulhoek, might have seemed at first sight
to be well matched, for the Bondelzwarts were a fighting tribe with
about 600 men of military age, while the Administrator of South
West Africa commanded a force of less than 400 police and volunteers. But the equipment of the two sides was unequal. Whereas the
Bondelzwarts had fire-arms of some kind or other for perhaps one
man in three, the government forces were sufficiently supplied with
modern rifles, machine guns, field artillery and aeroplanes. This
disparity of equipment explained the disparate casualty rates. The
tribe had 115 men killed in action but the government forces only

---

Misambwa movement in Kenya and its tragic outcome in 1948, of which he writes: 'This
episode seems to me really very close to your Bulhoek one—and it took place twenty-five
years later.'

  * The published symposium on *Millennial Dreams in Action* (ed. Sylvia Thrupp, The
Hague, 1962) covers a wide range of space and time and suggests by contrast the sociological and historical darkness in which academic persons such as Loram, not to mention
politicians such as Smuts, had been compelled forty years earlier to think and act.

  † In a speech in the House on 23 May 1923 Smuts said that he was called the Butcher
of Bulhoek in Moscow.

  ‡ The government referred to 'the Bondelzwarts rebellion' and some of the government's critics, both in South Africa and overseas, denounced 'the Bondelzwarts massacre';
but the Permanent Mandates Commission deliberately chose non-tendentious terminology.

two. Bombing from the air, although it was not mainly responsible for the Bondelzwarts death roll, decided the campaign. On Sunday 29 May the Bondelzwarts warriors were defending the ring of hills which surrounded Guruchas, the headquarters of their tribe. At Guruchas the old men, women and children were gathered together with their cattle and sheep, horses and donkeys. At 3 o'clock in the afternoon two aeroplanes flew in over the hills, circled the valley and dropped their bombs. The flocks and herds were their target but women and children of the tribe were at work or play among the animals.* The aeroplanes returned at sunset and dropped more bombs. They returned again at dawn the next day. Those attacks achieved their object—carnage amongst the animals, terror amongst the people and the capitulation of Guruchas. Nevertheless, 250 warriors of the tribe had slipped away during the night into the desolate mountains and kloofs southwards towards the Orange River. It was their purpose to fight against South Africans the same long and bitter guerilla war as they had fought eighteen years earlier against Germans. But history did not this time repeat itself. Thanks chiefly to aerial reconnaissance and bombing, the campaign ended one week later with the total subjugation of the Bondelzwarts tribe.

It was the bitter end of a long struggle for survival and dominance in a harsh lunar landscape. Over the vast tablelands of South West Africa the human population was spread thin: north of the Tropic of Capricorn Hereros and other Bantu tribes; south from the Tropic to the Orange River Basters, Bondelzwarts and other clans of Hottentot and mixed blood.† The original Hottentots of the Territory, the Nama folk, had hunted and killed the aboriginal Bushmen; but from the late eighteenth century onwards they had to defend their mastery of water and rough pasture against the Orlams, invading Hottentots from Cape Colony. The Orlams in their turn were moving ever northwards under pressure from the trekking Boers. Yet it was not conflict all the time between Hottentots and Boers. In their common struggle for life in a harsh environment they worked with each other

---

* In evidence before the Permanent Mandates Commission Major Herbst stated the casualties from the bombing as two children killed, seven women and children wounded.

† The census of 1922 gave the following enumeration of the Territory's population:

    177,462   Natives
     30,845   Half-breeds
     19,437   Whites (of whom 7,855 were Germans who stayed on after the war)

and learnt from each other. From the Boers the Orlams received fire-arms and the Bible, waggons and the *taal*; from the Orlams the Boers learned new skills in the tracking of Bushmen and animals, in the digging of edible roots and in the building and furnishing of their round, reed-roofed huts. The Boers fathered children on Orlam mothers. The Orlams fathered children on Nama mothers. From this medley of military conflict, economic co-operation and racial inter-mingling the Bondelzwarts tribe emerged.

Bondelzwarts families had Afrikaner, or, occasionally, English names. They spoke Afrikaans. They were Christians. As a tribe they were independent and liberty loving or, as the Europeans said, inso-lent. They produced brave fighters and skilful leaders. On the fringes of nomadic civilization they could hold their own with their Boer counterparts; but they failed to withstand the weight of power which Imperial Germany brought to bear against them. In the Herero war of the early twentieth century they had been among the first to fight and the last to stop fighting. Some of them, rather than submit to the Germans, went into exile across the Orange River. There they lived for the next ten years and more, nostalgic for their tribe and the land of their tribe, sadly diminished though the land was.*

Among the exiles were Jacobus Christian, the Captain† of their tribe, and Abraham Morris, the indomitable leader of their feints and ambushes in the Gungunib Kloof and its surrounding mountains. In 1915, when Botha and Smuts invaded German South West Africa, Morris joined their forces as a scout. The Bondelzwarts welcomed the South Africans as liberators and looked to them for restitution of the land, independence and pride which the Germans had taken from them. They had reason for pitching their hopes high, for Smuts already had in his head his case against German colonial rule: namely, that the Germans had maltreated their Native subjects. The statement of that case pointed forward to the Mandatory principle, that the well-being and development of peoples such as the Bondelzwarts constituted a sacred trust of civilization.‡

To fulfil such high expectations proved politically impossible. What

* In 1906 the Germans confined them within a Reserve of approximately 174,000 hectares—only a small fragment of the land which, in the view of the Bondelzwarts, belonged to them.

† 'Captain' was a title adopted under Boer influence and subsequently recognized by the Germans.

‡ Smuts, however, had not originally intended that Mandates should be established in Africa. See *Smuts: The Sanguine Years*, pp. 491, 499, 507.

the tribes of South West Africa and the Aborigines Protection Society in England expected was incompatible with what the white settlers expected—to begin with, the German settlers; nearly 8,000 of them stayed on in South West Africa and the Union government treated them on the principle of *parcere subiectis*.* Meanwhile, 10,000 or more South Africans were seeking advancement for themselves in the conquered territory. They enjoyed their government's strong support, for Botha had been insistent from the start that he must strengthen his position as war leader by opening South West Africa to Afrikaners in search of land and jobs. Unfortunately, too many of the men who got the jobs, in the police especially, were unqualified for them. There was disquieting evidence of that in the letters which the military Administrator wrote to Smuts from Windhoek in the latter years of the War.†

South West Africa remained under martial law until October 1920, when Smuts chose G. R. Hofmeyr to inaugurate a civil régime. Subsequently the choice aroused criticism but when Smuts made it he had good motives and good reasons. Hofmeyr was a Cape man of liberal education and outlook and of wide administrative experience in the Cape, the Transvaal and the Union. Throughout the previous ten years he had been the respected Clerk of the Union House of Assembly. He had come to Smuts originally on the strong recommendation of John X. Merriman and had always proved himself trustworthy and intelligent. In sending him to South West Africa Smuts gave him the support of two experienced senior colleagues, Major Herbst as Secretary of the Administration and Major Manning as Native Commissioner.

All this, however, was far above the heads of the Bondelzwarts. After five years of South African rule in one form or another they were finding that life remained for them pretty much as it had been before. To be sure, their South African rulers were milder or laxer in small things than the Germans had been, but they maintained intact two basic rules of the German system: every male Native over the age of fourteen must carry a pass; and he must be in the service

* The Union Government not only respected the private rights of Germans in South West Africa but patiently negotiated with the German government for a mutually acceptable political settlement. By the agreement of October 1923, the Germans were to become citizens of the Union, except when an individual opted specifically for German nationality. By the same agreement, the German community was guaranteed a large measure of cultural autonomy.

† See *op. cit.* p. 401.

of a white master unless he possessed visible means of support. To the Bondelzwarts, visible means of support meant land; but their new masters were not restoring the land that the Germans had taken away; on the contrary, they were encroaching—so the tribe asserted —on the remnant of land that the Germans had left them.* At the same time they appeared determined to impose perpetual exile upon the tribe's lost leaders. Year after year the tribe petitioned for the return of Jacobus Christian and Abraham Morris and for the reinstatement of Christian as hereditary Captain; year by year they were told that their petition could not be granted for the time being. At last, in August 1919, Christian took matters into his own hands and returned across the Orange River, with about forty of his followers and their animals, without asking leave. The police told Christian to report to the magistrate but then arrested him while he was on the way. They also confiscated the arms which he and his men had brought with them. The Administration subsequently released him and allowed him to remain in the Reserve, but did not reinstate him in the Captaincy. It had already appointed a headman of its own choosing, a half breed called Timothy Beukes who had no connection at all with the tribe.

That was a flagrant error of what in those days was called Native Administration. Hofmeyr, when he took office as Administrator, recognized the error but did not rectify it, although he was well aware that Christian's influence was paramount in the tribe. He found himself under immediate pressure from European settlers who for some years past had been scared of Native risings; but he thought that they had no sufficient reason for their fears and was prepared to believe that the Natives had real grievances. In February 1921 he visited the Bondelzwarts and listened to their complaints. In May of the same year he instructed Major Manning to pursue the inquiry further. Manning spent three days in the Reserve and produced an illuminating report.[7] Its most prominent feature was the evidence it contained of the tribe's extreme poverty. In the light of that evidence, Manning was able to understand their bitter sense of grievance against the tax they had to pay on their dogs. They needed the dogs for the protection of their small stock and they used them for hunting; but white men held the strong conviction that hunting was a bad

* On instructions from Hofmeyr the Surveyor-General investigated the Bondelzwarts' allegations of encroachment on their land and reported them to be unjustified.

thing for Natives; they ought rather to work for the settlers. A money tax was a strong inducement for Natives to look for work; but the dog tax had been fixed so high* that the Bondelzwarts could not earn the money for it, either in paid employment—which anyway was not easy to find—or by any other means. As they put their difficulties to Major Manning—'They had never refused to pay but had no money. Their stock was usually in quarantine and when any could be sold they only got a few shillings for them. They were only permitted to sell grass to the storekeepers, who only gave small prices and these in the form of "goodfors" for goods. The young men were willing to work if given an opportunity.'

Manning took their economic grievances seriously and he was just as much impressed by their political grievances. He felt no doubt at all that they regarded Christian as their rightful and actual chief and that they disregarded the alien headman who had been foisted on them. He found no evidence of hostility or insolence on Christian's part. He censured the police for the trick they had played on Christian when he returned from exile and declared that it had destroyed confidence between the tribe and the government. He recommended that dealings with the tribe should so far as possible be removed from police control and entrusted to the civilian authorities. This recommendation, like the others which Manning made explicitly or implicitly, was sound; but the ensuing action at administrative headquarters was tardy and ill-considered. Moreover, Manning had made no mention at all of one outstanding grievance of the tribe— the continuing ban on the return of Abraham Morris from exile. In May 1922, Morris returned without leave.

When Morris and his companions crossed the river they knew that they were breaking three administrative regulations—by entering South West Africa without leave, by bringing in livestock without a permit, by bringing in fire-arms. Nevertheless, Morris had some grounds for hoping that the authorities would deal with him tolerantly, as they had dealt tolerantly two years earlier with Jacobus Christian. He made no attempt to conceal his arrival at Guruchas

---

* The tax was £1 for the first dog, 30s. for the second, £2 for the third. A year later, Hofmeyr reduced it by 50% but meanwhile many members of the tribe were prosecuted and punished for non-payment. Another financial burden on them was the 30s. they had to pay for branding irons. Unlike the Europeans, they were compelled to leave their branding irons with the police instead of taking them home, and this discriminatory treatment rankled with them.

and on the demand of a police officer, Sergeant van Niekerk, he readily surrendered his rifle. Next morning van Niekerk returned under instruction to arrest Morris. Even then, Morris might have gone quietly; but the tribe would not let him go. A protesting crowd forced the policeman and his prisoner apart. Up to then van Niekerk had been patient and tactful but now he lost his temper. He mounted his horse and before he rode away he turned round and shouted, 'Now the government's lead will melt on your hides.'*

The tribe interpreted this outburst as a threat of war. To the Administration, the tribe's behaviour seemed a threat of rebellion. On 10 May a telegram from the local magistrate to Major Herbst denounced Morris as 'a dangerous person' and told an alarmist story of events since his return. On 12 May a senior police officer, Major van Coller, arrived from Windhoek with instructions to investigate the trouble and, if possible, to settle it peacefully. Van Coller approached Christian, whom he rightly recognized as the tribe's real head, through two intermediaries, Mr Northout, the recently appointed Superintendent of the Reserve and Mgr Krolokowski, the head of a neighbouring Roman Catholic mission.† The intermediaries exchanged letters with the nervous and wary Christian and after a day or two went out to see him at Guruchas. There Northout made a promise which he had no authority to make and which his superiors refused to honour. If the men wanted gave themselves up, he said, everything would be forgiven and forgotten.‡ Christian put that promise upon record: 'I, Jacobus Christian, declare herewith that the five men will immediately report themselves to the magistrate at Warmbad when I have received an assurance, in writing, from the Administrator at Windhoek, that if these men surrender everything will be forgiven and forgotten and that no further steps will be taken against my people as told us by the Commissioner.'

Hofmeyr made no reply to that communication but instructed van Coller to demand the surrender not only of the wanted men but of all arms and ammunition, and at the same time to warn the Bondelzwarts that any further resistance on their part would produce

---

* Van Niekerk subsequently denied that he had used these words; but two out of three members of the Commission of Inquiry (see p. 537 below) found his denial unconvincing.

† Morris had joined the Roman Catholic Church when he was in exile in Cape Province.

‡ Northout denied, but without carrying conviction, that he had used these words.

serious consequences not only for individuals but for the whole tribe. Meanwhile Hofmeyr speeded up the organization and deployment of his assault force. Van Coller made various attempts to induce the Bondelzwarts to yield, but on 23 May he received the following letter:

To Major van Coller

I, the undersigned Captain J. Christian, in re five men and the rifles.

Dear Sir, it is very difficult to surrender my property because the rifles and the five men are my lawful property. The men did not steal anything and the rifle was handed by Abraham Morris to Police Sergeant van Niekerk. Further I see, as pointed out by Sergeant van Niekerk, that the troops are assembling in Warmbad and Kalkfontein, and I see no chance of surrendering the rifles and the five men. Further I have no rifles to hand over. I am still waiting for my rifles which I handed to the Government in 1919, and I pray that same may be returned to me.

Your friend,
J. Christian, Capt.[8]

Hofmeyr thought Christian's letter insulting but he sent him a message to say that he was willing to meet him. He received no reply. That clinched the affair. For the past six years or more, Hofmeyr wrote later, the Bondelzwarts had been growing ever more insolent and the Europeans more panicky. He felt that the whole country would become ablaze unless a settlement were announced or a decisive blow struck. He had not, he protested, sought the use of force; but the time had now come 'to inflict a severe and lasting lesson'.[9]

Hofmeyr took personal command of the armed forces. Journalists jeered at him, but he conducted a successful punitive expedition. When it was over Captain Prinsloo, the man who hunted Morris to his death, rebuked one of his troopers for his vindictiveness against the Bondelzwarts. 'We are not here for revenge', Prinsloo said, 'but to put an end to this rebellion and that's all.' After a short silence a friend of Prinsloo's commented, 'This isn't pleasant work. These people are fighting for the same thing as we fought the English for twenty years ago: freedom. That's all they want.'*

Apart from his use of air power, Hofmeyr had followed the established practice of Colonial governments in Africa. For the past three decades, to go no further back, punitive expeditions, sometimes

---

* Prinsloo's friend was the volunteer Toon van den Heever, a young lawyer from Windhoek who later became a judge of the Supreme Court and a leading Afrikaans poet. This story is told by Richard Freislich. (See General Note on Sources.)

closely akin to the Bondelzwarts affair, had been the normal and—so the administrators and soldiers usually maintained—the necessary concomitant of the establishment or re-establishment of European authority. If the punitive expeditions in Kenya between 1890 and 1910 had been marked on the map, there would have been few, if any, blank spaces except in the desert areas. If a record had been compiled of punitive expeditions in the Lango district of Uganda from 1910 to 1920, there would have been few, if any, blank years. Forty years later, the historian of the King's African Rifles* recorded, for the reign of Edward VII, the issue of thirty-four separate clasps, additional to the General Service Medal. Each of these clasps commemorated a military expedition in East, Central or West Africa. Sir Charles Eliot, when he was British Commissioner in the East Africa Protectorate, once made the ironical suggestion that every British officer should be given three medals as soon as he landed at Mombasa, on the understanding that he would have to surrender a medal for every punitive expedition in which he took part. Some of these expeditions inflicted heavy losses of men and animals on African populations. To be sure, they became less frequent with the years; in the reign of George V only ten clasps were issued to the King's African Rifles. Nevertheless, severe punitive expeditions took place in Kenya—to mention only one of Britain's many African territories—in 1925 and again in 1929.†

The Bondelzwarts affair was not abnormal; but it received abnormal publicity. That was the inevitable consequence of South West Africa's status as a Mandated Territory. From 5 September 1923, when the Union Government took the initiative in reporting the recent happenings to the League Assembly, up to 12 May 1924, when Hofmeyr made a personal appearance before the Permanent Mandates Commission, the Bondelzwarts affair remained in the limelight at Geneva. Throughout the same period it received wide publicity in the British press, particularly in dailies like the *Manchester Guardian* and weeklies like the *New Statesman*. That was significant. By the early 1920s the stream of pro-Boer sentiment in Britain was

* Colonel H. Moyse-Bartlett.

† In the above paragraph I have drawn upon a memorandum kindly written for my use by Professor D. A. Low. Needless to say, this memorandum is unemotive. Professor Low demonstrates that the use of force played a more important part than most British historians have recognized in the establishment of colonial rule; but he is well aware that other essential elements of authority were co-existent with the use of force.

rapidly drying up and the stream of pro-Native sentiment was rapidly rising. Publicity about the attack on the Bondelzwarts reflected and no doubt accelerated this long-term change of direction in British public opinion.

Public comment in South Africa was significant chiefly in short term. A notable feature of the parliamentary debates of May 1923 was the almost total silence of the Nationalists. It must have irked them not to take up this new stick for beating Smuts with, but they could hardly run the risk of branding themselves in the *platteland* constituencies as the champions of Hottentots. Most of them absented themselves from the House. They felt able to do so because they had friends in the Labour party ready and eager to flail Smuts. Thomas Boydell portrayed him as 'a cold pitiless man to be trusted to kill if necessary'. R. B. Waterston denounced him as 'the bloody Jeffreys of South Africa'. 'Tonight', Smuts commented, 'the whole fire seems to have been concentrated on me. It leaves me cold.' A Labour member interjected, 'Murder always does.'[10]

In the *Pretoria News* of 4 June 1923 Vere Stent, a journalist of wide experience and sharp perception, made the following comment on this vituperative campaign:

I was with General Smuts during the East African campaign. I sat at Defence Headquarters...during the attempted revolution of 1914. I was at Headquarters at Johannesburg during the revolt of 1922. And I may, perhaps, as an eye witness be allowed to say this: At no time did I ever see the General show the slightest sign of vindictiveness or even anger. He is instinctively a calm, kindly, sympathetic man: as far from a bloody-minded 'Butcher' as it is possible to imagine. His demeanour during a crisis is that of a man playing chess. It is impersonal, grave—as that of one knowing the issues at stake should be. It is the frightened man who commits cruelties and butcheries, not the collected, cool soldier. The General was always the latter, and no one knows it better than Col. Creswell.* Let us hope that he has by now the grace to be ashamed of his friends' hysterical outburst.

Smuts could have defended himself with some effect if he had wanted to. The Governor-General, in a despatch enclosing reports of the debates of late May, put on official record Smuts's urgent appeals to Hofmeyr to use every effort towards a reasonable settlement. Smuts could have cleared himself, the Governor-General said, by publishing his

* Creswell was again leading the Labour party in the House of Assembly, following his victory in a recent by-election.

telegrams to Hofmeyr; but he chose to shoulder the responsibility himself rather than to sacrifice a subordinate officer.[11] The responsibility belonged properly to Smuts in his public capacity; but his secretary, E. F. C. Lane, could hardly endure to see his chief submitting to gross personal slander. Writing to Mrs Smuts on 28 May, Lane enclosed one of the telegrams and asked her to keep it carefully, with his letter, in her collection of 'biography papers'.[12]

CHAPTER 6

NATIVE AFFAIRS

SMUTS was the Union's fifth Minister of Native Affairs; but whereas the first three between them had held that office for only three years,* the fourth, Louis Botha, had held it continuously for six years. Botha evidently saw sense in the custom of the Cape, where Native Affairs had been usually the personal responsibility of the Prime Minister. The trouble was that the Prime Minister always had so many other things to do. Smuts found himself constrained after some years to delegate some of his departmental duties to F. S. Malan. Thereupon the cry was raised that the country needed a full-time Minister of Native Affairs. Nevertheless, most M.P.s supported John X. Merriman in the strong plea that he made for still imposing upon the Prime Minister of the day individual responsibility for Native Affairs.[1]

When Smuts took office the Department of Native Affairs had a European headquarters staff of less than forty and a European regional staff of less than 500. The regional staff was divided 50-50 between 'the districts' and the 'labour districts'; all the officers assigned to the latter were, as the name implied, specialists. In the former also there was a sizeable specialist staff concerned with the administration of the land law, agricultural practice, health regulations, taxation and education—although the last-named function belonged principally to the Provinces. In the general oversight of peace, order and good government administrative methods varied from district to district: at one end of the spectrum was the Transkei, which academic observers customarily acclaimed as a model of 'indirect rule'; at the other end was the whole area of the Transvaal, where the Department of Justice exercised direct authority over the Native population. Yet even in the Transvaal salaried chiefs and headmen performed subordinate administrative functions. In the Union as a whole, nearly 2,000 chiefs and headmen were on the

* H. Burton (May 1910 to June 1912); J. B. M. Hertzog (June to December 1912); J. W. Sauer (December 1912 to September 1913). Perhaps I should here point out that in writing about Native Affairs and Natives I am following contemporary usage. On p. 482 below I record the growth of dissatisfaction with this usage.

pay-roll of the Native Affairs Department when Smuts took charge of it.[2]

Both the headquarters and regional staffs had so much routine work to do that they found little or no time for sustained thought about the principles of policy. Nor could they find any help worth mentioning in the academic community of that time. Missionaries were still the main pioneers of ethnographical and anthropological research.* In the universities, the disciplined study of African cultures did not gain a firm foothold until 1920, when the University of Cape Town appointed A. R. Radcliffe-Brown to its new chair of Social Anthropology. After a few years, Cape Town's example began to be followed elsewhere. Possibly the shock of Bulhoek had something to do with that.

For Smuts, the timing of these new developments was unfortunate. In 1919, when he took charge of Native Affairs, he had still to depend for advice and criticism chiefly upon the practical men of his department. They in their turn were bound to depend heavily upon his driving power and thought. The driving power they could take for granted; but the thought was still in large measure an unknown quantity. Throughout the nine years that had elapsed since the inauguration of the Union, Smuts's silence in the debates on Native policy had been total.

He had, however, put some of his ideas upon record in a speech that he made on 22 May 1917 in London.[3] Possibly he conceived that speech as a pendant to his widely acclaimed exposition, only eight days earlier, of the nature of the Commonwealth. He had been speaking then to a parliamentary audience; but now he was addressing a joint meeting of the Imperial Institute and various South African societies. He told them that the Commonwealth in general and South Africa in particular had a civilizing mission to perform in Africa. Some people, he admitted, considered it an open question whether or not South Africa's white people would succeed, even within their own boundaries, in establishing a firm base for civilization. South Africa was not only white man's but also black man's country; white civilization would stand or fall there with the success or failure of the whites in their dealings with the blacks. For the

---

* Most notable among them was H. A. Junod, a Swiss missionary in Mozambique who had published a famous book, *The Life of a South African Tribe*: vol. I, *The Social Life* (London, 1912); vol. II, *The Psychic Life* (London, 1913).

definition of white–black relationships Smuts stated two fundamental axioms. First, 'there must be no intermixture of blood between the two colours';* secondly, the white people must build their conduct upon what Lord Cromer had called 'the granite bedrock of the Christian moral code'. He admitted that his own nation was no more consistent than other Christian nations were in practising that code; nevertheless, they accepted it as axiomatic. He only wished that they could discover some correspondingly clear-cut political axiom.

But although in this regard [he continued] nothing can be taken as axiomatic, we have gained a great deal of experience in our history, and there is now shaping in South Africa a policy which...may have very far-reaching effects in the future civilisation of the African Continent. We have realised that political ideas which apply to our white civilisation largely do not apply to the administration of Native affairs...and so a practice has grown up in South Africa of creating parallel institutions—giving the Natives their own separate institutions on parallel lines with institutions for whites. It may be that on those parallel lines we may yet be able to solve a problem which may otherwise be insoluble...Instead of mixing up black and white in the old haphazard way, which instead of lifting up the black degraded the white, we are now trying to lay down a policy of keeping them apart as much as possible in our institutions. In land ownership, settlement and forms of government we are trying to keep them apart, and in that way laying down in outline a general policy which it may take a hundred years to work out, but which in the end may be the solution of our Native problem. Thus in South Africa you will have in the long run large areas cultivated by blacks and governed by blacks, where they will look after themselves in all their forms of living and development, while in suitable parts you will have your white communities, which will govern themselves separately according to the accepted European principles. The blacks will, of course, be free to go and to work in the white areas, but as far as possible the administration of white and black areas will be separate, and such that each community will be satisfied and develop according to its own proper lines.

Thirty years later, Smuts would have had a rough passage with any London audience had he spoken to it in that strain; but his audience on 22 May 1917 held the same views as he did. When he proclaimed his doctrine of parallel institutions and separate development he was able to cite the authority not only of Cecil Rhodes but of Lord Selborne, who that evening was taking the chair for him.

---

* Smuts made no reference to the large intermixture of blood that had produced the Cape Coloured people.

More than twenty years ago [he said]...an experiment in native self-government was begun by Cecil Rhodes in the old Cape Colony which gave local institutions to the natives in Glen Grey reserve. That principle has been extended over a large part of the old Transkeian territories, and so successful has it been that when we came to framing the Act of Union an Appendix was added about the future administration of the Protectorates when they should be incorporated in the Union. This Appendix was largely the work of our chairman, Lord Selborne. He fought with extraordinary tenacity for that Appendix, and I am not sure, although I did not see the importance of the matter in those days, whether in the distant future the South Africa Act will not be remembered as much for its Appendix as for its principal contents. This Appendix laid it down that the native territories in South Africa should be governed apart from the Parliamentary institutions of the Union and on different lines which would achieve the principle of native self-government. Subsequently... the trend of opinion has hardened in that direction.

In giving Lord Selborne these good marks—as he and his audience assumed them to be—Smuts did not forget other meritorious servants of the British Empire. He made particular reference to Sir Godfrey Lagden, whom Milner had chosen in 1903 as chairman of the South African Native Affairs Commission—a body of ten, predominantly expert and overwhelmingly English-speaking. In 1905 the Commission recommended the separation of black South Africans from white South Africans both as occupiers of land and as voters.

The report of the Lagden Commission was destined to survive for three decades as the main blueprint of Native policy in South Africa. In 1913, Botha's government implemented its recommendations with regard to land. But the implementation proved incomplete. A decision of the Supreme Court in 1917 laid it down that Natives in the Cape Province still retained unrestricted freedom of land purchase, because that was one of the ways whereby they were able to qualify as voters in the Cape.* To General Hertzog that imperfection of the Union's land legislation appeared an outrageous blot. There was only one way, he maintained, of getting rid of it, namely, to abolish the Cape's franchise for Natives. Because that franchise had been entrenched in the constitution of the Union, the constitution would have to be amended as soon as the requisite two-thirds majority could be achieved. That would finally settle the land question and

---

* Act No. 27 of 1913 (The Natives Land Act) declared that no provision of the Act which might prevent anybody from qualifying as a voter should have legal force in Cape Province.

at the same time settle the franchise question, which in Hertzog's view was more fundamental still. Like the Lagden Commission, Hertzog believed that the whites and the blacks should not only live in separate areas but also vote on separate rolls: otherwise the day would surely come when the black voters on the common roll would outnumber the white voters: and that, Hertzog said, would mean the end of white civilization in South Africa.[4]

Smuts had once told Merriman that he did not believe in politics for Natives; but he and Merriman had subsequently worked out the compromise which enabled the Cape's colour blind franchise to co-exist in the constitution of the Union with the all-white franchises of the former Republics.* He believed it prudent to leave that co-existence undisturbed. To be sure, Imperial authority had sanctified the doctrine of separateness for the franchise as well as for land ownership; but Smuts did not push his advocacy of that doctrine to the limit. His attitude to it was experimental and pragmatic: if collisions should occur between the doctrine and the facts, he would be prepared to modify the doctrine.

The doctrine was static; but the facts of economic and social life were dynamic. Long before Smuts became Prime Minister and Minister for Native Affairs, that contradiction had created trouble for Botha, particularly on the issue of land apportionment. The Natives Land Act of 1913 made it illegal for black people to purchase or lease land in white areas and it ordered the eviction of 'squatters' habitually resident in those areas. In form those prohibitions appeared equitable, because they were balanced by equivalent prohibitions upon white people who might wish to purchase and occupy land in the black areas; but in fact they proved inequitable and in large measure unworkable because they collided with statistical fact. To send the blacks back to their own land might have been possible if the blacks had possessed enough land to be sent back to; but the black areas 'scheduled' in the Act could barely hold their existing populations, let alone hundreds of thousands of evicted squatters.

* See *Smuts: The Sanguine Years*, pp. 221, 253–4. Smuts's words to Merriman are frequently quoted out of context, with the implication that he was stating a principle which he believed to be universally valid and from which he never budged. In fact, he was doing no more than refuse to attempt the politically impossible task of sponsoring a revolutionary alteration of the time-honoured franchise of the Transvaal. He made no corresponding demand on Merriman to alter the time-honoured franchise of the Cape. For the evolution of his ideas on the franchise see pp. 213, 227, 264–6, 490 below.

The Act itself recognized that fact by making provision for the 'release' of additional areas for Native purchase. That was an unconditional pledge by the white parliament to its black subjects; but twenty-three years were destined to go by before parliament became ready—and then only upon new conditions—to honour the pledge. By that time, overcrowding by people and animals was creating desert conditions in many black areas, and more than half of South Africa's six and a half million black people were already earning their livelihoods in the so-called white areas.*

The frustration which dogged the Natives Land Act was not merely statistical but at root political. Botha did his best to honour the pledge which the Act contained; but parliament refused to release additional land for Native occupancy.† On the other hand, parliament was not yet ready to accept Hertzog's contention that Natives in Cape Province must surrender their franchise on the common roll before Natives anywhere in the Union were granted the additional rights of land purchase which had been promised to them. Botha tried in vain to force a passage through these obstacles of political interest and dogma. In 1917 he introduced an omnibus measure with the misleading title of Native Administration Bill; it attempted to settle at one stroke all the disputed issues of Native policy with the exception of the franchise. After it had suffered severe amputation in a select committee, Botha let it drop. His Native policy had come to a dead stop. But the contentions about Native policy continued. Inside parliament, Hertzog missed no chance of attacking the Cape franchise. Outside parliament, the emergent, if small, class of educated

---

* The Native Economic Commission of 1932 [U.G. 22, 1932, paras. 71–3, 80, 89, 96, 116] painted a sombre picture of denudation, donga-erosion, deleterious plant succession, drying up of springs and destruction of the soil in many Native Reserves. The 1936 census figures of the distribution of the Native population were, in round numbers:

'Native' areas (rural)	2,962,450
'European' areas (rural)	2,195,750
Urban and semi-urban areas	1,361,200
Alluvial diggings	24,650
Construction gangs	43,200
Unclassified	9,650
Total	6,596,900

† A Commission under Sir William Beaumont, after three years of work, recommended 'releases' of additional land which would have made the Native areas equivalent in the aggregate to approximately 13 % of the total land surface of the Union. When parliament rejected that recommendation, Botha appointed five local commissions. Their recommendations for 'releasing' land to the Natives were in the aggregate less than those of Sir William Beaumont; but even so, Botha did not venture to submit them to parliament.

Natives was continuously active—although with little effect—in the politics of the Union.

In January 1912 a few leaders had established the South African Native National Congress.* The leaders bore a common stamp. They came from a wide variety of tribes but from a limited range of groups and callings: the lawyers, the teachers, the interpreters, the chiefs' advisers, the journalists, the Methodist clergy. Many of them had received a good educational grounding at Healdtown or Lovedale, the Wesleyan schools of the Cape, and some of them had received further education at American or English—not yet South African—universities. Very few of them were without a strong religious affiliation. Some of them were related to chiefs and others maintained close relations with chiefs; but nearly all of them lived up to the name National, which they had put in front of the word Native in the constitution of their Congress. They conducted their proceedings in the main Bantu languages† but at the same time asserted their common identity and interests as black South African citizens. They stood for the Cape's 'colour blind' régime of civil liberties and voting rights and aimed at making it Union-wide. But they were destined always to fight rearguard actions. At the foundation of their Congress in 1912 they protested against the colour bar which had made the Union's parliament all-white. Next year they sent a deputation to London to contest the Natives Land Act. As loyal subjects of King and Empire they suspended their activities during the war but when it ended they sent a second deputation to London and on to the Paris Peace Conference—not that they had any secessionist demands to make in Paris, as Hertzog's deputation had; their specific protests were against racial discrimination in national and local legislation and in the constitutions of the Union and three of its Provinces. They recognized Hertzog as an arch enemy but believed that Botha and Smuts were tarred with the same brush. Specifically, they repudiated the doctrine which Smuts had expounded in his speech of 22 May 1917.[5]

They were the products of economic and social change in the

* Later called the African National Congress. Prominent among the early S.A.N.N.C. members were P. K. I. Seme, A. Mangana, G. Montsioa, G. Msimang, J. Dube, S. Msane, G. T. Plaatje, W. Rubusana, T. Mapikela, D. Letanka, S. L. Makgatho, R. S. Thema.

† The four leading Bantu languages were used in sessions of Congress and in the newspaper *Abantu-Batho*. Jabavu's *Imvo*, on the other hand, used Xhosa and English.

Union and they were sensitive to the complaints of their people in the cities; but as middle class constitutionalists they never got close to the emergent black proletariat.* Its discontents after the war began to explode in strikes: in late 1919 and early 1920 the Native sanitary workers of Johannesburg, the dockers of Cape Town, the drivers of Kimberley and the mine-workers of the Rand came out on strike in quick succession. Police repression and scabbing by white workers—so much for proletarian solidarity—quickly broke the strikes.[6] Nevertheless the black workers, in disregard of the unfriendly white trade unions, were taking their own first steps towards organized trade unionism. In 1919 a Nyasalander, Clements Kadalie, founded the Industrial and Commercial Workers' Union, an ambitious organization which numbered among its members many who did not strictly belong either to commerce or to industry. For some years the I.C.U. was the spearhead of protest against racially discriminatory laws and practices. In October 1920 at Port Elizabeth the I.C.U. had its first martyrs. Eighteen months later, Hertzog cited the Port Elizabeth shootings in his indictment of the man whose footsteps—he said—were dripping with blood.

As Minister of Native Affairs Smuts had inherited a great heap of confusion, frustration and anxiety. During his first six months at the Ministry he showed no visible sign of attempting to cope with it. Secession and inflation were the burning issues of the parliamentary struggle and of the elections in March 1920; if Smuts was getting to work on his departmental tasks, nobody outside the department yet knew it. When the elections were over, the outgoing Bishop of Pretoria warned him in an open letter that Native policy was drifting dangerously. The Bishop laid heavy emphasis upon the rapidly growing race consciousness of the Natives. They had learnt from Europeans, he said, what the word exploitation meant and they were applying the word to their own condition—to their economic, social and political grievances as wage earners, slum dwellers, pass bearers and unrepresented taxpayers. They were picturing themselves as 'a voiceless people': white politicians made the laws; white officials and policemen enforced them; the black people were never consulted. The Bishop pleaded with Smuts to call them into consultation

* Their nearest approach to unconstitutional action and to leadership of the masses was in their 'down with the passes' campaign in Johannesburg early in 1919.

before it was too late. He enumerated the consultative institutions which he had in mind: at the centre, three expert and independent Commissioners for Native Affairs; in every Province, one or more Native Advisory Councils. He believed that these Advisory Councils might later on be developed both downwards and upwards: downwards to the roots of local government; upwards to a Native Advisory Council for the whole Union. Such developments, he thought, would in the course of time convince the Natives that they were no longer 'voiceless'. Meanwhile, the government should adopt the practice of introducing two separate sets of estimates: first, for European revenue and expenditure; and secondly, for Native revenue and expenditure.[7]

The Bishop of Pretoria believed that he was expressing the moderate and reasonable aspirations of the South African Native National Congress. In some respects his belief had good grounds; but not in all respects. The Congress was prepared to welcome consultative institutions; but it also knew the meaning of sovereignty. To it, 'voicelessness' signified above all the exclusion of Natives in three of the Union's four Provinces from a share—if only a subordinate share—in choosing the sovereign legislature. In retrospect it seemed curious that the Bishop made no mention at all of the Cape franchise, which was the most prominent symbol of Native aspirations; but in the early 1920s many humanitarians and liberals took it for granted that 'parallel institutions' contained the main heads of an answer to the question of colour.*

Smuts did not let much time go by before he squarely faced the Bishop's challenge, such as it was. On 26 May 1920 he moved the second reading of his Native Affairs Bill. It made provision for the establishment of a three-member Native Affairs Commission with power to make recommendations over a wide field of affairs affecting the Native population, and with power to submit the relevant papers to parliament, in the event of the Minister not accepting its recommendations. The Bill also made provision for the establishment of Councils in areas where the Native population predominated, and it empowered these Councils to levy a rate and to spend the proceeds on certain specified agricultural, health and educational services. Finally, it authorized the Governor-General, on the recommendation

* This assumption found systematic expression in *The History of Native Policy in South Africa* by Edgar H. Brookes (2nd edition, Pretoria, 1927). The distinguished author subsequently adopted the opposite assumption and, as a Senator representing the South African Natives, acted on it.

of the Native Affairs Commission, to convene Conferences of Chiefs, members of Councils and other representative Natives.

These proposals, and the speech which Smuts made in their support, were in close accord with the Bishop of Pretoria's proposals and arguments. Smuts admitted at the outset that reform was long overdue and that many evidences could be seen of the sense of grievance and distrust which was rife in the Native population; amongst these evidences he cited the petition of the deputation recently in Britain. The Natives, he insisted, must be given a constitutional outlet for their grievances; as things were, they had the vote only in one Province, and nowhere in the Union did they have the machinery for giving expression to their views and bringing them to the attention of the government. This was the main cause, he said, of a growing estrangement between black and white which boded ill for the future of South Africa. He hoped that the Conferences which his Bill proposed would prove the starting-point of a happier relationship. For the present, his motto was one step at a time. He was well aware that the Bill excluded many important issues which Botha's Bill had included; but the Native Affairs Commission would study those issues and make recommendations for dealing with them.

That disclaimer did not deter members from dragging the excluded issues into the debate. Creswell and other Labour speakers wanted total territorial separation between black and white. Nationalist speakers made the same plea and some of them went on to demand electoral separation—in other words, abolition of the Cape franchise. Speaking on 13 July, Hertzog demanded it as 'a matter of self-preservation for the White man'. Meanwhile, he supported the Bill because he thought it pointed towards that goal. Tielman Roos, on the other hand, was afraid that the proposed Conferences would prove the prelude to a vote for Natives everywhere in the Union. He wanted to see the segregation principle acknowledged and applied in the Bill. He attacked Smuts for dealing with the Native question piecemeal. Smuts, in his reply, reminded the House—as he might well have reminded the Bishop of Pretoria—that the Cape franchise was entrenched in the constitution of the Union. They would have to wait a long time on the Native question, he said laconically, if they waited until the Cape franchise was abolished.[8]

The Bill became law. Circumscribed though it was, it was the first piece of progressive legislation since Union and contained some genuine promise for the future. Lord Buxton, until recently the Union's Governor-General, hailed it as 'a significant advance' and congratulated Smuts on the speech in which he had introduced it.[9] The *New Statesman* called his speech 'masterly' and called his Bill 'wise and generous'; 'a measure of the first importance'; 'the beginning of a new epoch in the relations of the white and the native races.'[10] Two years later, British radicals and humanitarians were still applauding Smuts. J. H. Harris, the secretary of the Anti-Slavery League and Aborigines Protection Society, took note that Smuts had appointed to the Native Affairs Commission men who 'at various times had been classed as agitators'. After reading the Commission's first annual report, Harris felt confident that it was getting into its stride. He looked forward to the Native Conference which it would soon organize as the beginning of 'an Elective Assembly for the Natives of South Africa'.[11] 'Parallel Institutions' again: indeed, they were the orthodoxy, and not least the Liberal orthodoxy, of that time.

The Commission proved dilatory in organizing Native Conferences.* Possibly it had too many other things to do. Smuts made it the instrument of his endeavour to achieve a peaceful settlement at Bulhoek and he appointed it to conduct the inquest on the Bondelzwarts tragedy. Apart from these crisis commitments, it had a standing commitment to conduct inquiries and make recommendations on 'any matter relating to the general conduct of the administration of Native Affairs, or to legislation in so far as it may affect the Native population'.† Possibly it found such wide terms of reference unconducive to concentration on anything in particular. Nevertheless, Smuts had given it a lead. His speech of May 1920 had shown one notable advance upon his speech of May 1917: in the three-year interval he had discovered that contemporary African society was not static but alarmingly mobile. He now laid heavy emphasis upon the breaking up of the old tribal life and upon Native participation in the new industrial life. Natives, he said, were being dumped down in the huge centres of population away from their tribes and families. Many of the consequences were pernicious and were bound to grow worse unless action were taken in time. In the next ten or twenty years

* The first Native Conference in terms of the 1920 Act met in 1925.
† In contrast, the terms of reference proposed for the Native Affairs Commission in Botha's abortive bill had had a narrow territorial restriction to matters concerning Native areas.

there would be a huge industrial development in South Africa. In this development white South Africans would be using Native labour to serve their own economic purposes. He thought that one of the most useful functions which the Native Affairs Commission could perform would be to study the conditions of Native life in the great urban agglomerations.

It took the Commission two years to complete this study and embody it in the Native (Urban Areas) Bill.* That, possibly, was not after all slow work, in view of the complexity of the problem and the intricate discussions which it required. Smuts told parliament that never before had so much consideration and consultation gone to the making of any Bill. The Commission had faithfully performed its duty of explaining the Bill clause by clause to representative bodies of Natives. Before reaching that stage of its labours, it had spent prodigious effort in hacking a path through the South African jurisdictional tangle. In every Province, responsibility for the living conditions of urbanized Natives belonged to the municipal authorities; but the laws and regulations defining this responsibility varied widely from Province to Province and even within the same Province. There existed, besides, a jurisdictional conflict between the Provinces and the Union; control of the municipalities was a Provincial function but Native Affairs belonged to the Union. A decision of the courts settled that issue in the Union's favour; but a good deal of time went by before the Union government made up its mind to impose any strict control on the municipalities.

Laissez-faire was the municipal rule of life. Everywhere in South Africa the city fathers had allowed poor whites and poor blacks to come in and settle wherever they pleased; or, rather, wherever they could. In Johannesburg they settled cheek by jowl with each other in the slums of Sophiatown, Martindale, Newton and Newclare. Nevertheless, segregation by colour became step by step the custom of the cities. In 1904, an outbreak of plague in the Johannesburg slums spurred the city fathers to action; they cleared the Natives from the infected area and dumped them into a location near a sewage farm at Klipspruit. At the end of the First World War, an outbreak of influenza spurred them a second time into action: they cleared more Natives from the slums and dumped them into another location

---

* The Bill embodied a good deal of the work of the Transvaal Local Government Commission (chairman, Adv. C. F. Stallard) which reported in 1923 (T.P. 1–1922).

near another sewage farm.[12] These two locations were products of imposed segregation; but most locations in most South African cities were products of a spontaneous self-segregation. Natives, when they came to town, commonly sought the company of their own kind in the rapidly growing locations on the fringes of the cities. The city fathers ran these shanty towns in a haphazard way and usually made a profit by running them. That, at any rate, was the conclusion of the Tuberculosis Commission of 1914. The Commission did not believe that the inhabitants of the locations were getting much of a return for their money. It said that most of the locations were a menace to the health of their own inhabitants and of the white citizens; that the dwellings, with few exceptions, were 'a disgrace... nothing more than hovels, constructed out of bits of old packing-case lining...and other scraps and odds and ends'. It went on to say that it could imagine no better breeding grounds for tuberculosis than these insanitary, overcrowded hovels.[13]

Nine years later Smuts quoted this scathing denunciation of municipal neglect.[14] Introducing the Native (Urban Areas) Bill on 7 February 1923, he put the blame not so much upon the callousness as upon the ignorance of white South Africans. They had allowed themselves to be taken by surprise. When he was a young man it had been a very unusual thing in this part of the Cape to see a black man; but in recent decades there had been an immense increase of the urban Native population everywhere. There had been no corresponding increase of the services which the new population needed.

The Natives [he said] have come to our towns unprovided for...They have picked up diseases, and have found our white civilization a curse to them. The result of this neglect to deal with the situation has been harmful in the extreme to both the white and native populations. It is a matter that is very urgent, and it is a matter that is not beyond solution.

The Native question is so large. We know so little about it, we know so little about certain factors which seem almost beyond human control. There are such aspects of the Native question, but this is not one of them. Although this proper housing and proper control of Natives in urban areas is a difficult question, it is manageable even at this late hour if we undertake the task with energy and good will. If this House can lead in the right spirit, and the country will respond, as I have no doubt it will, we may remove one of the biggest blots resting on our civilization in South Africa.

He made it plain that his government was prepared at need to take drastic action. The responsibility for town planning still lay, as it had always lain, upon the urban authorities; but if any such authority failed in its duty, the government would step in and do at the town's expense what the town itself should have done.

He then enumerated the measures of town planning which the Bill made mandatory. Clause I laid it down that every town must establish a location for its Native inhabitants. For the majority of towns, which had their locations already, there was nothing new in that; but there was a good deal that was new in what followed. Everything must be done, Smuts insisted, to ensure that the Natives who were playing a part in the economic life of a town were provided with proper accommodation. The Bill, he said, made a distinction between different types of Natives: those who were emerging from barbarism and those who had already emerged from it. For the former, locations of an ordinary type would be provided; for the latter, Native villages would be provided. In these villages the standard of housing would be higher and Natives would be encouraged to acquire their own plots of ground and put up their own houses. Smuts expressed the hope that the villages would grow in size and multiply in numbers as more and more Natives came to realize their attractions. Meanwhile, the Bill made realistic provision for the common needs of ordinary people—of the people, for example, who were coming to the cities for the first time; hostels would be provided to see them through their settling-in period.

The implications of the Bill were segregationist. Smuts laid emphasis on that. Whites and blacks who had been milling around with each other in slum areas would find themselves living apart as the blacks moved off to the new villages. Under section 5 of the Bill, the government would have the power to move them compulsorily: or, more precisely, it would usually have this power; for, in the Cape particularly, there were exempted Natives, such as the owners of property and the registered voters. Smuts insisted that the government must continue to respect all established rights. At the same time he expressed the hope that the Natives who possessed those rights would respond spontaneously to the attraction of the newly provided services and amenities. In so far as that happened, residential segregation would be achieved, because both the whites and the blacks wanted it.

The Bill bore the stamp of authoritarian, paternalistic planning; but it also left some room for common consent and individual choice.

The municipalities retained their authority over the locations. The central government took authority to see that the municipalities performed their duty. It proposed to make its authority effective not only punitively but preventively; it would license the superintendents of locations and establish a staff of inspectors. All this was from the top downwards; but consent working upwards found expression through the establishment of Native Advisory Boards. Smuts insisted that the municipalities would have no power to make regulations relating to the locations unless and until they had held prior consultation with the Native Advisory Boards, That, he said, would give the Natives a voice in their own affairs, which was very necessary. He also wanted the Natives in the locations to run their own shops and brew their own beer.*

But the authoritarian element revealed itself again in his exposition of the control which the municipalities would exercise over settlement in the locations and villages. The municipalities were being compelled to spend more money on Native welfare than they had ever before dreamt of spending and were terrified lest the new amenities would attract to the towns more Natives than they could cope with. Smuts reported their argument as follows: 'We are prepared to do this service in so far as the locations are subsidiary to the needs of our towns. We are not going to have an unlimited black township next door to us, and pay for it.' The government, Smuts said, accepted that argument and was meeting it, partly in the present Bill and partly in a supporting Registration Bill; the two Bills together would establish complete control over the comings and goings of Natives.

Thus the principle took shape that Natives were 'surplus' in the urban areas whenever they failed to find jobs'.†

As Minister of Native Affairs Smuts had achieved in four years more legislation than his four predecessors had achieved in a dozen years. His achievement won wide acclaim; the British humanitarians

---

* It had been common for municipal councils to prohibit the brewing of 'Kaffir beer'; kill-joys thought it wrong; municipalities sometimes made a profit by providing the intoxicant themselves.

† The report of the Transvaal Local Government Commission had laid it down as a principle 'that the Natives should only be allowed to enter urban areas, which are essentially the White man's creation, when he is willing to enter and to minister to the needs of the White man, and should depart therefrom when he ceases so to minister'.

praised it even while they were denouncing the slaughter of the Bondelzwarts. Smuts felt at times that he was cutting a straight and safe road through the heap of frustration and fear which he had inherited. In December 1923 a spirit of hope inspired his Christmas message to South Africa:

White and black both have a proper place in South Africa. Both have their human rights, and let us in a fair and humble spirit approach the difficulties which arise out of them and labour to make this land a home in which both races can live together in peace and friendship and work out their salvation in fairness and justice.

That message was an improvement upon his austere maxim, four years earlier, about the white man building his conduct upon the granite bedrock of the Christian moral code. This time he was not preaching exclusively to the white man but was proclaiming human rights and the essential reciprocity of race relationships. His words contained human warmth. Some sections at least of the Native population responded to them with the same warmth.[15]

The fact remained that a parliament exclusively white in its membership and responsible to an overwhelmingly white electorate enacted the laws which governed race relationships. In doing so, it paid lip service to the ideal of 'keeping the Native question out of politics'. When Smuts won massive bi-partisan support for his important Bills of 1920 and 1923 he flattered himself that he was achieving precisely that. He too easily forgot the Bills that he dared not introduce, among them a Bill to honour the unfulfilled pledge of 1913 with regard to Native land.* He also forgot the Bills which Hertzog proposed to introduce when he got the chance, among them a Bill to remove Native voters from the common roll of Cape Province. Parliamentary action could not avoid bringing the Native question into politics if and when it attempted to get to the roots of racial relationships.

Whether it would ever succeed in getting to those roots was a different matter. The parties of opposition appeared to believe that their slogan of segregation contained all the solutions to all the problems. Not a session went by without Hertzog, Creswell and other

---

* His government followed the administrative practice of permitting Natives to purchase land in the areas recommended for 'release' by the Beaumont and local committees, where their recommendations coincided. However, as Smuts pointed out later (see p. 214), additional rights of land purchase could make only a small dent in Native land shortage so long as they lacked governmental financial support.

Nationalists and Labour men upbraiding the government because its policy was un-segregationist or insufficiently segregationist. In his speech of 8 July 1920 Hertzog declared that the Native Affairs Bill was good enough so far as it went but that it did not go far enough; segregation and in particular the segregation of voters was a matter of life and death for white civilization. On 24 June 1921 he declared that they had arrived only at the threshold of the segregation policy and that they had only two alternatives to choose between—social equality and mixing up or the opposite of all that. On 7 February 1923 he gave a mild blessing to the Native (Urban Areas) Bill because it made provision for residential segregation in or around the cities; but he attacked the clauses of the Bill which permitted Natives to acquire 'white man's land'; before long, he said, they would be demanding the white man's vote. When Hertzog sat down W. H. Stuart, an S.A.P. man from the Cape, did his best to inject some precision into the debate; he would be prepared, he said, to produce seventeen separate definitions of segregation: at one end of the scale, social segregation or separation, which was just as much desired by the Natives as by white people; at the other end of the scale, General Hertzog's absolute segregation, which was beyond attainment. Creswell, the Labour party's leader, denied that absolute segregation was beyond attainment. If they proceeded along the lines of the present Bill, he declared, they would have great black cities around their industrial centres and their white civilization would wither at the root. They must stop this drift before it was too late if they wanted to preserve themselves as a self-respecting, dignified and European civilization in South Africa.[16]

Segregation, obviously, was a powerful war cry. Whether or not it contained a solution to South Africa's complex economic, social and racial problems, it was at least a potential election winner.

CHAPTER 7

PEACE-MAKING AND A QUARREL

FROM the time of the Rand rebellion up to his fall from power two and a half years later Smuts had no good news to give his friends overseas about the state of South Africa; but he frequently reminded them, as he reminded himself, that the world was in a worse state.

Political conditions [he wrote in August 1922] are most difficult. I have never worked harder or amid more friction and trouble than at present. This is indeed a most difficult country to rule...However, I always console myself with the reflection that rulers of other countries are infinitely worse off. Who for instance would like to govern Ireland today?...Or who would like to stand in the shoes of Ebert or Wirth? Germany seems rapidly going under...God have mercy on this poor soiled world![1]

He tried to persuade his fellow South Africans that the state of the world and of Europe in particular was of concern to them; if Europe went under, they would have no chance to save their skins.[2] Europe's danger, he believed, was immediate and extreme. Nevertheless, he made a distinction between the ephemeral and the enduring consequences of the war and of the peace settlement. He had faith in the Covenant of the League. That faith inspired his message to America on 4 February 1924, when news reached him of President Wilson's death.

Wilson's untimely eclipse [he wrote] was due to temporary and accidental circumstances. As these pass away his heroic figure will stand out ever more clearly and his work will be recognized as among America's greatest contributions to the world.

He had long since forgotten his protests to the President in May and June 1919. In a telegram to Mrs Wilson he said that the world shared her grief at the departure of a prince among the sons of men.[3]

But America had repudiated Wilson. Smuts considered American isolationism a main impediment to economic and political recovery. Not only had it got the League of Nations off to the worst possible start: it had removed a balancing factor which Europe badly needed for her stability. At Paris, President Wilson had been willing to join with Britain in a joint guarantee of French security; but America refused that obligation. Britain would not shoulder it alone. In consequence, the French made up their minds to seek their own security by their own methods—that is to say, by alliances in eastern Europe, combined with political, military and financial pressure upon Germany. By 1923, those methods had brought Europe to the verge of chaos.

Smuts understood America; but he failed to understand France. He was fertile in suggestions for persuading the Americans to return to policies of co-operation; but he had no suggestions to make for exorcising French fears. Whenever the suggestion came up of any commitment to France, he showed himself just as much an isolationist as any politician of the Middle West. That did not inhibit him from denouncing the French when they went their own way. At the Imperial Conference of 1921 he denounced them for using the Reparation chapter of the Peace Treaty as the instrument of their domination in Europe. The British Commonwealth, he declared, must stand up to France. He did not explain how the Commonwealth was to do this.

Curzon pictured Britain as going about arm in arm with France but with one hand on her collar. To Smuts, that seemed an unlikely contortionist feat; he thought it more likely that France would drag her partner along with her. Early in 1922, when Lloyd George had hopes of clinching a deal with Briand—a British military guarantee to France, in exchange for French support of British reconstruction plans for Europe—Smuts protested that the price was too high. Later on, he warned Bonar Law against continuing Lloyd George's policy of marrying the reprobate with a view to his reformation.[4] Nevertheless he felt no joy in October 1922, when news reached him of Lloyd George's downfall.

It is a Tory reaction which has knocked him over...And I fear the new government will adopt a Francophile policy which will be even more fatal than George's vagaries. We mean to keep out of it all. But we want to see others keep out too.[5]

He seemed to think that Britain and the Commonwealth could be at one and the same time both non-interventionist and authoritative.

He wanted non-intervention; but he hated retreat. For example, he hated the idea of buying peace in Palestine by favouring the Arabs at the expense of the Jews. He suspected the Tories of wanting to do just that and tried his best to stop them. From the historical and moral point of view, he said, the Jewish National Home was one of the outstanding results of the Great War and one of the greatest acts of reparation in the history of the world. He appealed urgently to his friends in the new government to stand by the National Home.[6]

On the European issue he appealed to Bonar Law as his colleague and friend in the war years.

Foreign policy [he wrote] is going to be the acid test of your rule. And there I frankly fear that your Government may lean too much towards France. French policy was for centuries the curse of Europe and it was only the rise of Germany in the first place that changed her attitude. Now Germany is down and out, and France is once more the leader of the Continent with all the old bad instincts fully alive in her. Let the Germans be made to pay what and when and how they can. But let the Reparation question not be a cloak for the dismemberment of Germany and the sowing of the dragon's teeth afresh for the world. The French are out for world power; they have played the most dangerous anti-ally game with Kemal; and inevitably in the course of their ambitions they must come to realise that the British Empire is the only remaining enemy. We had better keep a sharp look-out in that direction.

This interpretation of the French past, present and future was highly disputable in its wide sweep; but it correctly appraised the immediate trend of French policy towards Germany. Even so, an anticlimax followed. The only specific advice which Smuts gave Bonar Law was to resist the pressure that would be put upon him for a security pact with France. If Poincaré persisted in his policy of breaking Germany up, he pleaded, let him do so on the responsibility of France; but let the hands of the British Empire remain clean. That was a weak conclusion to his bold argument.[7]

He had a clear view of the ends of policy but no clear view of the means. He had appointed Lord Robert Cecil to represent South Africa at Geneva and had instructed him to press for the admission to the League first of Germany and secondly of Russia. 'If this is not done', he said, 'there may be two dangers; either Germany sinks into the abyss and emerges later as a militant Monarchy, or she pulls through now and snaps her fingers at the West and proceeds to consolidate Russia as a German annex.' But if, he continued, it were done, it would help to undercut the main argument of the American isolationists—that there was no sense in trying to co-operate with the European nations so long as they remained so hopelessly divided.[8]

Certainly, to bring Germany and Russia back again into the comity of nations was a thing worth doing; but a small country like South Africa could not do it. No more could Great Britain do it, even if she had the will, so long as France called the tune at Geneva. France under Poincaré was in a far stronger position than Smuts realized. Unlike his predecessor Briand, Poincaré had no interest in a British military guarantee for France; the only guarantee that interested him was one that would support the entire structure of French alliances in eastern Europe. He did not expect to get all that from the British. Consequently, he took what he wanted without asking British leave. In January 1923, French troops marched into the Ruhr. Belgian troops marched with them. In Cape Town, the Franco-Belgian adventure gave occasion to some sardonic comment.

Yesterday [Smuts wrote on 1 March] the Belgian representative here came to speak to me about the Ruhr position. His point was that without Reparations Belgium was bankrupt. I told him that the only advice I could give the French and Belgian governments was to increase their armies very largely and to prepare for the next war which their action was making a certainty. He appeared much disconcerted. Poor devils, they know not what they do.[9]

The Reparation Commission had declared the German government to be in default on its payments. Consequently, the French and Belgian governments claimed legal justification for their invasion of the Ruhr. The German government denounced the invasion as an illegal act. The legal advisers to the British government agreed with the Germans. Nevertheless, the British Government allowed the French troop trains to run through the British occupied zone of Germany on their way to the Ruhr. Smuts believed that Britain was conniving at French policies ruinous to the prospects of a reasonable reparations settlement, of European recovery, of the world's prosperity and peace. He affirmed his views in personal letters to Churchill and other friends and in official communications to the Prime Minister. Still, he never expected to achieve much good by bombarding London with his letters and telegrams. He was looking forward to action at the coming Imperial Conference. In April 1923 he told a South African audience that the last Imperial Conference had opened the way to peace in the Pacific and that the next one had the chance 'to speak the great word' which would bring peace to Europe. In September he wrote to his wife mid-way on his voyage to London:

To me the future is as dark as night. Nowhere do I see a solution, nowhere light. I mean that I see nothing with which others will agree. And still I am an optimist. I feel there will be rescue.
(*Ik voel er sal redding komen.*)[10]

He landed in England a day or two before the opening of the Conference and found a situation which superficially appeared hopeless but contained beneath the surface a few elements of hope. The financial and economic structure of Germany was in ruins; but Stresemann, the new German Chancellor, had called off passive resistance and had committed the Germans—provided they were given the chance —to the 'policy of fulfilment'. That meant the end in Germany of inflationary subventions to the occupied territories and the beginning of a determined effort of economic and financial self-help.* Because Germany had almost no foreign credit, her effort could not succeed without help from outside; but fortunately, the American government had declared itself ready to seek means of helping, provided the European powers would work with it to that end.† There was the impediment. The French government was still using force to assert its financial claims and to achieve its strategical ambitions; when the Imperial Conference met, the secessionist movement in the Rhineland was close to its climax. Confronted with a French government which knew its own mind, the British government showed a divided mind.

That certainly was the impression which Baldwin gave on 1 October, in his opening address to the Conference of Prime Ministers. He quoted Disraeli on Britain's role as 'a moderating and mediatory power'. The British government, he said, did not share the view of the French and Belgian governments that they had a right to move into the Ruhr; but it had strained every nerve to preserve solidarity with them and to follow a policy of neither helping them nor hindering them. Smuts, when his turn came in the series of complimentary speeches, spoke suavely but with a glint of steel. The

---

* Stresemann's predecessor, Cuno, had followed a policy of 'passive resistance' which frustrated the French, but also caused a runaway inflation that brought Germany to the verge of economic and political disintegration. When Stresemann called off 'passive resistance' he instituted drastic financial reforms, symbolized by the new Rentenmark.

† The American Secretary of State, C. E. Hughes, had accepted this qualified commitment in a statement of 29 December 1922.

world, he said, was in a bad way; but the British Commonwealth was still there and it had no need to speak with bated breath. Two years ago it had opened the way to peace in the Pacific and now it was called upon to make a great united effort to bring peace to Europe. That was its duty. That also was its self-interest. Very adroitly, Smuts took up Baldwin's reference to his recent debt settlement with the Americans. He welcomed it as a splendid example of Britain's fidelity to her pledged word; but Britain, he said, might fail to make her pledge good unless peace and prosperity were restored to the world. 'What you have done', he told Baldwin, 'should therefore be followed up with equal decision in a great attempt to restore the trade conditions of Europe.'[11]

On 5 October the Conference started to debate foreign policy in detail. Curzon, in his opening statement, made no response to Smuts's challenge. He arraigned the French as bad allies; but he clung to the French alliance. He welcomed the end of passive resistance in Germany as the opportunity for a new start in Europe; but he left it to the French to make proposals—or not to make them—for exploiting that opportunity. A few days later, Mackenzie King made a statement which from Smuts's point of view was even more depressing. In effect, he said that the British Commonwealth could not possibly possess a common foreign policy; its separate governments in their separate regions had their own separate policies; Europe belonged to the British region; what Britain did in Europe was of no concern to Canada. Smuts rejected those deductions from the doctrine of equal status. The constitutional question, he said, was not on their agenda that day; but they were all signatories of the peace treaties and were all concerned with the aftermath. He saw no reason why Belgium should have a voice but Australia* no voice at all on issues of paramount importance to the world's prosperity and peace. They had all fought the war to uphold the sanctity of international obligations. The French invasion of the Ruhr was in violation of international obligations. He thought it a mistake not to deal honestly and frankly with France and not to stand up to her when she was in the wrong. The policies she was following were ruinous to Europe and the world and even to the prospects of receipts from reparations. He made some specific suggestions both about the

* No doubt he cited Australia because S. M. Bruce, the Australian Prime Minister, had vigorously rejected Mackenzie King's thesis.

content of a reparations settlement and about the means of achieving it. He hoped that America could be induced to attend a conference which would settle both reparations and inter-allied debts. If France refused to co-operate, he said, the conference should meet without her. Meanwhile, he thought it urgent to get the French out of the Ruhr. Unless that illegal act were undone Europe would be undone.

Smuts was looking all the time to America for support. Since his arrival in England, he had been in telegraphic communication with Bernard Baruch, the intimate adviser on problems of international finance and politics to successive American Presidents.[12] He had some reason to believe that Baruch's efforts were proving fruitful. On 9 October, it was announced from the White House that President Coolidge endorsed his predecessor's proposals for American participation in the financial rehabilitation of Europe.* This announcement, hedged though it was by conditions, became the occasion for an important British move. In a Note to Washington on 13 October, the British government declared its intention of enlisting the immediate co-operation of its European Allies in an invitation to the United States government to assist in an inquiry into the reparations question and related problems. The Note started the round of negotiations which led two months later to the Dawes Committee and to a workable—at least, a temporarily workable—reparations settlement.

The log jam had been broken; but at the time nobody knew it. The United States government made a favourable reply in principle to the British Note, but in practice remained insistent upon European unity as the condition of its participation in European affairs. The French government gave no immediate sign of offering any concessions at all for the sake of European unity. Whether or not the British government was any more willing than in the past to challenge French intransigence remained to be seen. Smuts made up his mind, as he said, to bell the cat. On 18 October he wrote to his wife—

I have spoken little in public, but have made a serious study of the German–French question. I intend speaking about it at the South African dinner next Tuesday and I shall not be surprised if what I say will cause

---

* It is not suggested that Baruch's (and indirectly Smuts's) pressure was the sole cause of this announcement; on the contrary, the counter-isolationist pressures in operation at this time were various. They came from many groups which had a strong interest in German and European recovery, and they included wide publicity for a speech-making tour by Lloyd George.[13]

a great fuss. Germany is fast going to pot [*gaat vinnig naar de maan*] and the thing must be tackled with all seriousness. But nobody will bell the cat. I am going to do it—and damn the consequences.[14]

His friend Keynes heard a rumour that he was at work on the arithmetic of reparations and implored him to have nothing to do with it. 'No action now has any value', Keynes declared, 'except something that frightens France or encourages Germany or both.' But Keynes had no need to worry. Smuts had finished his financial explorations and was not proposing to discuss 'imaginary milliards'. The speech that he had in his head was political.[15]

He delivered it on 23 October, to the South African Luncheon Club in London. That gave him the right platform, because he wanted to make the point that he was speaking on nobody's account except his own. He felt a plain personal duty, he said, as one of the two or three signatories of the Peace Treaty who still remained in power. Moreover, as a South African he had expert witness to give.

Small and comparatively unimportant as we are among the nations of the world, we have yet a rich and unique experience in the sort of trouble through which Europe is now passing. We also had our age-long contention between the white races in South Africa, which culminated in a great war, with all its horrors of loss and suffering. We also had our devastated area, which covered not merely a small strip of our own land, but practically the whole of the interior of South Africa. Defeated, broken, utterly exhausted, my little people also had to bow to the will of the conqueror. But it was not an impossible peace...The Boers were not treated as moral pariahs and outcasts. Decent human relationships were re-established and a spirit of mutual understanding grew up. The human atmosphere improved until in the end simple human fellow feelings solved the problems which had proved too difficult for statesmanship.

Four or five years after the conclusion of the war a new settlement was come to, based on mutual trust and friendship between the races. And South Africa today is perhaps the most outstanding witness in the realm of politics to the value of a policy of give and take, of moderation and generosity, of trust and friendship, applied to the affairs of men... Human nature is the same in all continents, and what could be done for the descendants in Africa can surely also be done for the parent peoples in Europe.

Those sentences contained his message to Europe. The message, he insisted, was urgent. Four years had passed since the peace treaty with Germany, but there was no peace yet. The war between the peoples had merely been transferred to the economic sphere, and the economic war was proving even more devastating than the military war had been. Europe had not much time left, he said, to save herself. He proposed an immediate conference of the Powers which were mainly interested in the reparation question.

I know that negotiations are afoot [he continued] to bring about such a conference, and shall therefore refrain from saying any more about it except this: I have no reason to think that any of the Powers concerned would decline to come to such a conference but I am clear in my mind that the absence of one or other Power should not prevent the rest from meeting and dealing with the situation to the best of their ability.

It is, however, in my judgment, vitally important that the U.S.A. should be there as an active member and bear her full weight, which, under the circumstances, may be more decisive than that of any other Power.

There was the declaration that Keynes was looking for—'something that frightens France'. Smuts was serving notice on the French that they were likely to find themselves isolated unless they mended their ways.

He expounded his proposal systematically. Reparation payments, he said, would be the main issue at the conference. About these payments he made two points: first, that the fantastic total fixed by the Reparation Commission in May 1921 could not possibly be paid; secondly, that a realistic total could be fixed and must be paid. But that could not begin to happen, he said, until the French evacuated the Ruhr. So long as Germany's industrial heart remained severed from Germany's body, the German government would remain incapable of paying anything. He denounced the Ruhr adventure not only as economic and political folly but as an illegal act. The French government, he said, regarded the Ruhr as 'a productive pledge', to be worked by the occupying authorities in order to make good the German government's default.

This is the official French viewpoint. But see what it means. It is not merely a bare occupation to exercise pressure on the German Government. It is a direct exploitation of German territory, entirely unprovided for in the Versailles Treaty. It cannot be squared with the Reparation provisions of the Treaty. It means the substitution by France of her own scheme for that which is contained in the Treaty... In the recent correspondence, the British government have stated their view that the occupation is illegal... We are back in August 1914. It is again the scrap of paper.

His final argument was prudential. He saw many disquieting signs that Germany was going to pieces. Her collapse, if it were not staved off, would prove more calamitous than the collapse of Russia six or seven years previously. Britain and the Commonwealth, he said, could not stand by and watch that calamity happening. They must give Germany the moral support which she needed in her hour of adversity. They must tell France in friendly but unmistakably frank terms that they intended to safeguard their own interests. Smuts protested that he felt no hostility to France. He recognized her just claim to security; but he did not believe that she could achieve that security by her adventure in the Ruhr and by trying to perpetuate her military domination over Europe.

I sympathise with France. But I am equally moved by profound pity for Europe, and horror of the fate to which she seems to be moving. And that fate must in the end affect France too. You cannot be a patriotic Frenchman unless you are also a good European.

In Paris, Pertinax of *L'Écho de Paris* and most of the other French commentators disputed Smuts's qualifications to tell them how to become patriotic Frenchmen and good Europeans. They saw him— and some of them never stopped seeing him*—as the declared enemy of France. Nevertheless, his speech shook them. He had dragged into the light of day doubts that had been gnawing at their own minds. Despite some superficial appearances of success in the Ruhr, the French were still no nearer than they had ever been to making the Germans pay. On the contrary, with each successive month of their Ruhr adventure the franc fell further.† Worse still, Smuts's speech contained the threat of a move to isolate France politically. Many Frenchmen suspected the Foreign Office of being behind that move. Smuts might protest that he was speaking for himself alone; but they did not believe him. No doubt they took note of the scepticism which his disclaimer was arousing even in the British press.

Whether or not Westminster and Whitehall had possessed any foreknowledge of what Smuts was proposing to say, many influential persons there and elsewhere congratulated him after he had said it. Curzon told him that his speech was 'most important and most helpful'. Hankey told him that it would do 'a lot of good' and added

---

* See p. 410 below.
† In January 1923 the franc exchanged for 7⅝ cents; in December for 5 cents. In this descent some oscillations occurred from time to time.

—'After six years with Lloyd George... I thought myself case-hardened against speeches, but I must confess I was moved by yours'. From the offices of the Union of Democratic Control E. D. Morel wrote: 'I want to express my admiration of your magnificent pronouncement which may, at the eleventh hour, save Europe, and save a future Anglo-French war which, unless our diplomacy speaks and acts now, I regard as absolutely inevitable.' From America, Bernard Baruch cabled to tell him that his speech had made the 'most profound impression' and Roderick Jones of Reuters cabled to the same effect. From Germany, Gustav Stresemann wrote him a letter of gratitude and resurgent hope. From Cornwall, Emily Hobhouse telegraphed—and this perhaps was the message that moved him most—'Three Cheers!—Bravo, dear Old Oom—The World will breathe a bit easier'.[16]

In the British press the speech made front page news. *The Times* printed it as a pamphlet. Almost all the London dailies reported it at length under laudatory headlines, such as 'Clarion Call', 'Vision At Last', 'The Hour and the Man', 'The Man and the Moment'. The provincial dailies were equally laudatory. So were the weeklies and the religious journals. Discussion on the speech continued in the correspondence columns for a fortnight and more. Except in the Rothermere press, the great weight of comment was behind Smuts. British opinion, it seemed, was crystallizing in a manner which the French government was bound to find disquieting.

Nevertheless, the French government still insisted on impossible conditions both for the international conference* and for the expert inquiry which the British government put forward as an alternative proposal. In consequence, the United States government still held itself aloof from the troubles of Europe. That was the position in mid-November, when Smuts took ship for Cape Town. His parting shot was a letter to *The Times*, calling on the British government to summon a conference and invite the Americans to join it even if the French refused to come. So drastic a move did not prove necessary. By the time Smuts reached South Africa the French were showing signs of a willingness to compromise. Within two months of his return, the Dawes Committee was at work on the reparation problem. It did what was necessary at that time. Smuts—although his own

---

* Poincaré definitely rejected the proposal for an international conference on 28 October.

plan had been a different one—deserved some of the credit for this dawn of a new hope in Europe.[17]

Smuts won acclamation as a peace maker—but more of it in Britain than in South Africa. In India, as in France, he won not acclamation but its opposite.

Indians and their friends in Britain told Smuts that he would do well to practise among his own people what he preached to other peoples. In a letter to *The Times*, Sir Valentine Chirol accused him of maintaining a double standard of political morality: for the nations of Europe, justice and mercy; for the Indians of South Africa, injustice and humiliation. While *The Times* was acclaiming Smuts as a peace-maker, Chirol denounced him as a peace-breaker; his policy in South Africa had been the original cause of Gandhi's anti-British evolution and his persistence in that policy was endangering the peace of India and the survival of the British Empire. Chirol quoted a warning which an Indian delegate to the Imperial Conference had addressed to Smuts on 23 October—that is to say, on the very day of his famous appeal for peace in Europe. 'I tell him frankly', Sir Tej Bahadur Sapru had said, 'that if the Indian problem in South Africa is allowed to fester much longer it will pass beyond the bounds of a domestic issue and will become a question of foreign policy of such gravity that upon it the unity of the Empire may founder irretrievably.' Other people besides Chirol took note of that warning and criticized Smuts when he rejected it. The criticism found its way into a leading article of the *Daily Herald*, which denounced Smuts for treating the Indians as Kruger had treated the *Uitlanders*. 'Yet he will go on, we doubt not', the leader writer continued, 'prating about moral justice and urging others to act upon principles which he treads underfoot himself.'[18]

Compared with all the front page reporting and editorial praise of Smuts's pronouncements on Europe, these dissentient views of his policy and character made only a small impact upon contemporary opinion. Nevertheless, they were ominous for the future. They signalized the reopening of a quarrel which twenty years later proved ruinous to Smuts. He had once flattered himself that the quarrel was finished with. From 1907 to 1914 he had been continuously in the thick of it; but his agreement with Gandhi on the eve of the First World War contained the promise—so he had thought—of permanent reconciliation between South Africa and India. That promise withered in the after-war years.

The Smuts–Gandhi agreement had been on a narrow front and could not have achieved permanent peace except by its progressive enlargement. Gandhi had been well aware of that. From the time of his entry into politics in the 1890s he had protested against all the disabilities which his fellow countrymen suffered in South Africa; but in his campaigns of non-violent resistance he had fought for strictly limited objectives. He had not fought for the franchise which Indians in the Transvaal had never possessed and which Indians in Natal—less fortunate than their brothers in the Cape—had lost. He had not challenged the laws which excluded Indians from land ownership and restricted their rights of residence in the Transvaal.* He had not challenged the administrative practices which cramped their commercial opportunities in Natal. He had not demanded unrestricted entry for Indians into South Africa or unrestricted movement for them from Province to Province. What he had done was to repudiate and resist some specific laws or clauses in laws which appeared most flagrantly symbolic of racial discrimination. His victory on this narrow front found legal embodiment in the Indian Relief Act of 1914.†

Gandhi knew that many of his followers had expected a far more substantial victory. He knew them to be dissatisfied not merely with the Indian Relief Act but also with the correspondence in which he and Smuts had recorded their agreement on matters of administrative practice—their agreement, for example, that there would be some relaxations of the immigration laws, both externally and internally, in favour of educated Indians; that the Indian community would in future be consulted at the drafting stage of legislation which affected its interests; that existing legislation would be administered in a just manner and with due respect to vested rights.

* Most notably the South African Republic's Law 3 of 1885 (which also excluded Indians from the burgher right) and the Transvaal's Gold Law of 1908. However, legal interpretation and administrative practice eased in many ways the restrictive effects of these laws. In Natal, where no legal restrictions existed on Indian rights of land purchase, residence and trade, the opposite often happened: for example, the municipal councils were entrusted with the power to issue trade licences and in the exercise of that power showed a bias against Indian traders.

† For the conflict between Smuts and Gandhi and their agreement in 1914 see *Smuts: The Sanguine Years*, ch. 16. At the climax of his non-violent campaign, Gandhi's main targets were the discriminatory £3 tax in Natal and the invalidation of certain Indian marriages—grievances which the Indian Relief Act removed.

By vested rights Gandhi understood 'the right of an Indian and his successors to live and trade in the township in which he is living and trading, no matter how often he shifts his residence or business from place to place in the same township'. He said subsequently that respect for vested rights, by his interpretation, meant also that no new law would be passed imposing fresh restrictions on Indians. No doubt he would have done well to make that interpretation explicit in the formal correspondence; but he had faith in the spirit, not merely in the letter of his agreement with Smuts. He believed that the white South Africans, freed from their fears of an Indian influx and of Indian political ambitions, would discover the will to deal justly with Indians as individuals. He looked forward to a régime of equality before the law which would be achieved not at a single stroke but by progressive stages of reform.[19]

Complete satisfaction [he reminded Smuts] cannot be expected until full civic rights have been conceded to the resident Indian population.

I have told my countrymen that they will have to exercise patience...
I shall hope that when the Europeans of South Africa fully appreciate the fact that now as the importation of indentured labour is prohibited, and as the Immigration Restriction Act of last year has in practice almost stopped further free Indian immigration, and that my countrymen do not aspire to any political ambition, they, the Europeans, will see the justice and indeed the necessity of my countrymen being granted the rights I have referred to.

In 1914 and for the next three or four years Smuts shared Gandhi's confidence that the spirit of their agreement would progressively achieve embodiment in South African law and custom. At the Imperial War Conference of 1917 he stated the grounds of his confidence in terms which Gandhi had used three years earlier.

In South Africa [he said] there has been this fundamental trouble, that the white community have been afraid of opening the door too wide to Indian immigration... I have always felt sure that, once the white community in South Africa were rid of the fear that they were going to be flooded by unlimited immigration from India, all the other questions would be considered subsidiary and would become easily and perfectly soluble.[20]

No doubt Smuts had also in mind the second reason for confidence which Gandhi had stated: 'my countrymen', he had said, 'do not aspire to any political ambition.' That, however, was no longer the situation when the war ended. Rights of franchise had already by then found a place on the Indian political agenda. *Per contra,* new restrictions of the civil rights of Indians had found a place on the agenda of white South Africa. India and South Africa were set once again on a collision course.

Political changes in India impinged on South African politics; Indian nationalists who were demanding a free and equal status for their country made the same demand on behalf of their countrymen overseas. Smuts did not possess the power to satisfy their demand. In August 1919, when he arrived home after two and a half years of absence, he found already on the statute book the Transvaal Asiatic Land and Trading Amendment Act, a discriminatory Act which did its best to slam doors of opportunity which hitherto had been open to Indians in the Transvaal. Earlier laws, as he and Gandhi had recognized, had appeared severely restrictive; but legal interpretation and administrative custom had tempered their severity. For example, Law 3 of 1885 had laid it down that Indians could not acquire fixed property in the Transvaal, except in such places as the government might assign to them; but Indians had in fact been permitted and at times even encouraged to acquire land by various devices of indirect ownership. Again, the intention of Law 3 had been segregationist; but its application had proved conformable with the growth of an extremely mobile Indian trading community.* The new Act closed these customary loopholes. It gave additional legal protection to the European shopkeepers who believed themselves to be threatened by Indian competition.

Krugersdorp had started the anti-Indian drive by launching a successful legal action and by founding the South Africans' League, a propagandist association which within a few months had vigorous branches in all the main centres of the Transvaal and Natal. The League enumerated as follows its complaints against the Indians: they sent money out of the country; their habits were insanitary; they depreciated the value of property; their standard of living was low; their methods of competition were unscrupulous; they closed important avenues to white employment; they produced nothing; they consumed Indian rather than South African products; they were a bad influence on the Natives; they were unassimilable; they were immoral; they were too familiar. That list of Indian short-

---

* A legal decision in 1904 had settled one hitherto contentious issue: namely, that the segregation contemplated in Law 3 of 1885 was residential only, not commercial.

comings was submitted in evidence to the Asiatic Inquiry Commission, which Smuts appointed towards the end of 1919 in the hope that it would make reason rather than passion the arbiter of policy. The Commission's chairman was a judge of the Supreme Court, Sir John Lange, and he had the assistance of Sir Benjamin Robertson, a senior official whom Smuts had borrowed from the Government of India.* In its report, the Commission rejected the sensational evidence of the South Africans' League and offered a cool, non-alarmist diagnosis of Indian activities. It rejected the proposals submitted to it for the wholesale expulsion of the Indian population or for its compulsory segregation. On the other hand, it favoured voluntary repatriation and segregation. It also recommended that the existing legislative controls over Indians in the Transvaal, including the law recently passed, should be retained. For Natal, it proposed new legislation to debar Indians from buying agricultural land outside a 20- or 30-mile wide strip along the coast.

No logical connection was visible between some at least of those recommendations and the cool diagnosis which preceded them. Presumably, the Commission made concessions to the hot politics of the Indian question. Those concessions calmed no passions. In parliament, members of Smuts's own party led the hue and cry against the Lange Report. It was the weakest document, Sir Abe Bailey declared, that any Commission had ever produced; it might satisfy the Indians who were eating into the vitals of South Africa but it would not satisfy a large contingent of South Africans who meant to assert themselves and show the Indians that they were not wanted. G. Heaton Nicholls, the S.A.P. representative of Zululand, wanted to know what was going to happen to white Christian civilization in Africa and painted a terrifying picture of the Asiatic influx into the East African territories. Two S.A.P. men from Natal, J. S. Marwick and H. G. Mackeurtan, demanded the compulsory segregation of Indians on grounds of sheer self-preservation. Speaking for the Labour party, T. Boydell pointed out that the Indians were competing not only with white shopkeepers but also with white wage earners; they were invading the tailoring, cabinet making, painting and French polishing trades; he did not want to see their prosperity interfered with

---

* Six years earlier, Sir Benjamin Robertson had been attached as an observer to the Solomon Commission, which produced the proposals embodied in the Indian Relief Act of 1914.

but neither did he want to see the prosperity of Europeans interfered with. Speaking for the National party, C. G. Fichardt wanted to see 'repatriation of the whole lot'; it was a matter of self preservation, he said, and the world had taught them in the last few years that when it came to that there was very little question of justice. Speaking for himself alone in that tempest of passion, J. X. Merriman reminded previous speakers that they had received their Christian religion from Asia. He warned them that they might receive something else from there unless they were careful. But Merriman by now was a very old man and nobody any longer paid attention to the strange things that he sometimes said.[21]

These proceedings in parliament were Smuts's send-off to the Imperial Conference of 1921. There the Indian delegates reminded him of what he had told them in 1917, namely, that his people would find it easy to do justice to the Indians in their midst now that they no longer had cause to fear an unmanageable Indian influx. The time had come for him, they said, to make his words good.[22] They demanded still more than that. Srinivasa Sastri moved a resolution claiming for Indians in the Dominions 'all the rights of citizenship'. All the Prime Ministers except Smuts received that resolution sympathetically. Smuts rejected it. He reminded Sastri that the Smuts–Gandhi agreement contained no reference to the franchise. Gandhi, he said, had known South Africa too well to raise that thorny issue. White South Africans were an entrenched minority in the black mass of the population. Inequality was their constitutional and political bedrock. If they gave equal political rights to the Indians they would have to give them to the Natives. No South African government which accepted Sastri's resolution would last a fortnight. If that were really so, Sastri retorted, there was not much chance of keeping India a contented member of the Empire. His passionate advocacy swayed the Prime Ministers to his side. They broke their own rule of unanimity. A resolution of the Conference declared that in the interests of the British Commonwealth it was desirable that the rights of Indians to citizenship should be recognized. The same resolution recorded South Africa's dissent and India's protest against South Africa's dissent. A commentator in New Zealand remarked sardonically—'If the people of India will not stay in the Empire unless they are granted full equality, and South Africa will not stay in if they are, there is a tough proposition ahead of the Empire.'[23]

Smuts was doomed to fight the same battle all over again at the Imperial Conference of 1923. His prospects of fighting it to any useful purpose did not improve during the interval. In India, Gandhi went to gaol. Indian politicians who believed in co-operation with the British Raj felt all the more constrained to prove that co-operation paid dividends. Sastri made a propagandist perambulation of the British Empire. His complaints against South Africa—the only Dominion which he did not visit*—made front-page news. To Smuts it was no consolation to see him putting the Colonial Office into the dock alongside South Africa. The Colonial Office had been taking it for granted that white supremacy was the natural order of affairs in East Africa. It gave the Kenya settlers a strong contingent of elected members in the Legislative Council. To the Indians of Kenya it proposed at first to give nothing at all. Thereby it let loose a violent war of words. The whites declared that Kenya belonged to them. The Indians demanded an equal share of white privileges. The Africans were dumb. Neither the whites nor the Indians paid much attention to them. The Government of India joined battle on the Indian side. From 1919 to 1923 the battle swayed this way and that. Its din reverberated throughout India, Britain, East Africa and South Africa. The spectacle of 10,000 white settlers setting out to create their own Kenya in the image of white South Africa made Indian Nationalists see red. The spectacle of Indians in any African territory setting themselves up as the equals of white people made South Africans see red. The men of Durban and Krugersdorp stood up to show India and the whole world that South Africans were masters in their own house.[24]

On 9 May 1922 H. G. Mackeurtan, the S.A.P. member for Durban-Umbilo, moved a resolution requesting the government to introduce legislation for the compulsory segregation of Asiatics. Mackeurtan considered himself a moderate man because he did not take up the popular cry for shipping all the Indians back to India. In his view, segregation was the middle course between the two alternatives of compulsory repatriation and doing nothing. Sir Abe Bailey, the S.A.P. member for Krugersdorp, was not content with that middle course and moved an amendment calling on the government to increase its efforts to ensure the departure of Asiatics from

---

* Sastri believed that the official and private treatment which he was offered in South Africa would prove humiliating.

the Union. Every Indian in South Africa, Bailey said, took the place of a white man, took his livelihood away and forced him to leave the country. What was to become of the 43,000 children born last year? What was their future and what hope was there for them? Were they to be the salaried clerks of Asiatics or the aliens of South Africa? Lord Milner would not have stood for that! Bailey denied that there was any room at all for Indians anywhere in Africa. But the next S.A.P. speaker, Brigadier-General the Hon. J. J. Byron, did not think that Bailey's amendment went far enough. Byron wanted compulsory repatriation of the Indians *en masse*. So the debate went on, until old Mr Merriman reminded the House of the repeated warnings that he and others had given the country against bringing in the Indians and against keeping them after they had served their indentures. But the people of Natal had always insisted that they needed the Asiatic to produce sugar. Now, having got all they could out of him, they wanted to kick him out. 'Perish the Empire but save Natal' seemed to be their cry; but they had brought these people in and must treat them in a humane and reasonable way. Besides, the notion that so small a community as the South Africans could settle such momentous issues without regard to the rest of the world was foolish. When Merriman had made his protest, Duncan wound up the debate. He did what he could to take the heat out of it.[25]

Smuts did the same at party conferences. He deprecated impractical proposals which would do South Africa no good and might do the Empire much harm. In his capacity as Prime Minister he fended off some of those proposals; for example, he refused on three separate occasions to advise the Governor-General in Council to validate a Bill of the Natal Provincial Council depriving Indians of their municipal franchise. Nevertheless he had to bow to the storm. In a party conference at Maritzburg in July 1923 he announced his government's decision to introduce new segregationist legislation which would—he protested—do strict justice both to the Indians and to the community as a whole. From segregation he passed to the Sastri campaign for equal political rights.

Mr Sastri has been going about the British Empire criticizing South Africa. I am not going to follow his example. All I can say is that with regard to the franchise, we see no reason to make a distinction between Indians in this country and Natives in this country. There is the coloured line which is in existence today. Right or wrong—I do not argue about that. It is a clearly marked line you can follow, but once you cross that line we see no reason why there should be any distinction between Indians and Natives. And if Indians have to have the franchise, I see no reason why it should not be given to the Natives. Well, we all know what the effect of that would be... Three years ago, at the last Imperial Conference, I took up that attitude, and you know how I stood aside from the representatives of the other parts of the Empire on that question.

He left his listeners in no doubt that he was ready to do the same again.[26]

While Smuts was conferring with his party in Pietermaritzburg Sir Tej Bahadur Sapru, an antagonist far more formidable than Sastri, was already quietly at work in London. Whereas Smuts came to the Imperial Conference only at the last minute and with Europe, not India, in the forefront of his mind, Sapru spent four consecutive months in London in total concentration upon one single objective— upon justice as the Indians saw it. Yet almost at the start Sapru's plans came close to foundering on the Kenya rock. The Colonial Office, having made the brilliant last-minute discovery that Kenya was 'primarily an African country', issued a White Paper which proclaimed the paramountcy of African interests. That doctrine, taken by itself, was a blow not so much to the Indians as to the Europeans, who now saw the South African and Southern Rhodesian road to white supremacy closed against them. The Indians, however, were thinking not about African claims in the future but about their own immediate claim for equality with the Europeans. They had demanded the common roll, but the White Paper put them second to the Europeans in a system of communal representation.* They had demanded the right to buy land anywhere, but the White Paper preserved the highlands for Europeans only. They denounced the White Paper. In India, all the politicians and the entire press denounced it. Above the din a cry arose to boycott the Imperial Conference.

After a hard struggle with his political colleagues in India, Sapru got leave to stay on and fight in London.[27] There he had trouble with Lord Peel, the Secretary of State for India. Because he held no official position in the Government of India but was merely a 'representative

---

* Europeans 11, Indians 5, Arabs 1. This was better from the Indian point of view than the representation in the Legislative Council stipulated by Lord Milner on 21 May 1920: Europeans 11, Indians 2. On the other hand, it was not so good as the Wood–Winterton proposals in 1922 for a common roll.

of British India', Lord Peel seemed to think at first that he should be seen and not heard at the Imperial Conference. But he had strong support from Lord Reading, the Viceroy, and in two or three interviews he won the confidence of Lord Peel. Before the Conference met, it was agreed between them that he would be India's main champion in the battle for equal rights. From July to October he spent his time with officials, politicians, newspaper editors and ecclesiastical dignitaries. Quietly but effectively he annexed the territory which hitherto had been Smuts's territory. When the Dominion Prime Ministers arrived in London he made appointments with them one by one and received assurances of support from all of them—with the exception of Smuts.

Sapru met Smuts three times. Their first meeting, on 3 October, was cordial and at its conclusion Smuts said, 'I will be faithful to you if you will be faithful to me.' Their second meeting, on 20 October, had a smooth beginning but a rough ending. Smuts spoke in praise of Gandhi, protested his own zeal for Indian self-government and offered his services to expedite its progress. Sapru politely declined that offer. After those preliminaries, the two men got to grips with the matters immediately in dispute between their countries. Smuts warned Sapru to expect no concessions at all from South Africa. If that was the position, Sapru said, it meant war between their two countries. Smuts remained good tempered and asked Sapru not to present him with an ultimatum. He promised to consult his colleagues in Pretoria. Three days later he met Sapru again and repeated what he had said before, that South Africa could do nothing to meet the Indian demands. Once again, Sapru told him that this decision meant war. Both men knew, of course, that it could be no more than a war of words, unless and until India took over from Britain the control of her foreign policy and her armed forces.

Next day, 24 October, the war of words began in the Imperial Conference. The Secretary of State opened proceedings with a 20-minute speech. Sapru followed with a speech of 1 hour 47 minutes. He had been working on it for days past and he achieved an oratorical triumph. He struck the note of allegiance to the Crown. In India, he said, that allegiance was a living thing, but if it were shaken the consequences to the Empire and to humanity would be incalculable. India was the main bridge between the races of Europe and Asia and her incorporation in the Commonwealth was the world's main hope for peace. As loyal subjects of the Crown, Indians were fighting for a place in the household of their King and would not be content with a place in his stables. So the speech moved to its climax, India's confrontation with South Africa. Anti-climax followed when Sapru's colleague, the Maharajah of Alwar, addressed the Conference. The debate was adjourned until 29 October. Then the spokesmen of all the Commonwealth countries except South Africa announced one by one their willingness to start practical discussions with India on the ways and means of implementing the equality resolution of 1921. But Smuts flatly rejected the Indian proposals and the theory on which they stood. The Crown, he declared, was the binding link between the parts of the Empire but it was not the source of civil and political rights; a citizen derived his rights simply and solely from the law of the State in which he lived. He insisted once again that equal rights for Indians in South Africa would lead to equal rights for Natives and that would mean the end of South Africa. 'We are up against a stone wall', he said, 'and we cannot get over it.'

When the Conference was over Sapru made a press attack on Smuts.[28] He had been suffering from oyster poisoning and moral indignation, ills of the body and spirit from which Gandhi was immune. Even so, he should perhaps have been content to let well alone. His campaign to isolate South Africa had proved brilliantly successful. To be sure, a dependent India could do the South Africans no harm; but independent India, a generation later, led the hue and cry against them at the United Nations. Smuts, if ever he looked back from 1946, must have remembered Sapru's performance in 1923 as the portent of trouble for his country.

CHAPTER 8

DEFEAT

His own countrymen applauded Smuts when the British press criticized him; but when it acclaimed him they gave him a mixed reception. At the first session of parliament after his return Hertzog assured him that he had the appreciation of the whole country for the stand that he had taken against India; but the Opposition parties expressed no appreciation of his stand on reparations and the Ruhr. A battle of cartoons broke out. The *Rand Daily Mail* pictured him flying to darkest Europe on angel's wings with 'the lamp of common sense' in his hand; but a Labour cartoon parodied that picture: to be sure, it gave him the angel's wings and put into his hand a top hat full of the flowers of brotherly love; but in the same sky it showed an aeroplane marked S.A.P. dropping bombs on Johannesburg. The caption read—'Smuts showering peace and goodwill on Europe but bombs and frightfulness on South Africa'.[*][1]

For Labour to make its propaganda not only in English but also in Afrikaans was a new portent and one that was ominous for Smuts. Yet he might have anticipated it. In politics and industry the Labour leadership still remained English-speaking; but the industrial rank and file was becoming increasingly Afrikaans-speaking; at the time of the Rand explosion, the white labour force of the mining industry was approximately three-quarters Afrikaner. Whatever language the white miners spoke, they were at one with each other in the hatred they felt for Smuts. They saw him as a puppet who moved his arms and legs when Hoggenheimer pulled the strings. Twenty years earlier, the Hoggenheimer symbol,[†] although Smuts himself had been too fastidious to exploit it, had served his cause well: in particular, it had provided cement for building the bridge between Het Volk and the Responsible Government Association, the two parties which opposed Milner. Now it

---

[*] Also in Afrikaans: 'Smuts strooi vrede en liefde oor Europa maar bomme en ve-skrikking oor Suid-Afrika.'

[†] On the Hoggenheimer symbol see p. 70 above.

was providing the same cement for bridge builders in the two parties which opposed Smuts. There was no good reason for Smuts to feel indignant or even surprised at this turn in the wheel of his fate. He himself had given the wheel a decisive push when he joined forces with the Unionists, notwithstanding the capitalistic taint which still clung to them. The National party and the Labour party, for their different reasons of xenophobic impulse and socialist ideology, throve on anti-capitalist slogans. In political logic, a bargain between those two parties was the appropriate reply to Smuts's bargain with the Unionists.

It was not, however, the inevitable reply. The Nationalists had no love for socialism, Labour had none for secession: if Smuts enjoyed good luck, incompatibilities of temperament and of ultimate purpose might possibly prevail over the short-term inducements towards a deal between Nationalism and Labour. But from the Rand rebellion onwards, all the luck ran consistently against Smuts. For example, it was a piece of bad luck that a delegation of Rhodesians should arrive in Cape Town right in the middle of the debates on the Rand rebellion. The delegates were sitting in the visitors' gallery of the House of Assembly on the day Hertzog denounced Smuts as the man whose footsteps dripped with blood. They heard the abuse which orators in both the Opposition parties hurled at his head. Rhodesians, they might reasonably have concluded, would best preserve their interests and peace of mind by keeping themselves separate from such rancorous neighbours.

The Union of South Africa Act had laid down a procedure for the incorporation of the Rhodesians into the Union. Smuts had set his heart on bringing them in. Unfortunately for him, the white settlers of Southern Rhodesia were given the option in 1922 either of joining the Union or of managing their own affairs as a separate self-governing Colony. They were to make their decision in a referendum; but before making it they needed to know what terms the Union would offer them. That was their purpose in sending a delegation to Cape Town; but the delegation returned at the end of April without a firm offer. There were so many complications to unravel that Smuts had to move step by step.

But just now [he wrote on 27 April] I am rushed almost beyond endurance. The usual Parliamentary grind is going on, and you have seen what that is. Besides I have just finished with the Rhodesian Delegation who came to see me on the question of incorporation into the Union. I am now busy with the Chartered Company in order to see whether we can arrive at an agreement on the expropriation of their assets. The work really means a financial review of the history of Rhodesia. And over and above all this, the Portuguese Delegation have arrived from Lisbon to negotiate a new Mozambique Treaty. I am now like an Oriental Despot giving audience to suitors from the ends of two continents. All very interesting but very exacting. It does not look like achieving success either—the Rhodesian or Mozambique business. But I am going to try very hard. It would be a great thing to round off the South African state with borders far flung into the heart of the continent. But I fear I am moving too fast, and patience will be necessary.

'Wider still and wider' was his dream for South Africa; but if he failed in his Rhodesian attempt he would fail everywhere. On the other hand—so he believed—if he succeeded in bringing the Rhodesians in, he would hold the whiphand over the Portuguese in Mozambique; he would be in a position to establish South African control over the emergent copper industry in Northern Rhodesia, if not in Katanga; he would be able to build economic and political bridges between all the territories of white settlement as far north as Kenya.[2]

The Opposition parties did not share his expansionist exuberance. They accused him of trying to bring in new supporters for his own party and of trafficking with foreign financial interests 'for the purpose'—so Creswell put it—'of securing to the Union the immense privilege of continuing to be governed by the present Prime Minister and his Cabinet'.[3] Creswell was referring to the negotiations which Smuts was conducting with the British South Africa Company for the expropriation of its assets. Smuts argued that he had to bring those negotiations to a conclusion before he could define his offer to the Rhodesian settlers. To reverse that order of procedure, he explained, would put the Union very much at the mercy of the Chartered Company, which then would be able to say: 'The Union Government is bound, and we shall raise our terms.'[4] That, probably, was a realistic appreciation of what the negotiation required, but it made parliamentary trouble for Smuts because the negotiation dragged on until after the end of the session. Consequently, Smuts was not in a position to tell parliament what terms he would offer to the Rhodesians. In constitutional law there was no reason for him to do so—section 150 of the South Africa Act gave parliament merely the *last* word*—but politically he laid himself open to the charge of following his own secret paths and of failing to consult the nation on an issue of supreme national importance. Not that it made much difference in practice; whatever his proposals might be and whenever or however he might publish them, the Opposition parties would give them at best a cold reception. No doubt the Rhodesians took note of the fact that they were not very much wanted in South Africa, except by the party which appeared, on the evidence of successive by-elections, to be close to the end of its term of office.

Nevertheless, Smuts began to feel hopeful of success. At the end of July he told the Rhodesians what terms his government could offer them for their entry into the Union as a fifth Province. The terms included: ten Rhodesian representatives in the House of Assembly with a progressive increase up to seventeen as their population rose; unencumbered ownership and control of Crown lands and a Rhodesian Land Board to allocate the lands for settlement; a guarantee to the Rhodesians that their labour would not be recruited for industries elsewhere in the Union; an assurance to them that the Chartered Company's mineral rights would be acquired later on; the immediate assurance of strong financial support for the development of their transport system and other public works. On top of all this—so it seemed to Smuts—he was offering them a secure future within a large and strong state. He found it hard to believe that they would deliberately reject that security in exchange for the precarious satisfactions of self-rule within a small state of problematical viability.

Some time previously he had agreed to go to Rhodesia in August to open an agricultural show. He now decided to take his wife with him and to spend two or three weeks going about the country and getting to know people. When he and his wife set out the prospects for his side appeared unpromising; but he was aiming —although his visit was ostensibly 'non-political'—at winning the Rhodesians over.

I hope they will vote to come into union [he wrote on 31 July] but I am told that the great current of opinion is still the other way. They are afraid

---

* Section 150 provided that on receipt of addresses from both Houses of the Union Parliament, the King-in-Council would be able to admit into the Union any additional colonies or territories, 'including the Territories administered by the British South Africa Company', on the conditions set out in the addresses.

of our bilingualism, our nationalism, my views of the British Empire. In short they are little Jingoes and the sooner they are assimilated by the Union the better for them and for us.

He and his wife allowed themselves just a little relaxation, he at Zimbabwe, she at Victoria Falls. Nevertheless their tour was strenuous. When it was over, he felt confident that it had served its purpose.* He wrote on 22 August: 'It has been a most interesting and busy time. I have done good work and I think the Referendum will now probably go in favour of entry into the Union.'[5]

It went the opposite way. By a majority of nearly 3,000 in a poll of approximately 22,000 the white men and women† of Southern Rhodesia decided to work out their own destiny as a separate self-governing colony. Smuts refused to recognize their decision as final. Within a few years, he told Bonar Law, they would bow to the inevitable and come into the Union. They would be in the Union already, he protested, if only Churchill had not been in such a hurry to offer them responsible government.‡ Even now, it might be possible to postpone that gift and persuade them to think again. Or if not, they must at any rate be made to swallow the fruits of their own folly. Smuts lectured Bonar Law on the tasks of British policy.

But I must add [he wrote] that it would not be good policy to extend any financial favours to Rhodesia, as she ought to seek relief for her financial troubles in the Union. Indeed, finance would be one of the principal causes to bring her into the Union, and the British Government should not in any way lessen the force of that cause. For the entry of Rhodesia into the Union is not only in her own interest and that of the Union but also in the interest of the British Empire. Rhodesia as a separate state struggling vainly with her impossible task is certain to become an embarrassment to the British Government in the end.[6]

Even if he was right, there was nothing he could do about it. The collapse of his Central African policy in October 1922 proved final, and of conspicuous historical significance in long term, certainly for Rhodesia and possibly for South Africa.

* He underestimated the persuasive powers of Sir Charles Coghlan, the leading advocate of responsible government for a separate Southern Rhodesia, and the reluctance of ordinary Rhodesians to enter a unitary South Africa (largely the creation of Smuts himself) as distinct from a looser federal structure.

† About one in three of the voters were women.

‡ As Colonial Secretary, Churchill had appointed the Buxton Committee to report on a scheme of responsible government for Southern Rhodesia. Smuts believed that Churchill's predecessor, Milner, had stood for a more cautious policy.

In short term, his defeat took additional shine from his prestige and demonstrated once again the effective, if still unacknowledged, partnership which the two Opposition parties were forging for his downfall. Precisely at this time, Hertzog and Creswell made up their minds to explore, systematize and in due course publish the terms of their partnership. At an important meeting on 15 July 1922 they took the essential first steps towards an electoral pact between their two parties. Plans for a pact had been for some time past in Tielman Roos's head and he had talked about them with a number of Labour politicians; but Hertzog would not suffer a person he considered irresponsible to pose as the party's pace-maker. His own pace was deliberate; but by April 1923 he and Creswell were ready to make a public statement. In a long letter of 12 April Creswell recorded four essential heads of their agreement:

(1) That the present government was acting as if national and 'big financial' interests were one and the same thing: consequently, that it was damaging the country's welfare and jeopardizing its future 'as a civilized people'.

(2) That any splitting of the anti-government vote in three-cornered contests was clearly undesirable at the next elections.

(3) That pro-government propaganda had created the 'secession bogey' as a means of confusing the real political issues and of frustrating electoral co-operation between the Opposition parties. The same propaganda, Creswell pointed out, had also created a Bolshevik bogey; but this was far less scaring to Afrikaner voters than secession was to English-speaking voters. He told Hertzog that the secession bogey would have to be laid if their two parties were to achieve effective co-operation at the next elections.

In this regard [he continued] you said that while no member of your party could be expected, any more than any member of the Labour Party, to renounce his freedom to express, inside and outside of Parliament, any views he may hold on this or any other matter, you were able to give this explicit undertaking to electors at the next general election, viz. that in the Parliament that will then be elected, should a Nationalist Government come into power, no Nationalist Member of Parliament will use his vote to upset the existing constitutional relationship of South Africa to the British Crown. We agreed that under these circumstances we could quite properly recommend to our respective Parties election co-operation on the lines indicated in paragraph 2 of this letter. This co-operation would indicate that we both appreciate the urgent necessity for the next

Parliament to devote itself single-mindedly to domestic measures required to promote the prosperity of the country upon lines more congenial to its people than those at present followed.

By this crystal-clear statement on the secession issue, Creswell and Hertzog sank the ship which had brought Smuts triumphantly to port in the elections of 1921. It only remained for them to record their agreement on one important practical matter.

(4) That the co-operation of Nationalists and Labour men in the constituencies at the next elections would not impinge upon their separate allegiances to their own parties.[7]

In his reply of 19 April 1923, Hertzog confirmed that Creswell's letter correctly stated the substance of their conversations. Later in the year, provincial congresses of the National party endorsed the election pact. The Labour party endorsed it at its annual conference in January 1924. *Die Burger* acclaimed the pact as the portent of Smuts's downfall and of the downfall of capitalist domination in South Africa.[8]

Smuts himself had been conscious for some time past that his fortunes were declining. Ever since the Rand disaster he had seen his majority progressively eroded by defeats at by-elections. Among them, the defeat of a strong S.A.P. candidate by Creswell in July 1922 was a particularly heavy blow. Smuts wrote:

I have just lost a by-election at Durban, Creswell, the leader of the Labour Party—who fell out at the General Election—having beaten a very good man of ours. That stupid elector, Hard Times, is all the time against me. My majority of 22 in 1921 has dropped to 13, which is not a very promising number.

By March 1923 his majority had dropped to eleven. By April 1924 it was down to eight. He was a tenacious fighter but he asked himself at times how much fighting strength he still had left. He was suffering from rheumatic pains and extreme physical and mental exhaustion. Towards the end of the second parliamentary session of 1923 he told Margaret Gillett—

The pace is terrific...How I shall get through it I don't know. The grind of politics is really more than one can bear. Times are hard, everybody is cursing the government, and I know nobody will do better than we do.

Those sentences were not the mood of a leader looking forward to victory.[9]

Victory could not reasonably have been his expectation after holding office for seventeen years,* of which the last three had been years of economic slump. Some people said that he and his capitalist masters had made the slump, but by a more plausible diagnosis its origins were overseas. Its effects on South Africa's national income, public finance, economic activity and employment were catastrophic. They were aggravated by three successive years of drought which accelerated and dramatized the flight of Afrikaners from farming. The ruined farmers and *bywoners*—'poor whites', as people called them—had to try to find city jobs at a time when industrial and commercial employment was everywhere contracting.

The government was certain to suffer opprobrium no matter what policy it followed in fighting the depression. Smuts proclaimed a policy of economic development under three salient heads:

1. Increased use and development of the country's material resources by way of (*a*) encouragement to agriculture, (*b*) founding of new industries.
2. Controlled immigration of Europeans of good quality and economic status.
3. Improvement of the quality of the existing white population, especially in the lower ranks.[10]

These were admirable objectives in long term but in short term the conditions for their realization were unpropitious: agricultural re-deployment required money and time and meanwhile low prices and drought were afflicting farmers; industrial development required capital and meanwhile the basic industries were fighting to keep themselves solvent; immigrants looked forward to bettering their condition and meanwhile white men in their thousands were leaving South Africa because they could not find jobs; education cost money and meanwhile the Provinces were cutting teachers' salaries.† How to pursue an expansionist policy in times of slump was an urgent but, in the 1920s, an unanswered question, not only in South Africa but everywhere. Hertzog and Creswell got no closer than Smuts did to finding an answer; they called on the government to spend more money on subsidizing white wages, raising teachers' salaries and

* Since March 1907, when he took office under Botha in the Transvaal.

† Education was a Provincial responsibility; but the Provinces were financially dependent upon Union grants. Union–Provincial financial relations were hotly debated in the early 1920s by politicians and publicists; but in 1924 they aroused very little interest in the constituencies.

similar humane purposes; but at the same time they censured it for failing to balance its budget.

The Smuts government established Union-wide electrification under public control. It passed an Industrial Conciliation Act and improved the apprenticeship system. It instituted a Board of Industries. It made plans for a national iron and steel industry.* Unfortunately for its own prestige, it failed to make those plans effective. Success would have required, among other things, large sums of capital, which in those years of slump could not possibly have been raised either by taxation and borrowing at home or by borrowing overseas or by any combination of financial expedients. South African and overseas investors were not likely to risk their money in ambitious new ventures of industrial expansion unless and until the existing basic industries were once again firmly on their feet. To put them on their feet meant, amongst other things, cutting costs.

Towards the end of 1922 the Mining Industries Board reported to that effect. It laid especial stress on the need to cut labour costs. It admitted that this would require some substitution of black for white labour, not in skilled employment (which would, it said, remain exclusively the white man's sphere) but in semi-skilled occupations. It went on to argue that a profitable and expanding mining industry would produce far more employment for white workers in other sectors of the economy than the small curtailments of employment—at most two or three thousands—which it made in the mines themselves. To quote its own words on the linked problems of costs, expansion and employment—

If, by a reduction of costs, low grade mines are able to continue working, if low grade ore in rich and poor mines alike is brought within the sphere of profitable exploitation, if mines which are standing idle today, because their ore is poor, are reopened, and if new mines are started on hitherto unpromising areas, more work will be provided for Europeans than by any artificial expedients which might be adopted for that purpose.[11]

The commission which submitted this diagnosis was composed of a Judge of the Appellate Division, a Labour Adviser to the British Board of Trade, the Government Mining Engineer and the Vice-Chancellor of the University of Cape Town.† These men were not

* See p. 63 above.
† Sir William Solomon, Mr William Brace, Sir Robert Kotze, Sir Carruthers Beattie.

Hoggenheimer's hirelings; but they were prescribing for South Africa's ills the unpleasant medicines of economic orthodoxy.

Equally unpleasant was the austere economizing of Burton, the Minister of Finance, and Jagger, the Minister of Railways. By 1924 the mines were expanding once more and an efficient transport system was giving good service to the nation. South Africa was well poised for the approaching economic upswing. But it came too late to save Smuts. When parliament met in January 1924 unemployment was still rife among white South Africans, while blacks were holding jobs which properly belonged—the Opposition parties said—to 'civilized labour'.

Proceedings in this parliamentary session foreshadowed Smuts's downfall by demonstrating the practical efficacy of the Nationalist–Labour pact. The Opposition leaders reversed their customary roles: Creswell attacked the government on the ground of Commonwealth doctrine;* Hertzog attacked it on the ground of employment policy. Of these two attacks Hertzog's was the more formidable. White South Africa, he cried, had no future unless it made employment for civilized labour. The white man must choose whether he was going to barter his European civilization for uncivilized labour or whether he was going to stand by civilization. The white man in South Africa had a right to existence. He could not exist on 2s. a day. Hertzog produced a confident answer to the question—what remedy did *he* propose? He proposed a *skeidsmuur*, a line of division between civilized and uncivilized labour. In the public service the government should adopt the rule that the work was there for civilized labour. On the railways it should insist that civilized labour had preference. In its dealings with private industry it should grant no privileges to any company or individual except on the condition that opportunities would be created for civilized labour and that uncivilized labour was not to be used solely because it was cheap. 'The native', Hertzog conceded, 'can be used to advantage; but I say that native labour must not be used where the services of the white man can and ought to be used, that is, where the white man of South Africa can make a living.' He meant—although he did

---

* Smuts had suggested that the new Labour government in Britain was bound to grant the trade preferences to which its predecessor had pledged itself at the recent Imperial Economic Conference. Such a contention, as Creswell rightly pointed out, was inconsistent with the doctrine of the unfettered freedom of each sovereign parliament of the British Commonwealth.[12]

not spell out his meaning in the terms of economic argument— a subsidized living.[13]

'Civilized labour' was a powerful incantation. Its magic created unity between the separate followings of Hertzog and Creswell and at the same time exposed the conflicts within Smuts's camp. The Smuts government was spending money to employ white men on work which black men could do more cheaply; but J. W. Jagger was trying to run the railways in accordance with what he called economic laws.* These contradictions of economic doctrine and policy divided the South Africa party as much as its reputed class solidarity united it. The party's contradictory attitudes towards Native policy had long since been patent to the world and were a root cause of the government's difficulties at Geneva over the Bondelzwarts affair.† Only on the Indian issue did government supporters seem able to speak with one mind, and even then they found it easier to speak than to act. Patrick Duncan introduced a segregationist measure called the Class Areas Bill; but before it could get beyond the second reading Smuts announced the prorogation of parliament and a general election with polling day on 19 June 1924.

The defeat of his party at the Wakkerstroom by-election of 5 April precipitated that decision. Some party members, then and later, reproached him for failing to take counsel sufficiently with his colleagues. Possibly they had good grounds for that complaint. They also felt that he had lost patience; he could have hung on, they complained, until the tide turned. But the Wakkerstroom defeat had special political significance. The S.A.P. candidate, A. G. Robertson, was a man of character and brains who had resigned his post as Administrator of the Transvaal for the express purpose of fighting the election. The Nationalist candidate, A. S. Naudé, was an almost unknown man. Naudé's victory demonstrated the electoral efficacy of the Nationalist-Labour pact, for Naudé could not have won without the strong support that he got from the railway workers

* According to Hertzog (5 February 1924) the government was spending an inadequate £3 millions in combating white unemployment. According to Jagger (6 June 1924) it was wrong to pay a white railway worker 9s. 3d. a day for work which a Coloured man would do for 4s. 6d. a day. At the same time, Jagger denied the accusation that he had dismissed white workers to make room for Coloured ones at reduced rates of pay.

† The Permanent Mandates Commission censured the Union government for its failure to state any conclusions of its own upon the highly conflicting evidence, both documentary and verbal, which it and its officials submitted.

of Volkrust and other Labour voters. As Smuts put the issue in his explanation to the House on 7 June:

The government also considers it an election of crucial importance. Although nominally only a by-election, all the surrounding circumstances give it a very special significance...After Wakkerstroom the government is doubtful whether it still enjoys the confidence of the country. We still have a parliamentary majority. But that is not enough. We are dealing with far-reaching questions of policy...Under these circumstances the government is of the opinion that the country should be consulted as soon as possible and that a fresh parliament should be elected.

In a telegram to Walton he put the issue more tersely:

Challenge of Pact parties had to be accepted and we must now fight it out.[14]

He felt no assurance of victory. He told Amery that he hoped to win but, failing that, hoped to come back strong enough to act as a check on the wreckers. He wrote to the Gilletts—

I have once more gone and done it, and another General Election is pending. The trouble with us is that the business lasts 2 months instead of a week as with you. And by the time that the end is reached everybody is half or quite dead. I hope I shall survive, in more than one sense. But you will know that a little spell of political rest will not be unwelcome to me personally. The indications are that I shall get it.

The Gilletts prayed God to grant it to him; but as the news reached them of his whirlwind tours in every Province of the Union, his confrontations with mobs that howled him down,* his day by day performances on public platforms and in press interviews, they began to doubt their prayers being answered. 'We begin to be almost afraid', Margaret Gillett wrote to him, 'of your gaining the victory, you are such a terrible fighter! and we would so much rather have you free.'[15]

They need not have been afraid. He never had a chance of winning. The fighting efficiency of his party was at a low ebb. In January 1924, when nobody had reason to suppose that a general election was imminent, the *Cape Times* published a series of articles

---

* For example, they howled him down at Bloemfontein on 28 May and at Durban * three days later. *Die Burger* and other responsible organs of the Opposition appealed for fair treatment of S.A.P. speakers; but T. Boydell, in an open letter to the *Guardian* (the Natal organ of the Labour party), told Smuts he himself bore the blame. 'Your own record', he wrote, 'has been one of disorder and violence.' Boydell's letter was quoted in the *Cape Times* of 7 June 1924.

on political conditions throughout the Union. From the Witwatersrand to the western Cape Province the reports that came in from widely diverse constituencies told the same monotonous story: in the S.A.P., lethargy and a decrepit organization; in the Opposition parties, good organization, great enthusiasm and the will to victory.[16]

The Opposition parties took the offensive. They attacked the government on its record. They pictured it as being at one and the same time violent, irresolute and incompetent.* They reiterated Hertzog's indictment of Smuts as a man whose footsteps dripped with blood.† They insisted at the same time that Smuts had no real will of his own. A cartoonist in *Die Burger* (6 May 1924) depicted him as a tiny figure crushed in the huge fist of Capitalism. Other cartoonists exploited the Hoggenheimer myth. Throughout the two months of campaigning, orators and journalists of the Opposition parties day by day drove the moral home: the electors must make their choice between 'the People and the Mine Magnates'. Equally, they must make their choice between irresolute government which could not even balance its budget‡ and resolute men who knew what they wanted and knew how to get it. It was for the electors to decide: economic stagnation or economic progress; unemployment or civilized labour; South Africa a huge black compound for the big capitalists or South Africa a prosperous white man's country. 'If the present national policy continues for another five years', Tielman Roos asserted, 'it will be impossible ever to have a large white population. If you don't wish to save yourselves, save your children.'§

The slogan, civilized labour, contained all this emotion and argument. It also contained one ambiguity: whereas Hertzog took pains to point out that the Cape Coloured people, whose votes he was soliciting, stood on the civilized side of the fence, many of Hertzog's followers wanted to put the Cape Coloureds on to the other side with the blacks: to them civilized labour meant white labour. Still, opinion in the National and Labour parties was unanimously in

* *Die Burger* (12 June 1924) systematically listed the government's sins of commission and omission under the three heads, *Geweld, Verwaarlosing en Geknoei.*
† At Potchefstroom on 3 June Hertzog himself reiterated it.
‡ On the eve of the election Burton, the Treasurer, announced a balanced budget; but the Opposition parties accused him of juggling the figures. Burton also was the main scapegoat for the deflationary policy pursued by the government from 1920 onwards.
§ Roos, at Springs on 7 May. Cf. Creswell at Brakpan on 22 May.

favour of the *skeidsmuur* or fence; indeed, it wanted two fences, a tariff fence to protect South African industry against foreign competition, and a racial fence to protect South African whites against black (and Coloured?) competition. Industrial protection and racial segregation—so ran the argument—were desirable things in themselves; they were also the road to civilized labour. Day after day, the Opposition parties contrasted their own purposeful march along this clear straight road with the government's tortuous shuffling towards the nation's dead end.

In combatting this propaganda Smuts and his party tried various tactics. They tried, first and foremost, to persuade the electors that the issues to be decided were quite different from those that their opponents emphasized: in the present election, as in its predecessor, secession was the essential issue. Unfortunately for them, clause 3 of the Nationalist–Labour pact contained a convincing answer to that argument. Hertzog, Roos, Malan and other prominent Nationalists assured the electors again and again that secession was a false issue: Creswell told them that it was moth-eaten. Smuts and his followers could not escape battle on the ground their enemies had chosen. They tried to mount a counter attack in the sector of segregation. How could industry survive, they asked, without black labour? How could farming survive? But those rhetorical questions hardly needed answering. Nobody believed for one moment that the mine managers and the farmers would lose their black labour. Segregation was not a precisely defined programme but a slogan with as many meanings as anybody could want. It meant one thing in one place, another thing in another place. Government speakers, including Smuts himself, failed to pin its meaning down. Quite often, they found themselves protesting that they too were segregationists. 'Bless me', exclaimed one of them in answering an interjection, 'General Hertzog has not got a monopoly of segregation.'*

On every disputed issue the challengers demanded an answer in the terms of either-or; but the defenders responded in the terms of more-or-less. Such a response was psychologically ineffective. It created the impression of a government which could not or would not take a firm stand on anything. In his election manifesto, Smuts assured the country that he stood for a bold industrial policy; but he did not give the same bold assurance of tariff protection for South

---

* Colonel Stallard at Roodepoort on 9 May.

African industries. Whereas Hertzog and Creswell promised Protection with a capital P, the most that Smuts promised was 'discriminating protection for those industries especially suited to the country'.* Even that proved too much for J. W. Jagger. On 19 May, he announced his resignation from office on the ground that his well-known views as a free trader were bringing into question the government's sincerity in its advocacy of industrialization. But of course, the Opposition parties said, the government could never have been sincere while it had a man like Jagger in it; moreover, it still remained subservient to the ex-Unionists who thought the same as Jagger did. What could be expected of a party and government so divided and so irresolute? The Opposition parties, on the other hand, knew their own mind. They had solutions for every big problem— the industrial problem, the Native problem, the Indian problem.†

The electorate gave them their chance to try out their solutions. The swing of votes was not sensational. On a 78·7 per cent poll the S.A.P. was approximately 5 per cent down, the Labour party 3 per cent up and the National party as before. Unfortunately for the S.A.P., it won more than half its seats in Cape Province, which had an abnormally high proportion of voters per constituency.‡ Moreover, most of its victories in all four Provinces were in urban constituencies which were similarly 'loaded' in comparison with country constituencies. Consequently, it won far fewer seats than it would have won if each vote had possessed the same value. So Hertzog took office with a Nationalist–Labour majority of twenty-seven. At Pretoria West, Smuts lost his seat. For him, the general election of 1924 was a smashing political and personal defeat.

He smarted under it but managed on the whole to take it philosophically.

As the cables will have told you [he wrote to the Gilletts] your wish has been gratified and I have been beaten. Yesterday I resigned and for the present it is all over. For two months now I have worked my hardest to

* At Johannesburg on 13 May.

† Hertzog, in point 4 of his policy speech at Smithfield on 3 May, promised a 'solution' of the Native question—with proper consultation, if necessary, of the entire people. Creswell, in point 5 of his policy speech at Durban on 30 April, said that the Asiatic problem would be 'solved'.

‡ The reason for the Cape's high quota was that the allocation of seats to the four Provinces was based on the European adult male population: for this purpose the non-European voters in Cape Province, numbering 41,086, were not taken into account.

fight this last battle. Well you know the rest. It will take me some time to adjust myself to the new situation. But first and foremost I want a bit of a rest and hope I shall get it now.

He told Alice Clark that the taste he had had of political life for the past twenty-six years was enough for any mortal, but that he still remained in politics as leader of the Opposition. Perhaps later on he would find his way out. Meanwhile, he had some free time at last for his botany and books. [17]

PART II

OUT OF POWER, 1924–1933

CHAPTER 9

CONSOLATION OF PHILOSOPHY

AFTER his defeat Smuts had to go to hospital to get an immense carbuncle cut out of his neck. That trouble, which his doctor ascribed to overstrain, affected him intermittently during the next three or four years and prompted Emily Hobhouse to write him a solicitous letter. His blood, she told him, must need a thorough purification.

You could however give yourself the 'Lemon Cure' and very efficacious that is. You begin with *one* lemon in the day, two the second day and increase by one daily till on the 11th day you take 11 lemons; then in like manner you decrease till you get down to one and it is over. The cure takes about 3 weeks you see. Take them on an empty stomach and not mixed up with indigestible things—lemon water when you awake, lemon, not milk, in your tea—lemon juice, not vinegar, with your salad. A *whole* lemon, rind also, put thro' the mincing machine and reduced to a pulp is *very* nice and sweetened well with honey *not sugar*. Most refreshing. You try.

Smuts replied that the cure did not sound to him very cheerful and that any way he had no serious worries over his health. It was her state of health that worried him. He pleaded with her to come out to South Africa and give her friends the joy of caring for her. He pictured her sitting under the huge old willows at Doornkloof where he and she had gone picknicking together in the far away past. The farm, he told her, was very beautiful now, all the lands along the river under cultivation, the hillsides covered with plantations of about a million trees, the flats smiling with the maize, and the fat Friesland cattle lying down in the sunshine. 'And you sit in Tor Gardens', he exclaimed, 'and contemplate the Universe at a distance, when it is so beautiful close by! No dear, you must really come out if your health will in any way allow it...' But she was locked in her last battle with the crimes and follies of mankind and the infirmities of her own much-suffering body. She died in June 1926. *The Times* printed an abominable obituary notice of her but her ashes were brought to South Africa for burial at the foot of the

Women's Monument in Bloemfontein. In his funeral oration Smuts recalled the death roll of Afrikaner women and children in the Anglo-Boer war. 'And then', he continued, 'one small hand, the hand of a woman, was stretched out to us. At that darkest hour, when our race almost seemed doomed to extinction, she appeared as an angel, as a heaven-sent messenger. Strangest of all, she was an Englishwoman.' He told her friends in England, 'We buried her like a Princess.'[1]

His old friend John X. Merriman died a few weeks after Emily Hobhouse. Meanwhile at Street in Somerset William Clark and his wife* were suffering the worst afflictions of old age.

A more glorious old couple [Smuts wrote] I had not seen in my days. I firmly believe that the universe is good and friendly, but it has very dark patches and the dark places are often close by the bright ones. But what is the use of moralizing when one is face to face with such human agony? One...can but look on in dumb sympathy, very much as a dog stands by its dead master.

He was mindful of his own mortality.

So the years mount up [he wrote in his fifty-seventh year]. What pathetic things we humans are. Like the 'Langbeinige Cicada' in *Faust* we make our sudden spurt and then sink back into the eternal grass to which we belong.

This day 11 years ago I took Taveta in East Africa where the Germans had dug themselves in for 18 months. It makes my blood glow to think again of those wild doings...And it is all dead and gone, and only the memory survives in the minds of those still living. Time flows over it all, obliterating the little mole hills of our efforts, and in a few years no trace is left.

He recalled that the tall East African grasses had so quickly overgrown the tracks of his great army that he had found it impossible, even a few months later, to retrace them. So much for the permanence of human achievement! Yet he ended those sombre reflections by proposing a combined Smuts–Gillett Expedition to East Africa 'for botanizing and birding'. As always, the glow of joyous anticipation swept away the mists of his nostalgia. He felt that he still had a life to live.[2]

* They were the parents of Margaret Gillett who—before her marriage—had first introduced Smuts into the family. Her sister Alice Clark gave up her work in order to look after the old people in their house 'Millfield' in Street.

His trouble was that he wanted to cram too much into it. He wanted at one and the same time to be a roamer and a stay-at-home, a thinker and a man of action. He wanted uninhibited personal freedom. He wanted to do his duty. When he first heard the news of his defeat at Pretoria West he told himself that this was his great chance to cut loose from politics; but as the news came in of the slaughter among his cabinet colleagues and in the party rank and file he knew that he could not cut loose from them except by running away. 'And so', he wrote, 'I am now member for Standerton, leader of the Opposition in a House where we are outnumbered by a larger majority than that ever seen in South Africa and with most of my important old colleagues gone. It will once more be a hard political grind.' He resented the grind. Politics, he exclaimed, were Purgatory, a desert of the spirit in which he had been wandering not for forty days, but nearer forty years. Still, they happened to be his job, and a man had to do his job, whether he liked it or not.[3]

After nearly two decades continuously in office he had some big adjustments to make in his way of life. The material ones did not much worry him; but they worried other people. His banker became deeply worried at seeing him spending as if he were still drawing the Prime Minister's salary; within less than three years his overdraft soared to well over £8,000.* The Gilletts worried over the dismal life that he was leading at the Civil Service Club in Cape Town during parliamentary sessions. He had never thought his club dismal —at least, he had never complained about it—but he gratefully accepted the space and privacy of 'Tsalta', a house in Claremont which the Gilletts bought for his use.† This new-found suburban peace doubtless eased the adjustment that came hardest to him— to have to live the life of a politician without the satisfactions of political power. He felt that the waste and friction of such a life were out of all proportion to the real work done.

* He had estimated his overdraft at about £5,000. Conspicuous items of his expenditure at this time were book-buying (as always) and the education of his children at school and university. As the owner (at this time) of ten farms he considered that the rises of land values would take care of his overdraft; whenever he became too hard pressed for money, he sold one of the farms.

† 'Tsalta' is 'At Last' written backwards. It was conveniently situated within easy reach of Kirstenbosch and the Skeleton Gorge way up Table Mountain. Finding the right house had taken time and Smuts did not move into it until February 1928. The Gilletts wanted him to accept it as his own house; but he insisted that they must be its owners and he merely the user, pending the time when they might wish to use it or the money they could realize by selling it.

Our parliamentary work [he wrote] is very strenuous and I find my duties as leader of the Opposition almost as exacting as formerly those of Prime Minister. From early morning till late at night one is continually busy, often with small things; but the big things are never far away. I manage to get in a certain amount of reading but that can only be done by the severest economizing of my time. What I regret most is that I find no time to write. There are a number of things I could say now, but I have no time. And old age will soon be there...I believe the only thing that could save me would be a long sentence of deportation or detention. Will some kind God not have me deported from this sad state in which I live?[4]

'If only I had more time' was the continuous refrain of his letters from Cape Town; but when the session was over he found time, glorious time, waiting for him at Doornkloof. There in his own home he felt 'the peace of God' descending on him.

I again sleep outside and in the early dawn the birds come to look for seeds quite close to my bed invisible behind the netting. They are most charming. The Hoopoes come now to feed at the kitchen in the morning. Many strange and beautiful birds put in an appearance. To them this place is Come to Good.* So it is now to me. I enjoy every day. I attend to a minimum of political business and read and read and read; and think and think and think. It is all so restful and satisfying. My soul had begun to dry up literally in these years of arid politics. But now I begin to feel at rest again. And God is very good. Of course I continue to attend to a heavy correspondence in which Joan† is useful. Ten to twenty letters every day is a lot for me. But I have time now to read and to ride and not to feel on edge all the time. Is it not a good feeling to be dead to the world? The family is very happy...

By now the children were well forward with their schooling and three of them were at, or ready for, the university; but Smuts and his wife could not hope for some years yet to have grandchildren coming to stay with them. The youngest creatures at Doornkloof were Sally the lioness cub and Kathleen de Villiers, a little girl whom they had taken into the family.[5]

At Doornkloof Smuts spent some hours every day out of doors, walking very fast except when he stopped to look through his magnifying glass at a flower or a grass and put it carefully away in his botanical press. Now at last he was able to take a big stride

* Come to Good was the name of an ancient Meeting House of the Society of Friends near Falmouth which the Gilletts had described to him.

† Joan Rowntree (later Boardman). When she married, Miss Sally Richardson took her place as a voluntary part-time secretarial assistant.

2. Doornkloof

forward with his botany. He had skilful and willing teachers: at
Doornkloof his neighbour I. B. Pole-Evans, the chief plant pathologist
of the Department of Agriculture; at Cape Town Rudolf Marloth,*
the teacher of his student years and now the grand old man of
South African botany, still game in his seventies for a strenuous
collecting expedition. Smuts at this time collected with ardour but
still had a lot to learn about naming and arranging his collections.
Yet even while he was lamenting his poor grounding in systematics
he had the good fortune to find an enthusiastic teacher, Dr Harriet M. L.
Bolus of the herbarium in Cape Town.† Back at Doornkloof he
had on his shelves most, if not all, the reference books that an African
botanist could reasonably ask for. Thus by one means and another
he reached the position where no more than half a dozen professionals
could compete with him in naming at sight the grasses of his country.‡
Moreover, he possessed a first-rate memory, a lively ecological flair
and a driving curiosity. In December 1927 two American botanists
who had climbed Kilimanjaro told him how surprised they had been
to find that the plant nearest to the snow line was a grass—but they
could not remember which grass. Smuts at once named three grasses
which grew on the plateau between the peaks, among them *Festuca
Abyssinica*. Yes, the Americans exclaimed, that was the grass they
had seen! Thereupon Smuts took down from his shelves Engler and
Prantl, *Die Naturlischen Pflanzenfamilien...*, and produced the relevant
references. He happened at this time to be in pursuit of a theory.
'It is very curious', he wrote, 'that the high Alpine flora of Africa
is Cape and not Mediterranean. I believe the Sahara sea cut off
Africa from Europe for long geological periods.' The questions that
he was asking about the distribution of plants led him to ask further
questions about Africa's geological and climatological record. Those
questions in their turn suggested to him still further questions about
distribution, including the distribution on this planet of man, or
man's hominoid ancestors. In February 1927 he wrote to Professor
Raymond Dart—precisely on Dart's birthday, as it happened,
which seemed to the professor a happy augury—a letter of warm

* Marloth died in 1932 at the age of 77.
† Smuts used to call her, and her husband Frank, 'the Boli'. He was the son of Harry
Bolus, who had started the herbarium in 1865. He got to know plants (particularly
grasses) by helping his father; but birds were his first love. She was an academically
trained botanist.
‡ This considered opinion has been given to the author by Dr John Hutchinson of
Kew.

congratulation on his discovery of the Taungs skull. A few years later Jannie Smuts, the second son of the family, began to explore South Africa's most ancient creations in stone of *homo faber*. That gave a new interest to their joint expeditions into the bush; the father collected plants, the son collected artefacts and each discovered that he had something to learn from the other.[6]

The time came for Smuts to make a systematic statement about his assorted explorations, questions and hypotheses within the area of South African scientific interest. It came sooner than he had foreseen. In April 1925 he was still lamenting that he had no time for writing. A month later he sent to Pole-Evans a composition 8,000 words or more in length, the draft of his presidential address to the South African Association for the Advancement of Science. Pole-Evans read the draft critically and advised him to abridge the geological section in order to make more room for botany; otherwise he proposed no alterations. Smuts delivered the address on 6 July 1925.[7]

Science in South Africa, he said, need not be provincial. Admittedly, Europe was the home land of the modern scientific spirit and the northern hemisphere possessed the bulk of the world's scientific man-power and resources. But the problems of scientific investigation need not and should not be correspondingly space-bound. 'Northerners' were apt to follow a north–south axis of investigation; but Smuts suggested that a west–east (or east–west) approach would prove equally rewarding. Given that approach, South Africa would find herself not on the periphery, but at the centre, of some important scientific explorations. The Wegener hypothesis of continental drift encouraged such an approach.

For us in this part of the world the most interesting feature of the scheme is that in it Africa assumes a central position among the continents; it becomes, in fact, the great 'divide' among the continents of the Southern Hemisphere. It appears as the mother-continent from which South America on the one side and Madagascar, India, Australasia and their surrounding areas on the other, have split off and drifted away, have calved off, so to speak.

He admitted, indeed he insisted, that the Wegener hypothesis still fell far short of scientific demonstration; but he believed that a rigorous probing of it would prove rewarding, and in the meantime he accepted it as a promising starting point for comparative study of the scientific problems of the countries in the southern hemisphere, with South Africa at their centre. He ran quickly through a list of geological problems which seemed likely to repay study. Then he settled down to his botany. South Africa had two distinct floras, the one clearly of tropical origin, the other a temperate flora confined chiefly to the seaward side of the mountains of Cape Province, although it also had outliers extending to the north along the mountain systems into the tropics. According to the orthodox view, both these floras were immigrants from the north; but Darwin had made an alternative suggestion about the origins of the temperate flora. Smuts quoted a letter of 1881 from Darwin to Hooker: 'I have sometimes speculated', he had written, 'whether there did not exist somewhere during the long ages an extremely isolated continent, perhaps near the South Pole.' Smuts called that speculation 'a wonderful guess'. It led him back to the hypothesis of a Gondwanaland, an immense land mass from which the existing continents of the southern hemisphere had split off, whether in the way that Wegener suggested or in some other way. He cited the palaeobotanical evidence which supported the Gondwanaland hypothesis and supported at the same time his own conception of a southern, not a northern, origin for Africa's tropical flora. He threw out the idea that the Cape floras might have had their origins even further south, in an antarctic or sub-antarctic flora which had perished in the climatic changes of the past. Yet all the time he insisted that palaeobotany, palaeontology, and the other related sciences were still only in their infancy in the southern hemisphere. He was trying to convey to his audience his own vision of the dazzling research opportunities which awaited men of science in South Africa. Not least in the investigation of human origins. He made that investigation his concluding theme. He approached it by a careful review of the present position and future prospects of meteorological and climatological research. Then he reported on Raymond Dart's work in connection with the Taungs fossil skull. 'This great discovery', he said, 'has brought South Africa right into the centre of the picture...Who knows whether South Africa may not yet become the Mecca of Human Palaeontology?'

He was aware, of course, that the lay members of his audience were unlikely to feel excited at the prospect of their continent achieving recognition as the cradle, or at least one of the cradles, of the human species. Consequently, he made the appropriate appeals to wealthy men and to the government to provide the ways and means of scientific research. There was profit in it, he told them, because science held the key to progress in agriculture and industry and was South Africa's real pioneer and *voortrekker*. As president of the S.A.A.A.S. he was bound to show a realistic awareness of the money bags. But he was speaking first and foremost to men of science in South Africa. His reporting of fact, given the state of knowledge at that time, was accurate. His discussions of hypotheses were discriminating and helpful. His proposals for further research were imaginative and judicious. In the judgment of critical scientists in the 1960s, his presidential address was memorable when he delivered it and still worth reading after the lapse of more than four decades.[8]

Meanwhile he was at work on a far larger task—not a lecture of 8,000 words but a book of 140,000 words. He called it *Holism and Evolution*. By September 1924 the plan of it was in his head; by September 1925 he had finished it.[9] During those twelve months parliament was continuously in session—except for a six-day recess at Easter—from 13 February to 25 July; if Smuts, as he protested, could not combine writing with his parliamentary duties, he was left at most with 29 weeks in which to write his 140,000 words. A few of his contemporaries, G. D. H. Cole for example, would have considered that task well within their competence. Still, Smuts was proposing to cover an unusual amount of ground. His purpose, as he stated it in September 1924, was to 'devise some simpler scheme to explain the unitary character of time, space, matter and all physical appearances and activities'. In the course of his writing he expanded that scheme by bringing into it mind and personality. Twenty-nine weeks was not much time for such a wide-ranging exploration. When Smuts had finished his book he called it a 'preliminary canter over the ground'. To some other people it looked more like a wild gallop, with some conspicuously rough riding.

He finished his last four chapters in a six-weeks' spurt infuriatingly interrupted by two political tours. He was in the mood of now or never. His leisure, such as it was, seemed to him a fragile boon which a turn of the political wheel could at any moment destroy. Within a day or two of finishing the book he sent it to E. F. C. Lane* in

* Lane had been his official secretary up to his fall from power.

London with instructions to find a publisher for it. He would perhaps have done better to hold it back for a few months while one of his scholarly friends studied and criticized it; but he had done that once before and had received for his pains the advice to write his memoirs instead of trying to write philosophy.* By now he had grown less deferential to scholarly opinion than he had been twelve years earlier. Naturally, he remained aware of his own limitations; or of some of them. By profession he was not a scholar but a politician. Politics had left him scant time for keeping himself abreast of philosophical and scientific discussions. He did not use libraries. He did not take notes and references and arrange them in card indexes, envelopes or folders. He was altogether dependent upon the books in his own study and upon his own memory, imagination, experience and thought. Thus there were plenty of reasons for him to make a cautious approach to publication. Nevertheless he felt unable any longer to keep bottled up in his head the ideas which for so many years past had been exploding there.[10]

The first intimations of them had come to him half a century ago on his father's farm, a little boy discovering his kinship with the stones, plants and animals of that small universe. In his uncle's church at Riebeeck West he had learnt that the farm and its creatures and its people and he himself all belonged to a great universe, created and governed by God. In his student years at Stellenbosch he learnt that science had a different story to tell. Or was it the same story, told in a different way? *Eenheid*, unity, became his philosophic quest. He set out in search of the place where impersonal law encountered 'the person'. Which of those two, he asked himself, was sovereign in the universe? In his first philosophic essay he gave his decision for personality; in his second he gave it for science. At Cambridge, as earlier at Stellenbosch, he oscillated between those two opposites. In September 1892 he began a long essay with the intent to prove that physics and chemistry held the key to the problems of life and mind; in January 1893 he crossed out 'mind' and discontinued his essay. His craving for *eenheid* was now finding its nourishment not in science and its philosophies, but in poetry—in the poetry of

* This had been the advice of H. W. Wolstenholme in 1912, after reading three chapters of the typescript of Smuts's *Inquiry into the Whole*. In 1925 Smuts allowed Gilbert Murray and C. C. J. Webb to see a typed copy of *Holism and Evolution* before it was published, but not before he had made his decision to publish it. *Note:* all the quotations in this chapter will be from the first (1926) edition of *Holism and Evolution*.

Goethe, which he had first read with Isie Krige at Stellenbosch; later on, in the poetry of Walt Whitman. He asked himself what kind of men these poets were. As he studied their works and lives, he discovered them to be 'whole' men. In London, where he was reading in the Middle Temple after taking his double first in the Law Tripos, he wrote a long biographical study of Walt Whitman. Midway in that study he made an exhilarating discovery:* 'wholeness' was the stamp not only of persons, but of matter, life, mind— of the universe and everything that it contained. In 1911, while he was fiercely concentrated upon political tasks which apparently left him no time at all for any other work, he wrote his *Inquiry into the Whole*, a book which ranged over the wide territories of epistomology, philosophy of science, philosophy of religion, politics and ethics. His friend Wolstenholme told him that it was unfit for publication. He put it back into the drawer and left it there. The book that he wrote in 1925 was not a refurbishing of his old *Inquiry* but a new exploration of a more restricted territory, the philosophy of science. That, at least, is what he said and intended. Nevertheless, *Holism and Evolution* contained by implication the entire history up to that time of his intellectual and spiritual Odyssey.[11]

The reading public that he had in mind was rather like the audience he had recently addressed in Oudtshoorn, a mixed gathering of experts and intelligent laymen. That conception of his audience governed his style; for the sake of the laymen he would need to use metaphors, analogies and similar devices for communicating his thought; for the sake of the experts he must aim at linguistic and logical precision. Perhaps he under-rated the difficulties of that stylistic combination; but he made a brave beginning in his first chapter, which he called *The Reform of Fundamental Concepts*.

The sciences of matter, life and mind, he declared, were organized as if they were separate kingdoms or even separate worlds; but this excessive separateness was man-made and an unnecessary drag upon the advancement of learning. To break it down two things were requisite: more knowledge and a new outlook. New outlooks, he insisted, had in the past contributed at least as much to the advance of science as new observations and experiments had done; that had been true in the time of Copernicus and again in the time of Darwin;

---

* Perhaps his reading of Bradley and other British Idealists helped him to make that discovery.

178

in the age of Einstein it was no less true. Unfortunately, men as thinking creatures were resistant to new outlooks and were apt— when at long last they appeared to accept them—to distort them by partial and partisan interpretations. The acceptance of evolutionary theory, for example, was still impeded by the persistence in some quarters of the false Cartesian dualism between the thinking mind and the material stuff (including the human body) which the mind contemplated. An equal impediment, in his view, was the dispute between two partial and partisan monistic interpretations, mechanism and vitalism, the one insisting that physics and chemistry contained the ultimate explanation of all phenomena, the other insisting that mind contained it. He believed that both these interpretations bore the stamp of an outmoded concept of causation, which envisaged cause and effect as two separate, sharply-defined entities confronting each other at a distance: which further envisaged the effect as a thing that could not possibly contain anything more than was in the cause. So rigid a concept of causation, he submitted, was in flat contradiction with the multitudinous novelty that was observable throughout the evolutionary process. He suggested a more flexible and, he believed, a more realistic view.

Conceive of a cause as a centre with a zone of activity or influence surrounding it and shading gradually off into indefiniteness. Next, conceive of an effect as similarly surrounded. It is easy in that way to understand their interaction, and to see that cause and effect are interlocked, and embrace and influence each other through the operation of their two fields. In fact the conception of Fields of force which has become customary in Electro-Magnetism is only a special case of a phenomenon which is quite universal in the realms of thought and reality alike. Every 'thing' has its field, like itself, only more attenuated; every concept has likewise its field. It is in these fields and these fields only that things really happen ...Things, ideas, animals, plants, persons: all these, like physical forces, have their fields, and but for their fields they would be unintelligible, their activities would be impossible, and their relations barren and sterile.*

The formulation of abstract concepts with sharp outlines and hard contours was not, he said, sufficient for knowledge and understanding; thought should also do its best to imitate the fluidity and plasticity of nature. 'We have to identify ourselves', he wrote, 'with

---

* Smuts was unable to read A. N. Whitehead's *Science and the Modern World* (Cambridge, 1925) before his own book was already in the press. After reading it, he still thought his own concept of 'fields' a better way of getting 'away from the idea of *simple location*' than the way Whitehead offered in his new analysis of space.[12]

the point of view of matter, so to speak. We have humbly to get into that closed cage; we have to take our post on that plane circular rotating disc. We have to interpret matter from the inside, from a point of view which is that of matter and not remote from and indifferent to it.' That was one of the refrains of his book. 'In order to understand Nature,' he wrote again, 'we have to proceed more modestly and in closer touch with our ordinary observation of her ways...I wish to get as near as possible to what one might call Nature's point of view in our explanation of her. To understand Nature we must take one of her own units, and not an abstract one of our own making.' Here and throughout his book he admitted, indeed he emphasized, the legitimacy and fruitfulness of conceptual abstraction and analytical study; but he insisted that they were not by themselves enough. 'The error of analysis', as he called it, was to mistake the analytical elements for the real operative entities, and thereby to envisage the natural world as 'a mere collection of *disjecta membra*, drained of all union or mutual relations, dead, barren, inactive, unintelligible'. The proper movement of thought, he said in effect, was not only analytical but synthetical. Vision of a whole situation or thing was the point of departure for an exploration of its parts.

In his second chapter he discussed *The Reformed Concepts of Space and Time*. Whether anybody could profitably discuss them without the aid of mathematics was a question to which intelligent people gave different answers. On the one hand, Schrödinger once prepared a difficult course of lectures without using mathematical symbols, not—he said—because the subject was simple enough to be explained without mathematics, but because it was too complicated to be fully accessible to mathematics. On the other hand, C. E. Raven used to tell Smuts that his explanation of Relativity *must* be oversimplified, because it was the only one which he, Raven, could understand.[13] Raven, probably, was more interested in 'the before and after' of relativity theory than in its precise formulation. To that extent at least he could accept Smuts's guidance. Smuts illuminated 'the before' in a short review of the Euclidean, Newtonian and Kantian concepts of space and time: Euclid had envisaged space as an objective, homogeneous, timeless entity; Newton had conceived both time and space as separate objective entities; Kant had conceived them as two necessary forms of man's sensuous perception—as characters imposed by the mind on what it perceives. But in the system which latter-day philosophers had adumbrated and latter-day physicists had mathematically described, space-time became both one concept and one reality, with its roots not only in the subjective mind but also in the objective universe. Smuts wrote:

Our whole conception of the universe is altered. Instead of conceiving the Universe as consisting of material bodies floating in a medium of uniform homogeneous 'space', we now look upon the vast variable masses of 'matter' associated with high-speed energies as developing huge 'fields' called Space-Time, in which the curves of the lines can be calculated and the course of events happening in them can be predicted...But these lines are not mere empty form. They are not mere curves of beauty; they are real and causal, for they determine the course of events in the universe. The peripheries of rotating bodies are such curves, the planets move round the suns in such curves; light is propagated along such curves; in fact these curves are the pathways of the physical universe which all physical events must follow.

The universe, as Smuts saw it, represented both structure and action.

He called his third chapter *The Reformed Concept of Matter* and recited the roll of honour—Thomson, Becquerel, Planck, Rutherford, Böhr—of the men who were revealing atomic structure as the manifestation of high-velocity activity. His exuberant welcome to the new physics found expression in metaphor and analogy. 'The quanta', he wrote, 'follow a scale somewhat similar to the notes of music, and we may therefore think of light as the music of the spheres, in which the total harmony or light effect is made up of definite discontinuous notes instead of continuous variations of light.' 'The alchemists', he wrote again, 'were then not so far out when they guessed that mercury could be transmuted into gold!' After that flight he returned once more to matter-of-fact reporting and reminded his readers that attempts at the artificial breaking up of matter were as yet only in the beginning stage. Like the lawyer that he was, he cross-examined the evidence of the physicists and their methods of reasoning. For example, in reviewing the 'planetary' hypothesis of atomic structure, he took pains to insist that it was not a record of observations; for nobody had directly observed an electron or the particles of a nucleus.

The observed phenomena [he wrote] are light effects of various definite qualities and quantities; the rest is theory or hypothesis, in which the elements of quality and quantity in the sensible phenomena are so minutely analysed and translated into elements of time and space as to result in the structure of the atom above given. And this structure is then tested by all the phenomena which call for explanation, and it is only finally accepted when it affords a complete explanation of them all. The electrons, the nucleus, the revolutions of the electrons round the nucleus, the sudden leaps of the electrons from one orbit to the other: these are not observed realities or sensible phenomena, but they all rest on a basis of sensible light effects, which have been most meticulously determined and tested by reference to other observed phenomena. They are therefore not sensible realities but scientific relatives.

His moods of imaginative ardour and methodological rigour alternated with each other. Possibly the first mood predominated as he cast around for the path which inorganic matter had followed in its movement towards the state known as life. He began his search by insisting once again that matter and life could no longer be conceived as contraries: that the difference between them could no longer be envisaged as the distance between deadness or absolute passivity on the one hand and activity on the other—a distance so great as to constitute an impassable gulf in thought. Matter itself, as progressively revealed in the new physics, was both action and structure, a mass of seething, palpitating, structure-building energies and activities. He dared to call those energies creative.

I am going to make a more daring suggestion and to indicate that in another even more important respect matter approximates to life. The structure of matter indicates that matter is also in a sense creative—creative, that is to say, not of its own stuff, but of the forms, arrangements and patterns which constitute all its value in the physical sphere. It is creative in a sense analogous to that in which we call life or mind creative of values...Once we get rid of the notion of the world as consisting of dead matter, into which activity has been introduced from some external or alien source; once we come to look upon matter not only as active, but as self-active, as active with its own activities, as indeed nothing else but Action, our whole conception of the physical order is revolutionized, and the great barriers between the physical and the organic begin to shrink and to shrivel.

He was playing once again the opening bars of his dominant theme. At the same time he was still casting about for a path across 'the barrier'. He suggested, with some citation of authorities, that matter in its colloidal state was a promising sign-post. In that state, one substance was dispersed throughout another in minute particles which yet were larger than molecules. The state was widely recurrent in the air and on the earth. More to the immediate point, it appeared to be distinctive of all life forms. It was the organizational state of the protoplasm of organic cells.

Matter in its colloidal state, Smuts suggested, showed a behaviour which seemed in some ways—he enumerated them item by item—to anticipate the processes and activities of life in its primitive forms. Nobody had found the path across the barrier; nobody, he said, might ever find it; but in his imagination he saw matter 'reaching up to the very threshold of life'.

He called his fourth chapter *The Cell and the Organism*. He thought it possible that before, after or in-between the organization of atoms and cells—those two fundamental structures of the universe—other structures might have arisen in the course of cosmic evolution; but if so, they had passed away. Man, in his search for the basic character of the universe, could only scrutinize such clues as had survived. Scientific scrutiny of the cell had had only a brief history; he rapidly traced its course from Robert Hooke's crude microscope in the second half of the seventeenth century to the sophisticated appliances and methods of contemporary cytology. He began to review the trends of cytological research and in doing so changed his angle of approach. Up to now he had emphasized those features of inorganic matter that pointed forward to life; but now he emphasized those features of the cell which seemed to him a new departure in cosmic evolution. The cell, he said, marked the point where matter or energy aroused itself from its slumbers and became active from within; where it became in some inexplicable way endowed with special characters of selectiveness and reproduction, of self-help and self-control. These were the phenomena of life, and they represented a fundamental innovation.

It is very difficult to realize it, and yet it is the fact, that the little microscopic or ultra-microscopic cell probably does all or most that the plant or animal is known to do. It literally breathes or respires; it takes in, manipulates, digests and assimilates its food; it reproduces its kind; it grows, decays and dies; it heals itself when sick and restores itself when a breakage takes place. It develops special means and mechanisms to assist it in carrying out these operations, and it co-ordinates and regulates all its manifold activities in a way which implies some wonderful central control of all these functions.

After that he reverted to a matter-of-fact mood and spent about 1,000 words on a detailed description of metabolism, the activity which above all distinguished living from non-living matter. He then allowed himself to speculate for a few pages on the origin of the cell—that is to say, the origin of life—although he admitted that nothing definite was known about it. Those speculations merged into a discussion of the phenomenon of reproduction. When he had finished that, he reviewed the differentiations which had taken place among cells, in particular, the differentiation which had led to the divergence between plant and animal forms. He was certainly galloping over the ground, but he slackened his pace as the end of his chapter came into sight. He had three crucial questions to ask and three considered answers to give.

He asked in the first place: 'Is the cell and are cells in an organism a co-operative system, in which the parts and their functions are so ordered and arranged that they co-operate for common purposes, and do not merely subserve the separate ends of the individual parts?' After answering that question affirmatively, he decided that his second and third questions would have to be asked and answered together. Was co-operation within the cell and between the cells of an organism merely the upshot of their multitudinous individual reactions, or did it express the activity of some co-ordinating factor? And if such a co-ordinating factor was at work, was it merely an external factor acting on the cell and the organism, or was it also an internal factor, performing its regulative function inside the cell and the organism? Those questions, he admitted, were both complicated and controversial; but he could not merely 'describe the facts' without offering any interpretation at all of them.

And looking at the facts in an unprejudiced way, and without a bias in favour of any particular theory, one cannot help being struck by the way in which the cells in an organism not only co-operate, but co-operate in a specific direction towards the fulfilment and maintenance of the type of the particular organism which they constitute. At this stage we have to steer clear of all ideas of plan, purpose or teleology in the organic procedure. But, even so, the impression is irresistible that cell activities are co-operative, that they are inherently or through selective development co-ordinated in a specific direction, and that the impress of the whole which forms the organism is clearly stamped on all of the details...And in some indefinable way this whole is not an artificial result of its parts; it is itself an active factor like its parts, and it appears to be in definite relation with them, influenced by them and again influencing them, and through this continuous interaction of parts and whole maintaining the moving equilibrium which is the organism.

In exemplification of the regulative functioning of organic wholes he referred to the self-restorative action of some simple organisms —plants, for example, and newts—after they had suffered mutilation in their parts.

He depicted an organism as 'a little living world in which law and order reign'. This little world, as he saw it, bore a threefold stamp. First, individuation: among cells and organisms, he said, differentiation was the rule; there were no repetitions but uniqueness everywhere. Secondly, co-operation: mutual-aid was the law of life within the cell and within the organism. Thirdly, internality: cells and organisms were not merely the objects of external pressures: they were self-acting subjects. As he looked backwards, he saw the structures of inorganic matter foreshadowing—but not yet reaching —the structures of life; as he looked forwards he saw the activities of life approaching—but not yet achieving—the activities of conscious mind and human personality. Once again, his vision expressed itself in the language of imagery.

When there was achieved the marvellous and mysterious stable constellation of electrical units in the atom, a miracle was wrought which saved the world of matter from utter chaos and chance. But a far greater miracle was wrought when from the atomic and molecular order there was evolved a still deeper and subtler order in the inner co-operative creative harmony of the cell. These two fundamental structures are the great abiding achievements in the course of Evolution, before the advent of Mind...And when we find the two to be not utterly different but expressions of a somewhat similar inner progressive tendency of nature, and when we find later, on the mental and spiritual levels of development, still clearer expressions of a similar tendency, we shall be justified in concluding that we are face to face with something real and causal in the form of a natural operative factor of a fundamental and universal character. The impression becomes so strong that it is not so much a matter of speculation as a recognition of clear simple facts before us.

He had now reached a stage of his story where two roads were open to him. On the one hand, he could move straight ahead into those chapters of the story—on mind and personality—of which he had already given due notice. On the other hand, he could stop the flow of his story while he paused awhile for reflection: what direction and shape, he might ask himself, was his story taking? He chose the second course.

He began his fifth chapter, *General Concept of Holism*, by reiterating his main conclusion—so far—on the course of cosmic evolution: namely, that the concepts and the natural orders of matter, life and mind successively approached each other and overflowed into each other's domain. That conclusion prompted him to ask whether some universal principle was operative in this succession of concepts and orders, and if so, what that principle was? In the religious, philosophical and scientific thought of mankind it had almost always been taken for granted that a principle of uniformity or order did exist; but the nature of that principle had been conceived in two opposite ways. Some people, 'the preformationists' (although Smuts did not call them by that name), believed that all things in the universe had been present from the beginning: either literally present, as in the first chapter of Genesis, or present as potentialities, awaiting what Smuts called their 'explication', that is to say, their unfolding and progressive realization. Other people believed that all things were not present at the beginning, but that new things arose in the course of evolution. According to this view, which Smuts called epigenesis, creation was not a once-for-all event but a continuing process.

As a fervent follower of Darwin, Smuts opted for epigenesis. He attacked Paley's preformationist conception of the universe as a giant mechanism, designed and set in motion for all time by an all-knowing artificer. 'It does not', he wrote, 'go like a clock, completely manufactured, and once for all wound up at the beginning to mark a time fixed and predetermined for it. It is slowly making itself, it is slowly winding itself up, it is slowly making its own time.'* No matter what form preformationist thought took, he was resolute in rejecting it. Hegel's metaphysical Idea, he declared, was just such another attempt to discover the whole universe 'in the past, at the beginning'.

Opting for epigenesis, however, was no more than the preliminary of his search for a fundamental principle operative in the distinct but intermingling worlds of matter, life and mind. That search, he said, required two kinds of activity, both the investigation of particular

---

* Throughout his life he showed a particular antipathy to Paley, who had been compulsory reading for young men when he was a student at Cambridge.

things, and the formulation of general concepts. By and large, men of science were active in the first way and philosophers were active in the second way. Unfortunately, men of science and philosophers usually knew and cared too little about each others' explorations; the former were apt to lose themselves among the trees; the latter were often satisfied with a distant view of the wood. Consequently, they were both almost equally prone to the error of oversimplification. He saw that error exemplified in the contention between mechanistic and vitalistic theories. Mechanists oversimplified the complex phenomena of life, mind, and personality, by 'reducing' them to the operations of physics and chemistry. Vitalists fell into the opposite error of inventing a life force to drive the physico-chemical machine. Smuts called a plague on both their houses. Their battle, he said, was quite unnecessary, a sham battle between entities or pseudo-entities artificially abstracted from the 'wholes' to which they belonged.

He was trying, he said, to explain Nature 'by reference to herself and her own standards'. He repeated what he had said just now about the cell and the organism: they were not simple, but composite of many parts; they were not an aggregation but a synthesis of those parts: in short, they were wholes. He assigned to them an intermediate position in Nature's hierarchy of wholes. They showed, he said, 'a family resemblance' both to the simpler wholes that had come before them in the cosmic process and to the more complex wholes that had come after them.

Not only are plants and animals wholes, but in a certain limited sense the natural collocations of matter in the universe are wholes; atoms, molecules and chemical compounds are limited wholes; while in another closely related sense human characters, works of art and the great ideals of the higher life are or partake of the character of wholes...Artistic creations are, in fact, mainly judged and appraised by the extent to which they realize the character of wholes. But there is much more in the term 'whole' than is covered by its popular use. In the view here presented 'wholes' are basic to the character of the universe.

He made a brief enumeration of some wholes which had become observable in the process of cosmic evolution: chemical compounds; plants; animals; human persons; human societies; values of the spiritual world.

Whole-making was the fundamental principle that he had set

out to find. Indeed, he had found it many years earlier and had also found his name for it: *holism*.* 'I do not much like the word', Gilbert Murray told him, 'but still it is properly formed and I do not see how to improve upon it.'[14] Murray might perhaps have warned his friend against giving the word too much work to do. Sometimes Smuts used it as a descriptive term, embracing 'all the small natural centres or empirical wholes' observable in the course of cosmic evolution. At other times he used it to express his theory of the evolutionary process. At other times still he acclaimed it as the prime mover of that process. *'Wholes'*, he wrote, 'are not mere artificial constructions of thought, they point to something real in the universe; and Holism as the creative principle behind them is a real *vera causa*.' That was his climax; but he seemed not to realize it.

Smuts finished his fifth chapter with the feeling that he had a great deal more to say. When he finished his book a few months later he still had the same feeling. In his last chapter and in his preface he gave advance notice of a second book on the holistic theme, if ever he could find the time to write it. He wanted to explore the realm of values. Mind and personality, which occupied three chapters of *Holism and Evolution*, would have made a good point of departure for that exploration. He might well have kept those three chapters in his drawer for the present and have made life— the cell and the organism—his immediate terminus. Had he done that, he would have written both a shorter and a more powerful book. He would have left many of his readers impatient for the sequel.

That idea did not occur to him. In his mood of now or never he felt that he had to cover as much ground as he could as quickly as he could. He left himself no time for revision. After 29 weeks of hard writing he made a parcel of his typescript and sent it straight off to London. Inevitably, his book from chapter v onwards bore the stamp of haste. Sometimes he became repetitive and diffuse. At other times he showed himself inadequately informed about contemporary trends of research and reflection. He discussed genetics without mentioning T. H. Morgan and the other pioneers of the Mendelian renaissance. He discussed mind with only a passing reference to Pavlov. He discussed personality with no reference at

* From ὅλος = whole.

all to Freud, but with some proposals of his own for a new science of *personology*.*

He was aware that he was offering a wide target for criticism but he was ready to run all risks. If he felt any need at all for personal reassurance, Gilbert Murray satisfied it. Murray told him that his book bore the stamp of life and was the most interesting philosophical work that he had read for very many years. What was more, he had handed his copy of the typescript to J. A. Smith and enclosed a long, critical, but warmly welcoming appraisal of it by that Crocean philosopher. Meanwhile, Lane had written from London with the news that A. D. Lindsay had read the book for Macmillans and strongly recommended it. In May 1926 Smuts was at work on the last proofs. In October his book appeared simultaneously in London and New York. He said that it must now fend for itself. It fended very well: within less than half a year Macmillans were asking him to prepare a new edition of it.[15]

Meanwhile he had been receiving an extensive fan mail. Winston Churchill told him that he had peered into the book with awe; Leo Amery discussed it with him in a long and thoughtful letter; Julian Huxley argued some of its main points with him; Lloyd Morgan argued some more points but acclaimed the book and said that he would be reviewing it in *Philosophical Studies*.[16] And all this time Macmillans were sending him press cuttings of the long reviews his book was attracting in the daily newspapers, starting with *The Times*; in important weeklies such as *The Times Literary Supplement*, *The Nation and Athenaeum*, *Discovery* and *Nature*; in *The Review of the Churches*, *The Nineteenth Century* and other leading monthlies. To be sure, the book did not attract such extensive notice in academic journals; but among the philosophers or men of science who reviewed it were A. D. Lindsay, John MacMurray, George Conder, Wildon Carr, Lloyd Morgan, F. H. A. Marshall, Arthur Keith and Graham Kerr. Finally, J. S. Haldane discussed it at length and with admiration as Gifford Lecturer on *The Sciences and Philosophy*.

---

* Biographical studies of creative individuals, he said, would be the foundations of this new science. To this, a reviewer in *Discovery* objected that there could be no science of the individual, because science deals not with individuals but with quantities, to which it seeks to apply general laws. A second, and possibly less disputable, objection may be mentioned by the present writer. As a biographer of Smuts, he has in the course of years got to know him intimately; but he doubts whether his knowledge can be called scientific. For example, he does not know, and has no means of getting to know, Smuts's genetic inheritance.

As a leading physiologist of his time and, like his statesman-brother, a philosopher in the idealist tradition, Haldane had good qualifications for expounding that theme to an audience of his fellow Scots. Throughout his two courses of lectures he had Smuts's recent book constantly in mind. Here and there he registered some dissent from its argument,* but most of the time he found himself in full agreement with it. 'The very nomenclature of biology', he said in his fifth lecture, 'embodies the conception that life, in whatever form it may occur, occurs as a specific whole, in which the parts and actions are related to one another, and cannot be isolated without destroying their nature. The working hypothesis of biology is that this wholeness exists, and this working hypothesis has carried biology forward just as successfully as the Newtonian conception has carried physics forward.' In his eighth lecture, he acclaimed *Holism and Evolution* as a book remarkable not only for its understanding of biology but for its wider scientific and human understanding.

The Gifford Lectures of 1927–8 recorded the high-water mark of Smuts's reputation as a philosopher of science. Next year the reputations both of Smuts and of Haldane came under a withering fire which they themselves had invited. The British Association was due to hold a meeting in South Africa. Haldane proposed a symposium in which he and Smuts, with Eddington and some others—including, if possible, a representative of the mechanist outlook—would discuss the nature of life. Smuts wanted to bring some South African scientists into the discussion; in particular, he proposed Lancelot Hogben, a convinced mechanist who had come recently to the chair of zoology at Cape Town.[17] The symposium duly took place. Smuts read a paper which he never published; Hogben read a paper which within the next twelve months grew into a book, *The Nature of Living Matter*. It was a masterpiece of polemical prose.

Hogben maintained a thesis, namely, that scientific method was one and the same thing in physics and in biology. If anybody objected that biology had also a special method of its own, he answered: 'Tell us it then.' He did not assert that physico-chemical hypotheses and techniques would some day provide the complete explanation of all animal and human behaviour; but he did assert that no limit could be foreseen to their progress in that direction. Their progress, he said, was creating alarm and despondency among

* See p. 196 below.

backward-looking theologians, philosophers, and even scientists in their anti-scientific moods. For example, as an investigator of respiratory physiology, Dr Haldane practised physico-chemical techniques; but as Gifford Lecturer he ground his ontological axe. 'Dr Haldane', he wrote, 'finds it so easy to point out the inadequacy of the mechanistic outlook. In the light of Pavlov's work we can now envisage the possibility that the methods of physical science will one day claim the whole field of what can properly be called knowledge.' Haldane, Whitehead, Eddington, Smuts came successively into Hogben's field of fire. He made Smuts his main target: he was the sort of man who summed up the universe in a monosyllable, and under the downy wing of his holism all the superstitions huddled. 'Of holism as a philosophy of biology', Hogben concluded, 'enough has been said elsewhere. It contains within it no promise of future progress.'

Hogben insufficiently doubted his own infallibility; but he was a rigorous logician with a superb gift for *saeva indignatio*. His assault left the holistic philosophy badly battered. It did not, however, sink it. Plant pathologists still encouraged their pupils to see their research problems both in the terms of functional efficiency—which meant seeing them as wholes—*and* in the terms of physico-chemical processes. Physiologists still from time to time delivered the Gifford Lectures. That, Hogben had said, was something that Sherrington would never do; *he* respected, even if Haldane did not, the line of demarcation between his 'public' life as a man of science and his 'private' life as a poet and philosopher. Alas for that prognostication: Sherrington's Gifford Lectures of 1937–8 were suffused not only with poetry but with holistic vision.* Not that Sherrington used Smuts's word: quite possibly he had not even read his book. But R. A. Fisher, the leading statistical geneticist of that time, not only read the book but in November 1950 made its argument about causation a main theme of his Eddington Memorial Lecture. Smuts never read that lecture; he had died two months before Fisher delivered it. Possibly he never knew that men of science in his old university still found merit in the book that he had written at headlong speed a quarter

---

* Chapter IV of *Man on his Nature*, with its wonderful description of the co-operative action of the hundreds of millions of the 'seeing elements' of the eye, was essentially holistic in thought and feeling. 'Earth's Reshuffling', an image that Smuts had used, was the title of Sherrington's chapter V, which suggests that he may, after all, have read Smuts's book.

of a century ago. He never met Agnes Arber, a Cambridge botanist pre-eminent both in plant morphology and in her genius for explaining what it means to be a biologist. In *The Mind and the Eye* she wrote:

When we try to trace the concept of wholeness as it develops in a man's mind, we realize that, as an infant, his vision of the surrounding world posseses a certain primitive unity since, in a sense, it forms a whole, not yet discriminated into components. At the opposite pole is the kind of unity achieved by mature thought, in which fully analytical observation of individual things, and the differentiation of individual ideas, has been followed by a synthesis which has reconstructed unity from diversity. Between these two poles—the first unconscious, and the second self-conscious—lies the whole developmental sequence of the intellectual life.

Evidently, the debate of 1929 between Smuts and Hogben was still continuing a generation later.[18]

In the scientific world, then, *Holism and Evolution*, after too easy a passage at the beginning and too rough a one later on, seemed likely to finish as well as Smuts could reasonably have hoped. But in the philosophical world the book did not fare so well. Those philosophers who acclaimed it on its first appearance belonged to a school which was going out of fashion. Philosophers of the rising generation were rigorous analysts who lived in perpetual terror of being called metaphysicians. In their tight little province there was no room for cosmologies or for synthesizing speculations of any kind. For a period of nearly thirty years, R. G. Collingwood was the only philosopher of note, at any rate in Britain, who considered 'the idea of nature', including Smuts's contribution to it, a fit subject for discussion. The fashion did not change until after Smuts was dead. But from about the mid-1950s, synthesis, even in its form of cosmological speculation, became once again a permissible philosophical activity. That turn of the wheel made it respectable to put *Holism and Evolution* back again on the book shelves of scholarly and thoughtful people.* There, however, it lived inconspicuously in the company of better known books by Alexander, Lloyd Morgan, Whitehead, and other philosophical exponents of 'emergent evolution'.† Such particular atten-

* See, for example, the introduction by E. W. Sennolt to the Viking Press edition (1961) of *Holism and Evolution*.
† When *Holism and Evolution* was published, some reviewers expressed surprise that Smuts made no mention of ideas similar to his own in the published work of Alexander, Lloyd Morgan and Whitehead. They did nevertheless give him credit for thinking his

tion as it attracted was chiefly on account of the logical contradictions which some critical philosophers imputed to it. P. H. Partridge argued that Smuts could not in logic combine the monistic metaphysic that he wanted and the pluralistic epigenesis that he asserted. He could not have at one and the same time both a *vera causa* and a procession of new evolutionary entities. If he wished to save his wholes, Partridge said in effect, he would have to sacrifice his holism.[19]

That word, which had displeased Gilbert Murray as a man of taste although it satisfied him as a philologist, made trouble for Smuts, both in England and in South Africa. In England, Karl Popper made the word his symbol for everything that he hated in totalitarian thought and practice from Plato to Hitler. It might seem strange that Popper, the man who proclaimed the open society, should inflict such hurt upon Smuts, the man who proclaimed the open universe; but in his political, as distinct from his philosophical, writings Popper was slapdash in his choice of words. Seemingly he did not even take the trouble to look up holism and its exemplifications in the *New English Dictionary*. Meanwhile in South Africa, nationalist propagandists had been attacking holism not as a totalitarian but as an imperialist word. A. C. Cilliers, a Stellenbosch physicist who had studied in Germany under Heisenberg, criticized Smuts's book, when it first appeared, in a long article of some academic quality; but he returned to it years later with the ardour and animus of a political pamphleteer. He had discovered in the interval that holism was 'British', the mental construct of a man out of love with his own nation and in love with the imperial super-state.

If it were to materialize externally [Cilliers wrote] and General Smuts's dream be realized in the triumph of the idea of the British Empire in a holistic State, it would mean the merging of the South African Nation into the larger British Empire Nation. This larger nation is bound to have eventually, one language and one culture only. That language and that culture is scarcely going to be Afrikaans. Following the ideal of General Smuts leads inevitably and indisputably to the extinction of Afrikaans as a language...A British Holist can't be an Afrikaans Holist at the same time.

Invincible ignorance of what Smuts actually had done, written and said (including what he had said to Cilliers's own students) was

own thoughts. In that they were right. In his unpublished book of 1912, Smuts had systematically explored the idea of emergent evolution although he did not use the phrase. Lloyd Morgan's *Instinct and Experience* was published the same year; Alexander's *Space, Time and Deity* not until 1920.

the only possible explanation of the imperial super-state story;* but political propaganda and personal animus kept that story alive, along with its twin, the myth that Smuts was out of love with his own country. To be sure, he was also in love with Europe and from time to time he let slip phrases which might suggest to a one-track mind that he considered South Africa to be merely a European outpost. In 1927, in the preface that he wrote to Monsignor Kolbe's book, *A Catholic View of Holism*, he let slip just such a phrase when he pictured himself writing *Holism and Evolution* 'in this far-off corner of the world'. To the distinguished Afrikaner poet and critic N. P. van Wyk Louw it seemed self-evident that only a man with a 'colonial' outlook could call his own country 'far-off'. Yet the original context of the phrase was quite different; in August 1925, when Smuts was on the eve of rushing his book to the publishers, he excused its imperfections by saying that he did not have the time and was 'too far away' to consult the experts in the various sciences whose progress and methods had been his theme. By and large, in spite of the talks that he had on botany with his neighbour Pole-Evans and the talks that he might have had on zoology and physics with Hogben and Cilliers, that was a plain statement of fact.[20]

Moreover, among the experts whom he needed to consult was an expert on God. To be sure, he was doing his utmost to keep God out of his book; but he could not keep God out of his mind. Ever since his student years, when the idea of the book first took shape, God had been its starting-point. Unfortunately, his thoughts about God were so personal and experimental that he did not care to discuss them, except sometimes with a particularly close friend; for example, Alice Clark. Thirty years earlier, he had been able to discuss them in Stellenbosch with Professor J. I. Marais; but Stellenbosch no longer bred theologians of the Marais stamp.† The Roman Catholic Church, if only he had realized it in time, still bred them, and one of them was living in Cape Town. F. C. Kolbe, the son of a Protestant minister, had gone to London in the 1870s to study law, but had undergone conversion to Catholicism and joined the priesthood. He was 16 years older than Smuts but had

---

* See pp. 38–49 above and pp. 200–2 below. Smuts spoke to the Stellenbosch students about holism in May 1927.

† In 1932 Johannes du Plessis, a pupil of J. I. Marais and Smuts's contemporary at Stellenbosch, was dismissed from his chair there on a charge of heresy.

many things in common with him: he was a student of biology and philosophy; he was a mountaineer and a lover of mountains; he had a zest for ideas; he was, despite his deafness, a charming companion. When he heard that Smuts was writing a book of philosophy he suggested that they should discuss it together, but Smuts told him that it was already in the press. 'I will send you a copy', he added, 'and then you can tell me where I am wrong.' When Kolbe received the book its 'divergencies and convergencies' with his own thought fascinated him. He warned Smuts that *De Kerkbode* would disapprove of it; but he added: 'On first reading the book I said to a friend, "This is a *deeply* religious book".'[21]

Six weeks later, Smuts saw himself under indictment on the charge of atheism. His accuser was A. Wyatt Tilby, who devoted six pages of a twelve-page article in the *Nineteenth Century* to exposing the wrong-headedness of a writer who tried to explain the design of the universe without reference to the designer. That gibe did not trouble Smuts intellectually; but it troubled him emotionally. He did not want to go to heaven in Paley's company,* but neither did he want to be branded an atheist. He wrote Wyatt Tilby a long letter in his own defence.[22]

Unfortunately for his peace of mind, he had other accusers, although some of them were ready to let him off lightly. He received a letter from the office of *The Baptist Times* enclosing a review of his book. 'I wonder', his correspondent wrote, 'if someday you will add a chapter? I think you have done a considerable thing, but I am not sure that the top of the apex is not missing.'[23] In other words, he could clear himself of the charge of atheism by introducing Deity as the culminating epiphenomenon of cosmic evolution. Alexander and Lloyd Morgan had done something like that; but Smuts did not expound an evolutionary process leading up to God. Nor did he, as the Book of Genesis did, find God 'in the beginning'.

Where was the Spirit [he asked in his last chapter] when the warm Silurian seas covered the face of the earth, and the lower types of fishes and marine creatures still formed the crest of the evolutionary wave? Or going still further back, where was the Spirit when in the pre-Cambrian

---

* Smuts did not like even the defenders of his theism to use the argument of design, and was displeased when Graham Kerr appeared to use it in a sentence of his review in *Nature*, discussing the power behind all creation: 'Some, with General Smuts, will spell it Holism: some will spell it God.'[24]

system of the globe the first convulsive movements threw up the early mountains which have now entirely disappeared from the face of the earth, and when the living forms, if any, were of so low a type that none have been deciphered yet in the geological record? Where was the Spirit when the Solar System itself was a diffuse fiery nebula?

Mind or Spirit, he answered, was not present at the beginning, either implicitly or explicitly. His answer shocked many people, including that staunch Hegelian, J. S. Haldane; but Smuts would no more accept the Absolute than the Super-Person as his God. On the evidence of his last chapter, it was hard to see him accepting God in any conceivable guise. Nevertheless he had written in his fifth chapter:

Is life or mind implicit in matter, and are the characters just referred to an appeal of the human mind to the mind imprisoned in matter? Has Science gone so far in her long search for truth that at last mind greets mind in the inner nature of things? Have the rescuers reached the imprisoned in the long dark tunnel of Nature?

That sounded as if he was half expecting to find God somewhere along the curves of space-time. Theologically, as well as logically, his thought was full of unresolved contradictions.

Those contradictions did not trouble Kolbe.* When he called *Holism and Evolution* a deeply religious book he had in mind not its argumentation but its feeling. From his point of view as a scholarly and serene Christian the book appeared muddled; but he recognized its author as a man searching for a straight path of thought. He did not want to push Smuts into the Catholic path; but he did want to help him find his own path. He pointed to the resemblance between Smuts's 'wholes' and the 'substantial forms' of Aristotle and Aquinas. Smuts grew interested and made up his mind to read those authors. Kolbe suggested that he might also find it worth his while to re-read the first chapter of St John's Gospel. About ten years later, when Kolbe was dying, that advice began to bear surprising fruit.† Meanwhile, Smuts and Kolbe enjoyed a friendship which enriched both their lives.

Whatever his friends and enemies might say about *Holism and Evolution*, the writing of it was a major event in Smuts's life. In those

---

* No more did they trouble C. E. Raven, who in his second series of Gifford Lectures (1952) called himself a holist and called Smuts a theist. See Note III to Raven's *Experience and Interpretation* (Cambridge, 1953).

† See pp. 305–7 below.

twenty-nine weeks of intense concentration he did not define the universe; but he did define himself. By an effort of his self-conscious mind he re-enacted his imaginative experience as a boy on his father's farm. He re-discovered himself as of the earth earthy; yet at the same time a person with full title to his own thoughts, affections and loyalties. Man, he declared in his concluding pages, need not feel himself an alien in time; behind his striving towards the good was the entire weight and momentum and innermost nature and trend of the universe. He told Gilbert Murray that his book contained his creed. Without that creed, he said, he could hardly have lived.[25]

CHAPTER IO

LEADING THE OPPOSITION

THE general election of June 1924 had made it plain to Smuts that
his party organization needed overhauling. That was a task jointly
for himself as the party's leader, and for Louis Esselen as its secretary.
Esselen was a well-educated Transvaaler of sound Afrikaner stock, a
progressive farmer who had pioneered the citrus industry and remained
throughout his life a zealous and intelligent advocate of soil conserva-
tion. He had been a staff officer to Botha during the Anglo-Boer
war and to Smuts during the South West African and East African
campaigns of the First World War. As secretary of the South African
party and subsequently of the United party until his retirement
from office in 1940, he worked for two decades or more behind
the scenes in South African politics, the counsellor of politicians
and senior civil servants, the go-between of parties in times of
critical negotiation. In 1920 he had played an influential part
in the abortive *hereniging* discussions and subsequently in the
negotiations which brought the Unionists into the South African
party. In March 1922 he had been under fire with Smuts in their
dangerous drive through Fordsburg when Smuts was making his
way to military headquarters in the last phase of tumult on the
Rand. Smuts always found Esselen a good man to have with him
in difficult times.

In the aftermath of the 1924 defeat their joint labours were
undramatic. Esselen reported to his leader the sad state of the party's
finances. In the Transvaal he was doing his utmost to recover
a debt to the party of £90 on the sale of a second-hand Ford car.
To cut down office expenses and at the same time to improve
discipline he was absorbing the Transvaal administration into the
central administration of the party. Smuts, nevertheless, was chary
of carrying centralization too far, and gave anxious thought to the
chairmanship of the party in the Transvaal. He realized that bad
organization was merely one cause of his recent defeat: weak leadership in the middle ranks was a second, hesitant and contradictory
propaganda was a third cause. To clarify his party's thought on

critical issues, he appointed committees of the parliamentary membership to study and report upon each of the main matters which Hertzog's government was likely to raise. These reports, he thought, might provide the material for a consolidated statement of the party's policy.[1]

He was anxious to make rapid headway with his party work because he expected, before very long, to have to fight a new election. He did not think the Pact government would last many years and told his wife in February 1926 that he could not risk accepting a pressing invitation to visit America for fear that Hertzog might spring an election on the country while he was away. He told Lane that the two parties of the Pact would sooner or later start quarrelling and that their doctrinaire fanaticism would land them in economic trouble. In the event, he had to wait four years for the fulfilment of his first prophesy and seven for the fulfilment of his second. His opponents made far better use than he had foreseen of the powerful economic upswing which was just getting under way when they achieved power. 'Great rains in the interior', he wrote, 'a general lifting of the depression and great platinum discoveries in the Transvaal gave them all the luck possible.' He did not altogether grudge them their luck. Not merely for himself, he reflected, but also for the country, it was time for a change; Hertzog and his colleagues would find the responsibilities of office educative. In May 1925, when the Prince of Wales visited South Africa, it fell to Hertzog to do the honours. 'Perhaps it is as well', Smuts wrote, 'that the visit came after a change of Government in this country. Instead of the Nationalists now standing aloof and pointing to us as jingoes and snobs, they have to do the job themselves with our approval, and the national unanimity of South Africa is therefore far greater than it would otherwise have been.'[2]

The third article of the Hertzog–Creswell pact ruled out republicanism for the immediate future. Hertzog was moving towards the conclusion that a free association under the Crown with the sister nations of the British Commonwealth would satisfy the aspirations of his people, provided they could be convinced that they possessed equality of status within the Commonwealth and in the wider society of nations. That, precisely, was Smuts's contention. Hertzog believed that South Africa should adopt her own national flag. Smuts believed the same. Government and Opposition agreed to consult with each other and with heraldic experts in designing the flag. Unfortunately, they failed to reckon with the explosive power of symbols. Government supporters refused to consider any symbolism which included the Union Jack. Opposition supporters refused to accept any symbolism which excluded it. Smuts maintained that South Africa must learn to live with her own history. He told his wife that he loved his old Vierkleur and could therefore understand his English-speaking friends loving their old flag; consequently, room must be found on the new flag for the Union Jack alongside the flags of the two Republics. In the event, that argument prevailed; but for nearly two years a violent contention of the parties and of the symbols raged in South Africa.[3]

Meanwhile Hertzog was coming to grips with the constitutional issues of national status. Among the papers which he inherited from Smuts was the memorandum of June 1921, in which Smuts argued the case for a General Declaration of Constitutional Right.* Both in its broad outline and its specific details, the Smuts memorandum anticipated almost every demand which Hertzog was proposing to make at the Imperial Conference of October–November 1926. Smuts had saved Hertzog an immense amount of work and had presented him with a superb tactical opening, but had also created some embarrassment for him. In his correspondence with Amery† and subsequently in his discussion with the Commonwealth Prime Ministers, Hertzog emphasized the wide area of his agreement with Smuts; but he knew that the republicans in his party would not thank him if the sovereign status which he offered them bore Smuts's trademark. Consequently, he had to persuade them, and if possible to persuade himself, that he and Smuts were at odds on some issue of fundamental principle. 'Where the honourable member and I differ', he told the House of Assembly on 22 April 1922, 'is that he cannot get free in his policy from a kind of super-authority, something that has authority over all, and an authority holding everybody by the throat, something like a super-authority and a super-state.' That accusation was fantastic in the light of what Smuts had done and of what he had said, over and over again, in public and in private,

---

* See pp. 44–8 above.

† Amery, as Secretary of State for the Colonies in the recently formed Baldwin government, promptly implemented the Smuts–Amery plan for separating the Dominions Office from the Colonial Office. Thereby he became the first Secretary of State for the Dominions.

from 1911 onwards. Once again, Smuts repudiated the super-state. 'I have', he declared, 'no such idea. My idea is an organization or a combination of equal states, and nobody superior...There is no super-state, no super-authority.'[4]

But the denial, no matter how often Smuts repeated it, never made the least impression upon Hertzog.* Smuts's mythical super-state was Hertzog's blind spot. Tactical necessities of the party-political struggle were in part the explanation; but not completely. Between Hertzog and Smuts some real differences persisted. They might sometimes look like differences of constitutional doctrine; but at root they were political differences. For example, Smuts often spoke of 'the common Crown'; whereas Hertzog, despite some linguistic lapses,† upheld the theory of the divisibility of the Crown, and from that theory deduced South Africa's right to declare her neutrality in the event of war. In opposition to that, many champions of 'the common Crown' were apt to argue that when the King was at war all his subjects were at war, no matter where they lived. It was tempting to foist that argument upon Smuts—tempting, but totally unjustified, because the Smuts–Botha letter to Lloyd George of 12 May 1919 was the most uncompromising assertion ever made of South Africa's absolute right to declare her neutrality if she so decided.‡ That letter was a political act, not a constitutional theory.

* No more did Smuts's denials make any impression upon Hertzog's biographers, C. M. van den Heever and O. Pirow. With disregard of the historical record, they re-iterated the allegation that Smuts's aim was an imperial super-state and/or 'holistic imperialism' (Pirow's phrase). As evidence, they were usually content with quoting Hertzog; but occasionally they quoted a sentence imputed to Smuts, without saying where, when and in what context Smuts uttered that sentence. Thus, van den Heever, in *Gen. J. B. M. Hertzog* (Johannesburg, 1943), p. 469, stated that Smuts said in 1917 'Whatever we may say or think, we are a subordinate province of England'. Pirow repeated that statement (p. 102). Neither author gave a precise reference. I have had to read scores of Smuts's speeches in 1917 before I could track down (in the report of the Imperial War Conference, Cd. 8566 of 1917, pp. 46–8) any comparable utterance. Its significance was the opposite of that alleged by van den Heever and Pirow. As in all his speeches on imperial relations, Smuts insisted that the relationship of sovereignty and subordination no longer existed and that freedom and equality were the present political realities. This was his reason for proposing the word Commonwealth in place of the word Empire. At the same time, he pointed out that legal survivals of the sovereignty-subordination relationship still existed side by side with the political reality of national equality. He identified those legal survivals in order to emphasize the need for having them cleared away.

Many other examples could be cited of partial and undocumented quotation in the books of these two writers. Their failure to give precise references creates unnecessary difficulties for serious historians.

† In 1926 Hertzog's speeches contained occasional references to the 'common Crown'; but they signified nothing more than a time lag of his phraseology in relation to his thought and feeling. ‡ See p. 5 above.

Whenever he could, Smuts steered clear of theorizing. The real difference between Hertzog and Smuts was that Hertzog looked forward to a South African declaration of neutrality as a great political triumph; but Smuts looked forward to it as a great political calamity. Hertzog and Smuts held conflicting political views of the Commonwealth of Nations. Smuts conceived membership of the Commonwealth to be a vital South African interest, and Hertzog was moving hesitantly towards the same point of view; but Smuts also acclaimed the Commonwealth, with its values of peace, order, good government and steadily expanding freedom, as 'a great cause'.* To the end of his life, Hertzog never did that.

And so he continued to misinterpret Smuts. Misinterpretation was conspicuous in a speech which he delivered at Stellenbosch in May 1926.† Purely as a descriptive exercise, the speech had great merit. It reviewed the attempt which 'the Empire group' had been making at successive Imperial Conferences since 1919 to assert its 'group unity' in the field of foreign relations. It recorded the successive frustrations of that attempt, culminating in the Treaties of Locarno. It reported Smuts's sombre reflections on Locarno.‡ All this was valuable political diagnosis; but Hertzog spoilt it by riding his hobby horse. He called 'the Empire group' a 'fictitious state, super-power or supreme state authority'. It was nothing of the kind. Nor was the Imperial Conference, as Hertzog alleged, 'a quasi-federal Empire'. Smuts had explained again and again in parliament that the Imperial Conference was a purely consultative gathering with no power to impose any obligations of any kind upon South Africa. But Hertzog, until he himself attended an Imperial Conference, remained blinded by his will to disbelieve.

In parliament on 28 May Smuts recognized the 'first-rate importance' of the Stellenbosch speech. He did not propose, he said, to discuss the controversial issues which it raised; but he asked the Prime Minister to clarify one important statement. He had given notice of his intention to press for a declaration of rights, not merely for the edification of the Commonwealth nations, but for formal

* See p. 324 below.

† C. M. van den Heever (English ed. p. 210) refers to this speech but does not mention its date; while O. Pirow (pp. 107–12) quotes from it at length and says that it was delivered 'in March 1926'. The *Cape Times* reported it on 17 May 1926.

‡ See p. 230 below, for his reflections on the alternative risks associated with the Locarno Treaties.

publication to the world. He had also said that the desire of one or more members of the Commonwealth to hold aloof from the declaration should not prevent the others from pressing ahead with it. Smuts now asked him whether it was the intention of his government, in the event of its failing to get from the Imperial Conference the declaration it wanted, to issue a declaration of its own. Reassuringly, Hertzog replied that that would be 'a very wrong and stupid thing to do'.[5]

Smuts's question had particular point because his own bid for a declaration had been frustrated five years earlier by his fellow Prime Ministers. But in 1926 the auguries were happy for Hertzog. The arch-obstructionist Hughes no longer spoke for Australia. Mackenzie King, Canada's spokesman, held ideas nearly identical with Hertzog's. So did Cosgrave and O'Higgins, the spokesmen for Ireland. So, in the main, did L. S. Amery, the Secretary of State for the Dominions. When all the work of drafting and re-drafting was finished, a document emerged—the famous Balfour Declaration of November 1926—which contained not only the principles that Smuts and Hertzog had upheld, but also a realistic programme for implementing them. At the closing session of the Conference, Hertzog declared that he had attained all that he wanted and, what was more, had attained it with the full co-operation and sympathy of all his colleagues.* Amery wrote that night in his diary: 'It really has been a great clearing up of outstanding points on a basis which eliminates friction, and leaves the way clear for future co-operation. It is true that it leaves the way equally clear to dissolution. That is a risk we have got to run, and if the will to unity is there we shall overcome it.'[6]

Hertzog's public statements in London and on his return to South Africa gave good ground for believing that 'the will to unity', as Amery interpreted it, was getting the upper hand of the separatist will. The National party, Hertzog declared, had achieved everything that it had striven for and was now 'absolutely content'. Roos, Malan and other prominent Nationalists made similar declarations. Smuts quoted some of them at a congress of his own party in the Transvaal. 'Well', he commented, 'I wish to say that the South African Party is also satisfied.' It was a pity that he could not have

* He had, however, failed to get his favourite word 'independence' written into the Declaration. Mackenzie King, mindful of North American history, said that the word would get him hanged when he got back to Canada. But when Hertzog got back to South Africa he used the word just as if the Conference had accepted it instead of rejecting it.

left it at that, for the times were surely propitious for South Africans to forget their past quarrels and make a fresh start. But Smuts no more dared to risk a party split than Hertzog dared; Hertzog had to placate his ex-Republicans, Smuts had to placate his ex-Unionists.* The Smuts party could not possibly stay silent while the Hertzog party claimed sole proprietorship of the Balfour Declaration. No, Smuts retorted, the Balfour Declaration embodied principles which the South African party had consistently maintained and the National party had persistently repudiated. To prove his point he quoted *verbatim* a long series of Nationalist pronouncements in favour of an independent South Africa separated from the United Kingdom and the British Empire. The South African party, he concluded, had stuck to its guns, whereas the Nationalists had turned a somersault.[7]

Amery congratulated Smuts upon his success in striking a balance between the just claims of his party and the requirements of national unity. From such a shrewd political strategist, who also knew far more than any other politician about the inside story of Imperial Conferences throughout the past ten years, that was an impressive tribute. Nevertheless, Smuts failed to control the firebrands of his party. He confessed his failure. 'Thus we have the admission of Hertzog', he wrote on 28 May 1927, 'that he had thought of leaving the Flag Bill in abeyance for one or two years on his return from London, but the Empire Group decided him the other way.' Wherever the blame lay, the contention over national symbols exploded again with a violence which might almost have destroyed the nation. 'This flag calamity', Smuts wrote, 'threatens to engulf everything.'[8]

It became almost impossible in such an atmosphere to achieve any rational discussion of South Africa's status as a member of the British Commonwealth and of the international community. On 14 March 1927, Drummond Chaplin opened the discussion in parliament by acclaiming the Balfour Declaration as the embodiment of everything that the South African party had always stood for. Thereupon Hertzog accused the South African party and its leader of standing for the imperial super-state. The Balfour Declaration, he said, had killed that monstrosity. It had vindicated his own contention ever since Union that South Africa was a sovereign

---

* He also had to placate some fervent champions of the indivisibility of the Crown, such as Stallard and Nicholls, who were not ex-Unionists but old S.A.P. men.

independent nation. He then went on to tell the House how Smuts himself had wanted in 1921 to win assent to a similar declaration—

AN HON. MEMBER: He surrendered.

THE PRIME MINISTER: Yes, that is quite right, because he never brought it up before the Imperial Conference. Before he got so far, he became afraid for some reason or other.

SIR THOMAS SMARTT: That is not usually his custom.*

Hertzog went on to tell the House that *he* had not been afraid. *He* had kept on fighting until his theory of the Empire was vindicated and Smuts's super-state was broken up; yet Smuts now had the audacity to pretend that the new Empire was his! After that, Hertzog continued raking up the past all the way back to his De Wildt speech of December 1912. Smuts in his reply spent just a little time in rebutting Hertzog's accusations: his alleged addiction to the super-state, he protested, was 'a misunderstanding' on Hertzog's part and in 1921 he had not run away; 'the circumstances' had been against him. But now the time had come, he continued, for looking forward instead of looking back, for laying the ghost of the past, for getting out of the bog in which they had been wandering for years. 'This is not an occasion for wrangling and quarrelling', he pleaded, 'but an occasion for rejoicing. We have been divided as a people for years...The differences have now been removed.'⁹

That appeal bore no immediate fruit. When parliament rose three months later Smuts wrote, 'It has been a horrid session, as the children would say. Nothing but unpleasantness and wrangling and vituperation...We are deteriorating politically in this country, and all standards are sinking.'¹⁰ That lament marked the low point. During the recess he and Hertzog worked together to stop the rot. In October they reached an agreed settlement of the flag controversy.†

Reason returned at long last to the South African political debate. In March 1928 Hertzog explained the content and significance of

---

* See p. 49 above.

† As Smuts acknowledged, Hertzog behaved handsomely in the final negotiations, which were conducted between only the two of them. The agreement received a better reception among his followers than among Hertzog's because his views, by and large, found expression in the National Flag. In addition, it was agreed that the Union Jack, 'to denote the association of the Union with the group of nations constituting the British Commonwealth of Nations', should be flown alongside the National Flag at appropriate times and places. That meant that South Africa had two flags. It also meant some intermittent wrangling about the occasions for flying them together.¹¹

the Balfour Declaration in a comprehensive and closely reasoned parliamentary speech which emphasized, amongst other things, South Africa's right to declare her neutrality in the event of war. Smuts, in his reply, steered clear of the theoretical issues, but emphasized the grave political significance of any decision for or against neutrality. The issue, he said, might have to be faced someday and he, for one, saw grave dangers ahead; but he believed that wisdom lay in choosing the course of policy most likely to prevent neutrality from becoming a practical question. To that extent, Hertzog and he were in agreement. Nevertheless, their two speeches had undertones of conflict. Hertzog seemed to be recommending neutrality not only as a theory but also as a policy. Smuts, on the other hand, gave plain notice that neutrality was unlikely to be his policy, if and when the time should come for decision. So long as the cause was good, he declared, the nations of the British Commonwealth would stand together in the future as they had stood together in August 1914.

In his letters to Amery, Smuts showed himself well aware of the differences of outlook and emphasis between Hertzog and himself. They felt the same about the sovereignty, but not about the solidarity of the nations of the Commonwealth. Hertzog in his speeches always emphasized the sovereign, the separate status. 'The note of co-operation and comradeship', Smuts said, 'he never or very seldom, and then grudgingly, touches.' Nevertheless, Amery saw grounds for hoping that the will to co-operate would steadily grow, now that Hertzog and his followers felt assured of South Africa's equality of status. He looked forward to the emergence in South Africa of a genuinely bi-partisan foreign policy. He also urged Smuts to join forces with Hertzog in achieving 'a real national settlement of the native question'.[12]

If Amery had studied the 1924 elections and the South African *Hansard* since then, he would have realized that there was only one way of achieving a bi-partisan Native policy, namely, for Smuts and his party to underwrite the Nationalist–Labour programme. Parts at least of that programme, as Smuts well knew, had a strong attraction for some members of his own party, especially for Transvaalers of the Stallard and Natalians of the Nicholls stamp; but they were repugnant to other party members, particularly to F. S.

Malan and his friends in the Cape. Consequently, Smuts had to move warily if he were to keep these diverse sections of his party in line with each other and with his own conception of what was desirable and practical. Throughout his first five years as Opposition leader he managed on the whole to strike a tolerable balance between what was due to his party, to himself and to South Africa.

One word, segregation, contained the ideology of Hertzog and Creswell. These leaders and their followers envisaged both a horizontal and a vertical line of division (*skeidsmuur*) between white and black South Africans: the horizontal line to define the base of their citadel of economic defence; the vertical line to define their long wall of political defence. The picture was dramatic in its broad sweep; but the attempt to fill in its detail revealed some significant divergencies of outlook and emphasis. The horizontal line, as embodied in the civilized labour policy, meant one thing to the National party and a different thing to the Labour party: the former had chiefly in mind the economic defence of 'poor whites'; the latter had chiefly in mind the interests of the white labour aristocracy. Similarly, the vertical line of political defence took different shapes in the minds of different people. Creswell envisaged it as a territorial border, all the blacks on one side, all the whites on the other, with total economic and political separation of the two races. That, at least, was the picture which Creswell painted in his speeches. Hertzog, on the other hand, showed some respect for quantitative fact; he knew that the South African economy depended upon black labour; he knew just as well that the black territories could not support all the blacks. His strictly limited proposals for enlarging those territories were conceived partly as a fulfilment of the 1913 pledge,* partly as a *quid pro quo* for the franchise rights which he proposed to take away from black voters in the Cape. To remove them from the Cape's common roll was his main objective. It was, he said, a fundamental principle.

The Pact Government went first to work on drawing the horizontal line. In October 1924 it published its definition of civilized and uncivilized labour, relating the former to standards of life 'tolerable from the European standpoint' and the latter to 'the bare...necessities of life as understood among barbarous and undeveloped peoples'. It made the newly established Ministry of Labour its

* See pp. 114–16 above.

main instrument for the defence of civilized employment. That Ministry set purposefully to work to create jobs for whites at rates of pay above the market rates. Government departments set the example; public utilities such as the South African Railways and Harbours Board followed it. The Department of Labour brought strong pressure to bear on the municipal administrations. It also made the new protective tariff an instrument of pressure upon private manufacturers; various benefits accruing to them under the tariff were made conditional upon their increasing the proportion of civilized labour in their establishments. Whether measures such as these were really efficacious in creating a higher national total of white employment could be disputed; but in specific undertakings they did undoubtedly create more jobs for white men through the displacement of Native, Indian and—from 1930 onwards—Coloured workers.*

Purposeful administration was the sufficient instrument of these activities in the defence of civilized labour; they did not require new legislation and did not figure prominently in parliamentary debate. But the trade union programme of economic defence was a different matter. In February 1925 that programme took legislative shape in the Mines and Works Act Amendment Bill. It was a single-clause, high-explosive bill. It specifically named Natives and Asiatics as persons who could be excluded by regulation from receiving certificates of competency in certain trades, and it specifically empowered managements to apply a racial classification of their employees when apportioning work among them 'in respect of mines, works or machinery'. In his speech on the second reading (25 February 1925) the Minister of Mines and Industries said that the Bill dealt with a great national question, the preservation and perpetuation of the white race. Self-preservation, he declared, was the first law of nature: whereas the original Mines and Works Act had pursued that end indirectly and ineffectively,† the amendments he was now proposing pursued the same end openly and effectively.

---

* Hertzog's conception of civilized labour did not exclude the Coloureds, and the Department of Labour officially insisted that the policy was non-racial. Nevertheless, it was commonly called, at times even by Ministers, the White Labour Policy. The report of the Economic and Wage Commission (U.G. 14 of 1926) and of the Carnegie Commission on Poor Whites (1932) suggest doubts of the policy's efficacy on the national scale.

† In the case *Rex* v. *Hildick Smith* the Transvaal Provincial Court had declared regulations under the Mines and Works Act 1911 to be invalid.

Considerable discussion followed on the historical origins of the Mines and Works Act of 1911 and its historical relationship to what was now proposed. Smuts contended that the present Bill went far beyond previous practice; that it went 'right into the blue'. He saw no practical necessity for it and saw it as the threat of grave danger to South Africa.

Let me say this, the Minister referred to 'blankedom' and said he thought he should claim me from previous speeches as one of the men who had stood for a white South Africa. Make no mistake my whole political effort and public life in this country has been to establish and render firm and secure white civilization in this country. But there are ways of doing it, and the question is whether this Bill and the statutory enactment of this colour bar in this wide and extended form with the disability placed here upon millions of our fellow subjects—whether this is the way to establish the white position in South Africa. I am very doubtful about it.

AN HON. MEMBER: It will greatly assist.

GENERAL SMUTS: No, I don't think it will assist. I think it is going to embarrass us in every way possible...and if we want to entrench our position merely as a white oligarchy by getting round us a ring fence of hate from all the other communities in South Africa, we shall have a very hard and difficult row to hoe in future. That is not the way to establish a white South Africa.

He reminded the House that under Dr Malan's Nationality and Flag Bill every inhabitant of the country would become henceforward a South African; not only the whites but the Natives as well.

While the Minister of the Interior is declaring every Native a South African, his colleague is bringing in a Bill under which we are going to declare to the Natives: 'You shall in future be debarred from rising above the level of hewers of wood and drawers of water.' I am all for the white man, but there is something in my breast that cannot stand this.

He went on to express his profound regret that the Minister had named Asiatics in the Bill. He saw nothing to be gained by flouting the feelings not only of black Africa but also of yellow Asia. Such unnecessary provocation could only increase the dangers which threatened white South Africa.[13]

Smuts pleaded with the government to 'narrow the issue'. He offered the co-operation of his party in passing a Bill to re-establish the legal validity of the old Mines and Works regulations. The government rejected that offer. After the House of Assembly had twice approved and the Senate had twice rejected the Mines and Works Amendment Bill, the government invoked clauses 58 and 63 of the Constitution to force the Bill through a joint session of the two Houses. There, in May 1926, Smuts continued his rearguard action. White South Africa, he declared, did not need or want the kind of protection the Bill purported to give it.

> AN HON. MEMBER: Say that at the next election.
> GENERAL SMUTS: Yes, I will say it at every election.

In a long and angry rejoinder which ranged from the iniquities of Bulhoek and Bondelzwarts to those of the nineteenth-century missionaries and their twentieth-century imitators,* Hertzog denounced Smuts's speech as contemptible, brazen, shameless and hypocritical. When the division was called, the government won by a majority of sixteen. That vote on 12 May 1926 made the industrial colour bar a fundamental South African principle.[14]

Plainly, it was harder than Amery imagined for Smuts to reach agreement with Hertzog on a bi-partisan racial policy. Nevertheless, the possibility existed that he might approve Hertzog's vertical line, as distinct from his horizontal line of division between whites and blacks. After all, he himself had proclaimed the principle of 'parallel institutions' and had embodied that principle in legislation. In doing so, he had won applause not only in South Africa but also in Great Britain.† 'The policy of differentiation'—which meant just the same as 'parallel institutions'—remained highly respectable throughout the 1920s both in political and in academic circles. Differences of opinion, when they arose, were not so much upon the point of principle as upon the problems of application.

Smuts, consequently, was in the mood to wait and see what Hertzog would propose. He was certainly ready to support any practical proposals, in conformity with the Act of 1913, for giving the Natives more land. On the issue of a separate roll for Native voters he was keeping an open mind. Communal representation did not seem to him inherently wrong. In the 1920s it was not yet a dirty word: on the contrary, it was British policy in India, Kenya and other dependent territories; in South Africa, British proconsuls and their expert advisers had strongly advocated it.‡ Their advocacy,

---

* Church leaders had sent in a petition against the Bill. Among the signatories Professor Johannes du Plessis was the only member of the Dutch Reformed Church.
† See pp. 120–1 above.   ‡ See p. 114 above.

however, had encountered resistance in the Cape, where voting on the common roll had provided three generations of political stability. The Cape's common roll was entrenched in the South African constitution. If Hertzog could offer the Cape voters, and particularly the non-European voters, something which they considered a fair exchange for their existing franchise, Smuts might support him; but if not, not. Smuts waited. What troubled him most was Hertzog's promise to produce 'a solution' of the Native problem. The slow and complex processes of social change and political adaptation could not, as he understood them, be expressed in the mathematical idiom of problems and their solution.

In July 1925 Hertzog gave Smuts notice that he would invite co-operation from him in solving the Native problem. In November, in an important speech at Smithfield, he expounded his own solution.[15] In December he explained it to a conference of Natives:* 'I hope you will agree', he told them, 'that no injustice is done when different grazing is given to sheep from that given to cattle.'[16] Meanwhile, he was pressing Smuts insistently to co-operate with him. After taking counsel with his senior colleagues, Smuts said that his party could not bind itself one way or the other without first seeing the Smithfield proposals expressed as draft Bills. Thereupon Hertzog accused him of making Native policy a party political issue. In a letter to Smuts of 23 January 1926, he declared their correspondence closed.[17]

Six months later Hertzog laid before parliament four Bills: the Union Native Council Bill, the Representation of Natives in Parliament Bill, the Natives Land Act (Amendment) Bill, and the Coloured Persons Rights Bill. They covered wide ground but they did not contain a solution of the Native problem: on the contrary, they raised some awkward new problems. Smuts spot-lighted them in a tightly packed memorandum of 7,000 words. To begin with, land: the government was proposing to 'release' more land, not necessarily for Native occupancy but for competitive inter-racial purchase. This, Smuts said, was more likely to increase than to diminish the territorial intermingling of blacks and whites. Simultaneously, the government was proposing new measures to eject hundreds of thousands of blacks from white farms; this, he said, would aggravate the congestion of the blacks in their own rural

* The conference had been called under Smuts's Native Affairs Act of 1920.

areas and would accelerate their rush to the cities. Next, he considered the government's proposal to remove Native voters from the Cape's common roll and to give the Natives throughout the Union seven white representatives in the House of Assembly, with limited powers of voting. This operation, he maintained, could not be carried through at one stroke; under section 35 of the Constitution, the rights of Native voters already enrolled in the Cape were inviolate. With regard to the new representation for Natives which the government was proposing, he pointed out that the electing bodies would be predominantly under government control; under circumstances which could easily be envisaged, they might even determine the balance of power in parliament.* Turning to the Coloured Persons Rights Bill, he admitted that it appeared at first sight to live up to its name, both by leaving intact the rights of Coloured voters in the Cape and by taking a first step towards the parliamentary representation of Coloured persons outside the Cape. Unfortunately, the proposals for compiling a list of Coloured persons were bound to create 'some interesting situations'. Some persons who had hitherto passed for white would find themselves Coloured when their pedigrees came to be investigated; within the same family, some children (if they were born before the Act was passed) would be Coloured; but other children (born after the Act) would be Natives. Smuts exposed the Coloured Persons Rights Bill as an unlovely product of muddled thinking and incompetent drafting. He thought better of the Native Council Bill, notwithstanding the misgivings he felt at some of its provisions. By and large, his conclusion was that parliamentary discussion and amendment could make the Land Bill and the Council Bill workable; but that the other two Bills should be submitted to 'a small National Convention' or, preferably, to a strong representative commission, rather like the South African Native Affairs Commission of 1903–5.[18]

Hertzog's Native Bills were running into heavy weather. In December 1926 Tielman Roos expounded them to another conference of Natives. They saw little good in any of them, except the Union Native Council Bill. They particularly resented Roos's at-

---

* Smuts did not expound, but no doubt had in his head, a more down-to-earth objection to Hertzog's franchise proposals: namely, that they were likely to reduce the number of seats held by the S.A.P. in the Cape. In a series of articles in the *East London Daily Despatch* in June 1926, Colonel Crewe expounded this objection.

tempt to make them trade the Cape franchise for the expectation—such as it was—of more land; on the contrary, they protested, parliament was unconditionally bound by its past promises to produce an equitable land settlement. Their protests did not particularly trouble the government; it had the simple remedy of not consulting them further.* But the parliamentary opposition required more careful handling. Hertzog had received a copy of Smuts's memorandum. Its devastating analysis of the Native Bills could not fail to give him pause. The Bills had their first reading in March 1927 and were consigned thereafter to a Select Committee. They did not re-emerge until the eve of the next general election.

The closest approach to a bi-partisan racial policy occurred during February and March 1928, when Hertzog and Smuts held a series of exploratory talks. At Hertzog's invitation Smuts gave a frank exposition of his personal point of view. What worried him, he said, was the attempt to settle the franchise piecemeal: one settlement for the Natives, a second for the Coloureds—with a third to follow, he asked Hertzog, for the Indians?

And it was a question [Smuts continued] which he should consider seriously, whether a more comprehensive solution should not be adopted. That is to say, a general franchise reform, constituting a common franchise all over South Africa based on occupation and income or salary which was to apply to all, black and white alike, and while not so high as to exclude the Whites, yet to be high enough to exclude the bulk of the Native population. In addition to this common qualification, there might then also be an eduction and civilization test, applied to all non-Europeans in future, the presumption being that the European was civilized and that the non-European had to prove his adoption of European civilization. Such a comprehensive scheme would be quite simple, would draw no colour distinctions at all in regard to qualifications, and would only apply a differential civilization and education test which was reasonably justified.

Hertzog promised Smuts to consider his suggestion carefully. At their next meeting, he told him that opinion in the North was not ripe for it. That, by and large, was what Smuts had told Merriman twenty years earlier.

Hertzog's particular proposals now became the focal point of discussion. Smuts told Hertzog that he was offering the Natives too

* In breach of the government's assurances, no further conference of Natives was summoned during the following four years.

little in exchange for the Cape franchise: in his Smithfield speech he had argued that the Native voters on the Cape's common roll were the determining factor in twelve constituencies; if that were so, they ought to be offered five or six seats in the Assembly,* without prejudice to the five seats in the Senate which Hertzog was now proposing to provide for the Northern Natives. Smuts also laid special emphasis upon the obligation to leave entirely untouched the rights of Natives at present on the Cape register; the only course, he said, was to allow them if they so chose to vote with the Whites for so long as they lived. Turning to the Coloured Persons Rights Bill, he reiterated his objections to the proposed list of Coloured persons. It would be far better, he repeated, to establish uniform franchise qualifications irrespective of race, supplemented by an educational test for non-Europeans. He went on to tell Hertzog that he was not enamoured of his Union Native Council; for the present at any rate, he would have preferred to develop the local councils and to hold the all-Union annual conferences which the Act of 1920 made provision for. Coming finally to the Land Bill, he said that it was far too complicated and it missed the main purpose, namely, the provision of additional land for effective Native occupancy. To release the areas defined ten years ago from the restrictions of 1913 upon the competitive purchase of land had little relevance to that purpose; rather, the government should arm itself with wide powers of expropriation and it would have to provide the necessary finance.[19]

Smuts was not lecturing Hertzog. Their talks together were spread over four leisurely meetings and were conducted in the spirit of free inquiry; each man said his separate say in turn and from time to time each reminded the other that their joint exploration was individual, and left their respective parties uncommitted. They must have found this personal exchange of views a refreshing change from their parliamentary confrontations. Possibly they forgot, while they were talking together, the confrontation in the constituencies which was already hanging over both their heads.

Hertzog had less reason than Smuts to fear that confrontation. He had behind him a united party; Smuts had not. Smuts had recently been taking counsel with fourteen members of his party

---

* In 1926 Hertzog's figure had been seven seats in the House of Assembly, but since then he and his party had had second thoughts.

who had made a particular study of Hertzog's Bills.* He found it
a rare occurrence if more than four of the fourteen shared the same
opinion on any one of the Bills. For example, on the franchise issue,
Jagger and three others were firm for the Cape's common roll;
Duncan and three others were firm for communal representation;
Nicholls was against any representation at all for Natives except in
the Senate; F. S. Malan and two others were advocates of a Union-
wide uniform franchise; the remaining two members, it appeared,
held no opinions. On the land issue, Nicholls maintained that the
Natives already had quite as much as they needed; Collins considered
their need of land so urgent that it ought to be satisfied in advance
of any decision about the franchise; between these two poles the
other members oscillated. Smuts might well have asked himself what
his chances were as the leader of such a deeply divided party.[20]

In February 1929 Hertzog fired the opening volley of his election
campaign. In a joint session of the two Houses of Parliament he
introduced the two Bills which required a two-thirds majority if
they were to become law; he had no expectation of winning that
majority, but it was his purpose to dramatize the peril of white
South Africa and the rescue which his party offered. His talks with
Smuts a year earlier had taught him some useful tactical lessons.
For the time being, he dropped the Council Bill and the Land Bill;
he also dropped his highly contentious proposal for annulling the
established rights of Natives at present registered on the Cape's
common roll. That concession apart, the content of his franchise
proposals was a good deal less liberal in 1929 than it had been in
1926. The Natives' Parliamentary Representation Bill provided (1)
for the indirect election of two senators to represent the Natives of
the two northern provinces, and (2) for the creation of a new
Native Voters' Roll in the Cape and for the election by voters on
that roll of two senators; later on, of three members of the House
of Assembly.† The Coloured Persons' Rights Bill made provision
for the appointment of a Coloured Voters' Registration Board in
each district, and for the election of one white member of the

---

* In particular, members of the Select Committee.

† Since there was to be no abrogation of the existing rights of voters on the common
roll, some time was bound to elapse before the numbers on the separate roll reached the
total requisite for the return of three members of the House of Assembly. The electors of
the two senators in the northern provinces were to be members of local councils and
advisory boards, and chiefs appointed by the government.

House of Assembly to represent Coloured voters outside the Cape Province.

The South African party fought the two Bills clause by clause, but did not propose any alternative policy. Smuts protested that he and his party were not bound finally or irrevocably to the Cape basis, but he insisted that the franchise was only one part of an extremely complex economic–political–racial situation. He thought it foolish to rush into partial decisions; instead, he proposed patient consultation with the Natives and the calling of 'a National Convention or Commission' to explore the ends and means of a comprehensive national policy. Hertzog congratulated Smuts and his supporters upon the particularly skilful way in which they had carried on the debate without saying anything at all. Hertzog felt no such inhibitions. 'I shall not retreat', he declared, 'in so far as the Cape franchise is concerned. It is a fundamental requirement that it shall be altered.' Members opposite, he declared again, were waiting for the day when equal rights would permeate South Africa: 'If that day dawns, hands up as well.'

That was Hertzog's clarion call to the electors.[21]

The joint session ended on 25 February 1929. Polling day was fixed for 12 June. That meant a long and strenuous campaign. Smuts told his friends that he would fight until he was dead or half-dead. He felt confident of winning.[22]

His main specific reason for confidence was schism in the Labour party. During 1928 it had split into two apparently equal halves; one half, led by Creswell, continued to support Hertzog; the other half spent most of its energies in fighting the Creswellites. It was predictable that the Labour vote, which had been decisive in 1924, would count for far less in 1929. What remained unpredictable was whether or not an increase of the Nationalist vote would make good the decrease of the Labour vote.

On 12 June the electors, in a heavy poll (80 per cent as compared with 78·7 per cent in 1924), answered that question as follows:

National party	South African party	Creswell Labour	National Council Labour	Independent
78	61	5	3	1

The National party emerged from the fight with a majority of eight over all other parties. Since it could count on the unquestioning support of Creswell's team, it had an unshakable parliamentary majority.

Nevertheless the South African party won the larger share of the votes*

	South African party	National party	Creswell Labour	The rest
Numbers	181,195	150,476	25,621	15,568
Percentage of Poll	48·60	40·36	6·8	4·17

If each vote had possessed the same value, the South African party would have had seventy-two seats in the House of Assembly instead of sixty-one; the National party would have had only sixty seats instead of seventy-eight. That would have given Smuts a comfortable parliamentary majority, even without the support of 'the rest', whose votes would normally be cast on his side.

The abnormal discrepancy between the support which Smuts won in the constituencies and the seats which he won in parliament was not merely a transitory accident. Nineteen years later, its consequences proved catastrophic. Smuts possibly should have paid more attention to the arithmetic of elections.†

The general election of June 1929 came to be called the 'Black Peril' Election. It deserved that name. Naturally, it was not entirely and exclusively a controversy about colour. To some extent at least it was a prosperity election. Hertzog claimed that he had fulfilled his economic programme: the year by year surpluses of Havenga's budgets, the protectionist tariff, the industrial and agricultural expansion, the defence of civilized labour—he contrasted all these achievements with South Africa's drift and misery under Smuts's government. Smuts retorted that Hertzog's government had reaped where its predecessor had sown; it had been lucky in its economic weather, but would reveal its ineptitude when the weather changed. Whatever truth that prophecy might contain, the South African

---

* The figures include not only votes cast but an estimate of votes for uncontested seats, as follows: 85 % of the poll (at the national average of 80 %) has been allocated to the party whose candidate was returned unopposed and 15 % to the party which refrained from contesting the seat. For all calculations of totals and percentages I am indebted to Miss Clodagh O'Dowd of the University of Cape Town.

† See pp. 505–6 below.

electorate, like most others of that time, was in the mood to believe that bright weather would last forever. Two years or even one year later its mood, and possibly its voting, would have been different; but in June 1929 it felt a natural inclination towards the government associated with good times.

Even so, the colour issue was dominant. The Nationalists staked their fortunes on a gigantic campaign to convince the constituencies that white civilization was in danger. It was in danger, they said, because Smuts stood for *niksdoen*, for 'letting the situation develop', which meant letting white civilization drift on to the rocks. Worse than that, the country was in danger because Smuts stood for *gelykstelling*, the equality of black and white. In support of that indictment they quoted some sentences he had used in April 1928 when addressing an audience of Coloureds: he had even dared to quote Rhodes's tag about equal rights for all civilized men. But those words were as nothing when compared with his monstrous utterance at Ermelo on 17 January 1929. He had said, or was reported as saying—

Let us cultivate feelings of friendship over this African continent, so that one day we may have a British confederation of African states...a great African Dominion stretching unbroken throughout Africa...That is the cardinal point in my policy.

He denied later on that he had used the words 'African Dominion',* but it was too late. General Hertzog, Tielman Roos, and Dr Malan, as leaders of the National party in their respective provinces, issued their famous Black Manifesto.[23] It denounced Smuts as

the man who puts himself forward as the apostle of a black Kaffir state... extending from the Cape to Egypt...and already foretells the day when even the name of South Africa will vanish in smoke upon the altar of the Kaffir state he so ardently desires.

Day after day from January to June the Nationalist politicians and journalists quoted his Ermelo speech against him. If he got his way, they cried, White South Africa would be drowned in the Black North: or, if not quite drowned, it would begin to look like a little spot on the point of the tail of a powerful pitch-black African

* As reported at some length in the *Cape Times* of 18 January 1929, he had used those words, but not in the sense imputed to him by his opponents. As in his Rhodes Lectures later that same year (see pp. 223–9 below), he was thinking rather vaguely of confederal rearrangements of British African territories, under White leadership.

dog.* The cartoonists of *Ons Vaderland* and *Die Burger* let themselves loose on that theme. A cartoon of 8 March in the former paper pictured a lone white couple in a crowd of blacks, all dressed in smart city clothes, with the caption 'If the S.A.P. gets its way'. A cartoon of 21 March in the same paper showed a Griqua soldier with a white bride on his arm; the caption explained that a victory for Smuts would bring the country to *that*. Cartoons conveying the same message could have been counted by the score. Among the most effective was one which *Die Burger* published a week before the election. It showed a farmer grazing with dismay at an election poster supposedly put out by the South African party.

S tem vir die S wart A frika P arty

That was the warning and the battle cry reiterated week after week and day after day on every Nationalist platform and in the headlines, leading articles and correspondence columns of the Nationalist Press. To vote for Smuts meant voting black. To vote for Hertzog meant voting white. *Stem wit vir 'n witmansland!* Vote White for a White South Africa!

That propaganda proved efficacious.

* *Die Burger* (21 Jan. 1929) pictured ''n sterk pikswart hond met 'n kolletjie op die puntjie van sy stert'.

CHAPTER II

'PROFESSOR JAN SMUTS OF OXFORD'

Smuts told his friends that he had worked very hard and had expected better things, but that Hertzog's black bogey had beaten him. He did not feel heartbroken. The Nationalists, he said, had enjoyed prosperous times throughout their five years of power but the economic weather would soon be changing and then they would 'come a cropper'. When his friends the Gilletts put it to him that he could find some better way of serving his fellow-men than by fighting South African elections, he agreed with them that younger men of fresh outlook and new methods—if they could be found—might well succeed where their elders had failed. 'But', he continued, 'it is not so easy to pull out with credit. One does not like being a *quitter* as the expression is.'[1]

Nevertheless he felt himself to be only half employed. While parliament was in session he had as much work as he could cope with; but for six months or more of the year he had time on his hands. He told Arthur Gillett that he did not yet, and perhaps never would, feel equal to writing another book; for the present, he was just filling in time by doing the things that he liked doing. He was thoroughly enjoying his solitude. When people saw an old bull grazing apart from the herd, he reflected, they always assumed that the younger bulls had driven it away; 'but'—he asked—'is he not half willing to go and be alone and by himself?' He found refreshment in solitary walking, plant collecting, sun-bathing, reading, thinking. But then his mood would suddenly change and he would whip up volunteers to go on safari with him. In July 1929 he organized a nine days' safari to the Zimbabwe ruins; twelve months later he organized a much more ambitious one to Northern Rhodesia and Nyasaland. 'Our expedition', he told Arthur Gillett, 'was perhaps on the whole too strenuous, and we crowded into five weeks what would, not many years ago, have taken a year or more and what took Livingstone almost a lifetime.' But there was so much that he had wanted to see and do. Before setting out he had told Sir Ernest Oppenheimer that he would be 'having a good look round' at the prospects of development in the immensely promising Rhodesian copper belt, as well as collecting plants for Kew. The pace he made in 'Arthur Ford', his powerful touring car, proved too exhausting for his distinguished fellow-collector, Hutchinson of Kew; but the two other botanists in his party, Margaret Gillett and her son Jan, survived it.*[2]

Smuts by now was on terms of ease and intimacy with the leading botanists of South Africa and Kew. Meanwhile he was improving his acquaintance with C. van Riet Lowe and other South African prehistorians, and was in correspondence with L. S. B. Leakey of Kenya.[3] Year by year his knowledge and love of Africa grew deeper. At the same time, his roots remained deep and strong in the mother continent of his civilization. After the past six years of uninterrupted struggle on the home political front, culminating in the defeat of June 1929, he felt a strong urge to rediscover Europe. Unexpectedly, a way opened to him.

He found himself in demand as a lecturer. Immediately on his return from the safari to Zimbabwe he received an invitation to visit Oxford in November 1929 as Rhodes Memorial Lecturer. When the news of his acceptance became known, other universities, learned societies and voluntary societies in England, Scotland, the United States and Canada rained invitations on him. Before long he found himself heavily booked for November and the next two months. Then, on his return home in February 1930, he received an invitation from the University of St Andrews to deliver the Gifford Lectures. That honour he declined; but he could not possibly decline another honour offered to him almost simultaneously—the Presidency of the British Association for the Advancement of Science in its centenary year. His acceptance committed him to the delivery, eighteen months later, of the presidential lecture. Around the appointed day, 23 September 1931, other commitments were soon clustering. In two successive years he undertook two strenuous and exhilarating lecture tours.[4]

---

* Jan Gillett was his godson, and could also fairly be called his pupil in botany. The previous year, while still a schoolboy, he had made his first visit to South Africa. On the day of his departure, Smuts, as he drove him to the harbour, pointed to another ship sailing out. 'There', he exclaimed, 'the ship is already gone!' The boy answered, 'I wish it had!' Hutchinson was also in a sense the pupil of Smuts and deeply grateful to him, as he publicly acknowledged, for dragging him from the herbarium and helping him to understand African plants as living individuals and societies.

Out of Power, 1924–1933

He had a good reception both in Britain and in North America; but he knew only too well that a South African who won praise overseas was liable to fall under suspicion in his own country. A shrewd political commentator in Johannesburg wrote to him towards the end of his first tour:

I have been trying to watch what effect your absence would have in the two camps. As regards our own, your reception overseas has been truly gratifying to most. But some have undoubtedly come under the influence of the oft told tale of the Nationalists that all would be well if only you were safely out of the way. The old trick: destroy the leader and the army will go to pieces by itself...

A typical result of your absence was the party's attitude to the Quota, commonly called the anti-Jew Bill. The Nationalists knew that our ranks were divided and that only you have the needed authority to give us a united lead. They relied on that, and rightly so, because our lot became like a lot of lost sheep fearfully looking to the right and the left...

Now, as regards the other camp, they have, of course, looked sourly enough on the appreciation you have received everywhere else but in your own country...In their papers Professor Jan Smuts of Oxford is now dubbed an Uitlander.[5]

Throughout the sixteen years from 1924 to 1939, Smuts was only four times absent from South Africa. One of those four absences—at the World Economic Conference in 1934—was on public duty. The four together fell a long way short of twelve months. Nevertheless, the myth took root that he was continually gadding to other countries. He did not ignore that tittle-tattle, but neither did he let it intimidate him. His sense of propriety rather than prudential calculations determined the times that he fixed for his journeys overseas. So far as he was able, he arranged the tours of 1929 and 1931 in the parliamentary vacations and he controlled their duration by packing them almost unbelievably tight with the things that he thought worth doing. On each of the two voyages to England, and even on the short voyage in December 1929 from England to America, he kept himself hard at work on lecture preparation. During the eighteen days of his American and Canadian tour he delivered twenty-six long addresses and conducted hundreds of conversations, almost non-stop. After that effort, he told his wife, he had to spend nearly a week of the return voyage in making good the sleep that he had missed.[6]

He was able to fulfil these packed programmes without disgracing himself because he was speaking on subjects which for many years past had been continuously in his thoughts. He had three subjects: Africa, peace and science. Surprisingly, it was only under the third head that he said anything of continuing significance. Under the first two heads events were destined to work out differently from his prognostications.

Smuts had an African axe to grind. For the past five years he had been grinding it in concert with his friend Amery. In November 1924, when Amery became Secretary of State for the Colonies in Baldwin's government, Smuts wrote to him—

You will have to watch the whole East African situation very carefully if that great territory is not to become a purely Native State with an Indian trading aristocracy in charge. All the highlands of Eastern Africa from the Union to Abyssinia are healthy for Europeans and can be made a great European state or system of States during the next three or four generations. It is one of the richest parts of the world, and only wants white brains and capital to become enormously productive. But the present tendencies seem all in favour of the Native and the Indian, and the danger is that one of the greatest chances in our history will be missed. The cry should be 'the highlands for the whites' and a resolute white policy should be pursued. The fruits of such a policy will be a white State in time more important than Australia. There is land enough for all the vast Native population on the flanks of the highlands. But the Natives by themselves will continue to stagnate as they have stagnated for the last ten thousand years. A great White Africa along the Eastern backbone, with railway and road communications connecting North and South, will be a first-class addition to the Empire and will repay all the capital put into it. It is an expansion of the Rhodes policy. Why should it not become *your* policy?

Those sentences contained by anticipation the main thesis of the Rhodes Memorial Lectures. Amery approved the thesis and hoped to see it stamped upon the political map of East and Central Africa. How this could best be done he did not feel sure. One method, he told Smuts, would be the expansion of South Africa to the Zambesi or even into Northern Rhodesia, with a federation of white-controlled states to the north-east; another method would be for South Africa to stay within her existing borders, for the two Rhodesias to amalgamate, and for another amalgamation or federation to take shape in East Africa. Either way, he felt sure that Smuts would play a dominant part in shaping the future.[7]

In the event, neither Smuts nor Amery played a dominant part. Each man was underrating the strength of political opposition in his own country. In South Africa, Smuts lost the 1929 election on the cry that he was trying to make his country the miserable appendage to a mammoth Kaffir state. In Britain, Amery found himself pushed this way and that by a positively schizophrenic public opinion. Ever since the confrontation of the 1830s between systematic colonizers and negro emancipators, British governments had pursued violently contradictory colonial policies: for example, in 1923 the same government had granted responsible government to the white colonists of Southern Rhodesia and had proclaimed the paramountcy of African interests in Kenya. The Kenya colonists, to be sure, paid scant attention to that pious profession. They continued to claim Southern Rhodesian privileges and to clamour for a 'Great White Dominion'. As a first instalment, they demanded a settler majority in the Legislative Council and a settler-dominated East African Federation. Their Governor, Sir Edward Grigg, gave them his backing.* So did Smuts. So also did Amery, in so far as he could. But the opposition proved too strong for Amery. In January 1929 he had on his table a powerful report which aimed at barring and bolting the door against the political ambitions of the white settlers.† In the few months of office still remaining to him, he temporized. His successor, Lord Passfield, the Fabian socialist widely known as Sidney Webb, could reasonably be expected to give his verdict against the settlers. Nevertheless, the verdict remained still undelivered in November 1929, the month fixed for the Rhodes Memorial Lectures. Smuts, possibly, had some hopes that he might help to sway the new Secretary of State back to the side of the settlers.

Smuts went into action under the banner of David Livingstone—that heroic Scot,‡ he exclaimed, who in his own person became 'the first, the greatest and the most beneficient of the new forces for

---

* The schizophrenia of British policy had found expression even in the choice of East African Governors: Sir Donald Cameron of Tanganyika opposed settler claims to political domination as strongly as Sir Edward Grigg of Kenya supported them.

† A divided mind was once again to be observed even in the *Report of the Commission on Closer Union of the Dependencies in East and Central Africa* (Cmd. 3234 of 1929): the Chairman, Sir E. Hilton Young, dissented on some crucial issues from the majority of the Commission, whose main driving force was J. H. Oldham, secretary of the International Missionary Council.

‡ Smuts gave his main account of Livingstone in an address delivered to Scottish audiences in Edinburgh and Glasgow on 21 and 22 November: the address was published along with the Oxford lectures.[8]

change and progress'. Those forces, Smuts insisted, were irreversible. Their gathering momentum since Livingstone's death had hurried Africa into two revolutions: the revolution in transport, with railways and the internal-combustion engine taking the place of head porterage; the revolution in mining, with its massive investments and their dramatic economic consequences. White settlement followed as the natural and—in Smuts's view—the beneficient consequence of these two revolutions. Missionaries and officials were too thin on the ground, Smuts said, to bear the burden of African advancement; for that purpose, the weight and the numbers and the example of settled European communities were indispensible.

For without large-scale permanent European settlement on this continent the African mass will not be moved, the sporadic attempts at civilization will pass, Africa may relapse to her historic and prehistoric slumbers, and once more only mining holes and ruined forts may ultimately remain to bear testimony to future ages of what once was. We shall have a repetition of the Zimbabwe, and not an enduring impression on and betterment of the peoples of this continent.

Smuts, nevertheless, was well aware that his gospel of white settlement was out of favour in the radical company which the new Secretary of State kept. The settlers were under indictment for appropriating land which should have been reserved for African ownership and use. Smuts admitted that the white people of South Africa had made that calamitous mistake; but he believed that the white people of East Africa had avoided it. He ran over the figures of population and area to prove that there was land enough and to spare for all foreseeable African requirements, with a large surplus in the highlands for a deep-rooted European community. And that, he reiterated, was the indispensable steel framework of the whole ambitious structure of modern civilization in Africa.

Granted the plentiful supply of land, the whites and the blacks would be able, in Smuts's view, jointly to develop the resources of their continent and, at the same time, to live their own separate lives in their own separate communities. Smuts recognized 'the African Personality'. Naturally, he did not literally anticipate that slogan of a later generation; but he declared: 'The negro and the negroid Bantu form a distinct human type which the world would be poorer without.' Yet he had learnt from the functionalist school of social anthropology that the culture of the Bantu, like the culture of similar 'types', was distressingly fragile when it came under pressure from a more highly-developed civilization. His second Rhodes lecture contained some observations on that theme which Malinowski might well have made.* 'For the natives', he declared, 'religion, law, natural science, social customs and institutions, all form one blended whole, which enshrines their views of the world and the forces governing it. Attack this complex system at any single point, and the whole is endangered.' From that premiss, he argued the case for a policy which still at that time enjoyed prestige among British colonial administrators and the academic students of their practical endeavours. The policy had various names: parallel institutions; indirect rule; administrative separation. Those names had idealistic connotations; but a fourth name, segregation, possessed some South African associations which did not please British radicals.†

Whatever name was chosen, it was hard to see how Africans could at one and the same time live their separate lives in their separate areas and still become participators in European progress. Smuts found himself impaled on that dilemma. For the sake of civilizing the Native, he was offering him employment in the white man's sphere; for the sake of preserving his culture, he was offering him shelter in his own sphere. Smuts tried to escape from that contradiction along the path of migratory labour. The civilizing purpose was sufficiently served, he said, when the black man went out to work for a white master; the traditional culture was sufficiently safeguarded when the man's wife and children stayed at home. 'It is this migration of the Native family', he insisted, 'of the females and children to the farms and the towns, which should be prevented.'

The time was to come when he would change his mind about that;‡ but in November 1929 that time was still far off. In his own

* Up to the early 1930s (although not afterwards) it was a fair inference from B. Malinowski's published writings that he favoured a policy which would shield African societies from external pressures: that is to say, a policy of protective segregation. See, e.g., his 'Practical Anthropology' in *Africa*, vol. 2 (1929), pp. 22–8. See also the chapter by H. Ian Hogben in *Man and Culture. An Evaluation of the work of Malinowski*, ed. Raymond Firth (London, 1957). Nevertheless, Malinowski would have seen no scientific value in the 'child race' interpretation of African society which Smuts once or twice injected into his Rhodes Memorial Lectures.

† Smuts (see p. 113 above) used the label 'parallel institutions'; Lugard had used the label 'indirect rule'. However, by 1929 a different label was in favour with Lugard. 'Administrative separation' summed up his recommendations (and those of Miss Margery Perham) for Kenya. See Margery Perham, *Lugard. The Years of Authority* (London, 1960), ch. XXIII.

‡ See pp. 475, 490 below.

country, he maintained, African workers, including the migratory workers, were responding well to the demands and opportunities of economic and social progress. Meanwhile, the system of indirect rule had taken deep root; he traced its growth from Rhodes's Glen Grey Act through the Transkeian Bunga to his own Native Affairs Act, and he looked forward to the day when the larger part of the Native population would be managing their own local affairs, and thereby training themselves 'for eventual participation in a wider sphere of public life'. Nevertheless, he had to admit that his hopeful picture of a gradual evolutionary process did not fit all the facts. Large numbers of South Africa's Native population no longer had their roots in the Native areas. 'They raise a problem', he confessed, '...as they claim to be civilized and Europeanized, and do not wish to be thrust back into the seclusion of their former tribal associations, or to forego their new place in the sun among the whites.' His solution of the problem was to recognize their claim to a share in the political rights of South African citizenship.

He took it for granted that their share would be subordinate. He also left open the method of defining their share—whether by communal representation or by admission to the common roll, subject to the imposition of a strict 'civilization test'. The first method had British proconsular backing* and was contemporaneously operative in India, Kenya, and other territories under British rule; more to the point, it was Hertzog's method. The second method had been operative in the Cape for three successive generations and Smuts saw no sufficient reason for changing it. Whether or not a change was made, two principles seemed self-evident to him: first, South Africa's territory and sovereignty were indivisible; secondly, the Native population must have representation in the sovereign parliament. As he put it—

I do not think there can be, or that at bottom there is, among those who have given the subject serious attention, any doubt that in the supreme legislature of a country with a mixed population all classes and colours should have representation. It is repugnant to our civilized European ideas that the weaker in a community should not be heard or should go without representation, either by themselves or through European spokesmen, where their interests are concerned. There can be but one sovereign body in a country, and that body should represent the weaker no less than the stronger.

* See pp. 113, 114 above.

15-2

The Rhodes Memorial Lectures made little impact in long term upon British opinion; but their immediate impact appeared considerable. The Sheldonian theatre was crowded for the first lecture and uncomfortably packed for the second and third. A scholarly and liberal-minded historian, W. P. Morrell, gave Smuts exuberant praise in the *Oxford Magazine*. What must have pleased him still more was an evening talk that he had with Lugard at the Gilletts' house in Banbury Road. Lugard discovered a close identity of views between Smuts and himself upon the subject of 'administrative separation'. Writing to Smuts after their talk, he asked leave to quote from it in public.[9]

Lugard, however, was missing the drift of Smuts's argument, namely, his advocacy not only of white settlement in East Africa but also of white political predominance. That could not be reconciled with the gospel of imperial trusteeship which Lugard himself and his friend J. H. Oldham had been propagating for the past six years and more. Oldham had a genius for working behind the scenes and at this very time was employing it to sway the new Secretary of State to his side. He was also a formidable controversialist. Without waiting for the publication of Smuts's lectures in book form, he wrote and published at high speed a little book of his own under the title, *White and Black in Africa. A Critical Examination of the Rhodes Lectures of General Smuts*.*

Oldham, as he acknowledged in his last chapter, was in sympathy with Smuts on some issues, but not on the immediately crucial issue. His main purpose was to frustrate the political ambitions of the East African settlers. East Africa, he maintained, was not and never would be a Great White Dominion. Smuts's 'highland backbone' was a figment of his imagination; there was only 'a chain of islands', with strictly limited capacity for supporting a white farming population.† For this reason alone—apart from the dictates of conscience —domination by the white minority must be ruled out. For practical reasons of equal cogency, the domination of a black majority must be ruled out. Imperial trusteeship remained. For so far ahead as Oldham could see, that trusteeship must continue unshared and unimpaired.

---

* Oldham's book fell short of 20,000 words; but for his qualifications as author see note on p. 224 above.

† Oldham's count of the then existing white farming population was as follows: in Kenya, between 5,000 and 6,000 men, women and children; in Tanganyika, no farmers at all but only planters; in Uganda, not even planters.

The Secretary of State endorsed Oldham's argument in a famous White Paper of June 1930. Smuts called it 'the stupid White Paper on Paramountcy'.[10] He refused to accept it as the British government's last word. The issues, he insisted, remained open. So, indeed, for two more decades, they did.*

A dinner in London for veterans of the East African campaign constituted the link between Smuts's lectures on Africa and his lectures on peace. The organizer of the dinner, Captain A. W. Lloyd, with the backing of his committee and of Smuts, sent an invitation to General von Lettow Vorbeck, Smuts's adversary in the battles and the long pursuit of 1916. Inevitably, this gesture of reconcilation became the occasion of indignant letters to the newspapers; but the old soldiers applauded it. On the evening of 15 October 1929, both generals were present and both made appropriate speeches; but Smuts had a wider audience in mind than the 500 officers and men who represented his old army.

Wars [he said] are the sport of youth. It is probable that wars are an indication of the youth of the human race. But we have now reached maturity; we have sown our wild oats, and I hope that the Great War will prove the last of its kind and that mankind has learnt its lesson and will go forward in the paths of peace and build up a better world than that into which we were born.[11]

His hopes for peace hung mainly upon the League of Nations. He told his audiences in Oxford and elsewhere that the League was one of the great miracles of history; that it was not merely a paper constitution but a living human society; that there would have been no World War in August 1914 if the League had existed then. His implication was that the League, as it now existed, would be able to prevent a second World War. Unfortunately, he did not always distinguish between the League as it existed and the League of his dreams.

He dreamt of an all-inclusive League; but he knew that Russia and America were out of it. Unless Russia joined the League, he

---

* Lord Passfield showed himself more effective in stating a principle than in taking action to make it effective; his statement of June 1930 became the prelude to more inquiries and reports which had the effect of whittling the statement away. Even after the Second World War, the Labour government in Great Britain not only continued to encourage white settlement in Kenya but also conceded an elective majority on the Legislative Council—the prize for which the settlers had been contending for a generation or more. To be sure, the prize fell short in practice of the settlers' hopes.

told a friend, he could see no chance of disarmament in Europe, because no protocols or guarantees could be of any avail to a disarmed Europe, face to face with the vast war resources of a resuscitated Russian state with over 100,000,000 people.[12] Despite that sombre pronouncement, he encouraged his British and American audiences to look to the League for peace in their time. Yet Russia did not join the League until 1934. America never joined it. Those facts did not destroy his optimism. 'But I do believe', he wrote in May 1929, 'that serious war is quietly becoming impossible. And if America under the Kellogg Pact will back League action under Article 16, the trick will be done.'[13] In other words, American association with the League would prove just as serviceable to peace as American membership of it. That, at any rate, was the impression which he conveyed to his American audiences.

He dreamt of a non-coercive League. At the Paris Peace Conference, the French had wanted to give the League military teeth that would bite hard; but he had opposed them. He had opposed the Geneva Protocol and every other attempt to extend the military commitments of League members.[14] Almost to the last ditch, he had opposed the potential military commitments accepted by Great Britain under the Locarno Treaty.* Nevertheless, he was finding it convenient to bracket Article 16 of the Covenant—the sanctions article—with the toothless Kellogg Pact. He felt justified in doing this because he did not expect the sanctions teeth ever to bite in any military sense. At need, some economic nibbling might be permissible; but he expected the mere threat of sanctions to bring would-be aggressors to the conference table. Over and over again he told his British and American audiences that conference, not coercion, was the League's technique for preserving peace.[16]

He favoured a revisionist League. Article 10 of the Covenant displeased him because it gave the League's blessing to the territorial *status quo*; Article 19 pleased him because it gave the League's blessing to the revision of outmoded treaties. A good deal of treaty revision had taken place during the Briand–Stresemann era of Franco-German collaboration; but Stresemann died before Smuts delivered his Rhodes Memorial Lectures. Nevertheless Smuts hoped for a continuance of treaty revising; above all, he hoped for a great

* Here his realism contradicted his optimism; he was afraid of the Commonwealth someday finding itself in schism on a major issue of peace or war.[15]

British effort, led by Ramsay MacDonald, to achieve a breakthrough in disarmament. That, he believed, was the crucial issue for the League and for world peace.

Two years after his Rhodes Memorial Lectures he told an audience in Sheffield[17] that disarmament was an obligation imposed by the peace treaties not only upon the defeated, but also upon the victorious powers. Nevertheless, he did not see how the erstwhile Allies could be expected to reduce their armaments at one stroke to the German level. It was the first step, he said, that counted. He hoped that the forthcoming Disarmament Conference would take that step. Evidently, his hopes at Sheffield in October 1931 were not so high as they had been at Oxford in November 1929. For that diminution he had sufficient reasons—the world economic crisis, the rise of Hitler, Japan's invasion of Manchuria.

By now he was whistling to keep up his courage. In his private correspondence he still said sometimes that war was becoming impossible. Nevertheless, the rumours of war were spreading through the world like an epidemic. He put the blame on journalist scaremongers; but his fears sometimes went deeper. He shrugged them off with phrases. In October 1931 he wrote, 'The worst never happens.' In October 1932 he dismissed the darkening situation with a quip—'desperate but not yet serious'.[18]

On his lecture tour in America Smuts had found some rest in the home of his friends the Lamonts. Tom Lamont was a leading Wall Street financier and had been the ally of Smuts and Keynes in their endeavour, eleven years earlier, to inject financial commonsense into the deliberations of the Paris Peace Conference. Florence Lamont was charming, intelligent and a great letter writer. From 1930 up to the war years she and Smuts wrote to each other half a dozen or more long letters every year. He did not share her interest in music and the fine arts: once, when she was planning a tour in Italy, he told her, 'As a boy I was brought up on Livy and on Hannibal's campaigns and always, when I think of that country, the thought of Hannibal and his glorious march through it comes before my mind's eye. You see cathedrals and I see battlefields in the haze of the past.' Nevertheless, he continued, he and she were both addicted to philosophical inquiry. Children asked the most enormous questions in the most matter of fact way, and what were they but grown-up children? 'I want an answer', he exclaimed, 'to the insistent question: how has value become a reality?'[19]

In his presidential address to the British Association at its centenary celebrations in September 1931, he sketched the outlines of an answer. In doing so, he announced the theme of the next big book that he wanted to write.* The universe which he had depicted in *Holism and Evolution* was structural in each of its successive evolutionary forms: values, he now suggested, belonged to the same structural order.

The free creativeness of mind is possible because, as we have seen, the world ultimately consists, not of material stuff but of patterns, of organization, the evolution of which involves no absolute creation of an alien world of material from nothing. The purely structural character of reality thus helps to render possible and intelligible the free creativeness of life and mind, and accounts for the unlimited wealth of fresh patterns which mind freely creates on the basis of the existing physical patterns.

The highest reach of this creative process is seen in the realm of values.

That statement came towards the end of his lecture and was the culmination of a long argument. He had announced as his title 'The Scientific World-Picture of Today' and had justified it by presenting *homo sapiens* to his audience as a picture-making animal, with a persistent disposition to make comprehensive pictures of his particular experiences: there had been, for example, the pre-scientific pictures of magic, animism and the early nature gods; subsequently, there had been pictures which deserved to be called scientific, in virtue of the disciplined observation which they embodied. Science, he suggested, had been closely related for some centuries past to commonsense, with its world of material stuff, of real separate things and properties acting on each other and causing changes in each other. This commonsense world-picture had been sufficiently realistic and spacious to stimulate, and in large measure to contain the prodigious scientific advances from Newton's day until close to the end of the nineteenth century; but since then it had been dissolving and giving place to a new world-picture. The point of departure had been reached, he suggested, when physical science began to dig down below the level of things directly observed and to find below this level things resistant to direct observation, but necessary to account for the facts of observation.

* The second book, which he long hoped to, but never did, write, will be referred to henceforward as *Holism II*. See pp. 341, 395–6, 427, 523–4 below.

So far, he had been recapitulating the argument of *Holism and Evolution*. He had been telling again at speed and in vivid prose his story of the evolving cosmic structure from the curves of space-time to the emergence of man; from matter through life to mind, from organization through organism to organizer. But now he suddenly collided with the second law of thermodynamics. The collision occurred along the road of his reflections about the contrasted characters of biological time and space-time. Biological time, he said, had a flow from past to future like the 'before' and 'after' of human experience; it was historical; it suggested a forward striving. But the space-time of physics was neutral as regards direction; it could be a plus or a minus. In the light of the second law of thermodynamics, it looked like a minus. That was what the astronomers seemed to be reporting. A confrontation had emerged between cosmic process and organic evolution, between the vast physical universe with its movement towards disintegration and the small organic world with its movement towards integration. Life could be pictured as a minority movement upwards in a universe where the majority movement was downwards.

The energy which is being dissipated by the decay of physical structure is being partly taken up and organized into life structures—at any rate on this planet. Life and mind thus appear as products of the cosmic decline, and arise like the phoenix from the ashes of a universe radiating itself away. In them Nature seems to have discovered a secret which enables her to irradiate with imperishable glory the decay to which she seems physically doomed.

Or, if one chose to express it more prosaically, life was off the main track of the universe.

Smuts was making a report upon beliefs which were prevalent not only in scientific circles but also, increasingly, in literary circles. Those beliefs fell short of proven scientific truth. To Smuts, they seemed a medley of tested theory, provisional hypothesis, debatable inference and ignoble panic. Even if the universe had started with a bang unnumbered millions of years ago, he saw no sufficient reason for any self-respecting man to start whimpering now.*

---

* In a prudent footnote, Smuts left open the debate about the cosmic origins and destiny. Sherrington, in delivering his Gifford Lectures nine years after Smuts's lecture to the B.A.A.S., found himself similarly confronted with the second law of thermodynamics. His way of escape was through the Cartesian dualism of mind and non-mind, which Smuts rejected. Smuts was not looking for a way of escape. Lord Cohen, in *Sherrington, Physiologist,*

He preferred his own picture of the universe as structure, making itself manifest in 'wholes' increasingly complex and integrated, all the way from space-time to values. To be sure, that picture was not strictly the product of scientific observation and reasoning; but no more was its opposite. Towards the end of his lecture, he staged once again a confrontation of the opposites:

Our origin is thus accidental, our position is exceptional and our fate is sealed, with the inevitable running down of the solar system. Life and mind, instead of being the natural flowering of the universe, are thus reduced to a very casual and inferior status in the cosmic order...According to astronomy, life is indeed a lonely and pathetic thing in this physical universe—a transient and embarrassed phantom in an alien, if not hostile universe.

To that lament on man's miserable estate, Smuts made his defiant answer:

The human spirit is not a pathetic, wandering phantom of the universe, but is at home, and meets with spiritual hospitality and response everywhere. Our deepest thoughts and emotions are but responses to stimuli which come to us not from an alien, but from an essentially friendly and kindred universe.[20]

His defiance was magnificent; but it was not science, as Professor Hogben had defined science.* Nevertheless, ten highly competent men of science, thirty-three years later, submitted Smuts's lecture to a rigorous examination. All ten gave him credit for descriptive accuracy in the wide fields of his scientific interest. Two of the ten denied the scientific character of his 'world picture'; it was, they admitted, a possible picture, but it was not the product of inductive reasoning; rather it was an interpretation of scientific fact and theory in the light of an already determined point of view. The remaining eight applauded Smuts not only for his accuracy but also for his interpretative insight. Some of them found his lecture just as much alive in 1964 as it must have been on the day of its delivery, 23 September 1931. In rueful agreement with that verdict, a distinguished physicist confessed that he had attended the lecture, but had not listened to it, because he had been wanting all the time to be back at his bench in the Cavendish Laboratory. He now wrote—

Philosopher and Poet (Liverpool, 1958), pp. 60–1, discusses some of the issues in a manner which suggests that Smuts had rational grounds for refusing to let the second law of thermodynamics intimidate him.

* See pp. 190–1 above.

Why didn't I listen?...

The reporting is excellent, and completely in accord with the atmosphere of the time. It certainly avoids flagrant errors, and identifies, far more clearly than most men of science did in that period, the significant trends of scientific evaluation. It suggests insights and interpretations which were not only worth considering at that time, but which are very much alive today...Dated? No! A living contribution to thought which deserves to become an indispensable part of the education of every man of science.*

To Smuts, 23 September 1931 was 'the great day'. He used those words in a letter the following day to his wife: *Gister was die groot dag*. He had still ahead of him then a good many more days of heavy presidential duty, and when at last the conference was over he confessed that he had found it exhausting to have to live for two hectic weeks with the potentates of science. Moreover, he confessed, the intense pursuit of the abstract was bound in time to exhaust any man.[21]

His craving by now was for something limited and manageable to think about. On the voyage home he read Leakey's latest book on East African prehistory and discussed South African prehistory with his travelling companion, van Riet Lowe. The idea of a new article or lecture began to take shape in his head.

I have also been much interested [he wrote from his ship] in Leakey's book, and I have worked out certain parallelisms for climate and man in South Africa, which I may write up later if I have time. It is a fascinating subject—the oscillations of climate with the appearance of man through the ages. The evidence from South Africa and East Africa supplements the European information in a curious way, and *vice versa*.

He carried the idea home with him and during the Christmas vacation at Doornkloof he wrote his paper, *Climate and Man in Africa*. Eighteen months later, he delivered it as a lecture in Durban to the South African Association for the Advancement of Science. The lay members of his audience must have found his argument and its supporting tables hard to follow; but he hoped that they had at least found his slides interesting. He had two hypotheses to

* The ten men of science whom I consulted were my colleagues at the Australian National University. I asked them the following questions. Did the lecture contain any flagrant errors, or was its scientific reporting reliable? Was it well constructed? Given the state of scientific knowledge in 1931, were the interpretations which it put forward sensible and suggestive? Finally, were its facts and interpretations out of date in 1964, or would the lecture still be worth listening to, despite the lapse of 33 years?

propose: first, that the pleistocene scheme of climatic change, as worked out in Europe, was applicable not only to East Africa, as Leakey and others maintained, but also to South Africa; secondly, that a similar correspondence between the three regions could be discovered, or at least looked for, in the field of archaeological and anthropological research. Given the primitive state at that time of climatological and archaeological research in Africa, he knew that he had to walk warily; but he hoped that scientific investigators might find his hypotheses worth testing.

And so they did. John Goodwin of Cape Town wrote to ask him for extra copies of the lecture, which was, in Goodwin's view, 'a landmark in the history of both geology and climatology in their relation to human history'.[22] Thirty years later, notwithstanding the great advances of research since July 1932, that still remained the widely-held opinion of South African geologists and archaeologists.*

It was appropriate that the last lecture in the 1929–31 courses of Professor Jan Smuts should have dealt with African material. In his first lecture, he had told his sophisticated Oxford audience that he had no other qualification for speaking to them except that he was an African.

---

* This judgment is based on the answers given to questions closely identical with those mentioned in the note on p. 235.

CHAPTER 12

REUNION

FROM 1930 onwards Smuts smelt victory; but in his day of opportunity he did not pluck the ripe political pear. In February 1933 he accepted office under Hertzog.

Many years later, his remarkable decision produced some remarkable comment. Looking back to 1933 with after-knowledge of Hitler's war, Oswald Pirow gave Smuts credit for uncanny foresight and superb manipulative skill. To be sure, Pirow said, he had been forced to eat his own words and to swallow such principles as he possessed; but he had reckoned all that a small price to pay for the great prizes in store for him—the disruption of Hertzog's party, the preservation of his own party, the destruction of his country's independent foreign policy, the triumph of his own holistic imperialism.[1]

But that retrospective interpretation of the politics of reunion had not occurred to contemporary observers and participants. Oswald Pirow himself, the politician who was closest to Hertzog throughout the negotiations of 1933, gave credit at the time to his own leader for political foresight and skill. The great majority of contemporary observers gave credit to both leaders for patriotism. As they looked forward into the still unrecorded future, they did not foresee, any more than Smuts or Hertzog did, the events of September 1939. As they looked back upon the recorded past, they saw a slow but sure convergence of the policies for which the two leaders had stood. Most of them welcomed that convergence. Most of them were ready for reconciliation. Most of them believed that it would prove permanent.

Hertzog and Smuts had been locked in political combat for the past twenty years; but their combat had been more about means than ends. They both affirmed South Africa's sovereign equality in the community of nations. With equal insistence, they both affirmed *Suid-Afrikaanse Volkseenheid*—the ideal of South African nationhood based upon equality between the two European cultures. Hertzog's rejection of the conciliation policy* had been a rejection of its

* See pp. 23–4 above.

timing, not its principle. He had feared a political sell-out to the dominant British Empire and a cultural sell-out to the dominant English language. In 1913 he had believed that he saw good grounds for his fears; but by 1933 he no longer believed it. The Afrikaans language* and the culture of Afrikaners were by now securely established. South African sovereignty was by now indisputable. There was no longer a single reason, Hertzog declared in 1930, why South Africans belonging to the two cultures should not feel and act together in the spirit of a consolidated South African nation.

In effect, Hertzog was announcing that he was ready at long last to adopt the policy of concilation. Whereas Smuts had made his journey to Damascus in 1906, when he encountered Campbell-Bannerman, Hertzog had made his journey in 1926, when he encountered the Commonwealth Prime Ministers. On his return home, he had told South Africans that secession from the Commonwealth would give them no more freedom than they possessed already: 'It would not be in our interests; it would be foolish, and I believe that if it were proposed not 5 per cent of the population could be got to vote for it.' Inevitably, Hertzog claimed the main praise of achievement for his own party; but sometimes he gave a little credit to Smuts for bringing *his* party to the right way of thinking. The South African party, he declared in 1928, had now become so nationalist that if it had always been like that the Nationalists need never have left it.[2]

Why, then, continue the ancient quarrel? Under the new circumstances, Afrikaners began to show a renewed interest in *hereniging*, reunion. The reunion of whom with whom? Different people gave different answers to that question. The Afrikaner Broederbond, for example, gave an un-advertised but clear-headed answer.[3] The Broederbond by now had far outgrown its humble origins.† While still keeping a strict check upon the increase of its members, it chose them carefully; they were all nationalist Afrikaners, in situations of influence. The Broederbond was now maintaining a network of cells and branches in every Province of the Union, with the exception of Natal. Its executive council had mastered the techniques of devolution and of interlocking control; in 1927, for example, those techniques had found embodiment in the Federasie van Afrikaanse

---

* Since 1925 the Afrikaans, not the Dutch language.
† See p. 26 above.

Kultuurverenigings, commonly called the F.A.K. In its turn, the F.A.K. practised the same techniques, thereby making itself the mother-ship of scores of smaller craft.* The entire cultural life of Afrikaners was beginning to bear the Broederbond stamp of *Afrikaner-volkseenheid*. Its meaning was that the Afrikaners were by themselves a nation. So indeed they were, in the linguistic and cultural meaning of nationality. But nationality possessed also a political meaning. If *Afrikanervolkseenheid* signified an Afrikaner political structure, with its own exclusive symbols and ideology, the consequence would be Milnerism in reverse, with South Africans of the English culture living on sufferance in their own country.†

Hertzog and Smuts were both insistent that South African nationality, in its political significance, must remain the common and equal possession of the two European cultures. As Afrikaner politicians, both of them in their different ways were practioners of the policy of partnership: Smuts was leading a bilingual party closely comparable with Canada's Liberal party; Hertzog's pact with English-speaking Labour had brought him to power. If reunion meant the establishment of a monolithic and exclusive Afrikaner party, both leaders would have to reject it. If, on the other hand, it meant no more than the healing of their own personal and political feud, they could both accept it. Even so, they would each be bound to scrutinize with close care the means proposed for achieving it. Neither would be willing to impose upon his own party the main costs of reunion while conceding to the opposing party its main profits.

Thus the Afrikaner political leaders, like the Afrikaner ideologues, had a clear idea of what they wanted, or were ready at need to accept. Other Afrikaners, without expending much thought upon the precise definition of ends and means, preached reunion-at-large as a good cause.

Gys Hofmeyr, the former Administrator of South West Africa, issued a public appeal for reunion in July 1926 and followed it up six months later with an open letter in identical terms to Hertzog and Smuts. He did not ask them then and there to dissolve their respective parties, but told them that the time had come for them

* By the early 1940s approximately 300 Afrikaner associations, cultural and economic, were affiliated to the F.A.K.
† See p. 330 below.

to rebuild Afrikaner unity.* How they were to do this he did not explain. Neither leader took action on his appeal and in February 1927 Smuts told Louis Esselen that reunion seemed to be quite dead.[4]

Nevertheless, Smuts reported later the same year that there was still 'a great deal of hereniging talk about'. Prominent among the talkers was Gys Hofmeyr's nephew, J. F. H. Hofmeyr—the infant prodigy, the Oxford phenomenon, the 22-year-old Professor, the 24-year-old Principal of a University College. As Principal, the young Hofmeyr had behaved on one occasion like a prig and an autocrat; but part of the blame could plausibly be put upon his inexperience, or upon his mother's interference; besides, if he had been foolish in making unnecessary trouble, he had also been courageous in coping with it. Smuts, at any rate, continued to believe in him and in his destiny as a South African statesman. In November 1920 Smuts had offered him employment as organizing secretary of the South African party; in February 1924 he appointed him Administrator of the Transvaal. Everybody was astonished at the elevation of so young a man to so exalted a position; but Smuts recalled that he himself had been younger still when President Kruger appointed him State Attorney of the South African Republic.† He told Hofmeyr that he had always wanted to bring him into political life and was delighted that the opportunity had come sooner than he had expected. Hofmeyr made good use of the opportunity. From 1924 to 1928 he won a well-deserved reputation not only as an administrator but also as a politician; in particular, he skilfully maintained his neutral position between the two parties. As his term of office approached its end, both parties made bids for his political services. He committed himself to neither of them. On Union Day 1928 he broadcast an appeal to both parties to wind themselves up and join their forces in a great new party of like-minded men.[5]

This new appeal for reunion was as high-minded and imprecise as the elder Hofmeyr's appeal had been; but it created more stir. However, the people who responded to it held conflicting opinions about the right road to reunion. Some people favoured reconciliation

---

* *vir die heling van die breuke onder ons Afrikanervolk.*

† Smuts recalled somebody's mocking exclamation when the old President chose him for high office—'*My God, het Paul nou sy kop verloor?*'

between the old leaders; others wanted the leaders to stand aside and leave the work to younger men. Some people expected the new party to lead the country towards liberal policies; others expected it to fight communism and deal firmly with the Indians and Natives. Amidst this confusion, the rival politicians continued to bid against each other for Hofmeyr's allegiance. Hofmeyr still kept them guessing. He spent nearly six months in fending off an attempt by Smuts to get him committed as the S.A.P. candidate for Barberton. Nevertheless, Smuts remained patient with him.

His sympathies [Smuts wrote to a front bench colleague] are strongly with us; but he is also a sort of 'hereniging's man', very much as Gys was a year ago. I think that is a point on which he is really troubled. As you know, the Hofmeyr mind naturally turns to Hereniging. I am for it also if we can call the tune, instead of playing second fiddle.

Smuts at that time was hoping to win the 1929 election. Nor had he yet quite given up hope that Hofmeyr would join the fight on his side. Hofmeyr, however, had gone away with his mother on a tour overseas. He returned in time to vote; not to fight. He did, however, declare himself at long last on Smuts's side, and in October 1929 he carried the S.A.P. flag to victory in a by-election in Johannesburg North. Another chapter of the reunion story had closed.[6]

Nevertheless, although nobody at that time realized it, a new chapter was already opening with the bitter economic blizzard which began to blow in 1929 and continued for the next three years to gather force and spread ruin. About the same time, the worst drought within living memory began to scourge South Africa.

And the drought [Smuts wrote in December 1930] becomes part of people's psychology—you see a dull expression and you know *that* is what all are thinking about. You see how the soft spots in character go and the mind hardens. The Arab character is desert bred; so largely is that of the Jews. The psychology of the desert is creeping over South Africa too.

He called to mind the valley of dry bones in the Book of Ezekiel. Meanwhile, the party zealots were wanting him to direct his mind to the dazzling political opportunities now arising from the economic disaster. The Nationalists, they told him, were riven by factions. Tielman Roos, despite his recent translation to judicial office, was pursuing a political intrigue. The whole crazy political fabric would soon be falling down like a pack of cards. Smuts took note of those prognostications but said that he was waiting until the mists cleared up.[7]

He continued waiting well into 1931. 'The government', he wrote in July, 'is rapidly proceeding to hang itself'; but he was still giving it rope. That remained his mood until two days before his British Association lecture, when the news broke that Britain was off the gold standard. 'The ark of the Covenant', he exclaimed, 'the pound sterling has gone.' That meant action at last. He cabled an urgent message to South Africa to leave the gold standard and join the new sterling area. After some hesitation,* his party fell into line behind him. At an emergency session of parliament in November 1931 the Opposition challenged the government to take the country off gold. The government said No. As a conservative, and until recently a fortunate Minister of Finance, Havenga had hopes of steering South Africa through the financial and economic storm by means of a primage duty on imports and a subsidy on exports. As a champion of South African sovereignty, Hertzog made gold his symbol. He set out to demonstrate his country's independence not only in the political but also in the economic sphere. Smuts considered Hertzog's worship of 'the golden calf' ruinous to the real interests of South Africa. He believed that he had a good cause to fight for.[8]

Even so, he could not completely dismiss the possibility that coalition, not combat, would resolve the crisis. Louis Esselen and Tielman Roos had been talking with each other. Pirow, certainly, knew about their talks. Esselen believed that Pirow was reporting them to Hertzog; and it was his hope to bring Smuts into them when he returned from the science congress. In a letter to Roos on 11 November 1931, Esselen put his plan on record.

Pirow has indicated to me that if it can be arranged by Oom Jannie [Smuts] he will meet you two so that matters can be discussed, and I may add that this has the concurrence of General Hertzog. Oom Jannie is quite willing and the only thing that remains as to [*sic*] how you want me to arrange the meeting. I would suggest that you and the Chief first have a conversation and he can then send for Pirow.

For the good of South Africa and all of us, I want to make an earnest appeal to you to help us in obtaining what you and I and many others have striven for for a long time. With a little give and take I feel confident

---

* Duncan and Hofmeyr took their cue at first from the mining industry; it was reluctant to leave the gold standard because that would mean a rise in money wages, which would not be easily brought down if and when South Africa returned to the gold standard. Fortunately for South Africa, that phase of economic thought did not last long.

that our efforts will be crowned with success. The new Party must come and the sooner the better, and I feel sure that in a year or two you will emerge a greater man than you have ever been before.[9]

That letter foreshadowed the kaleidoscopic changes which started twelve months later; but throughout the greater part of 1932 the two political parties followed a collision course.

In a whirlwind tour of the Union early in the New Year Smuts denounced the government for its ruinous obsession with the gold standard. He painted a vivid picture of the impending collapse of the public finances, the progressive strangulation of export industry and domestic trade, the sufferings of ordinary people. His speeches made a big impact, particularly upon his country audiences.

General [a Free State farmer wrote to him] please don't give them any rest until you get them to see daylight it still seems to me they don't know what is going on in the Country, here the town and District is like a grave-yard absolutely dead for days you can't see a farmer in town shops are closing Hotels are doing nothing farmers are killing sheep for the market and are selling at about 3/- to 4/- each. A farm that cost £7/10/0 a morgen 4 years ago last year was for sale and the offer was £3/15/0. Last month this same farm was sold for 37/6d a morgen the farmer cannot get a 1/- credit and the store-keeper is unable to meet his liabilitys. We are abso-lutely moneyless and going from bad to worse. On the 30 of Dec we had a meeting and passed a Resolution to come off the gold standard. This week they brought Pen Wessels and packed the meeting with backvelders, and appealed to their national feeling and got the vote reversed. It is a great pity you have not sent in men to tell them the truth. Please go on with the good work and get them to go off or go under for a good long time they will not be missed.[10]

When parliament met, Smuts denounced the government for bringing the country to the edge of ruin by its doctrinaire obstinacy, its politics of prestige and its economics of deflation. He won the upper hand in debate, but did not pitch his hopes too high.

We had great fun [he wrote on 12 April] last week in Parliament. I pro-duced a *sterling* budget (off gold) in which I showed no cuts, no retrench-ments, no new taxation and a good surplus—compared with the cuts and heavy taxes and deficit of the government's gold budget. People are im-pressed by an ocular demonstration like that, and the government are making frantic efforts to upset my budget. I don't myself view the matter too seriously, but it has been excellent fun and has had a good effect politically. Not that I am over anxious to upset the government too soon. If once we are in harness again it will be a slave's job.

But there was no immediate prospect of his getting into harness again. As he confessed six weeks later, his successes in debate had failed to shake the government.

It has been a barren and disappointing session. I had some vague hope of being able to turn the Government out during the session, but the Nats and a few Labourites hung together like thieves; and the suffering of the country continues. I don't know how long this will go on—perhaps till next session or longer. But somehow I feel that the country cannot stand this economic strain on the gold standard much longer and that the end may come sooner than one thinks.[11]

During the parliamentary vacation he had serious political trouble of his own with the devolution movement in Natal. At the same time, the government regained some of its prestige at the Ottawa Conference, thanks to Havenga's good performance as a negotiator of tariff preferences—although Smuts believed that the Conference would have done far more good if, instead of haggling over tariffs, it had fixed the £ at 12s. and thereby secured the higher price level which everybody was talking about. Smuts confessed to being disappointed, although on the figures he need not have been, by his party's failure to capture Colesberg at a by-election. None the less, he believed that the country was swinging his way. 'The Nats', he wrote after one of his speech-making tours, 'while still sticking to their party, are beginning to think that their policies may be wrong and I may be right. More than that I don't expect for the present.'[12]

But more, far more than that, was brewing. At the Germiston by-election in December 1932 J. G. N. Strauss, a young man whom Smuts had been wanting for some time past to bring into politics,[13] inflicted a shattering defeat on the Nationalists. That was the signal for Tielman Roos to go into action. Hitherto he had worked behind the scenes; but on Dingaan's Day he appeared on a public platform to denounce the gold standard and demand a National Government. Six days later (22 December) he announced his resignation from the Bench in order to fight for those great causes. The effect was dramatic. People rushed to the banks to get their money out of the country in the hope of finding themselves able before long to get it back again at a premium. The banks told the government that it was impossible any longer to defend the gold standard. On 28 December the government told the country that it was off gold.

Immediately, the country felt the weight of the depression lifting from off its back. That, precisely, was what Smuts had prophesied when he had expounded his sterling budget. But the people were no longer thinking about Smuts. Roos was now their prophet and hero, their Joshua whose shouting had brought down the walls of the gold standard. They expected him to keep on shouting until he had achieved his second miracle, the National Government. Roos was ready to oblige them.

Roos, as Smuts saw him, was a charlatan; but he had broken the log jam. 'The situation', Smuts wrote to John Martin, 'is now fluid, and we may just have the chance of achieving some lasting good.'[14] He meant lasting good for South Africa. But how to define it? More than a month went by before he felt sure of his definition. Meanwhile, he and his party had to face the challenge that had been flung at them: would they or would they not accept the leadership of Roos in a new political combination? Smuts's chief counsellors in the ensuing negotiations were Esselen, Duncan, Reitz and Hofmeyr. According to the record which Hofmeyr kept,[15] Smuts on two separate occasions declared himself ready to stand down if that was in the best interests of the party and the nation. His intimate colleagues would not hear of his standing down. In consequence, the negotiations became a debate about what Roos could offer to the South African party and what he wanted in exchange. Roos had won too much success too soon; the government's action in leaving gold had deflated his political value. He could offer the evanescent magic of his own name and the votes of about fifteen Nationalist politicians—sufficient for a short-term victory over Hertzog. In exchange, he wanted the leadership of the new government and half the ministerial portfolios. Under pressure, he scaled down these demands just a little; but when Smuts met him face to face in the third week of January 1933 the negotiations foundered. Smuts was prepared for that; he had told his wife two weeks before that the talks with Roos would never come to anything.[16]

All the same, he had been right to let them run their course. He had realized from the start that he would have to steer a passage through stormy cross-currents of national and party feeling. Reconciliation was the cry of the country; victory was the cry of the party. After eight long years of frustration, the S.A.P. rank and file could hardly bear to see their leader let slip this heaven-sent chance of bringing

the Nationalists crashing down. They demanded a party caucus.
Throughout two days of passionate debate Smuts listened to a
majority of his parliamentary followers upbraiding him for failing
to clinch the deal with Roos. Gradually, the debate swung to an
even balance and on the third day Smuts broke silence. He told
them quietly that he would never serve under Roos. What lasting
good, he asked them, could Roos bring to the country? Certainly,
he could bring about Hertzog's overthrow; but the price to pay for
that would be perpetual embitterment. Did they want national
embitterment? Or did they want national unity?

By a unanimous vote the caucus reaffirmed its confidence in Smuts
and gave him full powers to conduct any further negotiations. Now
that Roos had been put aside, the only person to negotiate with
was Hertzog. For Smuts to make an approach to Hertzog was asking
almost too much. He had too often felt the lash of Hertzog's tongue.
He and Hertzog were temperamentally at odds with each other.
'His is a strange mind', he told a friend, 'without a spark of humour,
that savingest of the Christian virtues.'[17] He could hardly see himself
coping as a colleague, although he could cope well enough as an
opponent, with the emotional oscillations of Hertzog: one day he
would be sweetly reasonable, the next day he would make violent
and unreasonable attacks on anybody who contradicted or criticized
him. Nevertheless, Smuts gave him credit for consistency of principle.
Despite his unpredictable gusts of passion, he followed a predictable
road. Smuts was ready to believe that his own long march and
Hertzog's march had led them at long last to the threshold of
reconciliation. After a hard struggle with his pride he put that
belief to the test. On 30 January he moved in parliament 'that the
Government should tender its resignation forthwith and so afford
an opportunity for the formation of a national Government'. He said
that he was appealing for a new start; but he did not make his
appeal persuasive. He could not forbear from reminding the government of its pledge to maintain the gold standard—yet there it was,
he exclaimed, still clinging to office after it had failed to make its
pledge good. No doubt he had to use words like those for the
satisfaction of his own followers; he had shamed them into renounc-
ing victory; but they would not forgive him if he sued too weakly
for peace. None the less, his words nearly destroyed the chance of
peace. They stung Hertzog into a passionate rejection of his ap-

peal, a torrent of self-justification, counter-accusation and insult.[18] By the time he sat down, Hertzog had to all appearances killed reunion.

Nevertheless, individuals in both parties still continued to work for reunion. Hofmeyr was the main intermediary. He told Smuts next day that Hertzog would welcome a second approach from him. After the insults of the previous day, that was a lot to expect from a proud man. But the good of the country? Let the National Government be formed, Smuts said, with his support but without his participation. Hofmeyr told him that it could not be done. Smuts promised to think the situation over. On 1 February he rose in parliament to wind up the debate. He expressed disappointment at its tone and the course it had taken. 'Perhaps I am to blame', he said. 'Perhaps I have handled the subject unskilfully...I did not want to start a general indictment of the government or a general dogfight.' He renewed his appeal for unity.[19] Now at last he had broken the log jam, more quietly but more effectively than Roos had broken it seven weeks before on Dingaan's Day.

Some time still went by before the old enemies met. Smuts had threshed the business out with his caucus but Hertzog had not yet called his together and when he did so he found it divided; he had a majority behind him for reconciliation but Malan, with a compact body of supporters, was fiercely against it. Hertzog told his caucus that he could not leave Smuts's appeal unanswered and on 14 February sent him proposals for coalition. Next day the two men spoke with each other face to face. Formal negotiations followed. On 28 February Hertzog informed the House that agreement had been reached to establish a coalition government 'on a basis more or less of equal participation and on the basis of principles laid down beforehand'.[20]

From the second week of February Smuts had been receiving letters expressive of the affection and respect his friends felt for him. Many people regarded with awe so unusual a sacrifice of personal ambition. The Governor-General wrote—

But what I particularly want to say to you now is how much I feel South Africa owes you...In spite of the general expectation of the success of yourself and your party at the next general election you put aside all personal and party advantages in favour of a step which, in your view, was in the best interests of the Union. This self-effacing act on your part...

this very grand thing you have done is a deed which will gloriously enrich the pages of South African political history.

More even than that letter Smuts must have treasured one which he received a month later from the widow of President Steyn. In the years of struggle against the British the Steyns and the Smutses had been close family friends, but politics had subsequently estranged them and Mrs Steyn had continued the estrangement after her husband's death. She now made a move to end it. She told Smuts that she would never have believed that he would agree to serve under General Hertzog, even if an angel from heaven had prophesied it. She told him that his great courage and self-sacrifice filled her with wonder.[21]

Smuts took office under Hertzog as Minister of Justice. In some respects, it was the same office as he had taken in 1898 under President Kruger. He cited that coincidence in a cool, self-mocking mood. 'It is really funny', he reflected, 'that I should be back at the very job I had 35 years ago...at the mature age of 28...And then they call this a Department of *Justice*!'[22]

PART III

SECOND MAN IN THE STATE, 1933–1939

CHAPTER 13

FROM COALITION TO FUSION

THE terms of coalition were contained in the seven articles of a public statement agreed by the two leaders.[1] The first three articles revealed the close, if not yet the complete, identity of their constitutional and political ideas—South Africa's sovereign status and its recognition in the Statute of Westminster; her territorial and jurisdictional unity, as symbolized by the national flag; at the base of it all, equality between the two linguistic groups of European South Africans. The fourth, fifth and seventh articles proclaimed an agreed national policy of economic development and social welfare, with specific mention of the civilized labour policy. But the sixth article suggested that the two leaders were not as yet of one mind on the colour question. Hertzog had wanted to get his own proposals for Native land and franchise written into the terms of coalition; but the most that he got was agreement to make an 'earnest effort' to solve the Native question along lines that would place the requirements of white civilization in the forefront, without depriving the Native of his right to develop, with separate political development of white and black. The promise merely to make an 'earnest effort' registered a check to Hertzog; but the specification of its direction gave him cause to hope that the check would prove temporary.

The costs of coalition to the two leaders and their parties were not yet predictable. Smuts had to face grumbling in Natal, where the lunatic fringe of S.A.P. members found even the Statute of Westminster anti-British, and in the Cape, where F. S. Malan and some other S.A.P. members resented the still-continuing dominance of the Transvaal contingent; but the party caucus remained solid in his support. Hertzog had to fight a hard battle in the Nationalist caucus. D. F. Malan had opposed the coalition talks from the start and he now publicly attacked Hertzog for conducting and concluding them without the backing of a united caucus. He found nearly thirty co-signatories for his manifesto; a formidable phalanx with a firm territorial base in the Cape.

Hertzog called these mutineers extremists and opportunists; but

251

he failed to take their true measure. His failure was understandable. In the temper of public opinion at that time, neither Dr Malan nor any of his followers would have stood much chance of re-election if they had flatly rejected the coalition. They refused any share of its responsibilities; but in the elections of May 1933 they accepted its ticket. Pirow complained later that it was 'not in the best of taste' for them to creep back to parliament behind a banner which was not their own;[2] but Pirow ought rather to have blamed his leader for not forcing them to fight on their own feet and under their own banner. Hertzog threw away his only chance of destroying the enemies who in the end destroyed him. Smuts showed himself no more far-sighted. When Malan was hard pressed in Calvinia, Smuts rushed to his rescue.

In this immensely distorting general election no candidate who stood aside from the coalition, except for two Roosites, two Natal Home Rulers and two Creswell-Labourites, won a seat. The real battles were fought later, when the country's coalition fever grew into fusion fever. When that trend became apparent, Smuts was in London with Havenga at the World Economic Conference.* From there he had to give such guidance as he could to Esselen, Duncan and other party managers. They told him that fusion was growing from the grass roots, particularly among Afrikaners. They welcomed but also feared what was happening. Amalgamation on the *platteland*, they said, might cause a breakaway on the Rand. Smuts recognized that danger, but felt that a move forward must be made. The party, he told Esselen, could not stand still; if the leaders tried to do that, they would soon find themselves without a party. Hertzog before long came out openly for fusion. When Smuts returned home, he found his party executive in the Transvaal already committed to it.

But the fact is [he wrote] that in the rural Transvaal the urge towards fusion is very great and the Executive probably had its hand forced. I shall see there is proper consultation and co-operation between all sections of the party. But of course I agree and believe fully that in the end there is likely to be fusion. Dr Malan and his stalwarts may soon split off, and that too may ease the position for many S.A.P.s.

---

* This was the only overseas mission entrusted to Smuts during his 6½ years' service under Hertzog. Apart from his brief appearance at St Andrews in 1934, Smuts did not again leave African soil until he joined Churchill in October 1942 on the eve of Alamein.

Nevertheless, Smuts did not wish to see the situation too much eased for his side at the expense of Hertzog's side. That, he told an English friend, would mean 'Sap predominance, with a Nat Prime Minister with a small following of his own. You have that situation in England and it does not work well.' He wanted a strong centre party which would shed its extremists—its racialists, as he called them—on both sides.[3]

He set out to steer that programme through congresses of his party in each Province. In Natal and the Cape he feared opposition; but his fears proved unfounded, at any rate for the time being. After the Cape congress he wrote—

Everything went well at that congress and it is clear that I have the full confidence of the party still. But I don't feel comfortable or easy when people show so much confidence and in effect shove their responsibility on to me. It only means that if anything goes wrong they also put the whole blame on me.[4]

But in 1933 nothing went wrong for him. A chastened Tielman Roos offered him support, which he no longer needed.[5] On the economic front, the coalition government was doing well. The drought broke and the country looked marvellous after the rains. By the end of the year he felt sure that he was through the danger zone.

But Hertzog was in trouble. At his party conferences, he carried the day by 591 votes to 9 in the Transvaal and by 74 to 29 in the Free State; but in the Cape Dr Malan beat him by 142 votes to 30. In October 1933 at Bloemfontein the Malanites repudiated Hertzog; in December they founded their own party. Afrikanerdom was again in schism. Sometimes the same family was split.*

Malan was doing to Hertzog what Hertzog had done twenty years before to Botha. The very name of his new party—*Purified* National party†—contained an indictment of the old leader; it made him out to be, although not personally corrupt, an errant, a lapsed Afrikaner.‡ This Malan sincerely believed. In his view, Hertzog was pursuing *vereniging*, not *hereniging*—a political combination

---

* 'The Steyn family', Smuts wrote in February 1934, 'is hopelessly split—Gladys and Colin are for Roos, Mrs Steyn is for Hertzog (and me), Emmie and the v. der Merwes are violently pro-Dr. Malan.'[6]

† *Gesuiwerde Nasionale party*. The italics of *Purified* are mine.

‡ *Volksvreemde Afrikaner.*

of incompatible elements, not Afrikaner reunion. But perhaps it was not too late even now to pluck the brand from the burning? In February 1934, Malan approached Hertzog and persuaded him to re-open the discussion. Malan was practising shrewd political tactics. His aim was to kill fusion or—better still—to turn it into fusion between a reunited National party and a breakaway section of the South African party.

Smuts commented sardonically upon the Hertzog–Malan talks and their outcome.

I have had this week [he wrote on 21 February] a most hectic time politically. General Hertzog took it upon himself to make peace with Dr Malan and to conclude the peace in an exchange of letters which left the poor S.A. party in the air. My little plan seemed all gone and I was beginning to make other plans for the future. But then I tackled the General with the result that he left the Doctor in the air and again returned to unity with the S.A. Party. A right about face in one week! That is how we carry on in South Africa. What Dr Malan is now thinking of it all lord only knows. But I am not yet rejoicing as there may be another somersault soon. The Malanites are determined to wreck the fusion of the parties and the coming together of the races. But Hertzog cannot now drop the S.A. Party without coming a nasty cropper, and I think he genuinely desires racial peace.[7]

Smuts was exaggerating; but the published correspondence did raise legitimate doubts in the minds of S.A.P. men. Smuts felt that he could not go ahead with fusion until he had secured certain specific and public reassurances. He had two interviews with Hertzog and in between them he held a party meeting. Finally, on 18 February, he wrote and delivered a letter which, although considerably toned down from its first draft, firmly stated the issues which had to be cleared up between the two leaders and parties. He understood, he said, that no change in the procedure of the negotiations was contemplated; but that he and Hertzog would still retain responsibility for negotiating fusion, subject to ultimate decision by their respective party congresses. Turning to matters of substance, he pointed out that the recent Hertzog–Malan correspondence appeared to go beyond the coalition agreement under three main heads: status, nationality and republican propaganda. In order to avoid misunderstanding, he proposed to state his own views under each head. (1) *Status:* He took note that Hertzog personally interpreted it as including the divisibility of the Crown, the right of neutrality and the right of secession. That was not his own interpretation. He understood that he and Hertzog agreed to differ on these matters; and that, in consequence, no pronouncement upon them need be written into the new party's programme of principles. (2) *Nationality:* Because of some indefinite references to this subject in the Hertzog–Malan correspondence, he felt bound to make it clear that he could not accept 'anything which would mean a substantial modification being made in respect of our common status within the British Commonwealth alongside our Union citizenship'. (3) *Republican propaganda:* 'While not desiring', he wrote, 'to impose restrictions on the expressions by members of the [proposed] party of their individual opinions as to the form of our Constitution, I consider it necessary that any references to this in the statement of principles should be governed by a clear declaration that the party as such stands for the maintenance of the constitutional position as laid down in the South Africa Act and the Statute of Westminster.'

On each successive issue Smuts stated his views firmly but also courteously. Hertzog, he recalled, had dealt reassuringly with all the points that he had raised during their private conversations. He hoped that he would feel able to repeat those reassurances in writing. His hope was realized. Hertzog wrote to him the same day, accepting his account of their conversations point by point.[8]

The road to fusion was now almost clear; the passing of the Status of the Union Bill cleared it completely. In supporting this Bill, Smuts demonstrated his pragmatic approach to the main issues of constitutional controversy, such as the divisibility of the Crown and South African neutrality in time of war. He had rejected any theoretical commitment on these issues; but he was willing to sponsor procedural innovations which made them subject to South African political decision. Under the new legislation,* it became plain beyond any question that the Parliament of the Union possessed sole legislative authority, and that the Government of the Union possessed sole executive authority, in foreign no less than in domestic affairs. Whether in any future war South Africa became a belligerent, or a neutral, or something in between, would depend solely upon the advice which the government of the Union tendered to the

---

* In terms of procedure, the stipulations of the Status Act were spelt out further in the Royal Executive Functions and Seals Act.

Governor-General. That in turn would depend upon the government's command of majority support in parliament.

During and after the passage of the Status Bill, Smuts had to fend off revolt among the 'jingoes' of his party. He sent back a hectoring letter which Kingston Russell, editor of the *Natal Mercury*, wrote to him:[9] he would not, he told Russell, accept such a letter from anybody. Angry people in Durban were denouncing the Status Bill as a repudiation of the Empire, and in a sense they were right; but it was just as much an affirmation of the Commonwealth, a reception of the Statute of Westminster into South African law. In the debate on the second reading, Smuts defended the Bill in a speech which one intelligent critic declared to be the greatest of his career.[10] When the division bell rang only seven members of the House voted against the Bill. Nevertheless, those seven were in the mood to go the whole way as rebels.

On 5 June 1934 Hertzog published the 'Programme of Principles' which he and Smuts had hammered out.[11] A short preamble acknowledged—as the Union's Constitution did—the sovereignty and guidance of Almighty God. It then proclaimed the guiding purpose of the new party.

Its object is the development of a predominant sense of South African national unity, based on the equality of the Afrikaans-speaking and English-speaking sections of the community, coupled with the recognition and appreciation by either section of the distinctive cultural inheritance of the other.

For Smuts and Hertzog alike, that sentence contained the fundamental principle, not only of their political *rapprochement* but also of South African nationality. In July 1934 they both looked forward with confidence to the progressive triumph of that principle. It appeared to have tough roots in South African society. Thanks largely to the widely prevalent use of both languages as media of instruction in the schools—for which the Education Acts both of Smuts and of Hertzog had made provision a generation earlier—South Africa was conspicuously and increasingly a bilingual country. It seemed reasonable to expect that the white children who worked and played together and spoke each others' language at school would grow up with the conviction of being brothers and sisters within the same nation. But the Afrikaner Broederbond did not hold that conviction. No more did English-speaking parents hold it when they insisted in Natal and elsewhere on sending their children to unilingual schools.*

The event was to prove that Smuts and Hertzog had been over-optimistic when they proclaimed their doctrine of two equal cultures constituting one nation. The event was also to prove, and far more quickly, that they had been over-optimistic when they agreed to differ about the right to neutrality, because at that time they thought it unlikely to become a question of practical politics. Having dealt in their recent correspondence with neutrality and the divisibility of the Crown, they saw no need to make a place for them in the articles of fusion. By and large, those articles were identical with the previously agreed articles of coalition. The main deviation was in article 6:

Native policy

(*a*) An earnest endeavour will be made to arrive at a satisfactory solution of the Native question along lines which without depriving the Native of his right of development, will recognize as paramount the essentials of European civilization.

(*b*) It is recognized that a solution of the political aspect of this question on the basis of separate representation of Europeans and Natives or otherwise, being fundamental in character and not having hitherto been a matter of party division, should as far as possible be sought through agreement, and should be left to the free exercise of the discretion of individual members representing the party in Parliament.

(*c*) The recognition of the Natives as a permanent portion of the population of South Africa under the Christian trusteeship of the European race is accepted as a fundamental principle.

Sub-clause 6 (*b*) called off the party whips. To Hofmeyr and some other S.A.P. men of liberal aspirations, this liberty for tender

---

* The rapid increase of bilingualism from Union up to Smuts's defeat in 1948 is shown (despite some hot controversy about the interpretation of the census returns) in the following figures:

Percentage of white population speaking both languages

1918	1926	1936	1946
43	61	66	69

According to a survey conducted by Dr E. G. Malherbe in 1938, covering 18,000 school children in Standards IV to X, 43% of the children's homes were in various degrees bilingual. The survey also demonstrated that bilingual education was on balance stimulating to young intelligences. See E. G. Malherbe, *The Bilingual School* (Longmans, 1943). It was Malherbe's major premiss that the second language was not 'foreign', but belonged to the cultural inheritance of South African children. However, following the fall of Smuts in 1948, the opposite major premiss became the basis of policy. By the 1960s, bilingualism was a steadily diminishing quantity, particularly in the Afrikaans-speaking section of the white population.

consciences was welcome; but Native voters on the Cape's common roll were afraid that it boded no good for them.*

Among S.A.P. men article 2 (*d*) was the only one that raised contention. It declared—

While the Party stands for the maintenance of the present constitutional position, no one will be denied the right to express his individual opinion about or advocate his honest convictions in connection with any change of our form of government.

Those words were a sop to the tender consciences of republicans. Smuts considered them a small price to pay for the resounding affirmation of South African nationhood in the preamble to the programme of principles; but Colonel Stallard and six other English-speaking M.P.s made them the occasion of their breakaway from Smuts to form the Dominion party.

That small secession did not much trouble Smuts. From June onwards he was hard at work upon the final tasks of bringing his S.A.P. following into the new United party. He told his friends that the work was going well.

There is a very good spirit abroad. English and Dutch† are coming well together, and now that the artificial political differences have disappeared, the fundamental points of agreement are emerging and pulling people together. If this progress could continue for some years this would be a different country from what I have known in my lifetime.[12]

His last sentence was an unconscious prayer for peace in his time.

* See pp. 259, 261 below.
† Both Smuts and Hertzog sometimes used this old-fashioned terminology.

258

CHAPTER 14

'A NEW UNSETTLEMENT'

'THE NATIVES', Smuts wrote in December 1934, 'are getting more and more suspicious and they think that Fusion means that they are now without champions and that the Nationalist viewpoint has won.'[1] That sentence reported the state of Native opinion—in so far as Smuts knew it—not only about the uncertain future, but also about the historical past. It asserted that the South African party had been hitherto, in Native eyes, the champion of Native interests and rights.

Within strictly defined limits, Smuts personally had been their champion. His steady resistance to Nationalist colour policies was on record in the parliamentary debates on the industrial colour bar and Hertzog's Native Bills.* Moreover, his public statements throughout the long years of parliamentary opposition had been consistently in accord with what he said privately. He called himself a Fabian, and with good reason. In the politics of culture-contact, as in everything else, he was temperamentally and philosophically an evolutionist. He believed it impossible for Hertzog or anybody else to produce any comprehensive, once-for-all settlement of the innumerable political, economic and social problems which confronted South Africa's diverse races and cultures. 'Hertzog's settlement', he wrote, 'is the beginning of a new unsettlement.'[2]

Hertzog taunted him with having no settlement of his own to propose; alternatively, he taunted him with proposing to turn South Africa into a Kaffir state. Those contradictory accusations became the dominant theme of Nationalist propaganda in the general election of 1929. Meanwhile, English liberals were lamenting his lack of a fighting spirit in the cause of racial justice. 'Hertzog', he reflected, '. . . will not see reason and no doubt looks on me as a White Kaffir. My English friends look upon me as a European reactionary; such is the world with its complexities.' The Gilletts were beginning to feel that he would never resolve his dilemma so long as he stayed in parliament; they wanted him to issue a clarion

* See pp. 208–14 above.

call for racial justice and then resign his seat. In effect, they invited him to change himself from a politician into a prophet.[3]

But he had no prophetic message. Hertzog had one. So, possibly, had Sir James Rose Innes, whose intervention in the last election had proved 'a godsend'[4]—so Smuts believed—to the Nationalists.* But no Fabian could turn himself into a prophet. Smuts stuck to his political grind. For example, in 1932 he fought Oswald Pirow's Native Service Contract Bill, which aimed at helping the white farmers in two ways: first, by tying the black labour tenants still more closely to the land; secondly, by driving the black squatters off the land.† In support of the first objective, the Bill made provision for the whipping of juvenile absconders. Pirow declared that it would also have made provision for the whipping of adults if he had got his way—and possibly he would have got his way had Smuts given up politics for prophesy. Smuts admitted that the strap had played a part in the history of South Africa; but he went on to say that it had been 'dead' since his childhood and that it had been left to the Minister of Justice to revive it. As to the thousands of squatters whom the Minister wanted to drive from the white farms, Smuts asked where they were to go. They could not go to the town locations.‡ No more could they go to the Native reserves; these were 'filled up'. Smuts insisted, as he had insisted in 1926, that it was both unjust and impracticable to drive Natives from the white farms unless and until parliament fulfilled its pledge of 1913 to enlarge the areas where it was legal for them to acquire land of their own.[5]

Smuts put up a bold front; but he knew that it was caving in behind him. Even before the 1929 elections the South African party had been deeply divided on Native policy;§ after the elections its divisions grew deeper still. In 1930 Smuts wrote gloomily about the

* During the election campaign of 1929 Rose Innes, Burton and some other Cape men had issued a manifesto calling for the Union-wide extension of the Cape franchise and severely criticizing Smuts's proposal for a national convention or commission on Native policy.

† 'Labour tenants', as their name implied, held land on white-owned farms in virtue of their labour services to the owner; the so-called 'squatters' paid rent of some kind. The occupancy of the former was more compatible than that of the latter with economic land use. Clause 9 of Pirow's Bill made a landowner in any 'proclaimed' area liable to a tax of £5 for every Native occupant on his land who had not, for a period of not less than six months, rendered him any 'service'.

‡ In 1930, an amendment to the Native (Urban Areas) Act of 1923 had drastically reinforced the controls on the movement of Natives into the cities and towns.

§ See pp. 214–15 above.

course of colour politics. Hertzog's Native Bills, he told his friends, were getting worse with each successive draft. Reaction was in the air; it was seeping through his own party; it was undermining his personal authority. 'In fact', he reported, 'we are pretty well split...Natal going even further than Hertzog...The Natives in the meantime are becoming more sullen and suspicious and have lost faith in the white rulers, and nurse their suspicions and resentments.'[6]

Hertzog remained set in his purpose to remove the black voters from the Cape's common roll. These voters were now a diminishing political quantity. In 1930, parliament passed the Women's Enfranchisement Bill, which gave votes to all women of European descent but gave no vote to any Native or Coloured woman: the immediate consequence was a devaluation of such electoral power as the Natives and Coloureds had hitherto possessed. The diminution of the Native vote, expressed in percentage terms, was as follows:

Native voters on the Cape's common roll as a percentage of all registered voters in Cape Province

1929	1931
7·5	3·10

Native voters on the Cape's common roll as a percentage of all registered voters in the Union

1929	1931
3·5	1·4

But that was only a first step. In the Cape as elsewhere the newly enfranchised white women were subject to no civilization test; but the Cape's franchise laws still imposed a civilization test upon all men, including the white men. That anomaly could not long survive. In 1931 the Franchise Laws Amendment Act did away with it, and in doing so put on the Cape's common roll approximately 10,000 new white voters. Contemporaneously, administrative measures were being set on foot to reduce the number of non-white voters on the Cape's registers. By 1935, Native voters in the Cape constituted only 2·5 per cent of the Provincial electorate, and only 1·1 per cent of the Union electorate.[7]

Plainly, white supremacy was in no immediate danger. Hertzog knew that;* but a merely factual white supremacy did not satisfy him: he held it to be fundamental doctrine that whites and blacks must never vote together. Smuts, by contrast, held Native representation to be fundamental doctrine but its mechanism a matter of circumstance. He had stated those two propositions with emphasis in his Rhodes Memorial Lectures.† At the same time, he had given some reasons for leaving the Cape franchise alone: it had been established for a long time; the Natives set great store on it; to take it away from them would unsettle them to no useful purpose. He might have added that it would unsettle and possibly unseat some of his parliamentary supporters in Cape Province.

But Hertzog, not Smuts, was calling the tune. He followed up his victory in the 1929 elections by summoning a Joint Session of the two Houses and getting it to appoint a Joint Select Committee of twenty-seven members to consider and report upon the Natives Parliamentary Representation Bill. This committee became his instrument for cracking the S.A.P. façade of unity. Smuts attended all its meetings and sat powerless while Heaton Nicholls and the Natal contingent, with strong support from Stallard and other S.A.P. men on the Rand, did Hertzog's work for him.

On 2 May 1930, Nicholls introduced a draft Bill 'to make additional provision for the representation of Natives in the Senate, and to prohibit the registration of Natives as Parliamentary Voters after the commencement of this Act'. Nicholls criticized the Prime Minister's draft Bill because of its insufficient adjustment of means to ends. 'My chief objection', he said, 'lies in the fact that the Prime Minister is not seizing this opportunity to ensure the complete and permanent dominance of the European.' For that purpose, he argued, it was essential to prohibit Natives from voting as individuals. It was no less essential to deny them representation of any kind in the House of Assembly; they would get their compensation in the Senate, not as individual electors, but as members of communities. 'We ought really to go back to the Native kraal', he said, 'to the Native family, to the tribe, to the tribal council before we arrive at representation in Parliament.' Nicholls's Bill did not go quite so far back as that; but it took elaborate pains to ensure that the four

* Dr Malan took particular pains to emphasize the gap between theory and practice in the Cape (*H. of A. Deb.* vol. 16, cols. 596–600). He reviewed the history of measures taken to ensure white supremacy whenever Native voters on the common roll seemed likely to grow uncomfortably numerous. † See p. 227 above.

Senators, who would become henceforward the sole representatives of the Natives in parliament, should hold their seats by indirect election. When Nicholls was writing his memoirs thirty years later, he took credit to himself for proposing that these Senators might be black men. But that proposal remained in the field for precisely seven days. On 9 May 1930, Nicholls became a consenting party to its excision.[8]

Tactically, the early manoeuvring on the Joint Select Committee had the aim of establishing the basis for discussion. Nicholls moved that his own draft franchise Bill should be adopted as the basis. Thereupon Senator F. S. Malan, in a long amending motion, proposed the enfranchisement of Natives throughout the Union on a civilization test and on the common roll. To that, J. H. Hofmeyr moved as an amendment the restriction of Malan's proposal to the Cape Province only, with the additional proviso that Native voters should never exceed one-tenth of the total voters' roll of that Province. Five days later Colonel Stallard, the S.A.P. member for Roodepoort in the Transvaal, came ponderously to Nicholls's support with a proposal for constituting a Grand Committee of the Senate as the focus of deliberation and action in the sphere of Native policy. The decisive day was 9 May. Hertzog moved 'that the Committee disapproves of the principle of common representation in Parliament for Europeans and Natives'.* The motion was carried by a majority of 18 to 8. The Nicholls–Stallard draft Bill was then adopted as the basis of discussion. Once again, the voting was 18 in favour, 8 against. Once again, Smuts voted with the minority.[9]

Those votes of 9 May 1930, as Smuts had foreboded and as Nicholls recollected in his old age, signed the death warrant of the Native franchise on the Cape's common roll.[10] Nevertheless the committee had much detailed work still to do in implementing the Hertzog–Nicholls–Stallard principles. It had also to prepare a Native Land Bill. Smuts attended its meetings assiduously and occasionally got some satisfaction from them;† but usually he found them depressing. In February 1931 he confessed that he disliked even

---

* Hertzog, nevertheless, accepted an argument which Smuts had first put forward in 1926, namely, that Native voters already on the common roll must be allowed to remain there so long as they lived.

† For example, on 16 March 1931 Smuts got satisfaction when the committee rejected Stallard's proposal to exclude Natives in towns and on white farms from any share in the indirect election of the four white Senators. He got more positive satisfaction from the programme that was taking shape for the extension and development of the Native Reserves. Under this head, Nicholls was now a convert to his ideas (see p. 215 above).

thinking about the committee. In May he wrote: 'It is a recurring decimal. And the end will be largely mischievous, I fear.' In June he wrote: 'The Native Bills Committee is getting worse and worse. We shall not arrive at an agreement and the Natives will be deprived of such scanty rights as they still possess.'[11]

That marked his low point. His hopes began to rise as the government began to wilt under its economic troubles. Mischief, he reflected, sometimes wrought its own cure; with so many anxieties of their own, the white politicians might for a time forget the black voters. He hoped for a breathing space—which was as much, he said, as anybody dared hope for.[12] The breathing space lasted for some years. Fusion followed it. As Smuts saw the situation, fusion could produce nothing worse than the Joint Select Committee decisions of 1930. It might conceivably produce something better.

Early in 1935 Hertzog set the Joint Select Committee to work again. In its final report it recommended two Bills: first, the Native Trust and Land Bill; secondly, the Natives Parliamentary Representation Bill. Smuts considered the first Bill a good piece of work and he considered the second far better than the Nicholls–Stallard draft Bill of some years back: in particular, he was pleased to see the end of Stallard's 'grotesque' Grand Council of the Senate. In its place the Bill made provision for a Native Representative Council which was, in Smuts's opinion, a big improvement upon the Council first proposed by Hertzog ten years earlier. The Natives, he said, were now being offered a voice in their own affairs which parliament could not possibly ignore. 'This', he continued, 'with a land Bill and improved educational and health facilities, may make a real advance.' Nevertheless, the advance seemed to him insufficient compensation for the loss of vested rights inflicted upon the Cape voters. He made up his mind to vote against the Natives Parliamentary Representation Bill.[13]

In his memorandum of 1926, in his talks with Hertzog in 1928 and in successive parliamentary speeches, Smuts had formulated a doctrine of *quid pro quo*: if the Natives lost their franchise on the Cape's common roll, he maintained, they must receive equivalent compensation. In his view, the present proposals did not give it to them. He had been keeping touch with Professor D. D. Jabavu,* the

---

* D. D. Jabavu, the son of Tengo Jabavu, was the product of three generations of 'acculturation'. He was a well-trained student of Bantu languages and a foundation

most prominent spokesman of the Natives. And then, all of a sudden, the proposals were recast. In mid-December 1935 Jabavu took the chair at an 'All-African Convention' in Bloemfontein. He had summoned the Convention with the specific purpose of fighting the Native Bills. The Convention appointed a deputation to seek an interview with the Prime Minister and convey to him its repudiation of the Bills. The interview took place towards the end of January 1936. Smuts was not present at it; but he had played a discreet and possibly a decisive part in bringing it about. Following that meeting, Hertzog made a *volte face*. The part which Smuts played in that, whether or not it was decisive, he was too discreet to put upon record.[14]

Hertzog now recast the Natives Parliamentary Representation Bill so drastically that he called the new version of it Bill No. 2. Bill No. 1 had already scrapped Stallard's contribution to the 'philosophy' (as Stallard called it) of the representative system; Bill No. 2 now scrapped Nicholl's contribution. In his speech of 2 May 1930, Nicholls had declared:

There should be no Native voters in the House of Assembly. Instead they should be given Senatorial rights...The House of Assembly is the House of Democracy. Every member there is sent by a direct vote of the people. The mere right to vote is recognition of the existence of democratic institutions, and I hold that those democratic institutions are alien to the Bantu race. The House of Assembly, too, is the Executive House of the country. In it lies all the power...To ensure European dominance it is essential that there should be no vote of any kind cast except by the European.

For the past six years, that doctrine had found embodiment in each successive draft produced by majority vote of the Joint Select Committee. It had found embodiment in Hertzog's Bill No. 1. But Hertzog's Bill No. 2 threw it on the scrap heap. The new Bill, while putting the Cape's Native voters on to a separate roll, made provision for them to vote, as individuals, for three white representatives in the House of Assembly. What still remained of Bill No. 1 was the useful element—Native representation in the Senate and the Natives Representative Council.*

member of the academic staff of Fort Hare. He was on easy and friendly terms with Smuts. In the early 1930s his daughter Nontando (Noni), while she was receiving her education at an English school, spent her vacations with the Gillett family in Oxford.

* The franchise provisions were to be 'entrenched' in the constitution: that is to say, they could not be destroyed—nor, for that matter, supplemented—except by a two-thirds majority of both Houses in joint session.

Smuts declared himself satisfied that Bill No. 2, together with the Native Trust and Land Bill, constituted the *quid pro quo* for which he had been holding out. But the spokesmen for the Natives declared themselves dissatisfied. Whether or not Jabavu and the other members of the deputation had encouraged Hertzog to make his new offer,* the executive committee of the All-African Convention rejected it. A generation later, Jabavu's daughter forgot Hertzog, Stallard, D. F. Malan and Heaton Nicholls, and remembered or misremembered Smuts as the destroyer of the Cape Native franchise.[15]

In the joint session of the two Houses, the voting was 168 in favour of Bill No. 2 and 11 against. Strange company was kept in the division lobbies. Smuts, when he voted Yes, had the company of Dr Malan, who during the debate had maintained four propositions: first, that the Natives should have no representation in the House of Assembly; secondly, that they should have no Natives Representative Council; thirdly, that they should have no more land; fourthly, that the Cape Coloureds should be put on to a separate electoral roll. Hofmeyr, when he voted No, had the company of Colonel Stallard, that doughty fighter in the cause of Native disenfranchisement. The only memorable speech made during the debate was Hofmeyr's. Possibly its most telling point was the one that Smuts himself had made six years before, namely, that Hertzog's Bills would produce, not a settlement, but a new unsettlement.

It so happened that the Gilletts were in South Africa during that critical time. They saw that Smuts was under great strain, but they no longer pleaded with him to exchange politics for prophesy. In their letters home, they reported his anxious preoccupation with Hertzog's Native Bills, Mussolini's conquest of Abyssinia, and the imminent danger to the League. They made no mention of another matter which was much in his mind at that time. Between the second and third readings of the Natives Parliamentary Representation Bill, Hitler moved into the Rhineland.[16]

* Hertzog said that the deputation had asked him to 'work back to 1929'. To some extent Bill No. 2 did that.

3. With General Hertzog outside the House of Assembly

CHAPTER 15

INTERNATIONAL TENSIONS

As Minister of Justice and Deputy Prime Minister Smuts administered his department, drafted legislation, spoke often and at length
in parliamentary debates and made missionary journeys through
the constituencies on the United party's behalf. If those heavy duties
on the home front had absorbed all his energies, Hertzog would
have made no complaint against him. Hertzog treated foreign affairs
as his own exclusive province. He did not normally circulate departmental papers about them or discuss them with his Cabinet colleagues.
Smuts, in consequence, had little inside information about his
country's situation in an increasingly dangerous world. He did what
he could to keep himself informed from unofficial sources. Throughout
the 1930s, foreign affairs loomed large in his private correspondence
and became at times a main theme of his speeches.

Like most of his contemporaries, he failed to see the shape of
things to come and fumbled his way forward through a fog. 'And in
this blankness and confusion', he wrote in August 1936, 'what is
our duty, besides carrying on in our own little circle?' His friends
overseas* made more than one attempt to get him to come to
Europe to work for peace; but he recalled his failures in 1919 and
saw no reason to suppose that he would do any better at a second
try. Yet how, he asked, could a man wash his hands of the fate of
the world? It was cowardly surrender of all other forces of public
opinion that had made Hitler the master of Germany. He quoted
Milton's sonnet on his blindness and told himself that he, Smuts,
was on the reserve, not doing anything useful but simply waiting
and staying at his post in case he should be needed.[1]

His reflections grouped themselves in phases around the main
landmarks of the international situation—the collapse of the Disarmament Conference, Italy's attack on Abyssinia, Germany's re-
occupation of the Rhineland and the rapid succession of consequential crises in central Europe, the Mediterranean and Asia.
In each new phase he recognized new problems, but conducted

* In particular, Lord Lothian and R. B. Mowat.

within his own mind the same debate: how best to pursue peace; how best to defend freedom. He felt the tension between those two opposites. Until the final crisis of August–September 1939, he still hoped and prayed that it might prove possible, all appearances to the contrary, to reconcile them.

By 1934, the Disarmament Conference was in ruins and Germany had followed Japan outside the League. Smuts had a long-standing engagement late that year to deliver an address on the occasion of his installation as Rector of St Andrews University. He accepted another engagement to speak at Chatham House in London. At St Andrews, his theme was freedom; in London, it was peace.

He told his London audience that Freudian neuroses were at the root of the world's troubles and that the remedy for them was to drag them into the open. Fear, the meanest of human motives, was the first and most dangerous neurosis; the remedy for it was to stop the war talk and to stop thinking of the League as a coercive body, which would bring aggressors to order by threatening them with sanctions. Conference, not coercion, must remain the League's technique. A second neurosis was the obsession with equality; it was Germany's present trouble and the remedy for it was to treat the Germans as equals; they would then soon come back to the Disarmament Conference and the League. He felt sure that the neuroses of Europe, although tiresome and obstinate, were curable, and that Europe before long would settle down peaceably. He did not have quite the same confidence about the Asian neuroses; but he stressed the need to avoid even the appearance of antagonism between East and West. Whatever happened, he declared, the Western powers must never depart from an attitude of friendliness and large human good will towards Japan. Yet, in a world where it was necessary to walk warily, they must also make prudent provision for their own security. Their sheet anchor, in his view, was co-operation between the British Commonwealth and the United States.

Events soon refuted Smuts's hopeful diagnoses; but Lord Lothian told him at the time that he could recall no speech which had made so profound an impression upon public opinion. *The Times* expressed only one regret—'that a statement so perspicacious and so wise, at once so imaginative and yet so plainly derived from hard experience in politics and war, should not have come from the lips of a member of our own Cabinet'. Nearly all the British newspapers were fulsome

in their praise of Smuts. On the other hand, Lord Cecil told him that
he had inclined too much to Germany's side; that he had failed to
recognize the strength of France's claim to security; that his views
on sanctions were dangerous doctrine for the League of Nations.
That was challenging criticism.[2]

Smuts was also his own critic. Notwithstanding his optimism at
the political level, his mind at a deeper level was full of forebodings.
Early in 1934 he had told Amery that peace depended upon what
was at the back of the German mind: specifically, at the back of
Hitler's mind. In letters to his friends throughout the year his
reading of that riddle was invariably pessimistic.

It is only when one sits down [he reflected] and quietly writes down the
account that one realizes that everything one has held dear in the past is
endangered at present.

Would Luther or Goethe be tolerated in the Germany of today?...Is the
decline of Liberty not an even greater threat to civilization than the
menace of rearmament and war? All this troubles me very much. There
seems to be a call for great action, but somehow we don't see the course
ahead and sit as it were paralysed in the face of the gravest dangers.

I look upon the destruction of liberty in all its spiritual forms as in many
ways a greater menace to civilization than even war itself. A barbarism
of the spirit...is steadily stealing on us...with its repressions and sup-
pressions and tyrannies. When will the day break again?

It was always said that the Germans were too highly cultured to imitate the
Bolshevists. But Nazi Germany seems to me even more repulsive in her
methods [he was writing after the blood bath at Nuremburg on 30 June
1934] than Russia ever was or than Fascist Italy was. I am deeply puzzled
over all this as it fills me with doubt and misgiving for the future. We can
continue to cultivate the good life in our private circle, but what is to
become of the world if this sort of madness continues to grow in public life?

War seemed to him almost inconceivable, but he admitted that in
Bedlam all things were conceivable. 'Pity the poor public men', he
exclaimed, 'who have to govern in these days!' Yet he was thinking
just then not so much about the public men, as about the students
whom he would soon be addressing at St Andrews. From early in
the year he had been asking himself what he could possibly say to
them that would be worth their while to hear.[3]

It so happened that he had been deeply concerned for some time
past with the difficulties and future prospects of some young friends

of his who were becoming converts to Communism and getting themselves into various scrapes and predicaments. In his dealings with them and in the counsel he gave their parents he blended sympathy with common sense. Communism as a system of thought and way of life was repugnant to him—

Still, there it is [he told one parent] and there is also their sincerity and disinterestedness...I can understand and most fully sympathize with you in your anxiety. And yet you must respect their personalities, and you must remain the same friendly comrade you have ever been.

Our children—so easily and comfortably launched in the old world, will have a very different situation to face in the new world now emerging. It is going to be harder all round, and that may be better for them. But it will not be half as pleasant.

No doubt the situation of these young people was in his mind when he chose the title and theme of his Rectoral address.[4]

Freedom was his theme. At St Andrews on 17 October 1934 he painted a sombre picture of the new tyrannies, disguised in patriotic colours, which were resurgent in Europe.

Although the ancient homelands of constitutional liberty in the West are not yet seriously affected, we have to confess sadly that over large parts of Europe the cult of force...has for the moment triumphed. Popular self-government and parliaments are disappearing. The guarantees for private rights and civil liberties are going. Minorities are trampled upon; dissident views are not tolerated and are forcibly suppressed. For those who do not choose to fall into line there is the concentration camp, the distant labour camp in the wilds or on the islands of the sea.

Intellectual freedom is disappearing with political freedom. Freedom of conscience, of speech, of the Press, of thought and teaching is in extreme danger. One party in the State usurps power, and suppresses its opponents and becomes the State. The Press is made to write to order and public opinion is manufactured for the support of the autocracy. Even freedom of religion is no longer safe...In many, if not most European countries the standard of human freedom has already fallen far below that of the nineteenth century.

Nevertheless, he told the students, as he had told the men of science three years before, that freedom had its roots in the order of the universe. It must be defended. It must prevail.[5]

The movement of his mind at those deep levels was ominous in long term for fusion in South Africa. Hertzog might possibly have thought that his Minister of Justice was doing no harm when he told Scottish students that freedom was a value worth defending, had it not been for the passages in the speech which appeared to accuse Hitler. Hertzog, according to Oswald Pirow, expected great things from Hitler. Some years before fusion, Pirow had listened to a conversation in the Prime Minister's office between Hertzog and Creswell.

They were discussing Communism and Colonel Creswell summed up the position by remarking: 'I wonder whether Russia is not destined to play Macedonia to Europe's Greece?'

Some years later Hertzog came back to this conversation and remarked: 'Creswell was right, unless Hitler can stop Russia.' The idea of Germany as Europe's bulwark against Russia thereafter became one of the main principles of his foreign policy.

Smuts, on the other hand, said straight out—though not in public— that Hitler had a bee in his bonnet about Russia.[6]

If Hertzog saw Hitler as the champion of European freedom, while Smuts saw him as its destroyer, conflict between them was unavoidable. Yet Hertzog, possibly, was not quite so clear-cut in his views as Pirow made him out to be; while Smuts, certainly, still hoped that he could resolve the contradiction between his mood at St Andrews and his mood at Chatham House. If his theory of the curable neurosis proved sound, the contradiction would resolve itself as Nazi Germany, in response to the appropriate treatment, became not only a peace-loving but also a liberty-loving nation. That was the firm conviction of Smuts's friend, Lord Lothian. In January 1935, Lothian made a visit to Berlin and returned with the news that Hitler did not want war, that he believed in self-determination, and that he could be trusted to keep the peace for the next ten years, provided the British negotiated with him in a spirit of frankness, firmness and respect for Germany's equal rights. Smuts accepted Lothian's diagnosis. If only the British would pursue 'a resolute policy of appeasement and reconstruction of the Peace', he declared, the effects would be far-reaching.[7]

Fifteen years earlier, at the Paris Peace Conference, Smuts had contributed the word *appeasement* to the vocabulary of international politics.* It had signified for him at that time a policy of magnanimity

---

* See *Smuts: The Sanguine Years*, pp. 512–13, for a brief discussion on the origins and later transformations of the word *appeasement*. This theme might prove rewarding to an historian closely acquainted with the diplomatic and political history of the inter-war years, and interested in semantics.

and prudent restraint pursued by the stronger party towards the weaker party. However, in the late 1930s, he discovered that appeasement was coming to signify the direct opposite, namely, a policy of propitation pursued by the weaker party towards the stronger party. He then stopped using the word. But as late as 1935 he was still using it in its original sense, because he was still taking it for granted that the victors in the First World War remained the stronger party. What most troubled him in 1935 was not the restoration of conscription in Germany and the rebuilding of the German air force, but the prospect of repressive action against Germany. From this point of view, he congratulated British statesmen upon restraining the French from 'evil'; he took pleasure in the weakness of the 'Stresa front' against Germany; he welcomed the Anglo-German naval agreement.[8]

He was aware that there was little point in his preaching appeasement unless he were prepared to state whom he was proposing to appease, and with what. In a negative way he clarified the issue by naming the powers whom he was not proposing to appease. They were Italy and Japan. Their elimination left Germany as the beneficiary of appeasement.

My own view [he wrote in February 1935] is that the colonial question as settled at Paris should be reopened and that some real effort should be made to satisfy Germany. But what can be done to satisfy Japan? And there is the greedy Italy to reckon with. If we could reach a stage of international appeasement when these matters could be calmly and objectively considered in a judicial spirit, a solution is perhaps possible. But today, in these noises and in this atmosphere of constant crisis and deep-seated distrust, one almost despairs of finding any way out.[9]

In those sentences he foreshadowed his reaction later that year to Mussolini's attack on Abyssinia.

On 9 October 1935 the South African representative at Geneva announced that his government would put into force against Italy all the sanctions which the Council of the League recommended. Hertzog and Smuts were in complete accord with each other upon that policy; but Smuts drew upon his head the reproaches of his friend Amery. The League, Amery said, was committing itself to a task beyond its capacity to perform. Its rule of unanimity would inhibit resolute action and its sanctions would inflict no dangerous damage upon Italy; but Britain, as their main advocate, would suffer a humiliating diplomatic defeat, or else be dragged into a war for which she was prepared neither materially nor psychologically. Amery reproached Smuts for repudiating the wise words that he had spoken only the year before at Chatham House; he had said then that the League was a conference table, but now he was trying to make it an international war office. To that last reproach, Smuts had no convincing answer. In 1934 he had said that Article XVI of the Covenant—the sanctions article—was vestigial. In 1935 he said that it was fundamental.[10]

His *volte face* had reasons both of the head and the heart. His head told him that a return to the age of military adventure and diplomatic manoeuvre in Africa was dangerous; his heart told him that it was outrageous. 'I am deeply moved', he wrote on the eve of Mussolini's adventure, 'by the prospect of a Christian nation, ranking among the Great Powers, now preparing to war down a native state in Africa which has so far maintained its independence through the ages.' At the same time he felt that the struggle to save Abyssinia was equally a struggle to save the League. He was hoping and praying, he said, that the League might survive: like the early Christian Church, she carried in her bosom a great and rich idea of human brotherhood. There spoke the League's evangelist; but Smuts was also a realistic politician, trying to diagnose the causes and the possible alternative consequences of Mussolini's gamble and the League's crisis.

After Manchukuo why not Abyssinia? And so we go on in the old ways. But if the League disappears it will leave the most dangerous vacuum imaginable in the world of today. The old system will not work, except by way of war.

It is quite clear that *this* is the vital test of the League, and failure here will be fatal for the League. Manchuria was too obscure a situation and too far away. But here the issue is clear and at our door.

Today it is a second class great Power like Italy, tomorrow it will be a first class great Power like Germany, trying to impose her will by high-handed action on other countries. The stand had to be made now.[11]

Not for the first time in his life, he was trying to find standing room between the 'old ways' of individualistic struggle, which had been the rule of foreign policy throughout the greater part of history, and the 'new ways' of the co-operative world order, as symbolized and partially embodied in the League. His friend Lothian, in a recent lecture, had set out to prove that this standing room did not exist. There were only two alternatives, Lothian said: either a sovereign state ruling the whole world, which signified peace; or an aggregate of separate sovereign states, which signified war. Since the League was neither one thing nor the other, it must be dismissed as a dangerous sham. Smuts read this Hobbesian pronouncement on 4 August 1935, the twenty-first anniversary of modern man's greatest calamity—so far. He recognized Lothian's logic; but he denied its application to the existing state of the world.

You say in effect [he told Lothian] that a half-way house like the League is a mistake because it leaves the real crux of national sovereignty unsolved. This disturbs me greatly. National sovereignty could only disappear in another world cataclysm worse than that of 1914–1918...I therefore am forced to set your solution aside as both impracticable and too dangerous.

He told Lothian that if the League failed there would be no use his dreaming of a World State—there might be no world left to organize into a State. He also invited him to come closer to the ground and to consider the consequences to the Commonwealth of the League's failure. The Covenant of the League, he pointed out, provided members of the Commonwealth with a common code of practice; if they lost that guidance their foreign policies might begin to follow divergent, if not opposite, paths. He could well have added that the same danger faced Hertzog and himself in South Africa, and that the collapse of the League, if it were allowed to happen, was likely to be followed, sooner or later, by the collapse of the fusion government.[12]

On 10 June 1936, Neville Chamberlain denounced the continuance of sanctions as the very midsummer of madness. A few weeks later, the Assembly of the League, responding once again to a British lead, called them off.*

So you have won [Smuts wrote to Lothian]† and sanctions are going, and the sanctions clause will no doubt go too. But what will remain of the League?...Two things had seemed to me to make the Peace worthwhile —German disarmament and the Covenant. But Prussianism is back on us in an aggravated form, owing to our delay in disarming ourselves. And now the Covenant is going too.

---

* South Africa and New Zealand, alone among the nations, voted for continuing sanctions.

† Lothian for a time had supported the League, and had said privately that Britain must be ready at need, even without the support of France, to cut Italian communications through the Suez canal; but later on he had reverted to his original attitude.

A week later he told Amery that the League's collapse boded ill for the Commonwealth.

Then again, if we come to consider Commonwealth foreign policy, the question with us is going to be the new basis. There is no doubt that the League was a great support to the immense Commonwealth system by binding all of them for external purposes through the same machinery and the same treaty. Commonwealth countries would always be fighting on the same side or all neutral together. Such was the immense value of the League to us... To me the road appeared clear so long as we were all bound by the League as the basis of our foreign policy, but once that goes, I see only dangers ahead and no clear daylight.

He felt bitter when he looked back along the road from September 1935 to June 1936—the British lead at Geneva, the British election, the Hoare–Laval pact, the repudiation of that pact, the final capitulation. 'But what', he asked, 'must be the position of people like me, far away, who have loyally tried to be loyal and friendly in the face of the heaviest odds, and who now find it quite impossible to defend British policy? What should one do?'[13]

The only thing to do that he could think of was to play for time, in the hope that somehow or other the world's peace and South Africa's unity might still be saved. Playing for time meant negotiating with Hitler.

In September 1935 Smuts had prophesied that a success for Mussolini in Abyssinia would encourage Hitler to go and do likewise. 'If Italy gets away with it', he wrote six weeks later, 'Germany or rather Hitler will follow suit within five years and the world will once more be convulsed from end to end.'[14]

On 7 March 1936 Hitler reoccupied the Rhineland with his armed forces. In doing so he went beyond his earlier defiance of the Versailles Treaty, for he had declared the previous October that Germany would continue to accept neutralization of the Rhineland as an obligation incumbent upon her under the freely negotiated Locarno Treaty. It would therefore have been understandable if Smuts had ranked Hitler equal with Mussolini as a disturber of the peace and had advocated equal treatment for both. He did the opposite. He thought coercion the right treatment for Mussolini but conciliation the right treatment for Hitler; he thought that the Italians should be bludgeoned, but that the Germans should be persuaded into peaceable behaviour.

18-2

Admittedly, it went against the grain of his temperament. 'It is a cursed spite', he said, 'that we have (for the sake of European peace) to support the ruffianly policy of Hitler.' He meant Hitler's ruffianly policy in his own country; he called it odious but did not think it incompatible with good behaviour by Hitler towards other countries. From the point of view of the Commonwealth, he saw a distinction between the Fascist and Nazi dictatorships: Italy, the friend of yesterday, had become a deadly and dangerous enemy; Germany, the deadly enemy of yesterday, wanted to be friendly.[15]

He was taking Hitler's words at their face value. Tacitly, if not in express terms, he accepted Hitler's plea that the Franco-Soviet pact had absolved Germany from her obligations under the Locarno Treaty. In positive terms he welcomed Hitler's offer of peace negotiations—for the limitation of air forces, for twenty-five year pacts of non-aggression between Germany and her neighbours, for Germany's return to the League of Nations. Like *The Times*, he saw 'a chance to rebuild'. He told Tom Lamont that the present crisis would prove to have been a blessing in disguise if it frightened statesmen at last into making a lasting peace. He told Lothian that the world was getting ripe for big things, both good and evil, and that the stage had now been reached when things could be done. His advice was to clinch quickly with Hitler's offer of peace pacts and of Germany's return to the League, and to proceed from that basis to a programme of negotiated co-operation in the spheres of economic and colonial policy. For example, arrangements might be made for assuring Germany of easy access to tropical raw materials and for returning Togoland and the Cameroons to her as mandated territories.[16]

But Hitler's peace offer produced no results. Smuts at first blamed the French for that anti-climax; it was just like them, he said: they had missed every opportunity since Versailles.[17] Yet only a few months later he was asking himself whether the opportunity that had seemed so clear to him in March 1936 had ever really existed, except in his own imagination. Hitler, it appeared, had not much interest in such colonial *douceurs* as Smuts thought appropriate for him: after all, they were merely titbits. Hitler claimed the return of every colonial territory which Germany had lost in 1919. Smuts, on the other hand, was determined to refuse lodgment to Germany's air force anywhere within bombing distance of the Rand. That meant a refusal by the Union to give South West Africa back to Germany, and a refusal by Britain to give Tanganyika back. On that issue Hertzog, as Prime Minister of the Union, and Pirow, as Minister of Defence, saw eye to eye with Smuts.[18]

Consequently, Smuts had no just cause of complaint when Nazi propagandists filled the air with the din of Germany's colonial grievances; but he did feel puzzled by all the other din that they were making at the same time about all their other grievances and hatreds. He found himself unable to form a clear idea of what they and their master really wanted.

If Germany really wants peace with Great Britain [he wrote in September 1936] why raise this colonial issue so prominently?...The line I have hitherto been inclined to take is that Germany really wants peace, but will not have it at the price of inferiority. But why this open and flagrant aggressiveness towards Russia?...*As things are today* any British government who agree to retrocession of German colonies will be hopelessly beaten, and they know it. While Germany is preparing to attack Russia and Czecho-Slovakia and what not, no British government dare make so unpopular a move, which may moreover be quite useless too. The fact is, I am getting more and more mystified over German policies. If they agree to a *general* settlement which will bind them for the future the question of the colonies will become quite soluble; but why surrender colonies when that will not secure peace in Europe?[19]

About this time he stopped using the word *appeasement*. His education in totalitarian power politics was by now proceeding fast. He was discovering their dynamism, their incessant thrust and overspill into new areas, issues and objectives. This dynamism was refuting the prudent calculations and counsels of his friends Amery and Lothian. Limited commitments, the localization of wars, the use of one dictator to restrain his neighbour and all the other time-honoured expedients of the balance of power had hitherto seemed realistic; but now they were beginning to look utopian. Similarly, it had seemed realistic hitherto to draw a sharp line of division between the internal constitution of a state and its external policies; but in the new flux and flood of power the line was becoming hard to hold, or even to locate. It seemed no longer to have significance for Hitler and Mussolini. The oligarchs were supporting the oligarchs, just as they had done in the days of Thucydides. Smuts was beginning to feel that the democrats would have to support the democrats.

He kept his feelings under restraint. He was aware that if he gave them free rein he would be committing himself to a crusade. The last thing he wanted was a crusade, or a war of ideologies, or a war of any kind. On the other hand, he was beginning to realize that *not* to have a creed and a cause might be just as dangerous for peace as having them; nations did not always march into their wars; sometimes they shuffled or drifted into them; or else they let themselves be pushed into corners from which they could not escape except by fighting. Smuts did not reason all this out in general terms; but on two specific issues he made up his mind that it was insupportable any longer to be pushed into corners. Palestine provided one of these issues, Spain the other.

Palestine was demonstrating the explosive chain reactions of totalitarian dynamism. The dynamic Hitler started a new Jewish exodus. For tens of thousands of Jews, Palestine became not only their promised land but their city of refuge. But Palestine was also an Arab homeland. The sudden advent of so many Jews terrified the Arabs and drove them to revolt. The British sent an army to Palestine to put the revolt down. Then the dynamic Mussolini moved into action. From his wireless station at Bari he spread propaganda against the Jews and the British throughout the Arab world. The British government began to consider the imposition of restrictions upon Jewish immigration into Palestine. The first rumour of that brought Smuts into action. He and Lloyd George were the two surviving members of the War Cabinet which had endorsed the Balfour Declaration of 1917 and had won international recognition for the Jewish National Home in Palestine. In 1930 he had rallied Lloyd George to his side in protest against the MacDonald government's 'incredible breach of faith'—so he called it—in regard to the Balfour Declaration. In 1936 he made a new appeal to Lloyd George for joint action to defend the National Home. It was not a time, he said, for deserting the sorely tried Jews and lying down before Arab agitation. Whatever the British did, the Palestine Arabs would be hostile to them; so why, he asked, should they also make an enemy of World Jewry?

But besides these considerations [he continued] there remains the deliberate policy decided on in the war in favour of the National Home. On that we should not weaken. We have given up so much of the fruits of the Great War that at least this little ewe lamb should not also be slaughtered. It is the imponderables that make history.[20]

That last reflection brought him no comfort when he shifted his attention to Spain. There the dictators, not the imponderables, were making history. He wrote early in the civil war—

It looks like an out and out struggle between Communism and Fascism. I must frankly admit that in this case my sympathies are with the government against the Fascists. It would be a double calamity if the rebels win, firstly because in that case yet another country would have to be added to the Fascist dictatorships, and secondly because the Roman Church, which is at the root of this business, has been a centuries old curse to Spain... Spain has been on a wrong tack ever since Inquisition days.

But of course he fixed his main attention upon the ideological and power conflicts of his own century. He saw the German and Italian interventions in Spain as a plain case of the oligarchs helping the oligarchs and as an equally plain bid for an important strategical objective—a position of strength in the western Mediterranean which would enable the dictators to threaten the British entry-point at Gibraltar and the French life line to North Africa. He thought it foolish of the British and French to tolerate non-intervention when it was clearly, in his view, a one-sided and most dangerous intervention. He insisted that they could have kept the Germans and Italians out of Spain if they had been resolute and clear-headed. Instead, they were receiving a demonstration of the new technology of war and its consequences for humanity.

You know I don't think anything so barbarous as the bombing of Madrid happened even in the Great War. We are becoming barbarized, and our acceptance of these things shows that the human fibre in us is deteriorating ...I think of Milton's sonnet on the slaughter of Piedmontese...I think Chaka was not worse in all his fiendish barbarities.

Spain is a portent. Think of an undefended city of a million inhabitants being shelled and bombed like Madrid...It is like Nineveh doomed to destruction.[21]

In the Spanish civil war he saw Hitler and Mussolini in action as a partnership. They announced the Berlin–Rome axis in October 1936. So much for Lothian's hopes of using Hitler to control Mussolini and so much for Amery's dreams of reconstructing the Stresa front. So much, Smuts might have added, for his own exposition, only a few months before, of Hitler's peaceful intentions.

It now occurred to him that Hitler's foreign policy was essentially the projection of his internal policy; that the Nazi bombings in

Spain were of one piece with the Nazi Jew-baitings. He asked himself whether anything good would come out of a country whose deliberate policy it was to persecute Jews and Protestants. 'A decent Germany', he wrote, 'might have been a good friend; it is difficult to think of Nazi Germany as safe company in the future.' Nor could he conceive how decent people could want to keep company with 'the unspeakable Mussolini'. He took note that the newspapers nowadays were always full of bad news.

It is like old times again. This morning's paper was full of the wild attack of Goebbels at Nuremburg on the Jews and the Bolshevists. It is really incredible that one great Power can publicly speak of another great Power in such outrageous terms. Years ago that by itself might have precipitated a first-class crisis...

I *do* fear Germany and that brutal ruthless mentality which is once more resurgent. Mussolini I don't fear. It is not in Italy to succeed far. But the Germans may dynamite our Western civilization yet, which they have so much helped to build up.

In a different mood, he tried to express his fears in the language of clinical diagnosis. The dictators, he said, could not rest upon their past achievements. Their fires required continual additions of fuel. Both Hitler and Mussolini must keep moving on.[22]

Towards the end of 1936 he saw them moving on from the Berlin–Rome axis to the Berlin–Rome–Tokio triangle. They had not yet achieved it or given it a name, but he believed that he could see the trend of their ambition. He saw the European oligarchs reaching across the oceans and the great Eurasian land mass to the Asian oligarch.[23] Looking back on 1936, it seemed to him to have been a year full of doom.

I see in the papers this morning [he wrote in the New Year] that Eden has said that 1937 will decide the future of our civilization. My fear all along has been that 1936 has been the decisive year, when in a moment of absent-mindedness or funk collective security was abandoned and the League virtually burst. I think then the step that counts was taken; and thereafter we were back on the old paths of war which might lead us anywhere. If 1937 is the decisive year we still have some months of grace. I hope it is not already too late. It is a curious feeling this—that mankind is drifting, drifting, and that nothing now can prevent the castatrophe. I resist the feeling as much as possible.[24]

From January 1937 until the month of Munich Smuts's two moods, the St Andrews mood and the Chatham House mood, waged

war against each other within him. Whenever he thought of the
Jews, Abyssinians or Spaniards he fell into his St Andrews mood and
told his Quaker friends that pacifism was not the answer to the
Hitlers and Mussolinis.

These gentlemen have to be confronted with the sort of argument which
alone appeals to them, and the force behind Democracy ought therefore
to be a match for that of the Dictators...The force of Right is still weak
and feeble in the world, and has to be helped out by the Right of Force,
if the world is not to be flung back into barbarism.

He admitted that he was borrowing those phrases from Churchill;
but he denied that Churchill was 'roping him in'; he did not, he
said, see himself in that picture. None the less, Churchill's defiant
speeches struck a deep chord in him. Here were Britain and France,
he exclaimed, the strongest naval power and the strongest land power
in Europe, allowing themselves to be blackmailed and browbeaten
by a pair of rascally dictators—

But we are afraid of our shadows. I sometimes long for a ruffian like
Palmerston or any man who would be more than a string of platitudes
and apologies. But this is perhaps only the old Adam in me!

Yet he managed to keep his old Adam under control. Lothian, not
Churchill, was steering him.[25]

Early in 1937 Lothian pleaded with him to come to Europe and
give the impulse for negotiating an Anglo-German agreement. What
Lothian had in mind was British disentanglement from Europe and
'a sort of Ottawa economic Mittel-Europa' for Germany. Smuts
did not come to Europe, but he wrote Lothian a long letter. Its
basic assumptions were optimistic. Great Britain, he said, was still
the greatest reserve force in the world and she was now arming
heavily; consequently, she was in a position to take the initiative
without incurring the imputation of weakness. Germany, on the
other hand, was in a far weaker position than appeared on the
surface; her Four Year Plan had proved a failure and she did not
possess the resources for carrying on a long war.

...Germany [he continued] has also made terrible mistakes, and the
worst of all is Hitler's obsession against Russia. Ten years ago an attack
on a ruined down-and-out Russia could still be a possible policy. Today
that has become mere midsummer madness. If Germany is now a power-
fully armed power, Russia is no less so, with far greater material and
mineral resources to sustain a prolonged war...Russian power thus
makes for peace in Europe.

Against this highly satisfactory background, which was in considerable degree the creation of his own imagination, Smuts made a list of Britain's bargaining counters. The British, he said, did not mean to hold on to *all* the German colonies; they knew that the *Anschluss* with Austria was only a matter of time; they knew that the régimes in Memel and Danzig were make-shifts; they knew that they could secure American co-operation in opening large economic and financial opportunities to Germany. He believed that all these inducements might be offered to the Germans for the sake of peace, provided two basic conditions governed the negotiation: first, it must exclude everything prejudicial to France and Russia; secondly, it must include and settle every contentious issue.

But it must all be done [he continued] for a lasting comprehensive European settlement which must include progressive disarmament, a resuscitated League with a revised Covenant, and a revised economic and fiscal policy which will re-establish European commerce on a normal basis.

I do not think this an impossible programme if properly handled.[26]

But Smuts was too sanguine. In May, Lothian attempted the task which he had wanted Smuts to undertake. He went to Berlin as a self-appointed emissary, held discussions with Hitler, Goering and Schacht and composed a memorandum of his conclusions. He said that the Germans, although difficult, were not unreasonable. They were nationalists, but did not want to dominate other nations. They were not jealous of the British Empire, but felt that the British were always frustrating them. If they were given the prospect of obtaining their just rights and a good living, the present abnormal features of life in Germany would pass away. There appeared to be good prospects of a successful British negotiation with Germany under the following heads:

1. Eastern Europe: that Germany should get possession of Danzig, Memel, parts of the Polish Corridor, Austria and the Sudetenland, with an agreement to safeguard the reciprocal rights of the nationalities on those areas.

2. The Colonial–Economic question: that Germany's economic needs, as stated by Schacht, should be met, and that some colonial territory should be ceded to her for the sake of her *amour propre*.

3. The League and Disarmament: after agreement had been reached under the two preceding heads, it might prove possible to get Germany back into the League, or into some Concert system, with disarmament to follow.

Smuts made no comment on the memorandum. He must have noticed how Lothian was saying 'might' where he himself had said 'must'; how he was proposing to give the Germans what he thought they wanted and only after that to wheedle them back to the League. Possibly he also noticed a contradiction of his own thought—his notion of achieving a comprehensive and permanent settlement with people whose essential dynamism he had so recently diagnosed.

Meanwhile, dynamic action was being let loose against the Chinese. Smuts wrote on 24 September—

But think of Canton being bombed to extinction by the Japanese. Think of similar devilment all over that huge immobile population. And then the British government declare their satisfaction with the Japanese Note that they have given strict instructions against bombing of civilians!

I really wonder what the world is coming to. For if this is permitted in China much worse will happen tomorrow in the West. I think the troubles and manoeuvrings in Europe are trifling compared to what is happening in Asia, where untold miseries are goading hundreds of millions into madness on a colossal scale for which mankind will have to pay...These things cry to high heaven, but fail to reach this poor helpless world in the west, which is impotent in its domestic squabbles. And Hitler and Mussolini are prancing about in Munich and Berlin. Only a Jewish prophet of old could do some sort of justice to this bedlam of a world situation.

He insisted that the war in China was more ominous by far than any event anywhere in the world since the Great War.

What an awakening for that slumbering civilization! But what will the giant yet do when fully released? I fear Japan has done a thing which may not only undo her yet, but which may threaten the West far more in the coming generations than anything that has happened in the East in the past. The heroism of the Chinese may yet shake the world.

He asked himself how the Chinese would use their power when the Japanese had thoroughly militarized them? Hitler, meanwhile, proclaimed the Berlin–Rome–Tokio triangle. Smuts noted that announcement as a new betrayal not only of Asia but of Europe.[27]

Germany, Smuts said, was doing irreparable wrong in revenge for the smaller wrongs which she had suffered after the last war. 'But even so', he went on, 'I would talk with the enemy in the gate—even if there is no more than talk.'* Talk to what end? To gain time. Time for doing what? For saving the peace. 'How

* Smuts was referring to the mission of Lord Halifax to Berlin in November 1937.

the situation will really develop', he told Amery, 'nobody can see...But whatever the evolution of the future may be, we should take every precaution that it develops peacefully.'* He faced the fact that peace was no longer obtainable except by recognizing German predominance in continental Europe. His recent assessment of the balance of power, he now admitted, had been proved fallacious; in particular, he had been far wide of the mark when he depicted Russia as an effective make-weight. If anybody had told him, he said, that Russia would sit still while Japan was securing the mastery of China, he would never have believed it. Only a few months later, he saw Russia once again sitting still while Hitler secured the mastery of central Europe.

Germany seems now to be in a fair way [he wrote in March 1938] to accomplishing all she ever dreamt of doing. Russia which was the only real check on her is paralysed and out of action...With the present impotence of Russia, Germany has a clear field, and she is deliberately marching on, at a great pace. Today it is Austria. Tomorrow there will be internal trouble in Czecho-Slovakia between Sudeten Germans and Czechs and once more Germany will step in for 'law and order', and I doubt whether anybody will raise a finger and so she will march on....It will indeed be a Napoleonic Empire once more.

As a free man, Smuts disliked that prospect; as a prudent man, he came to terms with it. 'All my instincts revolt', he exclaimed, 'against this racialism, this intolerance and persecution, this hatred of the things that are dear to me.' But he kept his instincts bottled up. Amery, late in the day, was trying to think out ways and means of calling a halt to Hitler; but Smuts told him that Britain would have to go it alone in any Continental adventure.

As regards the Dominions [he wrote] they will fight for Great Britain if attacked, they will not fight in the battles of Central or South-Eastern Europe. I even have my doubts whether they will fight again for France and Belgium. They are now out of that business under the Locarno Treaty and I think they will remain out unless the world situation changes very much from what it is today. Frankly I do not see what else there is for them to do after all the mistakes and *lâchetés* of the past.[28]

Of course, British sea power remained, and with it the Commonwealth. 'I...am all for our world-wide Commonwealth', he declared, 'as the last remaining—and, I hope, effective—bulwark of human

* Cf. p. 86 above.

liberty.' Looking far ahead, he declared his faith in the staying power of freedom, the survival of the Commonwealth and the re-establishment of a rational world order. 'Meanwhile', he wrote to Lothian, 'let us keep the peace as long as we can.'[29]

His correspondence with Amery and Lothian contained by antici-pation the apologia for Munich. South Africa's decision not to intervene in the event of war had been agreed upon informally by an inner circle of Ministers—Hertzog, Smuts, Pirow, Havenga—before Chamberlain arranged his first rendezvous with Hitler. How-ever, it was not until 28 September that the full South African Cabinet approved the decision. It was as follows:

Statement of the attitude to be adopted by the Union of South Africa in the event of war in Europe with England as one of the belligerents: The existing relations between the Union of South Africa and the various belligerent parties shall, so far as the Union is concerned, remain un-changed and continue as if no war were being waged, with the under-standing, however, that the existing relationships and obligations between the Union and Great Britain and any other of the members of the British Commonwealth of Nations in so far as those relationships and obligations are the result of contractual obligations concerning the naval base at Simonstown; or of its membership of the League of Nations; or in so far as the relationships etc., must be regarded *impliciter* as flowing from the free association of the Union with the other members of the Common-wealth, shall remain unaltered and shall be maintained by the Union; and that nobody shall be permitted to make use of Union territory for any purpose calculated to infringe the said relationships and obligations.[30]

That statement did not fit easily into any of the recognized categories of international law and practice. Neither neutrality nor non-belligerency would have been sufficiently accurate designations of it. The statement expressed South Africa's desire to assume the rôle of a semi-neutral. There would have been no obligation upon any belligerent power to recognize the existence of such a rôle and little likelihood that an aggressive belligerent would respect South Africa's desires when its own interests were at stake. Nevertheless, the document was a careful, honest and laborious attempt to express the realities of South Africa's international situation and of her internal political situation. In its content and style it bore the stamp of General Hertzog's mind. He had written it in his own hand, both in Afrikaans and English. After his Cabinet had approved it he kept both versions of it carefully among his papers.

Throughout his life Hertzog had always set great store upon documentary statements. They gave him political anchorage. He treasured the document which recorded his Cabinet's decision at the time of Munich. Consistently with his lifelong habit, he ascribed continuing validity to its propositions. Smuts, on the other hand, did not feel so sure that the formulae which fitted one situation were bound to fit the next. In a series of speeches both before and after Munich, he took pains to declare his conviction that South Africa would take her stand with Britain and the Commonwealth, if ever the day came when they had to fight for their lives. Hertzog made no similar public declarations. That contrast did not escape the notice of D. F. Malan. The fusion government, he insinuated, had a divided mind upon the fundamental issues of peace and war.[31]

CHAPTER 16

TENSIONS AT HOME

IN the early months of fusion Smuts felt it 'a joy and a happiness' to move about the country. South Africa, he exclaimed, had disbanded her political armies, she had turned the greatest corner in her history, she was entering a new era of national achievement. And yet this Eden still had its serpents. In April 1935 Stallard's Dominion party won East London in a by-election. Even so, Smuts felt sure that he could stop the seepage to Stallard. He did not feel so sure that Hertzog could stop the seepage to Malan. 'The Malanites', he wrote, 'have re-started the old bitter fight—this time mostly from hatred of Hertzog, who is now fought with the weapons and in the style in which he fought me for so long.' Smuts soon began to fear that Hertzog was losing control in the Free State, as he had already lost it in the Cape. His wife made a visit to the Steyns in Bloemfontein and returned home with mixed feelings. 'I think that type of people', Smuts wrote, 'are now very friendly to us, but still hate poor General Hertzog very much for being taken in by me! I—the real culprit—am kindly forgiven. There is no hate like love to hatred turned.' The hatred shocked him. 'Every attempt at peace', he exclaimed, 'miscarries.'[1]

But Hertzog fought back. At Smithfield on 7 November 1935 he made a three hours' speech* to the head committee of his party in the Free State, acclaiming South African unity and denouncing its wreckers.

What do we see [he asked] surrounding us today? Indefatigable, zealous attempts in all directions to provoke national disunity; to awaken irreconcilable aversion and hatred between the races; to prostitute our cultural assets, our language and religion, our history and origins, as hostile instruments of attack, with which to fight, slander and crush one another... What is concealed behind all these excesses?

The Afrikaner Broederbond, he answered, was concealed behind them. He denounced the Broederbond as a sinister secret society.

* Next day the Free State *Volksblad* reported the speech in two full pages and published a long editorial refutation of it. The *Volkstem* (United Party, Pretoria) also reported the speech at great length but commented on it only in a second leader.

He described in detail its organization at the centre, its local cells, its techniques of devolution and interlocking directorates, its penetration of the civil service and the teaching profession. Its aims, he insisted, were not merely cultural but essentially political. Its ambition was to rule South Africa. In support of that assertion he cited names, dates, facts and figures culled from the Broederbond's secret records. The Broederbond and the Purified National party, he said in effect, were the two opposite sides of the same penny: the Broederbond was the party in action underground; the party was the Broederbond pursuing its aims in public.

Hertzog named D. F. Malan as a member of the Broederbond. Malan admitted his membership, not apologetically but with pride. In Malan's eyes, Hertzog stood self-revealed and self-condemned as an enemy of the Afrikaner nation. It was war to the death between them. Malan and his parliamentary followers at the time numbered no more than 19 in a House of 150; but they felt no dismay on that account. Victory, they never doubted, would be theirs, no matter how many years they had to wait for it. Their self-confidence had arithmetical roots. First they made a demographical count: the count of Afrikaners. Secondly, they made a political count: the count of *ware Afrikaners*, by which they meant their own potential supporters. Their first count was a statistical exercise; their second count was a mixture of statistics and the will to believe.

By their reckoning, the statistics of the 1936 census revealed the following ratios between the two linguistic sections of the white population, as classified in age groups.[2]

Age group	English-speakers	Afrikaans-speakers
Over 21	100	115
7–21	100	185
Under 7	100	212

It took them some years to achieve that show of precision; but their demographical self-confidence from the mid-1930s onwards was firmly grounded. The progressive numerical ascendancy of Afrikaners in the white population was a fact. By contrast, the political ascendancy of *ware Afrikaners* was a prophecy. But the Nationalists were confident prophets. What they did not predict was the date when their prophecy would be fulfilled. That depended upon their rate of progress in the constituencies.

Traditionally, Afrikaner nationalism had drawn its strength from the country constituencies. Malan set himself the task of winning them away from Hertzog, just as Hertzog twenty years earlier had set himself the task of winning them away from Botha. In addition, Malan recognized the new and rapidly expanding opportunities which awaited his party in the urban constituencies. *Die trek na die stad* or, as it was called in English, the rural exodus, had been gathering momentum for the past quarter of a century and was now entering a period of dramatic acceleration. Between the censuses of 1936 and 1951 the net migration of whites, almost entirely Afrikaners, from the country to the cities fell not far short of quarter of a million.* Whereas in 1936 Afrikaans-speakers constituted 48 per cent of South Africa's white urban population, by 1951 they constituted 69 per cent of it. These urbanized Afrikaners became increasingly the target of Nationalist propaganda.

The new propaganda ran easily in the old grooves. For that there was a sufficient reason. Afrikaners were not the only people who were coming to town. Similar pressures and opportunities were creating a still more striking rural exodus of black Africans. The time was approaching when the blacks would outnumber the whites not only, as they had always done, in the so-called white farming areas but also in the industrial areas. These processes of change were economically and sociologically complex; but Afrikaner Nationalists saw them as the re-enactment of a legendary drama. The white man, cried Dr Malan, was facing the black man at a new battle of Blood River, but this time he had to fight for his life on the open plains of economic competition.† Afrikaner Nationalists saw some other battles to fight: against the British-Jewish capitalists who —they said—were exploiting the whites; against the British-Jewish agitators who—they said—were preaching Communism to the blacks. Here were the elements of a dynamic ideology to reinforce the time-hallowed Nationalist protests against subservience to Britain and participation in British imperialist wars.

In short term, the Purified National party pursued limited

* This high estimate of net migration of whites from country to city between 1936 and 1951 is justified by taking into account a natural increase of 165,000 in the white rural population. The absolute decline was 77,000 (from the 1936 figure of 553,000). Meanwhile English-speaking South Africans remained overwhelmingly urbanized. They also remained highly concentrated in a limited number of urban constituencies.

† See p. 296 below.

objectives. It saw no chance of winning the next general election, due to be fought in 1938; but it saw good chances of gaining valuable ground. As a parliamentary tactician, Malan prepared the ground skilfully. He probed the United party where it was weakest, at the point of junction between Hertzog and Smuts. He did this by saying the things which many of Hertzog's followers wished in their hearts to hear their own leader say. Thereby he confronted Hertzog with a dilemma: if he did not also say those things, he ran the risk of desertions from his supporters to Malan; if he did say them, he ran the risk of starting mutinies among Smuts's supporters. Smuts in his turn had to face a dilemma: if he refused to follow Hertzog when he drifted towards Malan, he would be risking the collapse of fusion; in so far as he did follow him, he would be risking desertions from his camp to the Dominionites, to the Labourites or possibly to a splinter party of Liberals. Time after time, Smuts found himself in situations from which he saw no way of escape except by unhappy compromises.

Jewish immigration to South Africa became the occasion of Nationalist probing. Malan was not personally anti-Semitic, but politically he drew profit from anti-Semitic feeling. Smuts was disposed to allow free entry to Jews in flight from Hitler. Consequently, a news sheet called *Die Waarheid*, published by the violently anti-Semitic Grey Shirts, lampooned him as the Jew King. Malan did not use comparable language but he made the same point in a parliamentary joke: Smuts, he said, was on the map of Palestine and if he were deleted from it he would no longer be on the map of any country. Malan refused to have official dealings with the Grey Shirts; but his party showed where it stood when the Transvaal and Free State Conferences adopted new rules excluding Jews from membership. Throughout 1937, individual Nationalists conducted a violent agitation against Jewish immigrants. Yielding to pressures such as these, the government introduced legislation which in fact, if not in form, discriminated against Jews. Thereupon, Smuts's Jewish friends blamed him for making a weak surrender to the anti-Semitic agitation. Mrs S. G. Millin, a gifted authoress and recently Smuts's biographer, believed that his fear of the agitators held him back as Minister of Justice from appointing her husband to the Bench.*[3]

* Smuts appointed Philip Millin a judge the following year.

Meanwhile, progressive-minded people had begun to say that Hofmeyr, not Smuts, was the man to trust on the disputatious questions of colour policy. Notwithstanding Hertzog's attempt at a 'final settlement', many things remained unsettled. From 1936 onwards there were hot debates, for example, on mixed marriages, racial segregation in the universities and factories, and Indian land purchases in the towns. These debates followed a repetitive pattern: a Nationalist speaker would propose new restrictions; a United party speaker would try to outbid him and would perhaps introduce a private Bill; Hofmeyr would say No on the government's behalf. Usually, it was the accident of office that made Hofmeyr the government's spokesman;* but it so happened at this time that he was moving steadily to a more liberal point of view, while the majority of his colleagues were moving in the opposite direction. Hertzog must have asked himself whether Hofmeyr's statements were not putting too heavy a strain upon the cohesion of the United party. In February 1937 Smuts asked the same question:

We have had some difficulty in Parliament and the Cabinet [he wrote] over some Colour Bills introduced by private members of our Party. First it was some Bill against mixed marriages which however has for the moment been sidetracked. Then it was two Bills against Asiatics employing white girls etc. Hofmeyr took a strong line against the Bills, while I have temporized, as not only public opinion but opinion even among our reform social workers is much against such employment and the social evils to which they lead [*sic*] or may lead. A Select Committee is now enquiring into them. I think there is a good deal to be said for control of such employment and am prepared to consider a fair compromise. But Hofmeyr continues very stiff. These colour questions are more and more trouble, and are partly no doubt exploited by our opponents in order to foment differences of view in the United Party. You will probably see references in the press to these troubles, hence my reason for writing about them to you. If Hofmeyr were to leave the government it will be a great loss and a distinct blow to me, as he is one of my most promising young men and the reactionaries don't like him. He is a good liberal with a fine human outlook. Unfortunately he is also somewhat academic and exaggerates things and aspects of no real importance. And his mother is no help to him in the difficulties as she wants him to go out of politics— which would be a bad thing for the country and for him. I am doing my best to keep him with us, and to some extent sympathize with his standpoint, without thinking the actual points of difference as important as he does. Politics is the art of the possible and the practicable, and one has

---

* In his two capacities as Minister of the Interior and Minister of Education.

to give in on small things in order to carry the bigger things. But it is just in this comparative valuation that the snag lies.

That letter showed Smuts making excuses for himself but finding his excuses only half convincing.[4]

His dilemma by now was almost intolerable. Hertzog had given free rein to one of his followers, General Pienaar, who was set on proving that United party men were just as zealous for segregation as the Nationalists were. Hofmeyr, Hertzog's Minister of the Interior, confuted Pienaar. Thereupon Grobler, Hertzog's Minister for Native Affairs, confuted Hofmeyr. If Hertzog had not moved the adjournment of the House, Pirow, his Minister of Defence, would have taken sides with Grobler and Pienaar. And all this time Smuts kept silent. Hofmeyr told Mrs Millin that Smuts was weakly yielding to anti-Semitism, colour prejudice and the other forces of reaction. He himself, he said, was ashamed of the government of which he was a member. Nevertheless, he did remain a member of it. Smuts, still in his mood of unease, wrote on 10 April—

The difficulties with Hofmeyr have been finally overcome, but I fear not without leaving some aftermath of bitterness for the future. I have stood by him, as he is high principled and very able, and I don't want to leave him out for the future. He is now looked upon as the only liberal in the Cabinet, and I am looked upon with doubt by many. The way of the peacemaker is a hard one, and it has been my bitter lot for a long life-time. I don't mind.[5]

But of course he did most intensely mind, partly because he felt that his loyalty towards Hofmeyr had fallen under suspicion, partly because he recognized the instability of fusion—that is to say, of his lifework.

Actually, the concessions which Smuts made to keep fusion alive were not so large in fact as they were in appearance. The anti-Indian Bills were withdrawn for the time being, while Mr Justice Feetham pursued his patient, fair-minded investigations.* The Children's Act of 1937 contained benefits for all children of all races and colours. The credit of this legislation—or, as many Nationalists believed, the discredit of it—was specifically Hofmeyr's; but Smuts supported it. Smuts at this time was acquitting himself well as Acting Minister of Native Affairs. For example, when some policemen were killed in an African riot at Vereeniging, he dealt sensibly and humanely with the

* See p. 457 below.

aftermath. Opposition speakers had tried to fasten part of the blame on him.

My case had been made blacker [he wrote] by my releasing 400 Natives who had been caught in the round-up on Monday for being without passes or tax receipts. Politicians are exploiting this excitement all over the country for their miserable political ends...There is nothing that makes the European in this country so panicky as incidents of this kind, where Natives attack Europeans. My bad luck is that there is a sort of wave of this lawless behaviour—which is not confined to Natives. At Johannesburg a minor crime wave had led to a big mass outcry.

The whites are scared of Communism spreading among the Natives and look upon the Vereeniging incident as largely the effect of Communist propaganda among the Natives. There is however nothing in this view, and the Commission of Inquiry will report in that sense next week.

He went on to say that he felt sorry at having to hand the department back the following week to the Minister of Native Affairs, Grobler.[6]

Amidst so many tensions, Smuts took for himself at least one grain of comfort: the old disputes about status and the national symbolism appeared to be dead and buried. In the abdication crisis of December 1936, Hertzog performed a model operation on Statute of Westminster lines. Next year he carried through his long-matured plan of securing a South African as Governor-General. He failed, of course, to placate the Nationalists. They did not welcome Sir Patrick Duncan as Governor-General but thought that a home-born South African ought to fill the office—if it had to be filled. In their hearts they repudiated the entire symbolism of monarchy and thought the divisible crown only a piddling improvement upon the indivisible crown. They also thought it an infliction upon the nation that its representatives on occasions of state had to listen to God Save the King. Early in 1938 Hertzog conceived the idea of taking the sting from that grievance by applying once again the 50–50 principle: South Africa had two flags and why not two anthems? As a beginning (but no more than a beginning)* he proposed that Die Stem van Suid-Afrika should be played after God Save the King at the next meeting of parliament. The Cabinet adopted his proposal, much to the pleasure of Smuts and his wife; but Hertzog could not, perhaps he would not, let well alone. When parliament met and the two airs were played everybody seemed happy until—as Smuts told the story—

---

* Cabinet approval was asked and granted merely for a ceremonial innovation, not for establishing a second national anthem.

Some mischievous member then asked Hertzog in the House whether that meant that Die Stem had now become a national anthem. The simple answer was no, but Hertzog, who never can give a simple answer, went into a long disquisition to prove that God Save the King was not legally our anthem and that it was a mere invocation to God, and that Die Stem had much more of the character of a national anthem and might in time take the place as such of God Save the King. All perfectly unnecessary, but of course thereafter the fat was in the fire... What can you do with such leadership?...Of course I have to sit tight and save the work in national upbuilding for which I have been mainly responsible these five years.

It was small wonder that Smuts rejected the invitations he was receiving at this time to come to Europe and help set the world to rights. 'If I leave this show', he wrote, 'it may collapse, with far-reaching results.' He managed to patch up a compromise with Hertzog about God Save the King and Die Stem; but he wondered what kind of treatment the English-speaking voters would mete out to him on election day.[7]

They treated him well. Even the white miners on the Rand gave him a hearing, which from 1922 onwards they had never before done. A few of them made plans to break up a meeting which he had arranged at Doornfontein, whereupon party headquarters begged him to call it off; but he refused to be intimidated. When the day came, his inveterate enemies paraded the streets with placards— 'Come and hear the Murderer and the Traitor!' Four thousand or more people came to hear him—in the hall if they could get in, if not, in the grounds outside, over loudspeakers. A few demonstrators tried to shout him down; but the stewards in the hall dealt with them efficiently.* At the end of his address the immense audience gave him an ovation. Above all, the Doornfontein Jews applauded him. They had good reason.[8]

The elections were fixed for May 1938. From early in the year Malan had been fighting Hertzog with the weapons that Hertzog had used nine years before against Smuts. Malan told the country that the Purified Nationalists alone had the will to keep it white. He promised legislation against mixed marriages and the employment of whites by non-whites—the very legislation which Pienaar and Grobler had recently proposed and Hofmeyr had opposed.† He

---

* Among the demonstrators was Johanna Cornelius of the Garment Workers' Union. One of the women stewards removed her from the meeting after a scuffle.

† See p. 292 above.

promised to enforce residential segregation in the cities and occupational segregation, so far as it could be achieved, in the factories. He promised to put the Cape Coloured voters on to a separate roll.[9]

This time, however, the constituencies did not respond to the cry that white civilization was in danger. When the results were announced Smuts hailed them as a triumph for the United party.

Of the 150 seats in the House of Assembly [he wrote on 20 May] we have taken 111, with another result still to come in*...I almost feel as if we are at last through our racial troubles.† The last five years of close political co-operation in one Party by English and Dutch has [sic] been a wonderful heartening experience. This election has now cemented the close racial alliance...Knowing what a past we have, and what a commotion we have made in the big world, I am glad that there is at last this process of internal settling down and what we call Fusion. [10]

By and large he had cause for thankfulness. The final returns were as follows: United party 111, Purified National party 27, Dominion party 8, Labour party 6. The United party had lost only six seats. Nevertheless, Malan's followers had done far better on the count of votes than they had done on the count of seats. Hertzog had lost more ground on the Afrikaner *platteland*. Within the United party the Smuts contingent had increased its strength.

Hertzog acted as if the opposite had happened. He seemed if anything less resistent than he had been before to the magnetic attraction of his enemies. He made, approved or tolerated decisions which were bound to put a severe strain on fusion. The first of those decisions followed the elections within a week or two. People attending the ceremonial parade on Union Day found themselves the witnesses of a dramatic innovation. The military bands played Die Stem van Suid-Afrika. They did not play God Save the King. Hertzog could have foreseen—perhaps he did foresee, or perhaps Pirow did—that this departure from past practice was bound to rekindle the embers of conflict. Smuts chose to treat the affair as an accident; but a serious one.

These mistakes [he wrote] are heartbreaking, and I sit with the broken crockery, even if not with a broken heart! We must endeavour to carry on,

---

* He wrote in the margin 'Not won'. In speaking of 150 seats in the House of Assembly he was forgetting the additional three members returned under the Natives Parliamentary Representation Act.

† Smuts was still using the word 'racial' as he and Hertzog had used it throughout the past four decades (i.e. with reference to 'English and Dutch' relationships). But a change of usage was now impending.

but frankly I find it often most trying to work with my old Nat friends. They are more influenced by fear of Dr. Malan than of God.[11]

They had good reasons for fearing Dr Malan. He was riding the crest of a great Afrikaner wave which made the recent elections seem to many people a mere surface ripple. Almost everywhere in South Africa ox waggons, commemorative of the Great Trek, were moving from village to village in an intensely emotional pilgrimage along the roads which led to a high ridge outside Pretoria. There, on 16 December, Dingaan's Day, three Afrikaner women would lay the foundation stone of an immense monument to their heroic ancestors, the Voortrekkers. The government, after sponsoring this great commemorative drama and after voting large funds to build the monument, had allowed itself to be pushed aside. The Afrikaanse Taal-en Kultuurvereniging, a subsidiary of the F.A.K.,* managed the centenary celebrations. It permitted no descendant of the Voortrekkers, if he happened also to belong to the United party, to take any prominent part in them. When the great day came, Smuts was present simply as an Afrikaner. Hertzog stayed on his farm. Malan took the limelight, not indeed on Voortrekker Hoogte, but at Blood River. There he achieved his life's masterpiece of nationalist oratory.†

The Voortrekker celebrations gave the signal for a great leap forward of nationalist Afrikanerdom. Early in the year, while the ox waggons from the Cape were moving towards the Free State, an old and respected minister of the Nederduitse Gereformeerde Kerk, Rev. J. D. Kestell,‡ had called upon his fellow Afrikaners to join with each other in a work of rescue (*reddingsdaad*). The people who needed rescue were the Afrikaner poor, especially the poor who were flocking from the country into the city; the rescue party must include every Afrikaner who treasured his people's past and took thought for its future: 'We won't ask ourselves', Kestell declared, 'to which political party he belongs.' But the event worked out differently. The Reddingsdaadbond§ took shape in close association with the F.A.K. and as an exclusively Nationalist institution. Another Afrikaner society, the Ossewa-Brandwag, was brought to birth in the

---

* See p. 239 above.
† See p. 289 above.
‡ J. D. Kestell was an octogenarian with a record of courageous service as a chaplain in the Anglo-Boer War; he was also a well-known writer and co-editor of the records of the Assembly of the People at Vereeniging in 1902.
§ Rescue Action Society.

same exuberant times, to commemorate the trek of ox waggons. Its history was destined to be stormy.*

Hertzog, the main political creator of nationalist Afrikanerdom, now found himself totally an outcast from it. In the year following the Voortrekker celebrations his son Albert appealed to him to return to the fold; but he refused to recant any single proposition that he had stated at Smithfield on 7 November 1935. Afrikaners did not by themselves, he insisted, constitute the nation. Still less did the self-appointed Nationalist coteries constitute it. He declared that he would never lend his political aid to persons who were not prepared to recognize the equality and equal rights of the Afrikaans-speaking and English-speaking sections of the South African nation.[12] Hertzog when he took his stand on a principle—no matter whether he was right or wrong—sometimes came close to greatness. At other times he treated trivial matters as questions of principle. Hofmeyr, according to Smuts, was liable to fall into the same error. Soon after the May elections, the two men came into conflict with each other over the nomination by Hertzog of his friend Fourie as a Senator, within the category of persons possessing 'thorough acquaintance with the reasonable wants and wishes of the coloured races'.† Hofmeyr denied that Fourie satisfied that qualification, but Hertzog still insisted on nominating him. Thereupon Hofmeyr resigned from the government. In the House of Assembly he denounced Fourie's appointment as a prostitution of the constitution and a cynical expedient which made non-Europeans merely the pawns of the white man's political game. Hertzog answered angrily. Smuts kept silence. Hofmeyr told Mrs Millin that Smuts was now a prisoner to Hertzog and was no match for him in simple directness and straight-forwardness of purpose. On the other hand, he told Leslie Blackwell and some other people that Smuts was right not to resign. Smuts offered no explanation of his conduct, except perhaps obliquely; on one occasion, in comment upon an attempt to draw him out, he said—'Yes, the situation in Czechoslovakia is very serious'. It was the month of Munich.[13]

Some people hoped that Hofmeyr would start a new party to

* See pp. 335, 368–9, 381 below. Ossewa-Brandwag means Ox Waggon Guard.

† This category was defined in the constitution. It offered the only way that Hertzog had been able to find of getting Fourie back to parliament and thereby keeping him in the government, after he had lost his seat in the general election and had failed subsequently to secure a safe seat.

fight for liberal principles; but he decided to stay within the United party. That meant more trouble between him and Hertzog, and more humiliation for Smuts. In May 1939 Hofmeyr found himself compelled on grounds of principle to oppose the Asiatics (Transvaal Land and Trading) Bill.* Hertzog thereupon forced his resignation from the party caucus. Blackwell resigned with him. Smuts had pleaded in caucus for considerate treatment of his two friends; but Hertzog rejected his plea. Smuts submitted to Hertzog's will. Among liberal-minded South Africans, his reputation by now was at its nadir.

It was the time of Britain's guarantee to Poland.

* See p. 457 below.

CHAPTER 17

DECISION

TOWARDS the end of 1935 Arthur and Margaret Gillett went on a visit to Smuts in South Africa. They found him looking much older than he had looked only a few years before and asked themselves how much longer he would be able to stand the political grind. At times he asked himself the same question. In 1935 he admitted more than once that the effort he was putting into politics was disproportionate to the results he was achieving and more than he would be able to stand indefinitely. In 1936 he confessed that he was feeling irritable and dissatisfied with the run of things: 'With me', he said, 'overwork means a feeling of heaviness in the head, which gradually spreads and oppresses the whole system and spoils the temper and takes away the joy of life.' In 1937 he confessed that it took him nowadays a full week to recover from the exhaustion of a political speech-making tour. 'Years ago', he said, 'I could keep this sort of thing up for weeks at a time, but age tells.' It did not tell all the time: on 24 May 1936, his sixty-sixth birthday, he felt himself flooded with the joy and beauty and blessedness of the world. 'Oh what a day', he exclaimed, 'even at 66!...And yet the end cannot be far off and so one slips from one stage to another.' He was beginning to complain of loss of memory. In June 1938 he started work on his botany books in the hope of recovering the names of flowers which he said that he had been forgetting by the score; but early next year he found himself back where he had started.

I have done no work this weekend [he wrote on 29 January] except go through part of my Cape Botany in order to refresh my memory, as to names especially. My memory is becoming like a sieve and lets through names of plants which I know as well as my own. It is a deep humiliation thus to forget within six months, and if this continues much further I shall become unfit even for my political work, in which remembrance of facts, figures and names is vital. What can one do against these devastating inroads of old age?

Despite these lamentations, he knew in his heart that if he were really put to it he could still outpace and outlast anybody in South Africa.

He said that he could *think* by the hour without getting tired. Or he could *act*. Unhappily, most of his so-called work was neither one thing nor the other.

So much of the work is just unutterable drudgery, a weariness of the flesh and the soul. And yet this is the way of human affairs. I could do all this far better by myself in a tenth of the time. But the pace of our human army is that of its slowest unit, and we cannot get away from this grievous dispensation.

But there he was wrong. The time was at hand when he would get away from it and would make the pace both for himself and for South Africa.[1]

There was no serious diminution as yet of his physical powers. In May 1936 it took him 1 hour 30 minutes to climb Table Mountain by way of Skeleton Gorge; in June 1939 it took him 2 hours, but then he was just recovering from a painful chafing of his feet. His average time for the ascent was 1 hour 45 minutes.[2] Whenever he was in Cape Town for the parliamentary session he tried to make the ascent once every week, usually on a Saturday. Occasionally he ran risks. In August 1939 he climbed the mountain in defiance of a bad weather forecast, got caught in a cloud burst and was lucky to achieve a slow descent through the raging torrent of Skeleton Gorge. What a humiliation it would have been, he said, if search parties had had to be sent out for the Deputy Prime Minister! It so happened that he had been a passenger only a few days before on a dangerously damaged aeroplane; but the trouble had been discovered in time.[3] His good luck was bad luck for Hitler.

Table Mountain, he used to say, meant more to him than sticks and stones. 'Such a day behind me', he exclaimed, after one long Saturday of climbing and rambling in the autumn sunshine, 'and I thank the Lord for this gracious gift of Himself in his creatures animate and inanimate.'[4] That was the mood which Roy Campbell had mocked in his satirical quatrain. Smuts wanted to translate the mood into rigorous philosophical thought; but nowadays, he lamented, he could find no time for thinking. He felt that it would be an immense boon if he could get just six months free; but he was lucky if he could get six days. In 1938 he wrote a jejune and lifeless preface for the proposed German translation of *Holism and Evolution*. In recent years the book had been attracting a good deal of attention in Germany.* Professor Adolf Meyer of Hamburg conceived the idea of establishing an Institute of Holism. Smuts told him the idea was premature. Yet he soon found out that Germans could do worse things to his ideas than bury them in an Institute. *Ganzheit-Theorie*, as some Nazi writers were expounding it, shocked him. He thought it a monstrous parody of everything he believed in—'a queer compound of Holism, romanticism, racialism, ethics and religion...a ruthless scrapping of ideas and methods which we consider part of the moral and political heritage of the human race'.[5]

Abstract theorizing was becoming too much for him to cope with in his rackety life. It exhausted him almost as much as politics did because it was just another tangle of insoluble problems.

It is said that dogs go mad [he wrote] when they are subjected to experiments that are confusing to them. They make repeated efforts at a solution, and then become restless and aimless in their reactions and finally go quite mad. I suppose this would happen and does happen to us when we are left with nothing but tangles to which we see no way out...Here it is that the life of earth and family with its customary routine proves so helpful and healing to us.

Particular places and persons and things, not the Mountain or Man or Holism or anything else that he wrote in capitals, were the medicine he needed. Fortunately for his health and strength, he knew it.[6]

In the Cape, as well as in the Transvaal, he had a real home, 'Tsalta', the house the Gilletts had bought for his use.† It always seemed to be as full of children as Doornkloof was. Through his study window he could hear them at play. He said that he enjoyed the voices of the young—the younger the better; for after all, this was not a grown-up world; children made all the difference to it. He wondered where they got their endless energy from. He supposed that play was their way of learning and that grown-up people might achieve better results with less toil if they would sometimes take a leaf from the children's book. So he let his mind roam on, happily and without strain.[7]

He was a partisan for the children but he could be just as much at ease with the grown-ups, provided they were of the kind that suited him, either clever or simple, but not in between. The Gilletts saw a good deal of his relations with simple people because he liked to take them with him to his bushveld farm and sometimes arranged a

* During the war Hitler's government banned it. † See p. 171 above.

short safari for them when they visited South Africa.* He took them with him one day to the wedding of Leo, one of his black neighbours in the bushveld, and they enjoyed the dignity and friendliness of the occasion. In the Zoutpansberg he took them with him on a visit to the famous Rain Queen.† On safari he never stayed in hotels, because they made him feel like an animal in the zoo with the crowd gaping at him; the party always slept in tents. In the evenings, as they sat around the camp fire, farmers from the neighbourhood would often join them for long leisurely talks. One evening in July 1937 a farmer walked into their camp in the Louis Trichardt district. His name was Lemmer. Which family of the Lemmers? He said that he was a nephew of Commandant Lemmer, a comrade of Smuts in the Boer War days. The talk flowed—

I love to hear these genealogies gone into [Margaret Gillett wrote], it is all so friendly. It is a myth, this theory that Jannie is disliked and distrusted in his own country. There are those who dislike and distrust, but one sees when one goes about with him how general the friendliness is, and how easily the contacts are established when people are simple and natural. But it makes a story to work up, this myth of dislike and misunderstanding.

On their next safari about a year later three or four farmers walked one evening into their camp in the Clanwilliam district.

They were very nice people, the salt of their earth, and it was a pleasant and friendly little party, and he explained to them about the resignations in the Cabinet and about the European crisis, clearly and simply and easily, and it was full of humour and the goodness of things. People have a fable that Oom Jannie does not get on with people, but if they saw him with the country people they would never think that. It always seems to me that he is entirely at ease with people who have no nonsense about them and no sophistication, who will talk of the things they know.[8]

Not people in the mass but particular persons, not South Africa at large but particular places, delighted and restored him. He might say in one mood that Table Mountain meant more to him than sticks and stones but in another mood its sticks and stones and flowers and trees were magic to him; he knew thousands of them as individuals and kept discovering new ones on each new search that he made of

---

* Between 1935 and 1938 Mrs Gillett made three visits, twice with her husband and once with her sister, Dr Hilda Clark. In her letters home she gave full accounts of what Smuts was thinking and doing and of her own experiences.

† See p. 474 below.

4. Botanizing with Dr I. B. Pole-Evans in the Northern Transvaal

the plateau. In April 1936 he discovered twelve immense trees which he had never seen before, survivors of the primitive forest which now was crowded out by Forestry Department plantations of eucalypts and pines. He made a plan to clear the upper slopes from these intruders and make the mountain safe again for its original flora. At Cape Point, Vasco da Gama's most dramatic landmark, he struck another blow for the integrity of the ecological record.

Here we have at the door of this great metropolis [he wrote]*...a bit of wild nature very much in the same physical condition as it was hundreds of thousands of years ago. The game has unfortunately almost entirely gone. Some precious and rare plants have also disappeared. But the country itself looks very much as it appeared to the early Dutch settlers, as it appeared to Bushmen and Strandloopers, to the Fishhoek race who lived some 20,000 years ago, and to the still earlier Stone Age men and sub-humans who roamed this part of the sub-continent in the most distant part of our pre-human and sub-human origins.

Surely it must be a sacred trust to us of today to preserve this priceless relic of the past for the future generations.[9]

In the ecological record plants and trees were his particular favourites. 'Botany to me', he wrote, 'is what bridge or patience is to card players. Of course it is also much more.' According to his different moods he found different names for botany: it was his 'sweet opiate' when its images moved across his eyes as he was dropping off to sleep; it was 'poetry' to him when he was reading Marloth on Monocots; it was his 'companion' when he went on safari. In June 1935 he was planning a safari all the way to Nyasaland. 'My friends will shoot big game', he wrote, 'and I shall collect plants...I am so glad that I learnt botany when young—there is no better companion in the wilds.' It was just as much his companion in the paddocks of Doornkloof, his own highveld farm, especially when they were drenched by heavy rains after a long drought. Then he would go looking for the green shoots of grasses which for many years past had been lying dormant.[10]

At Rooikop, his lowveld farm, he enjoyed not only botanical but also archaeological pleasures. He mingled them with parental pride, for his son Jannie by now was winning renown through his studies of prehistorical implements, including the products of a great 'factory' that had existed at a bend of the Elands River near Rooikop.

* He wrote in support of a plan to buy back farms at Cape Point and make the whole area a Nature Reserve.

Those implements belonged to the Stellenbosch or Fauresmith culture—South Africa's equivalent of the Chellean and Acheulian culture of Europe. The men who had made the implements were precursors of *homo sapiens*. In his address to the South African Association in 1931 Smuts had made a spirited reconnaissance of this prehistorical territory and it now delighted him to find himself his son's pupil. Van Riet Lowe, whose appointment to full-time archaeological work he had promoted in May 1934, came down to Rooikop to help explore the implement factory. In Paris, the Abbé Breuil was taking note of Jannie's discoveries and theories. That proved to be the beginning of a happy and scientifically fruitful friendship.*[11]

Arthur Gillett told him once that botanizing and archaeologizing and camping in the bush were his way of escape from the hard realities of life; but he rejected that description. 'You mention the word "escape", he wrote, 'but I don't think we "escape" from our own world to this world of peace and harmony which seems so remote from ours. We *return* rather to the natural home of our minds and souls.' Return was literally the description of two pilgrimages that he made in 1937. In April he returned to Stellenbosch and walked along the identical footpaths among many of the same trees where he and Isie Krige had walked together so often half a century before. A month later he returned to Klipfontein, the Swartland farm where he had grown up.

Yesterday [he wrote] I saw the vast line of blue Winterhoek Mountains stretched out before Klipfontein with a beauty of colour and line and a majesty which made it even more to me than in the days of youthful romance in the far past. I could not think of anything more lovely in my long experience of scenery. And I blessed my good fortune in having been privileged to grow up in such surroundings, and with home associations which remain an unforgettable memory. The beauty of home life was fully matched by the beauty of the world around me. If anything has gone wrong since I cannot blame it on my associations of home or nature.[12]

Two years earlier he and Isie had returned together to Stellenbosch on a visit to the widow of Professor Johannes du Plessis, a student contemporary of theirs in the late 1880s at Victoria College. 'You will remember him', Smuts wrote, 'as the man who was excommunicated by the Dutch Reformed Church because he did not believe in Verbal Inspiration. He was a fine scholar and noble spirit

* See pp. 397–8 below.

and a dear companion of my youth.'[13] His death had left his widow in poor circumstances and Smuts discussed with her ways and means of educating her son. Perhaps he also discussed with her Johannes du Plessis's religious beliefs; certainly, he was thinking about them. And when he returned to Klipfontein it would have been strange if he did not recall the religious teaching of his uncle, the Reverend Boudewyn de Vries, pastor of the little church which he had attended every Sunday with his parents and brothers and sisters. In the eyes of a later generation of Calvinist theologians, his uncle's doctrine also was dangerously close to heresy; but Smuts doubted whether these theologians were closer to Christian truth than Boudewyn de Vries and Johannes du Plessis had been.*

Early in 1937 he started reading his New Testament again. This was a momentous act of return, although at the start he did not realize it. In a letter of 3 April, after recording his walk along the familiar paths at Stellenbosch and the memories it brought back, he wrote—

I have recently taken to reading the New Testament again in Greek, partly to recover some of my half-forgotten Greek but especially to see whether I can now get some fresh light on the Gospel story...We have put such a thick varnish of glosses and interpretations on the original account that a special effort has to be made to get back the simple intention of the original authors. So I am once more re-reading the wonderful story and have now done most of Matthew. I can only do a small bit each night...When I have done all four Gospels I shall try to clarify my mind and see whether any fresh conclusions are possible. When last I read the Greek Testament it was with very orthodox eyes, which I have no longer. And yet I am probably today more deeply interested to get at its meaning than I was in my orthodox youth.

Yet he was telling himself that the story meant more to him than the meaning. He loved its simplicity. Science, he said, dealt with general laws and theories; politics dealt with people in the mass; but the value of the Gospels was in their detail. Its vividness amazed him. He could hardly believe, yet he did believe, that there had been, once upon a time, an order of existence where simple men walked the earth filled with the spirit, however poor in all earthly things. They seemed so close to him that he had to keep reminding himself of their remoteness in time and place. They were primitive peasants. They lived in an obsolete Jewish setting. Jesus himself was a Jew who had died nineteen hundred years ago. Yet Smuts had the feeling that

* See *Smuts: The Sanguine Years*, pp. 20–2.

he knew Jesus and loved him, although in a different way, he said, than he had done as a boy.[14]

So for a time he surrendered himself to the story; but his nagging intellect did not leave him at peace for long. It intruded even upon his simple botanical pleasures; he re-read Goethe on the *Urphlanze* and studied the refutation of Goethe's theory in the books of Zimmerman, Bower and other post-Darwinian palaeobotanists. For a week or more he thought of nothing else.

I had almost forgotten the world. But...I suppose I shall soon be roused out of my botanic slumbers and be in the thick of the human struggle again. But it is pleasant for a short while to wander in the world of [say] five hundred million years ago, or more. Life was young but full of promise. Why should it not be even more promising now, in spite of the complications to which it has led?

Here he was restating his idea of emergent evolution; of *nisus*, or the upward thrust of successive evolutionary forms towards consciousness, personality and value; of immanence and inwardness in the processes of the universe. In his successive moods he saw the idea in the light of science, of poetry, of religion. He quoted Goethe's lines

> Was war ein Gott, der nur von aussen stiesse
> Im Kreis das All am Finger laufen liesse?*

In May 1939 he wrote—

The older I become, the more clearly I see that the Beyond that is Within is the only Beyond there is. It may be heresy but it is the nearest we shall ever come to the truth with our limited faculties of insight and expression.

Jesus, he said, had expressed that truth in seven words:

> The Kingdom of God is within you.[15]

In his letters Smuts returned again and again to that saying; yet he did not find it sufficient. He was beginning to doubt whether immanence, or continuous creation from the inside, or the Kingdom of God as an inner presence, was by itself a sufficient explanation of reality. It raised epistemological difficulties. For example, Eddington seemed to regard the order of the universe as a construct of the human intellect, but Smuts thought this view too flattering to *homo sapiens*; he believed rather that the universe, as a rational order,

---

*   What were a God who stood outside the whole,
     Spun at his ring and let it twirl alone?
                              (Lowes Dickinson's translation)

existed objectively, and that man was still in the early stages of exploring it. Similarly, Smuts looked upon man as the explorer, not the sole and original creator of moral values. Not only immanence, but transcendence, belonged to his world-picture. His trouble was to express the picture in words. 'We meet the Other', he wrote, 'we look into the Burning Bush which is not merely our own introspection.' That metaphor failed to satisfy him. He tried again. 'But surely', he exclaimed, 'there must be some "Other", and not my spiritual idealism merely...It is a nexus between two terms—the one "I", the other term—What?' He found no words to answer that question. Yet Jesus, he remembered, had made the mystery understandable in the simple imagery of a personal relationship: his 'other' was the Father; but he had also said 'I and the Father are one'.[16]

Smuts felt that mankind in his century was hanging in mid-air because it had nothing real and tangible to attach itself to. Religion, he said, was the anchoring of the personality to something steady and permanent and eternal in this transient turmoil; but his century had lost its anchorage and was being driven this way and that by fanatical ideologies and false Messiahs. He asked himself what the prospects were of a Christian recovery. Sometimes he thought that Christianity was too heavily incrusted with pre-scientific concepts to have meaning for modern man. At other times he thought that its meaning might still come through if it were sufficiently de-mythologized. At other times still he thought that story, metaphor and image were its proper and effective language. 'The Incarnation', he wrote, 'is just our attempt to undo our own mistake in separating God and Man.'[17]

The New Testament fascinated him but contained no direct answers that he could see to the political problems of his time. Nineteen centuries ago, he reflected, while Palestine was cultivating its own patch of the soul, Rome was bearing the almost intolerable burdens of world government. Jesus had lived within the shelter of the Roman peace. He had had no experience of the problems of power. Isaiah's portrait of the Suffering Servant* seemed to have made a deeper impression upon him than anything else in the old records.

---

* Smuts discussed 'self-suffering' in a study of Gandhi's technique which he wrote at this time for the volume of Gandhian studies edited by Radhakrishnan. See *Smuts: The Sanguine Years*, p. 346.

The Suffering Servant made no appeal to Smuts when he thought about Hitler.

Resist not evil? Yes, resist to the uttermost. But how? Shall we fight evil with its own weapons? Can we allow force to submerge everything without mustering greater force to stop it?

Up to March 1939, when Hitler seized Prague, Smuts was still withholding his answer to those practical questions. In August he was reading Kierkegaard's *Fear and Trembling*, a book which made Abraham's temptation the starting-point of a deep discussion of faith. By now, Smuts had decided that his own faith must be militant.[18]

From the time of Munich to the outbreak of war Smuts kept his friends informed from week to week about his views on the international situation. His letters expressed two intermingling moods: the mood of an observer, trying to understand events in the outer world and their significance for South Africa; the mood of a participator, trying to discover his own duty.

As an observer of the controversy in Britain after Munich he gave credit to Chamberlain. He did this most emphatically in a broadcast address for Armistice Day, 1938. He asked his listeners to consider the situation and prospects of world peace twenty years after the ending of the Great War. He examined at some length the setbacks which the League had suffered and emphasized their dangerous consequences. The choices last September had seemed stark— 'nothing but brute force or abject surrender'—until Chamberlain's intervention saved the peace and gave the world a second chance. Smuts insisted that ordinary people throughout the world expected their leaders to make constructive use of that chance. The intense relief which they had shown last September when the danger of war disappeared seemed to him a good augury for peace. On the other hand, the shock tactics which some national leaders had recently employed were a menace to peace and would lead to another world explosion unless they were stopped. Under present conditions, Smuts continued, rearmament and alliances were inevitable and might even exercise a stabilizing influence in short term; but their outcome sooner or later would be war. Peace, he insisted, must rest upon the rule of law and sound institutions. 'I am and remain', he declared,

5. On Table Mountain, February 1939

'a League man. What other alternatives are there before us?' He ended his broadcast by considering ways and means of restoring the League and making it, even at this late stage, a comprehensive and authoritative guardian of the world's peace.[19]

Neither publicly nor in private did he pay any respect at all to the plea, which even then was being made in whispers, that Chamberlain had served his country well by postponing war to a more convenient season. Not the postponement of war, but the safeguarding of peace was his objective. Up to the end of 1938 he still had good hopes of its being achieved; but early in 1939 his fears began to predominate over his hopes. He had been making plans with his American friends the Lamonts for a holiday in Nyasaland, but on 10 January he called the plans off. 'Everything', he wrote, 'seems to point to trouble coming to a head in south-eastern Europe next spring or summer. Russia is weak and Germany has apparently a clear field to move towards the Black Sea, and constitute a new Manchukuo in the Ukraine...Besides, there is a Nemesis behind these Dictators and they have to keep moving on.' He was afraid that they were proposing to move on not only in eastern but also in western Europe. Their victory in Spain was imminent and he feared that they would use it to threaten British and French communications in the Mediterranean. If they did, they would create a crisis worse than that of September last. Did Hitler think, Smuts asked, that the military position now was more favourable to Germany and Italy than it would be later on? That looked like madness; but nations had gone mad before, and they were not immune now, despite the warning of 1914–18. Yet perhaps it was all a great bluff? That thought brought Smuts small consolation; the bluff, he said, would not come off but would more likely create a situation from which honourable retreat was impossible. 'I think of London', he wrote, 'with its 12 million people under the devastation of air raids...But God took pity on Nineveh, and so He may take pity on these poor innocent people over whom the doom of destruction hovers.'[20]

Smuts prayed for peace. None the less he expressed concern about Britain's anti-aircraft defences. In Spain Franco won the war. Smuts feared the sequel there. It surprised him when the blow fell first on Czechoslovakia. He wrote on 17 March 1939—

So events have moved even faster in Europe than even I in my pessimistic mood had expected. While the papers were announcing improving conditions and both Chamberlain and Hertzog talked of the prospects of a long era of peace—based on preparedness—Hitler has made another of his stunning blows and another sovereign state lies prostrate before Germany. Hitler sits today in the old Castle in Prague where I found Masaryk in April 1919—revising his Czech or Russian dictionary! Freedom shrieked as Kosciusko fell. But today Freedom does not even get time to shriek, but is suffocated out of existence without warning. Nor do I believe this is the end...I imagine Italy will not be satisfied to be a mere onlooker while Germany swallows all the feast in Central Europe.

Yet for a few weeks more Italy still remained an onlooker.

So friend Hitler has once more gobbled up a province [Smuts wrote on 24 March]—Memelland this time. 'An apple a day'—a province per week. I can understand the perturbation all over Europe. But I am waiting to see what will be the next move by friend Musso. Surely he cannot remain naked and hungry while his partner has this gargantuan feast.

Mussolini waited until Good Friday. Smuts was in the Karoo that day, looking at some exciting irrigation projects. He wrote that night—

So much for the coming Eden. But in this world the serpent is never far off. So on reaching home we had to read of Mussolini's invasion of Albania. Sudden aggression of the type which Hitler has now made popular. Will Mussolini stop at Albania? It is too small a beginning to satisfy so great a greed...But the furies, the Erinyes, are gathering to avenge all this lawless greed—only how much more will be destroyed besides Mussolini and his new Empire.![21]

Smuts possibly paid too much attention to Mussolini. It was Hitler who made the pace. By seizing Prague he had broken his word to Chamberlain. When Chamberlain told the House of Commons what had happened, Smuts felt sorry for him.

What a feeble performance! Did British Prime Ministers ever before make such a feeble show? One cannot help feeling pity for him. His whole effort for peace has simply been set aside without further ado, and the naked reality stares him in the face. I have no doubt that his intention was good and that the first results (in securing peace last September) were all to the good. But how can one deal with these people if one genuinely wishes to avoid war?

He thought that Chamberlain was trying to rebuild collective security but would find building a harder task than pulling down had been; after all, it was he who had called sanctions midsummer madness and had dealt a final blow to the League. Smuts thought that the most Chamberlain could now hope for was a limited coalition, and even that would prove a difficult attempt. He was astounded when the news reached him that Chamberlain had drawn a line in eastern Europe and in effect had warned Hitler not to cross it.

Chamberlain's Polish guarantee [he wrote on 6 April] has simply made us gasp—from the Commonwealth point of view. I cannot see the Dominions following Great Britain in this sort of Imperial policy the dangers of which to the Commonwealth are obvious. We still remember Lloyd George's Chanak escapade…And in any case what a commentary on Chamberlain's previous disregard for collective security, and his calling League sanctions 'midsummer madness' in the case of Abysinnia! The real midsummer madness was letting the League down and rendering it useless for future co-operation in case of dire need. Chamberlain's League policy and flirting with Mussolini may yet produce other more dangerous consequences. Time alone can show.

Two months later he was still apprehensive about Chamberlain's European policy.

It is curious how Chamberlain has veered right round. He fought collective security—and called sanctions under the League 'midsummer madness'—and now he has given or offered guarantees to Poland, Rumania and I don't know how many others. He has really gone much farther than the League ever went. I don't find fault. Needs must when the devil drives. But it is a right about turn such as one has seldom even seen among politicians. I sometimes wonder however what chickens will in time come out of this brood of guarantees. Unless they can all be turned to a joint account of something in the nature of the League we may yet be sold an awful pup by countries who will in reliance on our guarantees drag us into one mess after the other. But perhaps this is just pessimism.[22]

The case for a more optimistic diagnosis depended, in his opinion, upon the outcome of the British negotiations with Russia. In early May he expressed doubts about their prospects; Litvinov's dismissal as Soviet Foreign Minister puzzled him; he asked himself whether Russia was turning to Germany and whether Hitler was re-insuring himself with Russia as Bismarck had done. 'Communism and Nazism', he reflected, 'are really close together.' Towards the end of May he rated higher the chances of an Anglo-Russian agreement.

The international situation [he wrote] looks slightly easier, with the prospect of an agreement with Russia. I have never liked entanglements with Russia which is to me an inscrutable country. But if that is the way to peace then for peace's sake let us have it. If a military agreement with Russia is concluded I believe the situation in Europe will be one of military stalemate, the opposing forces will be fairly balanced, and war may become unlikely. What is more, the continuance of the present intolerable situation of strained preparation will become senseless, consultations for a general settlement may ensue which may be the way out of the present dangers...

He continued his recital of possible happy events which might lead to yet other happy events—including a renunciation by Hitler of shock tactics against the Poles. This, he admitted, was 'just a wish thought', for even if an Anglo-Russian agreement were achieved, the dictators might still decide to get their blow in first. The predominance of his hopes over his fears was fractional and even so it did not last long. He wrote on 4 June—

Russia is hanging back, and Molotov talks casually of closer commercial relations with Germany while ostensibly pressing for the most far-reaching military agreement against Germany. What does all this mean—if not mere bluff to frighten the English and French into tying themselves hand and foot to Russia? Germany may see good reason to strike before this agreement is concluded, and secretly coquette with Russia to keep her quiet. Stranger things have happened...

Throughout the next two months all the news from Moscow seemed to him strange, to say the least of it. By early August he was growing alarmed at the apparent failure of the negotiations to make headway; peace seemed to hang on their outcome and if they came to nothing he imagined that war was a certainty. On 17 August he wrote—

What is happening in Moscow? Why this inordinate delay in fixing up an agreement? One feels all through that there are vital factors in the international situation which are hidden or unknown. And that makes one all the more uneasy and unwilling to form definite opinions.

A day or two later Ribbentrop and Molotov announced their agreement. Everything, or nearly everything, was clear at last. On 20 August Smuts wrote—

As you know I have been pessimistic for months about the European situation, and at last the great blow seems to be *about* to fall. I say *about* because *something* may still happen at the end. Hitler is to speak on Sunday and thereafter comes Nuremberg. It is just possible that war may still be prevented. But at present it looks like a moral certainty...

Hitler's speech the next Sunday made war a plain certainty. He demanded the immediate return to Germany of Danzig and the

Polish Corridor. But the world, Smuts said, was not in the mood for another Munich. He went on to make it clear that he himself was not in that mood.[23]

As an observer, he had no further comment to make on the course of events; but as a participator he had not yet spoken the irrevocable word. Before he could speak it he had to decide what his duty was. His formulations of that question had kept changing with the changes of circumstance. After Munich he asked himself: What can I do to help save the peace? After Prague he asked himself: What shall I do if war comes? After the Nazi–Soviet agreement he asked himself: What must I do when war comes? These phases of circumstance and of his self-questioning were not sharply distinct but overlapping. Even in his mood of profound relief after Munich he had realized that the danger of war, although averted for the time being, might return later on. In the aftermath of Prague he exclaimed one day that war had already come, except for the shooting.* Within his own mind he was already facing the question about his duty.

His friends could not possibly have doubted what his answer would be at the moment of decision. He would accept the commitment of war. Acceptance was a simple act of will; but its reasons were complex. Unconsciously, he revealed some of their complexities in the different connotations which he gave at different times to the first personal pronoun plural. 'We' meant for him 'We South Africans', 'We members of the Commonwealth', 'We free men', 'We humans'.

29 January: I cannot believe that we [= we humans] are fated with our own hands and with open eyes to destroy this civilization of ours.

10 March: If we [= we free men] do not go all out—by political action and if need be by fighting for our democratic principles—the Totalitarians are certain to win and reduce our civilization to a confirmed servitude. We cannot face that. I would rather die fighting than become passive [pacifist] and thus contribute to the downfall.

27 March: If we [= we humans, we free men] could once more hear the clear call of duty, and realize that the great human ideals are the only things worth living for, we may yet reconstruct this dying civilization on nobler foundations.

* He realized, of course, that war in the full sense of the word had already come to Asia. He paid close attention to the fighting in China and he watched Japan 'creeping south from week to week' along the coastline of Indo-China. He realized that Britain could not cope simultaneously with a European and a Pacific war and he welcomed Roosevelt's 'transfer of his Pacific fleet back to that ocean'.[24]

23 April: We [= we South Africans] have got drawn into this war business, and as a precaution against a Putsch I sent some 300 armed police to Windhoek to keep the peace, and at the same time introduced a Bill to take over the policing of S.W. Africa which hitherto has been left to an inefficient local administration. Of course I am accused of creating a war atmosphere, of siding with Great Britain, of dragging South Africa into war, etc. But I am quite right and shall not be deterred.*

8 August: Note the date of this letter. Twenty-five years after,† we [= we members of the Commonwealth] are once more facing the gravest situation in this poor old world. If war comes we shall eventually pull through once more, but I fear the initial go off.

In all these utterances, and in many more that he made throughout those months, he revealed his mood and purpose: not neutrality but participation, if and when war came.[25]

As the testing time drew near his spirits rose, as they had done in 1899. He took a short trip to Lake Kivu and watched a near-by volcano erupting and sending a river of red-hot lava into the lake. Why worry about the dictator spouters, he asked himself, when there was such a real and natural spouter in the world? None the less he cursed the mistakes of the past which now made it necessary to defy the dictators upon disadvantageous ground. For him personally the worst possible ground was Danzig and the Polish Corridor. He wrote on 6 July—

I see the German papers are making a great point of my having protested at Paris that Poland was being dangerously enlarged, and that the inclusion of Danzig was a grave mistake. Fate has so arranged it that Danzig may actually be the cause of the next world war. But it is a poor consolation to me that I have been a true prophet...For if Germany does fight for Danzig, she will deliberately fight for much more, and Danzig will be merely the specious excuse. It is pretty rotten to have my warnings of 20 years ago now twisted and used against us in this way. My own private feeling is that if necessary we shall now *have* to fight about Danzig...If Danzig follows Prague and Albania and all the rest we may as well put up the shutters of democracy.

But would his fellow citizens understand that? What, he asked, did Danzig mean to them? He wrote on 28 August—

With us there is no enthusiasm for Poland, and less for Danzig and the Corridor. Moreover, neutrality is even more firmly held as a faith than

---

* He acted in his capacity as Minister of Justice after making sure that he had his Prime Minister's support. They both believed that the action was urgently necessary and Smuts said later (to John Martin, 3 Aug. 1939) that it just forestalled a coup.

† Twenty-five years after the outbreak of the Great War (as it was then called).

in the Middle West of U.S.A. And on the other side (which happens to be my own) there is the difficulty to understand how in the long run we could possibly keep out of the fight, and how we could do so now consistently with our honour and vital interests...I had to face it 25 years ago and never thought of having it all over again. But such are the choices before us. The Germans, knowing my attitude at Paris, have published my notes to Lloyd George and Wilson protesting against the undue enlargement of Poland as a sure cause of future war. And now that my prophecy may come true I have to tell the people that it would be wrong for them to stand aside! And so wisdom is turned into the appearance of folly, and my conduct convicted of inconsistency. It is a queer world. I wish I were 25 years younger.[26]

He could better have written '40 years younger'. That would have made him 29, his age in 1899 when he went to war against the British Empire.

Hertzog, meanwhile, was standing fast—although Smuts at the time did not know it—upon the decision of his Cabinet at the time of Munich to declare South Africa a neutral or semi-neutral power.* From what he said in the House of Assembly on 4 September 1939 it became plain that he ascribed continuing validity to that decision, irrespective of changing circumstances. In his view, it was the duty of Smuts to give him plain notice, if and when Smuts ceased to feel himself bound by the principles which the Cabinet had accepted on 28 September 1938. In later years, Hertzog's biographers repeated and endorsed that reproach against Smuts. Pirow reproached him for a failure of frankness not only towards his Prime Minister but towards the South African public. Smuts, Pirow said, remained silent as the danger grew.[27]

Pirow was in error. Between 1 October 1938 and 23 August 1939 Smuts made twenty speeches which dealt at length with the international situation and its significance for South Africa. Each of these speeches was front-page news.[28] Together, the speeches constituted a clear record of what Smuts was thinking about the course of world politics and the interests and obligations of his own country. The trend of his public statements, like that of his private correspondence, was from guarded optimism to grave foreboding. Even in his mood of relief after Munich, he warned his audiences that the world's reprieve from disaster was conditional. He told them that the world was still dangerous, not least for South Africa. On 2 November 1938,

* See p. 285 above and p. 319 below.

speaking after Hertzog at a United party Conference in the Free State, he prayed that his Prime Minister might be proved right in forecasting a long period of peace—'but nobody', he continued, 'has a guarantee that things may not be different'. Like Hertzog, he accepted rearmament as a means of safeguarding the peace, but he was more insistent than Hertzog had been on its urgency for South Africa.

We have to look after ourselves [he declared] even if it costs millions... We are going to arm ourselves, even if it costs millions, simply because we want to keep what we have. We are not, through weakness or unpreparedness, going to allow an enemy to come to our shores and pluck South Africa like a ripe fruit.

At Potschefstroom on 28 April 1939 he and Pirow spoke from the same platform, and as regards land defences, to the same brief; but Pirow said nothing about his country's seaward defences. Smuts, by contrast, insisted in speech after speech that South Africa's safety was in the keeping of the Royal Navy.

9 December 1938, at Wemmerspan: When all is said and done the fact remains that the Royal Navy is and remains the sure shield of this country. That does not mean we have to be supine, neglect duty and leave all to the navy. But it is wise to recognize that fundamental fact in our defence situation.

27 March 1939, in Gardens constituency, Cape Town, after referring to Pirow's review of defence plans: But let me tell you that there are forms of defence which we cannot prepare in this country. And as things are today, and as they will continue for years, the best and the surest shield in this country for the independence of our people and the rights of this country will be the Royal Navy.

Make no mistake about it. I am not talking politics but fundamental sound sense. We have not a ship to protect our shores.

14 April 1939, at Malmesbury: We are lucky to have her [Britain's] fleet.

On foreign policy Smuts reiterated three linked propositions: South Africa could not isolate herself, but needed friends; her best friends were Britain and the other nations of the Commonwealth; she could not count on staying neutral.

12 October 1938, at Zeerust, referring to Malan's demand that South Africa should proclaim her neutrality in advance: We are a country worth conquering. Let us not lightly make a declaration which will place us in the greatest danger.

16 November 1938, at United party Conference at Pietermaritzburg: What is South Africa's lot in this cruel and Satanic world? To my mind there seems to be a curious delusion of safety in the Union. We look upon our 7,000 miles of distance as our protection...In the politics of South Africa you have this parrot cry of neutrality, a gospel which is being preached from many platforms in South Africa.

How will neutrality save us in days of danger? When we are in danger, are we to appeal to the aggressor for mercy?...Do not let us befool ourselves with talk of neutrality, but let us make up our minds that when danger comes to us we are going to fight for our country and its vital interests.

9 December 1938, opening Witwatersrand branch of the Navy League at Wemmerspan: These are solemn days for mankind. When people are thinking in terms of world domination, surely it is something that fills us with gratitude that the great sea power is still in the hands of the Commonwealth of Nations...

There are ignorant people in this country who speak lightly of cutting the painter, who talk glibly of neutrality in all circumstances and all cases. People who talk like that do not reckon with the facts and dangers which are on the move in the world today. No one can do South Africa a more serious disservice than make it possible for this country, in the hour of danger, to be deprived of the protection she has from the Royal Navy.

13 January 1939, at Ermelo: People who thought South Africa could be safe if a big war broke out were hopelessly misled. Even the United States would not be able to remain neutral, as it had been unable to do in 1917.

Early March 1939, interview with Negley Farson, reported in Rand Daily Mail, 6 March: As times of test approach we stick to our friends...It is not sentiment, it is an economic and defence necessity. Regarding South West Africa, our position is both legally and morally indefeasible. We shall keep it. Yes, we would even go to war. We will go to any extreme.

28 March, at Gardens, Cape Town: Other small nations like ourselves have gone under before now, and another thing which is essential, and which we have to do, is to keep in the closest touch possible with our friends and our associates in the British Commonwealth of Nations.

18 April, at Paarl: We have our friends in the world. We belong to the British Commonwealth of Nations.

Surely Pirow was careless, if not worse, when he accused Smuts— who by then had been dead for ten years—of having concealed his feelings and thoughts from the South African public. Pirow also accused him of concealing them from Hertzog. Presumably, Hertzog read the newspapers.

Hertzog seldom spoke about the world situation; but on 23 March 1939, after Hitler's occupation of Prague, he issued the following statement:

When and where the activities of a European country are of such a nature or extent that it can be inferred therefrom that its object and endeavour

are the domination of other free countries and peoples, and that the liberty
and interests of the Union are also threatened thereby, the time will then
also come for this Government to warn the people of the Union and to
ask this House to occupy itself with European affairs, even where the
Union would otherwise have no interests or would take no interest in
them.[29]

That statement was not trenchant; but Smuts possibly deduced from
it that Hertzog's mind about the foreign situation was moving in the
same direction as his own. If Smuts did make that deduction, it was
no more than a guess. Hertzog was not circulating important telegrams to his colleagues—at any rate, not to Smuts.* He was not
consulting his Cabinet. He had called it together at the time of
Munich; but he did not summon it when the Ribbentrop–Molotov
pact was announced, although that event must have shattered his
own assumptions—if Pirow rightly understood them†—about the
structure of world politics. When the Cabinet did at last meet
on 2 September the reason was in the main an absurd parliamentary accident.

On Monday 28 August Smuts described the accident in a letter to
the Gilletts.

Saturday was a busy day in office, as Friday had been; and added to the office
work a new tangle had turned up which has made us call precipitately
for a meeting of parliament. The Senate is due to expire next 5 Sep., but
the elections for a fresh Senate cannot be held till about the end of Oct.
And this at a time when the world is in wild uproar. Of course we cannot
leave this country without a full Parliament at a time when very grave
decisions may have to be taken; and so a meeting of Parliament for next
Saturday [2 Sep.] to prolong the life of the Senate had to be arranged.
Saturday last was spent in making these sudden arrangements, and in preparing the necessary legislation and other steps. . . It is curious that we should
have overlooked this hiatus in our parliamentary machinery. But the fact is
that nobody (except myself) has taken the European crisis very seriously.
It was looked upon as the usual Hitler bluff; and not calling for any
parliamentary action. Now of course the aspect of affairs has suddenly
become most sinister—hence this belated action to keep the Senate in
being.

* In various letters in 1938 and 1939 Smuts revealed, not with complaint, that he had
no official inside information about the international situation, apart from the summaries
circulated periodically by the Dominions Office to Commonwealth governments.[30] However, what has been said above about Hertzog's conduct of South African foreign policy
may call for revision when his private papers and the official records of his office become
accessible to historians.
† See p. 271 above.

And so the government had to summon parliament before it had any policy to put before it.[31]

Of the many stories told in later years about the fateful events of 2–4 September the most illuminating and vivid was Harry Lawrence's story.[32] Lawrence arrived at Cape Town on the morning of Friday 1 September, met Smuts and heard the news that Hitler had attacked Poland. Next day parliament met at 10.30 a.m. After the first formalities of the special session had been disposed of, Malan rose to ask the government what its attitude to the crisis was. Hertzog postponed giving an answer; he could not give one until he summoned his Cabinet. The House concluded its formal business. Smuts told Lawrence, as they walked away together, that there would be a meeting of the Cabinet at 3 p.m. that afternoon at Groote Schuur.

When the Cabinet met, Hertzog opened the proceedings. He spoke for an hour or more, striding backwards and forwards across the carpeted floor. He argued that Hitler was attempting nothing more than to free Germany from the fetters of Versailles and that South Africa should follow the policy agreed upon at the time of the Munich crisis. One or two ministers then spoke in his support, among them General Kemp, who declared that there would be a blood bath in South Africa unless the government maintained neutrality.

At last [as Lawrence vividly recalled the picture] General Smuts leant forward, his delicate hands ranging restlessly as was their wont in moments of emotion. He began by stating that the decision he had come to was the most serious he had been called upon to take in all his life; then he went on to say why South Africa should stand by the Commonwealth and declare war on Germany. Incidentally, he observed that he was Minister of Justice and that he had no reason to think that a declaration of war would lead to a blood bath.

Each one of us present at the meeting spoke that afternoon and expressed his views.

Seven members of the Cabinet were for Smuts and war, six for Hertzog and neutrality. Hertzog adjourned the meeting to the afternoon of the next day, Sunday 3 September.

Lawrence had breakfast next morning with Smuts at the Civil Service Club. After breakfast Smuts took Lawrence to his bedroom and showed him the rough draft of the motion he proposed to move next day in parliament. Then he went away to meet his daughter Louis and walk with her in the Kirstenbosch gardens. Many people saw them there, enjoying the wild flowers and shrubs. They drew comfort from his serenity.

Before the Cabinet met again on the Sunday afternoon Hertzog, although Smuts and his supporters did not know it, had received a message from Malan, promising his party's support for a motion of neutrality. The Cabinet meeting was short.

It was clear [Lawrence recalled] that there was a deadlock in the Cabinet, and General Hertzog declared that he would put the matter to the House. He was obviously convinced that he would have a majority for his neutrality motion.

It was in many respects a sad occasion, for we had reached the parting of the ways. After Colonel Reitz had thanked General Hertzog for the courtesy he had invariably shown those who had served under him, and expressed the hope that the personal friendships we had made would not be affected by what had happened, we all drank some sherry, shook hands, and left on our respective ways.

. . . General Hertzog had indicated that he would move his neutrality motion the next day; and General Smuts made it equally clear that he would come with a counter-motion.

That evening, Smuts met the ministers who had supported him in the Cabinet meeting and showed them the draft motion which he had shown in the morning to Lawrence. They accepted it.

Louis Esselen was also present at that meeting. As secretary of the United party he was in close personal touch with its members in parliament and was making a count of how they would be likely to give their votes next day. Colin Steyn, a former adherent of Roos who now supported Smuts, made a count of his own on Sunday evening. Some journalists made counts. Many stories were told in later years about these counts and their effect upon the minds of the two leaders. Possibly Smuts felt pessimistic at first, just as Hertzog felt optimistic. Possibly the estimates made by Esselen and Steyn caused him to rate his prospects of success higher. Nevertheless, neither he nor anybody else could predict the outcome of the debate with certainty.

On Monday 4 September the House met at 10.35 a.m. and quickly disposed of the Senate Bill. Hertzog then introduced his motion. As officially reported it was identical,[33] except for some unimportant verbal variations, with the proposal approved by the Cabinet on 28 September 1938.

That this House approves and accepts as the policy of the Government of the Union that the existing relations between the Union of South Africa and the various belligerent countries will, in so far as the Union is concerned, persist unchanged and continue as if no war is being waged: Upon the understanding, however, that the existing relations and obligations between the Union and Great Britain, or any other member of the British Commonwealth of Nations, in so far as such relations or obligations result from contractual undertakings relating to the Naval base at Simonstown or from its membership in the League of Nations, or in so far as such relations and obligations result *impliciter* from the free association of the Union with the other members of the British Commonwealth of Nations, shall continue unimpaired and shall be maintained by the Union; and no one shall be permitted to use Union territory for the purpose of doing anything which may in any way impair the said relations or obligations.

The core of Hertzog's argument was the equation he made between neutrality and independence. If South Africa joined the war on the British side, he declared, she would do so because a section of her people cared more for British than for South African interests. Such an outlook was incompatible with South African freedom and independence. If it prevailed, it would destroy South African unity. Hertzog spoke with passionate conviction and his speech, up to that point, had a powerful effect. He spoilt the effect by launching himself upon a tirade against 'the monster of Versailles' and protesting his conviction of Hitler's innocence.

Tom Naudé seconded the Prime Minister's motion and Smuts then rose to move his amendment:

To omit all the words after 'That' and to substitute 'this House declares that the policy of the Union in this crisis shall be based on the following principles and convictions, viz:

(1) It is in the interest of the Union that its relations with the German Reich should be severed, and that the Union should refuse to adopt an attitude of neutrality in this conflict.

(2) The Union should carry out the obligations to which it has agreed, and continue its co-operation with its friends and associates in the British Commonwealth of Nations.

(3) The Union should take all necessary measures for the defence of its territory and South African interests and the Government should not send forces overseas as in the last war.

(4) This House is profoundly convinced that the freedom and

independence of the Union are at stake in this conflict and that it is therefore in its true interest to oppose the use of force as an instrument of national policy.[34]

South African interests constituted the core of Smuts's speech. He took a different view from Hertzog of South African interests because he took a different view of Hitler and his policy. Danzig, he insisted, was only in appearance the cause of the war. The real cause was Hitler's refusal to admit any limit to his ambitions. The recovery of South West Africa was one of them and if South West Africa were lost the security of the Union would not be worth much. The time for defending the nation's independence and security was now, while the war was remote geographically and South Africa had loyal and powerful friends. If South Africa dissociated herself from her friends in the British Commonwealth the day would come when she would find herself isolated in a dangerous world.

Colonel Collins, the Minister for Agriculture and Fisheries, and Smuts's comrade forty years earlier in his fight against the British Empire, seconded the motion.* Then Heaton Nicholls rose and came close to destroying the effect of Smuts's speech. The whole debate, he declared in effect, was a sham because South Africa was already at war in virtue of the common allegiance which every British subject in every country of the British Commonwealth owed to the Crown. B. K. Long, until recently the editor of the *Cape Times*, saved the situation by repudiating that disastrous doctrine and insisting that the representatives of a free and independent nation were assembled that day to express the nation's will on its own destiny. In a moving passage of his speech Long pleaded that the natural affection of English-speaking South Africans for England should not be made a reproach against them: because of it they loved South Africa not less but more; as South African patriots they felt at unity in nationhood with their Afrikaans-speaking partners, who also were descended from a liberty-loving race. They believed that the freedom and security of their country lay in active comradeship with the other free nations of the Commonwealth. If South Africa stayed neutral, Long asserted, she would in effect be gambling upon a victory of the Commonwealth which she would have no part in winning. That would be ignoble; it would also be imprudent. Long sat down after making the most decisive speech, except for Smuts's,

---

* Despite his name, Collins consistently spoke Afrikaans in the House of Assembly.

in the debate. Malan followed Long. His speech was dignified but he added nothing to Hertzog's argument except his party's votes. He controverted the theory of national status which Nicholls, not Smuts and Long, had asserted. He endorsed Hertzog's justification of Hitler and insisted—in strange forgetfulness of Milner and 1899—that Germany's annexation of Czechoslovakia was 'a matter of safety' for her. The war, he insisted, was not a South African but a British war. If South Africa joined it she would proclaim herself 'a country of serfs'.

So the debate swung this way and that until nine that evening. When the division bell rang the voting was:

in favour of Hertzog's motion 67
in favour of Smuts's amendment 80

Smuts had carried South Africa into war by 13 votes.*

Strictly on the logic of *realpolitik*, Smuts deserved his victory. Hertzog's analysis of the European situation did not carry conviction. The Treaty of Versailles, which he denounced so passionately, still remained a memorable historical event; but after Prague and the Ribbentrop–Molotov pact it had lost such remnants of relevance for practical statesmen as it had retained up to 1939. Hitler, moreover, had given the South African government plain notice that he intended to demand the return of South West Africa. Hertzog had made an equally plain statement that the Union would never surrender that territory. Consequently, he could not convincingly argue that no South African interest was at stake in the conflict. In Smuts's argument also there were one or two unconvincing passages. He said there was no such thing in international law or in practical wisdom as the 'modified neutrality' which the Prime Minister proposed; but he failed to explain clearly why he had been willing the previous September to approve that middle course. He asserted that Germany was seeking to dominate the whole world by force; but that was a subjective judgment which might be, and indeed was, challenged. Despite those shortcomings, Smuts made a more coherent and convincing analysis of the national interest than Hertzog did.

A notable defect of Hertzog's speech had been the static conception

---

* Strictly speaking he did not carry South Africa into the war until 6 September, when the Governor-General, after refusing Hertzog's request for a dissolution, received his resignation, invited Smuts to form a government, and swore the new government in. The Governor-General made a careful record of each successive phase of these important transactions.

of politics and war which it revealed. The wild rush of events in 1940 would inevitably have shattered his painstaking formula for a modified neutrality. In retrospect, some wistful adherents of fusion argued that if he had been given time enough he would have brought a united South Africa into the war later on. The opposite would almost certainly have happened. Later on, as leader of the Opposition when France fell, Hertzog declared that Great Britain had already lost the war and that South Africa must save herself by making a separate peace. If he had been leader of the government when France fell he would hardly have chosen that time for scrapping his neutrality formula to bring South Africa onto the side of Britain and the embattled Commonwealth. Nationalist pressures in 1940 were so fierce that his policy would almost certainly have been to make a separate peace, with or without secession from the Commonwealth.*

Smuts therefore was right when he insisted that the decision to go to war had to be made once and for all on 4 September 1939. He counted the cost of that decision. Some of his opponents told him that it would mean civil war. He did not shut his eyes to that danger but took precautions against it. He knew that the decision to go to war would create bitter division in the country. But a decision to stay neutral would also create bitter division. The lines of cleavage were in different places. Smuts believed that the cleavage which Malan wanted and which Hertzog seemed to accept would do irreparable damage to the nation. He believed that the cleavage which he himself accepted could be repaired with time.

South Africa [he wrote] has a divided soul, but if we are faithful to the vision of forty years ago that soul will be one yet. Time is a causal factor and there has not yet been enough time. But in time it will come all right although we may not see it in our day.

Nevertheless he felt bitter grief when the head committee of the United party met for the last time at Bloemfontein. 'It was a tragic occasion', he wrote, 'and we separated almost in tears.'[35]

His counting of the cost of war for Europe and for the world was no less sombre. While orators and pamphleteers were already explaining how the war would lead to better things for humanity, he wrote to Tom Lamont—

Shall we never learn the lesson? There is no solution through war. This war, whatever the ultimate issue, will be followed by another peace which

* See pp. 350–1 below.

may be no peace, for after a devastating conflict there is no mood for a real and wise peace, as you and I found at Paris in 1919. Meanwhile civilization is falling back and the light of the Spirit is being dimmed... And so the caravan passes once more into the night. May God be with us and take the hands of His erring children.[36]

He did his utmost to free himself from illusions. He went to war because he could see no alternative. He saw a threat to values which in his view had to be defended. First among them was the security of his own country; in the early months of the war he made many speeches on that theme. He constantly reiterated his warning that the world was a dangerous place for small nations which had no friends. That always led him to the Commonwealth. He believed that South Africa had a vital interest in its survival. He also valued the Commonwealth for the promise of a co-operative world order which he saw foreshadowed in it.

For me personally [he wrote in January 1940] there was no other way. I am a firm believer in the Commonwealth, not only for its own sake and that of South Africa, but as the first tentative beginnings of great things for the future of the world. I was not going to desert or betray that great cause.[37]

He never made a comprehensive and systematic ennumeration of the things that he was fighting for but revealed them by flashes in his letters to his friends. Unconsciously he revealed his fighting spirit. Not merely his intellect but his temperament carried him into the war. One day he spent a little time looking at photographs of Chamberlain and Hitler. Chamberlain, he said, looked a good fellow, only undistinguished. But Hitler—

To me the wonder is how so small and commonplace a person can wield such influence for evil. His writings and speeches are the very acme of undistinction and vulgarity. And yet not Bismarck [he said later on 'not even Napoleon'] has wielded such influence. Great men have an air, a form about them which stamps them as apart from their fellows, but Hitler remains small, beastly and brutish...I certainly feel outraged by that [photograph] of Hitler. I suppose the Lord wanted to show our age how small we really are, by putting such a puny mortal in charge of us.[38]

Smuts was too much of an aristocrat to submit to seeing himself and his country and the Commonwealth and the world being put into Hitler's charge.

PART IV

WAR

CHAPTER 18

THE TWO FRONTS

HERTZOG had asserted in his speech to the House of Assembly on 4 September that South Africa could not possibly give any more support to the Commonwealth than his own proposals for modified neutrality made provision for.[1] Smuts was convinced that South Africa not only could, but must, give more support than that. His sombre forecasting envisaged a war of the oceans, quite possibly of the continents, into which South Africa must inevitably be drawn because of her situation on the map of world strategy.

He had no doubt that the enemy held the initiative. He called Hitler's pact with Stalin a pact between the Devil and Beelzebub and declared that it stamped Hitler at the outset as a morally defeated person; but so long as the two dictators held together they were a terrifying combination. If Germany should really get control of Russian resources the struggle would be grim. Even without that, he said, 'Germany has her hands free in the East and can mass all her resources at the vital points. In the air and on land she is very strong, and the ordeal for us will be fearful.' There was also Mussolini to be reckoned with. Smuts assumed that he had been promised gains in the Mediterranean to round off his Roman Empire. And so the war could very quickly come to Africa. It had already come to the Asian mainland and Smuts faced the possibility of its southward and eastward extension by Japanese attack. However, whenever he reached that stage of his gloomy speculations he always began to think of America. From the outset of the war he kept 'looking in that direction'. He regarded Washington as the key position in the diplomatic world and was delighted to hear that Lothian was being sent there as British Ambassador. 'The Americans', he reflected, 'are subject to violent gusts of public opinion, and if things go too badly with us, the Middle West mentality may suddenly disappear as it did in 1917. Let us woo and cultivate the U.S.A. They may yet be there before the end.'[2]

The immediate task, as he saw it, was to fend the Germans off in the west while the Allies built up their economic and military strength. He had no doubt that Britain and the Commonwealth possessed the material and moral power to play their full part as an oceanic combination; but he did not feel so sure of the French. Not that he anticipated their military collapse; it was their moral conviction and staying power that he mistrusted.[3] All the more reason, therefore, for South Africa to prepare herself for 'all eventualities'— to prepare herself, in particular, to join the battles that might have to be fought in Africa. In the debate of 4 September he had pledged himself not to send South African forces overseas. By his interpretation of this pledge, Africa was not overseas: it was the home ground.

Viewed from outside and comparatively, the South African war effort was not massive. Whereas the Australians, with an estimated population which in 1939 had not yet quite reached seven millions, achieved over the whole war period 926,900 full-time enlistments, the South Africans, with an estimated population which in 1939 already exceeded ten millions, achieved over the same period approximately 345,000 full-time enlistments.* The explanation of this contrast—as of the corresponding, if less extreme, contrast between the war-economic efforts of the two countries[4]—lay, of course, in the contrasting compositions of their populations. The Australians were homogeneous. They were able to use population and nation as interchangeable terms. The South Africans were not homogeneous. They made a distinction between *die volk*, the white people who constituted the nation, and *die bevolking*, the total population, most of which did not belong to the nation. Some of them made a distinction even more drastic than that. A leading Afrikaner intellectual wrote in 1941—

We reject the idea entirely that all [white] South Africans should together be considered as one people. For us Afrikanerdom is the People of South Africa, and the rest of South Africans are, as far as they are white, either potential Afrikaners, or aliens.[5]

Those concepts of population and nationality, with their precise numerical connotations, set strict limits to the targets of mobilization

---

* South African Enlistments:

European males	Non-European males	European females
186,218	123,131	24,975

South African Population (estimated, 1939):

Total	European	Native	Asiatic	Coloured
10,160,000	2,116,500	6,997,500	231,200	814,800

which Smuts could set himself. Although later in the war he declared himself ready at need to enlist non-Europeans for combatant service, he had no chance of getting parliament, or even his own Cabinet, to accept such a revolutionary proposal.* Opposition speakers constantly attacked him for enlisting non-Europeans even as non-combatants. They attacked him for bringing non-Europeans into war industry, or into employment of any kind where the concept of labour efficiency conflicted with their concept of race relationships. All these separate attacks supported their main attack against him for dragging South Africa into the war. They denounced it as a British not a South African war. They made it their constant endeavour to convince every true Afrikaner that service in the armed forces of the Union of South Africa was incompatible with his duty to the Afrikaner People.

In consequence, Smuts had to fight his war not only on the military but also on the home front. Throughout the whole war, politics inside the boundaries of the Union constituted the main impediment to military deployment beyond those boundaries and to civilian economic mobilization.

At the beginning of the war this did not greatly matter. The urgent need then was to achieve a limited mobilization at the maximum speed. South Africa was militarily naked when the war broke out. Although General Hertzog had been insistent throughout the fifteen years of his prime ministership upon South Africa's sovereign status, he had left it to the British navy to defend South Africa's coasts and trade routes. Apart from her hydrographic survey, South Africa possessed no naval establishment of any kind.† For air defence she possessed six modern machines (one Blenheim and one Fairey Battle bomber, four Hurricane fighters) and sixty-three obsolete general purpose machines (*Hartbees* and Furies). For her land-defence she possessed, first, a Permanent Force of approximately 260 officers and 4,600 men, distributed between the artillery, the air force and administrative or staff work; and secondly, an Active Citizen Force of approximately 950 officers and 14,000 men.‡ She

---

* See pp. 370–1, 412 below.

† She did, however, possess seventy officers and 900 men belonging to the South African branch of the Royal Naval Volunteer Reserve.

‡ The air force was not independent but was administered from Defence H.Q. in Pretoria as part of the Union Defence Force. The Active Citizen Force was based upon Smuts's Union Defence Act of 1912, which provided for the compulsory part-time training

did not as yet possess—apart from her Mint, where some important war work had recently been started—a munitions industry capable of supporting those sparse forces.[6]

For these alarming deficiencies Smuts put much of the blame upon Oswald Pirow, who for the past five years had been Minister of Defence under General Hertzog. Pirow's plans, Smuts said, had been great; but his performance had been more of a danger than a protection to his country.[7] Certainly, the gap between plans and performance, between the finance made available and the money spent, had been a large one; but perhaps it was unfair of Smuts to put the whole responsibility upon the shoulders of one man. Pirow's tenure of office had coincided with a period of boom during which neither the government, nor the industrialists, nor the people of South Africa were willing to contemplate any substantial switch of economic resources to military preparations.

Smuts may have exaggerated the making and breaking that he had to do, but as Pirow's successor in the Ministry of Defence he had to move fast—and he did. For naval defence he drew officers and men from the South African branch of the R.N.V.R. to man the guns of the coastal defences, the auxiliary cruisers fitted out at the Cape and the trawlers which were being rapidly converted into mine sweepers and patrol craft. By the second week of October he was ready to bring these forces together into a new organization, the Seaward (miscalled by scoffers Seaweed) Defence Force. He equipped the S.D.F. for air reconnaissance and anti-submarine work by taking over Junkers 86 aircraft from South African Airways. This, of course, was only a temporary expedient. For all aircraft—and the naval needs were small compared with the military needs—Smuts had to depend on what he could get from Britain or America. He pressed his demands urgently and in the meantime recruited the volunteer air crews which would man the fighters and bombers when they arrived. In training them he sought the close co-operation of the Royal Air Force; but he did not bring South Africa into the Empire Air Training Scheme.

He made all his preparations—at sea, in the air and on land—within the legal and administrative framework of the Union Defence

of all men of military age. In practice as distinct from theory it was a volunteer force, because the only men called up for training were those who, on registration, notified their willingness to be called up.

Act which he himself had fathered twenty-seven years earlier; but he did not use the powers of compulsion which the Act gave him. All his recruits were volunteers. In his plans for deploying them beyond the boundaries of the Union he doubly underlined the volunteer principle by providing a new form of attestation, whereby U.D.F. recruits could sign on for service 'anywhere in Africa'. The men who thus attested were given *rooi lussies*—shoulder flashes of an orange-red shade. They soon became a common sight in the cities and towns of South Africa. Before long almost all the soldiers and airmen were wearing them. It was as if they were saying, 'We are Smuts men'.*

In the first hectic months volunteers were given part-time training to begin with and after that four weeks of continuous training in camp. Then the volunteers for service 'anywhere in Africa' were drafted into the great training camps that were springing up everywhere in the Union. Before 1940 was half-way through the first battalions were on their way to Kenya. As mobilization and deployment proceeded the battalions were grouped into brigades and the brigades into two divisions, the first of which was ready, well before the end of 1940, to start on its long trek to Abyssinia, to Egypt, to Cyrenaica. This time, the trekkers were mechanized—a proof that the mobilization of war industry was keeping pace with the mobilization of fighting men.

All this achievement depended upon Smuts. His Cabinet of eleven contained some able and energetic men—J. H. Hofmeyr, Colin Steyn, Harry Lawrence, Claude Sturrock—but it also contained too many elderly, sluggish, backward-looking men. This may have been partly the fault of Smuts—his preference for familiar faces. Or it may have been the fault of circumstances—his inescapably narrow range of choice. Either way, it did not at the outset make much difference, for Smuts embodied the tradition of personal leadership which the Union had taken over from the Republics. South Africa had never completely absorbed British conventions of cabinet government; each successive government had always borne the personal stamp of its leader—of Botha, Smuts, Hertzog. Now that it was Smuts again people never troubled themselves to ask—What is the Cabinet doing? They always asked—What is Smuts doing?

* Of course the South African troops in Abyssinia wore them and there the Emperor Haile Selassie learnt their meaning. He gave them to the valuable Ethiopian battalion which served in Korea in 1952–3.

He did not often call Cabinet meetings. Instead he held frequent consultations with the individual persons, whether members of the government or not, upon whom he had devolved important powers. A realistic chart of South Africa's war government in 1939–40 would look, in bold outline, something like this:

Smuts

Parliamentary business:	*Finance:*	*Foreign Affairs:*	*Defence:*	*Party politics and Public Opinion:*
in his own hands, with main support from Hofmeyr, Steyn, Lawrence	in Hofmeyr's hands	in his own hands	in his own hands, with indispensable support from	in his own hands, with Louis Esselen as his closest adviser

Gen. Sir P. van Ryneveld (operations)   Dr H. J. van der Bijl (supply)

For the first four months he governed without parliament. His reason for keeping it so long prorogued was that he wanted time to build up strength both on the military and on the home front. But he was running a risk. He did not possess the statutory emergency powers which had been drafted under the previous government but had to take the powers he needed by proclamation in advance of parliamentary sanction. He had done the same sort of thing in the early days of the Union and had been denounced, by John X. Merriman amongst others, for his arbitrary behaviour.* No doubt he remembered that; but he had to weigh alternative risks and make his choice between them.

The recall of parliament was fixed for mid-January and there could be no doubt that the Opposition would then do its utmost to reverse the decision of September. It was swept along at first by a great wave of enthusiasm. To the twenty-nine members of the

* See *Smuts: The Sanguine Years*, pp. 368–73. In 1939 the imputation against Smuts of arbitrary action appeared still stronger in that his resolution for breaking off relations with Germany had been approved by the House of Assembly but had not been put before the Senate. With some justification, Smuts pleaded impossibility; but the constitutional issue was none the less tricky. It was debated in the Senate on 30 January and 1 February 1940. In *Trumpelmann and Du Toit* v. *Ministers for Justice and Defence*, the Supreme Court subsequently validated the emergency regulations contained in Proclamation 201 of 14 September 1939.

Purified Nationalist party it had been an exhilarating moment when thirty-eight members of General Hertzog's United party crossed the floor of the House to vote with them on the issue of peace or war. Nationalist Afrikanerdom hailed with joy this dramatic end to the *broedertwis*, the struggle of brother against brother which had been inflicted upon the people in 1934. *Hereniging*, the reunion of Afrikanerdom, was acclaimed a few days later with prayers and hymns and speeches at a great gathering in front of the Voortrekker Memorial outside Pretoria.[8]

But reunion still remained to be achieved, and there were obstacles in the way. First, the name of the reunited party: to take the original name might seem the simplest solution, but if the Hertzogites allowed themselves once more to be called Nationalists they might be putting themselves into the position of straying sheep received back into the fold—which was, indeed, how most of the Malanites regarded them. Secondly, the aim of the reunited party: the Malanites were demanding an independent republic outside the Commonwealth;* but the Hertzogites still shrank from so drastic a commitment.† Thirdly, the means to be adopted if and when the republican and secessionist aims were agreed upon: the Malanites, or at any rate a strong section of them, argued that a bare parliamentary majority would be sufficient, but the Hertzogites argued that the Republic could only be brought into being, and kept in being, upon the broad basis of the people's will.‡ Fourthly, the time factor: it was tangled up not only with the conflict about tactics but with a conflict far more deeply rooted in intellectual and emotional convictions. The Hertzogites, loyal to their own past, insisted that the English-speakers were just as much a part of the nation as the Afrikaans-speakers; consequently, if a broad national consensus were to be attained, they must be educated, persuaded. But this would take too much time, the Malanites claimed. They said in effect: Let us get the Republic as soon as we can and educate the English afterwards.

Whether the personal convictions of Dr Malan himself were quite so drastic as this could be doubted; but he was under extreme pressure from the Afrikaner zealots in the Ossewa-Brandwag and

* 'n vrye, onafhanklike Republiek, afgeskei van die Britse Kroon en Ryk.

† The Hertzogite commitment hitherto had gone no further than the admission of freedom to make republican propaganda.

‡ Op die breë grondslag van die volkswil.

other organizations who were in wild revolt against political compromise and the parliamentary system. At the outbreak of the war and for many years thereafter Malan and his lieutenants had to fight a stubborn battle to safeguard their political leadership within the constitutional framework established by the Act of Union. They had good reason to fear that the battle would go against them if they failed to achieve unity and discipline at the party-political level.

But they found it hard to reach agreement with Hertzog and his followers. The two phalanxes of Afrikanerdom met in conference at Pretoria in November 1939. Reunion was their common aim. They produced drafts and niggled at phrases but separated without achieving a common programme. Thereafter the Hertzogites formed a separate party, *Die Volksparty*. Among the laity of nationalist Afrikanerdom the disillusionment was bitter. Amateurs of politics rushed in to repair the damage. Reunion, they said, was too vital a matter to be left in the hands of professional politicians. They formed vigilance committees and reconciliation committees which appealed to the Afrikaner Volk over the heads of its parliamentary leaders. Driven by these high winds of feeling the politicians kept on trying. Towards the end of January they agreed to join forces in a single party under Hertzog's leadership. In summary, the heads of their agreement were:

1. Name of the party: Die Herenigde Nasionale of Volksparty.
2. Its aim: 'n vrye, onafhanklike Republiek, afgeskei van die Britse Kroon en Ryk.
3. Its means of achieving the aim: op die breë grondslag van die volkswil.*

The name was patchwork on a fifty-fifty basis; the statement of aim was a victory for Malan; the definition of means was a victory for Hertzog. Beneath the façade of unity, the basic conflicts of principle between Hertzog's followers and Malan's remained unresolved.

In contrast, the followers of Smuts were unshakeably at one in their immediate and limited aim of fighting and winning the war. Smuts himself was serenely single-minded. He said tersely, 'I know I am right.'[9] He felt compassion for 'the errant portion' of his people and for South Africa's divided soul. Time, he said, was a causal

* For English translations see p. 335 above.

factor and South Africa had not been given time enough to discover her single soul. It might not happen in his day; but if he in his day did his duty it would happen in the end.[10]

He envisaged the approaching parliamentary session as a decisive engagement in a long campaign. Despite his intense preoccupation with military mobilization he took upon himself a heavy burden of public speaking at national gatherings, at party conferences, at meetings in his own constituency and in the constituencies of his colleagues. He took heart from the results of some provincial by-elections which were fought in November 1939. The country, he felt sure, was moving in the right direction.[11]

Parliament met on 19 January 1940. Four days later Hertzog moved in the House of Assembly 'that this House is of the opinion that the time has arrived when the war with Germany should be ended and that peace be restored'. He said, as he had said in September, that the war was no concern of South Africa's and that she had been dragged into it simply because Great Britain had declared war; that Germany was merely redressing the wrongs done to her in the scandalous Treaty of Versailles; that equality, not the domination of others, was Germany's aim. He added that Hitler, after finishing his campaign in Poland, had offered to discuss peace with the Western Powers. By refusing his offer those Powers had put themselves in the wrong. By continuing the war they were committing a crime and South Africa should have nothing to do with it.[12]

Smuts rebutted those arguments and accusations and insisted that the Union could not make a separate peace 'without forfeiting its honour and sacrificing its vital interests'.[13] Hertzog's motion was put to the vote on 27 January. The voting was sixty-seven in favour, eighty against.

Smuts now moved the War Measures Bill to indemnify his government for the action it had taken under proclamation and to give it statutory authority for the action it would need to take so long as the emergency lasted. In the bitter debate that followed all the past—the ineptitude attributed to Hertzog and Pirow as well as the craftiness and autocracy attributed to Smuts—was raked over. The Opposition fought the Bill at every stage and by every means and tried to kill it by suffocation. The government replied at long last by imposing the procedure of guillotine—three days for the committee stage and one day each for report and for the third reading.

My opponents will not spare me [wrote Smuts to a friend], as I shall not spare them. But with the good assistance of guillotine passed last week, I shall not be drowned in endless floods of talk. How good it is for Democracy to have some of these weapons captured from the armoury of Autocracy! Democracy plus the guillotine is good for erring politicians.[14]

On 13 February the House approved the War Measures Bill by seventy-nine votes to fifty-nine; but there still remained a great deal of essential parliamentary work, including an Industrial Development Bill,* the budget and the departmental estimates. In each new debate the Opposition fiercely attacked the government's war policy. In all, there were four months of bitter parliamentary struggle. The days were few on which Smuts dare run the risk of absenting himself from the House. But the session came to a close at last on 14 May. Four days earlier, Hitler had launched his attack against Holland and Belgium.

NOTE: RESTRAINTS ON PERSONAL LIBERTY UNDER WAR EMERGENCY POWERS[15]

1. *The powers*

Emergency Regulation No. 15 of 14 September 1939 empowered the Minister of Defence (as amended later, the Minister of Justice), and certain officers responsible to him, to arrest and to detain any person whose detention was considered 'desirable in the interest of the State or in that person's own interest'. Since parliament was not then in session, this Regulation and the other issued at the same time rested originally not on statute but on a Proclamation (No. 201 of 14 September 1939) which declared that a state of emergency existed as a consequence of the war in which the Union of South Africa was presently involved. The legal validity of Regulation No. 15 was upheld by the Supreme Court in *Trumpelmann and Du Toit.* v. *Ministers for Justice and Defence.* When Parliament reassembled, Acts Nos. 13 and 32 of 1940 provided a statutory basis for the original War Emergency Regulations and for those subsequently issued.

War Measure 47 of 10 December 1941 further empowered the Minister of Justice to order the arrest and detention for questioning of any person whom he suspected on reasonable grounds of sabotage, or of the intention to commit sabotage, or of possessing information relative thereto.

* This was the origin of the Industrial Development Corporation (I.D.C.) which had an important future in South African economic development.

2. *The procedures*

A person detained for questioning under War Measure 47 could either be released, or charged in court, or interned under Regulation 15.

According to the Minister of Justice (*H. of A. Deb.* vol. 44, cols. 5296–7), the decision to intern any person was taken in each case only after a careful sifting of the evidence by the police, the local Control Officer, the central Control Officer and the Minister himself.

Regulation 15, unlike the United Kingdom's Regulation 18B, made no provision for appeals; but as an administrative measure an Appeal Advisory Commissioner was appointed. He was not a judge but a former Attorney-General (i.e. the permanent official in charge of prosecutions) of the Transvaal. The procedure of appeal was as follows. Within 14 days, if possible, the interned person was given a summary of the charges against him and was informed of his right to appeal and to obtain legal assistance and advice. He could reply to the charges in writing and could also obtain and present written testimony by others in his favour. These documents were then placed before the Appeal Advisory Commissioner (*H. of A. Deb.* vol. 43, col. 1533). Decision lay with the Minister.

Regulation 15 empowered the Minister or the Chief Control Officer to release an interned person either unconditionally or subject to conditions (in practice, conditions were invariably stipulated). A later amendment further empowered the Minister or Chief Control Officer, in lieu of detention, to impose restrictions upon a person's activities, as set forth in a document entitled 'A Certificate of Exemption from Internment'.

3. *The number of persons interned*

From time to time the Minister informed the House of the numbers interned and the numbers released within stated periods. It is not possible from these figures to enumerate precisely the grand total of persons interned during the war; but by subtracting the figures of releases from those of internments it is possible to state the number of persons in internment on specific dates.

From the Minister's statements it can be seen that the rise and fall of internments corresponded with the rise and fall of subversion and sabotage. The most critical period followed the Japanese attack on Pearl Harbour. On 6 April 1942 the Minister described War Measure 47, which had been enacted on 10 December 1941, as 'an extraordinary measure introduced to deal with an extraordinary and most dangerous situation' (*H. of A. Deb.* vol. 44, cols. 5297–8). On 16 April 1942 he announced that a list of members of a sabotage organization, the 'Stormjaers' (assault troopers), had been discovered; that members of the police had joined it; that bomb factories had been discovered and that bomb explosions had occurred, including nine in Potschefstroom alone (*ibid.* cols. 6324–5). It appears from the figures of internment that more than a year went by before the government felt justified in relaxing its vigilance. The following dates have been selected to show the ascending and descending curve.

Persons in internment on

19 Jan. 1940	1 April 1941	6 April 1942	22 Jan. 1943	31 July 1943	28 Nov. 1944	2 Feb. 1945	1 May 1945
76	193	232	366	582	376	66	2

The Minister's statements contained some information about categories of interned persons. As might have been expected, Germans domiciled in South West Africa, who under the legislation of that time had dual nationality, formed nearly half the total early in the war.* More surprising at first sight is the fact that totals later in the war included appreciable percentages of police, prison warders, public servants and railway employees.

4. *The conditions of internment*

Interned persons were kept at Ganspan to begin with and later at Koffiefontein. Opposition speakers alleged from time to time that their conditions of living were unsatisfactory. No doubt they were irksome; but Captain G. H. F. Strydom, an Opposition M.P. who visited Koffiefontein and interviewed various internees, appears to have been reasonably satisfied with the conditions of internment (*H. of A. Deb.* vol. 44, cols. 5291–4).

* By Act 35 of 1942 these persons lost their status as citizens of the Union.

CHAPTER 19

DEFIANCE

On 24 May 1940 Smuts turned seventy. Only twelve months before he had thought sixty-nine 'frightfully old' and had doubted whether he would ever find anything worth while to do 'in this dotage'; but now he felt young enough to fight Hitler. In a half jesting mood he allowed himself a few regrets for the book that he would never find time to write. 'And so much profundity', he said, 'will be buried with me! But the world will be none the worse, although it may be much the worse if we lose the war—that is the difference between thinking and doing.' Too old for thinking but not too old for doing—that was how he measured his age.[1]

His birthday fell at the centre of a tornado, two days before the Dunkirk exodus began and three weeks before Paris fell. Within ten weeks of that spring and summer Hitler conquered five nations.* 'The devil', Smuts said, 'knows that his time is short.' Although he would have liked to put back the clock to the time when he had positively revelled in fighting, he still felt 'exhilaration in doing a dangerous job like this'. He defined the job in a few terse words— to hold South Africa as a key position of the Commonwealth. That meant unrelenting struggle on each of his two fronts. He felt hopeful of seeing the struggle through. On 20 August he wrote, 'I have no doubt of holding my own.' On 1 September he wrote, 'One feels

---

* To save explanations in the text here is a brief chronology:

9 April	Invasion of Denmark and Norway.
8 May	'In the name of God go' (House of Commons debate).
10 May	Invasion of Holland and Belgium.
13 May	Churchill speaks as Prime Minister: 'Blood, sweat and tears.'
15 May	Dutch cease fire.
28 May	Belgians cease fire.
26 May–3 June	Operation Dynamo (Dunkirk).
11 June	Italy enters the war.
14 June	Paris falls.
22 June	French armistice.
3 July	Oran.
16 July	Hitler's first directive for Sea Lion (invasion of Britain).
13 Aug.–6 Sept.	Goering's operation Eagle (Battle of Britain).
7 Sept.	The attack on London opens.
17 Sept.	Hitler calls off Sea Lion.

that it is a good fight...I hope I shall be able to bear the strain as long as I am wanted—as I am very badly at present.'[2]

He allowed himself at times to feel surprised at all the work he was getting through. It was the work itself, he sometimes said, that carried him along. But he also recognized the roots of his strength. They were in his own body, in his home, in the love of friends and—this was his hard-won faith—in the spiritual constitution of the universe.

He took good care of his body and jestingly commended his example to his friends. 'Physical fitness', he told them, 'should be viewed in a religious light, and we should care for our bodies even more than for our souls. For if we love not our bodies that we see how can we love the soul which we have never seen?' He was moderate in food and drink and did not take tobacco. He knew how to rest. 'Sometimes', he admitted, 'I feel tired enough to know what it is to drop dead from fatigue. But after a good night's rest I rise fresh and fit for another bout.' If he woke in the night he did not toss and fuss but turned on the light and read until he felt ready for sleep again. He seldom if ever let a week go by without taking some hard physical exercise. By way of comment upon an assertion by Dr Malan that he was a physical and mental wreck he climbed Table Mountain rather faster than at his usual cracking pace. Climbing was his favourite week-end exercise and one Saturday afternoon in September it nearly brought him to his death on Devil's Peak, not by any slip that he made but from the folly of some louts who were rolling boulders down from higher up. After a stiff climb he would sometimes drive down to the sea for a swim and quite often on a Sunday he would collect a few friends and drive out to one of the lonelier beaches for bathing and a picnic lunch and a scramble in the hills behind the beach and possibly an hour of plant collecting. The Cape Peninsula was his playground while parliament was in session. Back in the Transvaal he would get up a good sweat dragging his 'Gestapo'—the policemen appointed to guard him—up and down the seven hills of Doornkloof or along the twisting paths through the thick scrub around Rooikop, his bushveld farm.[3]

Doornkloof was his home, his life's anchorage. It was his wife who made it that. In their great partnership the unexpected sometimes happened, as when the Oubaas one morning at breakfast quoted a verse from I Corinthians 13 and Ouma thereupon recited the whole glorious chapter in the original Greek.[4] No doubt there were

Defiance

sometimes other reminders of their intellectual companionship half a century ago at Victoria College, Stellenbosch. Now in their old age she was his comrade in the fierce struggle. She proved herself an effective leader on the women's side of the United party and a strenuous war worker, especially in the 'Gifts and Comforts' organization.* On one memorable occasion in 1942 she went with her husband to the Egyptian battle zone and spoke to the wildly applauding South African soldiers. With all this she never mistook her real war work. It was the same as her life work, simply to make a home for her husband and for their children and grandchildren and the friends they loved to have with them—but first and foremost, for him. He could never bear to set out for his day's work at the office unless she was at the door to wave good-bye to him. In the evening when he was returning home he knew that she would be waiting for him.

By now they had a round dozen grandchildren and a large contingent of them seemed always to be quartered on Doornkloof.[5] They liked their friends to visit them and Smuts would sometimes take a car-full of them with him to Rooikop, to archaeologize or botanize or just to do nothing. And then he would bring them back with him to Doornkloof, to share his joy in having a home. But the joy was destroyed for him when uninvited people from Pretoria and Johannesburg began to invade Doornkloof during the week-ends. They did it with the best intentions, to let the Oubaas know how much they thought of him and to cheer him up. Botha no doubt would have received them cheerfully, but Smuts felt a fierce resentment.

These Sunday parties after a heavy week make me really savage; but no means of making people realize the enormity of spoiling our only day of rest has yet been discovered...So many people do not know what to do with their own time and leisure and find it impossible to entertain themselves with books or other hobbies.

He called Sunday visiting a pernicious habit and a clear breach of the command to keep the Sabbath. He wondered how Isie could endure it—

but then she is a real lover of her kind, which I have never pretended to be. Is it not great to serve the world when you *don't* love it? God so loved the world that He could not help but send his son. But what if He had done so without loving the world?

* See pp. 391–2 below.

343

He let his tired mind run on until he felt that he had written enough 'metaphysical gibberish' for that day.[6]

He was being too hard on himself when he suggested that he was no lover of his kind. He loved his friends. He enjoyed his chance encounters with unpretentious country people. He endured with a good grace, even when he could not enjoy, the public meetings which were part of his duty.* What he could not endure was the aimless pressure of droves of people upon his privacy. He quoted A. N. Whitehead's definition of religion—'What a man does with his loneliness'. He went on to say that a man deprived of his loneliness must also be a man deprived of religion.[7]

The study at Doornkloof and the stoep at Rooikop were the symbols of his solitude. Its characteristic activities were reading, letter-writing and contemplation. Viewed in one aspect these activities were pure relaxation. By taking down a book from his shelves he could lose himself in a world of the imagination far removed from the struggles and strains of his working life. By taking up his pen to begin his weekly 'diary letter' to the Gilletts he could purge himself of last week's battles and anxieties by telling their full story, rapidly and without any corrections, just as it came into his head, along with the story of all the small and intimate things which belonged to his happiness—what his wife and children and grandchildren had been doing, how the weather was behaving, how the crops were growing— and how, he would ask, were the weather and the crops and the children getting on in Oxfordshire and Somerset? By taking his chair on to the stoep at Rooikop he could find in the benignity of nature the cure for his cares.

What a contrast between that world of mortal strife, and this peaceful brooding atmosphere which surrounds me as I write here on the sun flooded front stoep at Rooikop! Surely there is something in nature even closer to us than our own fellowmen and their tiresome strifes! What can be more akin to the soul stuff in us than this peace of God which surrounds us and supports us on an afternoon like this?[8]

Viewed in another aspect, these activities of his solitude possessed a concentration, point and purpose which could properly be called religious. Reading for him was at times a sedative—for example, when he read his botany books before going to sleep—but more often it was a stimulant, starting in his head a ferment of ideas which he

* His right hand was bleeding after all his handshakings at a meeting in May 1940.

carried from the world of the imagination back into the world of the practical.* Letter-writing was a means which he used of getting these ideas, along with all the others which came to him from his other activities, into focus upon the urgent question of where his duty lay. Meditation as he practised it was the very opposite of Words-worth's 'wise passiveness'; it was an unremitting and unrelenting battle which he fought within his brain between negation and affirma-tion, between denial and faith. The battle so absorbed him that he never had time to look at it from the outside or to think of giving it a name. As a lover of John Bunyan's prose, he might sometimes have envisaged himself as a man committed to a dangerous pilgrimage,† but he would never have allowed himself to be caught by Giant Despair, errant from the straight and narrow path and asleep; nor did he ever conceive himself to be in flight from the City of Destruc-tion, that is to say, from this world, which he accepted as his battle-field; nor did he long for life eternal in any Heavenly City. 'If you go all out in this life', he said, 'you are not so much concerned what happens to you individually thereafter.'⁹ He could enjoy the dramatic episodes of *The Pilgrim's Progress*, such as the battle between Christian and Apollyon; but its vision of God and man did not speak directly to his condition. He might rather have found in the Spiritual Exer-cises of St Ignatius Loyola, had he ever studied them, a purpose and a discipline not so far removed from his own. Psychologically, if not theologically, a resemblance existed between his endeavour and Loyola's. The first battle that they both had to fight was against the *deformata*.

From his student years onwards Smuts had always kept putting to himself the question: what kind of universe is this and what is the place of man within it? The answer which he had given in the early 1930s was confident, optimistic. As President of the British Associa-tion in 1931 he told his learned audience that this is a friendly universe; as Rector of St Andrews in 1934 he told the students that there is nothing in the universe which is alien to man in his striving towards the good.‡ Such aphorisms, torn from their context, could

* In addition to the Greek Testament which he made his constant companion, his reading during the first war year included books on politics (e.g. by Wells and Carr), palaeobotany (Darrah), physics (Millikan), the early Christian Church (Kirsopp Lane), as well as old favourites like the *Golden Treasury* and the *Antigone* (in Jebb's translation). He also tried to keep in touch with periodicals such as *Antiquity*, *Mind*, the *Round Table*, the *New Statesman*.   † On one occasion (see p. 439 below) he did so envisage himself.
‡ See pp. 234, 272 above.

have been mistaken for a demonstration by Dr Pangloss that everything is for the best in the best of all possible worlds. Smuts did not
ignore the power of evil; he had suffered from it in his own life and
he included it in his picture of the universe. But he was temperamentally disposed—he admitted it himself—to under-emphasize it.
In the summer of 1940 he could no longer do that. With Hitler
triumphant in Europe the *deformata* were staring him in the face.

In his endeavour to take their measure he oscillated, as his custom
was, between neo-Darwinian and biblical thought and language.
When the Nazis were over-running Norway he wrote:

> Nowhere in nature is there such cruelty. And why should man, the crown
> of nature, sink lower than the low beginnings from which we have emerged
> and have been moving for millions of years?[10]

Had evolution been in labour all these millions of years to produce
Caliban?

Six months later, when London was enduring its nightly torment,
he wrote:

> If we had been mere dull brutes this misery could have been dully endured.
> But we have that delicately sensitive structure of body and soul which
> multiplies the agony a thousandfold...It is no answer to say that we
> bring this misery on ourselves. The question remains about the order of the
> universe which renders possible and tolerates such a state of affairs. The
> writer of Job stated his solution of the problem, as it appeared to a fine
> spirit thousands of years ago. But that solution scarcely suits our case. We
> have learnt so much more of the order, the regularity, the harmony of the
> universe, that the anomaly presented by man becomes all the more
> glaring. Shakespeare dealt with individual men and cases and so wrote his
> immortal tragedies. But here it is Man himself, the Universe itself which
> forms the victim of himself, of itself. And the questions that now arise are
> far more searching, I may say far more blasphemous in appearance, than
> those that occured to Job or to Shakespeare's creations.[11]

Here he was putting into doubt the moral order of the universe.

In his endeavour to refute the doubt he drew what support he
could from the thought and language of science. He quoted Bacon—

> 'The mind of man turns upon the poles of truth.' To me that is not only
> a profound insight into the nature of man and of the universe but also
> a continual inspiration and consolation. Error, untruth is really alien to
> us as it is to the nature of things.[12]

Then why were tens of thousands of his fellow-Afrikaners listening
in night by night to Dr Goebbels's perversions of the truth over the

Zeesen radio? Smuts had his answer: truth needed time, it would prevail 'in the end'. He envisaged the *deformata* as a series of violent but transient explosions in the vast range of geological time.

The Great Rift Valley was formed in an age-long slow steady sinking and rising, which was from time to time punctuated by violent cataclysms and explosions. Is not that the sort of thing which is happening today? We are passing from an old dead order to a new unborn one, and the process is sometimes violently explosive.[13]

But Hitler could have said precisely that. If present historical explosions were similar in kind to past geological explosions one man's prediction of their outcome could be no better than another's. Smuts could not produce the refutation of his doubts except by demonstrating, at any rate to his own satisfaction, that a trend towards truth and all other spiritual values was operative within the universe. On the night the German army was coiling its springs for its leap across Holland and Belgium he found himself thinking of Samuel Alexander, that 'queer old patriarch' who believed deeply in Deity, not as a substance already existing but as one to which 'the universe was tending'. Smuts had expounded the same idea eight years before Alexander published *Space, Time and Deity*.* He still held to it and had for a good many years past been finding new support for it in the new evidence produced by palaeontologists and pre-historians.

Our progress so far [he said] has not been contemptible. 10,000 years ago we had not yet reached the neolithic stage. 20,000 years ago we were just trying to straighten ourselves in the Neanderthal form. In another 20,000 years we may almost reach the stature of the children of God. Today we are still with the Hitlers and Mussolinis, but we should not despair. Already we see all around us types and embodiments of beauty in mind and character which point the way to the future which is surely coming.[14]

But his own struggle with the Hitlers and Mussolinis was here and now. In this struggle an emergent Deity which had not yet arrived could not possibly help him. He needed a transcendent Deity, an I AM not only in the end, as Samuel Alexander said, but in the beginning, as the Book of Genesis said. And so he found himself groping towards the meeting-point, if it existed, of immanence and transcendence.

Man has no abiding city, except in the Eternal, however we picture it to ourselves. If only from this elemental struggle in time we could draw nearer to that world of spirit which surely is our destiny.[15]

* See *Smuts: The Sanguine Years*, pp. 302–4.

The universe must be seen as the organic structure that it is, instinct with Divinity, big with the inner spirit which is shaping and creating it, and of which it is but the progressive expression... It is so difficult to realize and formulate in thought the truth that that vast *Other*, not myself, is yet not really alien or different, but the Other of *myself*.

He saw this truth 'dimly foreshadowed' in the Christian Incarnation but felt that a new formulation of it, shorn of the ancient imagery, was required for the modern age. He re-read Spinoza's exposition of the highest love and tried to improve upon it.

The service of man, of the ideals which shine like the stars, seems to me to partake of this higher love which lures us on to great service. Here it is not *we* who love, but the force of the universe flowing through us and using us merely as vehicles. It is the love wherewith the universe loves itself— the absolute love, if I may so call it—the love with which God loves himself.[16]

He felt that he was getting too metaphysical. For the sake of his friends who liked his letters to be full of news and views but might grow tired of his philosophizing, for the sake of the ordinary un-philosophical people who looked to him for a lead, and not least for his own sake, he had to make a simpler statement of his faith.

One asks the question 'Is it possible that Evil can be so omnipotent and Good so feeble against it?' And then the Psalmist's sarcasm is remembered: The *fool* has said in his heart there is no God. One appreciates the wisdom of that retort. And so I shall await the issue between God and the Devil, between Christ and Anti-Christ, believing all the time that time is a form of the Divine Action and that we must give Him time. Evil is a short-range power, Good a long-range winner.[17]

He affirmed the sovereignty of God. Sometimes he seemed to go further and to assert that God was on his side against Hitler. But then he drew back from so presumptuous a claim. God was eternal and no finite person could know how He would exercise his sovereignty within a particular segment of historical time. The man Smuts might call Hitler Anti-Christ but God might have a different name for him. God might even see some purpose in a Hitler victory. In his heart Smuts could hardly believe that, but in his brain he accepted it as a possibility.

I keep believing in God, but I don't forget that He favoured the English more than the Boers, although then, too, we thought He would stand by our righteous cause. I hope He won't favour Hitler this time; indeed I cannot believe it.[18]

Anyway, whatever God's plan might be, He could not expect a man made in His own image to throw away his capacity of choosing between good and evil and of fighting for the good as he saw it.

No, I am in the same mood in which I was 40 years ago. Fight it out until you are really and truly beaten. In that way you may lose the fight but you save your self-respect and your soul and your future. God will sweep away this Hitler abomination all right, but we must help him to the utmost of our power to do so. Otherwise God may win without us, and we shall only be left with remorse at our own cowardice. It paid the Boers to hold out to the very end, and their effort turned defeat into eventual victory. I cannot see this world return to slavery and barbarism. But we must keep the banner of the spirit high throughout the struggle. That is faith.[19]

It was in some ways a highly idiosyncratic faith. Smuts was saying that a man would suffer in his self-respect if he failed to give God a hand while He was asserting his sovereignty. A nation similarly might suffer in its self-respect. His thought turned to the poor Americans and their policy of cash and carry.

What a creed, when the western world is reeling on its foundations! Cash and carry! However, perhaps I am unfair. We are really all much alike.

I hope the day is not far off when America will really bear her share of the intolerable burden, even if she does not send an army to Europe. If Britain and the Commonwealth win alone, America will never forgive herself; if they are beaten she will be even less able to bear the intolerable stigma. It is a most awkward fix for a really pacific nation...It is like poor Peter sitting in that vestibule near the fire, and denying his Master. Nor will it be good for the British to win single-handed. They are already inclined to be uppish.[20]

But just then he was loving British uppishness. When news came through of the first air battles he exclaimed—'Truly the Channel is now like the pass of Thermopylae, and those who die there give their lives in the dearest of all human causes. It makes my old blood tingle to listen to Daventry.' Six weeks later, when news came through of London's fortitude, he exclaimed: 'Is London not grand? And the R.A.F. is doing what the Fleet used to do in Britain's past. Hitler will not pass there.' He went on to put a question pertinent to his own action. 'Will he then come to Africa? It looks like it.'[21]

He had finished his long debate with himself. Its conclusion was contained in two propositions. The first was general: 'I believe', he said, 'in the moral government of the world, but that is inseparable

349

from *our* moral backing.' The second was particular: 'Necessity is laid on us', he said, 'and we cannot draw back from the task.' He meant that necessity was laid on *him*: '"Spend and be spent" is the order of the day, and like a soldier I must obey.'[22]

A cynic might have thought Smuts's spiritual exercises superfluous, because all the time he was resolving in action the problems which were torturing him in thought. Despite all the agonizing questions he kept putting to himself there was never a shadow of doubt about his answer to them. When he heard of Italy's entry into the war he exclaimed, 'So we know the worst, and that is often the beginning of the better. It all depends now on us, and on such support as we draw from a great cause. And so on to the end.'[23] He recognized at once the effect of Mussolini's action upon his own country. Closure of the ocean passage through the Mediterranean would restore the Cape route to the geopolitical pre-eminence which it had possessed throughout the three and a half centuries between Vasco da Gama and Ferdinand de Lesseps. South Africa would thus become indeed a key country of the Commonwealth.

Smuts answered Mussolini's challenge by two symbolic acts: a declaration by the Union of war against Italy and the assumption by himself of supreme command over the Union's armed forces. He had a new uniform made for himself but he had no intention of reverting to his old rôle of *vechtgeneraal*, the leader of his troops in battle. All the same, he was not making an empty gesture. As Commander-in-Chief (as well as Prime Minister, Minister of External Affairs and Minister of Defence) he was able in the years ahead to answer with an immediate Yes or No all proposals put to him by Churchill or by local commanders for the employment of South African forces in the field, and he was able with the same freedom to make proposals of his own. No comparable concentration of political and military power in the hands of one man existed anywhere else in the Commonwealth.

On the home front the government's declaration of war against Italy produced immediate effects. It enraged the Nationalists and injected new passion into their campaign against the war. Smuts had quite miscalculated the effect which Hitler's spring aggressions would produce upon them. He had expected them to be dumbfounded and dismayed by so dramatic a vindication of his argument last September that no small nation would be safe so long as Hitler was at large.[24] But on the contrary: when the fate of Holland came into debate just before parliament rose, the Opposition stuck to its former arguments and carried them further: they saw nothing to choose between one side and the other; all the belligerents were equally aggressive and unscrupulous; let them fight their own battles; let South Africa look after her own interests; let her withdraw from the war.[25] During the days of Dunkirk and the fall of France, Nationalist speakers all over the country let loose a violent propaganda against the war. Meanwhile, the Ossewa-Brandwag was drilling.

Smuts took the initiative. In a letter to Hertzog on 13 June he said that some mutual friends had made suggestions for a truce between the two parties. For his part he would accept a truce upon the following conditions: first, cessation of political meetings which made embittering party propaganda; secondly, cessation of embittering press propaganda. The truce would not, of course, affect the government's duty to conduct the war and to maintain law and order. On 17 June Hertzog wrote Smuts a letter based on very different assumptions. It attacked him for bringing South Africa into the war against Germany and now against Italy. It asserted that the war was 'hopelessly lost'. It called for an immediate peace.

Smuts told a friend that Hertzog's letter was poisonous, and that he had replied to it with less than his usual charity. That was putting it mildly.

This dishonourable proposal [he told Hertzog] was already submitted by you yourself to the House of Assembly in its last session and was decisively rejected by it...You surely cannot as a democrat expect from me that I shall solely on your personal pressure violate the decision of Parliament.

The reason which you urge for this singular request is 'that the war has already been hopelessly lost by the Allies'. This may be your opinion but it is not a fact...The groundless and false supposition on which your entire argument is based, is that the Union could have kept out of danger if we had remained neutral towards Germany. Has not Germany herself exposed the falsity of this argument? What has the neutrality of Denmark, Norway, Holland and Belgium profited them? Why should the Union, which incidentally holds a mandate over a former German Colony, and against whom she has shown her malice by continuous hostile propaganda and the formation of a fifth column, have been able to save herself if she also had remained neutral? Your argument has been refuted by the action of Germany herself.

351

You then point to the folly of our declaration of war against Italy. You omit to mention that Italy had first declared war against our friends Britain and her colonies—Kenya, Northern and Southern Rhodesia— which form our best line of defence. These three colonies are not in a position to defend themselves against the preponderance of power of Italy in Abyssinia and North Africa. Is it your view that we must just allow Italy to conquer these countries and march on the borders of the Union with her powerful air force? And should Italy's ally Germany also be allowed to do the same? What would in that case happen to the independence of the Union?...

Finally you fall back on threats. You refer to the pressure which your supporters exercise on the party leaders, and anticipate 'mass protests' which may perhaps follow. Even 'far-reaching disorders among the people' are mentioned.

We live in grave times, which remind us of other grave times in our history. It is to be hoped that the party leaders whom you refer to will realize their responsibility towards the people, and will avoid situations whereby the people may be involved in calamity through party political propaganda and mass protests, for which the main responsibility will rest on the leaders.

Smuts ended his letter by asserting the determination of his government to maintain law and order and to defend the independence and vital interests of the Union. For these purposes and in defiance of all threats it would employ the legal powers constitutionally entrusted to it by parliament.[26]

Nevertheless he gave his opponents plenty of rope. This proved to be good policy, because it soon became apparent that different sections of them were pulling in different directions. The majority of them were clamouring for immediate action to end the war, to proclaim the Republic and to secede from the Commonwealth. They believed that Hitler would win the war within a few months or even a few weeks. When that happened South Africa would receive no more mercy than she had earned as the foolish ally of a defeated Britain. Her only hope was to cut the British connection while there was still time. As Malan put it in a long and closely reasoned speech to his constituents, the choice confronting South Africa was 'a Republic or Hitler'.[27] That choice had to be made now. The crisis was far too urgent for any more time to be lost in the slow business of educating the minority. The formula agreed to last January—'on the basis of the people's will'—no longer had any sense...But that was where Hertzog dug in his toes. Up to the first week of July he had been solid with Malan in supporting the anti-war and secessionist demonstrations which were being organized everywhere in the Union; but next week his paper, *Die Vaderland,* warned Afrikaners against attending a monster meeting promoted by a Council of Action in the Orange Free State. When *Die Transvaler* supported the meeting, the widening breach between the Hertzogites and the Malanites was brought into the open. About the same time a whispering campaign was started against Hertzog; it was said that a box of documents had been found which proved him to be a collaborator, just like Smuts, with British-Jewish plotters. 'Poor Hertzog!', Smuts exclaimed. 'He is like Father Time finding his children devouring him.'[28]

Smuts at this time was getting ready for a short parliamentary session due to begin on 24 August. He said that he did not fear the coming fight and he had no reason to fear it. He secured a resolution for continuing the war, additional powers under the amended War Measures Act for maintaining internal order and an additional forty million pounds to spend on the war effort. On 16 September he celebrated the end of the session by climbing Table Mountain.[29]

Amongst his opponents the dissension grew fiercer. It came to a head in the first week of November at a party meeting in the Orange Free State. Hertzog demanded a comprehensive and unambiguous affirmation of equality under the proposed republican constitution between English-speaking and Afrikaans-speaking citizens. The voting went heavily against him. He resigned his leadership and membership of the Free State party and walked out of the meeting followed by Havenga and two others.[30] His enemies gave him no quarter. When the Transvaal Congress met it put a new clause into the party programme, to the effect that a simple majority in parliament was sufficient to bring in the Republic. Here was the repudiation of everything that Hertzog had always stood for. For him it was the end. On 12 December he resigned his seat in parliament. After serving his country for close on half a century he retired upon a meagre income. Smuts wrote—

To the honour of South Africa her political leaders generally retire poor men. And that in a land where there is endless opportunity for graft. I wish this honourable tradition could be maintained for ever. We may be wrong-headed but we are not thieves.[31]

The damage which the Nationalists suffered from these dissensions proved to be smaller than Smuts had anticipated. Next January, when General Edwin Conroy announced the formation of the Afrikaner party to uphold General Hertzog's principles, less than a quarter of the old guard in parliament rallied to its support.* In the elections of mid-1943 not a single member of the Afrikaner party was returned. It was not against moderates of the Hertzog stamp but against the zealots of the Ossewa-Brandwag that Malan had to fight his hardest battles. Malan's victory over them a few years later boded no good for Smuts in long term. But so long as the war lasted the conflicts which rent nationalist Afrikanerdom made him secure on the home front. He told his friend Amery that the attacks of the Opposition, virulent though they were, did not seriously interfere with the war effort and that he paid little attention to them. All the same he thought it timely to make a show of power by sending a mechanized column—the Steel Commando, he called it—through the Union.

They have had the most tumultuous reception ever given to a trek in South Africa and even in small villages people have come up in their thousands to see the show...People were deeply interested and amazed to see what a mechanized war unit of today is, and it has been an eye-opener to all. Everything made in our workshops except the parts of the aeroplanes.

On the home front the year of danger and defiance ended well.[32]

Nationalist propagandists had made a bad mistake of military forecasting. In June, when France left the war and Italy joined it, they had put their money heavily on an Axis victory. In September, after the Battle of Britain, that gamble began to look uncertain.

Meanwhile the balance of military power had been swinging in Africa. From the Commonwealth's point of view the situation could not possibly have been worse than it was in June. The scattered forces in Kenya, the Sudan, Egypt and Palestine fell a long way short of 100,000 men. Suddenly those forces found themselves bereft of French support and under immediate threat from two large Italian armies in Libya and Abyssinia. Smuts thought it certain that Hitler would send forces of his own to fight alongside the Italians. In some 'cogitations' which he telegraphed to Churchill at the end of June he faced the eventuality of having to give up Egypt. All the more urgent was it, he said, to build up bastions of defence further south. The Cape route must be safeguarded at all costs; the Empire had

* 10 out of 37.

been founded on it and the Commonwealth could not survive without it. Churchill approved Smuts's history but improved upon his strategy. In his reply he made clear his determination to keep the fleet in the eastern Mediterranean and to fight for Egypt.[33] On 9 July Admiral Cunningham won the first of his astonishing naval victories over the Italians. At the end of July the first Hurricane fighters, desperate though the need for them was in Britain, arrived in Malta. At the end of August, while Hitler's invasion threat was still at its climax, an armoured division embarked for Egypt by the Cape route. It arrived in September. Throughout these same months air and ground reinforcements from Britain were reaching Gibraltar and Malta and large forces were converging upon Egypt not only from Britain but also from India, Australia and New Zealand. Kenya was the staging post of the South African forces. Churchill would have preferred them to go straight to Egypt but Smuts refused.[34] He was already under political attack for stretching too far the formula, 'defence of the Union', and he would have been hard put to defend himself if he had moved his troops to the northern side of the undefeated Italian army in Abyssinia. Besides this, he believed that an attack from the south would prove the most effective means of overthrowing Mussolini's East African Empire. Wavell agreed with him and the event proved him right.

By the end of the year Wavell had 350,000 men on his ration strength. Meanwhile Smuts had been proved wrong in his forecast of Hitler's intentions: it was not until January 1941 that German bombers established themselves in Sicily and not until February that Rommel landed at Tripoli with the vanguard of the Afrika Corps. That delay* gave Wavell time for winning his victories in Egypt and Cyrenaica.

At the end of October Smuts had flown north to meet Eden and Wavell in conference at Khartoum. To his delight, the flight took him over 'the great craterland of East Africa' which he had not hitherto seen and gave him the chance of meeting his son Jannie, serving with his unit 'in one of the hottest most forbidding parts of this continent'.[35] He was more delighted still by the plans of attack agreed upon in Khartoum—operation Compass to drive the

---

* Its reasons were: first, that Hitler had already put Russia next on the list of his victims; secondly, that Franco refused Hitler passage through Spain; thirdly, that Mussolini wanted to win his own victories and refused such limited help as Hitler then offered.

Italians out of Egypt, operation Canvas to overwhelm them in Abyssinia.

No sooner was he home from Khartoum than news began to come in of Mussolini's misadventures with the Greeks. For Smuts it was exhilarating news: five years ago the Great Powers had sacrificed the League to propitiate Mussolini but now a little nation was giving him his deserts.

Hitler is bad enough, but that bounder brigand in Rome whose whole policy has been based on deceit and treachery—in Abyssinia, in Albania, in Greece and his entry into this war at the moment when France was down and out—and one feels comforted to see his bluff called, and by Greece of all people whom he has thoroughly despised.

I think the ironic spirit is never absent from history. How the Gods must laugh at Musso pushing out his ass's chin![36]

Then Wavell attacked at Sidi Barrani. With his two divisions he routed the Italians' seven. Smuts welcomed his victory as an acceptable Christmas box and a good augury for the battles still to come; but he did not forget Mussolini's formidable partner.

What a sell for that bully Mussolini! I only wish that similar treatment could be meted out to the other axis rascal. If this smashing defeat on two fronts could only be the end of Musso! But I fear his case will be like that of Austria in the last war, and the Germans will soon be in control of Italy.

All the more reason for going all out while the going was good. It so happened that his Quaker friends had just asked him what his war aims were. In his reply he recited the names of the battlefields in North Africa and Greece.

I look upon Sidi Barrani and Bardia, on Koritza and Santi Quaranta as essential war aims. And I hope more, much more of the same sort is coming. I love these war aims. The defeat of the devil is almost as much as the triumph of the Lord—though not quite the same. I wish that Hitler could also be thus unmasked. But he is a tougher devil.[37]

It occurred to him occasionally that he had a good deal of the devil in himself.[38] He hated war but when it came he smelt gunpowder. The exhilaration that he felt in face of danger was perhaps the closest bond between him and Churchill. He loved the exuberant greetings which Churchill sent him when the fight was hottest. They were on trek together, they were on commando together, they were shipmates together on an unsinkable ship.

CHAPTER 20

YEAR OF DESTINY

On the evening of 21 July 1940 millions of radio listeners throughout Great Britain heard the voice of Smuts coming from another hemisphere into their homes. It had a different sound from what most of them would have expected—friendly but just a little foreign, not at all dramatic or rhetorical but meditative, as if Smuts were thinking things out as he went along. They felt that he was close to them in their small island but at the same time distant, a detached observer charting the deep oceanic currents which were already, so he told them, flowing in their favour. They felt reassured and no longer so desperately alone.*

The next time they heard his voice was on New Year's Day 1941. Once again they felt him as a friendly, reassuring presence in their homes and once again they found themselves ranging the whole globe in his company. He began by quoting to them the ancient saying that the Gods lavish on those they love infinite joy and infinite sorrow. That had been their lot during the past year and would be their lot again in the year now beginning. But the year would also bring troubles for Hitler. People in the outside world no longer looked upon him as the certain or even the probable victor. He still held the initiative but he would run into great dangers however he used it. If he made a second invasion attempt against Britain he would find her much stronger than last year. If he carried the war into the Balkans and Middle East he would be over-stretching his lines of supply through hostile countries and would be unable any longer to ignore Russia. He had good cause already to look anxiously at America. Smuts said what no British statesman would dare to say—'I feel convinced that in the last resort America will not, as indeed she cannot afford to, stand out'. He made no attempt to forecast in detail what the Americans or the Russians or the Germans or anybody else would do during the coming twelve months; amidst all the kaleidoscopic possibilities of world developments he felt sure of one thing only: 1941 would prove to be a 'Year of Destiny'.

* Churchill to Smuts, 22 July 1940: 'We are all deeply grateful for your splendid and inspiring broadcast.'[1]

In his letters to his friends he developed the same theme. In October 1940, when he heard news of the Tripartite Pact between Germany, Italy and Japan, he wrote, 'The new Triple Alliance means that the U.S.A. and perhaps also Russia will yet come into this war which is rapidly shaping into a world war. And we may leave it at that.' In February 1941 he wrote, 'It almost looks as if the guns will go off all along the long line from the Far East to the West and as if the world war will be on next spring and summer.' How this would happen he did not attempt to forecast; but he believed it to belong to the logic of events.[2]

His attitude towards Russia was cool and watchful. He regarded Hitler's deal with Stalin as a bargain between the Devil and Beelzebub and he shared the general abhorrence at the Russian attack on Finland; but he did not allow himself to be swept away by moral indignation. He saw real difference between a system which might yet outgrow its savageries and one which of set purpose was turning back to pogroms.

Nazism...destroys the very soul of our civilization...I have not taken the same grave view of Bolshevism, for it never was clear to me that Bolshevism, in spite of its brutalities and cruelties, really threatened the essentials of our ethical civilization. And after all it was a revolution of a semi-barbarous people against a rotten government and an effete church. But Nazi-ism in highly cultured Germany is a very different affair.[3]

Such moral distinctions apart, he could see no real solidarity of interest between the frightened Russians and the overbearing Germans. They were uneasy bedfellows and might yet, in some way which he could not foresee, find themselves in conflict with each other.

In contrast, his attitude towards America was positive and confident. He believed that a moral solidarity existed between America and the British Commonwealth; they shared the same freedoms, they stood for the same values. He believed also that a solidarity of interest existed between them and that America could not for her own safety stand aside when the Germans, Italians and Japanese were in a combination to destroy the Commonwealth. For these reasons he welcomed even the most faltering forward steps of the Americans, such as the destroyers-bases deal of August 1940. In the presidential election at the end of the year he took issue with his friends in New York by backing Roosevelt as a more forthright friend of the Commonwealth than Willkie. 'Let America come in', he exclaimed,

'. . . I do not think we shall win without her. We could prevent Hitler winning. But that is not enough.' He believed that Roosevelt in his heart felt the same. At the end of March, when Roosevelt proclaimed Lend Lease, he exclaimed: 'Hitler's doom is sealed.' He looked forward to a deepening partnership between America and the Commonwealth which would continue after the war and establish 'the real peace, whatever the peace treaty may be'.[4]

He was allowing his hopes to leap too far ahead of the facts. The Commonwealth and the Greeks remained alone against the big battalions. Still, they made what use they could of the brief respite remaining to them. On 6 March 1941 Commonwealth forces, with the South Africans in the van, entered Addis Ababa. Smuts once again recalled the timid, and, as he believed, the unnecessary desertion of Abyssinia and the League only a few years earlier.

To think that Hoare and Baldwin could have been bluffed in 1935!. . .To me the whole business appeared as incredible then, as events have proved it to be since. But in the meantime the League was allowed to be torpedoed, and Europe put at the mercy of Hitler, and the stage set for this terrible world war. So great things turn on small things, and small men bear their share in shaping the course of history.[5]

He took some comfort from the thought that South African valour was vindicating in 1941 the stand which South Africa had taken in 1935. But he did not spend too much time in looking backwards. He was looking forward to Hitler's 'deadly counterstroke'. It might come any day now, in the Balkans and North Africa. Wavell had been freed none too soon from the danger to his rear in Abyssinia. Smuts thought that he had better not extend his forces too far in the western desert. Tobruk was far enough.[6]

In the first week of March Smuts went to Cairo to meet Eden and Dill, who had just completed their political and military soundings in the Balkans. The question to be decided was whether or not Commonwealth forces—Australians and New Zealanders predominantly— would cross the Mediterranean to fight side by side with the Greeks against the Germans. With some reservations, Smuts favoured taking the risk. His views, as quoted in part to the New Zealand prime minister, may have had some effect upon the decision. On the other hand, the inter-governmental consultations were approaching their end by the time he reached Cairo. In all probability, he did no more than endorse a decision which was already almost made.[7]

On 6 April Hitler unleashed on the Balkans his operation Marita. Even before that Rommel had begun to probe Wavell's thin forces beyond Benghazi. By the middle of April the whole of Cyrenaica was in German hands. By the end of April the swastika was flying over the Acropolis. The navy rescued from Greece 50,000 of the 62,000 men whom it had so recently landed there. Three weeks later it re-enacted the same drama on the beaches of Crete. At the cost of heavy losses it rescued 18,000 out of 32,000 New Zealanders.

It was a shattering demonstration of the new restrictions imposed upon naval power by air and land forces operating from a continental base. Once and for all, Smuts digested the lesson.* Characteristically, his first application of it was to the long-term problems of peace and freedom.

Whatever shall we do in future? The nation that does not arm continuously is lost—as France has been lost, as Britain will be lost but for the Grace of God. In this mechanistic age mere bravery and improvised organization at the last moment will not help. The only alternative is a League of the Nations or of some nations strong enough to withstand aggression ...As things are today disarmament is *not* the way to peace as we had imagined, indeed just the opposite. It could only be the way to peace if there is such a coercive union of the nations that it becomes impossible for any one of them to arm without being at once dealt with. And so close and coercive a union may also be destructive of liberty and national self-determination.[8]

But he had not much time to give to these distant peacetime problems when the immediate war problems were so urgent. His letters to Wavell at this time were an admirable blend of sympathy, realism and encouragement. He backed his words up by deeds. He ordered the first South African Division to move immediately from conquered Abyssinia to threatened Egypt and he worked 'neck or nothing' to get the second division ready for deployment and action on the same front. 'All our South African eggs', he said, 'are going into that basket. So I too have taken my fate in both hands.'[9]

He felt confident in Wavell's ability to hold the Germans in the Western Desert and at the same time steal a march on them in the Middle East by taking control of Iraq and Syria. Between May and July he saw this programme carried through and recorded with satisfaction the sinking of the *Bismarck* and the melodrama or farce

* See p. 364 below.

of Rudolf Hess's flight to Britain. 'We are sometimes conscious of
our own troubles', he reflected, 'but do not know what are the
other fellow's. Hess is a sign of what is passing in that amiable family.
And so much more may be brewing than we are imagining.'[10]

All the same, Hitler's attack on Russia took him by surprise. He
could not make up his mind whether it was a carefully calculated
enterprise or a demonstration of Hitler's fatalistic, somnambulistic
temperament. Either way, there was a chance this time that Hitler
had overreached himself. That would be the end of him. But Smuts
was on his guard against putting too much trust in Stalin. In the
light of his double-dealing in 1939, his poisonous propaganda since
then and his enigmatical attitude towards the Poles, Stalin did not
appear a reliable ally. Let it suffice for the time being that Russia
was absorbing, far more successfully than the experts had forecast,
the main shock of the German war machine. In late August Smuts
declared publicly that he blessed the arms of Russia. Thereupon
the Nationalists denounced him with renewed fury as the ally of
Bolshevism. But he did not recant. 'I bless Russia', he wrote, 'not
for having come in, because she did not...Hitler has forced her
into the fight. He has done us that signal service by the mercy of
God.'[11]

It fretted him, as it did Churchill, that the Commonwealth forces
in North Africa and the Middle East appeared unable to use this
heaven-sent opportunity of mounting an offensive. In August he
went north for discussions with Auchinleck, Wavell's successor in
the command. He spent some happy hours with the South Africans
in the Western Desert, but Auchinleck convinced him that Crusader,
the offensive which he was planning there, could not possibly be
launched for some months to come. Smuts consoled himself with the
thought that there would still be time for it before the Germans
regrouped their forces after knocking out the Russians—if they did
knock them out. Early in the Russian campaign he had seen two
champion liars trying to outlie each other in their military com-
muniqués and had not known which to believe, but as winter approached he felt confident that the Russians were doing far better
than knowledgeable observers had forecast. They were proving
themselves the real surprise of the war. The Americans, on the other
hand, were proving themselves the real disappointment.[12]

From his point of view the Year of Destiny which he had envisaged on New Year's Day would become a caricature of itself if it ended with the Russians, but not the Americans, as comrades in arms of the Commonwealth. In his gloomy moments that was the end that he expected. His exhilaration at the news of Lend Lease grew dim two months later when the Germans demonstrated their immense preponderance of power in Yugoslavia, Greece and Crete.

It is now all a question of time. *Too late* is (*sic*) the most awful words in all language. It *could* have been done; it *could* have been prevented; but the effort, the help etc. came too late. On these words hang the history of the world. With our power of endurance I trust however that formula will not apply in this case. We shall hang on grimly to the end—be it victory or defeat.

In August, news of the Atlantic Charter did little to cheer him up; the Americans, he said, were most singularly outspoken and also most anxious to keep out of the war. In September, he remarked sardonically that the Germans would turn on 'us' when they had knocked out the Russians and turn on the Americans when they had knocked out 'us'—'but I don't think we shall be knocked out, and we shall give the dear Americans as much time as they wish to come in and win the war—as last time'. In November, he said that the Americans had talked and talked until everybody was sickened but had proved most tardy in action.

In fact that blessed amendment of the Neutrality Act (which should never have been passed at all in any sensible country) is even now not yet through Congress. One can never find out what exactly America is doing. Vast sums have been voted but even now in the third year of the war scarcely one per cent of it all has been spent on munitions for her friends who are fighting her battle as much as their own. Wonderful speeches by the President—magnificent. But time is passing, and time lost cannot be bought with all the vast wealth of America. Perhaps I should not write with this impatience...

But his nerves at this time were getting frayed. As he observed the French giving free passage to their conquerors through Tunis for the supply of Rommel's Afrika Corps, he exclaimed: 'If God would only send them a woman, another Joan of Arc, for her men have failed her.'[13]

He could perhaps be forgiven these emotional outbursts because they did not disturb, except perhaps momentarily, the cool detachment with which he studied and appraised the developing situation.

He believed that American participation in the war belonged to a logic of events which was immediately operative in the conflict of strategical interests between America and Japan. He wrote in July—

Japan is at last coming into the open. Germany's attack on Russia was the first great surprise after the fall of France. Now Japan moves in the Far East, and the repercussions may be even more serious. The U.S.A. will now be forced to take action which will sooner rather than later lead her into the war. Hitler has brought Russia most unexpectedly on our side. Now Japan is going to force the U.S.A. to take an active and not merely an economic part in the war. So Evil defeats itself, and however powerful and clever works its own undoing...May it be so and not mere wishful thinking.

In mid-October he noted the fall of the Japanese Cabinet and felt sure that the new government would soon bring Japan into the war. At the end of November he saw the Gordian knot being cut. On 7 December he wrote: 'Destiny is writing a new chapter in our tangled human story.' That same night the Japanese made their first landings on the coast of Malaya and attacked the American fleet in Pearl Harbour. Next day the United Kingdom and the United States declared war on Japan. Three days later Germany and Italy declared war on the United States.[14]

For Smuts the tension was over. His prognostications twelve months earlier of the Year of Destiny had fulfilled themselves.

CHAPTER 21

THE STRUGGLE FOR AFRICA

SMUTS welcomed American belligerency as a great deliverance, paradoxically proclaimed to the world by great disasters. As he put it, America's entry into the war had established the pattern, but the way she entered it had upset the time-table of victory.[1]

The disastrous aftermath of Pearl Harbour did not take him by surprise. Seventeen years before, when the Singapore base was being planned, he had argued that it would be dangerous for the British to divide their fleet when they were at grips with a real crisis. Only a few weeks before, he had sent a telegram of warning to Churchill: if the Japanese were 'really nippy', he said, there was the prospect of a first-class disaster.[2] By that he meant a first-class disaster not only to the Royal Navy but also to the United States Navy. The American concept of naval deployment had found expression in maps which confined American responsibility within square boxes extending into the mid-Atlantic and mid-Pacific, while leaving to the Royal Navy, desperately over-extended though it already was in the Atlantic and Mediterranean, sole responsibility for all the rest of the world's salt water. By contrast, Smuts maintained that the danger zone extending from 'the Malaysian barrier' to the islands north of New Zealand ought to be a combined American–British responsibility. If it were not, each navy might suffer a separate defeat.

The event justified his forebodings, yet only once did he allow himself the indulgence of saying that he had told them so. On 31 January he wrote—

Practically everything happening now in the Far East was predicted by me, put on paper, passed on to the responsible authorities, who no doubt put the tiresome stuff in the patient pigeon-hole. If the British fleet at Singapore and the American fleet at Pearl Harbour had been together somewhere in the Pacific Japan might never have entered into this war,* at least not now, and both we and America would still have had our big battleships, now at the bottom, and the prospect before Hitler would

* But then no more (according to Smuts's own political analysis) might the Americans have entered it.

364

have been one of unrelieved gloom. First Japan has a great innings and Hitler need not only think of the Second Moscow.*[3]

In public he uttered no word of recrimination. On the contrary, his heart was altogether with Churchill, now under notice to defend his conduct of the war against snipers and underminers in the House of Commons. He saw Churchill as a man whose survival from the pre-war era to lead the Commonwealth through this crisis was providential. He acclaimed the service he was even now rendering to his country and the world by hammering out in Washington the British–American war partnership; yet no sooner was he home than he found himself under the fire of faint-hearted politicians.

All interesting to read and to contemplate as a human drama. But to think of all his energy thus absorbed, and taken off the grim business of war which is his real job. Democracy does really involve a cruel waste. How can a man find time and proper concentration for some of the hardest and most fateful problems of all time, when he has continually to pause and prepare for and make speeches which surely involve an immense amount of physical and mental energy? I think not so much the war as his own people are consuming him, literally eating him up...

But Smuts was showing more concern for his friend than the situation called for. He was imputing to him his own abhorrence of the parliamentary performances which Churchill, to the great profit of his nation, not only endured but enjoyed.[4]

What did completely satisfy Smuts at this time was the order of strategical priorities agreed between the Americans and British while Churchill was in Washington: victory in Europe first, victory in Asia to follow. From December to April he watched ruefully but without dismay the rushing torrent of Japanese conquest in Malaya, Singapore, the Philippines, the Solomons, Indonesia, Burma and Northern New Guinea. 'All a very bad business', he said, 'which we shall have to endure before the turn of the tide.' By the end of February he felt sure that the tide was approaching high water. He did not believe that Japanese resources or communications would stand the strain of massive assaults on Australia or India. In mid-March he told parliament that Japan had committed the greatest act of national folly so far recorded in history and that it was better so: she was an evil influence and if there had to be a show-down for and against evil, let it be world wide. On 21 March he wrote, 'Japan

* To Smuts the First Moscow meant Napoleon's.

was bound to have a great run and has had it too. But I hope she is now coming up against our main defence where she will first be stopped and later be rolled back with disastrous effect. If only America will hurry on the end of the Japanese advance will soon be reached.' America was indeed hurrying on and so was Britain. In the first week of April the Japanese suffered a check in an air battle over Ceylon. In the first week of May the battle of the Coral Sea halted their advance towards Australia. A month later, the battle of Midway destroyed their naval preponderance in the Pacific. The pattern of victory in Asia was now demonstrated and all that remained in question was the time-table.[5]

Smuts had been expecting this. Throughout these dangerous months his main anxiety had been the imminent German offensive against Russia. Trying to put himself into Hitler's mind, he imagined a pincers movement of the German land forces driving through the Caucasus into the Middle East and the Japanese naval forces joining them in the region of the Persian Gulf. He did not believe that so ambitious a strategical plan—if Hitler had in fact conceived it— possessed any foundation in reality. The Japanese could not possibly fulfil the rôle assigned to them. But the Germans might come close to fulfilling their rôle. Smuts wrote on 12 April—

If Russia is pushed beyond the Urals we shall have a long and difficult road to go to victory and much sorrow and loss may still be in store for us before the end. But even then I feel confident of victory. I have not reckoned on the Russian front holding as a *certainty*... We can win without Russia, though I admit it will be a most arduous business. If Russia holds we shall have victory in Europe before it is reached in Asia. If Russia is beaten back to Siberia, we shall have victory in the Far East and the collapse of Japan before it is reached in Europe. *This* is how the future looks to me. Of course it is all surmise and speculations. But our defeat does not enter into my speculation... This is not wishful thinking; it is *purposeful* thinking![6]

Within the agreed order of strategical priorities, the action which seemed most purposeful, not only to the Russians and to British left-wingers but also to large sections of public opinion in Washington, was an immediate second front in western Europe. Operation Sledge-hammer, a mainly British blow to secure lodgement across the Channel in 1942, and operation Round-up, a British–American offensive in 1943, were put on paper by the planners. They remained for a brief time the symbol of Russian demands and of American hopes; but the British distrusted them and Smuts totally disbelieved in them. To him they seemed a piece of wishful thinking, for nothing of any use could be achieved in western Europe until American deployment across the Atlantic was on a massive scale—and that would be 1943, at the earliest. Meanwhile, he insisted, the Americans and British could not possibly leave all the hard fighting to the Russians. On 19 May he despatched by personal messenger a letter to President Roosevelt. 'To me', he said, 'the all-important consideration is our time-table. It is 1942 that matters most. No doubt we can develop and deploy huge resources in 1943 and 1944, but we must first pull through 1942.'[7]

To him, 1942 spelt Africa.

From all his global explorations he kept returning to Africa, that is to say, to his own immediate business—on the home front, to begin with, for unless he held that secure the Cape route would be lost to the Commonwealth and its allies. Looking back upon the course of home politics since the breach between Hertzog and Malan late in 1940 he had good reason to feel moderately pleased. The Opposition in parliament was now divided into two camps. The larger camp under Malan continued for a time to call itself Die Herenigde Nasionale of Volksparty, but gradually it appropriated the simple name Nasionale party. The smaller camp under General Edwin Conroy called itself the Afrikaner party. It had some intellectual and moral weight, with a man like Havenga to speak for it and a man like A. C. Cilliers to pamphleteer for it and a well-established newspaper, *Die Vaderland*, to spread its news and views. What it lacked was ideological and organizational cement. Hertzogism without Hertzog, and without an effective party machine, was not likely to prove an enduring rival to the Nationalists. The real challenge to their leadership came from the extra-parliamentary and anti-parliamentary organizations which were now in a dangerous state of frustration and ferment.[8]

Some of these organizations were merely froth on the wave, the conceited posturings of academic busybodies who felt sure that they could do better than the professional politicians. For example, the Handhawersbond (League of Upholders) had no new ideas, no new policies, no workable machinery, but only a wonderful collection of

slogans—anti-khaki, pro-Monument, Boerdom, 'de Wet Afrikanerdom', 'Vegkommando', 'die Pad van Suid-Afrika'—a balloon of rhetoric which was punctured within a few months of its being pumped up.
Early in 1941 its leading spirits were looking for homes in other
organizations. Some of them found what they were looking for in
the New Order Group. This organization was ostensibly no more than
a study circle, devoted to the elucidation of the principles contained
in Oswald Pirow's *Nuwe Orde vir Suid-Afrika*, a pamphlet which, in
seven editions between December 1940 and May 1941, proclaimed
the gospels of Christian Republicanism and National Socialism. The
New Order Group spread its net widely but made only a disappointing catch of small fish, academic nonentities and ex-Hertzogite politicians who had stopped short of joining the Afrikaner party. It
never dared challenge the leadership of Dr Malan. The break, when
it came (August 1941), came on Malan's initiative.

By that time the National party was in open collision with a far
more formidable organization, the Ossewa-Brandwag.* Founded in
October 1938 to keep alive the patriotic fires kindled by the Voortrekker celebrations, its sphere of action was intended to be commemorative and symbolic of Afrikaner traditions and destinies.
Politics were supposed to be barred. But they could not be barred.
The zealous affirmation of Afrikaner cultural identity had political
and even military implications. It was not long before the O.B.
established a para-military organization under a Commandant-
General. Thereupon Pirow, as Minister of Defence in the Hertzog
government, forbade members of the Union Defence Force to belong
to the O.B. After September 1939 Smuts prohibited all government
servants from becoming members of it. The O.B. replied with a
recruiting campaign of its own which challenged the official recruiting campaign for the Union's armed forces. In December 1940 it
elected a new Commandant-General, Dr J. F. B. van Rensburg, who
took no pains to conceal his National Socialist convictions and his
contempt for the parliamentary constitution. Van Rensburg's
stormjaers began to look disquietingly akin to the Nazi stormtroopers.
Smuts did not prohibit them from playing soldiers but he made
certain that they played that game without weapons. By an emergency
regulation he called in the rifles and reissued them only to such
persons as would enlist for service in the government's non-permanent

* See pp. 296, 335 above.

home defence force. Presumably, he did not expect any enlistments from the O.B.

By Afrikaner tradition it was an outrage upon a white man to take away his rifle. Nevertheless the protests which Nationalist politicians raised appeared perfunctory. The reason was that the O.B. was becoming almost as much a challenge to the parliamentary Opposition as it was to the government. In the hectic months of mid-1940 it had adopted a constitution and established an organization intended to draw into its ranks every nationalist-minded Afrikaner. But this was already the purpose of the National party. Two Union-wide organizations, each claiming to be representative of Afrikanerdom, now confronted each other. The pacts of mutual non-interference which they made from time to time always broke down. The trouble was that each organization saw itself as the embodiment of Afrikanerdom in its entirety; the National party could not disinterest itself from Afrikaner culture, the O.B. could not stay aloof from Afrikaner politics. In mid-1941 the O.B. took it upon itself to distribute in tens of thousands a document based upon the *Konsep-Grondwet*—the draft constitution drawn up for the Afrikaner Republic. But so momentous a decision belonged, surely, to the political leaders? They decided that they could no longer postpone the struggle for power. They began by launching an attack against Pirow's New Order. Van Rensburg sprang at once to Pirow's defence. In doing so he made claims for his own organization which Malan could not possibly accept—'The O.B. for the whole nation', he cried, 'it covers the whole front'.* A month or two went by with the opposed forces sparring at each other and the conciliators trying to patch up the quarrel; but cracks began to appear in the O.B. and the party's champions pressed their advantage home. In early October *Die Transvaler* issued an urgent summons to all Nationalists to break loose from the O.B. Meanwhile the Nazi broadcasting station at Zeesen was joining the fray on the side of van Rensburg—a clear demonstration, the party leaders declared, that the O.B. was not truly national but a foreign excrescence on Afrikanerdom. Throughout the aftermath of Pearl Harbour these small but bitter battles were fought without truce and without as yet any conclusive result but with the O.B. getting such a battering that Harry Lawrence†

---

* Die O.B. vir die hele volk—hy dek die hele front.[9]
† Minister of the Interior.

exclaimed, 'Instead of the Government having to ban the O.B. Dr Malan has done it for us.'[10]

In long term Smuts had more to fear from a disciplined parliamentary Opposition than from an extra-parliamentary movement spotted by foreign ideologies and marred by sporadic sabotage.[11] Even in short term he found the Nationalists, despite their quarrels with the O.B., even more vehement than they had been in their attacks on himself. This perhaps was not surprising since he kept giving them new targets to shoot at. When he sent the first division to Egypt they asked him with scorn whether Britain's war in Egypt was part of South Africa's defence. They asked him further whether he had it in mind, in defiance of the resolution passed by the House of Assembly on 4 September 1939, to send South African troops overseas. In his reply he made it quite plain that he did have this in mind and at the appropriate time would come to parliament to seek release from the restriction embodied in what had been, as everybody remembered, his own resolution.[12] On top of this provocation he was soon publicly blessing the arms of Russia and thereby proclaiming himself, the Nationalists said, a champion of Bolshevism.[13] Six months later they saw him bring new dangers upon South Africa by his declarations of war against Japan, Bulgaria, Hungary, Roumania and Finland. In their eyes there remained only one act of recklessness for him to commit. He committed it on 11 March 1942 when he declared in parliament that he would be ready, if the Japanese attacked the Union, to arm the Natives and the Coloureds for the defence of their country.

Scores of thousands of them, of course, were already in uniform as volunteers for non-combatant service. Moreover, emergencies had more than once arisen in the battle zone where arms had been issued to some of them. By and large, however, the distinction between combatant and non-combatant had been maintained. Smuts knew that his Native and Coloured soldiers felt this distinction as a slight.

The Coloured people at the front [he wrote] have behaved magnificently. And the Natives who serve as motor drivers, orderlies, cooks, stretcher-bearers, even gunners and the like, have also done very well, and are being infiltrated into our army to make up for our lack of European manpower. They all clamour for weapons and full status as fighters, but I have not yet ventured to go so far in the face of a difficult public opinion.

At the same time he recognized the danger which might arise, now or in the future, from their continuing frustration. He had been told that some of them were saying, 'Why fight against Japan? We are oppressed by the whites and shall not fare worse under the Japanese.'[14]

This precisely was the point which many Nationalist journalists were unconsciously making in their comments on the collapse of the British Empire in south-east Asia. The bluff of British propaganda, they said, had at last been called by the proof given to the world by the Malayans and Burmese that they did not think their white rulers worth fighting for. The Nationalists seemed not to envisage the possibility of black people in South Africa ever thinking the same about their white rulers. Smuts, by contrast, took note of the unpleasant possibilities for South Africa inherent in the shifting balance of power between Europe and Asia, not merely in a problematical future time but, quite possibly, here and now. Despite his expectation that the Japanese would soon reach their high-water mark of aggression, he was compelled in prudence to consider the situation which would face South Africa if their penetration of the Indian Ocean continued unchecked. In March 1942 he had on his desk a memorandum from Colonel P. B. van der Westhuizen arguing the case for a massive enlistment of Native and Coloured troops on the ground that existing military manpower was inadequate for the defence of the Union's 1,500 miles of coast. If the government did not arm the Natives for defending their country, van der Westhuizen argued, the Japanese could be trusted to arm them for conquering it.[15]

Obviously, Smuts was not stumbling into an ill-considered improvisation when he made his statement to parliament about arming the Natives and the Coloureds. He was moved both by a genuine appreciation of their loyal service and also by a hard-headed estimate of South Africa's situation and real interests. Nevertheless he held back from pressing the debate to a clear conclusion.[16] A direct Japanese attack on South Africa, he said in effect, was so far only a contingency. Meanwhile, the army needed non-combatants as well as combatants. There was no reason as yet to grasp the nettle. Next year, when he did make a move towards grasping it, his colleagues in the Cabinet refused to accept the political risk.*

* See p. 412 below.

Although no action followed from his statement of March 1942 it was none the less a red rag to his enemies on the home front.

This has been manna from heaven [he wrote] for our wretched Opposition who have seized greedily at this opening to inflame passions and exploit prejudices. Fancy arming the Natives who are likely to use their weapons against the Whites! Think of arming the Natives after I had *disarmed* the Europeans only a year or more ago! Manifestoes are raining, the Church has been mobilized to pass angry resolutions and a campaign of meetings is being arranged. It is of course all purely party politics.[17]

Inevitably, the target which was offered at this time by the combination of British and American disasters, the Russian alliance, the Black peril and Smuts's wild recklessness—as they judged it to be—proved irresistibly attractive to his political enemies. In the early months of 1942 their propaganda reached its crescendo—at one and the same time anti-war, anti-British, anti-Bolshevik, anti-Commonwealth, anti-Smuts.[18]

Yet it appeared that Smuts had no great need to worry when the conflict on the home front came to its crunch. A bare five weeks after Pearl Harbour Dr Malan had moved in the House of Assembly a motion embodying the programme which nationalist Afrikanerdom, in the midst of all its fierce dissensions, had hammered out. The motion declared that the highest interests of the nation could be served only by converting South Africa into a republic dissociated from the British Crown and Empire and independent of any foreign Power. It demanded that this republic should be based on the traditions of the former republics of South Africa and should repudiate the false and dangerous elements contained in British liberalistic democracy; it should be Christian-national in substance and character and should observe the equal language and cultural rights* of both sections of the European population; it should be made safe for the European race and civilization in accordance with the guardianship principle; finally, it should be protected against the capitalistic and parasitical exploitation of its population as well as the undermining influence of hostile and unnational elements. In the long speech with which Malan supported this resolution he said very little that the House had not heard many times before. Nor did Smuts in his reply have anything new to add except for one significant

---

* Hertzog had broken with the Malanites when they refused to add equal political rights to this stipulation.

inquiry. He asked who were the parasitical exploiters alluded to in the resolution. Were they the Jews? An Opposition member exclaimed, 'You yourself.' Smuts seized his chance. He and his party, then, would be branded in the proposed republic as unnational elements. A republic so intolerant and sectionally minded, he declared, would never be achieved. He moved an amendment approving the government's recent declarations of war and reaffirming South Africa's membership of the British Commonwealth of Nations. On 17 January, after four days of debate, his amendment was carried by 81 votes to 56.[19]

He had by now almost doubled the majority with which two and a half years earlier he had carried South Africa into the war; but he might not have done so if he had sought a clear mandate from parliament to arm the Natives and Coloureds. Still, in some provincial by-elections which were held soon after his hypothetical statement on that issue his party won a handsome majority of the votes.[20] He kept telling himself that his Afrikaner kith and kin would sooner or later rally to him and the ideas for which he stood. Even the parsons, he said, would come round.[21] He said that in April 1942, when the war in Africa seemed to be going well. In June, when news came of the disaster at Tobruk, he wrote, 'My opponents, who were down and out, have once more raised their miserable heads and voices.'[22]

Only a few weeks before he had felt so confident. In his letter to President Roosevelt on 19 May he had sketched his design for victory, not as theory remote from present facts but as action already under way and pregnant with dazzling opportunities if reinforced and followed through. At the very worst—that is to say, if Hitler won success in his summer offensive against the Russians—victory in Africa would give the allies a firm base from which to counter the German thrust that could then be expected towards the oilfields of the Middle East and the Persian Gulf. And if things went well in Russia it would give them the chance of striking from Africa across the Mediterranean against 'the weaker members and hangers-on of the Axis', in preparation for the great assault against the Germans to be launched from the British Isles in 1943.[23]

Smuts felt sure that the first movements of this grand design were already unfolding themselves satisfactorily. In May, the seizure of

Diego Suarez in Madagascar scotched the fear that the Vichy French would give safe passage for Japanese submarines into the Mozambique channel, thereby endangering the supply lines of the Egyptian base.* In May, Auchinleck was getting ready to launch from that base the new offensive which this time, Smuts felt sure, would finish Rommel for good. Admittedly, Auchinleck had had indifferent luck with operation Crusader, the offensive he had launched the previous November. Although he had made good its unpromising start and had pushed it to the western limits of Cyrenaica, his overstrained lines of supply had made it impossible for him to hold all his gains. From February to May his forces and Rommel's faced each other in a state of equilibrium on the Gazala front about thirty miles west of Tobruk. Smuts thought this situation sound enough for the time being. He knew, of course, that his South African troops were critical of their British leaders; in February his son Jannie had written to him from the front urging him in heaven's name to come and take command himself, for this was a war of movement and what the army needed was a modern version of Boer War tactics. It was a flattering estimate of his military capacities which was re-iterated a few months later by Sir Miles Lampson, the British ambassador to Egypt.[24] But Smuts was not impressed. He had great confidence in Auchinleck. In the second week of May he flew north to hold conference with him and his senior officers, as well as with Lyttelton, the British Minister of State, and his administrative and supply officers. He took his wife with him and together they spent two days visiting the South Africans in the desert. He felt that their visit was a great success, above all *her* success. He was also satisfied with the upshot of the official conferences. His only doubt was whether Rommel might not strike first in the desert; but even if he did it would make no difference; Rommel this time was facing his Waterloo.[25]

Rommel did strike first and he struck hard, but the early news of the battle was good and Smuts felt exhilaration at the thought of his son being in the thick of it. Gradually, however, it became clear to him that the battle was going badly. By 16 June he was willing to

---

* Smuts may well have exaggerated this danger, but he recalled that French sub-servience to the Japanese had opened the way for the conquest of Malaya and he believed that the French were even now facilitating the supply of Rommel's forces through Tunis. He advocated the complete occupation of Madagascar and made available a South African brigade for this operation, which, however, was not carried out until September.

'grin and bear it' if the South Africans were forced back on Tobruk, provided they were not left isolated there. He telegraphed to Auchinleck for reassurance and on 18 June received a satisfactory reply. But only two days later the 'thunderbolt from the north' hit him. Tobruk had been overrun and among the 32,000 prisoners taken were 10,000 of his own South Africans.[26]

He took the blow like a soldier. It fell only a week or two before the rush to Durban for one of the main racing events of the year. He turned that coincidence to good account. As soon as the races were over a squadron of armoured cars roared round the track. Each of them carried a large placard, AVENGE TOBRUK! Loudspeakers broadcast a message from Smuts calling immediately for thousands of volunteers to make good the army's losses. There were bigger races in Egypt, he said, and their stakes were the future of South Africa. Within the first week his recruiting campaign brought in 5,000 men, amongst them his eldest son Japie who, as a key engineer in the Premier Mine, had hitherto been reserved from military service, much against his own will. From his younger son Jannie he received graphic news of the Eighth Army's defeat and his own adventurous escape. Some old memories awoke in him. He told a friend that he was really a creature of the Boer War and that he liked his children to go through the same experience—'What an experience! I am so glad that he has had this fire baptism and this taste of retreat. It is so different from the victorious advance and bites so much deeper into the soul.'[27]

In view of the misleading reports and forecasts which had been sent him so recently he had good ground for complaint; but that was not his view of how a soldier should behave when the battle was going badly. As soon as he heard the news of Tobruk he sent a signal to Churchill and Auchinleck saying that this was not the time for conducting post mortems but for making secure what we still held. Throughout the headlong retreat of the last two weeks of June he kept silence. In the first week of July, when Auchinleck stood at last to fight on the El Alamein line, Smuts sent him a signal to say that he had full confidence in him and would be with him heart and soul in the coming battle. When the battle had been fought he instructed his representative, General Frank Theron, to tell Auchinleck that the confidence placed in him had been fully justified; by his courage and tenacity he had won a battle which might well prove to be the turning point of the war.* Smuts gloried in the part which his own soldiers had played in it. 'The men of Abyssinia, of Amba Alagi, of Sidi Resegh', he wrote, 'once more rose to the occasion and did what I expected them to do. The First Division may yet avenge the Second, lost at Tobruk.' Throughout the following months, when he was playing a major part in the reorganizations which brought victory in North Africa, that was a thought that never left his mind—that his own soldiers would release their captured comrades and bring them home.†

Not until the crisis was over did he permit himself to make a critical appraisal of what had gone wrong. He then examined, as Churchill and his advisers were doing in London, the shortcomings of equipment, of tactics and of leadership which had come so close to destroying the Eighth Army. He rated lowest the shortcomings of equipment and believed that they would soon be made good by British and American factories. The shortcomings of tactics, as his son had said with emphasis in his letters from the front, appeared more obdurate; but he believed them to be derivative. In his view, leadership had been the main shortcoming and it remained the main problem. If the right answer could be found to that, everything else that was amiss would soon be set right.

Leadership seemed to him in part a problem of organization and in part a problem of personalities. The commander-in-chief, whoever he might be, had far too large an area to look after and far too much business coming on to his desk in Cairo; nobody knew this better than Smuts, who had been insistent throughout the past two years upon the need to stand on guard in Syria, Iraq and Persia as well as in the western desert. By now he was in the mood to welcome drastic changes in the structure of command. He was equally in the mood to welcome drastic changes of the commanders. He had stood staunchly by Auchinleck so long as the army was in danger but now that it was safe he expected him to show a spirit of aggression.[28] That was what Rommel had done when Auchinleck's supply lines had been overstretched; but Rommel was now being given time to build up his resources at Alamein, a position uncomfortably close to Cairo and of great natural strength‡ which the Germans could exploit just as easily

---

* No doubt Smuts was exaggerating. The fighting went on until the end of July and ended in stalemate. † See p. 379 below.
‡ The impassable sands of the Qattara depression, to the south of the position, made it impossible for either side to win by a powerful flanking movement.

as the British had done. Could it possibly be that the British were still making plans for a flight from Egypt? In the third week of July Smuts received from General Theron a despatch which said precisely that. Theron gave a full and detailed summary of the plans. They included a retreat of the South African forces to Palestine, of all places. What a commentary that would have been on the pledge which Smuts had given that he would secure parliamentary sanction before sending South African troops outside Africa! But in his reply to Theron he did not niggle over details. It was the whole principle of this dismal planning that he boggled at. If the need should really arise to withdraw from Egypt, he wrote, he would be ready to face it realistically with his comrades in arms, in the spirit of close allies determined to stand by each other in face of a dangerous enemy. But he could see no reason at all for anticipating that the need would arise. To contemplate the possibility of losing Egypt was to contemplate the possibility of losing the war. He could not believe that the situation on the Alamein front gave any excuse for that. Meanwhile, his government had the right and the duty to demand full information about the situation. He was sending his Chief of Staff immediately to Cairo.[29]

Smuts would probably have agreed that it is the duty of a commander-in-chief, while hoping for the best, to prepare for the worst, provided that he does so without causing such alarm and despondency as will make it more likely that the worst will occur.[30] In the planning reported to him by Theron he could not see that this proviso had been observed. He considered the speculations of the planners to be excessively lugubrious. In July, following the defeat of Rommel's final thrust, an armoured division and an infantry division had arrived in Egypt. The 51st Highland division was due in August. Meanwhile, a great flood of first-rate equipment—tanks, anti-tank guns, aircraft—was flowing in from the United Kingdom and the United States. Yet planning for the worst was still proceeding. The commander-in-chief should surely have kept the time lags of his subordinates under tighter control. On 23 July, Smuts telegraphed to Churchill that his confidence in the existing leadership had been gravely shaken.* Churchill's response was an urgent request for

---

* I have been reporting, not necessarily endorsing, Smuts's train of thought. No doubt it is right for a commander-in-chief to keep what Wavell used to call a W.P.C. (Worst Possible Case) file; but not, normally, to allow its appraisals, whatever they may be, to become widely known.

Smuts to join him in the grand inquest which he was about to undertake in Cairo. He hoped that Smuts would also join him on the
second stage of his mission—his journey to Moscow to inform Stalin
of the strategical decisions which the British and Americans had
recently agreed upon.[31]

Those decisions were in close correspondence with the argument
which Smuts had addressed to Roosevelt only two months previously.
They were, of course, equally in correspondence with the thought of
the British Chiefs of Staff. For this reason, nobody would have been
able to define precisely what impact Smuts's thought had had upon
Roosevelt. In June, when the Combined Chiefs of Staff were meeting
in Washington, Churchill and Roosevelt had discussed the idea of
a British–American expedition to French North Africa. Four weeks
later (24 July) at a conference of the Combined Chiefs of Staff in
London, full agreement was reached on Torch, a joint British–
American descent upon French North Africa with forces strong
enough, in combination with the Army of the Nile, to do what Smuts
said must be done, 'to end this African see-saw once for all'.[32] What
would happen afterwards had still to be hammered out in argument
between the British and the Americans. For the present, their agreement of 24 July, limited though it was, provided a perspective broad
and clear enough for the decisions to be taken at Cairo in the first
week of August.

There emerged from the Cairo Conference two decisions which
were destined throughout the two following decades to be sufficiently
reported and discussed: first, the clear-cut definition of two separate
areas of command; secondly, the inauguration of the famous fighting
combination of Alexander and Montgomery. According to later
testimony from Churchill, Lord Alanbrooke and others, Smuts played
a major part in making those decisions. His satisfaction with them
found expression in his private correspondence. He looked forward
with renewed confidence to victory in North Africa as a decisive
turning point of the war. With Hitler condemned, as now seemed
probable, to spend another year in Russia, he saw the opportunity
at hand to clear the Mediterranean basin and build the springboard
for a fighting front in Southern Europe.[33]

From August onwards Churchill kept sending him urgent requests
to come to London and stay with him there over the period of decisive
actions. Smuts accepted the invitation reluctantly. He told a friend

6. With Churchill in Cairo, 1942

that he was growing more and more of an African and disinclined to breathe other air. When he did finally arrive in London he said that he must make it a short visit: for good or evil, things were always on the move in South Africa; it was a key post, it was *his* post. Actually he had not once left it during the past eight years, except for his brief visits to the fighting front. Now he allowed himself just five weeks in London, from 14 October until 19 November. It was the appropriate time for him to be there. On 23 October Montgomery launched his attack on Rommel. Six days later, with the decision not yet in sight, Smuts exercised a steadying influence on Churchill's impatience. The two friends did not have long to wait for glorious news. On 6 November the bells of Britain, which had been silent for so many years, were ringing from every steeple and tower in celebration of Alamein. Next day American and British forces went ashore in strength at Casablanca, Oran and Algiers. Churchill proclaimed 'the end of the beginning'. Smuts had already committed himself further than that. On 21 October, in an address to the two Houses of Parliament, he had declared that the defensive phase of war was over at last and that the stage was now set for the offensive phase—the final act, he called it.[34]

Churchill would have liked to keep him longer in London and would also have liked him to go to America and talk to Roosevelt 'as from one Dutchman to another'; but Smuts could not bear to be any longer away from Africa.[35] He wrote to Roosevelt begging leave to postpone his visit and putting a forceful case for carrying the war across the Mediterranean into Italy. Then he flew home. He had two urgent announcements to make, the first to his soldiers, the second to his constituents. He broke the journey in Egypt, reviewed his troops in the battle area of Tobruk and told them that they would be brought back to South Africa for their training and re-equipment as an armoured division.* When he reached home he began at once to make arrangements for a great political rally in Standerton, his constituency.

I there announced [he wrote a few days later] that South Africans will be asked, after this African warfare is over, to go anywhere in the world. I myself was prepared to go even to the gates of hell! We were going to release our boys captured at Tobruk and bring them home.[36]

* It had been agreed at the Cairo Conference that the First Division should be converted into an armoured division but Smuts's announcement that it would be brought back to South Africa was new and, to some senior British officers, unwelcome.

Next month he received the news that the Prime Minister and President and their Chiefs of Staff had agreed at Casablanca to follow up the conquest of North Africa by an invasion of Sicily, even though this would mean postponing the cross-Channel invasion until 1944. He accepted this decision as a welcome instalment of the strategy he had at heart. Not so welcome was the news that reached him of the slow progress being achieved in the conquest of North Africa. In February 1943, the month of Russian victory at Stalingrad, the armies in Tripoli and Algeria still seemed to be bogged down. The Russians, he reflected, did not appear so supine as their western allies in face of the far worse weather which they had to contend with. This gloomy brooding over the contrast between Russian achievement and British–American ineptitude, or at least the appearance of it, remained a recurrent theme of his letters for the next five or six weeks.[37] But by the end of March Montgomery had broken the Mareth line and Alexander's troops were on the move in Tunis. Smuts looked forward to 'another Zama', a victory comparable with Scipio's victory over Hannibal, won in the same place as had witnessed once before a turning point in world history.[38] He hoped that his own son, who had shared all the ups and downs of the African fighting, would be there at the climax.

When that climax arrived in early May, more triumphantly than even he had dared to prophesy, it was not Scipio but Cromwell who came into his mind.

It is the cleanest, neatest, most sudden and spectacular victory of the war, and in size is quite comparable to the German defeat before Stalingrad. In Africa it is a crowning mercy as Cromwell would have said...I am a happy man and deeply thankful for this great 'mercy'.[39]

Victory on the fighting front offered him his great opportunity on the home front. He seized it with both hands.

Last Saturday [he wrote on 17 May] I made my announcement that we are to have a general election on 7 July and this of course has started the ball rolling. At first we thought that it could be held somewhere in August but owing to departmental speeding up we have gained about five weeks. The Opposition profess to be furious as they say I am rushing into a khaki election. But I don't see why they should squeal so loudly as they have been challenging me for the last four years to go to the country and all that time they have—in the intervals of their quarrels—done nothing but make propaganda and prepare for an election. I think we are on a good wicket at present. The spectacular victory in North Africa has impressed the doubtful, who now wish to be on the winning side. None so keen as those who come up when the fight has been won![40]

There spoke the shrewd tactician, the wily politician whom friends and enemies alike, albeit in different tones of voice, called *slim*.

Smuts was appealing to a predominantly white electorate.* He could count on massive support from the English-speaking voters and he hoped to win to his side many more Afrikaans-speaking voters than had supported him hitherto. The election was a battle between him and Malan for the allegiance of the uncommitted, or half-committed, section of the Afrikaners.

Both men had some awkward problems to cope with. As leader of the National party, Malan claimed to stand for nationalist Afrikanerdom in its entirety; but he had to face quite a lot of competition. Fortunately for him the Afrikaner party, which was the only competitor of the Nationalists inside parliament, had been losing strength through a steady seepage of its supporters either to the side of Smuts or to the organizations which the Nationalists considered deviationist. These organizations were Pirow's New Order, which the Nationalists despised, and van Rensburg's Ossewa-Brandwag, which they saw as a presumptuous enemy. They refused to discuss electoral pacts with either organization and fought the election *op eie pote*, on their own feet.†

They were well aware that Smuts had put them at a tactical disadvantage. They denounced his khaki election and his particularly dirty trick in bringing the First Division home—they said—not for re-equipment and training but for electoral propaganda. In their own propaganda, they laid the heaviest stress upon those parts of the party's programme which they thought likely to make an appeal to middle-of-the-road Afrikaners. They did not recant their demand for a Christian National Republic separated from the British Crown and Empire, but neither did they advertise it. They made much of the price rises and other wartime inconveniences which they ascribed

* There were approximately 12,000 Coloured voters on the Cape's common roll, *plus* the separately elected representatives of the Natives, as provided for in 1936.

† In the event, neither the New Order nor the Ossewa-Brandwag put up candidates of their own; but their leaders and possibly a good many of their members nursed a grudge against the National party.

to mismanagement by Smuts. They also made much of the dangers he had brought upon the country by making it the ally of Soviet Russia. Communism, they cried, was already spreading its poison among the Natives, the Coloureds and the Indians. That cry did not take Smuts by surprise. He had prophesied before the campaign began that the Malanites would go all out 'against Smuts and Communism'.[41]

Smuts could not take for granted the solidarity of his own political front. He was the leader of a coalition government and had to keep three parties in line with each other. The Dominion party and the Labour party were both small, but each of them had vigorous roots in Natal. In the electoral pacts which Smuts made with them both,[42] he thought it necessary to deal gently with their susceptibilities.* At the same time he had to cope as best he could with some troublesome dissensions within the United party.† His strongest assets were the unity of his supporters in fighting the war and the trust which they put in him as their war leader.

In fighting the election he faced a risk, but it daunted him no more than any of the other risks that he had been facing ever since September 1939. In all his battles on the home front he followed from start to finish of the war one simple rule—

...not to mind my political opponents too much, rather to ignore them and to concentrate on my own war and governmental business. That is the positive way, and means least waste of time and energy. The negative way of controverting your enemies and countering their knavish tricks is exciting, but essentially barren. Whenever you can afford it, ignore your opponents, don't answer back, but give the public instead something constructive and positive of your own.[44]

Amidst the din and fury of electioneering he remained steadily at work on his task of reorganizing the South African forces for their new campaigns across the Mediterranean. He fought the election on his own terms. By what he said and by what he refrained from saying he defined it as a win-the-war election.

He was denied the aid of one portent, the British–American invasion of Sicily, which came just three days too late to help him on

---

* In particular, he dealt tenderly with the susceptibilities of Natalians about 'Indian penetration'. See pp. 459–60 below.

† Examples of tension within the United party were: (1) the bitter feud between Louis Esselen and Senator Conroy, chairman of the party in Cape Province, and (2) the contest for nomination in the Gardens constituency, where B. K. Long, a man of outstanding integrity and ability, had to yield place to an inferior candidate. In this affair Smuts played an unwilling and ineffectual part.[43]

polling day. Even so, he thanked his stars for giving him a spectacular general election and, he felt certain, a victorious one.[45] How great his victory was he did not know for some time, because it took over a fortnight to count the soldiers' votes and the full results of the election were not known until 30 July. In summary, they were as follows:

FOR SMUTS	Before election	After election	AGAINST SMUTS	Before election	After election
United party	72	89	Nationalist party	41	43
Labour party	4	9	New Order	16	—
Dominion party	8	7	Afrikaner party	8	—
Independents	—	2	Independents	1	—
Native Representatives	3	3			
Total	87	110	Total	66	43

His majority was sixty-seven. His own party, which hitherto had been dependent upon the support of the Dominion and Labour parties, now had a majority of twenty-five over all parties, both the friends and the foes. In every province except the Free State he had won spectacular victories not only in the cities but in the country districts which hitherto had been impregnable fortresses of his opponents.

The Nationalists, notwithstanding all this, had not done so badly as appeared at first sight. The slaughter had been not so much in their camp as in the camps of their competitors. Whereas the Afrikaner party had lost every one of its battles and the New Order and the O.B. had not dared to fight at all, the Nationalists had polled 36 per cent of the total vote and had won two additional seats. They had given Hertzogism its *coup de grâce*. They had freed themselves not only from the Laodiceans but also from the lunatic fringe of Afrikanerdom. They remained uncompromisingly republican, secessionist and anti-war; but nobody henceforward could accuse them of being subservient to foreign ideologies or dependent upon a Hitler victory. They no longer had any rivals to fear in their bid to bring all Afrikaners into a common camp. They possessed a formidable organization and a near-monopoly of the Afrikaner press. They possessed a future.

Smuts did not see it. He did not look into the middle distance, to the day five years ahead when he or his successor would hear the results of the next election. Instead he looked far back along the journey which he and Botha had begun together and looked far forward to his vision of a free, harmonious and strong South Africa steadily working out her destiny within a new League and within a continuing Commonwealth of like-minded nations. In this large perspective he felt satisfied with his achievement. He called it a famous victory and believed it to be decisive for all time for his country's future.

The results of the General Election [he wrote on 31 July] were finally known yesterday, and our victory is far greater than any of us had expected. The United Party under me is more than double the Nats, and in addition we have the Labour and Dominion and Native representatives, which give us in all a majority of 67 in the House, compared with the 13 with whom I went to war in September 1939...And when I think of my years in the wilderness...and at sunset I find such recognition of what I have stood for and suffered for, I feel that at last I have been repaid with more than compound interest...It is indeed a 'famous victory'! The political front is now secure, with a parliamentary majority which is an embarrassment. And we can go on with the job.[46]

By the job he meant winning the war and establishing a just and durable peace.

CHAPTER 22

THE SUMMIT

A VIVID portrait of Smuts as a close observer saw him at the crisis of the struggle for Africa was painted by Lord Harlech, then British High Commissioner to the Union, in a personal letter to Mr C. R. Attlee, then Secretary of State for the Dominions. Lord Harlech emphasized most heavily not the sophistication of Smuts but his simplicity.[1]

He is 72 years of age, still erect, spare of body, dapper in his clothing, and intensely full of vitality. He keeps himself physically fit by eating little, and taking long walks over his 2,000 acre country estate at Irene, some ten miles from Pretoria. He is a non-smoker and almost a teetotaler. He takes a great personal interest in his two farms...At Irene he leads a patriarchal Afrikaner life surrounded by his wife, daughters and many grandchildren. This ramshackle house was bought by him over thirty years ago and is completely 'unmodernized' and always gloriously untidy. There is no garden or formal amenity and the personnel of his domestic staff has gone unchanged for many years. He intensely dislikes having to sleep in or occupy the rather 'grand' new official residence of the Prime Ministers of the Union in Pretoria. When he is compelled to spend a night there to entertain guests he refuses to occupy any of the principal bedrooms but has had an iron bedstead and severely plain furniture put in the box room, which he declares is the only tolerable room in the house! Wherever he is he likes to retire to bed very early between 9.30 and 10 p.m. and like most South Africans he gets up in the morning with the sunrise for the perpetual glory of the first hour of the African day.

Lord Harlech admitted that Smuts was detached in many of his human relationships but not that he was unsocial; he hated flattery or obsequiousness and disliked being fêted, but he was always eager to meet ordinary people in his journeys around the country or young officers back from Libya and he was open to have anything at all said to him with complete freedom of speech. He had the knack of getting information out of the humblest people. He was a country-man, a son of the soil, an Afrikaner; and something more than that— an African, perhaps the greatest African that had yet appeared, for the whole map of Africa was imprinted in detail upon his mind and

385

he felt an almost mystical affection for the continent from whose loins he had sprung.

This spacious vision that Smuts had of Africa was something that the majority of his fellow Afrikaners could not understand; his policies were outward-looking, theirs were inward-looking; his impulse was *trek*, theirs was *laager*. Although Lord Harlech did not cite those traditional Afrikaner symbols[2] he understood the conflicting emotions and attitudes which underlay them. He understood also the loneliness of Smuts in those widely ranging philosophical, historical and cosmological speculations which were foreign, not only to his fellow Afrikaners but to almost all South Africans of both language groups. That loneliness found symbolic expression in the study at Doornkloof.

His personal sanctum... the disorder of which no one is allowed to touch, is a large library walled with books—with books and papers on every table and in most of the chairs which are uniformly uncomfortable. The range of books—continually being added to—is amazing, but the special lines are philosophy, history, botany and 'Africana'. But among this confusion one sees old 16th and 17th century volumes in Dutch and Latin—translations of the Greek classics—especially Plato. On the occasion of my last breaking into the sanctum with a telegram I found him concentrated on the new two-volume history of Anglo-Saxon England by Professor Hodgkin.

If Lord Harlech had kept on looking for descriptive names for Smuts he would have been compelled, on the evidence of the Doornkloof study, to call him not only an Afrikaner and an African but also a European. But then he would have had to find still another name for a man so passionately addicted as Smuts was to pre-history and to his Greek Testament, a man who felt himself so deeply concerned with the biological origins and the spiritual destiny of *homo sapiens* as a species. Harlech might, perhaps, have called him a Terrestrial.*

Afrikaner, African, European, Terrestrial—Smuts was all these; but he also had his special political capacity as Prime Minister of the Union of South Africa. In that capacity he brought all his reading and thinking into sharp focus upon his urgent wartime tasks.

He arrives at his office in Union Buildings not later than 9.30 every morning and often earlier, and leaves ordinarily for home at 4 p.m....He sits

---

* This is the name which Pierre Teilhard de Chardin used in private to express his feeling, so closely akin to that of Smuts, of being involved with all humanity as a single species. See his *Letters from a Traveller* (English trans., London, 1962), p. 133.

at his desk in a corner of the room facing the impressive super life-size bust
of President Kruger. The centre of the room is taken up by the Cabinet
table and chairs for the twelve Ministers. These are rarely and only
irregularly ever occupied for in this country Cabinet meetings are few.
Every day there is a stream of callers and visitors... and often quite a queue
waiting in the busy room of his imperturbable and always cheery private
secretary, Pohl. Pohl, a robust Afrikaner from the Free State, born and
bred close to the Basutoland frontier, has now been with Smuts for many
years. He looks like a Rugby football international, is a miracle of tact on
the telephone in rapidly alternating Afrikaans and English...a man of
remarkable efficiency, discretion, and confidential reliability...Smuts's
speed of work is truly remarkable. I am always struck with the pace with
which he can read and assimilate a long telegram, and by his immediate
grasp of the major points when he has done so. His memory is almost
infallible...

And the purpose of this terrific concentration?

...It is quite obvious that his interest in the internal politics and affairs
of South Africa is entirely secondary to his interest in the war in all
theatres. At this point the soldier has precedence over the politician in him.

He drafts all important and many unimportant letters and telegrams
himself in his own handwriting. He rarely if ever dictates to a stenographer. Most of my communications from him are in manuscript. His
mind is so much quicker than anyone else's in this country that he is at
moments impatient with people of slow or hesitating speech. He speaks in
short clipped sentences and with the manner of authority and decision.
His inherent intellectual gifts are obviously outstanding, and...his length
of experience of public life and of war is in fact unique in the world
today...

His Cabinet colleagues are obviously in some awe of him.

It was just here that an undertone of anxiety became apparent in
Lord Harlech's letter. The question, 'When Smuts goes?', was beginning to frame itself. Harlech did not believe any other member of
the Cabinet was worth serious consideration as the successor to Smuts.

He is in every way the pivotal figure of his country. There is no one else
within feet of his mental stature or capacity. The further contribution that
South Africa can make to the Allied cause depends all too absolutely on
the life, health and continued leadership of Field-Marshal Smuts.

There was no doubt in Harlech's mind of his determination to continue the struggle as leader of all those South Africans who desired to
retain any British connection; but the question had to be faced how
long he would survive to do so. Louis Esselen, who was perhaps
closer to Smuts than any of his fellow countrymen, told Harlech

that he had begun to show signs of fatigue and that it was now becoming imprudent for him to keep on overloading his programme.

Sometimes he admitted it himself. In letters to his intimate friends he spoke of the candle that was burning low within him and compared himself to the poor woman in Tom Hood's 'Song of a Shirt' whose life was nothing but stitch-stitch-stitch, a life of unending toil that could not possibly have any joy in it. 'I often feel', he wrote, 'as if my mind is coming to a standstill, but then something again jogs it, and the poor old machine rattles on like a worn out motor-car. And so on, world without end.' But there would have to be an end someday and it would be far better for him and for everybody else to take his ramshackle car off the road before it fell to pieces. That was something that his old friend Merriman had not had sense enough to do, with consequences that had been pathetic. And now he saw Hertzog repeating Merriman's mistake. Hertzog had always been prone to take colour from his audiences and now, in a bid that he was making to re-establish himself as a leader of Afrikanerdom, he seemed to be dancing to the tune of Pirow's, if not of Hitler's, New Order. 'Poor old fellow!', Smuts exclaimed, '...What an end to have come to!' When news reached him in November 1942 that Hertzog was dead he felt regret not only for the passing of his old antagonist and chief but for the manner of it—'Poor man, what an exit!...when he might have retired gracefully in 1939 and retained the halo of past glory'. Smuts promised himself never to make that mistake. In the flush of his victory in the 1943 elections he protested that they would be his last: five years from now he would be seventy-eight and that was too close to dotage to be called old age. The thought of handing over to a younger man was a recurrent theme of his letters throughout 1942 and 1943. But he knew that he could not do it until the war had been won. In March 1942 he wrote, 'But I can't. It is a case of bondage to the ideal, to the light one is compelled to follow, whatever the cost. Determinism and free will join hands here, and in being a slave one is really free.' In May 1943 he wrote, 'But one has no choice, and just marches on like a soldier in a battalion on the march. The marching orders of our time are very severe, but one can but inwardly groan and obey.'[3]

Despite his inward groanings he told his friends that he had nothing really to complain of and compared himself to the old Boer farmer who replied, when asked how he was getting on, 'I have just buried my wife, the locusts have eaten my crops, a fell disease is carrying away my cattle: things are however not so bad with me.' As so often in the past, he was finding that the job itself carried him along. 'It shows', he said, 'that while one is working one *can* work. It is the pause that proves killing, and I suppose when I stop I shall stop utterly. We move by our own *momentum*, as long as it lasts, and after that it is mere *inertia*, as the mathematicians say.' At other times he told his friends that he had a devil inside him to drive him along.

I sometimes sit back and think what it is that makes an old man like me, whose heart and head are in quite another world, continue untiringly and unrestingly in tasks like these. It is a question not so easy to answer. We are curious mixtures in which the high and the low blend, and we deceive ourselves if we put it all to the credit of our virtue or other good qualities. There is a good deal of the devil also in it. There is an elemental drive that will not give in...

But he knew that there was more to it than that. It always seemed to happen, even when he was half dead with fatigue, that he would feel the powers of recuperation miraculously at work within him and new strength flowing into him until at last peace and joy flooded his whole being.[4]

Most of all it was in his own home that the rest for which his tired nerves craved seeped into him and through him and re-created him.

Fortunately I can have it in this blessed place. No peace this side the grave like the peace of Doornkloof. The grandchildren are in bed, the mothers and the grandmother are attending to household chores in another part of the big house, and here I sit in the study hearing only the dull subdued hum of silence in my head. This hum is now quite usual with me, and I suppose it is a sign of age, as I did not notice it before. It sounds like cicadas in the bush in the distance on a hot day, really quite pleasant if you happen to notice it. It does not interfere with hearing which remains quite good. But it recalls me now and then to warm days in the open when the air was full of this humming of natural things and I walked the earth in the company of dear friends. What memories this hum recalls, what botanizing and birding...[5]

And so his mind would start working again upon its memories of the past, its hopes and fears for the future, its concerns in the present. Rest for him was not a passive state.

Friends whom he brought to Doornkloof for the first time were apt to ask themselves how in the world he managed to get any rest there at all. In July 1941 he brought there Sir Henry Moore, the Governor of Kenya, and his wife, who had flown south to see their daughter Deidre settled in as a student at Rhodes University. The Moores were habituated to the elegance and comforts of their station and she in particular had appreciated them in earlier visits that she had paid to Westbrooke, the Governor-General's residence in Cape Town, and Groote Schuur, the Prime Minister's residence there. She had also cast an approving eye upon Libertas, the offiical residence in Pretoria, which Smuts was so reluctant to use.

A beautiful house [she wrote, after she had been dragged away to Doorn-kloof]...but they prefer this tin hovel, crawling with screaming children and cluttered up with every sort of junk. It's rather sweet of them. Henry is a bit bewildered by this household. Besides the old people there are Sylma, her husband and two children, Santa and three children, Louis, the doctor daughter, now in the army, and Japie the elder son and his wife and children who drop in constantly. The din is incessant and terrific and apparently everyone likes it like this—bar us...You must know that Doornkloof is a wood and tin bungalow which was a British officers' mess in pre-Boer War days and was bought by Smuts and conveyed a consider-able distance to its present site on bullock wagons.

Having crossed the rickety verandah into the hall one finds the dining-room on the right which is sparsely furnished with oil-cloth covered tables, upright chairs and a few dilapidated sofas and arm chairs, most of which have broken springs. This is the 'living room' in every sense of the word, and when the Oubaas returns to his study the rest of the family—all three generations of them—make riotous use of it. I might add that the whole family, with the exception of Ouma and the youngest grandchild, lives in awe of Oupa and although he does not scold or admonish, or very seldom, a glance from his steely blue eyes is quite enough to quell any unruliness...

On the other side of the passage is the only other sitting-room, which is smaller and very full of heavy Victorian furniture and is never sat in by any of the family. Its walls are hung with every sort of oddment, from signed photographs of Royalty and other distinguished people (usually hanging awry) to pictorial calendars ranging from the 1920s, and fly-swats. The tables are cluttered up with books, trophies, illuminated addresses, etc., and the atmosphere of the room is dank and unloved.

But that did not matter, since the smaller room was never used, in Lady Moore's experience, except once, to entertain Greek royalty. And one member at least of the royal party succumbed to the charm of Doornkloof, despite its disorder and noise and aesthetic horrors and the bitter cold of the high veld which seeped in through the wood and tin. As for Lady Moore, she found the cold absolute hell; but even that did not prevent her from falling in love, like everybody else, with this unusual home. The place fitted the people. 'They are real darlings', she wrote to her mother, 'and quite the kindest people in the world, bless them. Ouma is an everlasting source of joy and amusement and he is, of course, invariably enthralling.'[6]

Smuts used to say that Isie—or Ouma, as almost everybody now called her—was the real cement of the house and that without her house and family would fall to pieces. And then, he used to ask, what would happen to him? Throughout the dangerous years of the war she was as unsparing of her strength as he was of his. Although she found herself moving with him into the wider world beyond Doornkloof she clung tenaciously to her simplicity. Sometimes she went with him to Cape Town for the parliamentary session because she felt that he needed her there, but in the grandeur of Groote Schuur she remained uncompromisingly the Boer wife and mother; the only innovation of dress that she consented to, as Lady Moore observed, was to wear shoes in the house; for parties, when she could not avoid them, she considered her two cotton frocks quite adequate. With this scanty wardrobe she twice joined her husband on his visits to Egypt and moved serenely in the company of ambassadors, ministers, admirals, generals, air marshals and their ladies, when they had their ladies with them. She did not conceal her astonishment at the habit which prevailed among these grand people of dining at 9.30, which was her usual bedtime, and of sitting late after dinner, which she refused under any circumstances to do. They were equally astonished, but in the end quite vanquished, by her simplicity. She, meanwhile, was set upon her own business—to meet and shake by the hand every South African soldier in every camp within reach.[7]

Smuts took great pride in his wife's successes as a public figure and although he said that her best memorials were her children and the place she held in the hearts of South Africans he compelled her, resisting violently up to the last moment, to sit to a South African sculptress for her portrait bust. About two years later he and she both sat to the English painter, Simon Elwes, who produced good portraits of them both—'but his picture of Isie', Smuts said, 'remains his masterpiece. It reproduces all her vivacity and suppressed fire...' Yet at this very time the fire was flickering. Towards the end of 1942 Isie was looking forward in high spirits to a mammoth collection for her Gifts and Comforts Fund in celebration of her seventy-second birthday on 22 December. Her husband was looking forward to

Degree Day at Witwatersrand University, where she was to receive an honorary doctorate. But suddenly she suffered an alarming collapse. She made a quick recovery and was able to celebrate the Gifts and Comforts triumph on her birthday and to attend the graduation ceremony; but from that time onwards Smuts thought it necessary to have one of her daughters constantly with her in the house. The family joined him in his conspiracy to prevent her from starting work again at the old pace and used to tease her by calling her 'little national treasure', a title recently bestowed upon her by a senior medical officer, Brigadier Orenstein. National treasures, they told her, needed looking after. She enjoyed the teasing and the affection which prompted it. At a slower tempo she resumed her old way of living. 'I hope', Smuts wrote, 'we shall keep her fit for many a year yet, and that she will survive this old slave companion of a lifetime.'[8]

Both of them had reached the age when they had to resign themselves to the loss one after another of the friends of earlier years, until few were left. In July 1943 Sir Patrick Duncan, the Governor-General, died. Smuts recalled his 'imperishable service' to South Africa in September 1939 and felt that his passing left a great blank; but he also reported an earthy family conversation on the day of the funeral.

Little Katusha of Japie just now asked me how I was going to be buried. I voted for cremation and she for ordinary burial, and then she asked me why I preferred cremation. I replied that I did not want to be eaten by worms and to smell. She said, 'then I want also to be cremated'. After a pause she added: 'but best of all is to be like Jesus and rise again the third day.' However, that honour will not be reserved for the likes of us, and so we plump for cremation, Isie most strongly of all.[9]

The talk and play of children had a place in almost every letter that Smuts wrote from his untidy tin palace which was 'so full of small grandchildren and of abounding love'. In his exuberant moments he would exclaim that there never had been anywhere or at any time better rains nor better grass nor better grandchildren than the ones that blessed Doornkloof. Sometimes he would ask himself what the magic was whereby children were able to heal his wounds and make him feel a whole man again. 'The noise of children', he said, 'is quite unlike any other noise, and if they happen to be your own, why, the noise becomes music.'[10]

He liked listening to their noise coming to him through his open window and sometimes he would join them out of doors with the proposal of some new game for them to play; but he never admitted any of them—except perhaps, by an extraordinary and fleeting act of grace, the youngest grandchild—into his study. That was the fortress of his solitude.

What he did with his solitude meant as much to him for healing as did his family life. Yet solitude was not, perhaps, the right word for the time he gave himself alone in his study, since he spent so large a part of it in writing to his friends. Above all, to the Gilletts. The origins of his correspondence with them could be traced back almost to Lord Milner's time and for the past thirty years and more he had been writing to them almost by every mail—long letters in which he set down at speed the full story of the past week just as it came into his head, without any thought that anybody outside the Gillett–Clark connection would ever read the story. In recent years, however, he had found himself compelled to look at this rich record of the years in a new light. Not long before the outbreak of war Margaret Gillett told him that she had kept all his letters to herself and Arthur and all the Clarks and that she had it in mind to put them into order. She sought his permission to do this. At first he disliked the thought of his most intimate letters to friends being pawed over someday by strangers, but after due consideration he gave her leave to do what she wanted. A few years later he told her that the letters which the Clarks and Gilletts had written to him survived at Doornkloof and that it would become possible someday to bring both sides of the correspondence into a single collection. He also approved a plan which she had put forward of collecting some background material.[11]

The question was bound to arise in both their minds whether this new way of looking upon an old correspondence would have any inhibiting effects in the future upon its free and spontaneous flow. It did actually happen that the correspondence ran not so long afterwards into some bare patches; but for this there were two or three explanations. To begin with, there was the rapid supersession of sea mail by air mail and the invention of the air letter, which might have been specially designed to kill the good old custom of spacious and gracious letter-writing; Smuts compared it to the short story superseding the three-volume novel. Then there was the progressive exhaustion of Smuts as the war approached its end. Then again there was the increasing frequency and length of his visits to

Europe, not to mention the long visits which the Gilletts made to South Africa soon after the war was over: Smuts did not write to his friends when he could talk with them.[12] Despite these various interruptions and impediments he still wrote to the Gilletts a great deal and most of the time his letters retained their old liveliness. Meanwhile, he was opening up lively exchanges of letters with some new friends, especially Lady Moore and the Crown Princess Frederika of Greece. By no stretch of the imagination could it have occurred to him that these letters would ever be pawed over by strangers.* Letter writing remained for him in his old age what it had been for half a century and more—the unplanned, unstudied, uncorrected outpouring of the feeling and thought which welled up spontaneously from within him.

As always, his letters contained the record of his reading; but as the war dragged on year after year he found himself ever more deprived of time and strength to read. In 1941 he was still, by some people's standards if not his own, not so badly off: he read a little science (a Cambridge symposium on recent trends in research and some lectures by the astronomer Shapley), a little literary criticism (Raleigh on Shakespeare), a little philosophy (Livingstone on Plato), a little botany (Verdoorn on Edible Wild Fruits of the Transvaal), and quite a lot of theology or near-theology, including books old or new by Renan, Seeley, Raven, Glover, Duguid, Deismann and Schweitzer. But in 1942 the drought began to set in: the only books he read that year were Browning's *Ring and the Book*, Aldous Huxley's *Grey Eminence*, an old book by Lowes Dickinson on religion and one or two ephemeral books about making a better world after the war; he also opened a new edition of Wordsworth's *Excursion* but decided that he could not bear to read it. In 1943 he read Raven's recently published book on John Ray and Julian Huxley's Romanes Lecture on evolution and ethics, but little besides. In 1944 the only books that he read, or at any rate noted as read, were Middleton Murry's book on Jesus and the last volume of Fisher's *History of Europe*.

Such impoverishment of mind and spirit was almost more than he could bear. He was living a submerged life, he cried; he was being

* His correspondence with Lady Moore, thanks to her generosity, is now in the Smuts Collection.

barbarized. The war as it approached its end was stretching almost to breaking point the tension which he had felt throughout his life between the active and the contemplative elements of his nature. To be a whole man, he needed to act; he needed just as much to think; but now it sometimes seemed to him that the grinding compulsions of action were destroying for ever all his capacities of thought.

By thought he meant disciplined thought, fit for presentation in a published book to a critical reading public. He did not set himself any impossible standard but neither could he consider a lower level of achievement than he had reached in the past. When the war was over he turned down an invitation to prepare a new edition of *Holism and Evolution* and to permit its translation into Spanish. 'The advance of physics and biology in the last twenty years', he said, 'has really been phenomenal, and my earlier chapters read like prescientific.'[13] Nevertheless he still longed for 'time to write my second volume, and let the first become antiquarian as it is practically antiquated'. It was his ambition to tackle the problem which in later years was much discussed as the problem of the two cultures. As he put it in a letter to the Master of his old College, science was the great revelation of the modern world but it was not the only revelation and the time had surely come for trying to bridge the chasm which now separated the different revelations, and thus to restore unity in the higher life of mankind.[14] Whenever he reflected upon the war-directed activities of science he felt convinced that bridge-building was an immediate and urgent need.

I don't suppose any first-class work in science is done now outside of the war work...Of course...science has fallen into discredit. It has brought no solution to our human problems, and has added greatly to our engines of destruction in this war. Not that science is to blame for this misuse, but people judge by results, and by that standard science has a heavy account to liquidate. Science so far has had far too much to do with the things of sense and of matter, and the things of the spirit have been by-passed. But can it be said that atoms are more real than souls? And souls we have left to the novelists, while atoms have been tackled by the highest brains which our century has produced...Did I say novelists? I should have said parsons—and mostly such parsons![15]

It might have seemed that he was about to make a plea for the social sciences, which even then were busily building their little academic empires. He shied away from that. He had got wind of the school of thought called behaviourism but considered its outlook and method insufficient for the purpose that he had at heart—to understand, not merely how a man behaves, but to what universe of values he belongs. 'To the lover', he said, 'the *behaviour* of love is quite secondary. Love itself is the matter. And so with all the great spiritual values.' In effect he was stating two propositions: first, that values are a proper object of study; secondly, that the methods of external observation and quantitative analysis do not suffice for studying them. At the root of those affirmations was his own emphatic and joyful recognition of the emotion commonly called love—love in all its manifestations, love of the natural world and its creatures, of another human person, of values and ideas.

After the rains it is a glory to walk and behold these great landscapes... Why is this earth so good? Why does it make something feel like leaping in us? The thing behind all emotion is in it...Language in vain tries to catch hold of it, and so in the end we use the language of human emotion and call it love...And to think that for the last two or three centuries this unfathomable nature has been reduced in our Science to matter in motion in time and space...The measurable is almost the least important aspect of it...One has to read Newton's *Principia* together with Wordsworth's *Prelude* and *Tintern Abbey* in order to get some vague idea of the real truth.[16]

Was it then to the poets, he asked, rather than to the novelists and the parsons that a man should go in his search for those elements of truth which he could not find in science? Perhaps, but that would still leave the chasm between the two cultures unbridged. He believed that bridge-building was a task for philosophers. He believed it to be a task for himself. He envisaged his *Holism II** as a work of philosophical bridge-building.

It took him a long time and it cost him much pain to bring himself to the point of admitting that he possessed neither the materials nor the tools nor the strength for so ambitious a task of intellectual engineering. Fighting Hitler was his job and it left him no time for philosophy. Sometimes in his letters he tried by a desperate short cut to reach truths which he believed to be waiting for him over the hill, but all he ever achieved was a stale repetition of things he had often said before. He felt that he was becoming almost as boring as the parsons and advised his friends to skip his sermons and read his letters merely for their news.

* See p. 232 above.

The Summit

In the spiritual desert of his war years he found two oases. They were small, particular and blessedly remote from the holistic immensities. Nevertheless he saw upon the clear surface of their quiet pools vivid reflections of the universal.

His first oasis was the study of African palaeontology and prehistory. By 1941 or 1942 his botanical rambles and reading were becoming a war casualty, but he managed to keep pace with the still scanty output of papers on prehistory, and to keep personal touch with some at least of the authors. In 1941 news reached him that the Abbé Breuil, a renowned palaeontologist and the greatest living authority upon the cave paintings of Europe, was living a distressful life in Lisbon as a refugee from Nazi-dominated France. After taking counsel with van Riet Lowe Smuts offered the Abbé employment in South Africa at £50 a month, in form as an officer of the archaeological department but in fact with full freedom to do whatever work he liked. In February 1942 he received a reply of joyful acceptance. That was good news not only for Smuts but also for his son. In December 1942 the two of them held an informal colloquium with the Abbé and van Riet Lowe.

It was a good time, especially for Jannie, who had taken leave for the day specially to meet the Abbé. Most of the time was spent over stones and things in his little crowded prehistory museum. And you may be sure that the discussions were animated. In the end the Abbé thought that Jannie was right in concluding that Pliocene man in Africa is proved, but some of Jannie's *oldest* implements might prove to be natural and not human... But Jannie's main point of the vast antiquity of man—far beyond the oldest Stellenbosch culture—is proved by Jannie's collections.

When Jannie returned to his army unit in North Africa he wrote to tell his father that he was re-writing his paper on Pliocene climates which the geologists hitherto had found too heterodox. Meanwhile there was no need to worry about the points of difference still outstanding between himself and the Abbé Breuil; he was right and within a year or two the Abbé and most of the other experts would be agreeing with him. So indeed it came to pass—'and so', said Smuts, 'he has pushed the history of this poor race of man at least another million years back into the past'. That reflection set his mind racing along a familiar track of thought.

Think of our human march from those ancient times—a million years ago, if not more—up to today, with all our achievements in science and art and religion! Need we despair of the future, in the mess which troubles our human affairs today? Is there not something Godlike in us, in spite of all the devilries?...God reveals himself not only in the supreme characters of our race—in the Son and sons of God—but also in the human average, slowly rising beyond and above the sordid animal origins which we have not yet quite outlived...And so Prehistory becomes a witness to the Divine character of this universe as a whole.[17]

The second oasis where Smuts found living water was his New Testament, which he continued to read in the original Greek with a wonder that never ceased to grow. He felt at one and the same time the immense historical remoteness of the Holy Land and its almost unbelievable contemporaneity because of the drama that had been enacted there. Within the mighty Roman Empire of two thousand years ago and in the perspective of all the states and empires recorded since then the petty province of Galilee seemed scarcely worth remembering; nor did its people seem worth remembering, if the disciples of Jesus were a fair sample of them.

What a poor lot they were and He knew them to be so. The only redeeming feature were those wonderful women who would accompany them and minister to His needs. I love them and thank God for them...And in the end it was the vision of Mary the Magdalene which founded the story of the Resurrection and of the Church...[18]

Smuts admitted that St Paul had failed to cite Mary Magdalene as his authority for the Resurrection story; but that, he said, would have been too much to expect from a man who held such peculiar ideas as St Paul did about women. But whether Mary Magdalene was or was not the fountain-head of the story which rallied the scattered disciples and made them believe that the Master was indeed risen and alive, she remained for Smuts 'a lovely woman anyhow with a wonderful record as saint and sinner alike'.[19]

But the men! Smuts found their cowardice at the crisis almost unforgiveable. Nor did he rate their intelligence much higher than their courage. If despite everything they rose at last to the occasion it was Jesus alone who achieved the miracle. It amazed Smuts. Without any intention of irreverence he fell into modern slang.

How ever did Jesus put it across to those simple folk, even that $\left.{little \atop much}\right\}$ that he did get across? Socrates had the advantage of the greatest literary craftsman of all time to paint his immortal picture. But these simple folk, with their primitive language like the story-telling of children. And yet the result is so immensely impressive. Not even a Shakespeare could have done that last phase of the Master better, and the heroic simplicity of it all becomes so telling that one can scarcely bear to read...

All in the simplest lisping language as of a child's fairy tale—and the tremendous effect on one's mind. How much *did* get across there, perhaps even more in some respects than there was; in other respects so much less. The whole thing looks like a miracle of human nature and experience. And yet always the impression remains that the truth is greater than the story.[20]

Smuts sought help at times from commentators and historians, but his response to the Gospel story was always intensely his own. For example, in 1941 and 1942 he was reading books by the high-minded Seeley and the sophisticated Renan; but neither of them satisfied his sense of wonder. Both of them in their different ways seemed to him to miss what really mattered, Jesus himself, the Person. He wrote after he had finished Seeley:

Were the Person of Jesus...and...his real or supposed resurrection from the dead, not both necessary to create the greatest revolution the world has ever seen?...Man the highest animal is not enough, his terminus is God, and the distance has somehow to be compressed into a span which the simplest can compass. And so one Man became the incarnation of God, and through him all can become divine.[21]

He wrote after finishing Renan:

But in the end nothing matters except the human soul and its problems, and there is nothing comparable to the New Testament in this field. These people in their utter simplicity and devotion to a great force and extraordinary personality seem to have reached heights which constitute a unique record. And yet I wonder whether I would have liked them in life! Jesus himself would probably have been the only one to attract me. The wonder of him still remains the wonder of our race. And why should we not worship him?[22]

Almost was he persuaded to be a Christian.

He used to say that the heart, not the head, contained a man's explosive stuff and it was in his heart that the Christian Gospel exploded. Still, he would not commit himself to any creed which failed to satisfy his reason. St Paul, whom he looked upon as the supreme reasoner of Christianity, had stated two explicit conditions of belief which he felt bound in intellectual honesty to take seriously. He found himself grappling with the Pauline doctrine of the Resurrection and the Pauline doctrine of Faith. Although he wavered from time to time he found himself in the end unable to accept either doctrine, as Paul seemed to intend it. On the Resurrection he wrote—

Is the Christian hope well founded? Who can tell?...To me in the deepest sense a man like Jesus can never die, but does live on in men's souls for ever. And those very souls are made alive or resurrected by his indwelling spirit and presence. So whether the tangible Christ remains (as for Thomas's hands) or the intangible spiritual Christ who rises for ever like a fountain in men's souls, I do believe in the Risen Lord.

But not as Paul believed in him. Smuts knew that Paul stood firmly for Thomas and the physically Risen Lord; whereas he himself, if pressed for an answer, would have to take his stand on the other side.[23]

In the debate which he conducted within his own mind about the nature of Faith, he came closer to passing the tests insisted upon by St Paul. Although he would not accept ideas which were in conflict with science he did accept ideas which went beyond it. Explicitly and emphatically he affirmed the reality of a transcendent unseen world, although in the location which he assigned to it he found himself at variance with St Paul and also—or so he believed*—with Christian theology in his own time.

The meaning of this world [he wrote] is not so much in what is seen or known as in the Unseen or Unknown. And it is therefore intelligible how people came to locate an 'Unseen World' as part of their geography of the Universe. But the Unseen is but the inner meaning and real heart of the seen, and not a world apart. All true philosophy tends to that view. And it is also the testimony of poetry and art, and of real religion itself. The secret is within and not beyond. Or one might say the Beyond is the Within...

By the way, you will remember how puzzled I was to find where the saying comes from—'In the world but not of it'. Well, it is nowhere put in that short form anywhere in the Bible, but it is taken from two verses in John 17. The whole prayer of Jesus is for his own who are in the world, though they are not of it...and how neatly and finely it expresses a great spiritual truth. So the new and higher evolves from the lower but is also beyond it, and immanence and transcendence meet.

Faith in God means a trust in the foundations of our moral universe, the rock whence we were hewn, and not the fulfilment of our prayers and wishes...And by God I mean something at the heart of things which we do not comprehend, whose thoughts are not our thoughts, whose plans are not ours, who inspans Evil as much as Good in accomplishing his far-off ends.

* He had no acquaintance with Tillich's theology.

Smuts was not writing a philosophical or theological dissertation but was flinging into his letters almost at random ideas which welled up within him as he read his Greek Testament. Always, his concentration was most intense in times of crisis. Whenever the visible became clouded over he vividly apprehended the invisible. In the aftermath of Tobruk he found strength in that sentence of the Epistle to the Hebrews (xi. 22) where St Paul speaks of *seeing* the invisible. 'Faith', he wrote, 'becomes so strong that it is no longer faith, no longer a longing and groping but a *seeing* of something real and present and waiting to be disclosed.' Nevertheless he remained in two minds about the Pauline doctrine of Faith. If it meant *credo quia impossibile*, the brute acceptance of a dogma against facts and against logic, he would have nothing to do with it. The wisdom of this world, if wisdom retained its usual meaning, could not possibly be foolishness before God. Yet in the end he gave Paul the benefit of the doubt. In October 1941, when Russia seemed to be cracking under the German onslaught while America still clung to her neutrality, he wrote:

Is this the case for 'Faith' in the Pauline sense?—When every odd is against us and yet we cling to faith in our cause and final victory? Though He slay me, yet shall I trust in Him. Is this the Pauline faith? If so I understand and agree.[24]

From the beginning to the end of the war his 'spiritual exercises' were a gymnastic for action, but they also foreshadowed *Holism II*, if ever he should be granted the time and the strength to write it. The main pillar of this second book would be philosophy of religion, confronting that other pillar, philosophy of science, which he had tried to build in *Holism and Evolution*. Between those two pillars he envisaged an arch strong enough to bear the weight of all the 'I–Thou' and the 'I–It' relationships.* The keystone of the arch would be Personality, which he wrote, as always, with a capital P. Personality to him was a phenomenon both of the natural world, with which science was concerned, and also of the spiritual world, with which religion, literature and art were concerned; it was the climax, so far, of evolution; it was also 'the point of departure in human regeneration'. In his endeavour to understand what Personality meant he accepted Jesus as supreme evidence. Without his Greek Testament

* Smuts died in 1950 without having read Martin Buber, but ever since the years of his boyhood his feeling and thought had always followed each of the two moods and modes which Buber describes in *Ich und Du*.

he could hardly have got through the war; it carried him, he said, from his little world not only into another little world but into the universe.[25]

He was fortunate in having friends to whom he could write without constraint about these things; but he needed somebody with whom he could talk about them. He was missing Father Kolbe, the only South African who had ever been able to draw him out on religion, philosophy, politics and everything else that he had in his heart and head.* And then, after nearly two years of war, he found, against all reasonable expectation, somebody to take Kolbe's place, not indeed on terms of equality but at least as an eager listener. She was the Crown Princess Frederika of Greece, a great-granddaughter of Queen Victoria, a granddaughter of Kaiser Wilhelm II, a daughter of the Duke of Brunswick-Hanover. She had four brothers fighting in the German army but she also had the best of reasons for loathing Hitler. In mid-1941 she arrived in South Africa by way of Crete and Egypt, a refugee from the Nazi conquerors of Greece. She was one of a large party of escaped Greek royalties: her husband the Crown Prince Paul and their two young children Constantine and Sophia, her husband's elder brother King George II of the Hellenes, his younger sister the Princess Katharine, his aunt the Princess Marie Bonaparte and her husband Prince George, their daughter the Princess Radziwell, and a large troupe of ladies-in-waiting, secretaries, valets and maids, besides an English nurse and a Greek nursemaid for the two children of the Crown Princess. She was then 24, her husband was 40. Next year they had a third child, the Princess Irene, to whom Smuts became godfather.†

Soon after the arrival of these distinguished exiles Smuts gave a luncheon party for them at Libertas. He found them pleasant company. Both the King and the Crown Prince made a good impression on him as intelligent and experienced commentators upon European politics; he thought the Princess Katharine charming and the Princess Marie, who had studied psycho-analysis with Freud, brilliant; above all, the Crown Princess Frederika appealed to him by her charm, her youth and her courageous response to the challenges which she had already faced and was ready to face again. He saw her as a symbol both of the tragedy and the hope of Europe.

* See pp. 194–6 above.
† For the sources and scope of the following narrative see the Note on p. 558 below.

In the weeks that followed his party at Libertas Smuts must have had other encounters with the royal visitors for on Saturday 17 July he announced nonchalantly over the lunch table at Doornkloof that they would all be arriving that afternoon for tea. He then went out walking and returned only just in time to see that everything was in order and to greet his visitors on the old-fashioned stoep. Meanwhile Ouma and her daughters and the guests who were in the house had been desperately at work clearing the small sitting-room so as to ensure seating place, at least for the royalties. That was quite a task because all the rooms and passages in the house were already congested. In the end things were frantically pushed under sofas and chairs in the hope that the furniture would not be moved by the guests. But of course it was. All the same, the tea-party was a success.

Shortly afterwards the King went to London, which remained his headquarters until victory in the Mediterranean and the brightening prospects of Greek liberation made it advisable for him to establish himself in Egypt. The Crown Prince did not go to London but to Egypt. From there he was able to take generous furloughs in South Africa, which remained for nearly two years the domicile of his wife and family and of the Princesses Marie, Katharine and Radziwell. The friendship between Smuts and the royal ladies, particularly the Crown Princess Frederika, continued to grow.

On 1 June 1942 Smuts stood sponsor at the christening of the three-month-old Princess Irene and held a dinner party at Groote Schuur the same evening to celebrate the event. It was the time of the 1,000 bomber raid on Cologne. Some of the talk after dinner was light—

But mostly we discussed war and peace, and through it all one could never forget that the pretty young mother [Crown Princess Frederika] was a granddaughter of the Kaiser. A shrewd and able good woman in addition to being a German. It was clear that she was a real good German who hated Hitler and all his works and thoughts and longed for a peace which would finish Naziism but spare her people. The others all hated both Germans and Nazis and had no qualms in showing it...I could make good use of the great parable of the Sower, and the sparing of the tares for the sake of the wheat, which I said embodied not only the essence of Christianity, but also of Greek philosophy which throughout is based on the idea of not going to the limit, not overstepping the bounds of moderation and fairness, and following the idea of the whole. Sophrosune is Greek for both moderation and wisdom. This brought us to Holism...[26]

And this, perhaps, was the moment in which the Crown Princess Frederika became a convert to holistic philosophy.

These delightful encounters were interrupted in October 1942 when Smuts went to London to be with Churchill at the crisis of the battle for Africa and the Crown Princess went to Egypt to visit her husband; but on the return flight from London at the end of November she became his fellow-passenger at Cairo. After a journey which included good entertainment at various Government Houses and a special flight over Victoria Falls she shared the welcome prepared for him on the aerodrome by his wife and family, the Cabinet and various notable persons. In December, when he went to Groote Schuur with his daughter Sylma and her two children, he found the Crown Princess already installed with her children and servants at Highstead next door.* Early in the New Year the Crown Prince joined her there while the party at Groote Schuur was augmented by the arrival of Isie, Jannie, who was now home again with his Division, his wife Daphne and Lady Moore from Kenya. Pending success in the search which the Crown Princess was making for permanent housing at the seaside, the two families joined forces in Groote Schuur. They were still together there in the first week of March, when the Crown Prince returned to Egypt. Shortly after that the Crown Princess succeeded at last in her search for a house, but so long as Smuts remained in Cape Town for the parliamentary session he and she continued to see each other almost every day. In his letters to the Gilletts at this time he almost always had news to give of children's picnics at the seaside, walks of the grown-ups on the slopes and sometimes the summit of Table Mountain and talks between the Crown Princess and himself about 'the war and the coming peace, and God's ways with man, and philosophy and Greece—indeed there was no end to these discussions'. But he knew that they would have to come to an end when victory in the struggle for Africa came into sight and duty called the Crown Princess to her husband's side in Egypt. That day arrived in the second week of June 1943.[27]

So unusual a friendship between a soldier-statesman in his seventies and a princess in her twenties was bound to create a sensation. To the admirals and other high-ranking persons who visited

---

* Highstead was the official house of the Minister of Native Affairs, then Major Piet van der Byl. Formerly the whole Greek royal family had been at Westbrooke, but one of their maids had unfortunately set it on fire by leaving an electric iron switched on.

South Africa it seemed that local society found a good deal more interest in the progress of their Prime Minister's idyll than in the progress of the war. The gossip stopped short of scandal but not of mockery; the Oubaas, many people said, was making a fool of himself by spending so much of his time with the young princess. Some people injected venom into their mockery; they said that he was kow-towing to royalty, neglecting his own people, neglecting his own family.

Inevitably, this gossip percolated into his home. It roused resentment there not only on his behalf but also against him and against his guests. From January to March 1943 some members at least of the family, while maintaining a formal correctness of bearing towards the Crown Prince and Princess, were counting the days until they moved from Groote Schuur with their children and attendants into a house of their own. But Isie Smuts did not belong to this rebellious faction. She loved having the Greek children with her and did not mind her husband spoiling them: after all, she had got used to his spoiling their own children and grandchildren. More than that, in the far-off days of Crown Colony government she had got used to his bringing into her home an attractive and intelligent young woman and thus putting what might have seemed too heavy a strain upon her tolerance as a wife. This time, at any rate, the young woman had a husband with whom she was deeply in love. Isie Smuts accepted with an amused tolerance the invasion of her home by 'Palo and Freddie'—the names invariably used by the family amongst themselves for the Crown Prince and Princess. As time went on her feelings towards them both grew genuinely affectionate. 'Dear Little Princess' became a title she began to use not only in referring to the young wife and mother, but sometimes also in addressing her.

Nevertheless, her husband hurt her by allowing himself to be made the target of mocking and malicious gossip and by some failures of common sense which put her into awkward situations. Conspicuous among those failures was his invitation to the Crown Princess early in 1943 to be present at the ceremony where his wife would be capped and enrolled as a Doctor of the University of the Witwatersrand. Fortunately, the Crown Princess decided at the last moment that she ought not to accept the invitation. If she had accepted it, she and Smuts would have become inevitably the focal point of everybody's attention and Ouma would have been humiliated. Smuts simply did not see it. It was not so much insensitiveness that blinded him as a curious innocence or naïvety. For weeks he had been looking forward to his wife's day of glory and as the day approached he composed a speech in her praise which so moved her when he read it out to the family that she felt unable to control her blushes and had to retire from the room. The last thing he wanted was that her glory on the great day should be in any way dimmed; on the contrary, he wanted the dazzling young Crown Princess to be a witness of it and by her presence to enhance it. He failed to realize that everybody else would see the royal presence in a different light. From that tragic and absurd anti-climax he had a fortunate escape.

He was bearing a burden heavier in one respect at least than that of any other war leader, for nowhere else had so bitterly divided a nation been brought into the war. As Lord Harlech had seen, everything depended upon him; but as year followed year of his war on two fronts he began to draw dangerously upon his reserves of strength. The Crown Princess brought him refreshment of spirit at the time when he most needed it. In all places and on all occasions her company was a delight to him, whether she was joining in his game of baboon with the children or climbing Table Mountain with him or sharing the talk, sometimes merry and sometimes serious, under the stars and around the blazing fire in the bush at Rooikop, or delivering with royal dignity and youthful fire her speech on Greek relief, while he sat behind her on the platform and approved the progress she had made under his coaching. By temperament he was a giver, and it was his joy to have discovered in his old age a young woman so attractive, so intelligent and so eager to receive, over the gap of nearly fifty years, his gift of the wisdom he had gathered in his spiritual and political odyssey. *Guru* and *chela*, Lord Melbourne and the young Queen—either of those comparisons would have been apt. It was his pleasure to teach her both the philosophy and the statecraft that she would need in the time of testing that awaited her. He died seven years later believing that she had proved herself an understanding pupil.*

Nevertheless there were some items on the debit side of the balance sheet. Although South Africa had a real interest in helping to save Greece, a country of great strategical importance in the Mediter-

* In 1950, when news of Smuts's death reached Queen Frederika of Greece, she expressed her deep feeling in an English sonnet. Its theme was the man and his philosophy.

ranean area, from being dragged by force into the Communist camp, Smuts from 1942 onwards devoted a disproportionate amount of his time to Greek affairs.* Moreover, he was doing himself some harm in the earthy politics of South Africa by appearing so much at ease with people in such high places—with the Crown Prince and Princess most conspicuously, but with others besides. Almost certainly, he had done himself harm in 1941 when he accepted the baton of a Field-Marshal in the British Army. From that time onwards the Nationalist press was punctilious in referring to him as Field-Marshal Smuts, not of course in genuine deference, but in irony and with the implication that he was a lapsed Afrikaner whose true home was with the British. He should perhaps have anticipated that; but he regarded the honour as one conferred upon his country and also as a practical convenience, for it gave him extra purchase in his dealings with the military commanders and also gave Churchill an extra excuse for filtering military and political secrets to him.†

He had his price to pay for not being a snob and for feeling so much at ease in the company of all sorts and conditions of men, including those in high stations. Time had mellowed him. Whereas during the First World War he had remained obstinately a lone wolf throughout the two years of his stay in Britain, this time he accepted the friendship freely offered to him during his short visits. On 1 November 1942, when he was returning from a visit to his daughter's family and the other Clarks of Street in Somerset, he made a call on Queen Mary at Badminton and when he had to leave she came with him to the gate to wish him farewell.[28] In the inner circle around Churchill he had been known from early in the war as 'a wise old bird' and as the war dragged on he became known and loved as a staunch comrade. To Sir Alan Brooke, Chief of the Imperial General Staff,

---

* Smuts's channels of communication on Greek affairs were:

(1) Officially to the Dominions Office, through the South African High Commissioner in the United Kingdom.

(2) Personal Smuts–Churchill correspondence.

(3) Letters and telegrams from Smuts to the King of the Hellenes in London, through the Union's High Commissioner there.

(4) Letters and telegrams to Prince Paul in Egypt and (later) Italy, through General Theron.

(5) Personal correspondence and conversation with the Crown Prince and Princess.

I have not had access to all this material but have read the correspondence through General Theron. Its bulk is formidable. My notes from it are voluminous; but in this book I have made no use of them.

† For example, the secret of the atomic bomb; see pp. 433–6 below.

it was an event to meet him in August 1942 when he went with Churchill to Cairo for the grand inquest into the Middle East Command. When that work was done Brooke went on with Churchill to Moscow and soon after his return recorded his impressions of two contrasted but equally interesting personalities:

August 23rd...It has been very interesting meeting men like Smuts and Stalin. Such a contrast! Smuts I look upon as one of the biggest of nature's gentlemen that I have ever seen. A wonderful clear grasp of all things, coupled with the most exceptional charm. Interested in all matters, and gifted with the most marvellous judgment. Stalin, on the other hand, a crafty, brilliant, realistic mind, devoid of any sense of human pity or kindness. Gives one almost an uncanny feeling to be in his presence. But undoubtedly a big and shrewd brain with clear-cut views as to what he wants and expects to get.[29]

Smuts enjoyed his friendships with Brooke, Tedder, Ismay, Anderson —above all, his friendship with Churchill; but he did not forget his friends in the world of learning. Nor did they forget him. In July 1941, C. E. Raven, the Master of his old College in Cambridge, wrote to tell him that the Fellows were proposing to depose Paley and elevate Smuts to the place of honour between Milton and Darwin in the row of College portraits. It so happened that Smuts had just been quoting Shelley's assertion that he would rather go to hell with Plato than to heaven with Paley; but he protested that the new honour proposed for him was rather beyond his deserts.

Your offer to make me one of the Trio [he told Raven] brought back to mind a joke I heard long ago. Some fool who fancied himself great said that three great men and three only had adorned the pages of human history. And then he went on to add: 'Jesus Christ suffered on the Cross. Julius Caesar went the way of all flesh.' And then after a pause he added quietly: 'I do not feel very well myself.' I am afraid in this Trio I would be the fool. However, after the war, when we have all recovered our mental balance, we may discuss the subject in the Common Room at Christ's if by that time it has not been forgotten.[30]

From the time when the Allied armies conquered Africa and invaded Italy he gave continuous thought to the chances of achieving at the end of the war a free and stable world. Towards the end of 1943, at Churchill's insistent invitation, he made his second wartime visit to London. There on 25 November he addressed a large meeting of the Lords and Commons under the auspices of the Empire Parliamentary Association. The newspapers called his speech 'explosive' but he maintained that it exploded nothing except itself. His son Jannie, who was now on his staff, said afterwards that he had never known him in better form. He spoke for an hour with a few notes in front of him and in a reflective, exploratory vein. He told his audience that he had no fixed opinions to put before them but wished merely to submit for their consideration some 'thoughts on the new world' which had been running through his head.[31]

His approach was characteristically global: world peace was his objective and he tried to formulate principles for restoring and maintaining it. The League of Nations had failed, he suggested, because the men who made it—himself included—had shut their eyes to the realities of power. Consequently, they had left the League leaderless. Leadership and power, he said, must go together. From this principle he deduced the need for a new world organization with effective peace-keeping authority vested primarily in the Great Powers. Who were they? Roosevelt about this time was speaking of 'the Four Policemen' who would keep the world in peace—America, Russia, Britain and China; but Smuts did not see in Chiang Kai-shek's China the greatness which he believed the Chinese people would some day assume.* For the present, he recognized only three Great Powers.

Great Britain, the United States and Russia now form the trinity at the head of the United Nations fighting the cause of humanity. And as it is in war, so will it have to be in peace. We shall have to see to it that in the new international organization the leadership remains in the hands of this great trinity of powers.

The rest of his address was essentially an attempt to justify the inclusion of Great Britain in the trinity. He examined the old map of power which the war was rolling up and the new map which it was unrolling. On this new map there would be a blank where three Great Powers of continental Europe—France, Germany and Italy—had formerly flourished. Across this blank would fall the shadow of Russia, that new Colossus. Another Colossus, America, was casting a long shadow across the oceans. Smuts hoped and believed that the Americans would cut loose at long last from their isolationist traditions and exercise a stabilizing influence on Europe. All the same he felt misgivings both for the freedom of Europe and peace of the world should these blessings be left dependent upon a state of equilibrium

* See p. 283 above.

between the two mammoth powers. He saw need for a third, a mediating power. As he studied his new map he felt confident in nominating Great Britain for this role, not merely or chiefly because she would be the sole survivor of the former Great Powers of western Europe but because she was the centre of a Commonwealth which in *posse*, if not in *esse*, could treat with Russia and America upon terms of equality. He concluded his address by speculating upon means which might be available for building up the strength of the Commonwealth. He envisaged applications for admission to it coming from the small democratic states of western Europe. He envisaged a grouping of the overseas dependencies into units large and strong enough to manage their own affairs without control from London but rather in close association with neighbouring Dominions. That was the way, he suggested, to iron out the schizophrenic distinction between Commonwealth and Empire and thereby develop to the full the Commonwealth's potential strength.

It was also the way, although he did not say it openly, to make South Africa not merely secure within her own borders but also the leading power in Africa from the Zambesi to the Sudan.* In effect, he was proposing a loosening, if not the complete elimination, of the imperial factor and a corresponding extension of South African influence. In November 1929, when he delivered his Rhodes Memorial Lectures, that had been his distant vision; in November 1943, when he spoke to the Members of Parliament, he saw the same vision as emergent reality. Ever since the outbreak of war, he had been exploiting to the full the Union's military primacy up to and beyond the Equator. At the same time, he had been fostering the rapid growth of the Union's industrial primacy. In November 1943 he was looking for the right man to take charge of the proposed Council for Scientific and Industrial Research, and thereby to establish the Union's scientific primacy.[32] Meanwhile he was keeping continuous contact with the heads of the neighbouring governments. One after the other they came to South Africa to seek his support. His wife found the social side of his diplomacy burden-

---

* One or two liberal-minded critics of his speech, for example, Margery Perham in a letter to *The Times* of 6 December 1943, saw the trend of his thought. A writer in the *Statist* (18 December 1943) also saw it and doubted the willingness of Africans to accept the hegemony of South Africa, in view of the 'exclusive aristocracy' which held political power there. By and large, however, the speech was called 'explosive' because of things which it said or implied, not about Africa, but about Europe: in particular, about France, which Smuts referred to in a few rather tactless sentences.

some, as when one night at dinner she tried to make conversation with the Governor-General of Angola—

MRS SMUTS: Do you like *biltong*?

GOVERNOR-GENERAL: I don't know him. Does he live in Cape Town?

Still, the dinners at Groote Schuur and Libertas were a help to her husband. He felt confident that the whole operation was going well.

On Sunday [he wrote] Huggins the Prime Minister of Rhodesia arrived to stay with us and we were glad to have him. It seems as if we have now to carry all the smaller fry of Africa on our backs...I make a point of it to help as far as we can, and a little farther, mindful of the advice of scripture to cast your bread upon the waters. We are quite popular nowadays, and hope that something greater may be built on these foundations ...They may yet be in the net. I am working on some such plan as that of the Pan-American Union of our Yankee friends.[33]

He felt such confidence still in all his plans—for re-establishing law and order in the world, for keeping the Commonwealth strong, for making his own country secure and influential, even for clearing 'the rubbishy pinaster trees' from the slopes of Table Mountain above Groote Schuur. In this last enterprise his ally was Dr Pole-Evans.

We are clearing large patches of pinetrees [he wrote] and putting in grasses as we both dislike the pine thickets which uselessly cover the estate and cut off the view of the mountain which forms the chief glory of this place. Besides, much soil erosion is resulting from the bare areas beneath the pinetrees which kill off the vegetation cover and cause a rapid run-down of the rain on those steep slopes. I hope in time we shall once more have grassy slopes with sparse silver trees in place of these useless horrid pines, the planting of which in the Peninsula has been a calamity. Nothing can be finer than our indigenous mountain vegetation, nothing more ugly than the monotonous imported flora of the pine tribe. The pine in particular has shallow spreading roots which kill everything underneath.[34]

But the Department of Forestry had different ideas about the future of Table Mountain. Similarly, the Russians had different ideas about the future of the world.

CHAPTER 23

THE UPPER CONTOUR PATH

DURING the first four years of war almost everything that Smuts did proved effectual; but during the last two years almost nothing. The watershed of his fate, although at the time neither he nor his friends nor his enemies saw it, was 1943.

From 1939 to 1943 his achievement was immense. If Hitler's image was not to be stamped upon this planet his country was geopolitically necessary and he was politically necessary. The Cape of Good Hope lived up to its name and assumed once again its historic primacy in oceanic strategy. Without the Cape route, the Commonwealth could hardly have survived the war; without the Commonwealth, the Russians and Americans could hardly have won it. But the victory in Africa changed all that. Henceforward the Mediterranean was open again and the Cape route, although still useful, was no longer indispensable.

It was the irony of fate that Smuts and his country should find themselves so much diminished by victories they had done so much to win. Smuts hated the diminishment. Early in 1944 he calculated that he had sixty to sixty-five thousand soldiers in North Africa and Italy. That total was insufficient even for the limited military commitments his country had accepted. In May 1944 he wrote from the Prime Ministers' Conference in London to say that the time had come for giving arms to Coloured soldiers. Hofmeyr, his Deputy Prime Minister, called a meeting of the Cabinet and recorded in his own hand its unanimous and strong feeling that the Prime Minister's proposal 'should not be proceeded with'. Any military good that it would do, Hofmeyr said, would be out of all proportion to the political damage it would do. The Cabinet preferred to explore alternative possibilities of military reinforcement.[1]

The alternatives were unpromising; but what South Africa did or failed to do no longer made much difference to the Allied cause. South Africa was shrinking to her normal military size. Contemporaneously, although not comparably, Britain and the Commonwealth were shrinking. Up to the invasion of Normandy they still had more divisions than the Americans had in fighting contact with the enemy; but that was the fruit of their past endeavours. The peak year of British mobilization was 1943. From 1944 onwards the British contribution to victory was bound to fall sharply in comparison with the American contribution. Already, the Americans had outgrown their early deference to British war experience: by the early months of 1943 Washington had become, in fact as well as in name, the centre of British and American decision-making. Moscow, of course, made its own decisions with scant regard either to the British or the Americans.

Nevertheless, Churchill still spoke with authority to the Americans and Russians and he still took counsel with Smuts. Thereby he encouraged Smuts to devote to the problems of grand strategy more of his time and energy than the event justified. Not that Smuts needed encouragement: by temperament he was a grand-strategical hot gospeller. As a member of the War Cabinet in 1917 and 1918, he had consistently argued that political decision should come first and military planning second: clear your heads, he had told his colleagues, about your political ends and then decide your military means. In the middle years of the Second World War he preached the same gospel. His speech of November 1943 contained a definition of political ends which he considered rational and realistic. Thereafter, his correspondence defined those ends further and tried to define the means of achieving them. His definitions took shape in two propositions about time and space: first, the British and Americans must go all out for victory in Europe by 1944; secondly, their road to victory must run not merely from west to east but also from south to north.

His insistence on the need for victory in 1944 had two roots: first, horror at the damage the war was doing to the fabric of civilization; secondly, alarm at the growing preponderance of Russian power. That alarm had no ideological taint. Smuts did not beat anti-Communist drums. He regarded over-mighty power as an evil in itself. In his own lifetime he had seen the British succumb to its temptations and after them the Germans. He feared that the same temptations might prove too much for the Russians. He wrote in September 1943—

It is no credit to us that the Anglo-American combine do not pull a heavier weight in this war. It is not good for us to appear inferior in our war effort. And it would be a disaster if it afterwards appeared that Russia won the war. It would make her the master of the world and this might go to her head.

He wrote in February 1944—

Abroad the war is not going well, except in Russia which now seems to be winning the war for us. . . . Now Russia alone advances and is much more the Colossus than ever before. How will she use her immense power and unprecedented position when the war is over? That is more and more becoming a subject of thought to all thinking people. We must work together, but does co-operation work well in an unequal partnership? These are the points I made in my *explosive* speech, and they are even more pointed now than 3 months ago.[2]

Where the war ended in Europe seemed to Smuts almost as important as when it ended. He asked himself where the British and American forces would be on V.E. day? He wanted to see them in positions which would give them an equal say with the Russians in the territorial and political settlement of Europe and the world: specifically, he wanted to see them firmly established in central and south-eastern Europe. On this issue his political and his military thought were harmonious with each other. For strictly military reasons he had been an advocate of the 'soft underbelly' strategy before he became its advocate for political reasons.

His advocacy was vehement, persistent and perpetually frustrated. The landmarks of his frustration were the British–American war conferences. The Casablanca Conference in January 1943 had raised his hopes by approving the invasion of Sicily; but the Washington (Trident) conference in June lowered them by its failure to reach any clearcut decision for the invasion of Italy, not to mention the seizure of the Dodecanese. In July, his hopes rose again. Early in the month the American and British Chiefs of Staff approved the invasion of Italy, although with a smaller force than he thought necessary; towards the end of the month Mussolini was arrested and Marshal Badoglio's government opened secret negotiations for an armistice. On 3 September British and American forces landed in Italy. On 8 September the Italian armistice was announced. It looked for a moment as if the soft underbelly of the Axis lay wide open. 'These are great days', Amery wrote to him, '. . . I think you and I can both not only be pleased at the result but to some extent congratulate ourselves on having consistently taken the view that the war was to be won in Africa and from Africa across the Mediterranean.'[3] But

Smuts was already in a mood of deep depression. Still another British–American conference, the Quadrant Conference at Quebec, had just given absolute priority in the allocation of resources to Overlord, the cross-Channel operation proposed for 1944, at the expense of operations already under way in the Mediterranean.[4]

Smuts attacked this decision furiously. 'We should immediately take South Italy', he told Churchill on 3 September, 'and move on to the Adriatic, and from a suitable point there launch a real attack on the Balkans and set its resurgent forces going. This will bring Turkey into the picture and carry our fleet into the Black Sea, where we shall join hands with Russia, supply her, and enable her to attack Hitler's fortress itself from the East and South-east.' He admitted that he had not done the requisite staff work but he did not think his programme of attack too ambitious. When news reached him of the Italian armistice he sent Churchill a fiery telegram, advocating among other things the immediate seizure of the Dodecanese and the invasion of the Balkans with a force of two to four divisions to prevent the Germans from disarming the twenty-five Italian divisions there, to stiffen the Greek and Serb forces, to build up a front against the Germans on the Danube and Save and possibly to bring in the Hungarians on the Allied side. 'I suggest', he said, 'that our victories in the Mediterranean should be followed up in Italy and the Balkans instead of now adopting a cross-channel plan, which means switching on to a new theatre requiring very large forces and involving grave risks unless more air softening has been done.' But that would have meant a complete reversal of the priorities agreed upon so recently at the Quadrant Conference. Churchill could not possibly fling such a challenge at the senior partner of the Western alliance. 'I hope you will realize', he telegraphed to Smuts, 'that British loyalty to Overlord is keystone of arch of Anglo-American co-operation.'[5]

It made Smuts furious to see the Allies fumbling their great opportunity, as he believed it to be, in southern Europe. The Germans, he explained, knew better how to make war. On 11 September they seized Rome. Next day they recaptured Mussolini. He set up a new Fascist government. They rushed reinforcements to Italy until they had twenty-five divisions on the Cassino front to keep the Allies out of Rome. At the same time they built up their strength in the Balkans and kept a firm hold on Greece. They liquidated the small British landing parties in the Dodecanese. By early October 1943, when

Smuts arrived in London, the soft underbelly of the Axis was already growing a hard shell.

Smuts argued his case with anybody he could get to listen to him—the King, Churchill, the Chiefs of Staff. He told them all that they had in the South of Europe a clear run to victory if only they would see it; he told them it was folly to throw away that certainty for the sake of an operation which could not possibly be mounted for another six months or more, even if there were no further postponements. Possibly his importunity wore them down. Possibly they were already having second thoughts about the decisions taken at the Quadrant Conference. Whatever the reason, they now began to doubt whether the war could be run successfully on the principle of lawyers' contracts. On 23 October Churchill proposed to Roosevelt another conference to review British–American strategy in the light of the recent changes in the situation. In preparation for that joint review, the British Chiefs of Staff prepared a paper which included a good many items of the Smuts programme—an advance in Italy up to the Pisa–Rimini line; aid to the partisans in Yugoslavia, Greece and Albania on a regular military basis; a bridgehead across the Adriatic; a triple bid to bring Turkey into the war, to open the Dardanelles, to create chaos and disruption for the enemy in the Balkans. If all this added up to the postponement of Overlord, the Chiefs of Staff said, that was a consequence to be accepted.[6]

Smuts felt that he was making progress. On his journey home in late November he stayed three days in Cairo while the British Chiefs of Staff were meeting their American colleagues. He kept close contact with Churchill and had dinner and a long talk with Roosevelt. His mood remained optimistic.[7] But he had not only the Americans but the Russians to reckon with. The President and Prime Minister and their advisers had an appointment with Stalin at Teheran. Stalin refused to budge from May 1944 as the date fixed for Overlord. Worse than that, he endorsed a proposal of American origin for the invasion of the south of France in support of Overlord. This operation, whose code name was Anvil, had the merits of providing an additional supply line, of broadening the Western assault on Germany, and of satisfying French pride; but it could only be mounted by bleeding the Allied forces in Italy of their fighting men and landing craft and thus condemning them to a bitter, frustrating struggle from the south to the north of the peninsula.

Smuts, like everybody else, had to recognize the dominance of the cross-Channel programme. He offered thanks for a few piddling relaxations of the order of priorities. But it went against the grain of his temperament. He continued to denounce the policy of 'too little and too late' in Italy and south-eastern Europe and at the conference of Commonwealth Prime Ministers in April 1944 he made one last bid for the soft underbelly strategy. His idea was to scrap the invasion of the south of France and substitute for it a drive along the line Trieste–Lubliana–Vienna. Thus there would be three main forces converging on Berlin: General Eisenhower's armies from the west, the Russians from the east, the Russians, British and Americans from the south-east.*

A case existed for scrapping Anvil. The original plan had been to synchronize it with Overlord and thereby compel the Germans to weaken their forces in Normandy; but when Overlord was launched in June the nearest date in sight for Anvil was two months ahead. Smuts contended that this would be too late to serve any useful purpose. Churchill and the British Chiefs of Staff gave him a good hearing in London[8] and on his way home at the end of June he stopped in Italy for consultations with Alexander and Wilson, the British commanders in the Mediterranean area. He found that they agreed with him. Thereupon the Prime Minister put the case to the President. It was turned down. For the sake of Anvil, or Dragoon as it was now called, the British and American forces in Italy were bled by nearly forty per cent of their strength. The landings in southern France took place on 15 August. Thereafter the Americans and French drove rapidly to Lyons and beyond without meeting any opposition. Smuts called their drive a futile joy-ride. Churchill did not dissent from that opinion.[9]

At the second Quebec Conference in September 1944 the Americans consented for the first time to discuss the comparative political advantages of alternative strategical plans.† For reasons in large measure political, the conference gave the green light to Alexander for an advance on Vienna, if he could manage it; but with his depleted forces Alexander could not even manage a break-through in Italy.

---

* I am reporting without necessarily endorsing Smuts's argument. He had never seen the high mountains and narrow valleys along the way from north-eastern Italy to Vienna.

† Among the reasons for this change of heart were Russian implacability towards the Poles, Russian military progress in south-eastern Europe and the defection of Roumania from the German to the Russian side.

The conference also made provision for two brigades to land in Greece when the Germans left the country; but two brigades, Smuts feared, were far too small a force. Throughout the autumn and early winter, Smuts conducted an urgent correspondence on Greek affairs.* He would have liked to see a synchronization between the military occupation and restoration of the monarchy; but he had to admit that Greek politics made that impossible. None the less he remained determined that the monarchical cause must not go by default. He supported the Crown Prince's plea for permission to enter Greece with the British forces, and when that plea was rejected he resisted the proposal to make Archbishop Damaskinos Regent. His interventions offended the British Foreign Office; but they did not offend Churchill. Loyalty to Churchill was Smuts's lifeline; in the midst of all his passionate advocacy, he never once let it go. At Christmas, when Churchill went to Athens, Smuts was torn between admiration for his courage and anxiety for his safety. What would happen if he were killed, that one essential man?

Smuts saw the Greek chaos into which Churchill had flung himself as an epitome of the chaos soon to descend upon central Europe. Victory, he feared, was coming too late. Winter was not stopping the Germans from launching their counterstroke in the Ardennes and was not stopping the Russian onslaughts in eastern Europe; but it appeared to hold dominion over the western allies. Or was it Hitler's will, he asked himself, which held the dominion? He imputed to Hitler a macabre death wish.

The Germans are letting the Russians overrun Germany from the East while keeping us out on the West. There seems some curious blunder over all this handing over of their country to the Russians rather than the English and Americans who after all have still some strain of mercy in them. Can it be that Hitler and Himmler prefer, in case of an Allied victory, to see Germany itself destroyed and made a funeral pyre for the Nazi war lords? It is a terrible thought—this idea of immolating your whole people for *your* spectacular death.

He could see no other explanation of the Germans stonewalling against the Allies in the west and their running before the Russians in the east.[10]

He saw happening before his eyes the immense shift in the balance

* See note on p. 407 above. I have decided to handle in one impressionistic paragraph Smuts's voluminous correspondence about Greece.

of world power that he had always feared. 'The footsteps of the Russian giant', he exclaimed, 'are being printed on the sands of time.' To the Russians would go the glory of victory and the power that victory would bring. He was afraid that Allied strategy would not be held up as an exemplar to the future.

But what a performance by Russia! If only she will continue to be co-operative and equally helpful in the difficult peace and post-war problems confronting us. I fear, I much fear. Power and success are intoxicating things, and it will only be human if Uncle Joe's claims are on the scale of his contribution to the victory. Poor Europe, with such a glorious past, and now reduced to the pass of having to be saved by the East or half East. Mind you I am not anti-Russian, but I find food for deep reflection in the present situation in Europe, and in what may happen after this war.

I know how dangerous the predominance of any one Power can be, and how liable such dominant power is to abuse. I remember British jingoism and the Boer War; and I know Russia has even less experience and human wisdom than the British. And so my faith in man does not extend to faith in Russia, with no check on her in Europe and Asia, and mistress of the continent of Europe.[11]

He told Dr Weizmann that victory would dawn over a bleak world, bled white with the loss of life and treasure. He told Tom Lamont, his friend since the far off days of the Paris Peace Conference, that the outlook for humanity was far darker now than it had been then. Not ideas, he said, but events were shaping the world, if chaos could be called a world. Politics by themselves could not possibly control the chaos. Nazism, Fascism and Communism were not merely political movements but counterfeit religions. In face of their terrific force, he asked, what will *our* religion be?[12]

In Europe he saw only a flood of hate drowning all religion, reason and pity. When the Yalta Conference was meeting he wrote—

We are evidently nearing the end in Europe, and settlements and discussions are approaching which will be in many ways more important than the great battles now being fought. One's mind keeps moving in that world where Destiny is weaving our future. God give wisdom and far-sightedness to our leaders and especially to the three leaders who are now at this moment deciding the pattern of the future so far as that is humanly possible. One also keeps thinking of that horror which has come over Europe and brought suffering on an unheard-of scale. There must be millions of Germans in flight before the Russian armies—in weather conditions and sufferings of all sorts of which we can form no conception. I don't think history has ever before seen horror on such a scale—women

419

and children and old and sick trudging over the snowfields from east to west, hungry, ill clad and dying in their thousands on the roads...Is there no Pity in heaven or on earth? The face of Destiny is veiled in utter darkness, and we pray into a void from which comes no response.[13]

The Nationalists said that they had told him so. After having blamed him in the early years of the war for entangling South Africa with a British defeat they now blamed him for entangling her with a Russian victory. Even if he were right in his assertion—and this they denied—that small Powers needed the support of large Powers, he had chosen the wrong supporting Power; by the time the war was over the support of Britain and the Commonwealth would not be worth having; Russia and America would be dominant throughout the world. They went on to say that America was at best an uncertain friend while Russia was a dangerous enemy to South Africa. Smuts, they said, had dragged his country not only into a British war but into a Communist conspiracy.

Still, their attack on Smuts and Communism had brought them little profit at the last general election. Smuts now had behind him the big parliamentary battalions. In his dealings with them he always appeared confident. At a conference of the United party in Johannesburg on 11 October 1944 he looked back with pride on the achievements of the nation and the party throughout the past five years of war and looked forward with resolution to their tasks of peacetime reconstruction.

It has been [he said] an astonishing national effort, and its effect on our name and standing in this world and our future is far beyond anything that we had foreseen. We shall reap great dividends from this national investment...

We have on the whole behaved greatly, let us continue to do so...Let us also remember that we ourselves have set a high standard in this the greatest crisis of our lives and of world history, and that we should be just to ourselves and continue to act up to this standard to the end and not get bogged in a quagmire of petty grievances and complaints and in a spirit unbecoming our grand performance and endurance as a people. That is our record as a people, and as a party carrying out a true national policy. By that record we are prepared to be judged.

Switching from English to Afrikaans, he reviewed the very different war record of the Opposition party and of the organizations which belonged to its sphere of influence. That brought him to the Broederbond. Like Hertzog nine years earlier, he denounced it as a dangerous anti-South African conspiracy. At the national conference of his party in Bloemfontein two months later he reiterated that denunciation and announced his government's intention to proclaim the Broederbond a political body, membership of which would be treated henceforward as a contravention of the law. Meanwhile, he declared that no Broeder would be permitted to hold a post in the civil service.[14]

Louis Esselen and his co-workers had given Smuts a complete dossier on the membership and activities of the Broederbond; but they disapproved the use that he made of it. In their opinion, he should have published the full story of the Broederbond in the newspapers for the information of South Africans and their consequential action. The Esselen group was afraid that Smuts's party political speeches would prove to be merely a damp squib. So indeed they did prove. Smuts's accusations and threats provoked I. M. Lombard, the secretary of the Broederbond, to write four informative articles which showed a startling similarity of thought and tone to Zionist writings of that time.[15] Smuts also provoked the resignations of a few civil servants, including Wennie du Plessis, the man who five years later fought and beat him in his own constituency. Otherwise, the effect of his fulminations was negligible.

A counter-attack that Smuts made on the educational front fared not much better. For many years past the Opposition had been making propaganda against the use of both the official languages as media of instruction in the schools.* That propaganda had its roots in the Broederbond doctrine, as expounded by I. M. Lombard, that the Afrikaners by themselves were a nation and—so it would seem to follow from Lombard's silences, if not his explicit assertions—that the two European peoples together were not a nation. From that premiss it followed that Afrikaner children should not be exposed at school to denationalizing English influences. Hertzog and Smuts, on the other hand, notwithstanding their many differences of opinion on other important issues, had consistently maintained the thesis that South African nationality was a civic and political partnership between the two co-equal cultural communities. In April 1944 Smuts brought into the open this conflict of national and educational doctrine. After a passionate debate which continued for many days and

* See pp. 256–7 above.

filled 500 or more columns of Hansard,* the House of Assembly on 24 May 1944 passed a resolution reaffirming the Smuts–Hertzog conception of national unity and defining its educational component. The resolution called upon the government, in consultation with the provincial authorities,† to consider, and where necessary to amend, the educational laws and regulations in order to give effect to the following principles:

(1) The child should be instructed through his home language in the early stages of his educational career.

(2) The second language should be introduced gradually as a supplementary medium of instruction from the stage at which it is on educational grounds appropriate to do so.

(3) That such changes should be introduced in the system of the training of teachers as are necessary to make the ideals of bilingualism and of national unity in the schools fully effective.[16]

The resolution laid it down that this basic national and educational task should be completed within the next five years; but when Smuts fell from power four years later the school system remained by and large as it had been on 24 May 1944. For this anti-climax there were two main reasons: first, the stubborn resistance of Malan's followers; secondly, the equally stubborn, if less vocal, resistance of Smuts's followers—at any rate, of large numbers of them. English-speaking Natal, for example, showed almost as much zeal for unilingual schools as did the Afrikaans-speaking Free State.

On some other important fronts of policy Smuts by now was finding his political following unreliable, if not downright mutinous. English-speaking Natal, with support (including Nationalist support) from other parts of the Union, sabotaged his attempt in 1944 to achieve a peaceful settlement of South Africa's quarrel with India.‡ Smuts did not misread that portent. For some time past he had been lamenting the disintegrative effects of victory upon his supporters.[17] The Dominion and Labour parties were preparing to break away from the wartime coalition. The United party was discovering its inner disunity on almost every crucial issue except the war. South Africa, Smuts said, had almost forgotten the war.

* The debate arose on a motion by Swart, to which Smuts moved an amendment. It proceeded on 22 Feb., 10 Mar., 27 and 28 Apr., 23 and 24 May 1944. Its intellectual quality was mediocre; but none the less it contained useful material for the comparative study of nationalist movements.

† Under the constitution school education was the immediate responsibility of the Provinces.   ‡ See pp. 463–4 below.

He, meanwhile, had to cope not only with the war but with innumerable problems of the approaching peace. Even before the end of 1943 he was working at the same time on the organization of American war supplies and on the problems of post-war civil aviation. A little later he was heavily engaged in the establishment of three new Ministries—for Economic Development, for Transport, for Welfare and Demobilization.* At the same time he was giving sustained attention to the international aspects of post-war reconstruction. By every mail he was receiving a flood of planning papers from London and Washington. He read them all. He read all the papers which his own departments were preparing. The Prime Minister of a small country, he sometimes said, had a heavier burden to bear than the Prime Minister of a large country. He did not have the help of large staffs of experts, but had to do most of the detailed work himself.[18]

Certainly, Smuts's burden of work was grievous. But he had Hofmeyr to help him. As Minister of Finance, Deputy Leader of the Government and Chairman of the Central Executive of the United party, Hofmeyr was carrying heavy loads. His mother believed that Smuts was killing him by heaping so much work on him while he, Smuts, went gadding about the world. Hofmeyr, despite some murmurings, loyally accepted and faithfully fulfilled every task that was assigned to him. Nevertheless he was not in every respect the Number Two that Smuts needed. Whereas in Britain Sir John Anderson took over from Churchill the oversight of the entire home front, Hofmeyr in South Africa took over from Smuts an uncoordinated aggregate of functions; Anderson performed the task of managing the British war economy, while Hofmeyr performed the narrower task of managing South African war finance. Hofmeyr's mind did not range so wide—to cite another comparison—as Smuts's mind had ranged when he was Number Two to Botha. Possibly the reason lay not so much in Hofmeyr's intellectual limitations as in his temperamental inhibitions. He was too much in awe of Smuts. That in part was Smuts's fault; he treated Hofmeyr too much as his junior. The two men were loyal to each other, but their relationship had a missing component, equality. They never achieved full comradeship.

Smuts felt his loneliness. In 1944 he lost two old comrades of the

* From 1943 onwards Mr Sidney Waterson, formerly of the diplomatic service, played a leading part in this work as Minister of Economic Development.

Anglo-Boer war, Deneys Reitz and Willie Collins. 'That old guard of the Transvaal Republic', he lamented, 'is thinning out and now few remain.' He appointed J. G. N. Strauss to succeed Collins at the Ministry of Agriculture and congratulated himself on bringing a young man into his government.* A few months later Louis Esselen died. 'They are dropping off one after the other', he wrote, 'and I am left a solitary monument of a past stretching away since 1895.' He decided that the time had come to set his worldly affairs in order. After careful discussions with his wife and family he divided his farms among his children. With that task completed, he felt happy in the knowledge that no contention about the inheritance could arise after his death and that the only things he still possessed were his bank account, his books and the love of his nearest and dearest. 'A chapter is closed', he wrote, 'and Isie's mind is easier.'[19]

Nevertheless he was not expecting death for some time yet nor was he contemplating an early retirement from politics, although he must have heard some of the whisperings which were rife at that time among his followers about the succession to him. Senator Conroy suspected an intrigue to make Havenga the next leader. Conroy's own favourite for the leadership was Hofmeyr. That support, possibly, was no advantage to Hofmeyr, because Conroy, although influential in the Cape and—despite his name—an Afrikaner, was in open conflict with the Dutch Reformed Church. He himself realized that the whisperings had better stop. 'Believe me', he wrote to Hofmeyr, 'General Smuts, and he alone, is the only cohesive factor that keeps the Party together today and Heaven only knows what will happen should he, which God forbid, fall away.'[20]

Smuts had to stay at his post whether he wanted to or not, but he asked himself sometimes how long he would be able to stay. During the last winter of the European war he came close to the edge of despair.

And Conferences [he wrote in November 1944] are the order of the day and of all days, so that one prays that the week-end may come as Wellington prayed for night at Waterloo—and did not know that victory would come before night. But victory will never come to me any more. It seems as if night will overcome me and my works.

He compared the drought of his soul to the drought which was scorching the Cape veld. As he watched the forest fires spreading over

* Strauss was then 44 years old.

his beloved mountains he cursed the human brutes who had started them. 'I now believe', he wrote, 'in the Church formula of "man conceived in iniquity and born in sin", if that is the right phrasing. But enough gall.' He felt his strength ebbing from him. His hand-writing was now so shaky that he wondered if his friends would be able to read it. On Sunday afternoons, when bathing parties were arranged for one of the Cape beaches, he sometimes found himself shrinking from the cold water. The ascent of Table Mountain was too much for him now. A walk along the easy gradient of the upper contour path was as much as he could manage.[21]

Still, the upper contour path was something. 'I browse on the lower levels', he wrote, 'and in Marloth's *Flora* in the sleepless watches of the night. There is beauty and joy everywhere and not only on high mountains.' Deep within him were springs of life which would flow again if ever the chance returned of a little rest for his exhausted body and mind. He knew that the state of the world was terrifying and his own impoverishment of spirit pitiable, but—

Surely, surely the spirit will visit us again and refresh our parched souls. I shall not be surprised to see angels unawares and to hear their footfalls where now only bombs or war propaganda is heard. The Voices will once more speak to us like long ago, and we shall once more feel at rest.[22]

CHAPTER 24

SOMBRE VICTORY

THE difficulties of making peace when victory should be achieved
seemed so appalling to Smuts that he found himself reciting the
prayer of the old Griqua Chief who once told the Lord that saving
the Griquas was no task for children and that this time it was not
enough for him to send His Son: He must come Himself.[1] Smuts, as
he studied his New Testament, asked himself a practical question:
'How does it translate into human affairs?' He could discover no
translation, at any rate no direct translation, that fitted the needs of
his own war-ruined world. Jesus had had no need, he said, to probe
the problems of social and political order because Caesar was there
to look after them; but historical circumstances were different
now.

I feel the tragedy of the situation [he wrote] as deeply as any Friend,*
and I do believe that under ideal conditions the Christian message is the
only answer to our difficulties. But of course the situation for Jesus was
much simplified by the existence of the omnipotent Roman Empire and
by his sound principle of leaving to Caesar what was Caesar's. *We*, on the
other hand, are in the position of Caesar, responsible for peace and war,
for the maintenance of social order against brute violence and aggression.
Ours is therefore a much more complex situation than that which Jesus
had to face. What would *He* have done if in Caesar's place...?

That question might have seemed surprising; but questions similar
in their meaning, if not in their phrasing, had been asked in the early
Christian Church. The Fathers of the Church had concluded, after
much debate, that *dominium* and *bellum justum* were necessary political
institutions, *propter peccatum*—or, as Smuts would have said, because
evil remained a persistent and intractable element of human
society.[2]

But Smuts could not leave the problem there. Human affairs in
the mid-twentieth century included scientific technology, totalitarian
politics and war economics. That combination made *bellum justum*
out of date. Confronted with the threat of unendurable destruction,

* I.e. member of the Society of Friends.

civilized man was now at last compelled to attempt not merely the regulation but the prevention of war. Somehow or other, he must create institutions capable of doing Caesar's work. Smuts spent a good deal of time during the middle war years discussing with Tom Lamont, Lord Cecil, the Gilletts and other friends what stamp these new institutions should take.[3]

Nevertheless he did not consider new institutions by themselves a sufficient response to the challenge now confronting the human species. The best constructed engine, he said, was of no use unless it had a head of steam to drive it. He did not see where else that head of steam could be generated except in the minds and hearts of individual men and women. He wondered how much Jesus had known about the institutions of the *Pax Romana* when he told his disciples that the Kingdom of Heaven was within them.

It is perhaps doubtful whether He knew much; but in Galilee...where Roman troops were stationed to keep the peace...He may have heard of the great Human Experiment of organization. The Jews were in any case looking forward to a worldly kingdom for their resurrection and rise from thraldom. And Jesus spread the message that not along those lines would the Salvation come. The Soul, Man's relation to God, the inner purification and the practice of the gentler virtues would herald...the Kingdom of Heaven. Is this thought not basic in the truest sense? Has mankind not first to find its Soul again before it finds the new Kingdom?

Smuts was stating very high the requirements for human survival. Two things, he said, were requisite: institutional reform and individual rebirth. He considered individual rebirth the fundamental requirement. 'The situation', he wrote, 'is at bottom a religious problem.'[4]

Looking at the world around him Smuts saw counterfeit religions in plenty. Racialism, Nationalism, Nazism, Fascism, Communism—all of them had steam enough to drive the engines of destruction. But where and how would steam be generated to drive the engine of world peace? Smuts accepted the life and teaching of Jesus as a convincing refutation of all the counterfeit religions; but Jesus had lived and taught two thousand years ago in a tiny peasant country which now was far remote from the imagination and thought of megalopolitan man. Even further remote was Christianity's immense incrustation of pre-scientific and anti-scientific dogma. Smuts thought of the young men he knew at Cambridge. Perhaps the New Testament

427

was unable any longer to speak to their condition? Perhaps their generation was awaiting a new revelation? 'Is it the Man of Galilee', he asked, 'or another like Him born from our distressful conditions, who will point the way out of this darkness in which we are milling round?' Still, he did not forget the parable of the room swept and garnished. He was afraid of false Messiahs. What he most longed for was to hear the Christian Gospel proclaimed again in such terms and such a tone as both to satisfy the reason and touch the heart of twentieth-century man. He asked himself: 'How can we picture the Highest which would absorb all our love and passionate devotion, and make our hearts once more burn in us as did the vision of Jesus to the two disciples of Emmaus?'[5]

The friend and teacher of his student years, Professor Marais, would have understood his question; but neither the theological nor the political outlook of Professor Marais remained acceptable to the Afrikaner churches. Their devouring passion was nationalism. Was it different, Smuts asked, in the European churches? 'Such parsons!' he exclaimed. He admitted that there were exceptions, for example, Pastor Niemöller. He blessed the Quakers and other good Christian folk who kept 'pegging away in spite of it all—in fact, because of it all'. That seemed to him the sensible thing to do. The world could not wait for the thing it needed most, the religious miracle of individual men and women being born again. The first moves in the struggle for human survival would have to be made at the institutional end. 'We must tackle the job', he said, 'according to our human lights and means, hoping that Heaven's blessing will follow in due course.' The job he referred to was the establishment of a World Security Organization. For this purpose a Conference of the United Nations was held at San Francisco from 25 April to 26 June 1945. Early in the year a rumour had been going around that Smuts would be President of the Conference. Smuts himself had no idea where or how the rumour could have started. 'It is of course', he said, 'preposterous. Russia does not like me, France distrusts me, even in British circles there is divided opinion and South Africa is too small fry for such exaltation.' Besides that, he thought it quite likely that when the Conference met the play would have been already written and that only the theatrical performance of it would take place on the San Francisco stage.[6]

Here he put his finger upon the chief contrast between the drafting of the Covenant of the League of Nations and the drafting of the Charter of the United Nations. At the end of the First World War, so little preparatory work had been done that the way had been wide open for his own individual *tour de force*. In the brilliant state paper dated 16 December 1918, with little previous work to draw upon except the report of the Phillimore Committee, he had enumerated and expounded the essential objectives, organs and procedures of the future League of Nations. A generation later, the situation was different. Two years if not more before the Second World War ended the expert and semi-expert participators in the task of charter-making could be numbered by hundreds or even by thousands. Washington, in particular, was a great ant-hill of busy workers scurrying around with pieces of paper to pile upon the ever-rising mound of typescript and print dedicated to 'the establishment of a wider and permanent system of general security'. In all this work, which was hammered into preliminary shape at Dumbarton Oaks in September 1944, Smuts took no share. He was merely a distant spectator.[7]

By and large he was an approving spectator. In the early years of the war he had hoped for the reformation and restoration of the League of Nations. But that proved impossible. America had never joined the League. Russia had been expelled from it. Both countries insisted on the need to create a new world organization and to give it a new name. The name United Nations was a product of President Roosevelt's flair for idealistic rhetoric. Smuts willingly conceded that it was a good name; but when he compared the Dumbarton Oaks proposals with the Covenant of the League, he noticed that the draftsmen had found it easier to change names than to change things. Charter instead of Covenant, Security Council instead of Council, General Assembly instead of Assembly, International Court instead of Permanent Court of International Justice—the institutions which he saw emerging, barring their trivial variations of title, were much the same as those contained in *The League of Nations: A Practical Suggestion*, the paper that he had written at white heat in his sick room at 102 Banbury Road, Oxford, at the end of the First World War. He did not find that a consoling thought. For the League of Nations had suffered disaster. If the United Nations were to escape the same disaster, the shortcomings of the old Covenant would need to be identified and they would need to be made good in the new Charter. Unfortunately, sharp differences of opinion existed as to what those shortcomings were. Some people said that the League had failed because it attempted too much. Other people said that it had failed because it attempted too little.

Among the former were two persons of great experience and intelligence, Walter Lippmann and L. S. Amery. Smuts possibly did not know that Lippmann was advocating a purely consultative world organization; but Amery told him more than once that any more ambitious plan would prove to be the height of wishful delusion. 'If we had not killed the League of Nations by sanctions over Abyssinia', Amery insisted, 'it might have been a real help in dealing with Germany over Munich and later on over Danzig.' He cited Smuts's own speech in 1934 at Chatham House.* At that time, Smuts had been on Amery's side, but the moral he drew from the Abyssinian experience was the opposite from Amery's. He made himself the advocate of an international organization 'with teeth'.[8]

He did not carry his advocacy of the coercive principle to its logical conclusion, that is to say, an international organization with its own armed forces under its own executive. That would have signified a super-state, which he considered neither desirable nor, under existing circumstances, feasible. In his 'explosive' speech of November 1943 he made a proposal—not wrapped up as yet in legal and constitutional forms—to vest responsibility for keeping the world's peace in his 'trinity' of Great Powers. Roosevelt had a similar conception. He added nationalist China to Smuts's trinity and believed that these 'four policemen' would be able to keep the world in order. When France was added later on, the policemen became five.

This conception of world order ran into difficulties. It appeared to contradict the principle of 'the sovereign equality of all peace-loving states' which had been promulgated in the Four Power Declaration of October 1943. Smuts did not think the contradiction insoluble. He had insisted throughout the war that small nations could no longer find safety in isolation and he believed that they would willingly accept the primacy of the Great Powers in the new system of world security.[9] The tenacity with which Australia and other small nations fought for their rights must surely have surprised him. His own government held itself aloof from such contentions. Probably he was reasonably satisfied with the compromise finally arrived at, which

* See p. 268 above.

did justice to egalitarian aspirations by giving the smaller powers some representation on the Security Council alongside the permanent members, and by laying emphasis upon the prestige and powers of the General Assembly (where all nations would enjoy equal representation) in every sphere *except* that of peace-keeping. In that sphere, the main responsibility was put upon the Security Council and, within the Security Council, upon the Great Powers. To Smuts, that was fundamental.

But supposing the Great Powers could not agree in diagnosing a threat to peace and in prescribing the measures to deal with it? Should all action be held up unless and until they reached unanimity? That raised the highly contentious issue of the veto, on which differences of opinion existed, at first between the British and the Americans and, later on, between the British and Americans on one side and the Russians on the other. This time, Smuts was not content merely to be an observer. In September 1944 the Russian representatives at Dumbarton Oaks almost wrecked the discussions by refusing to accept any limitations at all upon the right of a Great Power to veto decisions of the Security Council, even when the Great Power was itself involved in a dispute. On grounds of constitutional principle, Smuts considered Russia's claim monstrous; but he advised Churchill to accept it on grounds of political necessity. In a long letter of 20 September he depicted Russia as a mammoth power with an inferiority complex; she had been treated as a pariah in the past and was likely to behave as one in the future unless satisfaction were done to her *amour propre*. 'Should a World Organization be formed without Russia', he argued, 'she will become the power centre of another group. We shall then be heading towards a third world war.' In other words, he thought it necessary to pay a high price in terms of constitutional principle in order to bring Russia into UNO. Whether he was right or wrong, his intervention produced a strong effect upon Churchill. He showed Smuts's letter to Roosevelt. No doubt it played some part in promoting the reappraisals and compromises of Yalta and, consequently, in bringing UNO to birth.[10]

On the eve of the San Francisco Conference, Smuts made a second noteworthy intervention. The Commonwealth Prime Ministers were meeting in London to discuss, among other things, the proposals for the Charter which the experts had drafted at Dumbarton Oaks and the further proposals which the politicians had agreed upon at Yalta.

Smuts praised their work but still found something lacking in the draft Charter. It was, he said, too legalistic in tone. It needed words to touch the heart of the common man and make him feel that the Charter was not merely a piece of machinery but something truly great. Words like the following—

> 'We, the United Nations...
> 'We declare our faith in basic human rights...
> 'We believe in the practice of tolerance...
> 'We believe in the enlargement of freedom...
> 'We believe in nations living in peace...'

Smuts laid upon the table the draft of an eloquent declaration of humanity's hopes and faith. The conference of Prime Ministers agreed that it would make a noble Preamble to the Charter. But perhaps too noble? Perhaps 'not quite consistent in style and contents with the rest of the Charter'? That was the feeling of British ministers and their expert advisers. They called to mind some more modest proposals for a preamble lying somewhere in the Foreign Office files and suggested that these proposals should be conflated with Smuts's proposals. The job was done before the next morning's meeting. The story of how it was done and of how Smuts's draft, while continuing to bear his name, became in effect the Smuts–Webster draft was told a decade later by Sir Charles Webster.[11]

There was an ironic sequel. In deference to the diplomatic proprieties, the new draft began by identifying the legal persons subscribing to the Charter—not the United Nations, but the High Contracting Parties. Nothing could have been more correct; but gone were the force and fire of Smuts's opening statement. At the San Francisco Conference, reproachful American idealists complained that the Smuts draft, as everybody called it, was lacking in force and fire. The aspirations of humanity, they declared, deserved better treatment. An ardent academic lady, Dean Gildersleeve, proposed these opening words—

> 'We, the Peoples of the United Nations...'

Her proposal was adopted; but the juristic and diplomatic experts had the last word. The closing sentences of the Preamble embodied their scruples and left no doubt at all that it was the governments, not the peoples of the United Nations, who were the creators of the Charter and the subscribers to it.[12]

For Smuts's own country his idealistic initiative produced consequences still more ironic. It introduced 'fundamental human rights'
into the politics of the United Nations. Next year, at the first meeting
of the General Assembly, Mrs Pandit quoted those words against
Smuts himself. From that time onwards they became a stick with
which to beat South Africa.*

The San Francisco Conference proved to be the last international
gathering which Smuts attended with his reputation as a world
statesman still untarnished by the sins imputed to his country and
to himself as its Prime Minister. His role at the Conference, to
borrow Walter Bagehot's phrase about the British monarchy, was
dignified rather than useful. As president of the Commission on the
General Assembly and as a respected elder statesman he was able
once or twice to help the Conference over what he called, by a
delicious slip of the pen, its 'styles and hurdles'; but neither he nor
any other individual would have been able to make any big dent in
a document that had been so long and so carefully prepared. Not
that he wanted to make any big dent in it. When the Charter was at
last approved he told Amery that the Conference had done 'a fair
job of work'.[13]

A month later, when he heard the news of Hiroshima, he revised
that opinion. 'Something far more drastic has to be done', he wrote,
'than we have attempted at San Francisco.'

He had been let into the secret of Tube Alloys—the original British
code name for the atomic bomb project—during his visit to London
in the autumn of 1943.† He recognized the bomb as potentially a
war-winning weapon but became far more deeply concerned with its
potential effects in long term upon the destiny, for good and evil, of
homo sapiens and of all life upon this planet. On the morrow of Hiroshima he told the Gilletts that his most constant preoccupation
throughout the past two years had been the problem of human

---

* In the process of re-drafting, the adjective 'fundamental' was substituted for 'basic',
the adjective in the original Smuts draft. 'Fundamental human rights' are affirmed in
the Preamble to the Charter and referred to in chapters I (Purposes and Principles), IX
(International Economic and Social Co-operation) and XII (International Trusteeship
System). The Declaration on Human Rights belongs to the post-Smuts period of
UNO.

† There is no strictly contemporary evidence of this, but in July 1945 Smuts wrote:
'I knew about the bomb since 1943 and did my best to prevent its secrecy becoming a new
source of division and strife.'[14]

control over this terrific force newly let loose by the human intellect upon the world.

> How [he asked] to control this new danger for man incomparably greater than anything known before? The question is still unsolved and remains the greatest before us. Of course the industrial potentialities of the bomb are enormous, but that is a question for the future. Its destructive power is already clear.[15]

Historical accident brought Smuts into contact and after a time into friendship with a man pre-eminent in intellectual and moral standing, who throughout the same years was asking the same questions with an even sharper sense of urgency. This man was Niels Böhr, the Danish physicist, whose arrival in England on 6 October 1943—only one day after Smuts's arrival from Africa—was the climax to one of the most thrilling escape stories of the war.[16] Böhr's contribution to the fundamental theory of atomic physics, and in particular a paper on the theory of uranium fission which he and a fellow-physicist had delivered at Princeton just before the war began, had been a main point of departure for the work of British scientists on the atomic bomb. Böhr was nevertheless astounded when he arrived in England to find how fast and far his British colleagues had pushed the work forward. But the work of development was not keeping pace with the scientific discovery. With their war economy stretched to its limits, the British could not make available the vast physical resources required for manufacturing the bomb. However, they had insured themselves two years earlier against this blockage by handing over to the Americans their atomic secrets.* The Americans set to work to such good purpose that they soon began to regard British participation as expendable. In January 1943 they imposed a security clamp which cut the British scientists off from the papers and progress reports of their American colleagues. Churchill protested against this rough treatment and the Quebec Conference of August 1943 approved arrangements more compatible with the British–American war partnership. A few months later top-ranking British scientists were packing their bags for Los Alamos.

Niels Böhr went with them. He did not, however, regard himself merely as the member or an exclusive national team or, for that matter, of an exclusive Allied team. Although he was scrupulously

---

* Notably, the report of the Maude Committee.

obedient to the rules of the system—scientific, administrative, political—within which he was working, his thoughts and aspirations were neither nationalistic nor tethered to the short-term strivings of the Western Allies but, quite simply, human. As a physicist he looked beyond the atomic bomb to the development of the hydrogen bomb; as a responsible and imaginative human being he apprehended humanity's need to seek means of saving itself from the powers of self-destruction which the bomb was putting into its hands.

A convergence was beginning to take shape between the thought of Böhr and the thought of Smuts. Quite possibly, neither man became aware of it until the early summer of 1944. As in the previous year, the arrival of Böhr and Smuts in London coincided almost to the day. Böhr had come on a personal mission. It was his purpose to try and persuade the Churchill government that the time had come for it and the American government to share their atomic secret with the Russians. The proposal might seem startling; but if Böhr's premises were granted it was logical. Böhr was a brilliant but simple man who by following a straight line of thought arrived inevitably at the explosive centre of high politics. His starting-point was the conviction that humanity would be putting its survival into jeopardy if it allowed its new scientific knowledge to be channelled into the old grooves cut by the competition for power. He saw co-operation as the antithesis of competition and confidence as the condition of co-operation. He also saw that time was short. The Americans and British would possess the atomic bomb soon; the Russians possessed sufficient resources of science and technology to produce it later on. Possibly they had a shrewd idea already of what was going on at Los Alamos. Let them be told about it frankly, if only in general terms. A deliberate attempt to keep them in the dark would be destructive of confidence, that is to say, of the only firm foundation on which to build international co-operation and human survival.

Böhr argued humanity's case—as he believed it to be—without departing from the rules of discretion which it was his duty to observe and without incurring any reputation for crankiness among persons well qualified to assess his character and thought. He had good reason for believing that his argument had been put before the President and had been listened to with sympathetic attention. Lord Halifax, the British Ambassador in Washington, approved his going to London to put it before the British government. In London, Lord Cherwell and Sir John Anderson gave it their serious consideration. Anderson said that the international control of atomic energy was an urgent problem and that if it remained unsolved no plans for a new world order would be worth the paper they were written on.

But even if Anderson was right on that score it did not necessarily follow that Stalin ought straight away to be told about the atomic bomb. Churchill stated some cogent reasons for not telling him. Moreover, D-Day was imminent. Churchill had other things to think about than Niels Böhr's proposals. When Anderson and Cherwell insisted that they had to be taken seriously, he invited Smuts to examine them. Smuts accepted the invitation. He spent a considerable time in study and consultations and it was not until mid-June that he sent in his opinion. On the long-term problems of atomic power and its control he wrote incisively. Both for war and peace, he said, both for destruction and beneficial use, the new discovery was the most important ever made by science: if ever there was a matter for international control, this was it. On the immediate problem he wrote less incisively. He produced no answer to Böhr's question but confined himself to insisting that the answer would have to be given soon. The British could not give it by themselves. The Americans were the senior partners in the bomb and if the decision were taken to share its secrets with the Russians they would have to make the approach. Whether the final decision was Yes or No, it would have to be taken jointly by the President and the Prime Minister. They must not allow the matter to drift but must make up their minds soon. That meant that they must meet soon. They met three months later at Hyde Park, the President's home in New York State. Their agreement, dated 18 September 1944, contained no comfort for Niels Böhr. It opened the road to Hiroshima.

A few weeks after Hiroshima Niels Böhr returned to his home in liberated Denmark. He had failed in his self-appointed wartime task but he continued throughout the rest of his long life to pursue the same end with such means as were available to him. In doing so he sometimes remembered Smuts and turned to him for encouragement and support. His voice was probably the last from the world of science which Smuts heard.

It is with great anxiety [Böhr wrote in June 1950] that I have heard that you have been seriously ill, but I hope that you are now on good way to recovery and that in years to come you will still be able to offer the world such human wisdom and leadership in world affairs as you have given in the past. I need not say how much your encouragement and sympathy in the difficult war years meant to me.[17]

And yet it would have been strange if a complete identity of views had existed during those years between Böhr and Smuts. A meeting of minds took place between them, but each had separate anchorage in his own world of experience and responsibility. Smuts, unlike Böhr, had to take responsibility for political and military decisions in his own country and was a deeply involved participator in the British planning of grand strategy. Although he had no advance knowledge of the decision to drop atomic bombs on Hiroshima and Nagasaki he endorsed that decision after the event. When news came of the capitulation of Japan he wrote:

I dare say this sudden collapse was due largely to the Atomic Bomb, the effect of which, both physical and psychological, must have been shattering. From that point of view its use has been justified. But it has been even more than justified from the point of view of preventing war in future. Although much has been said in vague terms of the new weapons in preparation, people were thinking of trifles like V 1 and V 2 bombs. And now they have, *before* the end of the war, seen something infinitely more horrible and death-dealing. They would never have believed the warning about deadly weapons in future warfare unless there had been this actual display of them at the end of this war.* We are now forewarned of what is coming if war is not ended for good...At last a discovery has been made which should put war out of court for good and all.[18]

That optimistic forecast appeared to have at its base a crudely deterministic theory of human behaviour which Smuts had more than once put forward. He had written in January 1945:

To me it looks as if science will do what our statesmanship has failed to do. The war inventions are now becoming so effective that war will become annihilation in future and may not be faced by peoples any more. We are just reaching that stage that science is putting the finishing touches to her war job...So I am not without hope of the future even if that hope is based so to say on despair—human nature being at last *coerced* into proper behaviour, where no other appeal would do.[19]

Coercion into proper behaviour was not, however, an idea which could satisfy him for long. He did not in his heart believe that an

---

* Smuts probably had in mind some sombre references of his own to the harnessing of science to war in a speech he had made four months earlier at the Commonwealth Prime Ministers' Conference. These references were given generous publicity (e.g. in the *Daily Telegraph*, 6 April 1945) but Smuts did not believe that they had produced much impact on public opinion.

impersonal science would do for men the things that they could not or would not do for themselves. Science had brought them face to face with a challenge more urgent than any they had ever before confronted, a challenge which called into question their very survival. To cope with that challenge they would have to make the double response of institutional reform and individual re-birth. In the year of sombre victory, Smuts could see no sign that they were ready to make either response. 'Even the atomic bomb', he wrote at the close of the year, 'may not be enough to give us peace. It becomes a rivalry as to who can make the most dreadful and destructive atomic bomb. And so we muddle on to the edge of the volcano.'[20]

At the root of his foreboding was a feeling of outraged pity. Man's inhumanity to man, which had appalled him during the last winter of the war, appalled him still more as the first winter of the peace approached.

The war and its mechanical horrors were bad enough. But this milling round of millions of people in all lands, homeless, foodless, hopeless, rotten with disease and drifting like flotsam before the Wrath is a picture of misery more than one can bear...It is the religion of pity which we are most in need of today...'Have Pity upon us O Lord' seems to be the prayer rising from millions of hearts to a pitiless heaven.

He felt that humanity was living in 'a spiritual vacuum, an empty hollow into which all the devils of our subhuman mind have entered'. In a sardonic play upon words he contrasted the yearnings of credulous persons like himself for faith, hope and charity with the acrimonious exchanges that were taking place between the three Great Powers.

It is power, science, economics—these three. But Paul's Three—the real Big Three—I see little of.[21]

Exhaustion lay heavy on him. Some loyal and sensitive South Africans began to notice it. Whereas in 1943 they had still responded to the vibrant faith and vivid imagery of his speeches, they now found his words lifeless, vague, mechanical, repetitive—the words of a tired old man slipping down the grooves of his tired old tongue.

> Oh words, those words
> ...
> 'mighty' and 'infinite' and 'God'
> that grow too tall for right and wrong,
> do with the vanished isopards lie
> along that grooved old tongue.[22]

438

In his public appearances he tried to give the impression of vitality and alertness; that, he said, was good propaganda. In his private life he had deep reservoirs of faith to draw upon. He discussed with the Abbé Breuil the advance of mankind since prehistorical times and called for 'three cheers for the human race'. He read his New Testament and saw 'the great Fulfilment' at work alongside 'the great Frustration'. His conclusion was that man might still fulfil his destiny in evolution and as a creature made in the image of God if he could muster sufficient courage, patience and prudence to bring himself through the immediate danger zone.[23]

Whenever he could, he let himself sink into the peace of his own home. 'I wonder', he wrote, 'what I would have done without Doornkloof...All my wounds are healed, all my aches are gone, and I almost feel reborn in this atmosphere of peace and loving kindness.' After a week-end at home he never doubted his ability to cope successfully with the next bout of administrative and political business. All the same, he congratulated Churchill on getting his discharge from the British electors. No doubt it was a misfortune for Britain and the world—'But there it is', he told Churchill, 'and what cannot be prevented had better be enjoyed!' For himself he saw no such chance of release, 'no mercy for this sinner, this old sinner, who will have to continue to carry his burden—for the present at any rate'. Later on, perhaps, he would be able to hand over the reins to Hofmeyr; but the party and the country were not ready for that yet. He compared his role with that of one of Bunyan's heroes, Mr Holdfast, or Mr Standfast—he could not remember the name. In a more humdrum mood he saw himself 'back in the old harness pulling the old cart'.[24]

PART V

THE DARKENING ROAD

CHAPTER 25

THE SHIFT OF WORLD POWER

THE map of power which Smuts saw in the year of victory contained all the intimidating features of the map which he had drawn on a famous occasion two years earlier.* It contained none of the hopeful features.

As he had forecast, there was a power vacuum in Europe. Unconditional surrender was now the rule of life for the defeated. And for the victors? He saw only one victor. Already in 1943 he had identified Russia as a main inheritor of the defeated powers, a new Colossus relieved from countervailing pressures at the eastern end of her vast territories by the collapse of Japan and at the western end by the collapse of the three great Powers of continental Europe. In 1945, Russia's inheritance of power exceeded by far his most sombre prognostications. Month by month he had watched with fascination and dread her advance into Central Europe and her imposition of Communism upon the territories her armies occupied. He saw Europe's inheritance disintegrating and Russia taking over the liquidated property. Stalin, he exclaimed at last, remained the victor, the sole victor, of the Big Three.[1]

In 1943 he had identified America as a second Colossus, destined at long last to recognize foreign entanglement as a fact and to take the lead in establishing and maintaining a just equilibrium of power in Europe and the world. But in 1945 the Americans seemed to him uninterested in assuming the rôle he had assigned to them. They seemed to be too much in a hurry to bring their soldiers home from Europe. They seemed also to be in agreement with the Russians upon the salt-water theory, according to which it was meritorious for a state to fulfil its manifest destiny by overland expansion, but sinful for it to do the same thing by expansion overseas. If that really was their principle, it meant a grant of absolution to expansionist Russia and an incitement to anti-imperialist attacks upon the British Commonwealth. Smuts thought it astonishing that the Americans could so quickly forget their wartime comradeship with the British.

* See pp. 408–10 above.

In August he recorded their sudden closure of Lend-Lease. He congratulated his own country on having been able to pay in hard cash for most of the American war supplies. But the British, it seemed to him, were being made to suffer for having fought too hard to save the world from Hitler. The brusque termination of Lend-Lease, as he saw it, was a symbolic act, the repudiation of a glorious alliance.[2]

In 1943 he had identified the British Commonwealth as a member of the Big Three, strong enough still to play its part beside the two mammoth states in controlling and moderating the shift of world power; but in 1945 he had perforce to admit that the Commonwealth was falling short of the capacities and achievements he had envisaged for it. No applications for membership of the Commonwealth had been coming in, or were likely to come in, from the democratic states of western Europe. No integrative movements were apparent among the overseas territories; on the contrary, there seemed to be a drift towards fragmentation, if not disruption. Worst of all, the erosion of power at the centre of the Commonwealth had gone much further than he would have thought conceivable two years earlier—the erosion not only of economic power but also, he was afraid, of will power. That was his partisan interpretation of the British electorate's rejection of Churchill.

From whatever angle he looked at it, the shift in the balance of world power seemed cataclysmic. His imagination made impressionistic pictures of its effects upon three continents, Europe, Asia and Africa.

'What', he asked, 'is to become of Europe?* It has been such a grand continent, where man has risen to such stature and achieved so much to improve our lot and raise us above the brute level. Now a world of hate and sorrow and suffering which makes one almost despair of the future.' Still, he never quite let go his 'small spar of hope'. Europe, surely, would rise again from her ruins. But when?[3]

What was to become of Asia? Even before the war, he had seen foreshadowed in Asia a shift of power more momentous by far than any he could foresee in Europe.† Now that the war had loosened the European grip on Asia, he saw a violently erupting continent which

---

* His feeling that he belonged to Europe, as well as to Africa, found expression in the opening sentence of his speech (in Afrikaans) to the States General of Holland on 11 October 1946: 'The old Zealander who in 1692 left Middelburg in Walcheren to seek a home in the far south has the honour to address you today through his descendant.'

† See p. 283 above.

contained more than half the human race. The revolt of Asia, as he pictured it, was at one and the same time the breaking loose of subject peoples from the empires that had contained them; the resumption of a secular conflict between two historic ways of life; the repudiation by coloured humanity of its subjection to white humanity.

What was to become of Africa? He called Africa 'the home continent', 'the continent of my love'. He was an African of white skin, the leader of a small white nation living dangerously on the shore of an ocean of colour. For the time being—indeed for a good many more years than he had still to live—Europe retained control of Africa south of the Sahara; but disintegration in the European homeland seemed bound sooner or later to destroy that control.

Meanwhile, Asians were leading the attack on European world dominance. The Russians were inciting them; the Americans were caught in two minds between their strategical calculations and their anti-colonial impulses. The new United Nations Organization seemed likely to become the sounding board, if not the arena, of these conflicts. As early as the San Francisco Conference, Smuts was facing that fact. Equal rights all round, he told Hofmeyr in May 1945, would become the cry at UNO when it got going.[4]

He saw that his enemies in South Africa would put upon his shoulders the blame for that. For was it not he who had written 'fundamental human rights' into the Charter? He foresaw that they would arraign him as a main perpetrator of the world's evils. 'Here in South Africa', he wrote, 'I shall be held up as one of the warmongers who helped to precipitate these evils on mankind. And the charge has a certain measure of plausibility.' So indeed it had. The expansion of Soviet Communism, the collapse of Europe, the decline of Britain and the Commonwealth—all these portents had been foretold by the Opposition leaders. Their warnings were on record in official print. Their remedy also was on the official record. From the beginning of the war almost to its end, they had reiterated their call to South Africa to seek her own safety by making a separate peace and by seceding from the Commonwealth.[5]

Smuts did not believe that safety lay along that road. He foresaw the attempts that would be made to isolate South Africa. He could not foresee any gain she could get by setting out to isolate herself. On the contrary, he thought it sound policy for her to keep the friends she had, to support them in their efforts to rebuild their strength and, so far as possible, to increase their number. All this would take time. He used often to say that time was a *vera causa*: a malignant cause, if the tide of events was moving so fast that the most skilful navigation could not withstand or elude it; but a beneficient cause, if a courageous and intelligent crew could keep the ship afloat until the tide turned. In the aftermath of the war that was his main hope. 'It is all a question of time', he wrote. 'If one could manage to pull through till the turn of the tide.'[6]

For pulling through, the first requisite was courage; but Smuts set almost equal store upon prudence. At the Paris Peace Conference of mid-1946, he found the Americans in violent reaction against their mood only a few months earlier of complaisance towards the Russians. They were now denouncing the Russians as enemies. Smuts thought they would do better for the time being to keep their minds open.

But what [he asked] do we know about Russia, what materials have we for an opinion at all? I find here people who have spent years there, diplomats and soldiers whose business at Moscow it is to find out what really is going on behind the curtain. They don't know...

Did even Russia know? Was she moving back to Czarist imperialism or forward to international Communism? Both views, Smuts said, were tenable; but both might be wrong. His own inclination was to regard Russia as a continental power pursuing limited objectives—dangerous ones, admittedly; but he believed that the dangers could be contained by a *realpolitik* compounded of patience and firmness. For that reason he repudiated the anti-Communist crusade but welcomed the American return to an active policy in Europe. He thought it necessary for America still to retain sole custody of the atomic bomb; for some years ahead, he could see no other shield for western Europe. Nevertheless, he considered the polarization of power between America and Russia a dangerous threat to peace. As he put it, UNO had become DUO; but for the sake both of freedom and peace, he looked forward to TRIO.[7]

He was returning to his vision two years earlier of the Commonwealth's rôle as mediator within the 'trinity' of Great Powers. The vision had no substance. His own letters recorded from month to month Great Britain's continuing economic exhaustion and the approaching crisis of the convertibility of sterling. They recorded one after the other the retreats of Great Britain as an imperial power. In the eastern Mediterranean, which had been a special interest of his own in two World Wars, he found those retreats hard to bear. The Jewish National Home remained, as it had always been, one of his great causes: in April 1946, as the sole surviving sponsor of the Balfour Declaration, he gave forthright testimony on its behalf; in May 1947 he urged Dr Weizmann to accept the partition of Palestine *faute de mieux*; in April 1948, he lamented Great Britain's fumbling termination of her great redemptive mission. 'We can't scuttle', he told Amery, 'from responsibility before history.' Yet 'scuttle' there had to be, even from South African battlefields of the Second World War. In December 1947 he wrote—

If anybody had told me in the days of our Herculean toils that all that world was hopelessly lost to us I could never have believed it...I am making a hard fight for Cyrenaica at least...That bit of North Africa, of such poignant memories, should remain ours, whatever happens. But nobody knows what may not yet be surrendered where so much has been already jettisoned in this shipwreck of Empire.[8]

'Getting out of it anyhow' seemed to him the worst possible policy. 'Let there be', he exclaimed, 'the appearance of strength, even where the reality is lacking.' From that unheroic point of view, he could approve British policy in Asia. Even so, the approval came hard. 'Mountbatten', he wrote in March 1947, 'will liquidate British interests in India and thus open the way for the new All-Asia anti-European policies which will sow the seeds of the future world conflicts.' From India's point of view, he thought unity a high price to pay for independence. 'Poor India', he wrote in May. 'Poor East, which has been asleep these thousands of years and is now having such a rude awakening.' He commented sardonically upon the independence of Ceylon. 'Ceylon, a Dominion this year?', he wrote in April. 'Am I mad or is the world mad?' Ceylon's independence, he thought, would be less substantial and self-respecting than his own country's independence had been under the Statute of Westminster; but he supposed she would have to be given the make-believe freedom that she wanted. Up to the middle of 1947, that was the dominant note of all his comments—a grudging acquiescence in the inevitable. Yet even then, he saw some virtue in what the British were doing. As a realist, he gave them higher marks for their policy in India, Burma and Ceylon than the marks he gave the Dutch for their policy in Indonesia. And gradually he came round to the view that the British retreat in Asia contained a creative element. His friends the Moores, from their vantage point at Government House, Colombo, helped him to understand present-day realities in Asia. They believed that the British, provided they rose to the occasion in Ceylon and India, could make a long-term virtue of their immediate necessity. In August 1947, Lady Moore acclaimed the transfer of power in India as a creative act which was sending British pride and morale sky-high. 'What Mountbatten has done', she wrote, 'is to transform the picture into one of pride and dignity in which, with fanfares of trumpets, we hand to the Indians the powers which we have for so long exercised and which we no longer want.' Smuts was not completely receptive of that interpretation. It reminded him, he said, of the stories told by writers on comparative religion of how the victim selected for sacrifice was decked in flowers and gaudy colours and thus became an object of religious awe and glory. Still, he agreed that showmanship had its uses, particularly when a retreat had to be given the semblance of an advance. He congratulated the Moores upon achieving in Ceylon what Mountbatten was achieving in India. 'What might have looked like a stupid and blundering concession and retreat', he concluded, '...has now been converted into a veritable vision.'[9]

On the practical level, the achievement of independence without a 'cutting of the painter' seemed to him a useful contribution to the stability of the international community, the Commonwealth and, not least, the Asian countries themselves. Britain, he reflected, was not after all doing so badly in her task of picking up the broken crockery and piecing it together again. He lamented the liquidation of the old British Empire but he clung to his faith that a new Britain would arise with a new rôle to play in the drama of human liberty. In November 1947 he found inspiration in Westminster Abbey.

Sitting next to Winston in the Abbey at the wedding and watching that mediaeval scene and ceremony I said to him: 'Are we in the Middle Ages?' He replied promptly: 'No, we are in all the ages'. And he was right...At this ceremony, so in the wide world, we have to keep our perspective and to look at present events in the larger setting of all history.[10]

At this very time, so Smuts believed, Britain and the Commonwealth had before them a brilliant prospect of self-fulfilment within this larger setting. It was the year of the Truman Doctrine and the Marshall Plan. Those events were welcome to Smuts both for what they were and for the creative promise which he read into them. He acclaimed them as the augury of a threefold achievement: first, the Atlantic Community; secondly, European Union; thirdly, Commonwealth–Europe. He thought it inconceivable that Britain and the Commonwealth would let slip this opportunity of union with Europe.

The biggest thing now afoot in the world [he wrote in June 1947] is Marshall's speech and America's offer of lend-lease to Europe if she can work out a united plan for her economic recovery. I hope she will not miss this chance...It would be a glorious opportunity for Britain to put herself at the head of this great movement and put her weight behind Winston's vision of a European union. It is no use her wallowing in her own misery and frustration. Proudly she should once more resume her glorious role in world affairs, and in action find her solution.

By January 1948 he was feeling confident that the British government and people would rise to the great occasion. On 23 May, radio listeners in Britain heard his voice from Pretoria encouraging them to go forward without fear. It was the eve of Commonwealth Day and of his own birthday. It was, besides, the last time in his life that he was able to speak to them with the authority of office. Only three days later he became an ex-Prime Minister.[11]

CHAPTER 26

THE QUARREL WITH INDIA

WHEN the war ended Smuts had been continuously in office for twelve and a half years. For the whole period 1934–41 his absences from South Africa added up to barely four months; but for the period 1942–5 they rose to an average figure of between two and three months per year. In 1946 he was absent for a considerably longer time, first at the Peace Conference and afterwards at the General Assembly of the United Nations. Old Mrs Hofmeyr seemed to think that he was taking joy rides, but Smuts considered his journeys awkward, inconvenient and harmful to his political position in South Africa.[1]

Yet he saw no way of avoiding them. Mrs Hofmeyr, certainly, would not have thanked him if he had sent her son to face the music at the United Nations instead of facing it himself. UNO was getting off to a very different start from the one that he had anticipated. He thought that it was not much more than a battle ground for the mammoth powers and a talking shop for the smaller powers. 'On the other hand', he reflected, 'our paths in the world cross and re-cross, and if we go our own separate ways, there may be worse collisions than in UNO.' In view of the rough handling which the General Assembly was giving him, that summing-up showed considerable detachment.[2]

The Indians led the hue and cry against him. He had sufficient poise to see their point of view. 'I am suspected of being a hypocrite', he wrote, 'because I can be quoted on both sides. The Preamble of the Charter is my own work, and I also mean to protect the European position in a world which is tending the other way.' Not only to the Indians, but also to many South Africans, those two attitudes appeared contradictory. Smuts was to blame, they cried, for the avalanche of condemnation which was falling on their country. Once again, he saw their point of view.

The Opposition [he wrote] naturally rejoices and puts all this to my account and to the liberalism (!) with which I have led the world astray. Here is the author of the great Preamble of the Charter, exposed as a

hypocrite and a double-faced time-server! They are of course all right. . .
But look at this bad fellow who is responsible for it all![3]

Certainly, he was caught in a contradiction; but he was not its
creator. History had created it. During the nineteenth century,
economic demand in South Africa had brought into being a community of Indians, which grew within three generations to nearly
300,000 souls.* During the twentieth century, India, like the other
European dependencies in Asia, put herself firmly on the road of
national independence. From the 1880s onwards, Indian nationalism
insistently challenged the inferior civic status imposed upon Indians
domiciled in South Africa. Consequently, it was predictable that
India, as she moved to independence, would move also into collision
with South Africa. At the Imperial Conference of 1923, Sapru had
given Smuts plain notice of that.† There were only two ways of
avoiding the collision: either the British must perpetuate their imperial rule over the Indians, or else the South Africans must produce
a new deal for their fellow-citizens of Indian descent.

In 1917, the Imperial War Conference and the British War
Cabinet had once and for all ruled out the first possibility. The War
Cabinet committed the United Kingdom to 'the progressive realization of responsible government in India as an integral part of the
British Empire'. Smuts, meanwhile, was proclaiming his doctrine
that the Empire of sovereignty and subjection must give place—
indeed, that it was giving place—to the Commonwealth of free and
equal nations. Nothing less than that, he knew, would satisfy his own
country here and now; nothing less than that, he agreed, would
satisfy India in long term. He made that distinction within the time
factor because he believed that Indians would put their unity into
jeopardy if they tried to take short cuts to independence. That did
not mean that he saw merit in British procrastination. On the
contrary, he more than once warned his British friends against letting

* South Africa's Indian population at the 1946 census was approximately 282,000,
distributed as follows:

In Natal	228,000
In the Transvaal	37,000
In the Cape Province	16,900
In the Orange Free State	14

Of the Natal Indians, 113,400 were in the city of Durban whose white population at that
time was 124,492. Comparative birth rates in the Union were: Indians 37 per 1000;
Europeans 20 per 1000.

† See pp. 148–9 above.

themselves lag behind the time-table which thoughtful and patriotic Indians were urging them to follow.

In November 1931 he put himself informally, but helpfully, into touch with the key persons attending the Round Table Conference on India.* Ramsay MacDonald, Gandhi and the Viceroy took counsel with him. The Viceroy entreated him not to remit his efforts at bringing India and Britain into accord.

> Gandhi came to see me this morning [Lord Irwin† wrote to him] and I know how great your influence is with him. He told me of the interest you have been taking, and this is only to beg you to continue to exercise your good offices...
> ...I saw the P.M. today and I think he hopes to get hold of you without delay...
> But apart from Gandhi, the knowledge that you were interesting yourself in the matter would, I fancy, exercise a most useful and salutary effect upon the mind of the Conservative party, and of the British Public generally. What is needed is to get it into their heads that Great Britain and India simply cannot afford the risks to both of failure to reach agreement.

A day or two later Gandhi wrote to him.

> I duly received your affectionate letter. My observations since our last meeting lead me to the conclusion that you may not withdraw from the friendly intervention you began so happily last week. If necessary, you should postpone your departure to South Africa for a cause you rightly believe to be the world's cause.

Three weeks later, Smuts was back in his own crisis-stricken country. Six weeks later, Gandhi was back in India, in gaol.

Smuts did not believe that it was all the fault of the British. The disunity of Hindus and Moslems, he thought, was at the root of the Indian–British disagreement. He wondered at times whether unity in Europe would not come before unity in India? Nevertheless, he could see no future for the course of policy which Lord Willingdon, the new Viceroy, was following.

> It seems to me [he wrote in August 1932] a sheer muddle to put the Congress in gaol, to alienate the Moderates, and yet to think of going forward with the grant of a new constitution. Who will work this constitution and

* He had come to Britain in fulfilment of his commitment as President of the B.A.A.S. The second session of the Round Table Conference was held from September to December 1931.

† Later Lord Halifax.

who will have any responsibility for its success? I can understand frank
Reaction or the Strong Hand. I can also appreciate a more or less liberal
policy of Trust such as that of Campbell-Bannerman. But what is this
monstrosity...? Gandhi is and remains the best friend and should be
dealt with as such and strengthened against his extremists.

A month later he wrote.

Gandhi has made a great achievement.* He is really one of the wariest
calculators I have ever seen, and his threat of starvation has brought the
Hindoos to heel and sent his stock soaring up. I hope the Government will
let him out of gaol and get his co-operation for other aspects of their
constitutional scheme as well. What a waste to keep such a power and
influence for good in gaol at such a time! And without Gandhi's co-
operation the new institutions will never even begin to function properly.[4]

In his pessimistic moods he doubted whether even Gandhi could
make the new institutions work. Of all the Asian nations, he reflected,
only the Japanese had proved themselves, so far, skilful players of the
political game. When he studied the Government of India Act, 1935,
he felt that it was putting the political ball at the feet of the Indians;
but he was afraid that they would fail to take possession of it. Yet
that, he continued, would be, to some extent at least, the fault of the
British; they could have taken larger risks; they could have shown
more magnanimity. When the war came, that was still his conviction. He repeatedly warned Amery, the Secretary of State, and Linlithgow, the Viceroy, that holding back was more dangerous than
pressing forward. 'Dominion status in its full implications', he wrote
to Linlithgow in August 1941, 'should not be denied them, but rather
given freely and graciously, as it is in any case inevitable.' He wrote
next year, when the news reached him that Sir Stafford Cripps would
soon be going to India—

A declaration about India's future is at long last coming, but much too
late, in spite of my strong earlier advice...Why can't they act swiftly and
with Campbell-Bannerman's courage?

He wrote five weeks later—

The Cripps mission to India has been added to our already full programme. It is a great pity that India was not taken in hand months ago
when I strongly urged it, and that we have now to give away under
compulsion what should have been given as a free and generous gift.[5]

---

* Smuts was referring to the Poona Pact, which corrected the British government's
'communal award', in that it did away with the electoral split between Hindus and the
Scheduled Castes. Gandhi's fast had been instrumental in achieving the Poona Pact.

Linlithgow and Amery both told him that the difficulty was not chiefly at the giving end of the political transaction with India, but rather at the receiving end. Linlithgow reported a conversation in which Gandhi had confessed to him that he had only recently read the Government of India Act and had found to his surprise that it could have been made the firm point of departure for Indian freedom. In view of all that had happened since the Act was passed, Linlithgow said, those were the saddest words that he had heard since his arrival in India. Amery made a more detached report on the difficulties of transferring power.

The essence, after all, of the Government's conception [he wrote in August 1942] is that a continent like India can only be governed democratically on the basis of agreement between its main elements and under a constitution generally acceptable to all of them. That is the principle upon which the United States and every British Dominion* have come into existence and continue to exist...Anyhow that is to my mind the only truly democratic solution, for democracy essentially depends, not on majority votes which are a matter of convenience under an accepted constitution, but on general acceptance of the constitution itself.

The other conception, that of Congress, is that as the largest and most effectively organized party, the leaders of that party are entitled to take over India from us and govern it as a unit...The claim, as applied to a continent like India, is impossible and could only lead to civil war and anarchy. On the other hand, in fairness to Congress, it must be said that it grew up naturally within the framework of an administratively unified India and has continued throughout to think of itself as the only mouth-piece of Indian nationalism against alien rule, and that those who differ from it are essentially interlopers who ought to keep their mouths shut in the interests of Indian freedom.

Amery at this time was writing to Smuts ten or twelve long letters each year. Smuts appreciated and in large measure shared his friend's cool realism. He considered Indian politicians deficient in practical foresight and even began to ask himself whether Gandhi was not outliving his political usefulness. 'His unique position', he wrote, 'and being a Hindu gives the Hindu majority too great a pull to leave much chance of a fair communal compromise.' That made things harder for the British. Perhaps they ought to cut the knot, if the Indians could not or would not untie it. Amery took this view. He told Smuts after the end of the war that he had tried to persuade the War Cabinet to proclaim Indian independence on V.J.

---

* Amery was forgetting the non-European elements of the South African population.

Day, leaving it to the Indians themselves to work out the details. That would have anticipated by two years the Mountbatten master-stroke.[6]

Smuts and Amery both knew that Indian independence must come. They both knew that its coming would put an intolerable strain not only upon the unity of the Indian sub-continent, but also upon Indian–South African relationships. As Secretary of State for India, Amery had transmitted to Smuts, sometimes with emphatic comment, India's complaints about the situation of the Indian community in South Africa; but when independence came there would no longer be a Secretary of State; the indirect pressure upon South Africa through London would become henceforward direct pressure from New Delhi. For Smuts, the nineteenth-century maxim 'liberal abroad, conservative at home' would cease to be serviceable. He would come face to face with a dilemma: either to let his country's domestic policy dictate its foreign policy; or else to bring its domestic policy into line with the requirements of its foreign policy. The former choice contained the risks of South African isolation; the latter choice might prove impracticable. For under no circumstances would Smuts be able to make a stronger bid for friendly and prudent relations with foreign nations than South Africa's white legislators and voters would sanction.

At the Imperial Conference of 1923 Sapru had manoeuvred Smuts into isolation; but South Africa at that time suffered no damage, except perhaps to her vanity.* On his return home, Smuts made no attempt to adjust his domestic policy to the requirements of his Commonwealth policy. He knew that his party expected the opposite from him and that he would have to fight an election before long. Early in 1924, Patrick Duncan, his Minister of the Interior, introduced the Class Areas Bill, an important prototype of segregationist legislation.† From the point of view of the Opposition parties—as indeed of many S.A.P. men—the Bill's chief fault was that it did not go far enough. In the election campaign of 1924, Hertzog and Creswell pledged themselves to remedy that fault. After their return

* See p. 160 above.
† In his speech on the second reading, on 2 April 1924 (col. 1279), Duncan denied that the Bill had any segregationist intent, but he was quibbling; the Bill reflected the segregationist philosophy of the Lange Commission of 1920. Before the Bill could become law Smuts fought and lost the election of 1924.

to power, their pledge found embodiment in Dr Malan's Areas Reservation and Immigration and Registration (Further Provisions) Bill. 'I must say', Dr Malan declared, 'that the Bill frankly starts from the general supposition that the Indian, as a race in this country, is an alien element in the population...'[7] Nevertheless, a *volte face* followed. On 17 December 1926, delegates of South Africa and India met each other at a Round Table Conference in Cape Town. On 11 January 1927, they announced that they had reached agreement. On the South African side, the conference had proved an unexpectedly successful exercise in the adjustment of home policy to the requirements of external policy.

The Cape Town Agreement of 1927 was not a treaty. Its provisions were announced by identical statements in the two legislatures. This method of procedure enabled the two governments to avoid the risks of seeking formal parliamentary ratification of their agreement. Nevertheless, it suited the Indian delegates to UNO two decades later to cite the Cape Town Agreement as an international treaty which South Africa, they alleged, had subsequently broken.*

The salient features of the Cape Town Agreement were: first, combined action of the two governments in an emigration scheme for such Indians as might prove willing to leave South Africa for India; secondly, a pledge by the South African government to promote the 'upliftment' of such Indians as might decide to remain. In the event, the hopes raised under each of these heads began soon to peter out. In 1932, a second Round Table Conference sponsored the unplausible plan of finding some tropical territory to receive *two* streams of Indian settlers, one from South Africa, one from India herself. Heaton Nicholls of Natal nominated New Guinea as the land providentially appointed to serve as South Africa's dump, India's Colonial Empire and Australia's Maginot Line.[8] By now, the Cape Town Agreement was becoming a fantasy. Its sole surviving achievement was the establishment on South African soil of an Agent-General or (as he was subsequently named) a High Commissioner for India.

The South African government could cite an escape clause in the agreement which left it free, if the emigration scheme failed, to seek as it saw fit its own solution of 'the Indian problem'. Its trouble was that the separate Provinces of the Union—not to mention the municipalities—all had their separate problems. This jurisdictional

* See p. 468 below.

tangle was among the basic causes of the disappointing sequel to the 'upliftment' declaration. Provincial and municipal councils were inevitably more concerned with the interests of their white electors than with the new policy which the Union government, without consulting them, had proclaimed. As the 1930s wore on, the white electors of the Transvaal grew mutinous. The Transvaal's laws and regulations restricting Indian residence and trade were chaotic. The task of reducing this chaos to order was entrusted to Richard Feetham, a patient, upright and humane judge; but his mountainous labours proved necessarily slow. Transvaal politicians and their constituents started a clamour for quick action to stop Indian 'penetration' of white areas. To satisfy them, Hertzog's government introduced the Asiatics (Transvaal Land and Trading) Bill of 1939. Its purpose was to pin down or 'peg' Indians to their existing residences and businesses in the Transvaal. Hofmeyr criticized the Bill. Thereupon Hertzog forced his resignation from the United party's caucus.* Smuts acquiesced in the Bill. Thereupon Gandhi rebuked him. 'Why is agreement of 1914', Gandhi telegraphed, 'being violated with you as witness? Is there no help for Indians except to pass through fire?'[9]

Two months later, Smuts was Prime Minister. The Commonwealth, he declared, was his 'great cause'.† In that cause, South Africa and India were comrades-in-arms. That was the situation as Smuts saw it; but the Dominion party saw it differently. By joining Smuts's coalition government, the Dominion party had destroyed its own *raison d'être*. Henceforward, all three parties in the coalition were equally committed to the war effort. There remained only one issue on which the Dominion party could speak with a voice of its own. Most of its members lived in Natal. So did most of the Indians. The Dominion party took up the issue of Indian 'penetration' into the white man's living-space. Thus it let loose an agitation which was dangerous, not only for the Commonwealth, but for South Africa herself. Before long, nearly all the white people of Natal joined the Dominionites in their Gadarene rush.[10]

The racial–economic–sociological situation of Natal was intolerably complex. Durban alone contained more than three times as many Indians as did the whole of the Transvaal. According to the law, these Indians—in contrast with their brethren in the Transvaal—were at liberty to reside, to trade and to buy land wherever they

---

* See p. 298 above.   † See p. 325 above.

pleased. In practice it nearly always pleased them to flock together with birds of their own feather. Their difficulties, like those of the white citizens, arose in large measure from Durban's dynamic growth. As traders, they had been living and working for half a century and more in the centre of Durban; as market gardeners, they had been living and working on the city's fringes. But motor transport started the usual suburban sprawl across and far beyond those fringes. It created Indian 'islands', both in the centre of the city and on its periphery. Meanwhile, the Indian population was growing rapidly and Indians were beginning to prefer family life of the western stamp to their own traditional joint family system. They had somehow or other to get houses for themselves; in consequence, they had to get land. Their situation contained an additional element of complexity. In virtue of their tradition* and—given their restricted economic opportunities—in virtue of their need, they regarded land purchase as an investment opportunity.

It was becoming impossible for all the Indians of Durban to stay congested within their own 'islands'. Nor was there any legal compulsion upon them to do so; although they possessed no votes, they did possess the right to buy land. Nevertheless, their prudence, as well as their preference for living with their own kind, made the great majority of them anxious to exercise their legal right with the least possible offence to the white citizens of Durban. That, most emphatically, was the policy of A. I. Kajee, a well-to-do Moslem who had come to the front in the Natal Indian Congress. For some years before the war, Kajee was informally but effectively damping down the Indian infiltration of white areas. On the eve of the war, a kaleidoscopic shift of communal politics removed him for the time being from his position of leadership;† but his successors continued his policy. For so long as they did so, Smuts was able to get on with the war without all the time looking over his shoulder at Natal. He deputed his Minister of the Interior, H. G. Lawrence, to hold a watching brief on his behalf. Lawrence formed a committee of Indian leaders and the Durban municipality to supervise, and so far as possible control, property transactions between Indian and Euro-

---

* Because of the Koran's prohibition of usury, the tradition was particularly strong in the Moslem community, to which many of the well-to-do Indians of Natal belonged.

† In the communal re-shuffle, a body called the Natal Indian Association, from which Kajee held aloof, assumed primacy over the Natal Indian Congress.

peans. Lawrence did his best; but after a few months his committee collapsed. For Smuts, its collapse was a calamity.

Smuts realized that any new legislative restriction of the rights of Indians in South Africa would reopen the quarrel with India which had been intermittently his curse for the past twenty-five years. He realized no less that a reopening of the quarrel would this time prove to be not merely a nuisance, but also a danger to the Commonwealth and to his own country. Nevertheless, the danger would be more immediate and deadly if he lost control of South Africa while Hitler still remained at large. He decided to play for time and if possible to extinguish the demogogic fires by a cold douche of fact. In 1941 he appointed F. N. Broome, a learned and respected Natalian judge, as chairman of a commission to investigate Indian penetration of European areas in Natal and the Transvaal during the period 1927–40.* The Broome Commission did its work thoroughly and reported towards the end of 1941. It put a spotlight upon the popular exaggerations of Indian penetration of white areas both in the Transvaal and Natal. In Durban, only 512 cases of Indian penetration had occurred during the 14-year period; of these, nearly two-thirds had been land purchases which did not lead to Indian residence.[11]

It appeared that Smuts had got the answer he wanted to the politicians who were demanding legislative restrictions upon Indian land purchase. Nevertheless, they continued their agitation. Indian penetration, they insisted, had been growing more aggressive within each successive month since September 1940, the terminal date of the Broome inquiry. Late in 1942, Smuts called once again upon Mr Justice Broome, this time as a one-man commission, to put that propaganda to the test of fact. Broome completed his task quickly and found the propaganda justified. Between 30 September 1940 and 28 February 1943, Indians had purchased 326 new sites in predominantly European areas of Durban. That figure signified an acceleration of Indian penetration at a rate which the white citizens would not tolerate. Judge Broome himself considered it intolerable.[12]

Only a few weeks earlier, Smuts had told South Africans that he was going to seek their consent for carrying the war across the Mediterranean and releasing the boys captured at Tobruk and bringing them home.† He was preparing to commit his future and

* Smuts chose 1927 as the base year because it had been the year of the Cape Town Agreement.   † See p. 379 above.

his country's future to the risk of a mid-war election. He dared not run the risk of allowing the story to spread through South Africa that he was selling white civilization in Natal down the river. When he received the second Broome report he went quickly into action.

For at the moment [he wrote on 15 April 1943] we are busy with a Bill to stabilize the Indian situation in Durban where there is wild excitement because rich Indians have been buying up properties on a large scale in the heart of Durban and panic has set in among the Europeans. You know the sort of situation and the fear which naturally possesses the whites on such occasions. There is nothing for it but to peg the position and forbid property transfers there for three years so that the whole position can be judicially inquired into. But this again has created commotion among the Indians here and in India and moved the Indian government to do its bit in the general hue and cry...I can never get away from this Indian tangle and the troubles of East and West.[13]

His decision to 'peg the position' fulfilled itself on 21 April, when the Trading and Occupation of Land (Transvaal and Natal) Restriction Bill passed its third reading. Thereafter it became notorious in India under its popular title, the Pegging Act. Before submitting it to Parliament, Smuts had dealt with a difficulty in his own cabinet. J. H. Hofmeyr submitted his resignation; but Smuts persuaded him to take it back again.* Hofmeyr was straining at the Witwatersrand gnat; but he swallowed the Durban camel. As he explained in his speech on the second reading, he approved the Bill's proposals for Natal but disapproved its proposals for the Transvaal, chiefly upon the ground that the former were conformable but that the latter were not conformable with the evidence and recommendations of Mr Justice Broome.[14]

Given Broome's premises, there was a good deal to be said in favour of pegging the position in Durban. In winding up the debate on the second reading Smuts quoted Broome but went beyond him. He made some points which he felt bound to make if he was to have any chance of winning the election: that Durban was a European city and would remain one;† that Indians in Durban would have done better to buy war bonds instead of land; that their appeals to

---

* Hofmeyr submitted his resignation and took it back in the same letter (7 April 1943).

† Durban was wholly European in its government, but in its population it was more or less a 3–3–3-aggregate of Europeans, Indians and Africans. In his speech on the second reading the Minister of the Interior had said that the Broome reports established a *prima facie* case against the Durban City Council for its failure to provide adequate services and amenities for the disfranchised Indian ratepayers.

India for political support were regrettable. 'But whatever mistakes they make', he continued, 'we are bound to remember that they are our people, born here; they have no other country, and we must be fair and just to them, and see that both in regard to land holding, housing schemes, amenities and all the rights which civilized people are entitled to, are also afforded to them, and that they have a fair measure of all this for themselves too.' In that determination, Smuts said, his government would institute a systematic investigation of all the difficulties of Indian life in Natal, and would produce remedies for them by the time the Pegging Act expired, three years from the date of its coming into force.[15]

The Act was 'an interim measure'; but it renewed the allegedly interim pegging that had been imposed four years earlier upon Indians in the Transvaal. In form, the Act was non-discriminatory, since its restrictive provisions applied reciprocally both to Europeans and Indians; but in fact it deprived Indians of legal rights which had been promised to them in 1865 and had belonged to them ever since then. Smuts had no ground for surprise at the furious denunciation which the Act provoked in India. He remained watchful for some way of escape from the cul-de-sac of one-sided restrictive legislation.

In a cabinet reshuffle after the 1943 election he appointed a level-headed Natal man, Senator C. F. Clarkson, as Minister of the Interior. Clarkson administered the Pegging Act so tolerantly that symptoms became visible in the Dominion party and elsewhere of renewed anti-Indian fever. Meanwhile Smuts had made good the pledge he had given during the April debate to institute a searching investigation into every aspect of the Indian situation in Durban. Once again he called on Mr Justice Broome, this time as chairman of the Natal Judicial Commission, an investigating tribunal with wide terms of reference and a reasonably balanced membership: two Indians to three Europeans. The Indians were A. I. Kajee and S. R. Naidoo. Another kaleidoscopic shift of communal politics had restored Kajee to his position as the main spokesman for the Indians.* Smuts considered that shift fortunate.

Kajee was an un-doctrinaire politician. Not theory, but the factual situation was his invariable starting-point in thought and action. The situation after the Pegging Act, as he saw it, contained elements

---

* Following an intervention of the High Commissioner for India, Sir Shafa'at Ahmed Khan, the Natal Indian Association had accepted absorption into the Natal Indian Congress.

461

both of danger and of opportunity: on the one hand, the white Natalians wanted to extend the Act to the whole Province; on the other hand, the Prime Minister disliked coercion and would work co-operatively with the moderate Indian leaders, provided he and they could hammer out some workable plan. Kajee set himself to that task. He started from two pragmatic ideas: first, to treat separately the problems of residence and land-ownership; secondly, to establish procedural collaboration between Indians and Europeans in matters of common concern. The second idea had already found embodiment in the composition of Judge Broome's commission of investigation. The first idea, Kajee hoped, ought to prove acceptable to the white Natalians, since they were all the time protesting that they wished the Indians well, but did not want them as neighbours.

On these bases, Kajee worked out the following plan:

1. In rural areas, the existing rights of farming, trading and residing would remain undisturbed.

2. In urban areas, Indians would possess unrestricted rights of land purchase and ownership; but they would voluntarily accept restrictions upon their rights of residence.

3. A mixed Board—two Europeans and two Indians under a European chairman—would exercise control over all dwellings in Durban: whenever a dwelling had been occupied by a member of one racial group, a licence from the Board would be requisite before it could be occupied by a member of a different racial group.

4. This machinery of control could be extended subsequently to other urban areas, but only after investigation and by decision of the Board.

From such consultations as he was able to hold, Kajee had cause to hope that moderate opinion both among Europeans and Indians would approve his plan. Smuts shared his hope. He arranged a conference at Pretoria on 18 April 1944: on the one side, the Prime Minister with four carefully chosen advisers;* on the other side, A. J. Kajee with six fellow-delegates of the Natal Indian Congress. The Indians had put their ideas into final shape during their night journey by rail from Durban to Pretoria. Smuts and his advisers accepted their memorandum without amendment. That same day, the Pretoria Agreement was proclaimed to South Africa and the world. Smuts sent telegrams to the Viceroy and the Secretary of

---

* His advisers were: Senator F. C. Clarkson, the Minister of the Interior; G. Heaton Nicholls, the Administrator of Natal; D. E. Mitchell, a member of the Executive Committee of the Natal Provincial Council; Senator D. S. Shepstone, a Natalian with a famous name, who possessed Smuts's confidence.

State—his friends Wavell and Amery—summarizing the Agreement and expressing his conviction that it would be as welcome to them as it was to him.[16]

Nothing so fortifying of Indian self-respect had happened in South Africa since Gandhi's departure thirty years ago. In Gandhi's time the Indians had practised self-help; now they were practising it again. Whereas the Cape Town Agreement of 1927 had been made over their heads, the Pretoria Agreement of 1944 was the embodiment of their own initiative. Kajee and their other leaders had shown imagination, moderation and tactical skill. They had made a large concession, but without surrendering a principle. By making that concession, they had drawn the teeth of the Pegging Act and had established the procedure of joint European–Indian action in matters of common concern. They had re-defined Indian politics in Natal as the art of the possible and had put them on to the path of ameliorative evolution.

For the Union of South Africa, all this was an immense gain. South Africa's quarrel with India, if it were to become endemic within the Commonwealth and subsequently within the United Nations, might make the politics of colour a matter of international controversy. In that controversy, South Africa might find herself with few friends. Such isolation, whether or not it proved damaging to her prestige, was likely to destroy the great opportunity of leadership in Africa which was now opening to her. Throughout the war, Smuts had kept that opportunity in the forefront of his mind.* The Pretoria Agreement of April 1944 removed a main obstacle to its realization. So at least it seemed.

On the morrow of the Pretoria Agreement, Smuts set out for the Commonwealth Conference in London and the charter-making conference in San Francisco. He set out in good heart; but he had cause, before long, to regret his unavoidable but untimely departure. 'Indeed', he told Wavell next year, 'the position has worsened since the Pretoria Agreement, which failed largely because of my absence from the country.'[17]

No sooner had he left the country than Natal rose in revolt against him.† At a packed meeting in Durban, D. E. Mitchell was shouted

---

* See pp. 410–11 above.

† To the honour of journalism in Natal it should be stated that the newspapers did not instigate this revolt; on the contrary, they commented calmly on the Pretoria Agreement.

down when he read a telegram from Smuts calling on his followers to rally to him in support of the Agreement. The Ratepayers' Association of Durban appealed to the Nationalists of the Orange Free State to come to the aid of Natal against the Asiatic hordes. It could have been counted to them for grace, perhaps, that they made no comparable appeal to the Ossewa-Brandwag.[18]

The white people of Natal blamed Smuts for not having consulted them; but in compensation for that mistake—if it was a mistake— he had put into their hands the power of veto. At the conference in Pretoria, a procedure had been adopted by common consent for giving legislative form to the Agreement: a special ordinance would be passed by the Natal Provincial Council; the Union Government would thereupon issue a proclamation to release Durban from the restrictions of the Pegging Act. The ball was now in the court of the Provincial Council. Its executive committee drafted the Occupational Control Ordinance. This Ordinance was in strict accord with the terms of the Pretoria Agreement; but the Provincial Council took the unusual step of referring it to a select committee. From the select committee's deliberations emerged the Residential Property Regulation Ordinance. It controlled not only the occupation but also the acquisition of property. In effect, it extended the Pegging Act for all time to the whole of Natal. In the judgment of Mr Justice Broome and of the Union Government's law officers, it contradicted the Pretoria Agreement. The Administrator of Natal commended it to the Provincial Councillors. They adopted it without amendment. These men had not set out deliberately to stab their leader in the back; but they were unable to think coolly on an issue which had become so heavily charged with emotion.

Inevitably, the Indians of Natal in their turn surrendered to the spirit of the herd. Moderate leaders of the Kajee type had for some time past been fending off the attacks of a politically-conscious younger generation which was repudiating the politics of compromise and taking its stand upon the abstract principles of justice. These rebels organized themselves into a new pressure group, the Anti-Segregation Council. After a few months of violent political warfare, they fought their way to domination of the Natal Indian Congress.* From that vantage point they proclaimed their demands in a ten-

---

* Kajee, however, was not yet quite finished. He retained an anchorage in the South African Indian Congress, that is to say, in the federal, as distinct from the provincial, organization.

point programme reminiscent of the Atlantic Charter. It could be summed up in two words: equality now. Those words became the battle-cry of their campaign and of the campaign which nationalist India unleashed against South Africa.

Smuts saw all around him the ruins of his endeavour. He advised the Governor-General to refuse assent to the Residential Property Regulation Ordinance; but he was bound to take more positive action than that, if only because the Pegging Act was due to expire on 31 March 1946. The Pretoria Agreement was now dead. The Broome Commission, following the secession of its Indian members, was dying. In a short interim report which bore the chairman's stamp, it put forward two suggestions for making a new start: a conference between the Indian and South African governments; a franchise for the Indians of South Africa. Smuts considered the first suggestion useless; but he made use of the second suggestion, albeit in a different manner from that contemplated by Mr Justice Broome.[19]

In a letter to Wavell of 14 December 1944, he explained the course of action that he had in mind.

It has not been easy to see a way through this welter of differences and prejudices...The Indians have moved more to the Left and have emphasized their standpoint more forcibly. The Europeans have become panicky for their future in Natal. The Indian Congress has elected a new Executive of a more uncompromising character who have pressed for their maximum programme—equal rights, equal franchise on a common roll, and all the other economic items of their programme. The break-up of the Coalition government has also made the position more difficult, as both Labour and Dominion Parties are inclined to exploit the Indian question in their own interests. My United Party is naturally in a difficult position with Natal opinion so excited and panicky. I refer to these matters to make you realize the political difficulties of the situation.

My idea is to introduce legislation into the Union Parliament which will give Indians in Natal and the Transvaal representation in both Houses of Parliament and in the Provincial Councils of those Provinces. I also wish to take further measures, mostly administrative, for Indians participating in municipal affairs, and receiving better appointments in the public and railway services and in educational and economic directions.

It is proposed...to provide for open or free areas in Natal, where ownership and occupancy will be open to everybody while in the rest of the Province ownership and occupation will be controlled by a board composed equally of European and Indian representatives under an official chairman.

He was distilling for Wavell's information the essence of his forthcoming Asiatic Land Tenure and Indian Representation Bill. He ended his letter with an expression of hope, even if it was a forlorn hope, that he might even now succeed in making a fresh start along the path of co-operation.[20]

No ground for hope existed. His one opportunity had been the Pretoria Agreement. He was deceiving himself if he imagined that the Indians would accept the parliamentary representation* which they would gain under the Bill as fair compensation for the rights of land purchase and residence which they would lose.

Even so, Smuts had to fight a hard battle with the Natalians and his party caucus to win their endorsement of his franchise proposals. The idea of *giving* votes to non-Europeans was certainly a dramatic reversal of the trend of South African thought for the past half century or more. In parliament it aroused a storm of protest. As spokesman for the Dominion party, Stallard declared that it was wrong in principle to give Indians representation in the House of Assembly. As leader of the Labour party—although it was divided—Madeley declared it wrong to give them representation in the House of Assembly, the Senate or anywhere else. As spokesman for the Nationalists, Malan denounced the Indian franchise and pledged his party to repeal it when they came to power. In the longest parliamentary debate that had occurred since Union, Smuts bore the main brunt. His party supported him, not in a fighting spirit, but in a mood of apologetic acquiescence.†

His victory in parliament did him no good with the Indians. Total justice was now their cry. They rejected his franchise offer as a miserable half loaf. They hated the whole Act. They called it the Ghetto Act. They started a campaign of passive resistance and succeeded before long in getting hundreds of their people put into gaol. In India, all the parties and all the newspapers acclaimed them as heroes and denounced their oppressors. Pandit Nehru's

* The franchise proposals were: (i) Indians in Natal and the Transvaal to be represented by two Senators (one elected, one nominated) and by three members of the House of Assembly: all to be Europeans; (ii) in the Natal Provincial Council Indians to have two representatives who need not be Europeans; (iii) voters for (i) and (ii) to possess specified qualifications of income and education; (iv) Indian voters to be on a separate roll.
    Judge Broome, in the *Interim Report*, had strongly recommended a 'qualification' franchise on the common roll, not a 'communal' franchise.

† Smuts himself piloted the Bill through the House, although that duty would normally have fallen on the Minister of the Interior. Hofmeyr declared the franchise chapter to be a sufficient compensation for the land chapter. The only speakers who criticized it were the representatives of the Natives. They rejected communal representation on principle and at the same time strongly attacked the land tenure sections of the Bill.

Provisional Government imposed an economic boycott against South Africa and recalled the Indian High Commissioner. On 22 June 1946 it made application to the Secretary-General of the United Nations to put the treatment of Indians in South Africa upon the agenda of the second part of the first session of the General Assembly. Sapru's warning to Smuts twenty-three years earlier had now fulfilled itself. South Africa's domestic policy had become at long last an issue of foreign policy. Smuts went himself to the centre of the storm. In his letters to Hofmeyr from London he made a realistic forecast of the rough passage he would have in New York.[21]

In London he took effective steps to secure the support of Great Britain and—he hoped—the other senior members of the Commonwealth. He wanted that support, not merely for fending off the Indian attack but also for winning international endorsement of his plan to incorporate South West Africa into the Union.

After the First World War, the Union had taken charge of South West Africa as a 'C' class Mandate. Under the terms of that Mandate, the Union government possessed the right to administer the Territory as an 'integral part' of South Africa; but it did not possess sovereignty. Smuts wanted that sovereignty; but he wanted it with the seal of international recognition. Not a dog would have barked during the Second World War if he had simply annexed South West Africa; but his old-fashioned respect for the legal fabric of the society of nations restrained him.* He was made to suffer for his self-restraint. At the San Francisco Conference notice was served on him that South Africa, like the other mandatory powers, would be invited to bring her mandate into the proposed trusteeship system of the United Nations. He stated some reasons to the contrary and engaged himself to submit them formally to the General Assembly when it was constituted.

Among those reasons geographical contiguity, ethnological kinship and mutual economic advantage were conspicuous; but the Union government insisted with equal emphasis that incorporation was what the population of South West Africa wanted. The European population had demanded it by a unanimous vote of the Legislative Assembly and the non-European population had approved it by

* The Russians went unchallenged when they followed a different fashion in dealing with the Baltic States.

a majority of 208,850 to 33,520. The British government declared itself satisfied with the procedure which the Administrator of South West Africa had followed in consulting the non-European population.* That, however, was not the conviction of the Indian government. When the General Assembly met, the Indian delegates took the lead in resistance to South Africa's claim. They made the counter-claim that South West Africa, like the other Mandated Territories, must be converted into a Trust Territory. On 14 December 1946, the General Assembly, by thirty-seven votes to none with nine abstentions, adopted a compromise resolution.[22] It did not insist upon trusteeship, but it rejected incorporation. Pending a final decision of the question of status, it requested the Union government to administer South West Africa 'in the spirit of the principles laid down in the mandate'.†

The Indian delegation fought Smuts on two fronts; it took the lead in thwarting his proposal for South West Africa and at the same time arraigned his government on the score of the Asiatic Land Tenure and Indian Representation Act. It denounced that Act as a segregationist measure which fell within the jurisdiction of the General Assembly on the grounds that

(1) it unilaterally repudiated the Cape Town Agreement between South Africa and India;
(2) it violated the Charter of the United Nations in respect of human rights and freedoms;
(3) it created a situation likely to impair friendly relations between India and South Africa.

The Indian delegation submitted a draft resolution which called on the Union government to 'revise their general policy and their legislative and administrative measures affecting Asiatics in South Africa, so as to bring them into conformity with the principles and purposes of the Charter'. The South African delegation submitted a counter-resolution proposing that an advisory opinion be sought

---

* The Prime Minister, Mr Atlee, told the House of Commons that Lord Hailey, who was engaged at that time on a research task in South West Africa, was satisfied with the procedure adopted for consulting the non-European opinion: namely, that each tribal Chief had a block vote equal to the number of tribesmen under him. Smuts, in his statement to the General Assembly, cited 56,790 (out of approximately 300,000) as the number of non-Europeans whom the Administration had not been able to consult.

† The question of status was temporarily settled by an advisory opinion given by the International Court on 11 July 1950, as follows: that the Mandate still stood; that the General Assembly had the same rights of supervision as the Assembly of the League had possessed (but no more); that the Union had no competence unilaterally to alter the status of South West Africa.

from the International Court of Justice on whether the matter in dispute belonged essentially, under Article 2 (7) of the charter, to South Africa's domestic jurisdiction.

The General Committee of the General Assembly referred the disputed issues in the first instance to the First and Sixth Committees (that is to say, the political and legal committees) of the General Assembly, meeting in joint session. To Smuts, this paraphernalia of committees, resolutions and speech-making seemed pseudo-legalistic, boring and futile. Temperamentally he was at odds with it all. Nevertheless he had to take it seriously. Between 21 November and 8 December 1946 he listened patiently and courteously to six successive speeches from the leader of the Indian delegation, Mrs Pandit. Five of the speeches were long; three of them were very long. They all expressed elevated sentiments; they all exposed South Africa's political and moral misdeeds.

Mrs Pandit took her stand upon the principles of justice which the Charter of the United Nations embodied. It was her main contention that justice was essentially non-discriminatory. By that standard, South Africa's racial policies were indefensible. By the same standard, Smuts replied, India's caste system and her communal conflicts were indefensible. His hearers made it plain to him that they considered such a reply to be in poor taste. Possibly he had been imprudent in letting himself be stung into making it. His main contention throughout the debate was that the Asiatic Land Tenure and Indian Representation Act belonged essentially to South Africa's domestic jurisdiction. South Africa, he argued, had broken no treaty with India; the Cape Town Agreement of 1927 and the joint communiqué of 1932 had created no treaty obligations. South Africa had violated no fundamental human rights within the terms of the Charter; there was not as yet any internationally recognized formulation of fundamental human rights. Nor had the framers of the Charter ever intended to elevate political equality to the status of a fundamental human right; to do that would mean the end of progress in countries where the less progressive races were in the majority. If peace were to be preserved in the world, Smuts continued, the fundamental principle was the one which Article 2 (7) of the Charter laid down: namely, that there should be no invasion of the domestic jurisdiction of any state. Whether or not the Asiatic Land Tenure and Indian Representation Act fell within the domestic jurisdiction of the Union of South

Africa was a question which could best be answered by the International Court of Justice.

Judged by the painfully achieved rules of diplomatic practice up to that time within the western world, Smuts's arguments were cogent; but the rules by now were obsolescent. A new precept for diplomats was coming into currency at UNO: if you have a good political argument, use it; if not, use a bad political argument; if you have no political argument at all, use a legal argument. Smuts was pinning almost his whole case upon a legal argument. It got him nowhere.[23]

In the last week of November, the First and Sixth Committees adopted a French–Mexican resolution which the General Assembly, on 8 December, passed by the required two-thirds majority: thirty-two votes in favour, fifteen against, seven abstentions. The resolution stated that, because of the treatment of Indians in South Africa, friendly relations between two Member States had been impaired and that they would be further impaired if a satisfactory settlement were not reached. It expressed the opinion that the treatment of Indians in the Union should be in conformity with the agreements concluded between the two governments and the relevant provisions of the Charter. It requested the two governments to report at the next session of the General Assembly the measures adopted to that effect.

The resolution proclaimed to the world the new diplomatic practice and the new distribution of diplomatic influence.* It proclaimed to the world the iniquities imputed to South Africa.

The world does not know or understand us [Smuts told a friend] and we feel this deeply, even when we are conscious that we are much to blame for it all. It is a good country and a good people, but the world sees its mistakes more clearly than its goodness or virtues.

I don't despair of the future, but it will not be easy to keep South Africa steady in this avalanche of condemnation which has so suddenly and un-

---

* Of the fifty-one original members of the United Nations Organization, twenty-seven were ex-colonial countries. Their preoccupations had found expression in chapters XI–XIII of the Charter, which dealt with non-Self-Governing Countries and Trusteeship. Inevitably, UNO and its Trusteeship Council became markedly more radical than the League of Nations and its Permanent Mandates Commission had been. In the vote of 8 December 1946, the line-up against South Africa was mainly the Soviet group, the Arab–Asian–African group (though the African members remained few in number throughout the next decade) and a fair number of Latin American States. This pattern, however, was not systematic: for example, France was a joint mover of the decisive resolution and Australia refrained from voting, much to Smuts's chagrin.[24]

expectedly overwhelmed it. People simply cannot understand it and are running over with resentment. It will be my part to keep them cool and if possible reflective, so that good may come out of this evil.[25]

His speeches on his return to South Africa gave on the whole an informative account of what had happened at UNO; but they contained too many phrases for unfriendly propagandists to seize upon. In a broadcast from Pretoria he laid stress upon the colour consciousness, the emotionalism, the demagogy and the lobbying which lay behind the vote of 8 December. His reporting on those matters, so far as it went, was accurate and relevant. Moreover, he tried to keep it in balance with other relevant matters.

You must realize all this [he said] and yet not despair.

Mankind has set out on a difficult road, a long road stretching far into the distant future. It is the road the United Nations Organization is now travelling away from wars towards peace and understanding. I fear that for many it is already a road to doubt and discouragement. We must realize all this and avoid wishful thinking or extravagant expectations.[26]

In view of the humiliation which his country and he himself had suffered, that passage might have been imputed to him for magnanimity. Instead, some of his phrases about the mischievous propaganda let loose in the multiple Assembly on the inflammable issues of race and colour were quoted or misquoted against him. He had not yet sufficiently learnt—and most of his fellow-countrymen had not even begun to learn—one elementary lesson of the new diplomacy: that the words of a politician in his own country are reverberant throughout the world and will certainly be seized upon by unfriendly propagandists as weapons of political warfare.

Nevertheless he proved a quick learner. During the nine months which elapsed before the next meeting of the General Assembly he managed to take some heat out of the ideological confrontation. He sent to the Trusteeship Council precisely as much information as had customarily been sent to the Permanent Mandates Commission. He side-stepped an attempt by Pandit Nehru to draw him into discussions upon the basis of the condemnatory resolution of 8 December; but he protested his readiness for genuinely exploratory discussions.[27] He cultivated his country's friendships. He provoked no new enmities. His conduct of foreign policy throughout those critical months was pragmatic, undoctrinal. He saw nothing to be gained by deliberately trailing his country's coloured coat. He saw a great deal to be gained by making his country less conspicuous upon the stage at UNO: after all, her main antagonists there had a great many other things on their minds besides South Africa. That, more or less, was the situation in September 1947, when H. G. Lawrence attended the General Assembly as South Africa's representative.

At UNO [Smuts wrote] the combat in the Council and the Assembly deepens. The language the U.S.A. and the U.S.S.R. hurl at each other in public is quite unprecedented...

Meanwhile our Indian trouble at UNO is less, and we may manage to patch up some arrangement which will look less scandalous than the quarrel which has been going on these last twelve months. Harry Lawrence is doing very well and treading the soft pedal—so is the wily Mrs Pandit who finds the atmosphere much less favourable this year at UNO.[28]

'To patch up some arrangement' was as much as he dared hope for. Since the torpedoing of the Pretoria Agreement three years before, he had never seen cause for pitching his hopes higher. Nevertheless, he continued to keep close and friendly touch with Kajee.*

In March 1946 he had received from India a telegram hotly denouncing his land and franchise proposals, but nevertheless ending—'your and South Africa's sincere friend, Gandhi'.[29] No matter what happened, his strange friendship with Gandhi remained indestructible. At the General Assembly in November 1946, a greeting came to him across the deepening chasm between their two countries. Its bearer was his main assailant, Mrs Pandit. Gandhi's parting words to her had been, she told him, 'that I should shake your hand and ask your blessing for my cause'.[30] Smuts did not fully understand Gandhi's cause. In February 1948 he felt deeply, but again did not fully understand, the tragedy of Gandhi's death. Gandhi, he wrote, was a strange phenomenon, an enigmatic figure, a prince of men.[31]

* At the time of his death late in 1947 at the age of 52, Kajee was trying to persuade Pandit Nehru's government to accept a Round Table Conference with Smuts's government without pre-conditions. At the General Assembly of 1946 he had attempted to play a conciliatory part behind the scenes; but he had not attended the General Assembly of 1947.

CHAPTER 27

COLOUR

By December 1946 South Africa's policies of colour were on the way to becoming the stuff and substance of her foreign policy. Perhaps that need not have happened. If the Pretoria Agreement had gone through in 1944 there need have been no Indian–South African quarrel two years later at the first General Assembly of the United Nations. Thereafter, the consequences of the quarrel became disproportionate to its causes; yet only by slow degrees. In 1946 and throughout the following six years the Indian government accused the South African government of denying justice to approximately 300,000 South Africans of Indian descent; but it made no accusations or demands on behalf of the many millions of black and 'coloured' South Africans. Not until Smuts had been two and a half years in his grave did the government of India and its allies at UNO mount an attack on the whole wide front against South Africa's policies of colour.*

Smuts, nevertheless, understood from the start the potentially universal significance of his particular dispute with Mrs Pandit.

Colour [he wrote on 17 November 1946] queers my poor pitch everywhere. But South Africans cannot understand. Colour bars are to them part of the divine order of things. But I sometimes wonder what our position in years to come will be when the whole world will be against us. And yet there is so much to be said for the South African point of view who fear getting submerged in black Africa. I can watch the feeling in my own family which is as good as the purest gold. It is a sound instinct of self preservation where the self is so good and not mere selfishness. What can one do about it, when (as Isie says) the Lord himself made the mistake of creating colour![1]

From some points of view he believed that the Lord, if only the politicians would let his work alone, had done a good job when He created colour. On 28 August 1933, half-way home on his first long journey by air, he had written from Khartoum—

* The attack was mounted in Resolution 616A of 5 December 1952. Two conspicuous landmarks along the road to this doctrinal confrontation were: on the UNO side, the Declaration of Human Rights in 1948; on the South African side, the Group Areas Act of 1950.

473

I smell Africa here...This is Africa, and I feel at rest. I have been much struck by the continuous graduations from the white type in Northern Europe to the African negro as this trip progresses—English–French–Italian–Greeks–Egyptians–Soudanese, and so on to the Bantu and the negro. The change of shading and of type is most marked. And the characteristics vary even more. I suppose all this variety is really an enrichment, whatever one may think of the comparative values of these types. I must say that after the Nordic I like the real African best; but that may be my continental 'provinciality', as Whitehead would call it.[2]

He felt the fascination of primitive Africa. It became embodied for him in the person of Modjadji, South Africa's famous Rain-Queen. A strange chain of circumstances led to their mutual acquaintance and understanding. In 1925 his daughter Cato and her friend Eileen Jensen had a motor accident in the neighbourhood of Modjadji's village and received great kindness from her. Smuts wrote to thank her, and his wife sent her a parcel of gifts in token of gratitude. A few years later, Eileen Jensen married Jack Krige, a nephew of the Smuts's. He and she were both social anthropologists and together they did field work among the Lovedu, Modjadji's tribe. Smuts became interested in their work and was also eager to see the famous hill of cycads, or Modjadji palms, in the neighbourhood of the tribe's head kraal. In 1936 he paid Modjadji a visit, which his niece recollected as follows:[3]

Oom Jan seemed instinctively to have the right touch. He was not put out by the fact that he was unacquainted with tribal procedure and Lovedu court etiquette. He behaved towards the Queen in much the same way, and accorded her as much dignity, as I imagine he might have in the case of any diplomatic dignitary in Europe. He stood up when she came in, went up to her and shook hands, exchanged greetings and during the course of conversation referred to her kindness to Cato in the past. Jack and I discussed the scene later and agreed that no advice which we as anthropologists could have given him, had we been asked, would have achieved what Oom Jan did by his natural, cordial manner. Oom Jan made a tremendous impression on the Lovedu court.

When war broke out and Smuts became Prime Minister, he received a letter from the Rain-Queen. 'We do not know', she told him, 'how to write to a man who now has the Crown of South Africa. All we can say is that we rejoice exceedingly because you are now a ruler over the whole country.'*[4]

---

* Smuts wrote a foreword to *The Realm of a Rain-Queen*, by E. Jensen Krige and J. D. Krige (London, 1943). Like the foreword he wrote in 1936 to Monica Wilson's *Reaction to*

Eileen Krige gave evidence that Smuts had never, in the whole course of her close acquaintanceship with him, treated the African as a child or an inferior. On the other hand, the Hoernles and some other members of the Institute of Race Relations criticized him on the ground that he cared chiefly for primitive Africans, to the neglect of the urgent problems of African urbanization. In 1929, when he delivered his Rhodes Memorial Lectures, that criticism would have had its grounds; but it did not have them in February 1942 when, with Hoernle himself in the chair, he addressed the Institute of Race Relations in Cape Town.[5]

Racial issues, he declared, had been too much clouded by theorizing; whereas they called for calm, scientific, factual investigation. Too many people wasted their time on arguments for equality or for racial superiority, whereas the main problems for scientific investigation were: first, the diverse and unequal levels of cultural advance; secondly, the integrative processes of economic development. Smuts took economic development and its social consequences as his main theme. He heavily emphasized South Africa's economic expansion, the labour-hunger of her industries and the rapid growth of her urban populations. These, he said, were observable facts. They refuted the theory that whites and blacks could live in separate territorial compartments. Rather too sweepingly, he equated that theory with the policy of segregation, which had originated—he said—in the white minority's fear of being swamped.

Attempts, as you know, have been made to get round this fear by the policy commonly called 'segregation'—the policy of keeping Europeans and Africans completely apart for their own self-preservation...The high expectation that we entertained of that policy has been sadly disappointed.

How can it be otherwise? The whole trend both in this country and throughout Africa has been in the opposite direction. The whole movement of development here on this continent has been for closer contacts to be established between the various races and the various sections of the community...

...Isolation has gone and segregation has fallen on evil days too.

But there are other phenomena springing out of these conditions... A revolutionary change is taking place among the Native peoples of

Conquest (London, 1936), it revealed his scientific interest in the tasks of the social anthropologist. It also revealed that he had grown during the intervening seven years, not only in scientific, but also in human, understanding. The correspondence between Smuts and Modjadji has been preserved among his papers. I am greatly in debt to Professor Eileen Krige for an illuminating memorandum which she wrote in reply to some questions which I addressed to her. I am similarly in debt to Professor Monica Wilson.

Africa through the movement from the country to the towns—the movement from the old Reserves in the Native areas to the big European centres of population. Segregation tried to stop it. It has, however, not stopped it in the least. The process has been accelerated. You might as well try to sweep the ocean back with a broom.

He went on to discuss the social implications of industrialization and urbanization. It was his main contention that the framework of social policy must be extended to include all races.

When people ask me what the population of South Africa is I never say it is two millions. I think it is an outrage to say it is two millions. This country has a population of over ten millions, and that outlook which treats the African and Native as not counting, is making the ghastliest mistake possible. If he is not much more, he is the beast of burden; he is the worker and you need him. He is carrying this country on his back.

It followed that the country was bound both in duty and in interest to satisfy his reasonable needs. Smuts enumerated those needs under specific heads: education, health, housing, nutrition, wages.

His address had its roots in his respect for fact; but in delivering it he made rods for his own back. The reactionaries seized upon his references to the failure of segregation as a demonstration of his intention to mingle the races indiscriminately in the big cities.* The radicals challenged him to make good as a politician his words as a preacher.

He went out of his way to invite radical criticism. In particular, he invited criticism from the seven M.P.s—four in the Senate, three in the House of Assembly—who represented the Natives under the Act of 1936. In an address to the Senate about Native Policy on 5 May 1941 he said—

The very fact that there are members here and also in the other place whose specific duty it is to attend to these matters marks an enormous progress in public opinion and I hope that it will be followed up. Do not mind being called agitators. Let them call you any names they like, but get on with the job and see that matters that vitally require attention, Native health, Native food, the treatment of Native children and all those cognate questions that are basic to the welfare of South Africa, are attended to.[6]

They took him at his word. As a team of critics during and after the war they proved themselves formidable. An immense disproportion

---

* He had specifically justified residential segregation, but he would have done well to remember that the word segregation as South Africans used it had many different meanings. His speech would have been less vulnerable to attack if he had taken pains to make clear which particular meaning he had in mind.

existed between their number and the impact they made upon parliamentary discussion. Three at least of the seven possessed outstanding ability.* Edgar Brookes, Donald Molteno and Margaret Ballinger, in their respective academic fields of public administration, law and economics, stood head and shoulders above the great majority of their fellow parliamentarians. Margaret Ballinger, in particular, achieved an extraordinarily high standard of parliamentary eloquence in the attacks she made, year after year and session after session, upon the government's shortcomings in the economic and social sectors of Native policy.[7]

According to her bill of indictment government action fell conspicuously short of the urgent needs of the Native population both in the country and the cities. In the Native rural areas, the government was failing to maintain the pace of land purchase under the Native Trust and Land Act of 1936.† In the urban areas, it was failing to provide houses for the black workers who were sucked into the war industries month by month in their thousands and tens of thousands. Mrs Ballinger drew her evidence from official government publications and the statements of Ministers. In 1943, the Social and Economic Planning Council estimated that 125,000 new houses were urgently required for non-Europeans. In 1947, the Native Affairs Department estimated the need at 159,000 houses, with additional accommodation for 106,900 unmarried workers. The Minister of Health admitted on 3 May 1946 that housing had become 'a crisis as well as a problem'; but year after year went by, Mrs Ballinger declared, without any effective government action to cope with the crisis. Similarly, year after year went by, she complained, without any constructive handling of the great labour migrations. The Urban Areas Act and the multifarious pass laws imposed restrictions upon the mobility of black labour, whereas the real industrial need, in her view, was more labour mobility and better guidance. She quoted the interdepartmental committee (the Smit Committee)‡ which in 1942 recommended a series of far-reaching innovations—

* A fourth very able representative, Senator D. Rheinalt Jones, resigned in mid-1942 in order to become full-time Director of the Institute of Race Relations. At the time of his resignation he wrote Smuts a letter of warm gratitude for the help he had given to the Native Representatives and their constituents.[8]

† Among the reasons for the slackened pace of land purchase was the loss of specialist officers to the armed forces.

‡ The chairman, D. Smit, was Secretary of the Native Affairs Department. A few years later he entered parliament as a supporter of Smuts.

relaxation of the pass laws, the establishment of labour exchanges, subsidization of the travel costs of Native workers. The government approved many of these recommendations but delayed putting them into practice.* Mrs Ballinger criticized its performance as invariably too little and too late. The Smit Committee, for example, had made various recommendations for raising the incomes of black workers and their families, and in 1943 the Lansdown Committee recommended increases of the wages of Native mineworkers; but Mrs Ballinger accused the government of implementing these recommendations only by halves.

The Native workers, she asserted, needed not only improved material conditions but more freedom, starting with freedom for collective bargaining. The Industrial Conciliation Act excluded Natives from its definition of 'employees' and, consequently, from the processes of industrial conciliation. The law did not recognize Native trade unions. To a request for recognition the Minister of Labour replied on 18 April 1942 with a flat refusal. That same year the government promulgated War Measure 145, which made it illegal for black workers (but not for white workers) to strike for better conditions. From one parliamentary session to the next Mrs Ballinger maintained an offensive against War Measure 145. In doing so she broadened the dispute about wages and welfare into a dispute about status. On 23 January 1947, after giving the government some credit for genuine improvements in the material conditions of Natives, she declared:

Behind our whole policy of social improvement and of social uplift lies the basic denial of human rights which destroys politically the whole virtue of that position. The essence of the situation, the essence of the criticism that we are facing in the world over our colour policies is in effect that none of our non-European communities in this country can look forward to anything that we can call real citizenship in South Africa. That is the real gravamen of the charge.[9]

The indictment was formidable. Mrs Ballinger and her colleagues superbly fulfilled the task entrusted to them of stating Native grievances. That was their *raison d'être* as Native Representatives; it was not to be expected that they should make out a case for the

---

* The Ministers of Native Affairs and of Justice did put into practice an important recommendation about the pass laws, namely, that no Native should be arrested unless suspected of a crime. Following a big increase of crime, the administration of the pass laws was tightened up again two years later.

defence. Nevertheless that case existed. The government had great difficulties to contend with—some jurisdictional and administrative, others strictly economic. Jurisdictionally—to cite only two examples —hospitals were a responsibility of the Provinces, houses a responsibility of the municipalities: to prod those authorities into action was the government's thankless task. Administratively, half a dozen or more departments of government—Native Affairs, Labour, Mines, Industry, Health, Education, Justice, Finance—exercised their fragmented responsibilities for the peace, order and welfare of the Native population. When policy recommendations—for example, the recommendations of the Smit Committee—arose out of interdepartmental investigation, the task of giving effect to them was widely dispersed among the separate departments. No single Minister held responsibility for co-ordinating and galvanizing all departmental activities within the sphere of Native policy. Smuts could not possibly shoulder that responsibility; his tasks as Prime Minister, Minister of External Affairs, Minister of Defence and Commander-in-Chief of the Armed Forces did not leave him time enough. Hofmeyr might have shouldered it had he stood in the same relation to Smuts as Anderson stood in relation to Churchill; but Hofmeyr did not take that view of his function on the home front.*

The administrative machine, even if it had been perfect, would still have had a near-impossible task to cope with. Between the censuses of 1936 and 1946 the Native population of South African cities rose from 1,141,642 to 1,689,053. That increase measured in a rough and ready way the expansion of industrial employment, particularly of war-generated industrial employment. By definition, such employment had its obverse, namely, the siphoning of economic resources out of the industries whose function it was to satisfy normal peacetime needs. Mrs Ballinger seemed sometimes to forget that there was a war on, and—when the war at last was over—to forget the time that must inevitably go by before the redeployment of economic resources could catch up with all the work that could not possibly have been done during the six years of war. In her speeches she seldom if ever referred to the comparable difficulties of other war-afflicted countries; yet all of them without exception discovered that house-building—to cite but one example—was inevitably and catastrophically a casualty of the war economy. Nor did she ever

* See p. 423 above.

make comparisons between South Africa's attempt to cope with the rush to the cities and similar attempts which other countries in other continents were making, or were failing to make. She appeared sometimes to assume both that South Africa had a monopoly of shanty towns and also that no justification could ever exist for influx control of any kind.*

Smuts admitted the shortcomings of his government; but in extenuation of them he pleaded the immensity and speed of the social changes and the impossibility of coping all at once with all the consequential problems. In no less than twelve speeches between March 1945 and 1948 he declared that of all the resources which were in scarce supply, time was the most scarce. For example, in discussing the control of population movements and the need for a system of labour exchanges, he said in the House of Assembly on 18 March 1948—

I hope we shall have a system like that. But now we are fumbling about; we are just trying to meet these problems by one expedient after another, and we do not find any real solution. I admit that—but be merciful; do not go too fast. We are cluttered up with problems; we hope to clear them up, the health question, the housing question, this question of migration. They will all have to be sorted out, and I hope they will be sorted out in a short number of years. But right now there is a congestion of these problems which is greater than the will of man can deal with...

In the meantime we have had to resort to these makeshifts, we have had to use these dodges—that is all they are—and I know that on the benches of the Native Representatives there is a great deal of impatience which is almost becoming intolerance, but the goodwill is there. The difficulty is in a very short time to meet situations which have come upon us all of a heap within a couple of years owing to conditions over which we have not had control.[10]

That appeal to the Native Representatives to show some understanding of the government's difficulties was not unreasonable. Moreover, the government had to its credit some substantial achievements. Hofmeyr's budgets of 1944 and 1945 extended social security beyond the barriers of colour by making old age and invalidity pensions the right of every South African, albeit at different levels of payment in accordance with the different social standards associated with race and colour. In 1945 a special Act made Native education, which

* This controversial issue was discussed both realistically and humanely by the Fagan Commission; see p. 490 below.

hitherto had been paid for in large measure by the poll tax, wholly a charge upon the central revenue. Actual expenditure on Native education increased during the period of Smuts's government from £909,340 in 1939 to £4,843,000 in 1947: of the latter figure, £854,000 was assigned to a school feeding scheme. Meanwhile, the Native College at Fort Hare was brought under the same rules of financial assistance as applied to all the other degree-giving institutions. In the fields of health and housing the government steadily stepped up its financial aid to the provincial and municipal authorities. In the field of wage determination, it made the cost-of-living allowances obligatory.

In her speech of 23 January 1947* Mrs Ballinger agreed that these achievements were substantial; but she went on to call them insufficient. In effect, she challenged the government to extend 'real citizenship' across the colour line. Smuts took note of that challenge but he did not see clearly how it could be met.

This and last week [he wrote on 6 February] I have been giving my attention to the next moves to be made in our Native and Indian questions —both at present in a jam which must be broken... The fact is that both Native and Indian leaders want *status*... Mrs Ballinger said the other day in Parliament that in social and economic advances we have a strong case, but the Natives want *rights* and not improvements. There we bump up against the claim for equality which is most difficult to satisfy except in very small doses which will not satisfy the leaders. I have so far done my best to follow the other line (of improvements) as less open to white prejudice and opposition. I must try again.[11]

His experience of recent years held out small hope of his new attempt proving successful. The Native leaders whom he had to reckon with belonged to two organizations, the African National Congress and the Native Representative Council, the former a voluntary political association, the latter an association officially established under the legislation of 1936. At the end of the war the African National Congress had a membership not far short of 5,000. Almost all its members were educated and deeply imbued with twentieth-century ideas of progress. In December 1945 they issued a Declaration of Rights which demanded item by item immediate and total equality between Africans and Europeans in law, politics and society.[12] Possibly they did not intend that declaration to be

* See p. 478 above.

taken *au pied de la lettre*; but their expectations, no matter how they might be scaled down, exceeded by far the concessions which any South African government would or could make to them.*

Far more disappointing to Smuts was the widening breach between the government and the Native Representative Council.[13] He had personally a vested interest in the success of that institution because he had accepted it as an important element of the *quid pro quo* when Native voters in the Cape were shifted from the common to the communal roll.† The new Council, he had said then, would give to the Natives a constitutional organ which they could use to ventilate their grievances and declare their interests. He had even looked forward to the day when the Council might become not merely 'the crown' of local self-government for the Native community but a legislative body on the national scale. Instead, the Council became a talking shop.

Its functions were:

(1) to consider and report upon such Bills, draft proclamations and other matters as were referred to it by the Minister of Native Affairs, and upon any matters specifically affecting Native interests;

(2) to recommend to Parliament or any Provincial Council such legislation as it considered necessary in Native interests.

Its composition was:

(1) six official members, including, as chairman, the Secretary of the Native Affairs Department;

(2) four Natives nominated by the Governor-General;

(3) twelve Natives elected indirectly by electoral colleges.

It was, in short, a purely advisory body with a conservative composition. Nevertheless, among the twelve elected members a few possessed cross membership with the African National Congress.

* Here some terminological observations may be appropriate. Originally (see pp. 117–18 above) the Congress had called itself the 'South African National Congress', but at a quite early stage of its history it had deleted the word 'South'. By the beginning of the war, if not earlier, the word 'African' had come to assume an emotive significance comparable with that of the word 'Afrikaner'. In 1939 the Native Representative Council passed a resolution requesting the government to use the word 'African' rather than the word 'Native'. Smuts personally felt no repugnance to that request; in his famous speech of 21 January 1942 he used 'African' and 'Native' indifferently. His first parliamentary use of 'African' occurred on 3 March 1947. It provoked queries and taunts from the Opposition benches but Smuts replied: 'They prefer to call themselves Africans and why not? I call myself an African. I do not see why people should not call themselves by the name they like, so long as you know what they are.' That point of view did not commend itself to the Prime Ministers who succeeded him. Nor did the word 'Native' long survive in official usage. For a statement of the reasons put forward in favour of the word 'Bantu', see W. W. M. Eiselen's article 'Harmonious Multi-Community Development', in *Optima*, March 1959.   † See pp. 264–6 above.

Colour

Hopefulness and a strong desire to co-operate constructively with the government were dominant in the N.R.C. during the early years of its short history; but thereafter it rapidly lost confidence in its capacity to fulfil any useful function within the existing constitutional framework of the Union. It became convinced that the real initiative in advising the government and preparing draft legislation remained where it had always been, namely, with the government departments and the government-nominated Native Affairs Commission. In 1943 it requested the presence of the Minister of Native Affairs at all future meetings of the Council, and the presence of other Ministers whenever the Council had occasion to consider the work of their departments. In 1944 it asked the government to abolish the Native Affairs Commission.* Meanwhile, it had come to two important constitutional conclusions: first, that its own numbers and functions must be enlarged; secondly, that African representation in parliament must be increased. Those two conclusions took shape in 1943 in the report of 'The Recess Committee on Representation'. Its main recommendations were:

1. adult male suffrage with direct individual voting (instead of the existing system of indirect election);
2. an increase in the number of electoral areas from 4 to 6;
3. an increase in the number of senators representing the Natives, *pari passu* with any increase that might occur in the Senate's total numbers;
4. an increase from 3 to 10 in the number of Native representatives in the House of Assembly;
5. enlargement of the Native Representative Council (to 48 instead of 12 elected members) and the assignment to it of such legislative powers as might, after due consideration, be thought fitting.

Those proposals were not revolutionary. They all fell within the framework of communal representation as established by the Act of 1936. The Act itself contained provision for enlarging the membership of the Native Representative Council. General Hertzog himself had intended originally to give the Council legislative functions. As for parliamentary representation, the proposed jump from three to ten members in the House of Assembly might seem shocking to some people; but those ten would have constituted only one fifteenth of the total membership. Hertzog's original draft Bill of

* As early as 1939 a resolution of the Council had expressed distrust of the Native Affairs Commission. This resolution followed tactless treatment of the Councillors by G. Heaton Nicholls, the then Chairman of the N.A.C.

1926 had made provision for seven Native Representatives. To add three to that figure after the lapse of eighteen years was a modest proposal.

Nevertheless, the Councillors from that time onwards grew rapidly more radical. In 1944 they carried resolutions calling for the total repeal of the pass laws and the scrapping of the segregation policy. In August 1946 Councillor Thema put the following resolution on their agenda:

This Council condemns the policy of segregation embodied in the Natives Land Act of 1913, the Natives Land and Trust Act of 1936, the Natives Urban Areas Act and its subsequent amendments, and the Representation of Natives in Parliament Act of 1936 as unjust and oppressive in that it has hopelessly failed to separate equitably Africans from Europeans, territorially, residentially and politically, but has imposed upon the African people disabilities which suppress their natural aspirations and the right to work out their own destiny. Further it entrenches the domination of European interests over those of Africans and prevents Africans from achieving the purpose for which they were created in God's image, namely to be co-workers with God in the creation of a better and peaceful human life.

In the opinion of this Council, the only policy of segregation which may be acceptable is the one that envisages the division of South Africa into two separate states—one for Europeans and the other for Africans; otherwise the policy of segregation should be abandoned, and the policy which is in keeping with the letter and spirit of the United Nations Organization Charter should be adopted and pursued.

That resolution was the product of crisis. Circumstances had never before been so disastrously unpropitious for a meeting of the Council. At Lovedale there had been student riots. On the Witwatersrand 50,000 African mineworkers had come out on strike. The police had fired into a body of the strikers and had killed some of them. Smuts had justified the police. Meanwhile the Councillors were taking train for Pretoria. On arrival there they found that their designated chairman, the Secretary of the Native Affairs Department, had been called away on strike business; a subordinate official was in the chair. They had to endure another humiliation. As far back as 1938, they had started petitioning the government for a meeting-place of their own. Their petitions had been in vain, but hitherto they had been given respectable accommodation in the Pretoria City Hall. In August 1946 that accommodation was denied them by the Nationalist majority of the Pretoria City Council. They found themselves shepherded into cramped quarters in the Department of Labour, where the lavatories were for whites only.

In those quarters they took stock of the frustrations of nine years:

We have reached a stage [Councillor Godlo said] when we feel that our coming to Pretoria and pretending to represent the people to place their grievances before the Government is just a waste of time.

Councillor Mosaka made the same point more argumentatively.

The experiment has failed [he said] because the Government, which is the author of segregation, and therefore the author of this Native Representative Council, never intended to honour its pledge—it has never bothered itself for one single moment about the Council...We have been fooled. We have been asked to co-operate with a toy telephone. We have been speaking into an apparatus which cannot transmit sound and at the end of which there is nobody to receive the message. Like children, we have taken pleasure at the echo of our own voices.

The Councillors spent the greater part of 14 August locked in procedural quarrels with the young official in the chair. On 15 August they scrapped Councillor Thema's motion. Councillor Moroka carried a more belligerent motion:

This Council, having since its inception brought to the notice of the Government the reactionary character of Union Native policy of segregation in all its ramifications, deprecates the Government's post-war continuation of a policy of Fascism which is the antithesis and negation of the letter and the spirit of the Atlantic Charter and the United Nations Charter.

The Council therefore in protest against this breach of faith towards the African people in particular and the cause of world freedom in general, resolves to adjourn this session, and calls upon the Government forthwith to abolish all discriminatory legislation affecting non-Europeans in this country.

The resolution of 15 August 1946 brought the Native Representative Council into step with the African National Congress and the Indian National Congress. 'It means', Hofmeyr wrote to Smuts,* 'that the (hitherto) moderate intellectuals of the Professor Matthews type are now committed to an extreme line against colour discrimination, and have carried the Chiefs with them. We can't afford to allow them to be swept into the extremist camp, but I don't see what we can do to satisfy them, which would be tolerated by

* Smuts had just set out for the Peace Conference.

European public opinion.' The government, Smuts replied, would have to liberalize its social policy, but it would also have to carry public opinion along with it. Now that the war was over he had hopes of making rapid progress with 'practical social policy away from politics'. Hofmeyr shared those hopes.[14] On 20 November he expounded them to the Native Representative Council when it resumed its interrupted sessions. His speech made no impression. The Council rejected 'social policy away from politics'. On 26 November 1946 it adjourned for the third and last time that year.*

Smuts, meanwhile, had been suffering a severe mauling at the General Assembly of the United Nations. The sequel in South Africa was an exacerbation of defiant feelings and extremist attitudes.

The fully publicized discussions at UNO [Smuts wrote on his return home] are having a great effect in all directions. We even hear about them from our domestic and farm Natives who really have nothing to complain of, but are deeply stirred by all this talk of equality and non-discrimination. I am so anxious to stay this rot and get a move on to better relations, but it is even more difficult now in view of these Native claims which have just the opposite effect upon European mentality. Both extremes are gathering strength.

South Africans are repelled into rebellion and say 'let us go our own way regardless of what an un-understanding world thinks of us'. UNO has accentuated the extremes...the bridge builder finds the chasm widening.[15]

Smuts had been born on Queen Victoria's birthday half-way through Queen Victoria's reign. It was the age of Charles Darwin, Bishop Stubbs, Walter Bagehot and the Fabian Society, an age which took for granted 'the inevitability of gradualness', not only in biological but also in social and political evolution. Smuts had grown up with the assumption that time was a commodity in plentiful supply; but now in his old age he saw time as a rushing torrent threatening destruction to his life's work. All the same he cherished the hope of being able even now to build a bridge across the torrent. In March 1947 he took counsel with his friends the Moores, who had an intimate knowledge of colour conflict in Africa and latterly had been gaining comparable knowledge of it in Asia. 'The world', he told them, 'is reeling between the two poles of White and Colour.' His own task was to keep South Africa steady—but on what basis,

---

* The Native Representative Council did not meet again until January 1949 when it was summoned to hear the death sentence passed on it by Dr Malan's government.

he asked them, and by what method? On the one hand, he was a humanist and the author of the Preamble to the Charter; on the other hand he was a South African of European descent, proud of his heritage of civilization and determined to maintain it. At UNO he had been branded a hypocrite. He rejected that accusation; yet how, he asked, was he to resolve the conflict of his loyalties?[16]

Lady Moore told him in effect that he could not resolve it.

I can see no possibility of compromise in the colour question; either the white race fights for its supremacy, confident of its superiority; or we admit that all men are alike under God and that Christianity and the other codes of ethics in which we believe make no distinction between a white skin and a brown, so why should we? The trouble is that the subject is one which it is difficult to be logical about because of the underlying fear, repulsion or whatever it is that the white man feels for the black and which to you in South Africa, with generations of colour-strife in your blood is an essential element of your characters of which you are almost unaware.

English people, with their copy-book maxims and their smug humanitarian theories, cannot understand the instinct inherited from forebears who have had to fight black races for their very existence...

How *can* you have a practical compromise?

Yet she knew that his public duty and personal character imposed upon him an exhausting and never-ceasing struggle.

Your personal problem [she continued] is so complex. Not only are there the two sides of your nature you speak of—the humanitarian and the South African—but there are the people by whose vote you rule South Africa, many amongst them hopelessly bigoted and deaf to reason on the colour subject but liable to turn extremist and ruin the future of South Africa should they lose their faith in you and your policies. You can't afford to come into the open with your real views; not for your own sake, for you don't care about that, but for the sake of the nation which for fifty years you have created and built up, cubit by cubit, with your own heart and hand and ceaseless toil. Isn't this true? I am sorry for you, for the conflict in your mind must exhaust you; but still more because, even if you come to conclusions that satisfy your own intellect and conscience, you may, from force of circumstances, have to compromise with yourself and say publicly not what *you* think but what it is best for people to hear.[17]

If that assessment of his situation was valid, his hopes of building bridges across the chasm of colour were self-delusive. Mrs Ballinger, however, submitted an optimistic assessment of his opportunities.

I want the Prime Minister to believe [she said in the House on 23 January 1947] that the volume of liberal opinion is much stronger than its vocal

The Darkening Road

support would lead one to suppose. There is a solid core of liberal opinion in this country that is prepared to take their stand on the basis of recognizing the rights of the Native population of this country to aspire to ultimate citizenship. There is a widening support for the principle of equal rights for all civilized men...I appeal to the Right Hon. the Prime Minister to integrate this movement of opinion.[18]

In effect, she was telling him that the electors would follow him if he led them boldly along the road towards racial equality. The evidence of previous elections hardly justified that prediction. In 1924 and 1929 the electors had followed Hertzog when he promised to lead them along the opposite road. To be sure, they had followed Smuts in 1943; but he had taken pains on that occasion to play up the war issue and play down the colour issue. His tactics on Native policy, as he expounded them to a friend, had been as follows—

Of course [he wrote] the Natives are not without a case. They are dreadfully underpaid and feel the economic stress very severely in the towns. I have urged our Wage Board to accelerate the determination of higher minimum wages for unskilled workers, but the needs and the demands are outpacing these reforms. Hence the unrest...I am going to do whatever is politically possible, and may even exceed the limits of political expediency. But I dare not do anything which will outpace public opinion too much on the eve of an election which may be the most important ever held in this country...I shall do as much of the right thing as possible, but always keep before me the paramount necessity of winning the election! Don't you agree that this is right? What will it profit this country if justice is done to the underdog and the whole caboodle then, including that underdog, is handed over to the Wreckers?

He could not have described more succinctly than in that last sentence the mechanics of the struggle for power within an electorate established predominantly upon the principle of racial discrimination.[19]

In so far as he accepted larger risks in 1948 than he had accepted during the war, he did so with his eyes open. His election campaign in 1948 was not a last-minute improvisation. In the New Year of 1947, after he had returned battle-worn from the United Nations, he set himself the almost impossible task of trying to restore mutual confidence between the government and the Native Representative Council. In May 1947 he held talks in Cape Town with Professor Z. K. Matthews* and five other members of the Council. It was

* Professor Z. K. Matthews, born at Kimberley 1901, educated at Lovedale, Fort Hare, Yale and London; was the first African graduate of the University College of Fort Hare

understood on both sides that the talks were exploratory; but Smuts submitted the outlines of a plan for making a fresh start with the N.R.C. He envisaged an all-African, all-elective Council of fifty members, meeting under its own chairman, spending its own revenues, and making laws within the sphere (still to be defined) of its own interests. He also envisaged the recognition of African trade unions and other wide extensions of African rights in the urban areas; but he said that he could not go into the details until Mr Justice Fagan and his colleagues of the Native Laws Commission had submitted their report.* He did *not* envisage any immediate extension of African parliamentary representation. That was the crux. Professor Matthews and his colleagues would not withdraw the demands that had been stated in 1943 by the Recess Committee on Representation. Mainly on that issue, the caucus of the Native Representative Council decided that the government's proposals in their present form were inadequate.† The negotiations, nevertheless, would almost certainly have been resumed had not Smuts fallen from power six months later. In the year of his death, his most formidable challenger from the liberal side, Mrs Ballinger, gave him credit for pursuing them in good faith and with courage.

But this [she told the House] I will say for the United Party Government, that when they had made that mess, they were prepared to see what they could do to clear it up...and the Rt. Hon. the ex-Prime Minister had at least got plans for discussing all these difficulties with the very people who, when Mr Hofmeyr met them, were not prepared to discuss the situation at all. And that is what I call statesmanship.[20]

and in 1936 became Professor of African Studies there; from 1941 to 1950 was a member of the Native Representative Council and in 1941 joined the African National Congress; in 1952–3 was Henry Luce Visiting Professor of World Christianity at the Theological Seminary in New York; in 1956, when Acting Principal of Fort Hare, was arrested on a charge of high treason and stood trial until 1958, when the charge was withdrawn; in 1960 was detained for approximately six months under emergency regulations but was not charged; in 1961 received an honorary degree from Rhodes University; in 1961 was appointed by the World Council of Churches as Area Secretary for Africa; in 1966 became the respresentative of Botswana at UNO.

   * Henry Allan Fagan (1889–1963) of Tulbagh in the Cape, graduated in Arts at Stellenbosch and in Law at London; was an Advocate of the Supreme Court in Cape Town, Assistant-Editor of *Die Burger* (1916–19) and Professor of Law at Stellenbosch (1920–33); in 1933 was elected an M.P.; in 1938 took Cabinet Office under General Hertzog; in 1943 was appointed to the Bench; from 1957 to 1959 was Chief Justice of South Africa; published poetry, plays and short stories in Afrikaans and was awarded the Hertzog prize for Literature. For the report of the Native Laws Commission ('the Fagan Report') see p. 490 below.

   † The decision of the caucus was made public in November 1947.

Still, Smuts could not continue to practise statesmanship unless he got himself re-elected. His parliamentary speeches from 1946 to 1948 revealed the risks that he would be running on polling day. In a speech of 17 April 1946 he told the House that the idea of trusteeship or guardianship, which he had thought sufficient four years earlier when he addressed the Institute of Race Relations, might not for ever contain all the answers. 'But the idea and the practice of guardianship also mean', he declared, 'that as those portions of the population who are under our guardianship develop, one must to a certain extent grant them political rights.'[21] That was a cautious intimation of his readiness to consider at some future time some limited improvements upon Native parliamentary representation as established in 1936; but it was not his programme for the approaching elections. 'Practical social policy away from politics' was as large an electoral risk as he dared accept. Still, he accepted it forthrightly. In speech after speech in and outside parliament he insisted that South Africa was a unitary and dynamic economy within which white and black South Africans had no option but to work together: 'we need them', he said, 'and they need us.' He warned his fellow citizens against the propaganda of fear: if they preached the black peril, the Natives would soon start preaching the white peril. Hope, not fear, he declared, was the proper attitude of mind. At an industrial exhibition in Pretoria on 18 August 1947 he reminded his audience of industry's immense achievement in conquering poverty in the white community. 'Is it too much to hope', he continued, 'that a similar achievement awaits industry in regard to another and no less grave problem—the reclamation of the poor Native, now floating like flotsam and jetsam to our great cities?'[22]

Towards the end of March 1948 the Native Laws Commission presented its report.[23] It embodied the social philosophy which Smuts had been expounding and gave him ammunition for his electoral campaign. Its major premiss was that black South Africans—not only the men but the women and children—must be accepted henceforward as a permanent part of the urban population. It declared territorial separation of the races to be a self-deceiving dream. It declared migratory labour to be an obsolete system. It did not deny the need for some controls over the movement of black people to the cities, but it rejected the time-honoured doctrine that they had no right to come to them or to stay in them except when they ministered to the needs of white people.* It did not propose immediate and total abolition of the pass laws, but it did propose their rationalization and relaxation. At the same time it made proposals more comprehensive than any that had been made hitherto for a system of labour bureaux which would help to get the right workers into the right employments. Comprehensiveness was a main virtue of the Fagan Report. Flexibility was another of its virtues. South Africa, it insisted, was a dynamic society in which the law must leave room for growth, change and experiment.

On behalf of the United party Smuts accepted the principles and proposals of the Fagan Report. Contemporaneously the National party accepted its own Sauer Report.† The first document tried to explain how South Africans who differed from each other in race and colour could live together; the second document tried to explain how they could live apart. The general election of 1948 was destined to become a battle between those opposite conceptions of social reality in South Africa.

* See p. 125 above.
† The Sauer Report was presented four days after the Fagan Report. It embodied the ideas of the emerging SABRA group. See pp. 500–1 below.

CHAPTER 28

ADVERSITY

WHEN the war ended Smuts was feeling anxious on his wife's behalf. 'She is rather frail', he wrote to a friend, 'and particularly weak in the legs, so that the least walking fatigues her. And you know how active she is by nature, and can understand our difficulty in restraining her from doing too much.' He met that difficulty by bringing his daughter Louis* to Doornkloof to look after her mother. He himself, if only he would have admitted it, needed some looking after. He was seventy-five years old and seriously run down. The scratches that he sometimes got when he went walking in the bush were taking a much longer time to heal nowadays than they had taken formerly. He told his friends that it was 'all the slow pace of old age'.[1] Looking back on the war years he asked himself at times how he had managed to keep going. The cause itself, he answered, had given him the momentum to win through.

In war, you have the danger and the exultation, the sacrifice and the *élan* of the spirit. But what supports you in the humdrum drudgery of ordinary life?...What is the new high incentive?...

He found no answer to that question. He said that he was doing his best—

But I do sometimes feel terribly tired, and fit only for bed when I get home in the evening...

You will see from this arid letter that I have a drought of the soul. One feels not only tired but parched and empty spiritually. I suppose we have to be patient and 'wait on the Lord', as the older generation said.[2]

Mercifully, he did not have a long waiting. In the New Year of 1946 he began to feel a new flow of strength and zest. On 16 January he again made the ascent of Table Mountain—not indeed at his old pace; but he made it.[3] He felt the strain of his overseas missions; but at UNO in November 1946 he took time off to explore museums in New York and to exchange ideas with America's leading pre-

* Louis (so named after Louis Botha) was the youngest daughter and a qualified medical practitioner. Her husband, Denis McIldowie, was an official in one of the mining houses and at the Peace Conference in 1946 acted as A.D.C. to Smuts.

7. Mrs Smuts launches the *Pretoria Castle* at Belfast by pressing
a button at Doornkloof, 19 August 1947

historians. Brief though the experience was, it enlivened him. Meanwhile he was looking forward to the delights of home-coming. Doornkloof was the gathering-ground of his children and grand-children; by now there were twenty of the latter, including four J.C.S.'s. 'So who can say', he asked, 'I have lived in vain?'[4]

From Doornkloof he sometimes made the hour and a half drive to Rooikop, the bushveld farm which was almost a miniature game reserve. In July 1947 he took a few days off to visit the real game reserve at Dongola, in the 10-inch rainfall zone of the northern Transvaal. His friend Pole Evans was its custodian and the two of them cherished the dream of making it a large co-operative venture of the Union, Southern Rhodesia and the Bechuanaland Protec-torate. That dream was for the future; but already there was much to enjoy.

My three days' holiday at Dongola [Smuts wrote] was a sheer joy. I stood within a few feet of a huge python who regarded me longingly and be-nignly with unblinking eyes. I was within twenty yards of a huge bull ele-phant whom I wished to film, but who trumpeted loudly and menacingly ...The film was not taken!...I had long walks, climbed the mountain, and slept unwaking through the nights.

That, for him, was the Africa which always set him going—as he put it—with infinite desire.[5]

He was recovering his zest for reading. Towards the end of 1946 he made a start on Shakespeare's tragedies. Of course, he had read them many times before, but never with the same awareness of their immediacy. What a mistake it was, he exclaimed, to foist them upon immature schoolboys.

Reading through this series I can see for myself (without any instruction) which are real Shakespeare plays and which are probably only retouched work of others. I could become a Shakespeare scholar if I had the time! But I am getting to know his style and language and thought to such an extent that I can notice (I think) where the stuff is not his.

Possibly he flattered himself; but before long he was at work on Dover Wilson's notes and essays; then back again to the plays, and from the plays to the sonnets. The news of his Shakespearian ardour somehow or other reached Leslie Hotson, who sent him his book on the sonnets. Smuts congratulated Hotson on his achievement—as he believed it to be—in dating them and thereby illuminating their biographical significance. He quoted Shakespeare's words about the prophetic soul of the wide world dreaming of things to come. They reminded him, he said, of St Paul's words about the whole creation labouring in anguish for the sons of God to come; they were not merely majestic poetry, but an insight into the heart of the universe. He could hardly believe that so young a poet had written them.[6]

Another of his discoveries or re-discoveries in 1946 was Emily Brontë. The delayed impact of *Wuthering Heights* upon his imagination was, he declared, like the impact of *Macbeth* or *Lear*. Again, he could hardly believe that so young a creature—only twenty-one or twenty-two years of age—could have written such a book. 'There is', he reflected, 'a secret about her, just as there is about Shakespeare—neither can ever be told, because they did not tell.' He read everything that he could get hold of about the Gondal story, but chiefly he read and re-read Emily Brontë's poems. Throughout the few remaining years of his life, they had their place with his Greek Testament upon the little table beside his bed.[7]

The rising sap of his energies and attachments found expression in his letters to old friends. Sometimes he reminded them of the past experiences which he and they had shared. Memory, he told them, gave those experiences a new dimension; it was like looking through a haze at mountains which to the direct gaze had appeared too stark. Memory, he said again, was a *present* experience, an incitement to look forward to new adventures and delights. 'But we shall *add* to them', he exclaimed, 'and so stretch the tale out as long as life lasts.'[8]

Nevertheless he knew that he could no longer live his life at the old pace. Although he congratulated himself on still being able to do as much work as men twenty or more years younger than himself, he was finding it hard to keep his former firm control over his working time; too often he frittered it away in profitless talk with visiting American journalists or eminent Englishmen in flight from the wrath of Sir Stafford Cripps. He was finding his days in the office too long for him. 'I find I can work at a good pace in the mornings', he wrote, 'but in the afternoons I feel the difference which the years have made, and at night I feel as if nothing has been left in me.' He felt himself even more dependent than in the past on his weekends for recovery from the strain of each successive week. His supporters, meanwhile, were all the time entreating him to grace with his presence their week-end conferences, rallies and socials. He

494

could not feel secure even on Sunday afternoons from the importunity of enthusiastic persons with good causes to plead; nor from their recriminations, if he begged to be excused from listening to them just then.* Yet he was far more submissive to all these encroachments upon his hours of rest and recreation than his medical adviser —had he consulted one—would have permitted.[9]

He kept away from doctors. In October 1947, when he was suffering from persistent gastric trouble, he tried to cure himself by starvation; it was the appropriate cure, he said, considering how much starvation was then going on in the world. About the same time he began to suffer severe pain from an arthritic leg, but he postponed calling in the doctors for fear that they would order him to bed for a week or two. He stayed at work and did his best to make everybody think that he was at the top of his form.

I am often amused [he confessed] to hear people remark how well and fit I look, when in fact I feel very near the end of my tether. Still, I dare say it is good policy to keep up appearances. In looking cheerful you make others cheerful and end by really feeling cheered up yourself. Besides, a smile is a healing process...I often notice what a pleasant effect smiling women's faces have...But really the fact is that I am too much living at the end of my physical resources.[10]

Sometimes he asked himself his old question, 'How long O Lord?' In 1946 his answer was: 'Long enough to see the royal visit through.' The King, Queen and the two Princesses arrived in the last week of February 1947. Mrs Smuts was not strong enough to go to Cape Town for the ceremonies of welcome; but the Queen insisted that they must all visit her at Doornkloof, and Smuts exclaimed, 'A Queen visiting a Queen!' His attitude to the royal visit was innocent. To him, the monarchy had long since ceased to be merely an institution. He felt that all South Africans, like himself, would find in its 'sheer humanness' the touch of healing they craved for.

It is a good and sound people [he wrote]...Our coloured people were specially pleased with the attention shown them...This is just the sort of thing which Kings and Queens can do and which give them a blessed and fruitful function in our human society...Nowhere is it more wanted than in this land of races and colours, and nowhere can it render a greater service. Politics runs too high with us, and as the King is above all politics he becomes the reconciler and peacemaker.

It was a wistful dream.[11]

* See reference to 'his own sheep' in note on p. 506 below.

To the question 'How long O Lord?' his answer after the royal visitors had left was: 'Long enough to see the general election through.' To fight and be beaten would, at any rate, win him an honourable release from politics. In some moods, he expected to be beaten. He told his friends that he had no claim to better treatment from the South African electors than the treatment which Churchill had got from the British electors. In former times, people turned to the Almighty in their troubles; but nowadays they put the blame on their governments. Wars, of course, bred troubles. 'So many things', he wrote in 1947, 'go inevitably wrong, there is a spirit of change about in the world. All other governments have fallen in this post-war time—why should I not fall too?' People, he wrote early the next year, did grow tired of the old faces and the old voices, and his own people had had to endure him for fifty years. He felt at times that it would be a benediction upon him if they would give him his release. But then his mood would change. If there had to be a fight, he exclaimed, he would be in the thick of it and he would win it. He would not permit South Africans to go the way of those Eastern peoples who—to reverse the biblical story—went out to find kings and found only asses. From his will to win he leaped to the conclusion that he was winning. One could never be quite sure, he admitted, that some new turn of events might not upset the apple cart; yet in nearly all his letters of the pre-election months he reiterated his assurance of victory.[12]

His advisers at party headquarters fed his over-confidence. If Louis Esselen had still been with them their calculations of the election odds might have been more sober. Esselen had never been afraid to tell Smuts unpleasant things about his party and about himself. He would surely have warned him against the danger that he was running in his own constituency on the Afrikaner *platteland*. For many years past, the electors of Standerton had seen very little of their representative. In December 1946 the party secretary at Standerton had told him in so many words that his presence in his own constituency was urgently required. Smuts replied that he could not possibly come yet; but that he had hopes of coming a few months later in company with the King and Queen. That, possibly, was an inappropriate reply. The Athenians, or enough of them to matter, had ostracized Aristides because they had grown tired of hearing him called 'the just man'. Similarly, the Afrikaners, or enough of them to matter, were growing tired of hearing so often about the eminent company which Smuts kept. The Afrikaners of Standerton not only heard about it: they saw it with their own eyes. Possibly they enjoyed the spectacle. Still, it was no substitute for the assiduous personal attention which they expected from their elected representative.[13]

Smuts's challenger at Standerton was assiduous in his attentions to the electors. He belonged to the Afrikaner Broederbond and had resigned his administrative post when Smuts gave public notice that every Broeder in government pay must choose between his allegiance to the Bond and his service to the State.*

Nomination day was 26 April, polling day 26 May 1948. For Smuts's men those dates more or less defined the campaigning season. For Malan's men they marked the climax of the sustained offensive that had been launched eighteen months previously at Hottentots Holland.

We have just lost Hottentots Holland seat [Smuts wrote in January 1947] in an important by-election—rather a bad defeat, as we had a first-class candidate (Sir de V. Graaff, son of the old magnate friend of General Botha). We were so certain of victory, and the enemy is now cockahoop... I feel very sorry for young Graaff who was nominated in 1943, would have been triumphantly elected, but instead was captured with the rest at Tobruk...and now when the seat is vacant again and he stands again, is again defeated—a real second Tobruk! But he will rise again, and be a Cabinet Minister and perhaps Prime Minister in time.

But the figures of the by-election were not a happy augury for that political resurrection. The Nationalists had converted their minority of 637 at the previous election into a majority of 1,228. J. H. Hofmeyr, they believed, had given them some timely, if inadvertent, aid. In an eve of the election speech on Graaff's platform, he had prophesied that the day would come when Indians and Natives would have representatives of their own colour in parliament. A Nationalist member called out, as the victorious candidate was being led into the House—'Hofmeyr should bring him in!'† Twelve months later, Smuts appointed Hofmeyr Deputy Prime Minister. He had delivered himself into the hands of his enemies.[14]

At United party headquarters the debacle of Hottentots Holland

* See p. 421 above.
† This, however, was not the opinion of de Villiers Graaff. He did not believe that Hofmeyr had lost him many votes.

made no noticeable impact. The party's organization was centralized, but too unwieldy for quick action; ten representatives from each province, together with all the Cabinet ministers, constituted the head committee. The provincial committees and local branches were, for the most part, lethargic. The party had few paid organizers. It had no youth movement. It was suffering from a hardening of the arteries. The National party, by contrast, was efficient and eager. At its base were the local groups or cells which the Ossewa-Brandwag had instituted and Malan in 1941 had imitated. In close association with those cells were the local branches of the National Youth League.* Higher on the ladder of party organization came the divisions, which corresponded with the parliamentary constituencies; higher still, the provincial executives. In theory, no central executive existed; in practice, the party's four provincial leaders constituted a formidably efficient directorate.† They had at their disposal a substantial force of paid professional organizers. Professionalism against amateurism, youth against age, attack against defence—that, by and large, was the contrast between the two parties. Moreover, Malan's men believed themselves to be something greater than a party. They believed themselves to be the Afrikaner Volk, fighting their battle to conquer and possess the South African State.[15]

Each of the contending parties had its subject allies. On the government side, a last minute pact with the remnants of the Labour party gave its candidates the free run of eight seats.‡ On the Opposition side, a carefully prepared pact with Havenga's Afrikaner party gave its candidates the free run of eleven seats.§ The former pact brought Smuts some small profit; the latter pact was a triumph for Malan. It healed or partly healed the great schism of 1941. Moreover, Havenga had the reputation—and not only among Afrikaners—of

* The Nasionale Jeugbond had been founded in 1936.

† The Federal Council of the party was its sole Union-wide organ, and in theory had merely a co-ordinating rôle; the four Provincial leaders constituted its steering committee. In fact, if not in name, they were the centre of power.

‡ John Christie was now the Labour party's leader. Madeley, the former leader, had announced in 1946 that race meant more to him than Socialism. His splinter group did not contest the election; but a second splinter group (the Central Group), led by the Rev. C. F. Miles Cadman, contested thirteen U.P. seats.

Meanwhile, the former Dominion party had re-named itself the South African party. It nominated candidates in eleven constituencies, but played no significant part in the election. Its leader Col. C. F. Stallard, in the debates of January 1948, had supported D. F. Malan on the colour issue.

§ The decisive agreement, ratified subsequently by the party congresses, was made between Malan and Havenga as early as March 1947.

pursuing realistic ends by reasonable means. Nationalist ardour and statesmanlike sobriety seemed now to be in unity with each other.

It was Malan's main purpose, after thus disarming the Hertzogite remnant, to make the largest possible dent in Smuts's Afrikaner following. It was his subsidiary purpose to win at least a small proportion—possibly, in some constituencies, a decisive proportion— of the English-speaking vote. The record of the eight elections since Union threw some light upon his chances.

	1915	1920	1921	1924	1929	1933	1938	1943	(1948)
National party	27	44	45	63	78	75	27	43	(70)

Those figures revealed some striking irregularities, most notably in the 1930s. The 75 Nationalists returned in 1933 held their seats by virtue of the Smuts–Hertzog pact of coalition; the 27 Nationalists returned in 1938 belonged to the 'purified' party which repudiated the Smuts–Hertzog fusion. Thereafter, the return of 43 Nationalists in 1943 was a demonstration—notwithstanding Smuts's wartime triumphs—that economic and international tensions need not for ever frustrate the Nationalist bid for power.

The figures revealed also some striking uniformities. From the Nationalist point of view, the elections had proved disappointing whenever they had been fought upon the issues of republicanism, secession or—more vaguely—Afrikaner isolationism. They had proved rewarding whenever the main issue at stake had appeared to possess a broader South African imprint: above all, the imprint of colour. That, particularly, had been the lesson of 1924, when Hertzog and Creswell launched their slogan of Civilized Labour; it had been the lesson of 1929, when Hertzog launched his Black Manifesto. After 1943 Malan read, marked, learnt and inwardly digested those lessons.

Even before the war ended, Nationalist propaganda began to change its tone and its target. The clamour for a separate peace, for a Republic, for a break with Britain and the Commonwealth suddenly died down. The party began to show anxious concern for the future well-being of the men in the armed forces. It began to send political missionaries into the English-speaking constituencies. It began publishing an English newspaper, the *New Era*. As the elections approached, Nationalist spokesmen insisted that republicanism and secession were not this time the issue. They made the specific pledge never again to force that issue, but to let it be decided by a referendum when the time became ripe. For extra measure, Malan's policy speech at Paarl on 20 April 1948 contained the assurances that a Nationalist government would honour all the promises that had been made to ex-servicemen and that it would *not* keep South Africa neutral in the event of war breaking out between the Communist and anti-Communist blocs.

After telling South Africans what the election was not about, Malan went on to tell them what it was about. 'Will the European race', he asked, 'in the future be able to, but also want to maintain its rule, its purity and its civilization, or will it float along until it vanishes without honour in the black sea of South Africa's non-European population?' That was a repetition of Hertzog's cry in 1929. Like Hertzog then, Malan now was accusing Smuts of *niksdoen*, of drifting, of doing nothing to save South Africa from the rising tide of colour. And there was something worse to follow. Smuts was grooming Hofmeyr as his successor. A Hofmeyr government was incompatible, the Nationalists asserted, with the survival of White South Africa.

As manipulators of the popular mood, the Nationalists showed brilliant flair. They produced a slogan and two bogeymen. Apartheid was the slogan. Hofmeyr was the first bogeyman. Communism was the second bogeyman.

Apartheid was a new name for the segregationist policies which all previous governments had pursued on this or that sector of the racial front, but never as yet along the whole unbroken front of racial theory and practice. A comprehensive theory was now emerging from the SABRA group, based on Stellenbosch University.* Whites and blacks alike, SABRA declared, had their separate and equally legitimate claims to civil and political liberty; but the whites would seal their own doom if they allowed the blacks to make their claim effective within South Africa's unitary jurisdiction and territory. From that premiss the conclusion followed that whites and blacks must achieve their separate freedoms within their separate jurisdictions and territories. Total territorial separation of the white and

---

* SABRA is short for Suid-Afrikaanse Buro vir Rasse-Aangeleenthede (South African Bureau of Racial Affairs). Although not registered in terms of the Companies Act until 1 December 1948, it had been taking shape for some time past. The Sauer Report (see p. 491 above) embodied its ideas in a National party document.

black races was the foundation stone of SABRA's theoretical edifice. 'By Separation', Professor Eiselen* declared, 'I mean this separating of the heterogeneous groups...into separate socio-economic units, inhabiting different parts of the country, each enjoying in its own area full citizenship rights...' That pronouncement was typically high-minded. No less typically, it was unquantitative.† Like Creswell before him, Eiselen was offering the blacks their own freedoms in their own areas. What areas? How many blacks? At what economic cost? Questions such as those would have brought into SABRA's field of sight that *pons asinorum* of segregationist aspiration, South Africa's unitary and dynamic economy. SABRA chose not to ask such questions.

Nevertheless, they could not be side-stepped indefinitely. The party leaders knew that; so they left room for themselves to explain later on that what they meant by apartheid was different from what the professors meant. 'The principles of apartheid', Malan declared in the House of Assembly on 2 September 1948, '...is that we have two separate spheres, not necessarily with an absolute dividing line, not separate territorial spheres.' Malan was already in power when he offered that explanation. So long as he was still fighting for power, he had taken care not to explain too much.

Apartheid was an appeal to faith. The bogeymen played upon fear. Smuts himself would never have made a convincing bogeyman; still, it was possible to make him look ridiculous. *Die Transvaler* called him *S.A. se grootste Brit*‡ and printed a cartoon of him riding on the back of a hippopotamus, surveying the distant horizon and exclaiming *Die toestand lyk my gevaarlik d-a-a-r*.§ The moral was that Smuts had an eye for distant dangers but no eye for the immediate danger of his own country. Hofmeyr, as the Nationalists chose to see him, was the personification of that danger. Between January and May 1948, *Die Burger* published twenty-two leading

* Professor W. W. M. Eiselen subsequently became Secretary of the Department of Bantu Administration and Development.

† How typical the pronouncement was can be seen from Dr Eiselen's article 'Is Separation Practicable?'; published in SABRA's *Journal of Racial Affairs*, January 1950; and in the resolutions of successive SABRA conferences, recorded in the pamphlet 'Integration or Separate Development?' (1952). The SABRA policy of total territorial and political separation was endorsed by a Congress of the Dutch Reformed Churches of Bloemfontein in 1950. I have reflected upon some later developments of the policy in my lecture 'Are there South Africans?' (*Hoernle Memorial Lecture*, Johannesburg, 1966).

‡ 'South Africa's greatest Britisher'.

§ 'The situation looks dangerous to me—*there*' (*Die Transvaler*, 12 May 1948).

articles on Hofmeyr. The articles portrayed him as a man of principle
—of the kind of principle that was death to South Africa. On polling
day, *Die Burger* published a cartoon of Smuts astride the map of
South Africa, casting a shadow not of himself but of Hofmeyr. Meanwhile, a list of Hofmeyr's alarming utterances over the past ten years
and more was circulating in pamphlet form. Its English title was
'Meet Mr Hofmeyr'.* The title might well have been 'Meet
Liberalism'.

Liberalism, the Nationalists asserted, was the slippery slope to
Communism. In face of that danger the National party's official
organ, *Die Kruithoring*, made a passionate appeal to all true patriots:
'Obliterate the red hordes. A vote for Jan Smuts is a vote for Joe
Stalin.'† That news would have astonished the Russians; but in the
context of Nationalist propaganda it appeared matter-of-fact. Smuts
was opposing Communism abroad; but what kind of people, the
Nationalists asked, were his supporters at home? First, the Springbok
Legion, an organization of war veterans which had Communists
among its leaders. Secondly, the Coloured voters,‡ whom Malan was
proposing to remove from the common roll of Cape Province; they
were being corrupted, the Nationalists asserted, by Communist in-
filtrators. Thirdly, the Labour party—but this time no Communist
taint was visible; Labour at the worst was pink. Still, that was enough.
On 17 May *Die Transvaler* published a cartoon of Smuts aloft and
alarmed on a horse. The animal was his own United party, but its
four legs were Communism, the Springbok Legion, the Coloured
voter, the Labour party. All four legs were on the one side.
Hofmeyr was heaving with a halter against the horse's weight,
while Smuts called out to him, '*Trek, Hoffie! Die ding wil kantel!*'
('Pull, Hoffie! The creature will tip over'.)

That propaganda continued non-stop in the Nationalist newspapers from the New Year up to polling day. The pro-government
papers, by contrast, appeared to take the line that South Africans

---

* The pamphlet's Afrikaans title was *Minister Hofmeyr, toekomstige leier van die
U.P.; sy verlede, sy hede en sy toekoms.*

† The *Cape Times* reprinted this startling appeal on 15 May 1948.

‡ The large increase in the number of registered Coloured voters in the Cape during
the five months preceding the elections (from 39,110 to 46,051) was attributable in part
to the United party's drive for registration. There were some statements from Coloured
spokesmen to the effect that there was little to choose between the two parties, and there
was even a proposal for boycotting the elections. Nevertheless, the majority of Coloured
voters probably came down on Smuts's side.

had many other things to think about besides the general election. In the Johannesburg *Star*, for example, the election did not become front page news until the last few days of the campaign. The *Cape Times* improved upon that performance by no more than a few weeks. Both newspapers, in contrast with their Nationalist contemporaries,

ALLES LINKS

Kenmerkend van die huidige verkiesingsveldtog is die feit dat alle linksgesinde organisasies die V.P. steun.

took pains to discuss public affairs, including the government's shortcomings, in a judicial spirit. Nevertheless they did in the end come down firmly on the government's side. The *Cape Times*, for example, warned the electors against the 'false front' of the Nationalist politicians. From mid-May onwards it published day by day an anthology of their wartime pronouncements under the heading 'Things they wish they had not said'. It published half-a-dozen or more articles with intent to prove from Mr Justice Fagan's figures that apartheid was moonshine. It defended Hofmeyr. To call him an assimilationist because he rejected apartheid, it declared on 19 April, was as untrue as to call Winston Churchill an anarchist because he rejected regimentation. Reasonable men, the *Cape Times* believed, would reject the over-dramatized *either–or* definition of the colour problem which Nationalism was trying to foist on them.

Smuts took that line. Speaking on 17 May in the Johannesburg City Hall he declared, 'The Nationalists do not want to see the middle way that South Africa has followed all these years.' In terms of politics, that middle way meant to him what it had meant twenty-one years before when he delivered his Rhodes Memorial Lectures: South Africa as a unitary state, within which the weaker races as well as the stronger must have electoral representation.* In terms of economics, it meant recognition of the hard facts set out in the Fagan Report, with implementation of the Report's proposals for coping with those facts. As Mrs Ballinger saw it, Smuts's middle way was too cautious; as Dr Malan saw it—or said that he saw it—it meant selling the pass to Communism. From whatever angle one looked at it, the impression it made was unaggressive.

Hofmeyr made one aggressive gesture. On 29 April he warned the country that apartheid must lead in logic to South Africa's territorial dismemberment, with a truncated white state ringed around by black states. Eleven years were destined to go by before a Nationalist Prime Minister validated that prophesy.†

Hofmeyr's gesture of aggression was no more than a flash in the pan. As polling day drew near he took increasing pains to prove that he did not stand and never had stood for racial equality. Some members of the United party, including Senator Conroy‡ and Smuts himself, defended Hofmeyr along those lines. Some other members, including the Ministers Strauss and Mushet, protested that Hofmeyr's views about colour were his own private affair and did not commit the party. One member at least, H. Sieberhagen, announced that he and thousands of other party men would join the Nationalists if ever Hofmeyr became Prime Minister. There was unity in Malan's camp; but in Smuts's camp disarray.

* See p. 227 above. In the election campaign of 1948 Smuts took his stand on the existing system of electoral representation as established in 1936.

† Dr H. F. Verwoerd validated it in an important speech in the House of Assembly on 19 May 1959.

‡ Senator Conroy made a public offer of £1,000 to anybody who could prove that Hofmeyr favoured equal parliamentary representation of Europeans and non-Europeans.

The election results were as follows:*

Members returned

For Malan		For Smuts	
National party	70	United party	65
Afrikaner party	9	Labour party	6
Total	79	Total	71

Malan's majority was eight—or five, if the three Native Representatives were counted. This was victory by a narrow margin. Still, at the previous election (1943) Smuts had won by a majority of fifty-four. The swing to Malan was immense.

Nevertheless, Smuts won more votes.

Votes

(including estimates for uncontested seats)

For Malan		For Smuts	
National party	420,447	United party	588,518
Afrikaner party	41,885	Labour party	32,164
Total	462,332	Total	620,682

Votes that were cast for small groups or for independent candidates were approximately 6 per cent of the poll. In the direct confrontation between Malan and Smuts the percentages worked out as follows:

For Malan		For Smuts	
National party	36·24	United party	50·72
Afrikaner party	3·61	Labour party	2·77
Total	39·85	Total	53·49

If each vote had possessed the same value, the apportionment of seats in parliament would have been as follows:

For Smuts	For Malan	Independents and others
80	60	10

By and large, the third group was pro-Smuts; but Smuts could have got along comfortably without its support. On the one vote one value basis, he would have won the straight fight with Malan by twenty seats, instead of losing it by eight seats.

* I owe these figures and calculations to Miss Clodagh O'Dowd of the University of Cape Town.

South Africa's most momentous election since Union was thus decided by a minority vote. The explanation of that paradox was twofold: first, the high urban concentration of the United party's supporters; secondly, the established rules and customs for delimiting constituencies and, in particular, for giving different weights to country and city votes. The urban concentration, with its consequent 'wastage' of United party votes, was a sociological phenomenon over which Smuts had no control; but his large parliamentary majority from 1943 onwards did give him considerable power over the rules and customs of delimitation. Some of his advisers in the United party discussed with him the ways and means of using that power; but Smuts cut the discussion short. The existing electoral arrangements, he said, damaging to his own party though they were, had their roots in the pact of good faith which had created and must still sustain the constitution.*

In retrospect, Smuts found no comfort in the reflection that he might have staved off disaster if only he had been crafty. He faced the bitter truth that Afrikaners in their tens of thousands had shifted from his side to Malan's side. The newly urbanized Afrikaners of the western Rand had become predominantly Malan's men. So had the rural Afrikaners of the western Cape, who up to now had been Smuts's men. So had the Afrikaners of Standerton, his own constituency in the Eastern Transvaal.† 'To think', he exclaimed, 'that I have been beaten by the Broederbond!' That exclamation contained some shrewd political reflection, but it did not fully express his personal hurt. He said to a friend, 'My old comrades have turned against me.' 'Oom Jannie', the friend replied, 'how could they turn against you?

* In 'Some South African Elections' (*Australian Journal of Science*, vol. 28, no. 3) I have briefly discussed the highly technical problems of delimitation, against the dramatically contrasted background of Australian experience. That discussion could profitably be extended to monograph length. For information about the discussions inside the United party, I am indebted to Mr B. Tucker, who had been in 1948 chairman of the party on the Rand. Here I may briefly mention a highly idiosyncratic explanation of the election results of 1948. In chapter IX of his fascinating book, *Old Four Legs* (London, 1956), Professor J. B. L. Smith says that the electors dismissed Smuts because he did not care for 'his own sheep'. He says that Smuts treated foreign scientists well but South African scientists badly. He gives an account of bad treatment which he believes he himself suffered, and asserts that Professor R. Broom suffered similarly. A very different account is given by Sir Basil Schonland in letters to the author of 2 January 1957 and 10 September 1963. Schonland, who was scientific adviser to Smuts and the first Director of C.S.I.R., declares that Smuts gave a revolutionary new deal to science in South Africa and to South African men of science. For this statement there is massive supporting evidence. With regard to the relationship between Smuts and Broom see p. 525 below.

† Smuts lost Standerton by 224 votes.

They are all dead.'[16] If that reply was comfort of a kind, it was also a devastating truth. It meant that Smuts and his ideas and his loyalties had lost their appeal to Afrikaner youth. It meant the end of an epoch; of his epoch.

Smuts drove into Pretoria to make his farewells to the officials who had so faithfully served him.

> We had all gathered [one of them recalled later on] in one of the committee rooms; the atmosphere was subdued when Smuts walked in, erect, grim, completely self-controlled. He stood for a while alone in the centre of the room. Nobody seemed inclined to disturb his thoughts until a senior official walked up to him and they exchanged a few words. Tea was handed round. Smuts accepted his cup, sugared it, and after stirring it for a while, left his teaspoon in it and hooked his thumb around it to prevent it toppling as he took a few sips. (He never failed to do this, to my knowledge, in any company.) Then suddenly his whole body seemed to sag, the military bearing disappeared and turning to his companion he sighed these words: *Ja Spies, so gaan dit* [literally, 'Yes Spies, so it goes']. He turned away, wandered about aimlessly for a few moments and then stood quietly against a table until asked to say a few words.

It was a sad leave-taking.[17]

His son Jannie tried to persuade him to take his final leave from politics; but on 31 May Senator Conroy came to see him at Doornkloof and in the end persuaded him that he could not quit. So he accepted the offer of Charlie Clark's seat in Pretoria East. There was no doubt this time of his getting back to parliament.

In some of his moods, the prospect of more fighting invigorated him; in other moods, it depressed him. He wrote in early June to Lady Moore.

> Yes, I have lost, but more than what you bewail. I have also lost the prospect of release, of some freedom at the end, and of quietly collecting my thoughts and gaining clarity in my own soul. One must view oneself at a distance and in a perspective, so to say, to understand what has underlain one's lifework and dark strivings. But my defeat in South Africa leaves me now no choice. If I go out of public life so much of what has been laboriously built up may be broken down again. I must defend my works—which means I must remain in the fighting line and continue to lead the Party. Hofmeyr has been too much under attack, and has been too severely wounded, to do this job—and I must continue in the leadership...[18]

He enjoyed one brief respite before returning to the firing line. Six months earlier, Cambridge had elected him Chancellor. Here was one more honour to damage his chances on polling day among people who disliked distinction; but he valued it above all his honours. 12 June was the appointed day of his inauguration as Chancellor. The Vice-Chancellor was Raven, his close friend and the Master of his old College. Raven found him so exhausted when he arrived in Cambridge that the prospect of his standing the pace of all the ceremonies and functions seemed doubtful, but when the two men went into the combination room Smuts at once fell into pleasant conversation with the Fellows. At the entrance to the hall he found the servants lined up to greet him. He shook hands with them and spoke to some of the older ones by name. As he entered the hall the undergraduates rose and cheered him. After lunch he took Raven for a fast walk around Cambridge. By the time they returned Raven was no longer afraid of the Chancellor not standing the pace of the next few days, but he was beginning to wonder whether the Vice-Chancellor would stand it. After the ceremonies were all over, Smuts declared that Cambridge had done him good and had made him feel once again that he was a man and not a worm.[19]

On his return home, he received a great welcome from his supporters. He appreciated their generous intention of doing their best to make amends to him for his defeat and humiliation; but he found it hard to cope with all the speech making they expected from him. 'Well', he said, 'that is politics, and it is my job.' He took possession of a quiet suite on the third floor of the Mount Nelson Hotel and set to work in preparation for the parliamentary session. On 7 August 1948, after a lapse of fifteen years, he took his old seat on the front Opposition bench.

It all sounds very dreary [he admitted] and is even drearier than it sounds ...No longer the struggle over constructive problems and positive tasks which promised real results. Now it will be the less pleasing and less fruitful task of criticism, and of preventing others from doing too much that is wrong. I am never a good hand at this sort of negative performance...

After three weeks of it, he wrote again in the same strain.

I get so tired of mere opposition. I almost look upon it as a degradation and cannot understand how the English came to look upon it as an honourable role. If you can't be God, then be at least the Devil! That, I suppose, derives from the sporting spirit of the English, but sport has never appealed to me, and if I can't *do* things I like to be out of them altogether.

8. Chancellor of Cambridge University, June 1948

But he knew that he could not be out of them and that he had no just ground for complaining. Justice, he said, was not a system of prizes and penalties.

Neither the joys of heaven nor the punishments of hell belong to the realm of justice. Don't expect success, don't be disheartened by failure. You have your allotted part, and the doing of it is your reward, and the failure to do it your punishment. There is nothing else in the nature of the universe—the rest is man's fancies and embroideries and frills, whether they be theory or philosophy or religion.[20]

In that stoic mood he settled down to his work of leading the Opposition. When the session was over he set out on a political tour of the Cape. Ever since the outbreak of the war, he said, he had been too much of a mythical character, and he must now give the country people the chance of getting to know him again. When his tour was over, he went north to Doornkloof.[21]

There, shortly before midnight on 10 October, his elder son Japie died suddenly from cerebral meningitis. Next day Smuts poured out his grief in a letter to the Gilletts.

This date is a mark of calamity in my history. On it fifty years ago the Boer War was declared. On it at 12.30 this morning Japie passed away, after an illness of less than 24 hours...Japie was so much to us. Such a son, such a human, such a comrade—such a joy and pride of life. And some miserable invisible microbe has robbed us of him.

He recalled the optimistic phrases of *Holism and Evolution* and of his lecture to the British Association. The universe, he had then declared, was orderly. He had dared even to call it friendly. Such phrase-making seemed superficial to him now.

We can understand the aged going [he wrote] who have had their chance for good or evil. But this senseless thing is almost unpardonable, and looks like a blasphemy on the Universe...Through it all runs this strand of the accidental, the unaccountable, the outrageous, the unforgivable. It is almost as if the power of chaos is at the heart of things and what is highest in us is *not* responded to but outraged by a senseless accidentalism in what actually happens. The only excuse I can offer for the universe is that we do not understand, that the mystery is greater than our limited outlook can explain, and that humility rather than violent remonstrance becomes us. Words, words, words. How hollow it all sounds in the void of the human heart...

That was as close as he ever came to recantation.

But he kept the argument open. In his home as in public life he had others beside himself to think about and support. His wife was quiet and calm in her grief; too much so, he thought; he was afraid that she might lose interest in life. The demands of life on the living, he said, were so great and so insistent that a man could not allow himself to pause at the paralysing thought of death. The anniversary of Alamein came round.

I have just sent off a message [he wrote] to the Alamein dinner tonight in London. There is this memory of victory won at a fateful moment, snatched so to say from the jaws of defeat. It is a symbol of life itself, of not succumbing and accepting the inevitable, but of fighting back and in the end winning through.[22]

He was now seventy-eight years old.

CHAPTER 29

HOLD FAST

BARELY six weeks before the 1948 election a journalist named Tom Macdonald had published a book, *Jan Hofmeyr, Heir to Smuts*. The Nationalists themselves might have chosen that title. It made a main point of their election propaganda and, after 26 May, their victory propaganda. Many United party members agreed with the Nationalists on that point. Hofmeyr, these people said, was a liability which the United party would have to shed, or at any rate scale down.

Prominent among Hofmeyr's opponents in the party were men like Conroy and Barlow who up to polling day had been his champions. On 31 May, at a meeting of ex-ministers which Smuts did not attend, Conroy called upon Hofmeyr to resign as chairman of the party's central executive. But that, Hofmeyr answered, was a matter for Smuts to decide. The same day, Smuts made his decision to remain leader of the party and to accept personal responsibility for all its policies, achievements and misadventures. In a public statement on the eve of his departure for Cambridge he declared, 'If there is blame for the present failure let it be mine—as no doubt the heavy punishment will be.'[1]

Smuts was absent for about three weeks. On his return he had to cope with a revolt against Hofmeyr in the Transvaal head committee of the party. He was determined not to yield to the rebels. 'My successor', he wrote on 28 June, 'must not be killed in advance of his advent.'[2] He did not tell Hofmeyr that; nor did he make the ardent declaration of solidarity and comradeship which Hofmeyr was longing for. Instead, he played a cool game. It ended with a unanimous resolution from the Transvaal head committee thanking Hofmeyr for his services and calling upon all party members to work together in unity. A joint meeting the following week of the party's caucus and head committee ended the same way. In a convincing speech, Hofmeyr put it to the meeting that the United party would do serious damage to itself if it expelled him or forced him to resign. Smuts endorsed that argument. When the meeting was over Hofmeyr wrote in his diary, 'I think we have now got to the end of the witch-hunting episode.'

Hofmeyr, possibly, had good grounds for calling men like Barlow witch-hunters; but many of his critics and, for that matter, of his supporters were doing their best to reach the right answer to a serious political question: was Hofmeyr's proper place inside the United party, or outside it? In June 1945, as on various occasions in the past, Hofmeyr's liberal friends urged him to stand fast upon his own principles and, if need be, to establish his own political party. But Hofmeyr had no political programme of his own. Even if a liberal programme was implicit in the phrases that he sometimes used, it still remained nebulous. Yet the phrases by themselves had become a major political issue. In the recent crucial election, they had lost the United party tens of thousands of votes. It was not only the witch-hunters who considered that loss incommensurate with any gain that they could see.

These men believed it urgent to get the Nationalists out of power before they dug themselves in. For the time being, the new government was making no irreversible changes of public policy. To be sure, it was releasing wartime saboteurs like Robey Leibbrandt and making it permissible again for public servants to belong to the Broederbond. It was making South Africa's foreign policy a disputatious projection of the Nationalist ideology. But it was taking no definite steps to implement apartheid. The pinpricks which some people called *klein apartheid*—job reservation for whites, the shutting down of artisan training for blacks, the imposition upon Cape Town of separate racial railway carriages and post office queues—these things were already happening; but on the larger economic and social issues raised by the Sauer Report* the government was taking no action. There remained the party's pledges to abolish Hertzog's parliamentary franchise for Natives and to put the Cape Coloureds on to a separate roll. Malan was taking legal advice as to whether he could do these things—thanks to the Statute of Westminster—by a majority vote in parliament; or whether he must wait for the two-thirds majority of both Houses which the constitution stipulated. Even if he received the advice he was hoping for, he would still have to wait. When it came to the wrecking of Hertzog's work, the decisive word still lay with N. C. Havenga, the dutiful inheritor of the Hert-

* See p. 491 above.

zog tradition. Havenga's Afrikaner party had nine votes in the House
of Assembly. If Smuts could win over to his side those nine votes he
would be able to turn the Nationalists out of power.

Inevitably, discussions arose in United party circles about the
possibility of a Smuts–Havenga agreement. In a diary entry of
28 July, Hofmeyr called these discussions an 'intrigue'; but that was
unfair. To cite the name of one person: E. G. Malherbe, the Principal
of the University of Natal, was no intriguer, but a South African
patriot. Early in September he had a talk with Smuts in the lobby of
the House, told him that Havenga was unhappy in the Nationalist
kraal, and implored him not to miss his chance of toppling the Malan
government with Havenga's aid. Smuts told Malherbe that he was
not prepared to work with a 'lot of Fascists'. Malherbe considered
that attitude disastrous. On 8 September he stated his reasons in
a long and cogent letter to Smuts.[2]

Havenga, Malherbe said, notwithstanding the notorious flirtation
of his party with the Ossewa-Brandwag, was not a Fascist. The O.B.
itself was not Fascist, although some of its leaders had once deserved
that name. The *entente* between the Afrikaner party and the O.B.
was on both sides merely a matter of convenience. They both had
good reasons for hating the Broederbond and the party managers
of Nationalism. Havenga's reasons had deep emotional roots in the
love and loyalty he still cherished for his dead leader. He would never
forgive the people who had stabbed Hertzog in the back. He would
be ready and eager to play his part in bringing them down, if the
right approach were made to him. 'You and Havenga', Malherbe
told Smuts, 'must amalgamate and allow our little nation to strike
out in the right direction under your joint leadership.'

Malherbe insisted that the Smuts–Havenga leadership must mean
something more than a mere refurbishment of the United party.
South Africans, and young South Africans in particular, no longer
found the United party inspiring or even interesting. The party
had lost its capacity for rejuvenation. Its leaders, Smuts himself
excluded, no longer had any strong appeal to the great body of
patriotic South Africans. Smuts must therefore be prepared to deal
ruthlessly with individuals. That warning brought Malherbe to the
great problem of what was to be done with Hofmeyr.

I have the greatest admiration for his high ideals and administrative
capacity. He was by far the most competent member of your Cabinet...

The fact however remains that Hofmeyr will be an embarrassment in any effort to unite the great majority of the United party with the moderate elements which Mr Havenga will bring with him from the Nationalist party ranks. However much we may deplore it, we cannot get away from the fact that Mr Hofmeyr will be an indigestible lump in the make-up of such a group. This will unavoidably cause serious crises sooner or later and cause the disruption of the whole scheme. You will therefore be forced, for the sake of the preservation of our national unity, and on behalf of the ultimate fulfilment of the very ideals for which Hofmeyr is striving, to leave him out, unless, of course, he is prepared to come in without pushing his principles. I seriously doubt whether he will be prepared to do this. He will probably take a few liberal elements with him, but they will always be able to be relied on to vote with the central party, when it comes to a serious show-down with the extremist elements who are at present dominating the Government and who will, I am convinced, command the allegiance of barely one-third of the country's electors in the event of a new central party being formed under yourself and Havenga. In course of time the 'anti-Hofmeyr stereotype' will dim, and he will probably be able to come back. The realization of his ideals is a matter of the general education of the people and will, even under the most favourable circumstances, still take years to bring about.

For the present, Malherbe proposed a five-point programme which distilled the essence of Smuts's own programme; first, co-operation between the two linguistic groups of the European population; secondly, vigorous economic development; thirdly, a vigorous immigration policy; fourthly, the educational and economic upliftment of the non-European population; fifthly, the defence of constitutional freedom both against Communist and against Nationalist totalitarianism. Under his fourth heading, Malherbe declared: 'History has as a matter of fact proved that the only guarantee for the continued existence of any civilization is provision for its spread and propagation among those in whose territories such a civilization is established, as well as among neighbouring majority groups.'

Malherbe was no reactionary; nor was he ill-disposed towards Hofmeyr. His political diagnosis and prescription were identical with those that Hofmeyr himself had received from his radical friends, for example, from Leo Marquard. Moreover, Malherbe was not proposing to Smuts that Hofmeyr should be the only person to make a sacrifice for the sake of South Africa. Smuts himself, Malherbe said, might be called upon to make a still greater sacrifice. Fifteen years ago, he had saved South Africa by taking office under Hertzog.

Might it not be necessary for him today to take office under Havenga? Malherbe raised that question without presuming to answer it. He felt confident that Smuts was great enough to make any sacrifice which the honour and vital interests of his country required of him.

Smuts studied Malherbe's letter.[3] It failed to satisfy him on one essential issue: namely, what Havenga stood for and what he was prepared to stand for. On that issue, nobody, then or later, possessed reliable evidence. At the United party congress in November, the rumours grew insistent that Havenga was on the verge of a break with Malan. It was agreed that informal soundings of Havenga's state of mind should be taken. Hofmeyr, convinced at long last that this did not mean a manoeuvre against himself, approved the proposal. How the proposal was carried out and what the upshot was nobody ever revealed. Before the talks with Havenga took place, if ever they did take place, Hofmeyr was dead.

He died on 4 December in the knowledge that his party and his leader remained steadfastly behind him. At the annual party congress in November he had been elected chairman by unanimous vote and had received a splendid tribute from Smuts.

Hold fast to what we have. We have in Mr Hofmeyr a man of vision and thoroughness. I regard character as one of the greatest values in life. Ability, yes, but one could almost say that you buy that. But character is something different.

Hold fast to character, Smuts was saying, hold fast to courage. He had said the same thing to Churchill and Auchinleck when the news of the Tobruk disaster reached him—that this was no time for post-mortems but for holding fast to what we had.

Some people continued to say that the political price that had to be paid for Smuts's loyalty to Hofmeyr was too high.* Hofmeyr's mother, on the other hand, bitterly resented the intolerable burdens which Smuts had piled upon her son while he himself—she said—enjoyed his overseas trips. She imputed to Smuts a main share of the responsibility for her son's death. When he went to see her the day after the funeral, her recriminations shook him; but the letter that he wrote that evening expressed nothing except his grief for Hofmeyr and for his own and the country's loss.

* In the *Cambridge Review* of 8 May 1965, Mr W. H. C. Frend says once again that Smuts missed his chance of a deal with Havenga. It may be so; but evidence from Havenga's side has not yet come to light. Nor can it be taken for granted that Havenga was a big enough man for the role which Malherbe and others wanted him to assume.

He was our ablest and most high-minded public man, and was in a sense the conscience of South Africa. To me he was my right hand, and his going will add immensely to my labours—already as much as I can bear. He was only 54 and was my destined successor. The pity of it that I should have had to bury him.[4]

By a strange irony, the sharp increase of tension between Havenga and Malan became that same day a matter of public knowledge. Havenga announced that he would be no party to repealing by majority vote the entrenched clauses of the constitution which protected the franchise rights of the Natives and the Coloureds. The fissure between the two government parties, Smuts wrote, might transform the political situation. Meanwhile, the government was making heavy weather of its balance of payments troubles. Smuts expressed hopes of being able before long to oust it from power.[5]

But his hopes suffered frustration. He had looked forward to a come-back of his party in the provincial elections of early 1949, and when they were over he professed satisfaction with them; but their results at best recorded a stalemate. A by-election at Vereeniging in May 1949 recorded something worse. 'We lost Vereeniging', he wrote, 'by 16 votes, because a negligent party official had not registered a parcel of 350 votes for us. And the enemy is cock a hoop, and the party is downcast and blames the organization and the leadership...However, these things pass.'[6]

But they did not pass. Later in 1949 two things happened to carry Malan through the danger zone. The first was the devaluation of the pound sterling; Havenga as Minister of Finance did not repeat his error of the 1930s; this time, he followed London's lead and thereby opened the road to South Africa's financial and economic recovery. The second bonus for Malan was his own Act No. 23 of 1949, which brought six white representatives of South West Africa into the Union's House of Assembly.* Predictably, they were all Nationalists. Their advent freed Malan once and for all from his dependence upon Havenga.

Smuts had missed his chance, if ever it existed, of preventing the Nationalists from digging in. He came close, once or twice, to admitting that. 'My work', he wrote, 'is a labour of love for South Africa, and partly of faith too, but that faith is now clouded with

---

* The quota for a constituency was 4,000, against the average 9,000 in the Union. South West Africa's 26,000 whites were also given four Senators.

a doubt.' Yet most of the time he admitted no doubt. In March 1949 he compared himself to a general who had led his army to defeat but was still hanging on until he should be able to hand over a successful show to his successor. In August 1949 he looked forward to rounding off his tale of battles with one good victory. In February 1950, after congratulating Churchill on his recent success in the British elections, he added, 'Here the Nationalist Government are continuing to lose ground all round, and I look forward to my victory following yours in Britain in due course.' But when he made that prophesy he had ahead of him only six more months of life.[7]

In foreign as in domestic policy the words *Hold Fast* contained the essence of his thought. In all his correspondence the problems of foreign policy loomed large—too large, he sometimes admitted.

One feels interested [he wrote of the news from China and Indonesia] and yet there is nothing one can do, and the wise attitude is not to get too deeply involved in our inner world of feeling where one is so powerless in the outer world of happenings... There seems to be a principle of relevance in the world, and we must draw a line at the things which are *really* relevant to our position, and leave the rest to God...We know that hearts are breaking in China and a world seems to be foundering. But we...are so limited that, to be effective, we must confine ourselves to our smaller world.[8]

Even so, his own world was not conspicuously small. It included the Commonwealth. Its heartland was Europe. What happened to Europe, he believed, was the immediate, the crucial issue. At Cambridge on 10 June 1948, he spoke his mind on that issue.[9]

A young son of the veld, he told his audience, had come to Cambridge fifty-seven years before and had found comradeship there in one of the smaller colleges. He returned in due course to his own and within a few years found himself and his people at war with the British people. Yet that war did not completely put out the light which Cambridge had kindled in him. The former enemies learnt at long last to understand each other. An agreement pre-eminent in the history of statesmanship embodied their understanding. One of its architects, Winston Churchill, was still alive and would be honoured later in the day's proceedings by the award of an honorary degree. 'But...I would specially mention', Smuts continued, 'one whose name should never be forgotten...Campbell-Bannerman, the statesman who wrote the word *Reconciliation* over that page and that African scene, and thus rendered an immortal service to the British Empire, aye, to the cause of man everywhere.'

Behind the great desk in his study at Doornkloof Smuts had hung Campbell-Bannerman's portrait. Throughout the past forty years and more he had kept alive the memory of the man and in his letters and speeches had often recalled it to others.* On 10 June 1948 he told his Cambridge audience that his own presence among them that day was a tribute to Campbell-Bannerman's wisdom. The present-day world, he said, still needed that wisdom, the more so because it was so much more dangerous than the world of half a century ago. To diagnose the dangers, and to prescribe some remedies for them, was the main purpose of his speech.

He put small emphasis upon the danger of war. None of the great powers, he believed, was in a position to fight another war or wanted to fight one. In his view, war was only an incident of the contemporary world-upheaval; it was not the real thing. 'That strange phenomenon called the Curtain' seemed to him the real thing. There was no longer one world; it was divided into two halves, with one of its halves practising aggression against the other half. The technique of aggression, he thought, was something new in human history; not war but the threat of war in support of ideological propaganda and internal subversion. The objective was 'conquest without war'. That recently had been Czechoslovakia's fate. It would soon become the fate of other western nations unless they discovered effective answers to the new technique. Smuts proposed three answers: first, military preparedness; secondly, European co-operation; thirdly, holding fast to values. The peoples of Europe, he maintained, had built up a culture and a way of life which formed the most precious achievement of men and was a standard for the rest of the world to repair to and advance under. That claim brought him to his conclusion: that the task immediately ahead was 'the salvaging of Europe, materially, politically and spiritually'.

Three months later he gave some extra precision to that programme. In a long letter to Churchill on 27 September 1948 he said that he did not now feel so sure as he had felt at Cambridge that

---

* As Smuts grew older, and particularly after his defeat, his public references to Campbell-Bannerman grew more frequent. In June 1948 he contributed a fine article on Campbell-Bannerman to a special number of the *Glasgow High School Magazine*.

war could be ruled out; the western nations remained so unprepared that Russia might decide that her opportunity was now or never; alternatively, she might blunder into war. In this situation, he asked, what should the western nations do?

I almost hesitate [he answered] to have to confess it, but I am beginning to think more and more that the wise course for us is boldly and openly to integrate Western Germany with the West, and, instead of continuing to dismantle and cripple her, to put her on her feet again and make her part of our Eastern Defence Wall, as she has been for centuries...Instead of making peace with Germany and saving and securing her as an ally for the future equilibrium of peace, we have continued to break her down and expose her and ourselves and the world to this Communist menace. She should rather be saved, if Europe is to be saved...

My suggestion to you is this: now that Marshall is in Paris, will you not raise this matter with him? You may, if you prefer, put it before him, not as your but my suggestion, and put the onus on me if you like.

In a cable of 3 October, Churchill declared his full agreement with Smuts. In a cable of 9 November, he reported that he had had a long talk with Marshall and had shown him Smuts's letter. Meanwhile, Smuts himself had written to Marshall, urging him to bracket the defence of Greece with the defence of Berlin. Possibly his intervention produced results. Marshall, no doubt, was getting similar promptings from many other people; but on 17 December he told Smuts that he fully agreed with him upon every issue that he had raised. In particular, he told him that action was proceeding to sustain Greece and to make Germany a fully participating member of Western Europe and the Atlantic Community.[10]

Smuts gave the Americans full credit for supporting western freedom; but he gave his heart to the little groups of men and women, above all, to the Greeks and the Berliners, who were holding fast in the front line. They reminded him, he said, of Horatius holding the bridge in the brave days of old. Their courage heartened a man in these disheartening times. And it might mark the turning of the tide.[11]

He acclaimed another small people that was fighting for its life. Two days before polling day, he had announced South Africa's recognition of the state of Israel. That announcement, some people said, had lost him many votes; but he never repented it.

The only people winning through to day [he wrote in December 1948] are the Jews who richly deserve success, which indeed they have snatched from the very jaws of disaster. I have supported them at every stage, even when they were a little mad!

He wrote eleven weeks later—

The only line on the upgrade all the time is Israel—God bless them. The people that produced the prophets and Jesus and Paul should not go under and be swallowed up in the mass of the human commonplace.

In November 1949, at a time of strain when the very thought of travel was repugnant to him, he flew to London to launch an appeal for funds to plant a forest in Israel. It was to bear Dr Weizmann's name. Weizmann himself was the guest of honour and Smuts proposed his toast.

I have seen those bare hills [he said] when Allenby and I rode over the hilly country of Judaea in the First World War. They must have been covered once with the fig and the olive and the vine. They must remain bare no longer. And so the idea has occurred to friends of Dr Weizmann that part of that area should be set aside for a forest in perpetual honour to him. What more fitting honour and memorial to the man who led Israel back to those bare hills after such long absence?...

This unique little people which bequeathed to mankind the noblest spiritual heritage of all history, produced also some great historic leaders of men, foremost among them Moses, the mysterious Founder who first led them out of bondage to this promised land...To this select historic list we now add our own contemporary, Chaim Weizmann, the scientist, the great Zionist, the indomitable leader who, after his people had been all but wiped out in the greatest purge of history, assembled the remnants, led them back to the ancient homeland in face of the heaviest opposition, and welded them once more into a sovereign state among the nations. Surely his achievement bears comparison with that of Moses![12]

But let Israel never forget, Smuts told the Jews, notwithstanding the misunderstandings and conflicts that had arisen along the hard road of the Mandate, that she owed her existence to a great act of British policy. He went on to tell those Englishmen who were putting their money on the Arab horse that Anglo-Israel friendship would prove a stabilizing force in the eastern Mediterranean. Consequently, it was a major interest of the Commonwealth.[13]

Despite this partisan fervour, his prognostications for the Commonwealth were pessimistic. He thought it a misfortune when Ireland declared herself a republic and left the Commonwealth; but he felt unhappy when the Commonwealth found room for the Republic of India. On the eve of the Prime Ministers' Conference of April

1949 he published a warning against the kind of weak toleration that would drain away the Commonwealth's substance and significance.

> My personal view [he said]...is that there is no middle course between the Crown and the Republic, between in and out of the Commonwealth. You are either in, or out of it, and if you choose to be out of it, you are out of it entirely and not on terms which can be devised. It is a case of the excluded middle. If in some nebulous or muddled way you can be both in and out of it, the whole concept of the Commonwealth goes, and what remains is a mere name without substance, the grin without the cat of *Alice in Wonderland.*

After the Conference he took the Holy Roman Empire as his parallel. In a letter to Churchill he recognized the practical reasons for making a compromise with India but expressed the fear that the Commonwealth was now on the way to becoming a fictional entity. If that happened, humanity would be the poorer. Meanwhile, he said, the decision taken in London was producing repercussions in Cape Town. The Nationalists now saw ahead of them 'a tarred road to the Republic'.[14]

To the Nationalists, republicanism and secession had meant, hitherto, one and the same thing.* Some of them, Smuts knew, were talking now of a Republic inside the Commonwealth; but secession, he feared, was the only conceivable terminus of the Nationalist thrust. To him, secession signified irreparable loss both for the Commonwealth and for South Africa. A generation earlier, he had said that it meant the secession of one group of whites from the other group and of the blacks from the whites.† Notwithstanding the many changes that had taken place since then, he still saw it as a disturbance of the elements of cohesion and a potential threat to the integrity of the Union.

Nationalist fervour was immediately focused upon the Voortrekker Monument, due to be unveiled on Dingaan's Day, 16 December 1949. As the only surviving Boer General and as State Attorney under President Kruger Smuts had a right to be present and to speak on that occasion. His speech expressed a fervent, but also a reflective patriotism. In the history of his people he saw three centuries of heroic endeavour under Divine guidance. He extolled the heroes and in particular—as was proper on that day—he extolled the Voortrekkers; but he refrained from over-dramatizing them. Their story, he said in

---

* See p. 372 above. † See p. 18 above.

effect, was a story not only of conflict but also of co-operation. On their setting out from the Eastern Province they had the sympathy and support of the English settlers. In their fight for survival against Dingaan English blood flowed with their own. Their Coloured and Native servants fought and died with them. Their battles, besides, were episodes of the Great Trek but not its essence, seeing that their advance was into lands hitherto unoccupied or into lands which Moselekatse and Dingaan had laid waste. Their fighting was with the war lords, not with the mass of the people. They were pacifiers, not exterminators. Smuts recalled the time of troubles which had followed their heroic age. He recalled 'the colossal figure' of their reconciler, Paul Kruger. He quoted Kruger's last message to his people—that they should take from their past the good that it contained and use it for shaping their future. Their past, he again reminded them, contained not only conflict but also reconciliation, not only the wars of independence but also the Union of South Africa. The Union was a bridge that had been built from both ends by Afrikaners and English-speaking South Africans. Provided the bridge held firm, South Africa could be made for *all* its peoples a land of righteousness.[15]

The organizers of the ceremony had put Smuts last on the long list of speakers that morning. Many people in the audience had been up since 5.30 a.m., whereas Smuts's call did not come until 12.30. Inevitably, a number of people had to leave. The story was put about afterwards that these true Afrikaners chose deliberately not to listen to him. Yet the great majority of the people stayed and listened attentively.

Two months previously, in the Coetzenburg rugby stand at Stellenbosch, he had held the close attention of 2,000 Afrikaner students. The committee of the Students' Representative Council had invited him; but thereupon had been challenged to defend its actions at a special meeting of the student body. That meeting ratified the invitation; but the committee naturally felt nervous when the day came. Smuts arrived on time. 'He appeared rather frail', a member of his audience remembered, 'smaller than most of us would have expected him to be, his very white hair being blown across his head by a slight breeze.' On the platform with him was the Rev. A. F. Louw, who had been a prisoner at St Helena during the Anglo-Boer war, and in the audience were many old Cape rebels who had come to hear him. As he greeted them by name the students, to their surprise, began to see him in the role of a Boer hero. He defended the decision of 1899 to make war and the decision of 1902 to make peace; both decisions, he said, had been tragic, but both had been necessary to make South Africa a nation. He gave the students a picture of the war and, at greater length, a picture of 'the old President'. Leadership, he said, could be a diabolical, but also a creative force. Paul Kruger had been a creative leader. He had recognized and followed the *heilige linie** which ran through human history.

At the end of his address he received a standing ovation. 'I never knew', a member of the student committee wrote later, 'whether it meant anything to Smuts, but I am sure that for a while, anyhow, it meant a great deal to Stellenbosch.' But some of the professors took a different view. A professor of theology, in his opening prayer next morning, thanked the Lord that he believed in a Personal God and not merely in a Holy Line.[16]

His aloofness from the Dutch Reformed Church was a matter partly political and partly theological. A letter describing how he had spent the first Sunday of September 1941 revealed the political impediment. 'It was the King's day of prayer', he wrote, 'but I was free as my Church declines to pray for us or the Allies, and I don't like attending any other Church.' A letter seven years later describing one of his chance encounters out walking revealed the theological impediment.

I was discussing with two young Calvinist parsons the other day the concept of Holism, which they took as purely humanistic and a denial of the theistic concept. I explained to them that I did not agree with Calvin's legalistic conception of human alienation and depravity. With John's Gospel I believed in Incarnation—the Word become flesh—the divine immanent in the human, and in matter and its patterns as a revelation of the Divine. Holism is therefore the approach towards the theistic concept from the side of nature, and builds as it were a bridge between humanism and divinity. They looked impressed, but perhaps did not take it all in.[17]

In building the bridge, he reflected, feeling came before thought; the arches of the bridge were faith, hope and love, not merely

---

* In the *Cape Times* of 11 October 1949, these words were translated weakly as 'spiritual thread'. But Smuts always had in mind the etymological solidarity of the words 'whole' 'health', 'holiness', and of their equivalents in Afrikaans.

systematic reasoning. Nevertheless he had for twenty years past kept clinging to the hope of someday finding the time to reason the issues out and expound them in a book. Among his papers he had four draft studies for *Holism II** and in his head he had the outlines of all the chapters. As the 1947 election drew near he recalled that he had written his first book after his defeat in 1924, and asked himself whether he would be repeating that experience next year. He suffered the defeat but did not attempt the book. He would not, he said, repeat Clemenceau's mistake of working in his dotage upon a task that demanded the fullness of a man's powers.[18]

He disliked his philosophical frustration but said that he could 'take it'. He found consolation in what he called the spirit of acceptance.

There is [he wrote] a contrariety in things, a general refractory character in the universe and in life which we must accept, or otherwise go under in the friction and frustration. I believe faith has something to do with it— a vague sense of holding on in spite of it all. It certainly keeps me going.

He still from time to time read books like Whittaker's *From Euclid to Eddington* or Berdiaev's *The Human and the Divine* and still occasionally indulged himself in speculations on the cosmic scale, akin to the still-unpublished speculations of Pierre Teilhard de Chardin. He asked Gilbert Murray whether the world's peoples were not perhaps moving on to larger groupings, just as the earlier city states had moved on to the present-day nation states. It might be so, he reflected, but he and Murray would be dead long before there was any proof of it. Meanwhile, Murray was turning aside from world politics to write about his father and about his own beginnings in that far off world of Australia in a bygone age. That, said Smuts, was a healthy return to the common man, who after all was a very good fellow so long as he did not think that he was able to run the world.[19]

The philosophizing of other people struck an occasional spark in him. He repudiated Bertrand Russell's attempt, as he believed it to be, to reduce all experience to sense data and sensibilia. The self or personality, he retorted, could not possibly be derived analytically from items of experience of which it was itself the source and pre-

---

* The titles of his four draft studies were: (1) Sensation and Perception; (2) From Substance to Pattern; (3) The Nature of Holism; (4) Holism in Psychology. On *Holism II* see p. 232 above.

condition. In a letter to Sir Robert Kotze,* who had been his rival in the early 1890s for the Ebden scholarship to Cambridge, he said the same thing in simpler words. Kotze in his old age had become a believer in the transmigration of souls. That belief, Smuts declared, was inferior to the Christian belief in immortality, as expounded by St Paul in I Corinthians 15; moreover, it was wholly irreconcilable with the concept of human personality.

This transfer of the psyche from person to person, in which the psyche gains richer experience in an unending series of lives, makes no appeal to the individual at all. It does not satisfy 'my' sense of identity to learn that it has been the identity of A, B, C, D, and an infinite series of other unknowns. It is not mine, and has no sense or value for me...

Nor is it a substitute for the scientific concept of evolution. In fact there is nothing in biological evolution, as scientifically understood, which warrants this flitting about of the psyche or entelechy from person to person. Genes are transmitted and produce the inheritable qualities of the scientific biologist, but whole psyches or entelechies are not thus transmitted.

The Oubaas was standing no nonsense. In particular, he was not standing the nonsensical assertion that he, J. C. Smuts, was not a person but was merely a migratory soul or, alternatively, a bundle of sensations.[20]

In his personal life friends meant more to him than books. 'They are all dropping off one by one', he had lamented as Louis Esselen lay dying; but it was not his mood that day to count all the friends with whom he was still exchanging letters about politics, war, archaeology, botany, the joys and sorrows of everyday life. Among them was 'dear old Pug',† his close comrade in some of the worst wartime crises, to whom he wrote in December 1949, 'So much was so good, but the comradeship was the best.' Among them also was General von Lettow-Vorbeck, his adversary in East Africa during the first German war; after the second war he had tracked the family down in Germany and had found it half starved; he helped it and wrote to von Lettow and his wife a bare two weeks before his own fatal illness, 'Both of you are favourites in my family.' There was Professor Robert Broom, his 'octogenarian friend' who was, he insisted, still beating all records; to the end of his life he never failed to congratulate Broom on his latest pre-historical discovery or

---

* Kotze had served South Africa meritoriously as Chief Government Engineer.

† General (later Lord) Ismay, head on the military side of War Cabinet Offices and closely associated with Churchill in his capacity as Minister of Defence.

academic honour.* There was Mrs Bolus of the Cape Town herbarium, to whom he wrote on 9 May 1950 his last botanical letter, brimful of his interest and delight in the Cape flora.† There were the Therons, the Moores, the van Zyls, the Gilletts and so many other true friends; and of course their children and grandchildren. Once, when the Gilletts seemed to him excessively perturbed about the ideologies and other plagues of the contemporary world, he told them that he could see no sense in their worrying. 'The children in the sandpit', he wrote, 'are the real thing.'[21]

Towards the end of 1949 the Gilletts were planning a visit to South Africa, their first visit for the past ten years and more. 'It won't', Smuts warned them, 'be the old times, which never return, but it will be very good whatever it will be.' He and they were lucky to have the use of their legs and he was looking forward to some good walking with them. Yet he had to warn them of changes for the worse in some of the old places. The dirty finger of the vandal was beginning to smear the mountains of Cape Province and there was nothing that anybody could do about it; tarred roads, he admitted, spelt progress. But sub-marginal farms‡ spelt the opposite. He accused the Nationalists of destroying the Dongola nature reserve to make farms for poor whites, who would be poorer still after they had slaughtered the game.

The worst business in Parliament this week [he wrote in April 1949] will be abolition of Dongola. The Nats. have set their heart on killing it and the game on it and breaking it up for settlers, in other words, for poor whites. But think of the slaughter of game that will take place there in the coming winter months. My heart bleeds and I find it hard even to think about it. What pleasure it has given us, what a refuge it has been for the harassed wild creatures of this land! But there is no mercy and no end to folly and political vindictiveness. And so we must endure what we cannot prevent. You will not see Dongola again, nor shall I alas. 'Look your last at all things lovely.'[22]

But Doornkloof was lovely still, even though it had been pushed into some new shapes to make room for Japie's widow and her six children. The Gilletts spent Christmas there and shared the merri-

* See p. 506 above for a strange story that Smuts did not care for Broom. Fifty-three letters from Broom to Smuts survive for the period 1924–50. Copies of thirty-six letters from Smuts to Broom survive. They do not include those that Smuts wrote in his own hand.
† In his letter of 9 May 1950 to Mrs Bolus Smuts included the draft of his foreword to *Wild Flowers of the Cape* by Mrs Garrett Rice—the last foreword that he wrote.
‡ The market price of land in the neighbourhood of Dongola was said then to be 6*d*. per morgen.

9. The Eightieth Birthday Celebrations in Johannesburg

ment of the Smuts clan, of the black families on the farm and of the black children from the nearby schools who came later in the day with their teachers for refreshments and gifts. After Christmas Smuts went off with the Gilletts to their old stamping ground in the Zoutpansberg. It was the high spot of their holiday, even though they did not, this time, eat their meals around the camp fire and lie down to sleep under the stars.[23]

Suddenly their holiday lost its gloss. Smuts had to go to Cape Town for the parliamentary session and had to do battle there with acute sciatic pain from a slipped disc. The pain had been troubling him intermittently since September but did not become fierce until after Christmas. Then at last he consented to see a doctor. The Gilletts went off to Hermanus and he wrote to tell them that he was on the mend after being electrified, pummelled, turned upside down and inside out. 'This old dog', he said, 'has other fleas enough and needs no sciatic flea to keep him from brooding.' None the less he was suffering discomfort and at times great pain as he sat day after day through the debates. The Gilletts, when they returned to Cape Town, were grieved to see the physical and mental strain under which he was living. Sadly, in the last week of February, they took their leave of him for the last time.[24]

When the session was over Smuts saw ahead of him the usual public commitments, intermingled with some notable family occasions. First among the latter was the anniversary of his marriage with Isie Krige on 30 April, fifty-three years ago. Their life together, he reflected, like the lives of so many other people, had been an interweaving of tragedy and comedy, of good and evil, yet withal well worth living; but he was hoping that their life together in the world to come would reveal a different pattern, provided he was not expected to wear a crown and twang a harp. Meanwhile, as he looked forward to the immense public celebrations which were being arranged for his eightieth birthday, he could not help wishing that he could become for once a forgotten man. In his letters he was fixing his thought chiefly upon the quiet, small things of life, the things he called 'our particular'. The big things, he said, were becoming too hard to puzzle out. With only eight days still to go to the celebrations, he wrote to the Gilletts—

I wish I could see the way clearly before me, but partly ignorance and partly the inherent human tangle in its complexity proves too much for me. How much easier the way would be if one saw things in their simplicity and one's duty as a clean and straightforward affair. But it is only at certain times and seasons that a clear light shines on one's way, and the way becomes a joy to go.

That was the last letter the Gilletts ever received from him.[25]

In Johannesburg on 23 May three hundred thousand people lined the streets to do him honour.[26] He received the Freedom of the City and expressed his gratitude in a short speech. At the banquet in the evening he made a carefully prepared speech in a spirit which was similar, granted the very different audience, to that of his speech six months earlier at the Voortrekker ceremony. On the evening of 24 May he spoke again at a birthday banquet in Pretoria. That was his last public appearance. His heart was failing and on 29 May he suffered a coronary thrombosis. Next morning, following a medical consultation at Doornkloof, he submitted to being sent to bed. For the fifteen weeks of life still remaining to him Doornkloof was his world.

He rallied from the first attack. By the second week of July he was able to get out of bed, walk a few steps and sit on a chair. On 6 August he was able to take a drive in the country, in company with his physician, Professor Guy Elliott. 'He pointed out the numerous acacias along the roadside', Elliott remembered, 'naming them and giving their history as if they were also one of his family. There was a calm ecstasy about his contemplation of nature in these days.' For the rest of August he was able to spend the greater part of every day up and in the open air. He saw visitors and enjoyed above all the company of his grandchildren. On 25 August he insisted that he was strong enough to wheel one of the babies in her pram, but in doing it he suffered a severe collapse. He recovered, but Elliott explained to his wife that these collapses were like the switching on and off of an electric light: 'sometime the light would fail'. All the same she wanted him still to have the joy of his drives into his beloved country. On the afternoon of 11 September she was with him on his last drive. He returned in good spirits and took his place for the evening meal at the head of the family table. After the meal he went to his room accompanied, as usual, by two of the family. As he sat down to prepare for bed he sank unconscious and this time did not recover.

Guy Elliott heard the news by telephone and drove at once to Doornkloof. Isie Smuts met him at the top of the steps leading on to

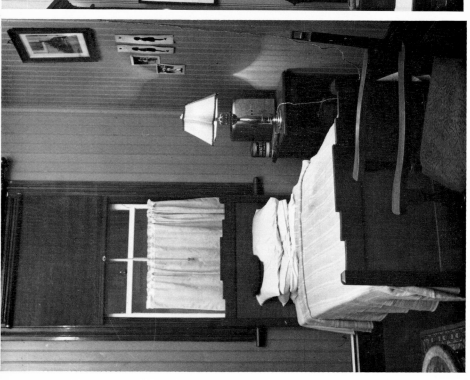

10. The bedroom at Doornkloof

11. The day before he died

the stoep. 'She was standing', he recalled, 'under a single rather dim electric light, for, she said to me later, she feared she might break down and that was unthinkable, particularly in front of her family, for was *she* not now the head of the family, and whoever heard of the head of the Smuts family breaking down?' Before going to bed that night she performed her usual domestic duties of ironing clothes, feeding the 'inside' and the 'outside' cats and washing up the evening tea cups, as she always did, because she said it was unpleasant for the servant to come in the morning and find a lot of dirty cups.

She did not go to the great funeral they gave him on 16 September. At supper two nights later a message was brought in to say that the teacher from the near-by African school was waiting outside with the children's choir. Could they come and sing, because the funeral train had gone through the station too fast for them to finish their song? She asked them to sing.

She answered in her own beautiful handwriting the letters of condolence that came pouring in to Doornkloof. On 5 October she wrote to Mrs Bolus of the Cape Town herbarium:[27]

But what I liked best in your letter was about the arrival of the Oubaas into the Presence on the other side and the welcome he received there amid 'the glorious burst of trumpets'...We are so thankful that he was at home with us all through his long illness...and that he was surrounded by his children and his grandchildren to the end. Louis was with us all the time...She was really the resident doctor and we had Dr Kelsey Loveday (our family Doctor) coming twice a day, while Dr Frank Forman from Cape Town University and Dr Guy Elliott from Wits University came over almost daily to see him. They were all very good and devoted to the Oubaas and had been old friends who would do anything for love of him. And sometimes he would be very well and sometimes he would collapse when there was a nasty clot in the blood near his heart, and we too would be in clouds one day and in the depths another day. And so it continued for several weeks. But the end came very suddenly and unexpectedly and he was gone before we could realize it...

REFERENCES

In the Smuts Archive, private letters are arranged in volumes with arabic numerals, official letters and memoranda in volumes with roman numerals, miscellaneous papers in boxes marked by capital letters. In referring to these series I have usually found it sufficient to cite the numbers or capital letters without further description.

CHAPTER I

1 See W. K. Hancock, *Smuts: The Sanguine Years, 1870–1919* (Cambridge, 1962), p. 522. All the retrospective passages of the present chapter, with their documentation, can be checked by using the index to that volume.

2 Vol. 26, no. 48, from W. S. Churchill, 7 April 1923.

3 Pierre Teilhard de Chardin, *Letters from a Traveller* [Eng. trans., London, 1962], p. 133.

4 Vol. 22, no. 255, to M. C. Gillett, 16 June 1919; vol. 98, no. 93, to Alice Clark, 25 June 1919.

5 Vol. 22, no. 153, 156, 158, to Isie Smuts, 20 and 27 May, 10 June 1919.

6 Vol. 98, no. 97, to Alice Clark, 21 July 1919.

7 Vol. 98, nos. 102, 106, to Alice Clark, 21 October 1919, 10 January 1920; vol. 24, no. 290, to M. C. Gillett, 7 April 1921.

8 Vol. 98, nos. 102, 131, 132, to Alice Clark, 21 October 1919, 24 March, 3 June 1922; vol. 23, no. 53, from Alice Clark, 23 November 1920.

9 Vol. 23, nos. 203, 229, to James Ward, 8 December 1920; to M. C. Gillett, 8 December 1920.

10 Vol. 24, no. 276, to M. C. Gillett, 3 January 1921.

11 Vol. 98, nos. 104, 108, 111, 120, to Alice Clark, 26 November 1919, 15 February, 18 March, 24 October 1920; vol. 25, nos. 307, 309, to M. C. Gillett, 5 and 19 May 1922.

12 Vol. 98, no. 129, to Alice Clark, 19 May 1921.

13 Vol. 23, no. 214, to M. C. Gillett, 27 July 1920.

14 Vol. 25, no. 299, to M. C. Gillett, 1 February 1922.

15 Vol. 24, no. 302, to M. C. Gillett, 20 August 1921.

16 Vol. 27, no. 349, to M. C. Gillett, 1 March 1923.

17 Vol. 24, nos. 296, 305, to M. C. Gillett, 20 May and 21 September 1921; vol. 27, nos. 203, 351, to I. Pole-Evans, 29 March 1923, to M. C. Gillett, Good Friday 1923; vol. 29, no. 188, from R. Marloth, 17 March 1924; vol. 30, nos. 85, 45, 145, to I. Pole-Evans, 26 March 1924, to R. Marloth, undated, to M. C. Gillett, 28 March 1924.

18 Vol. 24, nos. 301, 304, to M. C. Gillett, 16 August and 12 September 1921.

19 Vol. 23, no. 228, to A. B. Gillett, 6 December 1920; vol. 98, no. 112, to Alice Clark, 9 April 1920.

20 Vol. 22, no. 277, to M. C. Gillett, 4 October 1919.
21 Vol. 24, no. 279, to M. C. Gillett, 25 January 1921.
22 See W. K. Hancock, *Survey of British Commonwealth Affairs*, 1 (London, 1937), 79–80.
23 Vol. 23, nos. 192, 199, to Lady Mary Murray, January 1920, to Robert Bridges, 21 May 1920. (He was acknowledging the gift of Bridges's latest volume of poems, which was dedicated to him and personally incribed.) Vol. 98, no. 110, to Alice Clark, 8 March 1920; vol. 27, no. 356, to M. C. Gillett, 31 May 1923.
24 Vol. 24, nos. 279, 282, to M. C. Gillett, 25 January 1921, to A. B. Gillett, 15 February 1921.

CHAPTER 2

1 For the retrospective introduction to this chapter see *Smuts: The Sanguine Years*; its index will facilitate the tracing of quotations. I have also made frequent use of T. R. H. Davenport, *The Afrikaner Bond* (Cape Town, 1966) and N. G. Garson, 'Het Volk: The Botha–Smuts Party in the Transvaal, 1904–11' (*The Historical Journal*, IX, 1 (1966), 101–32).
2 See particularly Davenport, *op. cit.* pp. 264–9.
3 It need hardly be stated that I have had no access to the records of the Afrikaner Broederbond. Such knowledge of its history as I have gained is based chiefly on the materials listed by Professor Gwendolyn Carter in *The Politics of Inequality* (New York, 1958) supplemented by some miscellaneous gleanings.
4 From 1916 until 1923 South Africa's parliamentary Hansard was in abeyance. In studying the course of parliamentary discussion I have used newspaper reports, particularly those of the *Cape Times*, and the summaries of debates published in the *Journal of the Parliaments of the Empire* (*J.P.E.*). Occasionally I have had the good fortune to find the verbatim report of an important speech made by an unofficial Hansard-type agency.
5 Here and in what follows I am particularly in debt to Miss Clodagh O'Dowd of the University of Cape Town. She has written for my use memoranda on the elections of the early 1920s, and has included in them useful reports on the party discussions.
6 These assurances were given, for example, by D. F. Malan (see *Cape Times*, 26 January 1920) and F. W. Beyers (see the *Burger*, 17 February 1920).
7 Vol. 98, no. 110, to Alice Clark, 8 March 1920.
8 Actual votes cast for the Unionist party were only 38,944, but 6,776 votes have been added to this figure as an estimate of the support given to the Unionists in three uncontested seats. The estimate has been made by Miss Clodagh O'Dowd, on the assumptions (*a*) that the poll in these constituencies would have been the same as in the country at large (i.e. 65·58 per cent of the registered electors); (*b*) that 75 per cent of the

poll would have favoured the candidate who had been considered too strong to challenge.

9 Vol. 98, no. 117, to Alice Clark, 12 August 1920.

10 *Round Table*, vol. 11, p. 198.

11 *Cape Times*, 4 October 1920.

12 Vol. 23, nos. 187, 200, to T. Smartt, 30 September, from T. Smartt, 10 October 1920.

13 Vol. 23, no. 221, to M. C. Gillett, 25 October 1920.

14 Vol. 23, no. 222, to M. C. Gillett, 1 November 1920; vol. 23, nos. 201, 202, to J. H. Hofmeyr, 5 and 25 November 1920.

15 Vol. 98, nos. 125, 126, to Alice Clark, 11 January and 22 February 1921; vol. 24, nos. 243, 282, to L. S. Amery, 8 March, to A. B. Gillett, 15 February 1921.

16 The estimate for the uncontested seats is on the same basis as for the election of March 1920, referred to in note **8** above.

CHAPTER 3

1 Vol. 23, no. 221, to M. C. Gillett, 25 October 1920; vol. 98, nos. 120, 121, 122, 124, to Alice Clark, 24 October, 2, 23 and 30 November 1920; vol. 23, no. 203, to James Ward, 8 December 1920.

2 Vol. 23, no. 141, from Emily Hobhouse, 15 November 1920; vol. 23, no. 191, from Governor-General to Secretary of State (Smuts's draft, undated); vol. 23, no. 231, to M. C. Gillett, 26 December 1920; *New York Times*, 3 March 1921; vol. 23, no. 73, from Lady Courtney, 26 October 1920; vol. 23, no. 232, to M. C. Gillett, 1 November 1920.

3 *J.P.E.* vol. 1, pp. 540–51.

4 See W. K. Hancock, *Survey of British Commonwealth Affairs*, 1 (London, 1937), 22–3, for a review of this argument as presented by Lord John Russell.

5 Memorandum by Sir James Lambert, C.O. 532/155.

6 *J.P.E.* vol. 2, pp. 662–78.

7 Some account of the book's reception has been given by H. Duncan Hall in an article on 'The Genesis of the Balfour Declaration of 1926' in the *Journal of Commonwealth Political Studies*, 1, no. 3 (November, 1962), 169–93. Mr Hall quotes at some length from Smuts's Memorandum, which will be printed in full in the next instalment of *Selections from the Smuts Papers*.

8 See Cd. 8566 of 1917, p. 59, and *Survey of British Commonwealth Affairs*, I, 27.

9 Cmd. 1474 of 1921, p. 9.

10 This paragraph has been distilled from my *Survey of British Commonwealth Affairs*, vol. I, ch. IV.

11 Vol. 24, nos. 41, 69, 211A, from Tom Casement, 30 May, from Lady Courtney, 9 June, from Sir Horace Plunkett, 8 June 1921.

12 Vol. 24, no. 262, to Isie Smuts, 16 June 1921.

13 Royal Archives, Windsor Castle (R.A.), Series K 1702, 'Their

Majesties' Visit to Belfast to open the Parliament of Northern Ireland and subsequent efforts to bring about reconciliation in Ireland': no. 2, Smuts to Lord Stamfordham, 14 June 1921; no. 3, copy of letter from Smuts to the Prime Minister, 14 June 1921, enclosing the draft Declaration.

14 R.A. K 1702, no. 1, Sir E. Grigg to Lord Stamfordham, 14 June 1921.

15 The letter (R.A. K 1702, no. 1) is printed *in extenso* on p. 350 of *King George the Fifth, His Life and Reign*, by Harold Nicholson.

16 R.A. K 1702, no. 3, Memorandum by Lord Stamfordham, 17 June 1921. Sir Harold Nicholson, *op. cit.* p. 351, inadvertently gives 17 instead of 16 June as the date of Lord Stamfordham's representations.

17 For the complete text of the King's speech see Nicholson, *op. cit.* pp. 352–4.

18 R.A. K 1702, no. 7, Lloyd George to the King, 23 June 1921; no. 11, Memorandum by Lord Stamfordham, 25 June 1921.

19 R.A. K 1702, no. 15, Memorandum by Lord Stamfordham, 29 June 1921.

20 R.A. K 1702, no. 22, Smuts to Lord Stamfordham, 1 July 1921.

21 R.A. K 1702, no. 23, Lord Stamfordham to Smuts, 1 July 1921.

22 R.A. K 1702, no. 27, Memorandum (by Lord Stamfordham) of a conversation between the King and General Smuts at Buckingham Palace, Thursday, 7 July 1921. Smuts himself after his talk with De Valera on 5 July made some short jottings on 'De Valera's Position'. They are in the Smuts Collection, Box N, no. 89.

23 R.A. K 1702, no. 41, Lloyd George to the King, 21 July 1921.

24 R.A. K 1702, nos. 51, 52, Smuts to the King and Smuts to De Valera, both 4 August 1921.

25 R.A. K 1702, no. 54, copy of telegram from the King to Smuts, 5 August 1921.

26 Vol. 24, no. 299, to A. B. and M. C. Gillett, 8 August 1921.

27 Vol. 24, no. 305, to M. C. Gillett, 21 September 1921. The King's helpful intervention on 7 September is described in Nicholson, *op. cit.* p. 359.

28 Vol. 24, no. 315, to M. C. Gillett, 6 December 1921.

CHAPTER 4

1 Vol. 98, no. 127, to Alice Clark, 7 April 1921; vol. 24, nos. 262, 269, to Isie Smuts, 16 June, 14 July 1921.

2 Vol. 24, nos. 302, 305, 309, to M. C. Gillett, 20 August and 21 September, to A. B. Gillett, 18 October, 1921; vol. 98, no. 130, to Alice Clark, 14 September 1921.

3 C. S. Richards, *The Iron and Steel Industry in South Africa* (Witwatersrand University Press, 1960, mimeographed), ch. 3.

4 Vol. 25, no. 300, to M. C. Gillett, 7 February 1922.

5 Vol. 25, no. 302, to M. C. Gillett, 23 February 1922.

6 Vol. 25, no. 304, to M. C. Gillett, 24 March 1922.

7 Box H, no. 33. The report of the speech is marked: Blenkin and Ribbink, Official Verbatim Reporters and Shorthand Writers, 40 Bettleheim Buildings, cor. Simmonds and Fox Streets, Johannesburg.

8 Vol. 25, nos. 16, 325, from Lord Buxton, 21 November 1922, to M. C. Gillett, 20 December 1922; vol. 27, no. 340, to M. C. Gillett, 2 January 1923.

GENERAL NOTE ON SOURCES

In my brief references to the mining industry and its labour problems I have used my own *Survey of British Commonwealth Affairs*, volume II, part 2 (London, 1942) and materials there cited. Among works which I have read since then the following three have been of particular value to me: Sheila T. van der Horst, *Native Labour in South Africa* (London, 1942); Theodore Gregory, *Ernest Oppenheimer and the Economic Development of South Africa* (London, 1962); D. Hobart Houghton, *The South African Economy* (London, 1964).

In telling the story of events on the Witswatersrand from December 1921 to March 1922 I have made constant use of two scholarly theses written under the supervision of Professor J. S. Marais of the University of the Witwatersrand: Bernard Hessian, *An Investigation into the Causes of the Labour Agitation on the Witwatersrand* (1957) and C. R. Ould, *General Smuts's Attitude to White Labour Disputes between 1907 and 1922* (1963). Without the aid of these two theses I should have found the materials hard to cope with. On the one hand, there is a deficiency of official evidence: the Cabinet and departmental records for this period still remain in the 'closed period'; there is no printed official record of the Parliamentary Debates; the records of the Trade Unions and of the Chamber of Mines, in so far as they may still survive, have not been available to me. On the other hand there exists a formidable mass of print: very full newspaper reports and an extensive pamphlet literature; reports and minutes of evidence published by important government commissions; scores of books, some nearly contemporary, others published as late as the 1960s. A great deal of this literature is violently polemical. For example, on the eve of the 1924 election the Strikers' Legal Defence Committee published a passionate attack on the Smuts government entitled 'The Story of a Crime'. Thirty-seven years later the secretary of that committee, Ivan L. Walker, in collaboration with Ben Weinbren, told essentially the same story in a book entitled *2,000 Casualties*. Walker and Weinbren, who had had stormy personal histories in the early period of the white labour movement, drew chiefly on their own memories and on printed polemical material. To cite one example on the other side, the findings of the Martial Law Commission were hotly contested when they appeared, notwithstanding the Commission's judicial composition. Mr Hessian and Mr Ould, in the above-mentioned theses, have discussed all these materials critically and have compiled valuable bibliographies.

The fact that I wrote this chapter at a distance from South Africa has added to my difficulties. In studying parliamentary debates I have followed the method described in note 4 to chapter 2. I have read a good deal in libraries, both in London and Canberra, and have made constant use of microfilm. I have many times remembered with gratitude the late Mrs Smuts, who made a magnificent collection of newspaper cuttings and pasted them into her *Plakboeke*: these I have read on microfilm.

When the time came for me to write I decided to depart from the method which I have followed in most of my other chapters. My problem was to tell the story of a highly complex and controversial conflict within a single chapter of a book containing twenty-nine chapters. I did not have enough space to argue each particular point with reference to a particular document. I have given archival references only to Smuts's private correspondence, and even these references have been few, because in the stress of that time Smuts wrote fewer letters than usual. Such allusions as I have made to printed sources are incorporated in the text or in explanatory footnotes supporting the text. I have been careful to give the precise dates of important events, so that readers who wish critically to examine my treatment of them may readily trace the evidence in newspaper and other contemporary print.

Naturally, I have had no time to discuss controversial points of evidence; most of them have been carefully discussed by Mr Hessian and Mr Ould. Needless to say, these authors have no responsibility for any mistakes of fact or interpretation which I may have made. Nor need I say that I consider this chapter as subject to revision in the light of new evidence and new insights. Since I wrote it, Mr Norman Head's book, *1922, The Revolt on the Rand* (Johannesburg, 1966), has vividly illuminated the military operations.

CHAPTER 5

1 Quoted Bengt M. Sundkler, *Bantu Prophets in South Africa* (London, 2nd ed. 1964), p. 68.
2 For what follows see *Interim and Final Reports of the Native Affairs Commission*; and *Telegram from Commissioner, South African Police, Relative to 'Israelites' at Bulhoek and Occurrences in May, 1921*, pp. 1–11.
3 *Op. cit.* pp. 2–7.
4 *Op. cit.* pp. 9–11, despatch on 24 May of Colonel Truter, Commissioner of Police.
5 *Cape Times*, 26 May 1921, p. 7.
6 *Cape Times*, 25 June 1921, p. 8.
7 *Report of the Administrator to the Prime Minister on the Bondelzwarts Rising 1922* (U.G. 30–22), Annexure A, pp. 7–9.
8 *Op. cit.* Annexure D, p. 15.
9 *Op. cit.* p. 6.
10 *Cape Times*, 24 May 1923.
11 C.O. 532/239. File Dom. S/Africa 42480.
12 Vol. 27, no. 2, from E. F. C. Lane, 28 May 1923.

GENERAL NOTE ON SOURCES

Except for E. F. C. Lane's important letter of 28 May 1923 referred to on p. 110 above, and for the frequent references to the League of Nations discussions on the Bondelzwarts affair in the correspondence between Smuts and Sir Edgar Walton, South Africa's main spokesman at Geneva, there are in the Smuts Collection very few letters immediately relevant to the subject-matter of this chapter. As explained on p. 97, Smuts took ship for the Prime Ministers' Conference in London three days after the disaster at Bulhoek. By the time he returned the debate had been concluded. He may have talked about Bulhoek with the Gilletts and other friends but he had no opportunity for writing to them. With regard to the Bondelzwarts affair he had, as explained on pp. 109–10, a definite inhibition against writing, namely, his determination to say nothing prejudicial to Hofmeyr.

My narratives, consequently, are based almost entirely on materials outside the Smuts Collection. Here I have encountered some of the same impediments as I encountered in chapter 4: the official South African records were still in the 'closed period' when I wrote the chapter and there are no Hansard reports of parliamentary debates. I have used newspaper material in the manner described in my General Note on Sources for chapter 4. This time, however, I have been fortunate in having the following very valuable printed primary sources:

For Bulhoek

(1) *Interim and Final Reports of the Native Affairs Commission*; and *Telegram from Commissioner, South African Police, Relative to 'Israelites' at Bulhoek and Occurrences in May, 1921.* Laid on the Table of the House of Assembly on 30 May 1921. (A. 4–21. Vol. III of Printed Annexures to the Votes and Proceedings of the House of Assembly; First Session, Fourth Parliament.)

(2) Magistrate's Court Inquiry (of May 1921) into the circumstances surrounding the deaths of Edward Mpatane and other Israelites at Bulhoek on 24 May.

(3) The trial (before Sir Thomas Graham and two assessors at Queenstown, in November–December 1921) of Enoch Mgijma and others.

I should add that a great deal of oral testimony on Bulhoek awaits collection. For example, through the kindness of Sister Moore of Grahamstown, I am in possession of a valuable statement from one of the survivors, Evangelist M. C. Nkopo of Mcula.

For the Bondelzwarts conflict

(1) *Report of the Administrator to the Prime Minister on the Bondelzwarts Rising, 1922.* (Dated 22 June 1922. U.G. 30–22.) This Report has five Annexures, including the Report of 26 May by Major C. N. Manning and two Reports of 19 June by Major C. A. van Coller.

(2) Report of the South African Commission of Inquiry into the Rebellion of the Bondelzwarts (dated 19 March 1923, U.G. 16–23).

(3) The Administrator's Memorandum on (2) (dated 4 April 1923, un-numbered U.G. Parliamentary Paper).

(4) Permanent Mandates Commission. Report on the Bondelzwarts Rebellion submitted to the Council of the League of Nations and forwarded by the Council to the Assembly (dated 14 August 1923. L. of N. A 47 1923, VI).

Additional League of Nations material is listed by Arnold Toynbee on pp. 416–17 of the book cited below.

Secondary sources are scanty. With the exception of Eric Walker (*A History of Southern Africa*, 3rd ed., London, 1957, pp. 587–8) historians of South Africa have mentioned Bulhoek perfunctorily, if at all. For historical and sociological perspective, the following books are especially valuable:

Monica Hunter, *Reaction to Conquest* (London, 1935).
Bengt M. Sundkler, *Bantu Prophets in South Africa* (2nd ed., London, 1962).
Sylvia L. Thrupp (ed.), *Millennial Dreams in Action* (Comparative Studies in Society and History, Supplement II, The Hague, 1962).

The Bondelzwarts affair, because of its international repercussions, received some early attention from authors outside South Africa; for example, Arnold J. Toynbee in *Survey of International Affairs, 1920–1923* (London, 1927); Freda White in *Mandates* (London, 1926); and R. R. Buell in *International Relations* (London, 1926). South Africa's historians, with the exception once again of Eric Walker (*op. cit.* pp. 395–6), have neglected it until recent years: but I am indebted to A. M. Davey, *The Bondelzwarts Affair. A Study of the Repercussions* (Pretoria, 1961), and Richard Freislich, *The Last Tribal War* (Cape Town, 1964). Freislich studied the country, talked with surviving eye-witnesses and used the private papers of Colonel (in 1922 Captain) H. Prinsloo. Consequently, his highly dramatic story has value at times as a near-primary source.

Particularly valuable to me have been two memoranda which Miss Joan Bradley (as she was then) prepared for my use in 1964.

CHAPTER 6

1 *J.P.E.* vol. 14, pp. 170–2.
2 This sketch of the Native Affairs Department is based on a memorandum written for my use by Mr M. L. Chanock.
3 Smuts's speech of 22 May 1917 was reprinted in *Thoughts on the New World* (London, 1942).
4 See C. M. Tatz, *Shadow and Substance in South Africa* (Pietermaritzburg, 1962), ch. II, for a careful account of Hertzog's ideas on these issues.

5 This sketch of the first decade of the S.A.N.N.C. is based on a memorandum written for my use by Mr M. L. Chanock. For my brief account of the programme and point of view of the deputation of 1919 I have used a letter by one of its members, J. T. Gamede, published in *West Africa*, 27 January 1920. The deputation received scant attention in the British press—in *The Times*, none at all.

6 See Edward Roux, *Time Longer than Rope* (London, 1948), chs. XI, XII, XV.

7 Letter signed Michael Furse, Bishop of Pretoria, in the *Rand Daily Mail*, 22 March 1920.

8 *J.P.E.* vol. 1, pp. 543–63; vol. 2, pp. 210–16. Cf. Tatz, *op. cit.* pp. 34–6.

9 Lecture subsequently published in the *Journal of the Royal African Society*, vol. XX, no. LXXIX.

10 *New Statesman*, 31 July 1920.

11 *Evening News*, 24 June 1920.

12 See John Maud, *City Government, Johannesburg* (London, 1938), *passim*.

13 *Handbook on Race Relations in South Africa*, ed. Ellen Hellmann (London, 1949), p. 232.

14 I use the full report in the *Star*, 8 February 1923.

15 *Unitele wa Bantu*, 22 December 1923 (a long and appreciative leading article on Smuts's message).

16 *J.P.E.* vol. 1, p. 567; vol. 2, p. 212; vol. 3, p. 226; vol. 5, p. 195.

CHAPTER 7

1 Vol. 25, no. 318, to M. C. Gillett, 30 August 1922.

2 Address by Smuts to the S.A.P. Conference at Bloemfontein, 15 and 16 August 1923.

3 Vol. 30, nos. 58, 59, cables to *New York World* and to Mrs Woodrow Wilson, 4 February 1924.

4 Vol. 25, nos. 298, 300, 302, to M. C. Gillett, 18 January, 7 and 23 February 1922; no. 274, to Bonar Law, 20 November 1922.

5 Vol. 25, no. 322, to M. C. Gillett, 25 October 1923.

6 Vol. 25, nos. 277, 279, to W. G. A. Ormsby-Gore, 21 November and to L. S. Amery, 22 November 1922.

7 Vol. 25, no. 274, to Bonar Law, 20 November 1922.

8 Vol. 25, no. 242, to Lord Robert Cecil, 5 July 1922.

9 Vol. 27, no. 349, to M. C. Gillett, 1 March 1922.

10 Vol. 27, no. 350, to M. C. Gillett, 15 March 1923; no. 245, Governor-General to Secretary of State, 4 August 1923; no. 249, to W. S. Churchill, 13 August 1923; no. 265, to Mrs Smuts, 19 September 1923.

11 Imperial Conference, 1923. Appendices to the Summary of Proceedings. Cmd. 1988, pp. 3–11, 14–18.

12 Vol. 27, no. 271, to B. M. Baruch, 3 October 1923; vol. 26, no. 16, from B. M. Baruch, 5 October 1923.

13 I wish at this point to make special acknowledgement of the help given to me by my former pupil, Dr Bruce Kent, in elucidating the complicated politics of the reparations problem in the early 1920s.

14 Vol. 27, no. 282, to Mrs Smuts, 18 October 1923.

15 Vol. 26, no. 199, from J. M. Keynes, 21 October 1923. Cf. vol. 27, no. 93, from E. F. C. Lane to R. H. Brand, 6 October 1923. Brand had written to congratulate Smuts on his opening speech at the Conference. Lane, in conveying thanks from Smuts, reported him at work on an important memorandum on reparations.

16 Vol. 26, nos. 69, 156, 17, 42, 171, from Lord Curzon (undated), M. P. A. Hankey, 24 October, B. Baruch, 24 October, H. B. Carter (for Sir Roderick Jones), 25 October, Emily Hobhouse, 24 October 1923; vol. 27, nos. 29, 161A, from E. D. Morel (undated) and G. Stresemann, 29 October 1923.

17 *The Times*, 15 November 1923. The Dawes operation was carried out under the aegis of the Reparation Commission, which on 30 November agreed on a resolution setting up two expert committees. After that, it still took some time to get agreement on their terms of reference; but on 12 December the American government announced its willingness to appoint experts to serve on them.

18 *The Times* and the *Daily Herald*, both 3 November 1923.

19 See in general C. F. Andrews, *Documents relating to the New Asiatic Bill* (London, 1926).

20 Cmd. 8566, p. 1119.

21 *H. of A. Deb.*, 17 March and 3 May 1921 (press reports).

22 Cd. 9177 of 1918, pp. 195, 245–7.

23 Cmd. 1474 of 1921, p. 8; *Round Table*, vol. 13, p. 292. The writer was commenting not on the resolution itself but on a speech delivered subsequently by Sastri.

24 The story is told in some detail in W. K. Hancock, *Survey of British Commonwealth Affairs*, vol. 1 (London, 1937), ch. IV, section iii, 'Indians in Kenya'.

25 *J.P.E.* vol. 3, pp. 937–43.

26 The *Star*, 23 July 1923.

27 In what follows I make extensive use of despatches from Sapru to Reading on 10, 17 and 23 October and of a consolidating despatch which Sapru wrote in November during his sea passage home. I am indebted to Sapru's son, Shri A. N. Sapru, of the I.C.S., for permission to use photostats of these documents from the Sapru Papers (2nd series) in the Indian National Library, Calcutta. The published proceedings, including the main speeches on the Indian question, are in Cmd. 1988 of 1923.

28 *Daily Mail*, 10 November 1923.

CHAPTER 8

1 *J.P.E.* vol. 5, p. 201 (5 February 1924); *Rand Daily Mail*, 4 September 1923; cartoon published by S.A. Labour party (undated).
2 Vol. 25, no. 306, to A. B. Gillett, 27 April 1922; no. 271, to F. Holt, 20 November 1922. See also the *Round Table*, vol. 13, p. 206.
3 *J.P.E.* vol. 3, p. 924 (17 July 1922).
4 *J.P.E.* vol. 3, p. 671 (22 May 1922).
5 Vol. 25, nos. 316, 317, to M. C. Gillett, 31 July and A. B. Gillett, 22 August 1922.
6 Vol. 25, no. 273, to Bonar Law, 20 November 1922. Also nos. 271, 277, 279, to F. Holt, 20 November, Ormsby Gore, 21 November and L. S. Amery, 22 November 1922.
7 Margaret Creswell, *An Epoch of the Political History of South Africa in the Life of Frederick Hugh Page Cresswell* (A. A. Balkema, Cape Town, 1956), pp. 93–6; *Cape Times*, 21 April 1923.
8 *Die Burger*, 3 January 1923, '...dit die dood beteken van die Smuts regering en die val van daardie regering beteken die end van die kapitalis se heerskappy in Suid-Afrika'.
9 Vol. 25, no. 314, vol. 27, no. 357, to M. C. Gillett, 7 July 1922 and 14 June 1923.
10 *Round Table*, vol. 12 (1921–2), p. 900.
11 *Op. cit.* pp. 429–30.
12 *H. of A. Deb.* vol. 1, January to April 1924, pp. 7 ff.
13 *Ibid.* pp. 87 ff.
14 *Ibid.* p. 1345; vol. 30, no. 89, to Sir E. Walton, 8 April 1924.
15 Vol. 30, no. 146, to M. C. Gillett, 12 April; no. 100, to L. S. Amery, 7 May 1924; vol. 29, nos. 92, 109, from A. B. Gillett, 29 May and M. C. Gillett, 12 June 1924.
16 In my brief impressionistic sketch of the 1924 election I have the support of a scholarly memorandum prepared for my use by Miss Clodagh O'Dowd of the University of Cape Town.
17 Vol. 30, no. 148, to M. C. Gillett, 24 June 1924; vol. 98, no. 137, to Alice Clark, 22 July 1924.

CHAPTER 9

1 Vol. 30, no. 153, vol. 36, no. 225, to M. C. Gillett, 15 August 1924 and 23 March 1926; vol. 35, no. 178, from Emily Hobhouse, 11 April 1926; vol. 34, no. 87, vol. 36, no. 168, to Emily Hobhouse, 1 April 1925 and 6 May 1926; vol. 35, nos. 121, 180, from M. C. Gillett, 10 June 1926 and from L. T. Hobhouse (undated); vol. 36, nos. 197, 220, to L. T. Hobhouse, 15 June 1926 and to Oliver Hobhouse, 18 December 1926. See also *Smuts: The Sanguine Years*, pp. 180–1, and references.
2 Vol. 34, no. 292, vol. 36, no. 244, vol. 39, nos. 266 and 276, to M. C. Gillett, 4 August 1925, 3 August 1926, 5 January and 19 March 1927.

3 Vol. 30, no. 150, vol. 34, no. 273, vol. 36, no. 239, to M. C. Gillett, 9 July 1924, 19 March 1925, 30 June 1926.

4 Vol. 38, no. 63, from J. R. Leisk (Manager of the Standard Bank), 30 March 1927; vol. 34, nos. 278, 292, vol. 40, no. 214, to M. C. Gillett, 29 April and 4 August 1925, 18 February 1928.

5 Vol. 30, no. 156, vol. 34, no. 292, to M. C. Gillett, 17 September 1924 and 4 August 1925. Kathleen Mincher, *I lived in his Shadow* (Cape Town, 1965), p. 15.

6 From 1924 onwards references to botany occur by scores every year in Smuts's letters. The following are particularly illustrative of the story told on pp. 172–3: vol. 36, nos. 233 and 245, vol. 39, no. 330, vol. 40, no. 237, to M. C. Gillett, 19 May and 10 August 1926, 21 December 1927, 13 June 1928. The considered opinion of Hutchinson of Kew was reported to the writer by Hutchinson's colleague J. Gillett in a letter of 18 January 1957.

The references to primitive archaeology, though never so frequent as the botanical references, increase steadily from 1925 onwards. The following are particularly relevant: vol. 34, no. 5, to R. Dart, 4 February 1924; vol. 31, no. 136, from R. Dart, 10 February 1925; vol. 40, nos. 223, 244, 248, to M. C. Gillett, 12 April, 25 July and 25 September 1928; vol. 40, no. 189, to S. Richardson, 3 September 1928.

7 Vol. 34, nos. 278, 279, to M. C. Gillett, 29 April and 6 May 1925; vol. 34, nos. 122, 136, to I. B. Pole-Evans, 8 and 27 May 1925. The address, 'Science from the South African Point of View', was reprinted in *Plans for a Better World* (London, 1942).

8 Among South African scientists at work in the 1960s, with whom I have discussed the address, I am particularly in debt to Professor E. D. Mountain and Mrs Enid Du Plessis. They pointed out that research has taken some turns which Smuts in 1924 did not foresee: for example, he did not foresee the advance of palynology (the study of fossilized pollens).

9 Vol. 30, no. 157, to M. C. Gillett, 25 September 1924; vol. 34, nos. 215, 299, to E. F. C. Lane, 29 September and M. C. Gillett, 2 October 1925.

10 Vol. 34, nos. 202, 225, to E. F. C. Lane, 19 August; to Sally Richardson, 12 October 1925.

11 In 'The Theory of Holism', an address to Witwatersrand students on 21 September 1927 (reprinted in *Plans for a Better World*), Smuts told a good deal of the story of his holistic explorations. For their main phases see *Smuts: The Sanguine Years*, pp. 9–10, 28–9, 38–41, 47–51, 289–308.

12 Vol. 36, no. 258, to M. C. Gillett, 17 November 1926.

13 E. Schrödinger, *What is Life?* (Cambridge, 1944), Letter of C. E. Raven to the author, 12 February 1954.

14 Vol. 36, no. 30A, from Gilbert Murray, 1 March 1926.

15 Vol. 32, no. 188, from E. F. C. Lane, 17 December 1925; vol. 36, no. 30A, from Gilbert Murray, 1 March 1926; vol. 36, no. 233, to M. C. Gillett, 19 May 1926; vol. 39, no. 24, to Gilbert Murray, 25 February 1927.

16 Vol. 36, no. 28A, from C. Lloyd Morgan, 15 November 1926; vol. 37, nos. 7A and 50, from L. S. Amery, 2 February and W. S. Churchill, 21 February 1927; vol. 38, no. 41, from Julian S. Huxley, 15 October 1927.

17 Vol. 40, no. 83, from J. S. Haldane, 13 December 1928; vol. 43, no. 39, to J. S. Haldane, 6 February 1929. Smuts had interested himself, at Julian Huxley's suggestion, in the appointment of Hogben to the Cape Town Chair.

18 J. S. Haldane, *The Sciences and Philosophy* (London, 1929), esp. pp. 136–8; L. Hogben, *The Nature of Living Matter* (London, 1930), pp. 90–101, 243, 289–316; R. A. Fisher, *Creative Aspects of Natural Law* (Cambridge, 1950); Sir Charles Sherrington, *Man on his Nature* (Cambridge, 1953); Agnes Arber, *The Mind and the Eye* (Cambridge, 1963 ed.), p. 105 and *passim*.

19 R. G. Collingwood, *The Idea of Nature* (Oxford, 1950), esp. pp. 159, 173; P. H. Partridge, 'Logic and Evolution' in *The Australasian Journal of Psychology and Philosophy*, vol. XII, no. 4 (September 1934). I also wish to express my particular indebtedness to Professor John Passmore, the author of *A Hundred Years of Philosophy* (London, 1957), and to thank him for allowing me to read the draft of a supplementary chapter to appear in a new edition of that book.

20 See Karl R. Popper, *The Open Society and its Enemies* (3rd ed., London, 1956), vol. 1, p. 80; A. C. Cilliers, review in *Die Huisgenot*, 27 May 1922, and pamphlet *Britse Holisme of Suid-Afrikaanse Nasionalisme* (1938); Monsignor Kolbe, *A Catholic View of Holism* (Cape Town, 1928), p. viii; N. P. van Wyk Louw, *Liberale Nasionalisme* (Johannesburg, 1958), pp. 9–10. Also vol. 34, no. 202, to E. F. C. Lane, 19 August 1925.

21 Kolbe, *op. cit.* p. 48; vol. 36, nos 3A and 3B, from F. C. Kolbe, 23 October and 31 December 1926; vol. 36, no. 213 and vol. 39, no. 21, to F. C. Kolbe, 28 October 1926 and 22 February 1927.

22 A. Wyatt Tilby, 'General Smuts' Philosophy' in *The Nineteenth Century*, February 1927; vol. 40, no. 165A, to A. Wyatt Tilby, 27 April 1928.

23 Vol. 37, no. 50A, from J. C. Carlisle, 18 January 1927.

24 *Nature*, 26 February 1927 and letter from Sir Graham Kerr to the author, 26 October 1953.

25 Vol. 36, no. 142, to Gilbert Murray, 8 April 1926.

CHAPTER 10

1 Vol. 31, no. 185, from L. Esselen, 30 April 1925 and enclosure; vol. 34, no. 174, and vol. 36, nos. 114, 143, to L. Esselen, 26 January 1925, 18 February and 12 April 1926. But the Smuts–Esselen correspondence gives only a brief glimpses of their joint party work.

2 Vol. 34, nos. 68, 126, to E. F. C. Lane, 24 March, and Sir Maurice Hankey, 14 May 1925; vol. 36, no. 125, to Mrs Smuts, 25 February 1926.

3 Vol. 32, nos. 209, 115, from D. F. Malan, 28 August and J. B. M.

Hertzog, 23 November 1925; vol. 34, no. 238, to Sir T. Smartt, 12 November 1925; vol. 36, nos. 17, from D. F. Malan, 11 February, 184, to Mrs Smuts, 23 May 1926.

4 *H. of A. Deb.* vol. 7, 30 March–9 June 1926, cols. 2664–6.

5 *Ibid.* cols. 4294–8.

6 L. S. Amery, *My Political Life*, vol. II (London, 1953), p. 394; cf. H. Duncan Hall, 'The Genesis of the Balfour Declaration of 1926', in *Journal of Commonwealth Political Studies*, vol. I (1961), pp. 169–93. This article is definitive. For Hertzog's use of Smuts's memorandum see also C. M. van den Heever, *General J. B. M. Hertzog* (Johannesburg, 1943), pp. 483–91, 500–2.

7 *General Smuts on the Status in the Union, at the S.A. Party Provincial Congress of the Transvaal, 8 December 1926* (printed).

8 Vol. 37, no. 7, from L. S. Amery, 24 January 1927; vol. 39, nos. 20, 165, 167, to L. S. Amery, 22 February, to John Martin, 28 May, to I. B. Pole-Evans, 30 May 1927.

9 *H. of A. Deb.* vol. 8, 22 January–14 April 1927, cols. 1478–98 (14 and 16 March).

10 Vol. 39, no. 296, to M. C. Gillett, 27 June 1927.

11 Vol. 39, no. 316, to M. C. Gillett, 29 October 1927; vol. 40, no. 175, to L. S. Amery, 22 May 1928. Also Box N, nos. 92–104, a series of notes by Smuts which systematically record the successive phases of the flag controversy in 1927.

12 Vol. 37, no. 7, from L. S. Amery, 24 January 1927; vol. 40, no. 192, to L. S. Amery, 16 October 1928.

13 *H. of A. Deb.* vol. 3, 13 February–15 April 1925, cols. 266–74, 279–84. In the Hoernlé Memorial Lecture for 1966, *Are there South Africans?*, I have raised some questions about the relationship in the mid-1960s between the definition of South African citizenship and the facts of the South African economy.

14 *Joint Sitting of Both Houses of Parliament*, 7–12 May 1926.

15 Box N, no. 90, A Summary by Smuts (17 July 1925) of Hertzog's statement.

16 *Report of the Native Affairs Commission for the Years 1925–6*, U.S. 17, 1927, pp. 11–13, 20 ff. (Minutes of Conference summoned under Act No. 23 of 1920...on the 3, 4 and 5 December 1925.)

17 Box N, no. 90, Note by Smuts on Hertzog's proposals, 17 July 1925, vol. 32, nos. 112, 116, 117, from F. S. Malan, 11 September and from J. B. M. Hertzog, 1 and 18 December 1925; vol. 34, nos. 216, 244, 246, to F. S. Malan, 29 September and to J. B. M. Hertzog, 14 and 29 December 1925; vol. 35, nos. 159, 160, from J. B. M. Hertzog, 16 and 23 January 1926. Also U.S. 17–1927, *Report of the Native Affairs Commission for the Years 1925–6*, Appendix II. (Minutes of Conference summoned under Act No. 23 of 1920...on the 3, 4 and 5 December 1925.)

18 Box G, no. 7, 'Memorandum on Government Natives and Coloured Bills' by General J. C. Smuts, September 1926.

19 Box N, nos. 107–10, Notes by Smuts of his conversations with Hertzog on 13, 15 and 27 February and 12 March 1928.

20 Box N, no. 106, Political Notes *c.* January 1928.

21 *Joint sitting of both Houses of Parliament Natives' Parliamentary Representation Bill, Coloured Persons Rights Bill*, 12–25 February 1929, *passim*, and especially cols. 68–70 (for Smuts) and 34–6, 60, 126 (for Hertzog).

22 Vol. 43, nos. 36, 44, 103, to E. F. C. Lane, 22 January, to H. Montz, 6 March, to M. C. Gillett, 28 March 1929.

23 *Cape Times*, 29 January 1929.

CHAPTER 11

1 Vol. 43, nos. 44, 58A, 116, 117, to Col. Mentz, 6 March, to E. F. C. Lane, 28 June, to M. C. Gillett, 19 June, to A. B. Gillett, 19 June 1929. Also vol. 49, no. 270, to M. C. Gillett, 21 September 1932.

2 Vol. 43, nos. 104, 117, 120, to M. C. Gillett, 4 April, to A. B. Gillett, 19 June and 10 July 1929; vol. 46, nos. 66, 109, 212, to Sir E. Oppenheimer, 29 March, to Florence Lamont, 10 April, to A. B. Gillett, 16 August 1930.

3 Vol. 46, nos. 10, 165, to C. van Riet Lowe, 3 March, to L. S. B. Leakey, 29 May 1930.

4 Vol. 43, nos. 58, 122, to E. F. C. Lane, 28 June, to M. C. Gillett, 31 July 1929; vol. 44, nos. 30, 204, from the Secretary, University of St Andrews, 11 March, from Sir T. Holland, 24 January 1930; vol. 46, nos. 25, 110, to Sir T. Holland, 12 March, to the Secretary of St Andrews, 10 April 1930.

5 Vol. 44, no. 80, from Alfred Cohn, 19 February 1940.

6 Vol. 46, no. 6, to Mrs Smuts, 23 January 1930.

7 Vol. 30, no. 136, vol. 34, no. 192, vol. 39, no. 124, to L. S. Amery, 25 November 1924, 17 July 1925, 29 April 1927; vol. 37, no. 8, vol. 40, no. 2, from L. S. Amery, 30 March 1927, 1 May 1928.

8 The three Rhodes Memorial Lectures, together with three others, were published in the volume *Africa and Some World Problems*, by General J. C. Smuts (Clarendon Press, 1930).

9 Vol. 45, no. 59, from Lord Lugard, 24 January 1930.

10 Vol. 46, nos. 215, 228, to M. C. Gillett, 23 September and 25 November 1930. The White Paper Cmd. 3573 was entitled *Memorandum on Native Policy in East Africa*. It was supported by Cmd. 3574, *Statement of the Conclusions of His Majesty's Government as regards Closer Union in East Africa*.

11 Smuts's speech was fully reported in *East Africa*, 5 December 1929.

12 Vol. 34, no. 1, to Sir Henry Strakosch, 25 January 1925.

13 Vol. 43, no. 113, to M. C. Gillett, 31 May 1929.

14 Vol. 30, no. 137, to Gilbert Murray, 25 November 1924; vol. 34, nos. 1, 105, to Sir H. Strakosch, 25 January 1925, to Gilbert Murray, 23 April 1925.

15 Vol. 34, nos. 192, 230, to L. S. Amery, 17 July 1925, to Sir A.

Chamberlain, 21 October 1925; vol. 31, no. 13, from L. S. Amery, with enclosure from Sir A. Chamberlain, 8 August 1925.

16 Smuts's speeches in North America were taken down in shorthand and subsequently typed. They are in Box I, nos. 53–71.

17 The Sheffield address of 8 October 1931 was published under the title, *The Disarmed Peace*.

18 Vol. 46, nos. 225, 226, to M. C. Gillett, 4 and 12 November 1930; vol. 48, no. 72, to Florence Lamont, 2 February 1931; vol. 49, no. 245, to M. C. Gillett, 4 June 1932.

19 Vol. 46, no. 134, vol. 48, no. 108, vol. 49, no. 205, to Florence Lamont, 1 May 1930, 21 June 1931, 13 July 1932.

20 Smuts's presidential lecture to the B.A.A.S., and its reception then and later, have been more fully discussed in my lecture, *Smuts: Study for a Portrait* (Cambridge, 1965).

21 Vol. 48, nos. 136, 197, to Florence Lamont, 4 October, to M. C. Gillett, 2 December 1931; vol. 49, no. 259, to M. C. Gillett, 10 August 1932. Also letter from C. van Riet Lowe to the author, 19 April 1955.

22 Vol. 49, no. 108, from A. J. H. Goodwin, 5 December 1932.

CHAPTER 12

1 Oswald Pirow, *James Barry Munnik Hertzog* (Howard Timmins, Cape Town), pp. 160–1, 245. Smuts's biographer Crafford suggested similarly (p. 282) that Smuts had foreseen the events of September 1939.

2 C. M. van den Heever, *General J. B. M. Hertzog* (Johannesburg, 1943), pp. 432–3, 483–91, 500–2, 556–9.

3 My short account of Broederbond ideology rests upon evidence of a slightly later date (cf. note 3 on p. 531). On the assumption that I may possibly have antedated by a few years the emergence of the ideology, I should welcome criticism.

4 Vol. 35, nos. 187, 188, from Gys Hofmeyr, 6 and 10 December 1926; vol. 36, nos. 203, 221, to F. S. Malan, 6 August and 21 December 1926; vol. 39, nos. 1, 2, to F. S. Malan, 4 January, to Sally Richardson, 5 January 1927; Esselen Papers (67) (27), to Louis Esselen, 21 February 1927.

5 Vol. 39, nos. 250, 264, to J. F. H. Hofmeyr, 29 October and 14 December 1927. Also Alan Paton, *Hofmeyr* (London, 1964), esp. ch. 14.

6 Vol. 40, no. 95, from J. F. H. Hofmeyr, 20 November 1928; vol. 42, nos. 28, 29, 30, 31, from J. F. H. Hofmeyr, 12 March, 11 April, 8 May, 13 June 1929; vol. 43, no. 44, to Col. E. Mentz, 6 March 1929; vol. 43, no. 57, to J. F. H. Hofmeyr, 5 June 1929; Esselen Papers (3) (44), to Louis Esselen, 29 October 1929.

7 Vol. 46, nos. 230, 232, to M. C. Gillett, 4 and 17 December 1930; vol. 44, no. 80, from A. Cohn, 19 February 1930.

8 Vol. 31, no. 112, to G. B. van Zyl, 28 July 1931; van den Heever, *op. cit.*

pp. 556–9; vol. 49, nos. 177, 184, 281, 219, to L. S. Amery, 3 February and 9 March, to A. B. Gillett, 4 February and 24 March 1932.

9 Vol. 47, no. 55, L. Esselen to T. Roos, 11 November 1931. Entries in Hertzog's diary, quoted by van den Heever, reveal some knowledge and much resentment of what Hertzog regarded as Roos's disreputable intriguing.

10 Vol. 49, no. 12, from R. Brown, 15 January 1932.

11 Vol. 49, nos. 233, 242, to M. C. Gillett, 12 April, 24 May 1932.

12 Vol. 49, nos. 252, 260, 263, to M. C. Gillett, 13 July, 15 and 30 August 1932.

13 Esselen Papers (25) (65), to Louis Esselen, 17 March 1932. As secretary to Smuts Strauss had received some useful political education.

14 Vol. 50, no. 137, to John Martin, 6 January 1933.

15 Alan Paton, *op. cit.*, using Hofmeyr's memoranda as well as the earlier printed sources, has written a full account of these important events, thereby enabling the present author to write briefly of them.

16 Vol. 50, no. 138, to Isie Smuts, 11 January 1933.

17 Vol. 46, no. 232, to M. C. Gillett, 17 December 1930.

18 *H. of A. Deb.* 24 January 1933, cols. 31 ff.

19 *H. of A. Deb.* 1 February 1933, col. 318.

20 *H. of A. Deb.* 28 February 1933, col. 1066.

21 Vol. 50, nos. 20, 132, from Lord Clarendon, 3 March, from Mrs Steyn, 2 April 1933.

22 Vol. 50, no. 178, to M. C. Gillett, 4 April 1933.

CHAPTER 13

1 The *Cape Times*, 25 February 1933. Cf. van den Heever, *op. cit.* pp. 597–9.

2 Pirow, *op. cit.* pp. 159–60.

3 Esselen Papers (22) (81), (29) (84), to Louis Esselen, 11, 18 and 26 July 1933. Vol. 50, no. 29, from Patrick Duncan, 11 July 1933; vol. 50, nos. 172, 201, 202, to G. B. van Zyl, 4 September, to M. C. Gillett, 4 and 7 October 1933.

4 Vol. 50, no. 204, to M. C. Gillett, 18 October 1933.

5 Vol. 50, nos. 119, 121, Roos to Esselen, 11 November, and to Smuts, 5 December 1933.

6 Vol. 52, no. 149, to M. C. Gillett, 21 February 1934.

7 Vol. 52, no. 149, to M. C. Gillett, 21 February 1934.

8 Vol. 52, no. 101, to Hertzog, 18 February 1934; vol. 51, no. 145, from Hertzog, 18 February 1934.

9 Vol. 52, no. 108, from R. Kingston Russell, 24 March 1934.

10 Leslie Blackwell, *African Occasions* (London, 1938), p. 251.

11 The *Cape Times* of 6 June 1934 published the terms of fusion in full.

12 Vol. 52, no. 179, to M. C. Gillett, 12 August 1934.

CHAPTER 14

1 Vol. 52, no. 190, to M. C. Gillett, 10 December 1934.
2 Vol. 43, no. 104, vol. 46, no. 195, to M. C. Gillett, 4 April 1929 and 20 March 1930.
3 Vol. 44, no. 155, from M. C. Gillett, 26 March 1930; vol. 46, no. 200, to A. B. Gillett, 8 April 1930.
4 Vol. 43, no. 115, to M. C. Gillett, 11 June 1929.
5 *H. of A. Deb.* vol. 18, cols. 649–51.
6 Vol. 46, nos. 191, 192, 195, 203, to M. C. Gillett, 28 February, 7 March, 20 March, 30 April 1930.
7 The percentage figures have been taken from the detailed table compiled by C. M. Tatz, *Shadow and Substance in South Africa* (Pietermaritzburg, 1962), p. 64, and note 15 on p. 90. The figures refer to Native voters only, not Coloured voters.
8 *Reports and Proceedings on the Joint Committees on Native and Coloured Persons during the period 1930–4*, pp. 12–15. Also G. Heaton Nicholls, *South Africa in my Time* (London, 1961), ch. xx, and Tatz, *op. cit.* pp. 68–9.
9 *Reports and Proceedings . . .*, pp. 15–18.
10 Vol. 46, no. 203, to M. C. Gillett, 30 April 1930; Nicholls, *op. cit.* pp. 288–90.
11 Vol. 48, nos. 159, 181, 183, to M. C. Gillett, 19 February, to A. B. Gillett, 27 May, to M. C. Gillett, 6 June 1931.
12 Vol. 48, no. 183, to M. C. Gillett, 4 June 1931.
13 Vol. 53, nos. 194, 204, 205, to M. C. Gillett, 23 February, 28 April and 6 May 1935.
14 Vol. 52, no. 4, from D. D. Jabavu (undated); vol. 54, nos. 208, 210, to M. C. Gillett, 1 February and 30 March 1936. On the All-African Convention see Tatz, *op. cit.* pp. 87–9 and note 47 on p. 91.
15 Noni Jabavu, *Drawn in Colour* (London, 1960), p. 165.
16 Many letters of the Gilletts to members of their family, during their successive visits to South Africa, have been added, together with other background material, to the Smuts Collection.

CHAPTER 15

1 Vol. 54, nos. 231, 240, to M. C. Gillett, 6 August and 26 September 1936; vol. 55, nos. 152, 159, 174, 192, to M. C. Gillett, 7 January, 10 April, 8 October 1937; to Tom Lamont, 21 October 1937; vol. 57, no. 222, to M. C. Gillett, 16 March 1938.
2 *British Policy To-day. General Smuts Survey.* Reprinted from *The Times* of 13 November 1934, with leading article of the same date. Vol. 51, no. 36, from Lord Cecil, 15 November 1934; vol. 52, no. 30, from Lord Lothian, 20 December 1934.
3 Vol. 52, no. 99, to L. S. Amery, 1 February 1934; no. 172, to A. B.

Gillett, 1 July 1934; nos. 154, 157, 174, 177, to M. C. Gillett, 18 March, 3 April, 9 July, 28 July 1934.

4 Vol. 49, nos. 218, 245, to A. B. Gillett, 4 February, to M. C. Gillett, 4 June 1932.

5 Smuts's Rectoral address on *The Challenge to Freedom* was delivered on 17 October 1934 and subsequently published. Cf. *Notes of an Address* (Box I, nos. 84, 89) which he delivered in the chapel of Christ's College, Cambridge, on Sunday 21 October; his theme was basically the same, but with the politics left out.

6 Pirow, *op. cit.* p. 221; vol. 53, no. 151, to Lothian, 20 February 1935.

7 Vol. 53, no. 151, to Lothian, 20 February 1935; also J. R. M. Butler, *Lord Lothian* (London, 1960), chs. xi and xii, *passim.*

8 Vol. 53, nos. 197, 200, 202, 203, 205, to M. C. Gillett, 18 and 31 March, 14 and 22 April, 6 May 1935; nos. 198, 214, to A. B. Gillett, 23 March and 21 June 1935.

9 Vol. 53, no. 199, to M. C. Gillett, 23 March 1935.

10 Vol. 53, no. 4, from L. S. Amery, 3 October 1935.

11 Vol. 53, nos. 205, 215, 218, 229, to M. C. Gillett, 6 May, 21 June, 8 July, 30 September 1935; no. 214, to A. B. Gillett, 21 June 1935; no. 181, to L. S. Amery, 2 December 1935.

12 *Pacifism is not enough (nor Patriotism either)*, the Burge Memorial Lecture delivered on 28 May 1935 by Lord Lothian (London, 1935). See Butler, *op. cit.* pp. 207–9, for Smuts's letter of 5 August 1935 and Lothian's reply.

13 Butler, *loc. cit.*; vol. 54, nos. 173, 177, to L. S. Amery, 29 June and 23 July 1936; vol. 54, no. 223, to M. C. Gillett, 29 July 1936.

14 Vol. 53, nos. 227, 233, to M. C. Gillett, 10 September and 23 October 1935.

15 Vol. 54, nos. 210, 213, to M. C. Gillett, 30 March and 19 April 1936.

16 Vol. 54, no. 163, to T. Lamont, 24 March 1936; Butler, *op. cit.* p. 213, for letter to Lothian of same date.

17 Vol. 54, nos. 210, 211, 213, to M. C. Gillett, 30 March, 5 and 19 April 1936.

18 See Nicholas Mansergh, *Survey of British Commonwealth Affairs: Problems of External Policy, 1931–9* (London, 1939), pp. 240–52.

19 Vol. 54, no. 174, to Sir Maurice Hankey, 17 July 1936; nos. 238, 254, to M. C. Gillett, 12 and 23 September 1936.

20 Vol. 46, nos. 180, 181, 183, 184, to D. Lloyd George, 22 October 1930 (two cables), to Ramsay MacDonald, 24 and 25 October 1930; vol. 54, nos. 174, 179, 180, to Lord Hankey, 17 July 1936, to D. Lloyd George, 23 July 1936, to Rt Hon. W. S. A. Ormsby-Gore, 23 July 1936.

21 Vol. 54, nos. 228, 242, 247, 248, to M. C. Gillett, 27 July, 11 October, 12 and 22 November 1936; vol. 55, no. 158, to A. B. Gillett, 7 January 1937; no. 197, to M. C. Gillett, 29 October 1937.

22 Vol. 54, nos. 228, 233, 236, 238, 240, to M. C. Gillett, 27 July, 17

August, 12 September, 26 September 1936; to A. B. Gillett, 7 September 1936.

23 Vol. 54, nos. 5, 250, from L. S. Amery, 4 December 1936, to M. C. Gillett, 29 November 1936.

24 Vol. 55, no. 161, to M. C. Gillett, 18 January 1937.

25 Vol. 54, nos. 244, 250, to M. C. Gillett, 24 October, 29 November 1936; vol. 55, nos. 166, 167, 171, to M. C. Gillett, 21 February, 27 February, 21 March 1937.

26 Vol. 55, nos. 100, 143, from Lothian, 16 March 1937, to Lothian, 7 April 1937.

27 Vol. 55, nos. 188, 191, 192, 195, 197, to M. C. Gillett, 24 September, to A. B. Gillett, 2 October, to M. C. Gillett, 8, 23 and 29 October 1937.

28 Vol. 55, no. 155, to L. S. Amery, 9 December 1937; vol. 56, no. 10, from L. S. Amery, 18 March 1938; vol. 57, no. 118, to L. S. Amery, 28 March 1938.

29 Vol. 55, nos. 166, 178, 200, to M. C. Gillett, 21 February, 2 May, 13 November 1937; vol. 57, no. 144, to Lord Lothian, 20 May 1938.

30 Van den Heever, *op. cit.* p. 275; Mansergh, *op. cit.* p. 257.

31 *H. of A. Deb.* 25 August 1938, cols. 1676–80.

CHAPTER 16

1 Vol. 53, nos. 153, 189, 216, 223, to H. A. L. Fisher, 1 March 1935, to M. C. Gillett, 21 January, 1 July, 17 August 1935; vol. 54, no. 220, to M. C. Gillett, 6 June 1936.

2 *Die Transvaaler*, 26 April 1943, quoted by Michael Roberts and A. E. G. Trollip, *The South African Opposition* (London, 1947), p. 159.

3 Vol. 55, no. 160, to M. C. Gillett, 11 January 1937. On the anti-Semitism see the *Round Table*, vol. 27 (1936–7), pp. 440 ff.; Eric Walker, *History of Southern Africa* (London, 1964), pp. 656–7; Alan Paton, *op. cit.* p. 262.

4 Vol. 55, no. 167, to M. C. Gillett, 27 February 1937.

5 Vol. 55, no. 174, to M. C. Gillett, 10 April 1937. Cf. Alan Paton, *op. cit.* pp. 262, 267 ff., 291.

6 Vol. 55, nos. 188, 195, to M. C. Gillett, 24 September, 23 October 1937; the *Round Table*, vol. 28 (1937–8), pp. 197–9; Walker, *op. cit.* p. 641.

7 Vol. 55, no. 192, to M. C. Gillett, 8 October 1937; vol. 57, nos. 215, 218, to M. C. Gillett, 10 and 25 February 1938.

8 Communication to the author from Mr Morris Kentridge.

9 *H. of A. Deb.* 1 March 1938, cols. 750–60.

10 Vol. 57, no. 144, to Lord Lothian, 20 May 1938.

11 Vol. 57, no. 233, to M. C. Gillett, 24 May 1938; no. 148, to F. Lane, 11 July 1938.

12 Van den Heever, *op. cit.* pp. 272–4.

13 Vol. 56, no. 69, from Sir Patrick Duncan, 11 September 1938; Alan Paton, *op. cit.* pp. 287–92. According to Mrs Gillett (letter to the author, 27

May 1959) Smuts asked Hofmeyr after receiving notice of his intention to resign, whether he, Smuts, ought not also to resign. Hofmeyr answered that question with an emphatic No.

CHAPTER 17

1 From Mrs Gillett to her son Nicholas, 10 December 1935; vol. 53, nos. 213, 218, 226, 229, to M. C. Gillett, 15 June, 8 July, 9 September, 30 September 1935; vol. 54, nos. 218, 245, to M. C. Gillett, 24 May and 31 October 1936; vol. 55, no. 192, to M. C. Gillett, 8 October 1937; vol. 60, nos. 185, 206, 220, to M. C. Gillett, 29 January, 27 May, 28 August 1939.
2 Vol. 54, no. 216; vol. 60, no. 207, to M. C. Gillett, 10 May 1936 and 4 June 1939.
3 Vol. 60, no. 219, to M. C. Gillett, 20 August 1939.
4 Vol. 55, nos. 177, 192, to M. C. Gillett, 24 April and 8 October 1937.
5 Vol. 51, no. 24, from F. Brehmer, 28 February 1934, recommending Professor Meyer; vol. 52, no. 122, to A. Meyer, 20 September 1934; vol. 54, nos. 223, 234, 235, to M. C. Gillett, 29 June, 22 and 29 August 1936; vol. 57, no. 131, to Dr Helmut Minkowski, 8 April 1938, enclosing preface for German translation of *Holism and Evolution*.
6 Vol. 54, no. 254, to M. C. Gillett, 23 December 1936.
7 Vol. 57, nos. 208, 215, to M. C. Gillett, 3 January and 10 February 1938.
8 M. C. Gillett to A. B. Gillett, 21 July 1937, to Hilda Clark, 11 September 1938.
9 Vol. 54, nos. 211, 220, to M. C. Gillett, 5 April and 6 June 1936; no. 170, to L. Bolus, 26 May 1936; vol. 60, no. 49, to J. F. Metelerkamp, 2 March 1939.
10 Vol. 50, nos. 178, 210, to M. C. Gillett, 4 April and 21 November 1933; vol. 52, no. 179, to M. C. Gillett, 12 August 1934; vol. 53, nos. 195 and 170, to M. C. Gillett, 2 March, and to Florence Lamont, 15 June 1935.
11 Vol. 50, no. 157, to C. van Riet Lowe, 29 May 1934; vol. 53, nos. 216, 225, 226, to M. C. Gillett, 1 July, 2 and 9 September 1935; vol. 55, nos. 180, 200, to M. C. Gillett, 15 May and 13 November 1937.
12 Vol. 55, no. 158, to A. B. Gillett, 7 January 1937; nos. 173, 178, to M. C. Gillett, 3 April and 2 May 1937.
13 Vol. 53, no. 195, to M. C. Gillett, 2 March 1935.
14 Vol. 55, nos. 173, 192, 203, to M. C. Gillett, 3 April, 8 October, 30 November 1937; vol. 57, nos. 208, 232, to M. C. Gillett, 3 January, 15 May 1938; vol. 60, nos. 199, 207, to M. C. Gillett, 23 April, 4 June 1939.
15 Vol. 54, no. 234, vol. 55, no. 198, to M. C. Gillett, 22 August 1936 and 5 November 1937; vol. 57, no. 131, to Dr Helmut Minkowski, 8 April 1938; vol. 60, no. 203, to M. C. Gillett, 14 May 1939.

16 Vol. 55, no. 207, to M. C. Gillett, 23 December 1937; vol. 57, no. 234, to M. C. Gillett, 28 May 1938.

17 Vol. 54, no. 220, to M. C. Gillett, 6 June 1936; vol. 60, nos. 196, 203, to M. C. Gillett, 6 April and 14 May 1939.

18 Vol. 57, no. 208, to M. C. Gillett, 3 January 1938; vol. 60, nos. 193, 194, 201, 218, to M. C. Gillett, 17 and 24 March, 7 May, 18 August 1939.

19 Box I, no. 112, 'Twenty Years After'. Cf. vol. 57, no. 203, to Lord Cecil, 6 December 1938.

20 Vol. 60, nos, 38, 185, to T. Lamont, 10 January, to M. C. Gillett, 29 January 1939.

21 Vol. 60, no. 42, to L. S. Amery, 7 February 1939; nos. 190, 193, 194, 197, to M. C. Gillett, 5, 17, 24 March and 8 April 1938.

22 Vol. 60, no. 66, to Lord Lothian, 27 May; nos. 193, 196, to M. C. Gillett, 17 March, 6 April, no. 93, to E. Lane, 30 May 1939.

23 Vol. 60, nos. 201, 206, to M. C. Gillett, 7 and 27 May; no. 93, to E. Lane, 30 May; no. 207, to M. C. Gillett, 4 June; no. 215, to M. C. Gillett, 3 August; no. 111, to L. S. Amery, 2 August; no. 217, to A. B. Gillett, 17 August; nos. 219, 220, to M. C. Gillett, 20 and 28 August; no. 117, to Lord Brand, 29 August 1939.

24 Vol. 60, nos. 66, 199, to Lord Lothian, 27 March, to M. C. Gillett, 23 April 1939.

25 Vol. 60, nos. 185, 191, 66, 199, 111, 115, to M. C. Gillett, 29 January, to A. B. Gillett, 10 March, to Lord Lothian, 27 March, to M. C. Gillett, 23 April, to L. S. Amery, 2 August, to John Martin, 3 August 1939.

26 Vol. 60, nos, 212, 220, to M. C. Gillett, 6 July and 28 August 1939.

27 *H. of A. Deb.* 4 September 1939, cols. 19, 20; van den Heever, *op. cit.* p. 279; Pirow, *op. cit.* p. 242.

28 I have used a microfilm copy of the press cuttings pasted by Mrs Smuts into her *Plakboeke* and in giving 20 as the total of Smuts's significant public pronouncements on foreign affairs in this period have assumed that she did not miss any.

29 Quoted *Round Table*, no. 115, p. 637.

30 Vol. 60, no. 185, to M. C. Gillett, 29 January 1939; no. 42, to L. S. Amery, 7 February 1939.

31 Vol. 60, no. 220, to M. C. Gillett, 28 August 1939.

32 In the *Sunday Times* (Johannesburg) of 26 July 1964 Mr Vernon Barber published a reminiscent article, based largely on what other people had said to him on 2–3 September 1939, purporting to show that 'the credit for taking this country into the war' did not belong to Smuts. The article, which contained many patent inaccuracies, moved Mr Harry Lawrence, Q.C., to publish next week (*Sunday Times*, 2 August 1964) his own recollections, as the only member of Hertzog's Cabinet still surviving.

33 *H. of A. Deb.* 4 September 1939, cols. 17–24.

34 *Op. cit.* cols. 24–31.

35 Vol. 60, no. 230, to M. C. Gillett, 10 November 1939.

36 Vol. 60, no. 119, to T. Lamont, 6 September 1939.

37 Vol. 63, no. 3, to G. Dawson, 26 January 1940.
38 Vol. 63, no. 78, to M. C. Gillett, 30 June 1940.

CHAPTER 18

1 *H. of A. Deb.* 3rd Session, 8th Parl., vol. 36, col. 19.
2 Vol. 60, no. 223, to M. C. Gillett, 21 September 1939; vol. 60, no. 137 and vol. 63, no. 2, to L. S. Amery, 11 October 1939, and 16 January 1940; vol. 63, no. 3, to G. Dawson, 26 January 1940.
3 Vol. 60, no. 223, to M. C. Gillett, 21 September 1939.
4 Many articles on the South African war economy were published during the war in the *South African Journal of Economics*. A retrospective review by Professor H. M. Robertson appeared in vol. 22, no. 1 (March 1954) of that Journal. See also *Official Year Book of the Union of South Africa* (1956–7), no. 29, ch. XXIV.
5 From article by Professor L. J. du Plessis in *Die Transvaler*, 30 April 1941, quoted in *The South African Opposition* by Michael Roberts and A. E. G. Trollip (Cape Town, 1947), p. 15 (Afrikaans) and p. 228 (translation). Reference checked by author.
6 I have drawn this information about the armed forces and war industry from the published material referred to in note 4 above and from two volumes published by the O.U.P. for the Union War Histories Section of the Prime Minister's Department: *War in the Southern Oceans, 1939–1945*, by L. C. F. Turner *et al.* pp. 3–4; and *The Sidi Rezek Battles, 1941*, by J. A. I. Agar-Hamilton and L. C. F. Turner, pp. 71–2.
7 *H. of A. Deb.* vol. 38, col. 3440, 14 March 1940.
8 In this and the following paragraphs I draw freely on Roberts and Trollip, *op. cit.* ch. 2.
9 Vol. 63, no. 77, to M. C. Gillett, 24 January 1940.
10 Vol. 60, no. 162, to Robert Brand, 13 November 1940.
11 Vol. 60, no. 231, to M. C. Gillett, 16 November 1939.
12 *H. of A. Deb.* 23 January 1940, vol. 37, cols. 38–45.
13 *Ibid.* cols. 43–54.
14 Vol. 63, no. 85, to M. C. Gillett, 3 March 1940.
15 This note is based on a factual memorandum prepared for the author's use by Mr Donald Molteno, Q.C.

CHAPTER 19

1 Vol. 60, no. 206, and vol. 63, no. 120, to M. C. Gillett, 27 May 1939 and 14 October 1940.
2 Vol. 63, no. 20, to F. Lane, 31 May; no. 29, to L. S. Amery, 19 June; no. 42, to G. Dawson, 20 August; nos. 98 and 114, to M. C. Gillett, 3 June and 1 September 1940.
3 To M. C. Gillett, vol. 60, no. 224, 23 September 1939; vol. 63, no. 79,

9 February 1940; no. 88, 24 March; no. 105, 10 July; no. 110, 4 August; no. 115, 8 September; no. 119, 7 October; no. 133, 30 December 1940.

4 Vol. 63, no. 85, to M. C. Gillett, 3 March 1940.

5 Vol. 63, no. 118, to M. C. Gillett, 30 September 1940.

6 Vol. 63, nos. 98, 105, 120, to M. C. Gillett, 3 June, 10 July and 14 October 1940.

7 Vol. 63, nos. 96 and 124, to M. C. Gillett, 21 May and 13 November 1940.

8 Vol. 63, no. 110, to M. C. Gillett, 4 August 1940.

9 Vol. 63, no. 90, to M. C. Gillett, 7 April 1940.

10 Vol. 63, no. 92, to M. C. Gillett, 25 April 1940.

11 Vol. 63, no. 124, to M. C. Gillett, 13 November 1940.

12 Vol. 63, no. 120, to M. C. Gillett, 14 November 1940.

13 Vol. 60, no. 84, to M. C. Gillett, 29 February 1940.

14 Vol. 63, no. 112, to M. C. Gillett, 20 August 1940.

15 Vol. 63, nos. 84 and 94, to M. C. Gillett, 29 February and 9 May 1940.

16 Vol. 63, no. 105, to M. C. Gillett, 10 July 1940.

17 Vol. 63, no. 96, to M. C. Gillett, 21 May 1940.

18 Vol. 63, no. 97, to M. C. Gillett, 28 May 1940.

19 Vol. 63, no. 108, to M. C. Gillett, 21 July 1940.

20 Vol. 63, nos. 99 and 108, to M. C. Gillett, 8 June and 21 July 1940.

21 Vol. 63, no. 111, to M. C. Gillett, 12 August and vol. 63, no. 46, to John Martin, 21 September 1940.

22 Vol. 63, nos. 115, 122, and 123, to M. C. Gillett, 8 September, 29 October and 5 November 1940.

23 Vol. 63, no. 104, to M. C. Gillett, 2 July 1940.

24 Vol. 63, no. 95, to M. C. Gillett, 12 May 1940.

25 *H. of A. Deb.* 10 May 1940, vol. 39, cols. 7236, 7240–4; speeches by Dr N. J. van der Merwe, Eric Louw and Dr D. F. Malan. Hertzog, perhaps significantly, was absent from this debate.

26 Vol. 63, nos. 26 and 31, to General Hertzog, 13 and 20 June 1940.

27 *Cape Times*, 14 June 1940, reporting Malan's speech at Porterville the previous day.

28 Vol. 63, no. 111, to M. C. Gillett, 12 August 1940. Roberts and Trollip, *op. cit.* pp. 40–2.

29 Vol. 63, nos. 113, 115, and 116, to M. C. Gillett, 25 August, 8 and 17 September 1940.

30 Roberts and Trollip, *op. cit.* pp. 49–51.

31 Vol. 63, no. 133, to M. C. Gillett, 30 December 1940. Cf. no. 70, a warm personal letter from Smuts to Hertzog, 13 December 1940.

32 Vol. 63, nos. 66 and 128, to L. S. Amery, 9 December, and to M. C. Gillett, 8 December 1940.

33 W. S. Churchill, *The Second World War*, vol. II, *Their Finest Hour*, pp. 200–1.

34 Churchill, *op. cit.* pp. 376–8.

35   Vol. 63, no. 123, to M. C. Gillett, 5 November 1940.
36   Vol. 63, nos. 128 and 126, to M. C. Gillett, 8 December and 25 November 1940.
37   Vol. 63, nos. 68 and 130, to Wavell, 12 December 1940, and M. C. Gillett, 16 December 1940; vol. 66, no. 206, to M. C. Gillett, 6 January 1941.
38   E.g. vol. 69, no. 224, to M. C. Gillett, 10 March 1942.

CHAPTER 20

1   Vol. 61, no. 93, from Churchill, 22 July 1940.
2   Vol. 63, no. 119, to M. C. Gillett, 7 October 1940; vol. 66, no. 212, to A. B. Gillett, 14 February 1941.
3   Vol. 63, no. 95, to M. C. Gillett, 12 May 1940.
4   Vol. 63, nos. 113 and 119, to M. C. Gillett, 25 August and 7 October 1940; vol. 63, no. 56, to T. Lamont, 8 November 1940; vol. 66, nos. 206, 216 and 217, to M. C. Gillett, 6 January, 16 and 22 March 1941.
5   Vol. 66, no. 213, to M. C. Gillett, 16 February 1941.
6   Vol. 66, nos. 104, 207, 208, 210, to L. S. Amery, 18 February, to M. C. Gillett, 13 and 23 January and 2 February 1941.
7   New Zealand's war historians would appear to be at variance in some degree with their British colleagues in their interpretation of how the decision to intervene was arrived at. See especially *To Greece*, by W. G. McClymont (Wellington, 1959), ch. VI *passim*.
8   Vol. 66, no. 227, to M. C. Gillett, 2 June 1941.
9   Vol. 66, nos. 125 and 137, to Wavell, 19 May and 9 June; nos. 220 and 225, to M. C. Gillett, 14 April and 18 May 1941.
10   Vol. 66, no. 225, to M. C. Gillett, 18 May 1941.
11   Vol. 66, nos. 230, 233, 240, to M. C. Gillett, 25 June, 15 July and 2 September; no. 167, to L. S. Amery, 9 September 1941.
12   Vol. 66, nos. 233, 239, 241, 242, 248, 250, to M. C. Gillett, 15 July, 24 August, 8 and 15 September, 29 October, 10 November; no. 167, to L. S. Amery, 9 September 1941.
13   Vol. 66, nos. 225, 239, 241, 250, 252, to M. C. Gillett, 18 May, 24 August, 8 September, 10 and 23 November 1941.
14   Vol. 66, nos. 234, 247, 253, 254, to M. C. Gillett, 24 July, 19 October, 30 November and 7 December 1941.

CHAPTER 21

1   Vol. 69, no. 173, to Sir Robert Craigie, 11 September 1942.
2   Vol. 30, no. 136, to L. S. Amery, 25 November 1924. S. W. Roskill, *The War at Sea* (U.K. History of the Second World War), vol. I (1954), p. 558.
3   Vol. 69, no. 219, to M. C. Gillett, 31 January 1942.
4   Vol. 69, nos. 217, 219, 222, to M. C. Gillett, 17, 31 January and 25 February; no. 124, to John Martin, 26 February 1942.

5 Vol. 69, nos. 222, 223, 225, 226, 233, to M. C. Gillett, 25 and 28 February, 16 and 21 March, 7 May 1942.
6 Vol. 69, no. 229, to M. C. Gillett, 12 April 1942.
7 Vol. 69, no. 137, to President Roosevelt, 19 May 1942.
8 For what follows see Roberts and Trollip, *op. cit.* chs. iii–v.
9 *Ibid.* p. 95.
10 *Ibid.* p. 119.
11 Vol. 69, nos. 220 and 221, to M. C. Gillett, 7 and 14 February 1942, reporting a recrudescence of sabotage.
12 *H. of A. Deb.* 3 May 1941, vol. 42, cols. 8033 ff.
13 Vol. 66, nos. 230, 240, to M. C. Gillett, 25 June and 2 September 1941.
14 Vol. 69, nos. 236, 237, to M. C. Gillett, 1 and 7 June 1942.
15 Vol. 67, no. 41, memorandum from Col. van der Westhuizen enclosed in note to Smuts from Leslie Blackwell.
16 *H. of A. Deb.* 11 March 1942, cols. 3572–651.
17 Vol. 69, no. 226, to M. C. Gillett, 21 March 1942.
18 I base this sentence on a close study of *Die Transvaler*—its news, headlines, editorial comment and correspondence columns—from January to April 1942.
19 *H. of A. Deb.* 13 January 1942, vol. 43, cols. 33–50 (Malan), 50–7 (Smuts), and 532–6 (vote).
20 According to an estimate quoted in the *Round Table* (vol. 32, p. 426), the government secured 35,000 and the Opposition 20,000 votes in twelve provincial by-elections held at this time.
21 Vol. 69, no. 227, to M. C. Gillett, 3 April 1942.
22 Vol. 69, nos. 239, 240, to M. C. Gillett, undated and 29 June 1942.
23 Vol. 69, no. 137, to President Roosevelt, 19 May 1942.
24 Vol. 69, no. 229, to M. C. Gillett, 7 February; vol. 68, no. 82, from Sir Miles Lampson, 30 July 1942. Cf. vol. 69, no. 280, from General Theron, 8 September 1942, reporting that quite a number of other people had hoped that he would assume the supreme command.
25 Vol. 69, nos. 233 and 234, to A. B. and M. C. Gillett, 7 and 19 May 1942.
26 Vol. 69, nos. 236 and 238, to M. C. Gillett, 1 and 16 June 1942. See also I. G. O. Playfair, *The Mediterranean and the Middle East* (U.K. Official History), vol. iii, ch. x; J. A. I. Agar-Hamilton and L. C. F. Turner, *Crisis in the Desert* (S.A. Official History), part i; J. C. Smuts, *Jan Christian Smuts* (London, 1952), pp. 417–18; John Connell, *Auchinleck* (London, 1959), pp. 588–9. Playfair (p. 274) gives the following estimate of prisoners taken at Tobruk:

British troops	19,000
South African Europeans	8,960
South African Natives	1,760
Indian troops	2,500
Total	32,220

27 Vol. 69, no. 241, to M. C. Gillett, 10 July 1942.

28 Churchill, *op. cit.* vol. IV, pp. 386–7; telegram from Smuts, 7 July 1942.

29 Vol. 69, no. 277, from General F. Theron, 17 July; no. 159, to Theron, 21 July 1942.

30 See Playfair, *op. cit.* pp. 333–4, and Connell, *op. cit.* pp. 667 ff. and 702 ff.

31 Vol. 69, no. 247, to M. C. Gillett, 10 August 1942.

32 Vol. 69, no. 242, to M. C. Gillett, 12 July 1942.

33 Churchill, *op. cit.* pp. 412, 453; Sir Arthur Bryant, *The Turn of the Tide* (London, 1957), pp. 438, 440–1, 446–7, 449, 483; Sir John Kennedy, *The Business of War* (London, 1957), pp. 317–18. Also vol. 69, no. 161, to T. Lamont, 14 August; no. 268, from Sir A. Tedder, 1 September, no. 280, from F. Theron, 8 September 1942.

34 Vol. 69, nos. 249 and 254, to M. C. Gillett, 26 August and 1 October 1942; Kennedy, *op. cit.* pp. 317–18; Smuts, *op. cit.* pp. 423–5.

35 Vol. 69, no. 195, to President Roosevelt, 15 November 1942.

36 Vol. 69, no. 260, to M. C. Gillett, 14 December 1942.

37 Vol. 72, nos. 199 and 202, to M. C. Gillett, 19 January and 10 February 1943.

38 Vol. 72, nos. 75 and 209, to Sir M. Lampson, 29 March and M. C. Gillett, 31 March 1943.

39 Vol. 72, no. 215, to M. C. Gillett, 14 May 1943.

40 Vol. 72, no. 216, to M. C. Gillett, 17, May 1943.

41 Vol. 72, no. 209, to M. C. Gillett, 31 March 1943.

42 Vol. 72, nos. 98, 125, 223, to Col. Stallard, 17 May, to M. Ellis, 13 July, to M. C. Gillett, 11 July 1943.

43 For the correspondence between Smuts and the rival contenders in the Gardens constituency see vol. 69, nos. 159A, 169; vol. 70, nos. 40, 41; vol. 71, nos. 112, 113, ; vol. 72, nos. 77, 84, 90.

44 Vol. 69, no. 253 and vol. 72, no. 218, to M. C. Gillett, 24 September 1942 and 9 June 1943.

45 Vol. 72, no. 223, to M. C. Gillett, 11 July 1943.

46 Vol. 72, no. 226, to M. C. Gillett, 31 July 1943.

CHAPTER 22

1 For permission to quote from this letter (of 20 July 1942) I am greatly indebted to Lord Harlech.

2 They have been employed by Dr H. Brookfield in *Trek and Laager*; see *Frontiers and Men*, ed. J. Andrews (Melbourne, 1966), pp. 66–89.

3 Vol. 66, no. 238, to M. C. Gillett, 20 August 1941; vol. 69, nos. 219, 221, 224, 241, 253, 258, to same, 31 January, 14 February, 10 March, 10 July, 24 September, 29 November 1942; vol. 72, nos. 215, 222, to same, 14 May, 4 July 1943. For a tolerant account of Hertzog's last indiscretions see Roberts and Trollip, *op. cit.* pp. 129–30.

4 Vol. 66, no. 245, to M. C. Gillett, 6 October 1941; vol. 69, nos. 224,

260, to same, 10 March and 14 December 1942; vol. 72, no. 231, to same, 8 September 1943.

5 Vol. 69, no. 233, to M. C. Gillett, 7 May 1943.

6 I am deeply indebted to Lady Moore, who has allowed me to use relevant passages from her letters and diaries and has composed for my use a factual narrative as background to what she wrote contemporaneously. The passages quoted above are from letters which she wrote to her mother in England on 3 and 18 July 1941.

7 Again I am indebted to Lady Moore, who was with General and Mrs Smuts in August 1941 in Egypt. For the impact of Mrs Smuts upon 'society' there see Lord Chandos, *Memoirs: An Unexpected View from the Summit* (London, 1962).

8 Vol. 66, no. 222, to M. C. Gillett, 27 April 1941; vol. 69, no. 258, to same, 29 November 1942; vol. 72, nos. 198, 204, 207, to same, 13 January, 22 February, 14 March 1943; vol. 75, no. 202, to same, 6 July 1944.

9 Vol. 72, no. 224, to M. C. Gillett, 21 July 1943.

10 Vol. 69, nos. 219, 227, to M. C. Gillett, 31 January and 3 April 1942; vol. 75, no. 200, to same, 14 March 1944.

11 Vol. 60, nos. 215, 222, to M. C. Gillett, 3 August, 13 September 1939; vol. 66, nos. 221, 245, to same, 21 April and 6 October 1941.

12 But circumstances did not permit so many meetings or so much talk as they had during the First World War. See vol. 69, no. 258, and vol. 72, no. 223, to M. C. Gillett, 29 November 1942 and 11 July 1943. In 1944, a year of increasing exhaustion, there are fairly frequent references in Smuts's letters to his backslidings as a correspondent or to the erratic mails. [Vol. 75, nos. 198, 200, 202, 203, 211.]

13 Vol. 66, no. 208, to M. C. Gillett, 23 January 1941 ('Perhaps it was my function just to start the ball rolling'); vol. 77, no. 6, from Professor Adolf Meyer-Abich, 14 June 1945; vol. 77, no. 267, to M. C. Gillett, 9 November 1945.

14 Vol. 77, no. 128, to C. E. Raven, 3 January 1945.

15 Vol. 69, no. 244, to M. C. Gillett, 27 July 1942.

16 Vol. 75, no. 209, to M. C. Gillett, 24 October 1944.

17 Vol. 66, no. 97, to van Riet Lowe, 22 January 1941; vol. 68, no. 112, from van Riet Lowe, 9 January 1942, and no. 115, from Abbé Breuil, 7 February 1942; vol. 69, no. 117, to Abbé Breuil, 22 January 1942; vol. 69, no. 260, to M. C. Gillett, 14 December 1942; vol. 72, no. 226, to same, 31 July 1943; vol. 77, no. 242, to same, 21 January 1945.

18 Vol. 77, no. 255, to M. C. Gillett, 22 July 1945.

19 Vol. 75, no. 210, to M. C. Gillett, 1 November 1944.

20 Vol. 60, no. 239, to M. C. Gillett (undated: it was just after the fall of Tobruk), no. 241, to same, 10 July 1942.

21 Vol. 69, no. 223, to M. C. Gillett, 28 February 1942.

22 Vol. 66, no. 223, to M. C. Gillett, 3 May 1941.

23 Vol. 63, no. 90, to M. C. Gillett, 7 April 1940; vol. 66, nos, 207, 235, to same, 13 January and 28 July 1941.

24 Vol. 66, nos. 246, 248, 11 and 29 October 1941; vol. 69, no. 243, 22 July 1942; vol. 72, no. 226, 31 July 1943; vol. 77, nos. 244, 265, 3 February and 25 October 1945: all to M. C. Gillett.

25 Vol. 66, nos. 229, 243, to M. C. Gillett, 17 June and 22 September 1941.

26 Vol. 69, no. 236, to M. C. Gillett, 1 June 1942.

27 Vol. 69, nos. 252, 253, 258, 260, to M. C. Gillett, 18 September, 24 September, 29 November, 14 December 1942; vol. 72, nos. 198, 204, 205, 218, to same, 13 January, 22 February, 27 February, 9 June 1943; vol. 72, no. 107, to King George II of Greece, 4 June 1943.

28 From the diary of Mrs Gillett, who with her husband was with him on the drive to Somerset and back.

29 Sir Arthur Bryant, *The Turn of the Tide* (London, 1957), p. 483. See also Lord Tedder, *With Prejudice* (London, 1966), pp. 286, 321.

30 Vol. 66, no. 145, to C. E. Raven, 2 July 1941.

31 'Thoughts on the New World.' Address by Field-Marshal the Rt Hon. J. C. Smuts on 25 November 1943. Issued under the authority of the Empire Parliamentary Association.

32 Vol. 72, no. 172, to J. H. Hofmeyr, 28 October 1943: 'I think I have found our future director of scientific research. It is Professor now Brigadier Schonland...Do you approve my approaching him for post war appointment as our Director?'

33 Vol. 69, no. 219, to M. C. Gillett, 31 January 1942.

34 Vol. 69, no. 221, to M. C. Gillett, 14 February 1942.

GENERAL NOTE ON SOURCES

From the mid-war years until his death in 1950 Smuts wrote many letters to the Crown Princess (later Queen) Frederika of Greece, and she wrote many to him. Presumably she kept his letters, and after his death hers were restored to her, at her request, by Mr J. C. Smuts, the literary executor named in his father's will. I should like to think that some scholar, in some possibly distant time, will embody this material in a book which, by its sensibility and in some degree its theme, may invite comparison with Lord David Cecil's *Lord M. or the Later Life of Lord Melbourne* (London, 1954), chapters v and vi.

Meanwhile, my brief narrative derives from two main sources: first, the frequent and lengthy references by Smuts to the Crown Princess in his letters to other people; secondly, the testimony of persons belonging to or intimate with the Smuts family during the period of the Crown Princess's residence in South Africa. The testimony of Mrs Smuts herself, given to me in many conversations when I was her guest at Doornkloof some years before her death, has been of particular value to me.

It follows that the evidence which I have used has been in large measure not direct but reflected. Nevertheless, the reflections are vivid and, I believe, undistorting.

CHAPTER 23

1 Vol. 75, no. 40, to Hofmeyr, 2 May 1944; *ibid.* from Hofmeyr.
2 Vol. 72, no. 230 and vol. 75, no. 198, to M. C. Gillett, 1 September 1943 and 14 February 1944.
3 Vol. 70, no. 13, from L. S. Amery, 10 September 1943.
4 John Ehrman, *Grand Strategy* (U.K. Official Histories), vol. v, ch. II; Churchill, *op. cit.* vol. v, ch. vII.
5 Churchill, *op. cit.* vol. v, pp. 114–21; Ehrman *op. cit.* pp. 109–11 and Appendix vI, pp. 554–6.
6 Churchill, *op. cit.* vol. v, p. 220; Ehrman, *op. cit.* pp. 109–11.
7 Vol. 72, no. 233, to M. C. Gillett, 24 December 1943.
8 Ehrman, *op. cit.* p. 349.
9 Churchill, *op. cit.* vol. vI, ch. IV *passim*; Ehrman, *op. cit.* ch. vII and pp. 345–67.
10 Vol. 77, no. 242, to M. C. Gillett, 21 January 1945.
11 Vol. 77, nos. 129, 243, 244, 248, to T. Lamont, 4 January, to M. C. Gillett, 28 January, 22 February, 4 March 1945.
12 Vol. 75, no. 160, to Chaim Weizmann, 14 November 1944; vol. 77, no. 129, to T. Lamont, 4 January 1945.
13 Vol. 77, no. 245, to M. C. Gillett, 10 February 1945.
14 Box K, nos. 186, 189: speeches by Smuts at the Transvaal Congress of the United party on 11 October 1944 and at the Union Congress on 6 December 1944.
15 See *Die Transvaler*, 14, 20, 30 December 1944, 3 January 1945; and for comment on these articles, see *The Afrikaner Broederbond. A State within a State* (Johannesburg, 1945).
16 *H. of A. Deb.* 24 May, cols. 8183, 8184.
17 Vol. 75, nos. 196, 205, to M. C. Gillett, 4 January, 22 August 1944.
18 Vol. 72, nos. 218, 231, and vol. 77, no. 243, to M. C. Gillett, 9 June, 8 September 1943 and 28 January 1945.
19 Vol. 75, no. 159, to Admiral Evans, 3 November 1944; vol. 77, no. 159, to his daughter Santa (Mrs Weyers), 5 May 1945; nos. 250, 258, 260, to M. C. Gillett, 11 March, 16 August, 24 September 1945.
20 Vol. 73, no. 69, A. M. Conroy to J. H. Hofmeyr, 16 May 1944.
21 Vol. 75, nos. 209, 213, to M. C. Gillett, 24 October, 30 November 1944.
22 Vol. 77, no. 244, to M. C. Gillett, 3 February 1945.

CHAPTER 24

1 Vol. 72, no. 222, 4 July 1943.
2 Vol. 66, no. 258; vol. 69, no. 237, to M. C. Gillett, 31 December 1941 and 7 June 1942.
3 Vol. 66, no. 222, to M. C. Gillett, 27 May 1941; vol. 69, nos. 161, 192,

232, to T. Lamont, 14 August, to Lord Cecil, 10 November, to M. C. Gillett, 3 May 1942. Cf. pp. 359, 360, 409, 419 above.

4 Vol. 69, no. 161, to T. Lamont, 14 August 1942; vol. 72, nos. 216, 222, to M. C. Gillett, 17 May and 4 July 1943; vol. 77, no. 266, to same, 2 November 1945.

5 Vol. 69, no. 248, to M. C. Gillett, 20 August 1942; vol. 72, no. 226, to same, 31 July 1943; vol. 77, nos. 266, 267, to same, 2 and 9 November 1945.

6 Vol. 72, no. 216, to M. C. Gillett, 17 May 1943; vol. 77, nos. 245, 248, to same, 10 February, 4 March 1945.

7 *A History of the United Nations Charter*, by Ruth B. Russell (The Brookings Institution, Washington, D.C.), p. 215; 'Probably no other major governmental policy has ever been the product of so many minds as the American proposals for an international organization'. On Smuts's contribution to the Covenant of the League, see *Smuts: The Sanguine Years*, pp. 500–3, and *The Art and Practice of Diplomacy*, by Sir Charles Webster (London, 1961), p. 71.

8 Vol. 76, nos. 10, 11, from L. S. Amery, 9 February and 1 March 1945. And see pp. 360, 409 above.

9 Vol. 69, no. 194, to Dr T. Lie (of Norway), 12 November 1942; vol. 72, no. 216, to M. C. Gillett, 17 May 1943.

10 Churchill, *op. cit.* vol. VI, pp. 183–4; also *British Foreign Policy in the Second World War*, by Sir Llewellyn Woodward (United Kingdom Official Histories, London, 1962), pp. 451–9.

11 Webster, *op. cit.* pp. 11–12.

12 See *Many a Good Crusade*, by Virginia C. Gildersleeve (New York, 1954), *passim*; also Russell, *op. cit.* pp. 910–18, and Woodward, *op. cit.* pp. 532–5. My own allusions to this episode in *Four Studies of War and Peace* (Cambridge, 1961), p. 114, were too slapdash.

13 Vol. 77, nos. 121, 148, 174 (correspondence with E. Stettinius, the President of the Conference); nos. 251, 253, to M. C. Gillett, 8 May and 5 June 1945; no. 175, to L. S. Amery, 4 July 1945.

14 Vol. 80, no. 209, to M. C. Gillett, 24 July 1946.

15 Vol. 77, nos. 257, 258, to M. C. Gillett, 10 and 16 August 1945.

16 In what follows I rely heavily upon M. M. Gowing, *Britain and Atomic Energy* (London, 1964).

17 Vol. 96, no. 13, from Niels Böhr, 14 June 1950.

18 Vol. 77, no. 258, to M. C. Gillett, 16 August 1945.

19 Vol. 77, no. 293, to M. C. Gillett, 28 January 1945.

20 Vol. 77, no. 266, to M. C. Gillett, 2 November 1945.

21 Vol. 77, nos. 263, 274, to M. C. Gillett, 15 October and 28 December 1945.

22 From 'The General at Ottawa' in *An Unknown Border*, poems by Anthony Delius (Cape Town, 1954). Smuts made his Ottawa speech after the San Francisco Conference and Delius heard it over the air while he was on service with the South African Forces.

23 Vol. 77, no. 226, to Abbé Breuil, 27 November 1945; nos. 263, 264, 269, to M. C. Gillett, 15 and 18 October, to A. B. Gillett, 21 November 1945.
24 Vol. 77, no. 210, to W. S. Churchill, 10 November 1945; nos. 255, 258, 265, to M. C. Gillett, 22 July, 16 August, 25 October 1945; no. 269, to A. B. Gillett, 21 November 1943; no. 181, to Lady Moore, 31 July 1945.

1 Vol. 77, nos. 181, 192, 253, 256, 257, 262, to Lady Moore, 31 July 1945, to L. S. Amery, 27 September, to M. C. Gillett, 5 June, 29 July, 10 August, to A. B. Gillett, 9 October 1945.
2 Vol. 77, no. 259, to M. C. Gillett, 27 August 1945.
3 Vol. 77, no. 250, to M. C. Gillett, 11 March 1945.
4 Vol. 88, no. 44, to Lady Moore, 22 February 1948; vol. 77, no. 161, to J. H. Hofmeyr, 6 May 1945.
5 See pp. 351–2, 369, 372, 420 above; also *H. of A. Deb.* vol. 47, cols. 75–6, Dr Malan's speech of 25 January 1944.
6 Vol. 84, no. 116, to Lady Moore, 18 August 1947.
7 Vol. 80, nos. 112, 205, 209, 217, to J. H. Hofmeyr, 29 August, to M. C. Gillett, 23 June, 24 July, 3 October 1946; vol. 84, no. 202, to M. C. Gillett, 16 March 1947.
8 Vol. 80, no. 81A, Statement to the Anglo–American Committee of Enquiry into Jewish Immigration, April 1946. Vol. 84, nos. 56, 173, to Dr Weizmann, 29 May, 5 December 1947; vol. 88, no. 78, to L. S. Amery, 13 April 1948. And on Cyrenaica, vol. 84, no. 174, to Lady Moore, 10 December 1947.
9 Vol. 80, no. 205, to M. C. Gillett, 23 June 1946; vol. 82, no. 207, from Lady Moore, 6 August 1947; vol. 84, nos. 26, 33, 50, 76, 80, 116, to Lady Moore, 22 March, 17 April, 18 May, 14 June, 21 June, 18 August 1947.
10 Vol. 84, nos. 209, 128, 172, to A. B. Gillett, 14 September, to Lady Moore, 19 September, 28 November 1947.
11 Vol. 84, no. 80, to Lady Moore, 21 June 1947; vol. 88, no. 16, to Lady Moore, 25 January 1948; Box M, no. 252, 'The Changing Concept of the British Commonwealth and Empire', recorded for broadcast 23 May 1948.

1 Vol. 80, nos. 199, 205, 207, 211, to M. C. Gillett, 3 March, 23 June, 14 July, 23 August 1946.
2 Vol. 80, nos. 191, 200, 216, to M. C. Gillett, 10 January, 9 March, 24 September 1946; vol. 84, nos. 28, 131, to Florence Lamont, 31 March, to Lady Moore, 23 September 1947.
3 Vol. 84, nos. 191, 200, to M. C. Gillett, 14 January, 2 March 1947.
4 Vol. 47, nos. 8, 149, from C. F. Andrews and from Lord Irwin, 14 and 15 November 1931; vol. 47, no. 64, from M. K. Gandhi, 17 November

1931; vol. 49, nos. 212, 225, 260, 271, to M. C. Gillett, 5 January, 8 March, 15 August, 27 September 1932.

5 Vol. 53, no. 194, to M. C. Gillett, 23 February 1935; vol. 66, no. 135, to Lord Linlithgow, 4 June 1941; vol. 69, nos. 223, 227, to M. C. Gillett, 28 February, 3 April 1942.

6 Vol. 65, no. 87, from Lord Linlithgow, 13 July 1941; vol. 67, no. 12, from L. S. Amery, 10 August 1942; vol. 69, no. 229, to M. C. Gillett, 12 April 1942; vol. 72, no. 204, to M. C. Gillett, 22 February 1943; vol. 81, no. 18, from L. S. Amery, 6 January 1947.

7 *H. of A. Deb.* 12 June–25 July 1925, col. 6502 (23 July).

8 G. Heaton Nicholls, *South Africa in My Time* (London, 1961), pp. 310–15.

9 Vol. 58, no. 143, from Gandhi, 16 July 1939.

10 In this and the following paragraph I have drawn on the suggestive chapter VII of G. H. Calpin, *Indians in South Africa* (London, 1949). This is not to say that the author would necessarily approve my distillation.

11 *Report of the Indian Penetration Commission,* U.G. 39–1941.

12 *Report of the Second Indian Penetration (Durban) Commission,* U.G. 21–1943.

13 Vol. 72, no. 211, to M. C. Gillett, 15 April 1943.

14 *H. of A. Deb.* 14 April 1943, cols. 5394–5400.

15 *Ibid.* cols. 5438 ff.

16 Vol. 75, no. 28, telegram to L. S. Amery (presumably 18 April 1944). For the terms of the Pretoria Agreement and the press announcement, Calpin, *op. cit.* pp. 194–5.

17 Vol. 77, no. 235, to Lord Wavell, 14 December 1945.

18 Calpin, *op. cit.* p. 197.

19 *Interim Report of the Commission of Inquiry into matters affecting the Indian Population of Natal,* U.G. 22–1945.

20 Vol. 77, no. 235, to Lord Wavell, 14 December 1945.

21 Vol. 80, nos. 126, 142, 144, to J. H. Hofmeyr, 23 September, 15 and 17 October 1946.

22 Resolution 65 (1).

23 See T. B. Millar, *The Commonwealth and the United Nations* (Sydney, 1966), chapter IV *passim.*

24 Vol. 84, no. 15, to Chief Justice Sir J. G. Latham, 12 February 1947.

25 Vol. 84, no. 191, to M. C. Gillett, 14 January 1947. The General Assembly of 1947 reaffirmed the stand of the previous year, but in milder terms.

26 *Cape Times,* 19 December 1946.

27 Smuts called the telegrams exchanged between Nehru and himself 'paper bombs' (vol. 84, no. 98, to Lady Moore, 26 July 1947). They were printed, with other material relevant to the General Assembly of 1947, in 'Principal Documents relating to the consideration by the United Nations General Assembly of the Statement by the Government of South Africa and the Statement by the Government of India arising out of

Resolution 44 (1) adopted by the General Assembly on 8 December 1946, regarding the treatment of Indians in South Africa'.

28 Vol. 84, no. 131, to Lady Moore, 23 September 1947.

29 Vol. 78, no. 157, from Gandhi, 18 March 1946 (cf. vol. 80, no. 80, to Gandhi, 26 March 1946).

30 Nagantara Sagal, *Prison and Chocolate Cake* (London, 1954), p. 196.

31 Vol. 88, nos. 30, 44, to L. S. Amery, 12 February, to Lady Moore, 22 February 1948; vol. 88, no. 217, Henry Cooper to G. Shulka, 11 December 1948.

CHAPTER 27

1 Vol. 80, no. 223, to M. C. Gillett, 17 November 1946.

2 Vol. 50, no. 192, to M .C. Gillett, 28 August 1933.

3 Letter to the author from Professor Eileen Krige, 1 June 1966.

4 Vol. 59, no. 147, from Chieftainess Modjadji, 9 November 1939.

5 J. C. Smuts, *The Basis of Trusteeship in African Native Policy* (New Africa Pamphlet no. 2, 1942).

6 Senate Deb. 5 May 1941, col. 2214.

7 In what follows I shall be using material which Miss Joan Bradley (as she then was) prepared for me during intervals of her work in helping to get to the press the first four volumes of *Selections from the Smuts Papers*. At my request Miss Bradley produced the following memoranda:

    (1) Native needs and aspirations as stated by—

        (*a*) The Native Representatives in Parliament;

        (*b*) The South African Institute of Race Relations;

        (*c*) The Native Representative Council;

        (*d*) The African National Congress;

        (*e*) Mr Emil (Solly) Sachs;

        (*f*) The Smit and Fagan Reports.

    (2) What Smuts said in public.

    (3) What the Smuts government did.

    (4) Smuts and the Coloured People.

All these memoranda were comprehensive, informative and well documented. In using them I have decided not to clutter my pages with detailed references; but I have cited precise dates in order to facilitate checking from the published documentary material. I have also given precise references to some of the more important quotations, particularly to Smuts's private correspondence, which remains here, as well as elsewhere, my main original source.

8 Vol. 68, no. 67, from D. Rheinalt Jones, 13 June 1942.

9 *H. of A. Deb.* 23 January 1947, col. 11071.

10 *H. of A. Deb.* 18 March 1948, cols. 3475, 3476.

11 Vol. 84, no. 196, to M. C. Gillett, 6 February 1947.

12 Professor Gwendolyn Carter has printed this Declaration in Appendix IV (p. 485) to *The Politics of Inequality* (London, 1958).

13 In the following narrative I have made use of C. M. Tatz, *Shadow* *and Substance in South Africa* (Pietermaritzburg, 1962), ch. VII, and have been particularly indebted to the memoranda by Miss Joan Bradley mentioned in reference 7. I have also checked some quotations in the (mimeographed) proceedings of the N.R.C. which, in accordance with the 1936 Act, were laid on the tables of the House of Assembly and the Senate.

14 Vol. 79, nos. 30, 34, from J. H. Hofmeyr, 8 September, 7 October 1946; vol. 80, nos. 131, 144, to J. H. Hofmeyr, 28 September, 17 October 1946.

15 Vol. 84, nos. 195, 200, to M. C. Gillett, 1 February, 2 March 1947.

16 Vol. 84, no. 22, to Lady Moore, 2 March 1947.

17 Vol. 82, no. 194, from Lady Moore, 4 April 1947.

18 *H. of A. Deb.* 23 January 1947, col. 11071.

19 Vol. 72, no. 218, to M. C. Gillett, 9 June 1943.

20 *H. of A. Deb.* 15 February 1950, cols. 1329–30.

21 *H. of A. Deb.* 17 April 1946, col. 5743.

22 *H. of A. Deb.* 20 January 1948, cols. 81–90; *Rand Daily Mail*, 19 August 1947.

23 U.G. 28–1948.

CHAPTER 28

1 Vol. 87, no. 107, to Lady Moore, 23 August 1946; nos. 191, 194, 199, 200, to M. C. Gillett, 10 and 26 January, 3 and 9 March 1946.

2 Vol. 77, no. 266, vol. 80, no. 200, vol. 84, no. 213, to M. C. Gillett, 2 November 1945, 9 March 1946, 14 October 1947.

3 Vol. 84, no. 191, to M. C. Gillett, 14 January 1946.

4 Vol. 84, nos. 189, 40, to M. C. Gillett, 2 January 1947, to Lady Moore, 3 May 1947.

5 Vol. 84, no. 98, to Lady Moore, 26 July 1947.

6 Vol. 80, no. 216, vol. 84, no. 189, to M. C. Gillett, 24 September 1946, 2 January 1947; vol. 95, no. 205, to Leslie Hotson, 12 April 1950.

7 Vol. 80, nos. 209, 215, vol. 88, nos. 233, 244, 246, to M. C. Gillett, 24 July, 15 September 1946; 9 February, 5 and 20 May 1948.

8 Vol. 84, nos. 191, 207, to M. C. Gillett, 14 January, 21 April 1947.

9 Vol. 84, nos. 195, 201, to M. C. Gillett, 1 February, 5 March 1947; vol. 88, nos. 54, 72, 234, to Lady Moore, 6 March, 8 April 1948, to M. C. Gillett, 13 February 1948.

10 Vol. 84, nos. 128, 214, to Lady Moore, 19 September, to M. C. Gillett, 25 October 1947; vol. 88, no. 231, to M. C. Gillett, 16 January 1948.

11 Vol. 80, no. 225, vol. 84, nos. 199, 200, to M. C. Gillett, 26 December 1946, 22 February, 2 March 1947; vol. 84, no. 58, to H.M. the King, 2 June 1947.

12 Vol. 80, no. 191, to M. C. Gillett, 10 January 1946; vol. 84, nos. 98, 99, 142, to Lady Moore, 26 July and 12 December, to Florence Lamont, 29 July 1947; vol. 88, nos. 16, 72, 232, 237, 239, 241, 244, to Lady Moore, 25 January, 8 April, to M. C. Gillett, 24 January, 6 and 21 March, 2 April, 5 May 1948.

13 Vol. 80, no. 186, to D. W. du Preez, 30 December 1946; vol. 84, no. 204, to M. C. Gillett, 31 March 1947.

14 Vol. 84, no. 191, to M. C. Gillett, 14 January 1947; Alan Paton, *Hofmeyr*, chs. 36, 37.

15 This paragraph and the ensuing narrative of the 1948 election are based primarily upon a memorandum written for my use by Miss Clodagh O'Dowd of the University of Cape Town. The memorandum is one of a series which will, I hope, be worked up with a view to publication.

16 Communication from Dr E. G. Malherbe.

17 Letter of 27 October 1953, from C. F. G. Hirschberg to the author.

18 Vol. 88, no. 108, to Lady Moore, 8 June 1948.

19 Vol. 88, no. 113, to L. S. Amery, 2 July 1948. The late Professor Raven on various occasions talked to me about the inauguration of Smuts as Chancellor.

20 Vol. 88, nos. 250, 251, 255, to M. C. Gillett, 22 July, 8 August, 26 August 1948.

21 Vol. 88, no. 260, to M. C. Gillett, 29 September 1948.

22 Vol. 88, nos. 262, 264, to M. C. Gillett, 11 and 23 October 1948.

CHAPTER 29

1 *Cape Times*, 2 June 1948. Alan Paton, *op. cit.* chs. 39, 40, tells the poignant story of Hofmeyr's last six months of life. In what follows I shall draw upon the information contained in these chapters without giving page references.

2 Vol. 86, no. 143, from E. G. Malherbe, 8 September 1948.

3 Smuts made two drafts before replying to Malherbe on 13 September. He stressed the need to 'go warily' (vol. 88, no. 154). Malherbe wrote a further brief letter on 18 September 1948 (vol. 86, no. 144). The correspondence was in Afrikaans.

4 Vol. 88, no. 270, to M. C. Gillett, 6 December 1948.

5 Vol. 92, nos. 8, 9, 14, to M. C. Gillett, 20 February, 3 and 27 March 1949.

6 Vol. 92, nos. 12, 13, 22, to M. C. Gillett, 15 and 22 March, 22 May 1949.

7 Vol. 91, no. 129, to Lady Moore, 20 February 1949; vol. 92, nos. 7, 29, to M. C. Gillett, 12 February, 20 August 1949; vol. 95, no. 158, to W. S. Churchill, 27 February 1950.

8 Vol. 88, no. 273, to M. C. Gillett, 28 December 1948.

9 Box M, no. 256.

10 Vol. 88, nos. 166, 187, to Winston Churchill, 27 September, to General Marshall, 5 November 1948; vol. 85, nos. 123, 124, telegrams from Churchill, 30 October, 9 November; vol. 86, no. 151, letter from Marshall, 17 December 1948.

11 Vol. 88, no. 271, vol. 92, no. 7, to M. C. Gillett, 12 December 1948 and 12 February 1949.

12 Vol. 88, no. 221, to Lady Moore, 14 December 1948; vol. 92, nos. 9, 31, to M. C. Gillett, 3 March, 4 September 1949; Box M, no. 266.

13 Vol. 91, no. 347, to General Spears, 14 December 1949.

14 Vol. 92, nos. 14, 17, 18, 21, to M. C. Gillett, 27 March, 21 and 25 April, 13 May; and vol. 91, no. 207, to Winston Churchill, 21 May 1949. For the pre-Conference statement Box E, no. 13; for the speeches by Malan and Smuts in the House of Assembly, Nicholas Mansergh, *Documents and Speeches on British Commonwealth Affairs 1931–1952* (London, 1953), pp. 859–74.

15 Box M, no. 268.

16 The *Cape Times* of 11 October 1949 reported the occasion fully. In addition, its original promoter, Mr P. D. de Kock, has given me a detailed account of it; as has his then contemporary at Stellenbosch, Professor D. C. S. Oosthuizen.

17 Vol. 66, no. 241 and vol. 88, no. 258, to M. C. Gillett, 8 September 1941 and 8 September 1948.

18 Vol. 84, no. 98 and vol. 88, no. 172, to Lady Moore, 26 July 1947 and 17 October 1948.

19 Vol. 92, no. 13, to M. C. Gillett, 22 March 1949; vol. 91, no. 224, to Gilbert Murray, 13 June 1949.

20 Vol. 84, no. 196, to M. C. Gillett, 6 February 1947 and nos. 75, 196, to Sir R. Kotze, 13 June 1947; vol. 91, no. 350, to Professor H. Lundholm, 15 December 1949.

21 Vol. 91, no. 359, to General Ismay, 22 December 1949; vol. 95, no. 260, to General von Lettow-Vorbeck, 15 May 1950; vol. 84, nos. 123, 129 and vol. 95, nos. 143, 203, to R. Broom, 8 and 20 September 1947, and 17 February, 12 April 1950; vol. 95, no. 251, to Mrs Bolus, 9 May 1950; vol. 88, no. 251, to M. C. Gillett, 8 August 1948.

22 Vol. 92, nos. 14, 16, 32, to M. C. Gillett, 27 March, 10 April, 9 September 1949.

23 The visit of the Gilletts to South Africa (November 1949–February 1950) was fully recorded by Mrs Gillett, particularly in letters to her sister, Dr Hilda Clark.

24 Vol. 95, nos. 113, 279, 139, to Sally Richardson, 19 January, to M. C. Gillett, 21 January, to Mrs Pill, 16 February 1950; various letters and notes by M. C. Gillett.

25 Vol. 92, no. 15, vol. 95, nos. 288, 289, to M. C. Gillett, 3 April 1949, 29 April and 11 May 1950.

26 See J. C. Smuts, *Jan Christiaan Smuts* (London, 1952), ch. LXXXVII and Professor G. A. Elliott, 'The Last Days of General Smuts, by one of his Physicians', *U.C.T.* vol. II, no. 5 (June 1963).

27 Vol. 95, no. 68, Mrs Smuts to Mrs H. M. L. Bolus, 5 October 1950.

INDEX

Index

Index

Index

Index

Index